Bastions and Belligerents:
Medieval Strongholds in
Northumberland

John F Dodds

Photographs
by Eddie Ryle-Hodges

Keepdate Publishing

Published by Keepdate Publishing Ltd.
21 Portland Terrace, Jesmond
Newcastle upon Tyne NE2 1QQ

© John F Dodds
© Photographs by Eddie Ryle-Hodges

ISBN 1 899506 45 4

Designed and typeset by
Keepdate Publishing Ltd, Newcastle upon Tyne

My Gratitude

Over the past eighteen years while researching this book I have met and talked to literally hundreds of people, most of them country dwellers, and with but three unimportant exceptions, I have always been given the most friendly and helpful treatment. To encounter such kindness has been an encouraging experience, and I am indeed grateful to all concerned.

I wish to record my gratitude, also to the many professionals and experts who have helped me – local historians, various members of the University of Newcastle, the staff of Records Offices in Northumberland and London, the 'Lit and Phil', English Heritage, the National Trust, Northumberland County Planning Department and the Royal Commission of Historic Manuscripts and Monuments.

I cannot name them all so I shall name only one – my wife Irene, whose help and support I treasure most. To her I dedicate this book, with my love and thanks.

John F Dodds

Elsdon Motte and Bailey Castle. (p325)

Contents

Northumberland
Ten Areas and Ten Key Towns

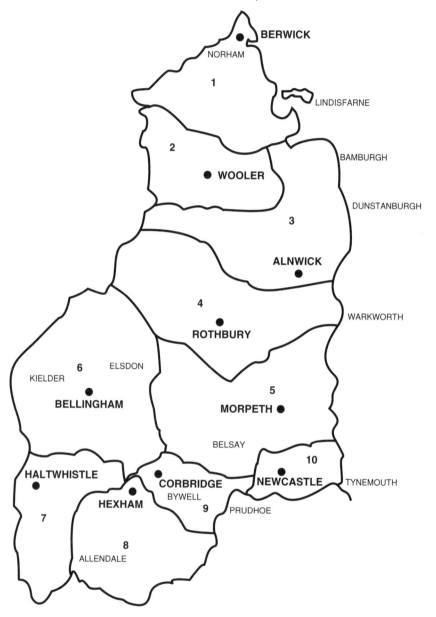

Note: *This map and those at the beginning of each area are indicatory only and are not to scale.*

The Vicar's Tower in the churchyard at Corbridge. (p438)

Introduction

Northumberland in the Middle Ages was the buffer, the no-man's-land, between two aggressive countries, Scotland, at first wanting more lebensraum, later its independence, and England, never understanding why such a small island should be divided. To the English kings the county was expendable; its barons and liberty lords were expected to stop all infiltrations, but if they failed it did not matter very much as intruders still had a long way to travel before they reached land of any value. Northumbrians had to look after themselves and could expect no help unless a large Scottish army came looking for a fight, so they did their best to defend themselves by making their homes as secure as finance and contemporary building techniques could make them.

They built a large number of strongholds of all types, from castles to fortified farmhouses, but just how many is not known, and probably never will be. Well over five hundred are covered in this study, their one time existence being verified by evidence on the ground and/or reference in old documents, but probably many more, specially of the more humble types, have been lost because they have been razed and their records, if they ever existed, have been lost or destroyed.

Of those we know about, roughly one-third have left us no physical traces. The rest survive today in every conceivable condition, from bumps in the ground to buildings still inhabited or utilised. Not surprisingly, however, considering their age, there are no strongholds still in their pristine, 'as built' condition. Some are ruins, some have been kept in repair over the years by frequent renovations and alterations, some have been partially rebuilt and are merely derivatives of the originals, while others have been absorbed into what are virtually new buildings.

Humble buildings were probably DIY jobs. The builders of towers and castles were directed by craftsmen called engineers who strove for strength and 'fitness for purpose' but not necessarily for artistry. Thus even the grand edifices lacked the architectural flair one sees in old churches, and as a rule their remains are of interest more to the historian than to the artist. In this study architectural description is confined to what the untrained eye can see, and no attempt has been made to rival the expert information in Pevsner*.

But while their stone and mortar may seem mundane to some, the stories of the people who lived in the strongholds are full of interest and emotion, an atmosphere this study endeavours to capture while outlining their history.

Hunter Davies, in the introduction to the first edition of his most satisfying book *A walk along the Wall*, tells us that as a child he was taken to see Roman forts and saw only "a load of old stones without a centurion in sight". Much later, when maturity and children of his own had sharpened his imagination, he was able to see the remains as living places, bustling with humanity engaged in activities which engendered his absorbing interest. By concentrating on people and events, it is hoped that this study will help to enliven Northumberland's great heritage.

Accuracy

No chronicler can stand up, put his hand on his heart, look you straight in the eyes and say "Every word I have written is the indisputable truth". History is the interpretation of past events, and very often more than one interpretation is possible.

There is an abundance of material lying around in the archives – wills, letters, minutes of court procedures, and so on, but it is seldom devoid of bias, vindictiveness or political partiality and must be read with these possibilities in mind. What the present writer has made of it frequently corresponds with other people's constructions, but differences do occur. As if deliberately to cause further confusion, the writer has on occasion filled in a gap in his knowledge with fragments of imagination, but such inexcusable flights are usually preceded by warning words such as 'perhaps' or 'may be'. Quite a lot of completely new material is incorporated, based on personal observations or discussions with local people who have bothered to delve deep into the history of their locale.

---

* Pevsner's *The Buildings of England* – Northumberland. See next page.

Extra Reading

References to original material are not provided in this work as it is considered they do nothing but disturb and annoy the normal reader, while specialists should know them anyhow. As compensation, there follows a short list of books which readers who have been stimulated into wanting more in-depth information may like to read. All are either still available to purchase or can be seen in most libraries.

History of Northumberland. 15 volumes of parochial history assembled by several editors between 1892 and 1940 and published by the Northumberland County History Committee.

History of Northumberland, by J. Hodgson. Covers the gaps in the County History. Published during the first half of the nineteenth century.

Comprehensive Guide to Northumberland, by W.W. Tomlinson. Contains a wealth of detail. First published in 1888 but has been reprinted many times since then.

Whittingham Vale and Upper Coquetdale. Two delightful and very detailed books by David Dippie Dixon which have been reprinted recently.

The Buildings of England – Northumberland. Nikolaus Pevsner's monumental volume has been revised and greatly extended by Grundy, McCombie, Ryder and Welfare, and was published by Penguin Books in 1992.

The Friday Books. Paul Brown's collection of articles which first appeared in the Newcastle Journal. Each one deals in a light-hearted way with one small area and the interesting characters who lived there.

From Border to Middle Shire: Northumberland 1586 – 1625. A carefully researched study by S.J. Watts of the University of Maryland.

A Dictionary of British History. Published by Pan Books in 1982. Indispensable to all who are concerned about dates and basic facts.

Excellent handbooks are available on site at the following historical monuments. They are published by English Heritage except those marked (NT) = National Trust, or (P) = private owner:

Alnwick (P), Aydon, Bamburgh (P), Belsay, Berwick, Cragside (NT) Dunstanburgh, Lindisfarne, Norham, Tynemouth, Wallington (NT) and Warkworth.

Perimeters

The Norman Conquerors introduced the castle to Britain, and the last battle on British soil, at Culloden, removed the final excuse for their maintenance as strongholds, so the designed limits to this study are 1066 and 1746. Some events and several families have precursors or appendages, however, which necessitate crossing these limits.

Geographically, only Traditional Northumberland, more or less as established at Carham in 1018 but including Berwick, is of concern.

Newcastle, which left the county in 1400, and the modern anachronism of North Tyneside are included. Thus is covered all the land from the River Tweed to the Rivers Tyne and Derwent, from Berwick to Blanchland and from Tynemouth to Thirlwall.

Arrangement and Order of Listing

For convenience, the county has been split into ten arbitrary areas, each one roughly embracing a recognisable terrestrial feature, usually a river system. A town or village within each area – one sure to be well known to readers and easily located on the map – has been assigned the title of 'Key Town' and is used as a location point from which to find all the other places in the area.

Within each area the Key Town is considered first, then the other places are grouped into small geographical sub-areas. The order of listing within these may seem rather nebulous but generally is related to their distance from the Key Town, the nearest first.

This zoning arrangement has been chosen in preference to an alphabetical listing for two main reasons, to enhance the natural relationship between near neighbours and to help those intrepid adventurers, be they walkers, motorists or armchair dreamers, who wish to study the strongholds at close quarters.

As a general rule, each stronghold is treated as a discrete entity, but there are exceptions where two or more are grouped as one item because of close affinity or sparsity of information.

Strongholds sorted out

Did you, by any chance, *butter* your toast with margarine at breakfast this morning? Perhaps you have been *Hoovering* your carpets with your Zippo vacuum cleaner before ransacking the *plastic* tin box for a biscuit at coffee time?

Colloquial English is full of such homely expressions which are well understood by most British people, although they must present some difficulty to foreigners. *Castle* is another example of a word popularly misused. We talk of Northumberland having hundreds of stone castles, but in fact there are, or were, only twenty and all the others are strongholds of a different sort. The error is exacerbated by the common use of the word in names of lesser buildings, perhaps for ostentation.

Normally this does not matter a great deal. The towers at Langley and Chipchase lose nothing by being called castles. But in this study, which deals with all manner of strongholds, it would be dreadfully misleading and complexing if we failed to differentiate between the types correctly, by the use of inappropriate nomenclature. So, at the risk of appearing to be pedantic, it has been decided always to call a spade a spade and never a trowel or shovel.

This decision leads naturally to the question of definitions, and here there is a problem as the British Standards Institution does not appear to have got round to establishing a 'Stronghold Standard'. There are, in fact, a multiplicity of so-called definitions, so it is necessary to establish a set which applies throughout this book.

Castles

Castle is not a general term for any type of stronghold, and there are fundamental differences even between the smallest castle and the largest tower or fortified manor-house. There are, however, a number of types of castles, although in battle-torn Northumberland we need discuss only four.

William the Conqueror introduced a very simple form of castle into England. Before he came the Britons had their hill forts, the Romans their stations, forts and walls, the Anglo-Saxons their 'burhs' or protected towns, but these were all communal strongholds and it was left to the Normans to think of defensive complexes belonging to one man. William is credited with bringing a couple of prefabricated castles with him when he crossed the Channel in 1066, and one is caricatured on the Bayeux Tapestry. What he probably brought was a load of cut timber with which to make palisades around convenient mounds at Pevensey and Senlac, and small huts, perhaps look-out towers as well, to put inside the palisades.

From these simple beginnings, more sophisticated earth and timber castles, which we call **Motte and Bailey Castles**, quickly developed for use by the king and the Norman aristocracy to control the numerically superior native population. They were built at strategic points to house a company of soldiers, to provide safe quarters for their lords and to publicise their dominance. The king and his top-drawer supporters owned several such places and travelled from one to the other, staying in each only long enough to eat all the food there. When the holder was not in residence, castles were left in the charge of governors, captains or constables, three names for the same officer.

We are lucky in Northumberland in having at Elsdon probably the most complete and unspoilt earthwork of a motte and bailey castle in England. A study of it is rewarding as it reveals the essential elements of all Norman-type castles, including those built in stone.

A convenient small hill or, as at Elsdon, the spur of a range of hills, was shaped by slave labour to form a level platform with steep sides all round. At some point on this platform a still higher mound was fashioned. Around this and around the whole complex were two or three rows of defences – earth ramparts topped by palisades, usually with a moat between. Access to the platform was by a ramp through a heavily guarded gate, and to the higher mound by removable stairs or gangway.

The large area on the platform was called the bailey, and here lived the soldiers of the garrison. They were accommodated in several timber buildings serving as sleeping quarters, cook house, brewery, stables and farrier, look-out bastions and chapel. The higher mound was called the motte; it carried a superior timber building for the lord's use, often built on stilts and covering a pit for rubbish and prisoners. The motte's extra defences were considered necessary in case the enemy overran the bailey or rebellious soldiers in the bailey became obstreperous.

Timber was used for both buildings and defences because it was readily available, easily and quickly fashioned and light enough to stay in place on unsettled, man-made mounds. It had two disadvantages, however – it was inflammable and it rotted. Quite soon the outer faces of the ramparts were being tiled with stone, and when King Henry II decided to strengthen the Border he decreed that all new castles should be built of stone.

Such strongholds were called **Keep and Bailey Castles,** a name which suggests they were similar to the earlier type except that the motte was replaced by a keep, the strongest part of the complex two or three storeys high and containing improved accommodation for the lord and his entourage.

The first stone castles were probably motte and bailey conversions. Harbottle Castle, for example, was constructed in 1157 by simply changing the building material one section at a time. Over the years variations crept in, especially to the size, shape and positioning of the keep. Alnwick's keep was more like a ring of towers, while Dunstanburgh's resembled two drums. In its original version, Dunstanburgh's keep guarded the entrance to the castle, being positioned in the line of the containing defences. Castles of this type became known as **Gatehouse Castles.**

A new concept in castle design reached Northumberland in the fourteenth century – the **Quadrilateral Castle,** sometimes in other parts of the country known as Concentric or Courtyard castles. The idea originated in the Holy Land and was brought to Britain in 1272 by the future King Edward I when he returned from misspending his youth on a crusade. These complexes consisted of a very strong curtain wall describing a quadrilateral, with turrets at the corners and at the entrance, and usually with a moat running all round the outer face. There was no keep but instead there was a more comfortable yet very strongly built hall or tower house, and this and all the usual accommodation for a garrison were built backing onto the wall, their fronts facing a central courtyard.

Most quadrilateral castles are in Wales; Northumbrian examples exist at Etal, Ford and Chillingham, all near the River Till. Etal is ruinous and the other two have been modified, so it is not easy to make out their original design.

Thus castles conformed to such a variety of plans and changing fashions it is difficult to find a definition which fits them all, never mind distinguishes them from large towers, for all successfully married garrison and barracks with secure residence. Fortunately castles had two common features absent from other types of strongholds – they were complexes of several buildings, and these were surrounded by 'live' defences. *The needs of the owner, his soldiers, his horses and his armament were housed separately and the whole was protected by a wall system which was manned constantly by sentries.*

Fortified Manor-Houses

Only eight of these are known to have been built in Northumberland, most of them in the less dangerous south of the country for they were not so strong as castles or large towers. Aydon Hall, near Corbridge, is our best example; it has been stabilised recently and English Heritage take care of it.

The name of this classification is rather misleading, for fortified manor-houses were not necessarily the homes of lords of the manor. Any rather grand mansion owned by a well heeled member of the public would do. Quite simply, they were houses which had been crenellated, or made as enemy resistant as was possible. The protection took the form of either battlements and other defensive appendages on the houses themselves, or of curtain walls and outer defences around the houses. Aydon Hall is a large hall house, stone built but not exceptionally strong, sited above a steep drop to the Cor Burn which protects three sides, and equipped with a sturdy wall – with a robust tower – along its exposed side.

Towers

A tower was a discrete fortification. It might have had a defensive wall round it, sometimes even a moat, but it relied heavily on its own thick stone walls, coupled with battlements and defensive accessories like arrow loops and machicolations.

It was discrete in having all accommodation and warlike paraphernalia under one roof, quite different from the multi-roofed castle. But it was not always alone. A few, like those at Welton and Halton, were built against already existing unfortified houses, while many gained companionship later in life when the building of an adjoining comfortable house became feasible.

Basically, towers were fortified hall houses set on end, with rooms piled one above the other instead of spread horizontally. They could be two, three or four storeys high, the ground floor being used only for storage. The roofs of the buildings were embattled, often pitched and sometimes with a parapet walk.

There was every imaginable size of tower. The larger ones were the homes of the nobility and could accommodate a garrison of twenty or thirty men. They filled the same roles as castles, but were not so impregnable or expensive to build and run. Langley, Chipchase, Ogle and Shortflatt were examples of this type, identified on some old lists as 'fortalices'. Small towers were often vicarages, or sometimes had been provided by benevolent landowners for the protection of their villagers.

Specialist towers included a bridge tower, which guarded the Coquet crossing at Warkworth, church towers specially strengthened for defence, as at Ancroft and Edlingham, watch towers as at Heiferlaw and gate towers as at Hexham and Alnwick Abbey. Yet another type was the camera, a name which presumably described their function rather than their design. Towers at Heaton and Tarset were so called because their owners retired to them for a bit of privacy.

As with castles, so much variety makes it difficult to find an all-embracing definition for towers. To say they "looked like towers" is not very scientific although to many it will conjure up – correctly – a picture of a rectangular or square building higher than its sides are long. To say that they were similar to a castle's keep is accurate for large towers but not for parsons' towers. Only one feature covers them all and separates them from castles: they were discrete strongholds, joined sometimes to unfortified houses but alone in the military sense. Everything required for defence was under one roof.

Bastles

Fortified farmhouses, the cheapest to build and offering the least protection of all Northumberland's strongholds. They owed their existence to an Act of Parliament of 1555 which made it compulsory for everyone living in the twenty mile wide Border Zone to build their own defences against reivers and cross-Border raiders. By no means everyone complied with the Act, but a few hundred did build strong houses, and the idea spread beyond the Border Zone.

Over two hundred bastles known, or considered very likely, to have existed are listed in this study. Probably a further two or three hundred were built but cannot be counted as no trace of them remains, either on the ground or in documented records. To historians, bastles are exasperating for they were occupied by plain, unsophisticated nonentities – with a few notable exceptions – who seldom did anything worth recording.

Bastles were quite remarkably uniform in design, almost as if the Wimpey of the day had won the contract to build them all. They varied a bit in size, proportions and detail, but all were oblongs, with the gable ends shorter than the side walls, all had just two chambers – store room downstairs, living room above it – and all had a high pitched roof. In all cases the walls were over three feet thick and made of rough, undressed stone laid in uneven courses, but their door and window frames and their large quoins, or corner strengtheners, were fashioned with some care. In most cases the ground floor entrance was in the centre of one of the gable walls, and was narrow – usually 27 inches – so that only one man at a time could enter. The upstairs door was in one of the long sides, reached originally by a removable ladder.

Foundations were not the sixteenth century builders strong point, but many bastles were built on plinths of large boulders, and these can be seen above ground, forming the first course of the walls. The ground floor chamber was a dark and airless place, either vaulted or with a timber ceiling supported on rough-hewn logs. The entrance was closed by a door – perhaps with a grill also – and this was locked with a crossbar from the inside. The man who did this could reach his living quarters through a trapdoor. With the door closed the only ventilation was provided by two small slits in the wall, so the chamber was totally unsuitable for live cattle or sheep, which (provided they could have got through the narrow door) would have died very quickly of suffocation and over-heating. As originally designed and built, the ground floor chamber was used mainly as a store for salted meat and grain.

The upper chamber did have a little light and air as one, sometimes two, small barred windows were provided near the door and provision was made for a fire. All the family lived in this one room, although in some bastles a small garret had been constructed beneath the roof timbers where small children could be bedded. The roof itself was sometimes tiled with stone flags, but, rather surprisingly in view of the fire risk, many were heather thatched.

Bastles as described were built in Northumberland from the 1550s to the early years of the seventeenth century. The protection they offered was necessary until about the middle of that century, then, when the risk of raids diminished, some bastles were modified slightly to improve their comfort and convenience. The most common improvement was to build an outside stairway to the first floor door.

By the beginning of the eighteenth century bastles were redundant and suffered one of three fates. First, many farmers, perhaps the majority, built comfortable farmhouses for themselves and razed their bastles, valuing the stones and the site more highly than their former home. Second, other farmers with the same aspirations kept their bastles but dramatically altered them to increase their ventilation and improve access so that the ground floor chamber could be used as a byer or stable. And third, other farmers converted their bastles into cosy houses, usually raising the roof a foot or two, adding windows, installing an internal staircase, blocking the doors and inserting a new door in one of the groundfloor long walls.

No bastles exist today in their original form, but many bastle derivatives can be found in the form of farm buildings or small houses. The nearest thing to a pristine bastle is Gatehouse North, but other interesting examples are to be found near the head of Tarset Burn, at Hole and at Woodhouses near Holystone. The latter and Black Middens are open for public inspection.

Strong Houses

Unpretentious vernacular houses which have been fortified or built with enough strength to resist attack but do not conform to basic bastle design are classified as Strong Houses. The most common difference between them and bastles are a second floor, more original windows and a protrusion or wing housing a staircase. A fine, though ruinous, example is at Doddington.

Other Defensible Structures

The word *Pele* or *Peel* is not used in this study, except as part of a name (eg, Staward Pele), in inverted commas or in its original meaning – a temporary encampment protected by palisades used by marching armies in the thirteenth and fourteenth centuries. The meaning has been distorted and pluralised over the years so is best left alone; to some people a pele is a small tower, to others a bastle or strong house.

A few self-explanatory military establishments such as **Forts** and **Gun Emplacements** or **Gun Platforms** were built within our perimeters. Examples are the Beblowe Fort on Lindisfarne, Clifford's Fort at North Shields and Codger Fort (a gun platform) on Wallington land.

Of the non-habitable type of defence, **Ramparts** and **Town Walls** are still in evidence – see both at Berwick. **Barmekyns,** seldom spelt the same way twice, were enclosures and their retaining walls which frequently surrounded or were adjacent to strongholds, but occasionally were on their own. They provided some protection for cattle and sheep – sometimes people too – against the opportunist raider.

Location Assistance

Each item on the ensuing pages begins with the name of the site and a line of light print, the latter having the meaning illustrated by the following example:

Norham

| L74 and L75 | P451 | NT906475 | 11km, 6³/₄ miles, south-west of Berwick |

| Sheet Number(s) of relevant O.S. Landranger maps. Scale 1:50 000 or 1¹/₄ inches to 1 mile. | Sheet Number of O.S. Pathfinder maps. Scale 1:25 000 or 2¹/₂ inches to 1 mile. | National Grid | Distance and direction from the area's Key Town. Distances are as the crow flies. |

Area 1
Tweeddale and the Northern Coast

Key Town: Berwick

Sub-Areas:

A   Up the R. Tweed
B   So-west from Berwick
C   South from Berwick
D   The Coast from
    Berwick to Budle Bay

This, the most northerly area, is roughly triangular in shape and correlates with North Durham with the addition of Berwick, Wark, Carham and a few small places in the south. Much of the area lies on or close to the Border and none of it more than eighteen miles from it.

The land is lush in Tweeddale, and the coastal plain is splendid agricultural country too, so there was plenty here for small bands of reivers to covet. It was the two way movements of armies and large raiding parties, English as well as Scottish, which did the most damage, however, and life in the area until the Union was harsh and precarious.

The main crossings of the Tweed were at Berwick, Norham, Cornhill and Wark, and strong defences were build there to try to control their use. Further from the Border, apart from a few homes of the very rich, small towers were the norm to protect isolated communities.

Key Town
Berwick upon Tweed
L75, P438, NT994534

If, as has been suggested, the name is derived from *Bere-wyke*, a grain settlement or homestead, then Berwick in Anglian times was probably just a focal point for those who tilled the fertile fields of the lower Tweed valley. The coastal promontary at Berwick, shaped rather like a marsh harrier's bill, makes a natural breakwater at the river's mouth, and this may have attracted some seaborne trade. But there was nothing of any military importance until Northumberland lost Lothian in 1018 and it became a Scottish frontier post.

Growing usefulness and importance caused Berwick to develop into a small town, so it was a valuable gift King Edgar gave to Bishop Ralph Flambard in 1097 for helping him grasp the Scottish throne. The bishop did not keep it long for, being an avaricious jingoist, he attempted to build a castle there, and this so upset the king the gift was taken back.

This little episode may have initiated a thought process in the minds of the Scottish leaders, for it is believed that King Alexander I, who succeeded Edgar in 1107, built a castle of some sort at Berwick shortly after his coronation. Its construction is not chronicled, but most likely it was a motte and bailey occupying the same high ground slightly to the west of the town later used for a stone castle.

No doubt a careful watch was kept from this castle for possible retaliatory moves when King David I invaded England repeatedly between 1124 and 1138. The danger did not hinder Berwick's rapid growth, however. It became the logical wool market for the whole of Lowland Scotland, and its port was recognised as being the most convenient from which to reach customers in England and on the Continent. In 1136 King David conferred upon it the prestigious title of Royal Burgh, aligning it with Roxburgh, Edinburgh and Stirling in the Court of the Four Burghs, an influential voice having the ear of the Scottish kings.

After David's defeat at the Battle of the Standard in 1138 there was peace on the Border until another Scottish king, William I The Lion, began to press his claim for more living space. He was captured in 1174, however, before he did much damage, and in order to obtain his freedom he had to pay homage to the English king, Henry II, and to surrender to him his castles at Roxburgh, Jedburgh, Stirling, Edinburgh and Berwick.

Berwick had little time to become anglicized before Henry's successor, King Richard I The Lionheart, sold all the properties back to William in order to finance his crusade against Saladin. So Berwick's castle was English only between 1174 and 1189, but in those fifteen years Henry rebuilt the place in stone and made of it a large and well-appointed fortress.

William renewed his claim to Northumberland after this, and John, the next English king, appreciating the danger his northern county was in, endeavoured to block one possible invasion route in 1204 by building an extension to a tower at the Tweedmouth end of Berwick's wooden bridge. William had the tower knocked down. John had the damage repaired. William knocked it down again. The two kings met eventually, in 1209, and John agreed to abandon his building programme in return for a financial inducement. By this time the bridge had been washed away and was not replaced for forty years.

King John was not the best of monarchs. He made a lot of barons very angry by dictating to them, by levying taxes in an unorthodox manner and by so carelessly losing some overseas possessions. The barons tried to control him by making him sign Magna Carta, but this had little immediate effect. Several Northumbrian barons decided they preferred the new Scottish king, Alexander II, to John, and they paid homage to him at Felton. John's reaction to such treachery was to raze the homes and crops of the guilty men, then, to punish Alexander, to perpetrate frightful atrocities on the inhabitants of Berwick

Fortunately, John did not occupy the town or damage the castle so his interference caused only a minor blip in Berwick's rising prosperity. During the relatively peaceful reigns of Alexanders II and III (1214 to 1286) it enjoyed its golden age as a major exporter and importer. Its most flourishing business was its wool trade with Flanders, the cloth-making centre of Europe. To lubricate this trade, many Flemish merchants lived in Berwick, occupying a palace-like building called Red Hall.

The death of Alexander III in 1286 heralded a dramatic change in Berwick's fortune. The king had outlived his immediate family and the only obvious heir to the throne was his young granddaughter, Margaret, the Maid of Norway, the last of the royal house of Dunkeld. Six guardians were appointed to govern the country while Margaret was sent for – she lived in Norway – but she died before she could be crowned. Thirteen hopefuls immediately stepped forward to take her place, so the guardians called for a competition and asked the English king, Edward I, to arbitrate. This, the 'Great Cause', suited Edward well but before accepting he got all concerned to agree to his condition, that whoever he selected should swear allegiance to him as his superior lord.

The competition, held at Norham, was scrupulously fair and the man with the best credentials was selected. John Balliol was crowned King of Scotland in the Great Hall of Berwick Castle in November 1292.

Had King Edward and King John Balliol been able to work together in harmony their two countries might have been united, to the benefit of both. But Edward was strong and ambitious and John was unable to stand up to his bullying for long. He did his best, but a ground swell of anti-English opinion forced him in 1294 to renounce his homage to the English king. A Committee of Twelve negotiated a mutual help treaty with France, the 'Auld Alliance'.

Edward came north to deal with this situation in his own inimitable way, but it was the Scots who opened hostilities by plundering and burning English ships in Berwick harbour in 1295. Berwick fell to Edward in the following year; most of its inhabitants were put to the sword, and the Flemish merchants in Red Hall were singled out for specially vicious treatment. At a stroke, the town's prosperity was cut to pieces. John Balliol was defeated at Dunbar soon afterwards.

The English invaders had found Berwick's town defences to be in a pitiful state so Edward ordered the construction of a wall and moat to enclose practically the whole peninsula. The castle was considered to be in remarkably good shape so it was restocked with food and ammunition so that it could be used as a base for Edward's army.

For thirty-three years the Scottish War of Independence dragged on, occasionally peaking as battles such as occurred at Stirling in 1297, when William Wallace was victorious, at Falkirk in 1298 when King Edward successfully retaliated and at Bannockburn in 1314 when Robert Bruce trounced an English army superior in numbers but handicapped by being led by King Edward II, but usually it was the steady grind of guerrilla tactics at which first Wallace then Bruce were adept. Berwick town and castle were captured by the latter in 1317. In 1328 King Edward III, Edward I's grandson, recognised the inevitable and abandoned all claims to feudal superiority over Scotland. He accepted Bruce as the Scottish monarch, and, as a seal of sincerity, a marriage was arranged between Bruce's son David and Joan, Edward's sister. The nuptials were celebrated in some style in Berwick Castle almost immediately.

Peace should have reigned for ever more – but it did not. When Robert Bruce died in 1329 the legality of David's succession was challenged by Edward Balliol, John Balliol's son. With considerable help from the English and some disinherited landowners, Edward was crowned king of Scotland in 1332. The crown sat uneasily on his head and he abdicated after only three months. King Edward III won a decisive battle against the Scottish clans at Halidon Hill, just north of Berwick, in 1333 and put Balliol back on the Scottish throne. Again he failed, and in 1356 he abdicated a second time, allowing David Bruce to be reinstated in 1357.

Thanks not only to Edward I but also to Robert Bruce, Berwick's town walls were now over ten feet high, stone faced and carrying nineteen towers, each nesting a timber fighting station. The castle, just outside the town walls, had been strengthened at its entrance and along its east wall, and the possibility of attack from the river bank had been reduced by the construction of the 'White Wall' from castle to the water edge. This precaution was tested in 1355 when a small force of Scots and French captured the town from boats in the river but failed to take the castle. The attack was serious enough to bring the English king to the scene, but there was no fighting: just the sight of his preparations was enough to send the raiders flying.

Two commando-style raids, in 1378 and 1384, proved the castle was still not immune against the tactics of opportunists. In the first of these the governor was killed and the castle occupied for eight days by only forty-seven Scots, but the Earl of Northumberland and his son, Hotspur, quickly regained control. The second raid was French inspired and was quite serious. The Earl, warden at that time, had his knuckles rapped for allowing it to happen, and this slur on his efficiency stung him into retrieving the castle by personally paying a large bribe.

Strangely, it was the Earl who caused the next attack on Berwick. He had sheltered there after participating in Archbishop Scrope's calamitous revolt in 1405 and King Henry IV had come after him with a large army well equipped with artillery which was used with some effect on the town walls.

Some repair work was done to the castle round about 1415 in anticipation of further trouble, but it was diplomacy rather than martial might which took Berwick from the English in 1461. King Henry VI, finally defeated at Towton in the Wars of the Roses, fled with his queen, Margaret, to Scotland and gave the town and castle to King James III in return for the promise of sanctuary and assistance.

Richard, Duke of Gloucester, the future King Richard III, forcibly returned Berwick to England twenty-one years later. Some low profile gun emplacements were added to the walls of both town and castle to help them cope with cannon fire, but in 1485 it was thought these would never be needed. In that year Henry VI and James III signed the Treaty of London which brought peace to the area and initiated discussions about the bounds of Berwick within which, both sides agreed, there should never again be any fighting. Berwick became a free town; a little later it became a free town in an independent state – of, but not in, England.

Berwick was not directly involved in King James IV's campaigns of 1496 and 1513, nor in the almost continuous cross-Border raiding to which the kings and noblemen of both sides gave their clandestine support, yet it remained a vital frontier post which the French might use to their advantage to distract the English forces from their objectives in France. None realised more clearly than King Henry VIII that a successful campaign across the Channel could be jeopodized by a diversionary battle at his back door, and he made sure Berwick Castle could handle such a contingency. His experts confirmed that its defences were satisfactory but they urged the relocation of its brew house, corn store and mill and armoury which were in the town and thus would be out of reach if the town was taken.

Whatever improvements Henry put in hand did not satisfy his daughter Mary, who came to the English throne in 1553. The Sieur d'Esse had arrived in Scotland with 6000 French soldiers, and they had not come for the scenery; she was convinced that Berwick was vulnerable. In January 1558 she lost Calais because of its poor defences and she was adamant that Berwick should not fall for the same reason.

Sir Richard Lee, a military architect fresh from a similar job at Tynemouth, was commissioned to survey and report. He recommended the abandonment of the castle, which in his opinion could never be made to withstand artillery bombardment, and the construction of new, low profile ramparts round the most vital parts of Berwick town. His ideas were approved and an order to proceed was about the last Mary issued before she died in November 1558.

In spite of its very high cost, the usually thrifty Queen Elizabeth was enthusiastic about the project at first, and appointed her cousin, Lord Hunsden, to the governorship of Berwick so that she might receive regular and reliable information about its progress. But within two years the likelihood of invasion from the north, and thus the need for elaborate defences, virtually disappeared.

The Treaty of Edinburgh was signed by Elizabeth and James VI in 1560. It ended the Auld Alliance and all French troops in Scotland were sent home. The Scottish nation became Protestant officially, like Elizabeth's England, and the only remaining contentious issues were local raiding and trading practices. Elizabeth's interest in her ramparts evaporated. Work on them continued to a modified plan until 1570, then was abandoned, the job neither as strong nor as complete as Sir Richard had intended.

After the Union of the Crowns in 1603 James the 1st of England and VIth of Scotland ordered the demilitarization of the frontier zone and Berwick moved theoretically from Border to Middle Shires. Its garrison was reduced to a hundred men, all its ordnance was shipped to the Tower of London and in 1607 its castle was sold as building material. Save for the very striking White Wall and a couple of gun turrets, there is little to see of it now.

The Civil War which started in 1642 brought a depressing return of militarism to Berwick. Oliver Cromwell invaded Scotland in 1650 and used the town as his base, moving stores, artillery and ships there. He went on to take the whole of Scotland (something neither the Romans nor Edward I had managed to do) and for the next eight years there was considerable prosperity and good order under the wise leadership of General Monck.

More troops were drafted into the town after the scares of the Jacobite rebellions of 1715 and 1745, but were not needed, so the Elizabethan Ramparts were never tested in battle. History was made in 1721 when the Ravensdowne Barracks were built, the first purpose-built housing for troops.

In 1746 Berwick was brought under the aegis of English law by the Wales and Berwick upon Tweed Act. Ninety years later, in 1836, Berwick, Tweedmouth and Spittle were made a county of England, so it is not true that Berwick is still at war with Russia because it made no separate peace after the Crimean War of 1854. From mid-eighteenth century for all practical purposes Berwick was part of Northumberland, but red tape slowed the legal process. Thus in 1885 it became one of Northumberland's Parliamentary constituencies. In 1889 Northumberland County Council accepted responsibility for its roads and bridges. It ceased to have its own police and education services in 1920, and in 1951 its own Quarter Sessions were discontinued. It was as recent as 1974 when the 1836 Act was repealed and Berwick stood in Northumberland officially.

Area 1, Sub-Area A   Up The River Tweed

Norham

L74 and L75   P451   NT906475   11km, 6³/₄ miles, south-west of Berwick

Capital of Norhamshire and Islandshire, the greater part of the Durham Bishops' County Palatine or northern territory. The village's Anglian name had been Ubbanford and, as this suggests, it was situated at the southern end of a ford across the River Tweed, the first above the tideway and thus of immense strategic importance.

The Bishops probably chose it as their 'northern home' because of this communication convenience, perhaps forgetting that fords could be used by the ungodly as well as the godly. The Bishops also held land north of the river, extensive estates which the Scots saw as remarkably like stepping stones to English domination in Scottish Church affairs. Rather cleverly, they removed this threat by having the estates transferred to the see of Glasgow in 1120.

This territorial loss alarmed Ralph de Flambard, bishop from 1099 to 1128. Would there be an attempt to rob him of his south bank estates as well? To prevent such an outrage, and also to try to deter an increasing number of Scottish raiders from using the ford, he built a small fortification on high ground a few yards downstream from the village.

The chosen site was naturally strong, with precipitous drops to the river on the north and to a tributary on the east. Only a limited amount of spadework would have been required to make moats on the other sides, yet the fortification which Flambard started in 1121 took seven years to finish; it would seem that he had in mind something superior to the usual motte and bailey, perhaps something faced in stone. Whatever it was, it failed to stop King David on at least two occasions in 1137 and 1138 when he used the ford to invade England.

King Henry II ordered the building of several castles along, or close to, the Border in 1157 to prevent further Scottish aggression, and Bishop Hugh de

Puiset was persuaded to start building a strong stone castle at Norham to replace what was left of Flambard's fortification.

The majestic ruins to be seen today represent a mix of dates, for the castle was repaired, altered or partly rebuilt several times during its long career. It is difficult to pick out traces of the original, but it seems fairly certain that it started as it meant to go on, as a typical Norman keep and bailey castle, made specially strong by massive walls. Nothing remains of the garrison accommodation; the keep, what is left of a three storey building, is mainly thirteenth and fifteenth century work.

Norham became the focus of much attention in 1291 as the place where the Competition to find a new Scottish king was held. Bishop Anthony Bek, or his predecessor, must have had a premonition as the castle had recently been extensively modified. It had become almost impregnable, with a 90 foot high tower, inner and outer wards, each with massive walls, a deep moat with a drawbridge, turrets on the outer wall and gates on the west and south sides guarded by flanking turrets. In addition, a splendid hall house, residence of the constable or his lord bishop but fit for a king, had been built in the inner ward.

This was where King Edward I stayed while hearing the claims of the thirteen competitors taking part in the 'Great Cause'. There is speculation, however, about where exactly the arbitration took place, for obviously the castle was too small. Upsettlington and Ladykirk across the river are possible sites, while Norham Church is favoured by many historians. One place which has not been given much consideration is Blount Island, in the middle of the river below the castle. It was convenient, within sight of trouble-watchers posted on the castle walls, easily accessible from both banks, large and flat enough to accommodate all the claimants and their retinues, and the irony of using a halfway house between his own country and the country he coveted would not have been lost on Edward.

Norham castle was continually manned during the Scottish War of Independence, when Sir Thomas Grey did frequent duty as its constable and Norhamshire's sheriff. After Bannockburn Robert Bruce besieged the castle on three occasions but never managed to gain an entry, thereby earning for Grey the Scottish leader's grudging respect.

A little light relief came to Norham in 1319 in the shape of a young knight called Sir William Marmion. His story has been well publicised by Sir Walter Scott, but for some unknown reason he set the lad's exploits against the backcloth of the Battle of Flodden which took place nearly two hundred years later. The real Marmion, it seems, attended a party in Lincolnshire with his girl-friend, a high-flyer of her time, who gave him a most conspicuous helmet with a "rich crest of gold". She told him that if he wanted her hand he must first prove his gallantry by bringing honour to the helmet in the most dangerous place in the kingdom.

Sir Marmion did want the hand and everything else that went with it, so off he went to Norham where, with Sir Thomas Grey's good humoured connivance, he was dressed in armour, helmet and all, set on a horse and sent out to meet a small raiding party. The Scots have a sense of humour too, but on this occasion they were perhaps stunned by the Belisha beacon careering towards them for, instead of killing him, they merely knocked him off his horse and left him for Grey to pick up later. That, unfortunately, is as far as the story goes; we are left to wonder whether he received a hero's welcome when he returned to his girl-friend, or whether he found her married to someone else.

A near miss in 1327 is on record. It was the night of King Edward III's coronation and the Scots expected the castle's garrison to be celebrating, too inebriated to notice a small party of rock climbers scaling the battlements, intent on opening the gates to their main force. The garrison was certainly in jubilant mood, but the sentries had remained sober and watchful. The scaling party was caught and the ingenious plan failed.

The Scots and their French allies made frequent sorties across the Border during the next century, but their strength was never sufficient to worry Norham castle unduly. The garrison did its policing job well but was not always successful. In 1355, for example, Sir Robert Ramsay of Dalhousie set fire to the village of Norham, causing the castle's constable to rush out – straight into an ambush.

The fourteenth and fifteenth centuries saw many changes made to the castle to improve its resistance to the sophisticated siege machines used by the Scots and French, and to render it a more comfortable place for the Durham bishops to visit.

During the Wars of the Roses Norham favoured the Yorkists at first and thus attracted the attention of King Henry VI's army, which lay siege to it in 1463. Lord Montagu relieved it after eleven days, but after he had gone the castle's constable voluntarily changed sides, backing the Lancastrians – a strange thing to do in the circumstances and Montagu came back to investigate. On the way he was stopped by a Lancastrian army led by the Duke of Somerset and Sir Ralph Percy. They had a set-to on Hedgeley Moor from which Montagu emerged the winner; he chased Somerset's men back to Hexham where the Red Rose withered terminally so far as Northumberland was concerned. Norham quietly surrendered to the Yorkists.

During the second half of the fifteenth century the castle's fabric and provisioning system were thoroughly overhauled. Improvements were made which probably saved it when King James IV attacked it in 1496 during an invasion which he claimed was to support Perkin Warbeck, a pretender to the English Throne, but was really to create a second front against the English and thereby take some of the sting out of their French campaign. James bombarded the castle with French artillery for a fortnight but the garrison held on until the Earl of Surrey brought relief.

1513 saw the same king invade England again, and again he attacked Norham. This time he had even bigger cannon, including the famous Mons Meg, yet it took five days of incessant bombardment to breach the castle walls and to force the garrison to surrender. This did not do James much good for he went on to his death, and his army's defeat, at Flodden, but it did serve to show that massive castles were obsolete, that masonry alone was no match for the new generation of ordnance. Immediately after the Battle of Flodden the Durham Bishop realised this and put in hand a quadrangular bastion called Clapham's Tower which was shaped so as to offer the minimum target to besiegers. Some smaller bastions, all with gun-ports, were built along the wall to replace gun turrets. Repairs were completed and the castle operational by 1515, but the new work was not finished until 1527.

The bastions were never given a full-scale test. The Crown took possession of the castle in 1559 when Bishop Tunstall forfeited his territory and Norhamshire and Islandshire became part of County Durham. The following year Queen Elizabeth signed the Treaty of Edinburgh which ended the Scottish and French 'Auld Alliance', so she saw no good reason for maintaining a defensive post at Norham, especially as she was paying so much for her ramparts at Berwick.

In 1571 the Queen granted the castle to Henry Carey, Lord Hunsdon, the Lord Warden of the Eastern March. It was not a gift Carey appreciated very much and he complained to Lord Cecil that it was uninhabitable and falling to bits. After the Union of the Crowns the castle had a succession of owners until, in 1923, it was given to the nation. English Heritage care for it now, and they invite visitors to its still impressive keep, gateways, walls and moats, all clearly indicating the essentials of a true Norman castle.

Newbiggin

| L74 | P451 | NT897456 | 12½ km, 7¾ miles, south-west of Berwick |

Groat Haugh

| L74 | P451 | NT890452 | 13¼ km, 8¼ miles south-west of Berwick |

The township of Newbiggin comprised East and West Newbiggin and Gret Hewghe, and its first owner was Eustice de Newbiggin. During the fourteenth century it became the property of a cadet branch of the Grey family, then before 1423 Robert Grey sold it to William Orde, a wealthy landowner whose main seat was at Ord, south of Berwick.

The survey of 1541 noted that Orde owned a tower at West Newbiggin. It was in good condition then, and later a barmekyn was built around it.

There are no visible remains, yet it seems fairly certain it was on the site now occupied by West Newbiggin farmhouse.

The same survey tells us that John Smythe has "newly made a strong house in a field called Gret Hewghe". This is taken to be the area now called Great Haugh. Smythe no doubt was a tenant, perhaps a farmworker, of the Ordes; there is no trace of his building now.

In 1748 the Orde fortune fell into the laps of three daughters who, between them, had five husbands (not altogether!). All got a share of the property, but who got what is not on accessible record.

Tillmouth

| L74 | P451 | NT870429 | 16 km, 10 miles, south-west of Berwick |

Twizel

| L74 | P451 | NT883434 | 15 km, 9½ miles, south-west of Berwick |

Long before the River Tweed became a frontier the few acres around its confluence with the River Till were considered to be strategically important – so important, in fact, that Osbert, a ninth century Northumbrian king, forcibly annexed them in 854 from St Cuthbert's Patrimony. This desecration got its just reward: the king was killed by the Danes soon afterwards and the land was returned to the Church, eventually to become part of Durham's Norhamshire.

The first recorded occupier of Tillmouth was a Norman, Jordan Rydell, a descendant of Golfridus Ridel, one time Seigneur of More, near Rouen, and veteran of the Battle of Hastings. The family prospered (in spite of being unable to decide how to spell its name) and in 1272, or shortly after, Sir William de Redel acquired Twizel. Tillmouth was retained but Twizel appears to have been the preferred residence.

By the fourteenth century the name had become Riddell and the estate had grown to include Duddo and Grindonrigg, plus other parcels of land closer to Berwick, all in the Bishop of Durham's shire. Sir William Riddell was styled 'Lord of Tillmouth', and when he died in 1325 his three daughters benefited from generous bequests. Isabella, the eldest, received Tillmouth, Duddo and Grindonrigg, while Twizel went to Constancia and the youngest got the outlying parcels.

Isabella was married to Sir Alan de Clavering of Callaly and his family retained his wife's inheritance for many generations, using Duddo as a residence for junior members, Tillmouth as a farming centre and Grindonrigg as a subsidiary farm. A village grew up at Tillmouth, inhabited by farm workers, and one of the Claverings built a chapel for them on the point of land between the two rivers – just about, according to legend, where the

Lindisfarne monks had rested during their long flight from the Danes in the ninth century.

Between 1415 and 1496 a small fortified tower was also erected at Tillmouth. It had a short but exciting life. It was "cast down, breached and defaced" during King James IV's invasion of 1496, and it sustained further damage in 1544 at the hands of aggrieved Scotsmen after the sacking of Leith and Edinburgh on the orders of King Henry VIII. In 1561 it was described as "a little tower or pile, much decayed", and was not mentioned again. It is alleged to have had a vaulted ground floor and a small barmekyn, but there is no trace of it or of the village now. Remains of the chapel can be seen still, but this is because it was rebuilt in the eighteenth century.

The Selbys bought Grindonrigg in 1510, but the Claverings held on to Duddo and Tillmouth – as freeholders after Bishop Tunstall lost Norhamshire in 1559 – until the end of the seventeenth century when Sir Francis Blake bought the former and a member of the ubiquitous Grey family the latter.

Sir William Riddell's second daughter, Constancia, shared Twizel with her husband, Sir John Kyngeston. Their son, Sir Thomas, who inherited in 1368, appears to have suffered from some progressive mental illness, for in 1385 two trustees were appointed to manage his affairs. They decided to sell the estate, the elevated part which looks down on the River Till, to Sir Gerard Heron and the 'Ville of Twizel' to Sir Robert Ogle (the fourth of that name who inherited in 1362). The two parts were not re-united until 1546.

Sir Gerard Heron, or perhaps his son, built a tower on the most visible part of his land before 1415, in good time for it to be savaged by the Scots in 1496 and 1544 just as Tillmouth's tower had been. In this case the intruders were not quite so thorough and something useful was left; the 1561 survey noted that a quarter of the building and the barmekyn were still standing.

The Selbys of Grindonrigg leased Twizel in 1522 and were still there in 1685 when the owners, the Herons received an offer for the place they could not refuse. They turned the Selbys out and sold to Sir Francis Blake of Ford – ironically the Herons' stronghold until the 1550s – who wanted a second property so that he could leave one to each of his two daughters when he died. This he did in 1717 and younger daughter Sarah inherited Twizel. When she married she did not have to change her name for her husband was her cousin, Robert Blake, probably a descendant of Sir Richard Blake, King Charles II's tailor. Their son, another Sir Francis Blake, inherited Twizel in 1734.

The new owner was a keen amateur architect with enough money and flair to produce some significant results. His first project was the rebuilding of the chapel in Tillmouth village, which he purchased for the purpose, selling it again as soon as he had completed the job. Next to receive his attention was Fowberry Tower, which he also bought. He planned, and started work on, a most ingenious scheme to totally envelope the existing medieval tower with a comfortable Georgian mansion – rather like fitting an embroidered cosy over an old teapot.

His most important project, however, was the up-grading of his own home at Twizel. Not being hampered by any uncontrollable need for self-effacement, he planned a blatantly ostentatious chateau which would reflect his social status. The ruins of the medieval tower occupied the most conspicuous position in the estate, so he decided to build around and above the old masonry, as at Fowberry.

Construction proceeded slowly and was unfinished when Sir Francis died, in 1780 or 1786. His son, yet another Sir Francis, inherited his father's property and his financial incontinence (in rather greater measure), but very little of his architectural skills. He left the building work alone at first while he made some ill-advised investments in real estate, including the purchase of Duddo from John Clavering in 1788 and Seghill Tower near Seaton Delaval soon after. Only in the 1790s did he decide to tackle his father's unfinished tasks at Fowberry and Twizel.

By about 1800 Francis realised his money was not going to last. To cut costs, he stopped work at Fowberry and sold the incomplete mansion to Matthew Culley, who finished off the job. Work at Twizel continued for a while, but it got more expensive as the professional, George Wyatt, had to be called in to help in 1812. By the time the building reached the fifth storey, with a further fifteen feet still to do, his suppliers and work force were making life really difficult for him. They seem to have taken exception to being paid with I.O.Us and began to hound him for real money – to such an extent that he had to flee from them to seek peace in a debtors' sanctuary at Holyrood in Edinburgh. There he died in 1818.

What the weather and vandals have left of the Blakes unfinished chateau still stands today, a pleasing folly set high above the tree-lined banks of the Till. It makes a memorable picture as viewed from Twizel Bridge, but it is sad that it is only a broken dream and not a true medieval fortification. That has been lost for ever.

Cornhill

L74	P451	NT854404 and	
	P463	NT857392	19 km, 12 miles south-west of Berwick

Cornhill was similar to Norham in being in Norhamshire, in having a twelfth century fortification and in being responsible for a Tweed ford, but Cornhill's ford was not very important in Norman times, and this was reflected in the size of its fortification.

The site of this fortification is in Peter's Plantation, clearly outlined by the absence of trees in the wood and by old moats along two sides. One other side drops steeply to a stream, while the important north side is almost a precipice with the old ford to Lennel at its feet. It is difficult to see how water could be brought to the moats and probably they were filled with thorn. The stronghold had undoubtedly been of the motte and bailey type, most likely strengthen with stone as at Norham.

Its effectiveness as a ford guard during the twelfth and early thirteenth centuries is not known, but the Earl of Fife had no difficulty in destroying it in 1335. As a new and improved ford was opened at about that time half a mile upstream, the stronghold was never repaired or replaced.

The village of Cornhill, half a mile to the south-east of the river, had its own fortification, a tower first mentioned in 1382. The village had been held by a family called Cornale but they forfeited it for some reason in 1328 and their land was divided into two unequal estates, the larger going to William Heron and the smaller to Robert Grey. The Grey estate passed by marriage to William Swinhoe of Scremerston in 1338 and it was his grandson who built the tower. It was still good for active service in 1415 and was worth repairing in 1496 after King James IV had knocked it about a bit. The Seiur d'Esse and a small army of French and Scotsmen found it worth attacking in 1549 but it was empty so they had to be content with stealing the provisions in it, including salted salmon. By 1631 it was in "indifferent good repair" but had acquired a barmekyn, and no more was heard of it.

The Heron part of the village passed to the Carrs when the main Herons lost their family seat at Ford. Much later, in 1670, the Carrs section was owned by the Armorers of Belford and the Foresters of Adderstone held the other section. Sometime before 1830 the whole village was united and in the hands of the Collingwoods of Lilburn.

There is no trace of the village tower now. W.W. Tomlinson says in his Comprehensive Guide to Northumberland that in his day (c1880) a large house at the end of the village street belonged to the Collingwoods, and he thought it occupied the tower's site. The present owners confirm this.

Carham

L74   P462   NT798384   25 km, 15½ miles, south-west of Berwick

Carham made its first mark on history in 838 when it staged a particularly bloody battle between a scratch army of Northumbrian Anglians and raiders from Norway. There was another important scrap there in 1018 when Malcolm II, King of the Scots, emerged victorious and the River Tweed became the eastern section of the Scotland/England Border.

So the area was no stranger to hostilities when English King Henry 1 granted it as a barony to Walter Espec, along with a more peaceful barony in Yorkshire. Espec, a loyal nobleman and soldier, built a motte and bailey castle at Wark, a couple of miles downstream, to guard a Tweed ford. At about the same time he founded two monasteries in Yorkshire – Rievaulx Abbey and Kirkham Priory – and granted Carham township (which included Wark) and parcels of land in the area to the latter. As control, he established a cell of 'black' Augustinian canons in Carham.

In 1151 Walter Espec entered Rievaulx Abbey and died there two years later. He had no children so his huge estates were shared amongst his three sisters, the eldest two obviously grabbing the most lucrative and leaving Carham for the youngest, Adeline, married to Piers de Ros. Their progeny lived in the barony until the end of the thirteenth century, always recognizing Kirkham Priory's right to maintain a cell there.

Inspite of having a castle just a short walk away, Carham had its fair share of trouble. In 1256, for example, a Scottish marauding party entered the canons' house and killed a Scottish cook they found working there. In 1296 the same building was plundered then burnt while most of the villagers were put to the sword. Goods and crops were taken in 1340, while in 1380 raids so destroyed the crops the land was regarded as 'waste' by the tax man. Strife was endemic throughout the life of the Auld Alliance, and sometimes the English reprisals against the Franco-Scottish raiders were just as damaging. Reivers from Redesdale knew the area also.

Rather late in the day – the early 1500s – the Prior of Kirkham Priory provided the villagers with a tower – "a little tower of defence against the Scots, of no real strength, without barmekyn or iron gate, intended for emergency refuge". It lasted less than fifty years.

The Crown assumed ownership after the dissolution in 1538. A watch and signal tower was built at Shidlaw (NT806380), on high ground a mile or so to the south-east of Carham, but this was of more use to the people of Glendale than to Carham villagers, being on a convenient route joining the two places.

The last recorded raid on Carham occurred in 1579. Fifty Teviotdale horsemen descended on the village in broad daylight and lifted cattle and a lot of household goods. In that same year Queen Elizabeth granted the church and the former canons' house to Sir Christopher Halton, and he hastily passed them on to Thomas Forster of Adderstone, in which family they resided until Thomas Forster, the Jacobite rebel leader, forfeited them in 1715.

The tower and its site are lost without trace. The site of Shidlaw's watch and signal tower is obvious but again there are no remains, the spot being occupied by farm buildings.

About three-quarters of a mile up-stream from Carham the Redden Burn flows into the River Tweed (NT790378). This is where the English/Scottish Border leaves the Tweed and starts its erratic course to The Cheviot. The confluence was a favourite spot for wardens meetings, where cross-Border justice was attempted.

Wark-on-Tweed

L74   P463   NT822386   23 km, 14 miles, south-west of Berwick

Walter Espec, the holder of Carham in the 1120s, chose to build his motte and bailey castle at Wark, a couple of miles downstream from the village, because it commanded a recognised ford and had an ideal site, the Kaim, a narrow ridge of gravel and boulders which had been deposited on an otherwise flat and marshy plain by ice-flow.

In the seventh century a large Anglian fort on the Kaim had been responsible for keeping Picts and other undesireables away from Ad Gefrin, King Edwin's palace at Old Yeavering, eight miles to the south. Espec's fortification was intended to keep Scottish raiders from entering King Henry I's domain.

When it was built the River Tweed probably flowed nearer to the Kaim than it does today, and it and marsh to the south would have provided some natural defences for the bailey, while the motte, the nerve-centre of the castle, sat atop the ridge. Even so, much in the way of man-made defences would have been needed, involving the local bondmen in considerable hard work. Perhaps this is why the site is called 'Wark', the phonetic spelling of 'Work' in the Border dialect.

David I, King of the Scots from 1124 to 1153, was the first to test Wark's strength. In 1136 he entered England via Coldstream and lay siege to Wark; the garrison held out for three weeks, then David lost patience and moved on to plunder to the Tyne. On another memorable occasion he sat outside Wark to await the castle's surrender while the main part of his army continued to the Tyne. At Warden it was annihilated by a scratch army of young Hexham men, so David felt obliged to leave Wark and exact payment for his loss from Corbridge. In 1137 David advanced through Northumberland to the outskirts of Durham City before unrest amongst his troops caused him to return to the Border. Morale returned when he got close to home, but again he was frustrated when trying to take Wark.

The taking of Wark became something of an obsession for David, and even after his defeat by King Stephen at the Battle of the Standard in 1138 he felt obliged to try another siege. On this occasion time was on his side; he was content merely to picket the gates to prevent supplies reaching the garrison within. He had to wait a long time, until everything edible in the castle – even the horses – had been consumed and until Baron Espec sent the beleaguered captain his order to surrender. To his credit, David was impressed by the garrison's endurance and bravery and allowed it to leave with full military honours. He even provided the men with horses. Then he razed the castle.

Wark remained in Scottish hands until King Henry II regained control of the Border in 1157 and decided to build castles to discourage further invasions. Espec's daughter Adeline and her husband Piers de Ros had inherited Carham barony in 1153, but the Crown retained Wark until a new stone castle was built on the Kaim. The sheriff of Northumberland was authorised to spend £373 in 1158 on the building. From 1160 until 1295 legal ownership descended linearly through Piers' side of the rather complex Ros family, but from time to time it was borrowed by the Crown for reasons of national defence.

The new castle was a Norman keep and bailey, almost certainly protected by a moat and extremely strong walls. The keep occupied the top of the Kaim while the bailey lay between it and the river.

King John confirmed the grant of the barony, but this did not stop Robert, Piers Ros's grandson, from joining the barons' conspiracy to restrain the king. His loyalty became so obviously fragile John installed his friend and staunch yes-man, Philip d'Ulcote, as captain of Wark castle. Little wonder that Robert was amongst the Northern barons who paid homage to Scots' King Alexander II at Felton in 1215.

Royal vengeance on these miscreants took the form of a blitzkrieg through Northumberland which left several castles and towers smouldering wrecks. Wark was lucky, for although set alight the fire was extinguished before too much damage had been done, and by 1227 it had been restored to full fighting trim, with the Ros's in control.

While King Edward I was travelling north in 1295 to deal with the situation caused by the death of King Alexander III, Robert's grandson, another Robert, suddenly switched to the Scottish side – for the best of reasons: he had fallen in love with a Scots lassie called Christine de Moubray. Edward deviated from his planned route to call at Wark, but when he arrived there he found a kinsman of Robert had already returned the castle to the English. Robert and his new Scottish friends had gone aplundering further south, assuming, correctly, that he had been branded a traitor and had forfeited his property. Edward stayed at Wark until he was ready, the following year, to take Berwick.

The castle remained in Crown hands until 1317, when it was granted to a Yorkshire branch of the Ros family. The new owners did not fancy the hazards of Border life and managed to exchange Wark for Crown land elsewhere. They would not have held it long anyway as Robert Bruce took it in 1318, and held it until it was handed over to King Edward III in 1328 in compliance with the terms of the Treaty of Northampton.

From this time forward, Wark appears to have been regarded as a separate entity, not connected with Carham barony. Thus in 1333 Sir William Montagu was granted the castle alone, as recognition of the valuable services he had rendered at the Battle of Halidon Hill. He was created Earl of Salisbury in 1337.

David Bruce rekindled his father's feud with the English in 1342. After one nearly tragic but fruitful incursion he rushed for home via Wark ford, passing on the way close enough to Wark castle to be seen by the Countess of Salisbury and Sir William Montagu, her nephew. The Earl himself was not at home or he may have laid a restraining hand on the young knight, who let the Scottish soldiers get passed without hindrance then, with the help of a few men, quietly guided the train of pack horses laden with plunder into the castle garth. David turned when this was reported to him, and was about to attack the castle when King Edward III arrived and chased him across the ford.

Edward, who had been trailing the retreating Scots all that day, stayed the night at Wark castle and was suitably entertained by the Countess. According to legend, she dropped a garter during after-dinner dancing; the king picked it up and, with due decorum, handed it back to the lady, an act of gallantry which caused some attendant courtiers to snigger. Edward rounded on them and spoke the immortal words, "Honi soit qui mal y pense" – Shame be he who thinks evil of it. The Latin became the motto of the Order of the Garter which was founded five years after this incident, and Jean Froissart, the French historian who for a time was Edward's wife's secretary, was one of many who believed this chivalric honour was inspired during that dance in Wark castle. Others, including F. Beltz who wrote Memorials of the Order of the Garter in 1853, claimed, with a touch more credibility, that the lady with the loose garter was Joan, the Fair Maid of Kent, who knew Edward much better than did the Countess and who, in fact, became his daughter-in-law in 1361.

The Montagus sold to Ralph Neville in 1397, and he, newly created Earl of Westmorland, exchanged it for Sir Thomas Grey's castle at Castle Heaton. His family retained Wark until 1920, except when Government troops garrisoned the castle, and he executed considerable repairs. These were not completed in 1399 and Sir Thomas's children and some tenants were carried off by marauders for ransom. Sir Thomas happened to be in London at the time, attending King Henry IV's first parliament – the first, incidentally, to use the English language – and the monarch felt it necessary to add insult to injury by reprimanding the poor man for maintaining an inefficient garrison!

The castle fell to French and Scottish raiders in 1419 but was retaken within twenty-four hours. Some servants managed to escape, amongst them a cook who knew the whereabouts of a sewer which ran from the kitchen to the River Tweed. He was able to lead a relieving force up this small passage and the castle was taken by surprise from within. According to W.W. Tomlinson, the remains of this useful sewer were found during nineteenth century excavations.

King Henry VI and his Queen Margaret took refuge in Wark castle on their way to Scotland after escaping from the Yorkist victors of the Battle of Towton in 1461, during the Wars of the Roses. Sir Robert Ogle and Sir John

Conyers attacked the castle to try to winkle them out, but the situation was saved by the prompt action of several squires of the Earl of Northumberland's estates.

The Scottish King James IV was no friend of Wark, sacking the castle in 1496 and again in 1513. King Henry VIII's advisers thought the building should be repaired and garrisoned to deal with the bitterness The Battle of Flodden had stirred up, but the Crown jibbed at the cost and only patchwork was done.

The last major attack on the castle occurred in 1523 and was led by the Duke of Albany, who had a large multi-national army under his command. The outer defenses were damaged by cannon fire, but Sir William Lisle, the resident commander, managed to prevent an entry.

Between 1538 and 1551, while John Carr of Ford was captain of the Government's garrison, the castle was thoroughly overhauled at a cost of £1846. It proved to be a waste of money; there was a puny attack in 1569 during the Rising of the Northern Earls – quickly put down by the king's men – then the castle's days of glory were over. In 1639 its armament was removed and its fabric assigned to nature and stone vandals.

Very little of the castle is visible today – just a few flattish stones which may have belonged to the keep's foundations at the top of the Kaim. Between there and the river is a flat field with no trace of the bailey or its outer defences.

Digression

North Durham and the Prince Bishops

Approximately one-tenth of geographical Northumberland did not come under the auspices of Northumberland County Council until 1844. Until the mid-sixteenth century this component was not even subject to the State laws while between 1559 and 1844 it was part of the county of Durham, although detached from it.

Blame King Oswald. When St. Aiden founded a priory on Lindisfarne in 634 he gave him and all succeeding bishops of Lindisfarne *in perpetuity* this huge plot of land in what was to become Border country. While St. Cuthbert held the see between 685 and 687 the grant acquired the name 'St. Cuthbert's Patrimony', a clever move for the respect and devotion this most famous bishop commanded ensured that ownership would never be forgotten or misapplied.

The grant comprised three 'shires', named later as Norhamshire, Islandshire and Bedlingtonshire. The first two were contiguous and formed a rough triangle with the River Tweed forming one side, the coast from Tweedmouth to Budle Bay another side and an undulating line from Cornhill towards the south-east the base. Bedlingtonshire was an irregular shape further south, between the Rivers Wansbeck and Blyth, containing Bedlington and Choppington. Berwick, Wark, Bamburgh and Ashington were not included in the grant.

In 875 the monks of Lindisfarne fled before Danish invaders. Led by Eardulf, their bishop at the time, and carrying their most treasured artefacts including the stone coffin containing St. Cuthbert's incorruptible body, they wandered around Northern England and Southern Scotland for seven hazardous years before settling in Chester-le-Street, where they built a cathedral church in a former Roman fortlet. While there Eardulf managed somehow to persuade King Alfred and Guthred, his Danish leader in Northumbria, to give him "and those who minister in my church, the whole land between the Wear and the Tine, for a perpetual possession". The grant was confirmed two centuries later and formed the basis upon which the County Palatine of Durham was established. In an era when land ownership was synonymous with wealth, Eardulf was a very rich man, and he became even richer just before he died, in 900, by annexing the vacant diocese of Hexham. This, however, was not 'perpetual'; in 1071 it was handed from Durham to York.

Further Danish invasions in 995 caused the Lindisfarne congregation to move from Chester-le-Street to Ripon, where they stayed a few years before making their final move to Dunholme, a peninsula-like prominence overlooking the River Wear. Here Bishop Aldene established the Durham convent and church in, or just before, 1018.

The coming of the Normans had little effect on religious beliefs in the North generally (although it had on religious buildings), but it made a profound difference in Durham. William the Conqueror appointed Walcher, the son of a Lorraine nobleman, to the bishopric in 1072. Although he was an ecclesiastic, this was primarily a political and military assignment, for William needed a loyal (ie French) and trustworthy leader in the north of his realm to defend the English/Scottish Border and to control the still rebellious native population. To do this job effectively, William realised, Walcher had to have executive power with the authority to act on his own initiative without recourse to the distant seat of government, so in 1076 Walcher was made Earl of Northumberland and, confirming and extending King Alfred's grant, the liberty-holder of most of what is now County Durham. Durham castle was built as a fortified residence for this exalted personage.

The castle did not protect Walcher from an angry mob in 1080 and he was assassinated. He was succeeded as bishop by William de St. Calais, but the Northumbrian earldom went to another Norman called Alberic. The County Palatine of Durham remained the bishop's liberty although it was still not geographically complete, a tract of land centred on the village of Sadberge and extending to Hartlepool in the north-east and nearly to Barnard Castle in the west remaining in Northumberland. This, the Wapentake of Sadberge, had been settled in the tenth century by Scandinavian laymen from Yorkshire, and their descendants were strong-willed enough to resist the grasping bishops until the whole of Northumberland was sold to Hugh Pudsey, the bishop at the time, by King Richard 1, the Lionheart, in the early 1190s. That king sold anything he could to get his travelling expenses for crusading. The Tweed to Tyne part of the sale was retrieved after four years, but the Wapentake remained in the bishops' possession.

It should be made clear at this stage that the Bishop of Durham had now, and until the sixteenth century, two quite separate roles to play. As a churchman he was the spiritual leader of a diocese covering Durham and, for some time, Northumberland, and he was the titular head of the Durham monastery. As the holder of the Durham liberty, or palatinate but popularly known as the bishopric, he had the powers of a feudal king. He appointed his own chancellor, sheriffs, judges and coroners, he administered civil and criminal law in his own name, he minted his own coinage and collected his own taxes. He claimed all the perks of royalty in matters of forestry laws, purveyance and wreck regulations. He was the Prince Bishop, the Viceroy, the ultimate authority within his province.

Like a king, he owned considerable demesne land, including what was now being called North Durham – St. Cuthbert's Patrimony This had been granted to the Durham bishops, not to the Durham Church, so it was his personal property. At the same time, of course, a lot of the bishopric was held by landed gentry for feudal type service. Throughout the Middle Ages Hartlepool was held by the Brus family, the kin of Robert Bruce, King of Scotland, and later by the Cliffords. Another Scottish royal family, the Balliols, held Barnard Castle from 1093 to 1306, the Lumleys had a castle near Chester-le-Street, the Hiltons held Hylton and the Eures had Witton-le-Wear. The most important from the local history standpoint were the Nevilles of Raby and Bracepeth who, in 1397, were raised to the peerage as the Earls of Westmorland.

The succession of Prince Bishops prospered for several centuries, but not so the Lindisfarne community. After guarding the shrine of St. Cuthbert for nearly four hundred years, they were disbanded in 1083 when Bishop St. Calais obtained papal permission to replace them with Benedictine monks from Jarrow monastery, which had been re-established just nine years earlier. The official reason for the replacement was the laxity of the old order of monks and their neglect of their vows, but, while this charge no doubt had some substance, it may be relevant that Jarrow was poor and unknown and badly needed the riches and the pilgrims Durham enjoyed. The monastic buildings at Durham were improved for the benefit of the newcomers, and work on the famous cathedral was started. The Lindisfarne monks were retired to pastoral duties in Darlington, Auckland and Norton. To their credit, the Benedictines tended St. Cuthbert's shrine with dignified respect, and paid a rich compliment to his memory by founding a new priory on Lindisfarne Island in 1093.

The Tudor kings were less indulgent with respect to Durham than their predecessors had been, partly because the need for a strong personality there was diminishing as Northumberland's defences on the Border were improving, partly because power in churchmen's hands was becoming unpopular and partly because the Prince Bishops' court was seen as distastefully lavish and extravagant. A series of events took place during the sixteenth century which completely changed the picture.

First, Parliament passed the Jurisdiction of Liberties Act in 1536 and Bishop Tunstall was deprived of his authority to try criminals. In that year, also, King Henry VIII, mindful of vox populi while following his own wishes, began dissolving the smaller monasteries and the writing was writ large on the walls of the larger establishments. The Pilgrimage of Grace, a rebellion partly supportive of Roman Catholicism, was very effectively squashed and Durham monastery was dissolved without trouble in 1539. It became a seminary for clerics of the English faith.

Bishop Tunstall survived all this, inspite of loss of palatine powers and the patronage of Rome, and he continued as a Church of England prelate for twenty more years. Then in 1559 he was required to swear the Oath of Supremacy to Queen Elizabeth – and this he refused to do. The Queen relieved him of all his remaining privileges and civil duties, and he died the following year.

The County Palatine of Durham became the civil County Durham, subject to the ordinary laws, customs and administration of an English shire. North Durham – Norhamshire, Islandshire and Bedlingtonshire – became a detached part of this. Some of the Bishops' private property was appropriated by the Crown, but a lot of it was retained as personal holdings. Thus, for example, Queen Elizabeth was quite in order when she granted Norham Castle to Lord Hunsdon in 1571, while Bishop Barnes was equally within the law when he leased Choppington Tower to Cuthbert Ogle in 1578. Over succeeding years much of both the Crown and the bishops' land was sold.

The final chapter in the saga of North Durham came in 1844 when Sir Robert Peel's government succeeded in getting Parliament to agree that "Areas lying within the geographical confines of one county yet are part of another county although physically separated from it should in future be part of the county to which it is physically attached". This clearly applied to North Durham, which thus was absorbed into Northumberland.

Area 1, Sub-Area B   South-West of Berwick

Thornton

L74 & 75   P451   NT946480   7 km, 4¹/₂ miles, south-west of Berwick

Some grass-covered bumps in a field by Thornton Cottage, 500 yards to the north-west of Thornton hamlet, look suspiciously like shrouds over the remains of a small medieval tower which was built during the latter part of the fourteenth century by the Herons of Ford.

Thornton manor was granted by the Bishop of Durham to William Heron of Ford in 1348. He installed his third son, John, there, and some years later built the tower, with barnekyn, for him. Part of the manor was held by Sir John Widdrington in 1443, but the tower remained Heron property until the Carrs took over Ford and its affiliated estates in c1558. By then it was ruinous, thanks to King James IV's pre-Battle of Floddon preparations in 1513.

In 1561 one corner of the tower had been repaired. it was sold by William Carr to Sir John Selby, gentleman porter in Berwick and owner of Shoreswood and part of Branxton. He willed his estates to his daughter and her husband, Sir William Forster of Bamburgh castle. Much later, in 1721, they formed parts of the Lord Crewe Charity Trust.

Shoreswood

74 & 75   P451   NT940465   9 km, 5¹/₂ miles, south-west of Berwick

This tower was amongst the many King James IV 'caste down' during his raid of 1496. The damage sustained was considerable and the building was never repaired, even though Christopher Dacre reported in 1584 that it was "very fit and convenient to defend the country and annoy the enemy". The cost of making it operational was estimated as £240.

At about this time the tower ruin and the adjoining 'gentleman's house' were owned by Sir John Selby of Berwick. He died in 1595 and nothing further is known about the place, save that in 1830 it belonged to the Craster family. No part of the tower has survived, and indeed the exact site is not known now.

Felkington

L74 & 75   P451   NT943442   10¹/₂ km, 6¹/₂ miles, south-west of Berwick

The Survey Booke of Norham and Islandshire of 1561 states: "In the town of Felkyngton is no tower or pile but one bastall house of small strength". It is possible the writer was referring to a bastle to our specification, for inceptive quantities were being built at that time, but more likely he meant what we would call a strong house – an isolated stone building designed to give some protection against raiders. Nothing remains today to help solve the question.

In 1631 the owner of Felkington was John Orde, who also had West Newbiggin. Both properties were still in the Orde family at the beginning of the eighteenth century, and William Orde built a mansion at Sandybank in Felkington. It was demolished in 1818 because it was thought to be haunted.

Grindonrigg

L74 & 75   P451   NT925431   12 km, 7^1/$_2$ miles, south-west of Berwick

First heard of as part of the Tillmouth estate held from the Durham bishops by the Riddells. During most of the thirteenth century it was sub-let to the Grendon family. Sir William Riddell, styled the first Lord of Tillmouth, left Tillmouth, Duddo and Grindonrigg to his daughter Isabella in 1325; she was married into the Clavering family of Callaly so Sir Alan de Clavering became the second Lord of Tillmouth. He regarded Grindonrigg as just another farm and the family held it to 1510, when it was sold to the Selbys.

The head of the Selby family built a tower at Grindonrigg while the lady of the house built a bridge over the River Till near Twizel. The former was small, in good condition in 1541 and was home to a farmer. The latter was completed just in time to carry the Earl of Surrey and his troops on their way to Flodden; it still stands, an elegant single span with a wonderful view, but now it is helped by an adjacent concrete structure. There is nothing left of the tower.

Surprisingly few raiders appear to have come Grindonrigg way, but there was a nasty moment in 1558 when a Franco-Scottish force came close. Fortunately the Earl of Northumberland and Sir Henry Percy, his brother, accompanied by a strong mounted contingent, were in the area and were able to chase the invaders away. It has been suggested that the Duddo Stones – which at NT930437 are nearer to Grindonrigg than they are to Duddo – were erected to commemorate this 'victory', but in fact they are relics of the Neolithic Stone Age; the four stones make a miniature henge which was built some three thousand years earlier.

The Selbys sold Grindonrigg in 1694 to William Strother of Fowberry and Kirknewton. He did not want to live in his new acquisition so he did nothing to the tower, but his grandson rather fancied the place and built a Georgian mansion, probably on the tower's site. There is a small estate of about half a dozen select houses there now.

Duddo

L75 & 76   P451   NT938425   12 km, 7^1/$_2$ miles, south-west of Berwick

Another part of the Tillmouth estate which went by marriage to the Clavering family in 1325. It was used to house, and to provide employment for, junior sons of the Callaly family for the best part of five hundred years – until Sir Francis Blake bought it from John Clavering in 1788.

There was no defensive building here until just after 1415, and then a tower was built which lasted only about eighty years before King James IV knocked it down. It was not replaced or repaired and the Claverings lived in an unfortified building at the east end of the village. They seemed to have been disdainful of the danger from Scottish raids, and in fact when one of them, William Clavering, was killed in 1586 it was not by the hand of a Scot but of a neighbour, John Selby. William was the innocent victim when John attacked Sir Cuthbert Collingwood, with whom he was in deadly feud.

The tower was still an abandoned ruin in 1561 but some years later it was rebuilt and a barmekyn added, perhaps as a result of Christopher Dacre's survey. It has suffered considerably since then, partly because of coal mining beneath it, and a single jagged tooth atop a three hundred feet rocky hill is all that can be seen today.

Castle Heaton

L74 & 75   P451   NT900418   14½ km, 9 miles, south-west of Berwick

Although sited above the left, or south-west, bank of River Till, this large estate nevertheless was part of the Durham bishops' Norhamshire until the middle of the sixteenth century. Originally it was called 'Heton' and it is only within the last one hundred and fifty years that the name has been changed, first to the phonetically more correct 'Heaton', then to 'Old Heaton' to distinguish it from 'New Heaton', a farm a mile or two to the south-west which had been detached from the main estate, and finally to 'Castle Heaton', presumably in recognition of its former status.

The bishops' first recorded tenants here were the Etons. Reversing the usual order of things, they appear to have given their family name to the place, taking an aspirate on board while doing so. By 1300 the family was calling itself 'de Heton', following the fashion of the time. They were medium ranking landed gentry, rich enough to lend money to Nicholas de Neubaud and shrewd enough to take the tenancy of Chevelyngham manor-house as collateral. Nicholas had inherited the Chevelyngham property from his uncle, lead an improvident life, could not repay his debts and suffered foreclosure in 1328. The de Hetons became 'de Chevelynghams' and Heton was sold to Thomas Grey, a member of a highly respected military family, two of whom were captains of Norham castle.

The Greys knocked down the building at Heton and in its place built a castle. Old records and plans tell us this was a very strong, square complex which included a keep and a great hold called the Lion's Tower as well as the usual garrison and household buildings, all contained within a wall with turrets at its four corners and southern entrance. There is no doubt it was a true castle and not just an elaborate tower: this is stressed because what is left for us to see today is nothing like a castle.

In 1398 another Thomas Grey and Ralph Neville, Earl of Westmorland, exchanged homes, Neville getting the new castle and Grey the battle-hardened fortification at Wark-on-Tweed. Neville had moved into Wark only the year before and had not liked it; he did not like Castle Heaton either and moved out before the year-end. Grey repossessed Castle Heaton while retaining Wark.

Meanwhile the de Hetons had been doing some castle building of their own, and by 1348 Chevelyngham manor-house had become Chillingham castle. Like Castle Heaton, it was a grand and secure home, no doubt the envy of many other landowners, yet the de Hetons did not hold it for very long. A page of history is missing here, but at some time between 1415 and 1440 the de Hetons disappeared and Sir Ralph Grey added Chillingham to his list of castles. His family lived in Chillingham castle until 1832 and retained it until 1982, they retained Wark castle until 1920 and Castle Heaton was theirs until the latter part of the sixteenth century.

Castle Heaton suffered more than Chillingham, and had less attention paid to it than had Wark. In 1496 and again in 1513 King James IV attacked it and left it a roofless, floorless ruin. The Greys obtained legal ownership in 1559 when the Durham bishops' jurisdiction came to an end, but they had no incentive to repair and they sold it to the resident farmer.

After the Union of the Crowns, 1603, the ruin was dismantled and the stones used to build a farmhouse and associated buildings. One part of the old castle, probably a section of the keep, was repaired and retained, however, and this is still in use today. It measures 70 by 17 feet and has a ground floor which serves as a stable and an upper floor, reached by external stone stairs, which makes a very dry grannery.

Area 1, Sub-Area C   South from Berwick

Ancroft

L75   P452   NU002451   8 km, 5 miles, south of Berwick

The medieval village was a short distance from the modern one, on the left bank of the Dean Burn (P451, NT996450), and was well known in its day for clog making. A family of cloggers had settled here at an unknown early date and a rewarding trade was maintained – even after clogs went out of fashion, for the villagers were able to adapt their skills to boot making and it is claimed that Marlborough's army marched not on its stomach but on Ancroft boots. There has always been a strong agricultural interest here also, and amongst the most affluent farmers was a family called Revelye.

Ancroft was in Islandshire, part of the County Palatine of Durham. When the bishops established their subordinate priory on Lindisfarne, Ancroft and a few other places on the mainland were given to it so that their corn tithes might provide a little wealth. The Church of St. Mary on the island was Ancroft's parish church, but as it was an impossible distance from the village the monks built a chapel-of-ease for the villagers, and installed a resident curate. The chapel retains much of its Norman original, inspite of a thorough renovation in 1870.

When new the chapel was a basic chancel and nave structure, but a fortified tower was added to its west end in the thirteenth century. This was the curate's lodging, but he was expected to share its protection with the villagers in times of raids or war. It is well preserved and still exhibits a vaulted ground floor and spiral stairs to two upper floors. Originally the only way in was from the church,but a door from the graveyard was inserted later.

No man-made defence had any effect when the dreaded plague attacked, however. Ancroft villagers suffered greatly, especially in 1667 when the disease was so devastating their normal funeral procedures could not cope. With special dispensation from the Prior, they carried the terminally infected people to an uncultivated field outside the village, there to await death under the cover of small bowers of broom. When the inevitable happened the bodies were cremated on the spot by setting fire to the broom. The field is called 'Broomie-huts' to this day.

Berrington

L75   P452   NU007431   10½ km, 6½ miles, south of Berwick

Many generations of the Manners family of Etal held this small Islandshire township from 1327 onwards. They built a tower in it before 1415 as a refuge for their tenants. By 1541, when the owner was the Earl of Rutland, the honour to which Thomas Manners had been elevated in 1525, the tower had fallen into 'extreme decay'. John Revelye started to repair it in 1561 but, whether or not he completed the task, there is nothing left now.

Barmoor

L75   P463   NT996398   13 km, 8 miles, south of Berwick

Stephen Muschamp, a young brother of the Wooler baron, started the Barmoor branch of the family in or about 1200. They lived in timber houses at first but in 1341 a descendant, Thomas Muschamp, obtained a licence to build a tower from King Edward III and the result was styled 'Barmoor Castle'. It failed to keep out raiders in 1367 when Thomas was relieved of eight men, two horses and a quantity of gold, silver and other valuables assessed at £20.

Barmoor occupied a key position on the Border as it gave direct access to all the Tweed crossings. It became a favourite place in which to muster armies, as did Earl Henry Percy in 1417 before marching to Roxburgh, the Earl of Surrey in 1513 before Flodden and the Earl of Surrey again in 1523 before attacking the Duke of Albany. The March wardens also used the place on several occasions as a raiding party assembly point.

In 1514 the tower was still serviceable and capable of lodging thirty horsemen, but by 1541 it was said to be ruinous, and the Muschamps did nothing to correct this. A century later they supported King Charles I and when the Civil War was over the fines imposed by Parliament ruined them. They had to sell Barmoor to William and Margaret Carr of Etal. By 1680 this couple had breathed new life into the tower by converting it into a comfortable home.

A succession of owners followed the Carrs and in 1791 the Sitwell family took over. In 1801 they commissioned a Mr Patterson of Edinburgh to build them a mansion. This architect did what Sir Francis Blake had started at Fowberry and Twizel – he left the Carrs' home as it was and built a very beautiful house around it.

For at least a century and a half this was the Sitwells' home, where in 1927 Brigadier-General William Sitwell wrote The Border from a Soldier's Point of View. During the 1980s, however, the mansion was empty and very much the worse for wear; many of its doors and windows were broken, part of the roof had disappeared and vegetation was colonising the ground floor.

But all was not lost. Young, energetic entrepreneurs took over the estate and by June 1990 they had opened the large garden as a discrete and uncrowded caravan park. A year later they had repaired the roof of the house and were laying plans to gut the building and convert it into holiday flats. They were in the business of inviting guests to take part in the rebirth of a historic Border hold.

Lowick

L75   P464   NU014396   13 km, 8 miles, south of Berwick

In the twelfth century, Lowick, like Barmoor, was a township in the Wooler barony. Two centuries later it had been split into two parts, one owned by the Hetons of Chillingham, the other had been granted to Lindisfarne Priory.

The lay part was bequeathed to his daughter Joan when Sir Alan Heton died and the title passed to her husband, Sir Robert Ogle. In 1399 he re-assigned it to his relative, John Ogle, of Whiston in Lancashire. He had little use for the property and eventually, it is believed, it was absorbed into the Priory's part.

Lowick was important to Lindisfarne as a hospitality halt for the many visitors to the priory who used the best roads in the district, the old Roman

Devils Causeway and its slip road to Beal. A chapel was built at the join and here the travellers rested until the tide ebbed sufficiently to permit a plodge to the island. It was a good place, too, to build a fortified tower, for unfortunately not all the travellers were friendly.

The 'when and where' questions about this tower can only be answered with possible clues. The building was standing in 1415 when Dom de Darcy, a Lindisfarne monk, was recorded as owner but it was not new then. The township suffered numerous raids during the fourteenth century, but they ceased after 1380, and one explanation for this was that the tower deterred raiders. A field name in the township could hint at where the tower was located: it is called 'Bastle Corner'. The building was not a bastle as we know them, but the word was often used for any fortified structure standing alone in the middle ages.

The monks used the tower until the priory was dissolved in 1537 and its property grabbed by the State. It was sold to the Swinburnes of Capheaton. By 1541 its roof was damaged. Christopher Dacre recommended its repair in 1581 but nothing was done and the building is not mentioned again.

Holburn

L75   P464   NU041361   17^1/$_2$ km, 10^3/$_4$ miles, south of Berwick

Here was another tower which served the Lindisfarne monks well in the fourteenth, fifteenth and sixteenth centuries before disappearing without trace. Holburn township covered quite a large area of Kyloe southern foothills: Holburn itself is a pleasant hamlet of a few cottages, a farm and an interesting water trough, but there is also Holburn Mill and Holburn Grange and any of these places could have been the site of the tower.

Once part of the Wooler barony, the township was granted to the priory in the twelfth century, and the monks grazed their cattle and dug the peat there. They were specially fond of the place because it included a memorial to their most cherished predecessor, St. Cuthbert. This is a cave above Holburn Grange (NU059352) where the great man was want to rest and pray from time to time. The tower is no more but the cave is still there, on National Trust land a short walk from a car park near the farm, and is well worth visiting if only for the view.

Raiders left the area waste in 1350 and this experience probably prompted the monks to build the tower. It was mentioned in the 1415 survey, and by 1514 it was said to be suitable for a garrison of twenty men. This did not stop more raiders from playing havoc in 1516 when practically everything moveable was taken, including livestock and several villagers.

After dissolution in 1537 the Crown sold the township to Thomas Holburne, a local man. By 1541 he had reconditioned the tower and built a barmekyn, yet more villagers and cattle were captured by raiders in 1553. The tower was abandoned to nature.

Area 1, Sub-Area D   The Coast from Berwick to Budle Bay
Tweedmouth

L75   P438   NT993525   ½ km, 600 yards, south of Berwick

There appears to have been two towers here, one built in the twelfth century and another in the sixteenth, both designed to impede Scottish invasions from Berwick.

The Durham bishops built the first, for Tweedmouth was in their Islandshire liberty. There is nothing today to indicate its site, but it is a safe bet it was constructed on the higher ground facing Berwick's first wooden bridge.

When Scottish King William the Lion became obstreperous after regaining Berwick and its new, English-made, castle, King John attempted in 1204 to extend and strengthen this tower. Twice his attempt was thwarted by William, and in 1209 John succumbed to a pecuniary inducement to abandon his building plans and to destroy the tower.

The second tower was mentioned in a report of 1541 without its owner's name. In 1555 Odnell Selby bequeathed to his wife Jannet "the tower we do dwell in". Selby was a name to conjure with on the Border so Odnell may have been the builder, or perhaps the Durham bishop provided it for him.

The ruins of the tower existed in 1753 – "lately the property of William Armorer, deceased" – but nothing remains of it today. It probably had occupied the first tower's site.

Spittal

L75   P438   NU005518   1½ km, 1 mile, south-east of Berwick

Spittal is an extension of Tweedmouth which grew round a leper hospital – hence its name – which King Edward I is given the credit of founding. In 1369 the master of the hospital was John de Bather, a cousin of the then Bishop of Durham, and he built a small tower for the protection of his staff and inmates. It was still in reasonable condition in 1541, and even as late as 1612 it remained an entry in court rolls, where it was called 'Bather's Tower'.

There are no remains to be seen today, and its site is not known for certain. The leper hospital was dedicated to St. Bartholomew, but so was the parish church so current use of that name is likely to relate to the church and cannot be used as a clue to the tower's position. The frequent discovery of human bones in an area which in the eighteenth century was part of Spittal Hall Farm is a more hopeful indication, however, but by no means conclusive. The farm was close to the mouth of the Tweed, in the north-eastern part of the town.

Scremerston

L75   P452   NU006493   4 km, 2½ miles south of Berwick

Scremerston started life as a farm, developed into a village, grew into a coal-mining town then settled down as a suburb of Berwick. The name comes from the original farmer, Skremerston, who leased the land from the Bishop of Durham during the twelfth century.

A story is told about a later farmer who styled himself 'The Lord of Scremerston'. He entertained Bishop Robert de Insula in 1274 and, as a good host should, he offered his guest a mug of the local country brew. Not wishing to offend, the bishop accepted the drink with gratitude although his palate was more attune to softed beverages. His first sip confirmed his worst fears: it was so terrible that honesty got the better of good manners and he had to tell his host he found the stuff quite unpalatable.

William Swinhoe got possession through marriage in the early years of the fourteenth century. Their son, William Two, married a daughter of Robert Grey and acquired part of Cornhill when his father-in-law died in 1338. When his own father died, in about 1360 he found himself the proud holder of both Scremerston and property in Cornhill. When he died one son, William Three, inherited the Cornhill estate and the other, John, the whole of Scremerston. He built a tower before 1402.

The family prospered when coal was found on their land and they invested in the holding of Behill, a part of Goswick, where a junior member set up home. In 1530 they teamed up with a Newcastle family called Lawson to buy Rock, a healthy farming estate just north of Alnwick. John Swinhoe, the last male of the Scremerston line, died in about 1538 and his heiress married Edmund Lawson, who thus became sole owner of the property. The Cornhill Swinhoes continued to about 1631 and the Goswick branch to between 1640 and 1650.

The Durham bishops were disenfranchised in 1559 and for a time Islandshire was Crown land. By 1561 the Lawsons had repaired their tower and had built a barmekyn, but they did not buy the freehold which, in 1601 was granted by the king to George Home, Earl of Dunbar. Twelve years later it passed to Lord Walden, Earl of Suffolk. The Lawsons were still residents but they neglected their tower which had decayed quickly since the Union of the Crowns.

Around 1625 the then current Lawson married a daughter of Sir William Fenwick, Meg of Meldon's son. He bought Scremerston from the Earl of Suffolk and gave the deeds to the young couple as a wedding present. In return they produced for him two grandchildren, who inherited jointly when their father died in 1655. One child, Catherine, married Sir Francis Radcliffe (the first Earl of Derwentwater to be) in 1660. The other, a son, sold his share to

Berwick Corporation, who wished to take advantage of the now flourishing mining industry. Sir Francis was rich enough, however, to buy out the Corporation, so Scremerston, once more united, became a Derwentwater property.

The plague struck Scremerston hard in 1667. As at Ancroft, victims fell too quickly for the normal funeral procedures and the terminally ill were carried to the coast at Cocklawburn, there to await death beneath flimsy shelters of bent grass.

All Derwentwater estates were sequestrated by the Crown in 1715 because of the third earl's participation in the Jacobite rebellion. In 1735 Scremerston was granted to Greenwich Hospital, and a trust set up by that body is still the principal landowner in the neighbourhood. It no doubt derived much financial benefit from the coal mines which supplied Berwick and Tweedmouth and all local places in the eighteenth century, and places further afield in the nineteenth century. In 1847 the Newcastle to Tweedmouth railway was opened, principally to distribute Scremerston coal, and in 1871 a new dock at Tweedmouth was commissioned to cope with the shipping of the coal.

No pits are working today; they are just memories encapsulated in a few disused air and mine shafts, and in local names like Old Colliery Wood, Deputy Row and the Miners' Arms. The foundations of the tower could be traced in a field on the north side of the village in the nineteenth century, but nothing that can be positively identified from ground level is there now.

Goswick

L75   P452   NU057452   10½ km, 6½ miles, south-east of Berwick

Closely associated with Scremerston through the Swinhoe family who arrived on the scene in the fifteenth century. Before then the township had been held jointly from the Durham bishops by Adam de Behill, Henry de Goswick and Patrick de Goswick. Each paid tithes on all their products except lamb to the Lindisfarne priory.

The Scremerston Swinhoes bought the Behill holding, probably that part around Beal, and installed a junior member there. The other two parts eventually descended to the Middlehams, but the three parts were united in the fifteenth century when William Swinhoe married a Middleham heiress. Their descendants continued to live in Goswick until 1640, when the estate was sold to Thomas Watson, a former mayor or Berwick.

Although there was no local fortified tower up to 1550, there was one on Thomas Swinhoe's land in 1561, quite a large one at that. It was frequently altered until it was knocked down at the end of the Watson dynasty in 1823.

Cheswick

L75   P452   NU031465   7 km, 4½ miles, south-east of Berwick

Cheswick lies between Scremerston and Goswick but is related to neither. The Lindisfarne monks owned three acres in the township around their tithe barn and the rest was held by farmers who were identified in the fourteenth century as John de Hagardestun, Patrick de Chesewic and his nephew, William de Chesewic. A little later there were four holders for Patrick willed his part to his two daughters, Matilda and Elizabeth.

John changed his surname to Haggerston and his family held their portion to 1631 as an extension to their main property two miles to the south. William sold his lease to Sir Thomas Grey in 1369 and they held the property until 1677. Matilda married Robert de Strangeways of Ketton, near Aycliffe and they held their share until the eighteenth century. Finally, Elizabeth married Robert de Manners of Etal so her portion went along the Rutland line until the seventeenth century.

In all this roll-call of holders, Robert Strangeways was the only one to build a tower. It was constructed just before 1400 on the north side of his estate and it lasted a hundred and fifty years. There is no trace of it now.

Haggerston

L75   P452   NU040436   10½ km, 6½ miles, south-east of Berwick

John de Hagardestun, a Scot who could trace his ancestry for at least a hundred years and who held a considerable amount of land in Scotland, chose to live here, south of the Border, when he joined the Scottish barons who swore fealty to King Edward I in 1296. He seems to have been well known in the English court, for in 1311 he gave hospitality to King Edward II, and it was here the king received the homage of Thomas Earl of Lancaster for the additional earldom of Lincoln. The double earl, the High Steward of England, was in the district looking for a good place to build a castle: Dunstanburgh was started two years later.

Robert, John's son, changed his surname to Haggerston. He obtained a licence to crenellate from King Edward III in 1345 and replaced his manor-house with a tower, said at the time "to be strong and square". A later Haggerston, Thomas, rather unusually was allowed to buy his vill from the Durham bishops in 1388; he was still owner in 1415 and the tower was well maintained. And so it was in 1538 and 1541, but it was badly damaged by fire in 1618. It was replaced immediately, but by a cowboy who, it was discovered later, built the walls of wood and wickerwork with only a thin facing of stone.

A later Thomas Haggerston distinguished himself in the Civil War as a colonel in the Marquis of Newcastle's army and was created a baronet by King Charles I in 1643. His son, a second Sir Thomas, married Jane, the heiress of Sir William Carnaby, and they had many children who started cadet branches of the Haggerston family. Perhaps it was because of this population explosion that yet another Sir Thomas built a mansion adjoining the tower in 1777. This did not satisfy his son, Sir Carnaby Haggerston, who in or about 1805 pulled down the tower and built a wing to the new mansion on its foundations, and another on its other side.

This complex must have been enormous, but it lacked the desired elegance and air of sophistication, so in 1889 Norman Shaw, of Cragside fame, was commissioned to improve its appearance. In about 1892 a close relative replaced the main family. He was Christopher John Leyland, who in 1897 commanded the Turbinia at Spithead Review.

The mansion was soon replaced after a disastrous fire in 1911,and this time the family's long history was reflected in the plans – they included a tall tower. The total building cost was said to be £250,000, a lot of money in pre-Great War days.

The family did not enjoy their new home. It was sold and the purchaser demolished the house in 1931, leaving only the mock tower to stand alone. It is not alone today: it is the central attraction in the Haggerston Castle Holiday Park and is crowded around with caravans.

Lindisfarne

L75   P452   NU126417   17 km, 10¹/₂ miles, south-east of Berwick

The church and monastery founded in 634 by St. Aiden with the assistance of his great friend and benefactor, King Oswald, appear to have had no man-made fortifications: the monks seemed to think their faith was strong enough to resist the enemy, but helpful also was the close proximity of the royal vill of Bamburgh, the tides which sealed off the island twice a day and the prominence of their position on the Heugh.

And indeed the enemy did not bother them for nearly a hundred and sixty years, throughout the golden era when Lindisfarne became Europe's foremost seat of learning and the arts, when Christian teaching spread out from it over most of England and when it was the domicile of St. Cuthbert, arguably our most celebrated saint. Nor was solvency a worry, thanks to St. Cuthbert's Patrimony and other gifts of real estate given to them by King Egfrid in 685 and King Ceolwulf in 737.

But the wealth of the community attracted the Danes. Their attack in 793 was so devastating that when news came of the approach of more Danes in 875 the monks decided that discretion was the better part of valour and left the island, never to return.

A new priory was founded on Lindisfarne by the Benedictine monks of Durham in 1093. They built their church first, about half the size but otherwise very similar to their new cathedral at Durham but sited on flat land just a few feet above sea-level. The monastic buildings were constructed intermittently over two centuries, parts being added as money became available and as accommodation requirements grew with the developing importance of the priory as a Mecca for pilgrims. One of the last buildings was a replacement prior's lodging, erected in 1341. The date is significant for it means that the monks knew what the Post-Bannockburn Scots and the rebellious Borderers had done on the mainland and could quite easily do on their island. For the first time they thought about fortifications, and some strength was included in the building plans. Strong, wide walls with a turret between were constructed along the two outer sides of the lodging, and a barbican was built onto the refractory's southern entrance from the courtyard. Some outer walls were strengthened and the main gate on the west side of the complex was provided with a 'yethouse' or gatehouse tower. The monks even looked beyond their walls and erected small watch towers overlooking the Ouse, one at Steel End and the other on the Beblowe, a sheer pinnacle of basalt rock.

While all this was going on the lay population of the island was growing steadily and a village appeared close to the priory. Most of the men were fishermen, but they and their wives made extra money selling victuals to the pilgrims. They were renowned, also, for salvaging property from wrecks. As one would expect on a holy island, they were seen often on their knees when a vessel sailed close to shore, but they were not praying for the safety of those on board; they were mouthing, "God send her to us".

The priory was dissolved officially in 1537 but the last prior, Thomas Sparks, and his monks were allowed to stay until 1541. Like the mainland County Palatine, the island outside the priory belonged to the bishop, but Bishop Tunstall forfeited it when he refused to take the Oath of Supremacy to Queen Elizabeth I in 1559. Then the Crown assumed responsibility as landowners and a captain was put in charge of Lindisfarne and the Farne Islands.

An Order in Council was issued in 1539 which made it compulsory for all havens to be "Fensed with bulworks and blockehouses". It made a lot of sense in Lindisfarne's case as the island was close to a sea lane used frequently by Scottish and French vessels and pirate ships, any of which could invade. By 1550 the watch tower on the Beblowe had been replaced by a sturdy-looking stone fort, built very largely with dressed stone taken from the deserted priory. It was garrisoned by twenty soldiers.

In 1604, as payment for overseeing a thorough enforcement of law and order along the Border, King James I of England and VI of Scotland conveyed large tracts of Northern England to George Home, the Earl of Dunbar. Lindisfarne, except the Beblowe fort, was included in this grant and thus was passed on to Theophilus Lord Howard of Walden (later the Earl of Suffolk) when Lord Home died in 1611 and his daughter, Lord Howard's wife, inherited.

The Beblowe fort remained as Crown property. It commanded a wide view over the sea approaches to the island, but it was considered to be too far from the Ouse to control vessels entering or leaving the harbour, so, in 1675, the old watch tower at Steel End, on the eastern tip of the Heugh, was replaced by a small fort which was within hailing distance of the harbour entrance. A small part of it, a featureless ruin, remains standing today.

The fortunes of the Beblowe fort are more interesting. It was repaired in 1555, perhaps extended too, for by the turn of the century it was housing a garrison of forty men. Thirty of them succumbed to the plague in 1639 and were not replaced.

By 1715 the number had dropped to seven – a leader and three watches of two. Thus it was easy that year for Lancelot Errington, the master of a Newcastle brigantine, and his nephew Mark to trick their way into the fort and to declare it a prize for the Jacobite rebels. It was a short-lived victory for they were ousted the next day by a detachment sent from Berwick.

Coastguards replaced soldiers in the nineteenth century, then even they were regarded as superfluous and the fort was left uninhabited until it was bought in 1902 by Edward Hudson, founder of Country Life. He commissioned Edwin Lutyens, architect of the London Cenotaph and Liverpool's R.C. cathedral, to convert it into a private residence, a job he did with great sympathy, partly by joining two turrets with a long gallery. The result is a most romantic-looking small 'castle' which rivals anything to be seen on the banks of the Rhine.

The substantial and beautiful ruins of the priory are cared for by English Heritage, who also maintain a small museum. The 'castle' and its contents of old Flemish and English oak furniture collected by Edward Lutyens are owned by the National Trust.

Fenham

L75   P452   NU086407   15$\frac{1}{2}$ km, 9$\frac{1}{2}$ miles, south-east of Berwick

Bishop St. Calais of Durham granted this Islandshire township to his new subsidiary priory of Lindisfarne in 1093 or 4 as one of its first endowments. Good use was made of the gift right up to 1537 when the priory was dissolved.

The monks quickly built a grange and a mill so that they could store and process the corn – mostly barley but some wheat – which they grew themselves or received as tithes. The mill was sited on the coastline, just a yard or two from the mud of Fenham Flats, now part of the Lindisfarne National

Nature Reserve. A stream which drained the fens further inland, the Mill Burn, was diverted so that its water could rush down onto the mill wheel.

Although the monks on the island seemed unperturbed about the danger of Scottish raids, here on the mainland it was deemed prudent to take precautions, and they built what is believed to have been a small motte and bailey castle on a slight elevation behind the mill. There is nothing to see now as the site has been made into a garden for the cottage which has replaced the mill.

The grange, or tithe barn, was built near a well a few hundred yards inland from the mill. Close to it, a manor-house was built to enable the monk in-charge to 'live above the shop'. The house was large and built of stone, but not really defendable until it was altered and strengthened in 1339. Then a 'tower chamber' with vaulted ceiling was incorporated within its walls. In 1385 it got a moat by further diverting the Mill Burn to swing round the building.

The mill and the grange became the stage for a thriving business. The corn was collected in the grange then carted in convenient loads to the mill where it was ground. The product was taken from there to Granary Point, a quarter of a mile up the coast, where a rough stone pier had been constructed – and can still be seen – to facilitate loading onto flat-bottomed barges. At high tide these took the grain to Lindisfarne, where the monks took what they needed for themselves and loaded the remainder onto ships bound for market, usually London.

After dissolution the estate became the property of Bishop Tunstall until 1559, when the Crown took over. In 1565 it was granted to William Reade, the captain of Lindisfarne and the Farnes. Before this appointment he had been captain of Berwick castle and had got to know King James VI well. He died in 1604, a very old but happy man for the king had dropped in to take some refreshment with his friend while on his triumphal journey south the year before to receive the English crown.

What happened to the estate after William's death is not know until William Tuffnell Jolliffe bought it and built Fenham farmhouses in 1784. The manor-house was allowed to decay and by 1826 only earthworks remained.

East Kyloe

L75   P464   NU059397   14$\frac{1}{2}$ km, 9 miles, south of Berwick

Kyloe was a scattered township on the slopes of the Kyloe Hills and occupied about a square mile of good agricultural land. Its tower was built in the south-east corner where East Kyloe farm now stands.

Eustace de Kilei, who was alive at the end of the thirteenth century, was the first recorded holder, but he lost all in 1327 for helping Robert Bruce. The owner, Bishop Beaumont of Durham, then granted Kyloe and adjacent townships to Robert Manners of Etal. Strangely, Kyloe was only a life grant so the place returned to the bishop when Robert died in 1354. Fifteen years later Sir Thomas Grey of Castle Heaton and Wark-on-Tweed obtained a heritable grant and his family held the place for over two hundred years. One occupier, David Grey, built the tower before 1450.

In 1589, after the Greys had bought the township, another Sir Thomas granted one of the farms to someone he called "my servant" yet who shared his name. The original main-line family, by now domiciled in Chillingham castle, had been so prolific over the years that 'Grey' had become a common name in Northumberland, and many who held it could claim only a tenuous relationship with the fount. Indeed the Greys who owned this estate at the end of the sixteenth century styled themselves 'Greys of Kyloe' and had no practical connection with Chillingham.

The tower which was their home was quite small – its groundfloor vault measured only 23 by 17 feet – but very strong, with eight foot thick walls of large stones held by good quality cement. It was in good repair in 1560 and was still habitable in 1630 when Ralph Grey bequeathed it to his uncle, Henry Grey of Morpeth. He had five daughters and the tower was very cramped, so in 1633 they moved to a mansion near Kyloe church. The five daughters eventually inherited equal shares of the estate, but all sold out. In 1705 Sir Carnaby Haggerston (the great-grandfather of the man with the same name who demolished Haggerston tower) held two-fifths and Captain Charles Bacon Grey held three-fifths, but this did not last very long as both proprietors sold small plots of their land to sitting tenants. There were seventy inhabitants of Kyloe and 'ye most part freeholders', wrote John Warburton in 1715. It is not known where East Kyloe farm and the tower fit into this apportionment.

The vault of the tower is still intact today but the upper storey has gone. Two of the groundfloor walls back onto farm buildings and the other two are practically hidden behind trees, but it can be seen that the arched entrance has been extended upwards by an unskilled hand, probably to allow the passage of farm machinery. There is no trace of a barmekyn.

There is no village at Kyloe; the nearest is Fenwick, a little to the east at NU066400 (P452), which should have a fortification of some sort – the 'wyke' or strong homestead on the 'fen' – but does not appear ever to have been thus encumbered. The family which lived there in the middle ages took its name from the place, just as the Fenwicks who lived near Stamfordham did, and the two families were not even remotely related. The northern family made history in 1281 by being one of the very few whose release from slavery is recorded. Bishop Robert de Insula, by deed dated at Norham castle, "manumitted and called from slavery to perpetual liberty Eustace fitz Eustace of Fenwick, with all his family and chattels". By way of thanks, Eustace arranged for a pound of wax to be given each year to Durham Cathedral to fuel the lamp which lit the shrine of St. Cuthbert behind the high altar.

Buckton

| L75 | P464 | NU081384 | 17 km, 10$^1/_2$ miles, south of Berwick |

Detchant

| L75 | P464 | NU087364 | 19 km, 11$^3/_4$ miles, south of Berwick |

Two ancient vills with towers recorded in the 1415 survey report. Although separated by only 2400 yards – within signalling distance – the building styles were quite different and the holders had nothing in common.

Buckton was in Islandshire, held by Willi Atkynson until at least 1460. His tower was quite small, and seems to have disappeared by 1581 when the farm alone is mentioned, owned by Brian Grey. He sold to the Haggerstons in 1637.

Detchant was in the Wooler barony, held by Hugh de Dichende in 1166. His family continued to live there for almost two hundred years, then became extinct when Sir John de Dichend died.

Richard Lilburne was the holder in 1415 and it was probably he who had built the tower, a large one, recorded as a fortalice which in old terminology was only slightly less important than a castle. As at Buckton, nothing remains today and the site is not known with any precision.

Roughly half way between Buckton and Detchant, by the side of the Great North Road, there used to be a walled group of fir trees which became known as 'Grizzy's Clump' to commemorate a young lady who played a part in the Monmouth rebellion of 1685. When the Duke of Monmouth denounced King James II as a usurper and backed his words with a force of 150 men, Archibald Campbell, the ninth Earl of Argyll, tried to help him by spreading the rebellion in Scotland. His efforts were quickly quelled, and one of his lieutenants, Sir John Cochrane, was captured and incarcerated in Edinburgh's Tolbooth to await the arrival of a warrant for his execution which had been issued in London.

By means of slipping £5000 into the right hands, a pardon was obtained, but to do any good, this had to reach Edinburgh ahead of the warrant. Cochrane's eighteen years old daughter, Bonny Grizzy, was determined that it would. She donned the costume of a highwayman and waited in the plantation for the mail coach carrying the warrant to arrive. When it drew abreast she stepped out onto the road, pistols at the ready, and held up the postman. Then "She's prie'd the warrant and away she flew, with the speed and strength o' the wild curlew".

Long before a replacement warrant could be dispatched, the pardon had been received in Edinburgh and Cochrane had been set free. Thanks to the wit and courage of his daughter, he escaped justice, but the principals of the rebellion, Monmouth and Argyll, were executed. The majority of the former's men were slaughtered by Government troops at Bridgwater, while the remainder were punished savagely by Judge Jeffreys at the 'Bloody Assizes'.

Elwick

L75   P465   NU115368   20 km, 12½ miles, south of Berwick

The dividing line between Islandshire, North Durham, and Bamburgh parish, Northumberland, ran through this small hamlet, splitting it into two estates. King John acknowledged this in a charter dated 1203. In 1415 the holders were Thomas de Elwyke in the northern half and Thomas Bradforth in the southern part. Both had built towers; they were in existence in 1561 but no remains exist nor clues to their whereabouts. During the sixteenth century the two estates combined and were farmed by the Younghusbands until 1630, when they moved to Tuggal Hall. The Earl of Tankerville, a Grey of Chillingham castle, was owner in 1852.

Easington Grange

L75   P465   NU118357   21 km, 13 miles, south of Berwick

The Anglian home of the Aesc family is a mile to the south-east of the Grange, which by comparison is quite modern. Very little is known about the place for certain, but it may have been contemporary with the strengthened grange at Fenham – say about 1340 – for it appears to have had an interior 'tower chamber' similar to that installed at Fenham. There is also an Easington Grange Mill a quarter of a mile to its north, so the possibility cannot be ruled out that this was another grain production scheme operated by, or on behalf of, the Lindisfarne monks.

The grange was destroyed when a farm was built on the site so we are robbed of material evidence. The farm was bought by the Culley Brothers in 1801.

Middleton Hall

L75   P464   NU094354   20 km, 12½ miles, south of Berwick

This is a geographically-inspired name and no one called Middleton ever owned the estate. In particular, it never had any connection with nearby Newlands which was owned by a Middleton at one time. The name is merely a corruption of 'middle town', although it is far from clear what it was in the middle of.

Actually it was part of Baron Muschamp's Wooler barony (nowhere near its middle!) from about 1107 until a Scottish family called Marescal – later changed to Marshall – purchased most of it in 1250. It appears that the Muschamps kept a little of it as their name is still connected with the estate a century and a quarter later.

The Marshalls gave assistance to King Edward III's enemies in or about the year 1330 and forfeited their estate, which was granted to Michael de Pressen, a page at the royal court, in 1335. At first the award was for life only and a rent of ten marks a year was charged, but Queen Philippa successfully persuaded her husband to make it a hereditable gift. Michael died in 1375, leaving a daughter, Margaret, who was married to Sir John Lilburn.

The Lilburns had plenty of land around Wooler and probably did not use their part of Middleton Hall estate, but the Muschamps, who still held a portion of it, did need it for a home for a very junior branch of the family. They built a tower which in 1415 was owned by William Muschamp.

Thomas Lilburn died in 1587 without legitimate heirs. The Muschamps relinquished their share of the estate at the same time to allow the Armorer family of Belford to buy the whole lot. It was theirs for nearly a hundred years, in which time they added wings to the tower, making a large mansion of it. In 1685 William Armorer died in debt and his creditors sold the estate to Abraham Dixon. Armorer's son and heir moved into Belford Westhall.

Dixon was a Newcastle merchant with plenty of money. In 1756 he commissioned James Paine to design something rather better than Middleton Hall for him, and he moved into the result, Belford Hall, in 1759, selling his old estate to Greenwich Hospital.

This most fortunate institution had no need to buy very much property in Northumberland for it had been granted the huge Derwentwater possessions in 1735. Scremerston, eleven miles to the north, had come to it in this fashion, but it had to buy Middleton which it wanted, presumably, because it complemented or extended Scremerston in some way. In the 1880s the old tower and its newer wings were demolished and replaced by a hall which still exists, although it has been converted into several self-contained apartments, administered by a trust set up by Greenwich Hospital.

Belford Westhall

L75   P465   NU103341   21½ km, 13 miles south of Berwick

The present building, Westhall Farm, built in the 1830s in a rather pretentious style, is set on sloping ground a few hundred yards west of Belford Village. There are obvious signs of a moat, however, and this and an ancient well suggest that the site has an interesting history.

It may have accommodated a motte and bailey in the eleventh century, but the first recorded building was a large manor-house, unfortified and built of wattle and plaster on a timber frame. Here King Edward III and his army spent a night in 1333 on their journey to Berwick and the battle of Halidon Hill.

By 1415 the manor-house had been replaced by the 'Castrum de Beleford', a strong tower, the property of Phillippi de Darcy and her son

Johannes. The moat was dug at this time as part of the building's defences: a pair of mid-fifteenth century bronze spurs have been found by its remains.

Much later, in the seventeenth century, the owner was David Graham, the Duke of Montrose's son who was created Earl Graham of Belford in 1722. He modified the tower extensively and it became virtually a manor-house once more. He rented this to the late William Armorer's son when creditors turned him out of Middleton Hall.

Newlands

L75   P465   NU115324   23¹/₂ km, 15 miles, south of Berwick

Newlands was the 'new lands' which were attached to Warenton (NU106304) in late Anglian days to make one large agricultural estate. The combination holds to this day, although two farms have been made of it, the Mousen Burn being the dividing line.

In the eleventh century King William II granted Odard, Vicecomes de Bamburgh, the Norman sheriff of the royal city, the barony of Embleton in which the Warenton/Newlands estate was included as an insular manor. Its history was Embleton's history until it was sold to John de Middleton of Belsay in 1296. He obtained a licence to crenellate from King Edward II in 1310 and built a tower at Newlands.

John had the misfortune to be related to Gilbert Middleton, leader of the notorious Mitford Gang. Although connivance was never proved, the worst was assumed and John's possessions were confiscated by the Crown in 1318.

King Edward III stayed a few days in Newlands tower in 1329, and although officially still a minor he evidently was empowered to grant Sir Thomas de Bamburgh, a clerk in chancery and rector of Embleton, permission to live in the tower. He and his family did so for some eighty years, and then the place was empty for a long time. In 1417 Robert Harbottle of Preston tower was bound by King Henry V to keep Newlands tower, also Dunstanburgh castle and the king's mill at Embleton, in good repair.

Brothers called Carr are alleged to have been tenants in the fifteenth century, but nothing more is known for sure about Newlands until 1663 when Mrs Weldon is on record as paying rent for it. In 1692 Thomas Forster appeared to have had some interest in it, and in 1747 John Forster emerged as part owner with William Pratt. But by this time the tower had disappeared and the superior type farmhouse which still adorns Newlands farm had taken its place. Both Warenton and Newlands farms are owned now by Eric Charles Graham of London. A Mr Sanderson took the tenancy of Newlands in 1910; he died in 1949 and his daughter, Cynthia, continued to manage the farm until she retired in 1990.

Newcastle Keep. (p467)

Area 2
Northern Cheviots, Glendale and the Till Basin

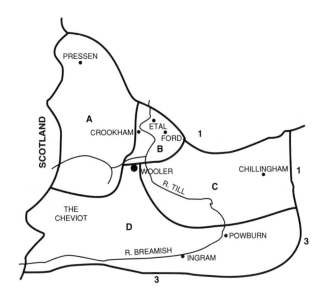

Key Town: Wooler
Sub-Areas:
A Glendale
B Down the Till
C Up the Till
D South from Wooler

PRESSEN

SCOTLAND

A
CROOKHAM
ETAL
FORD
B
1

WOOLER
R. TILL
C
CHILLINGHAM
1

THE CHEVIOT
D
•POWBURN
3

R. BREAMISH
INGRAM
3

A topographical mishmash of bleak mountains, gently rolling hills, rich arable land, rough sheep country, a sand and gravel plain, rushing torrents and meandering streams. The whole was in the Border military zone, so there were plenty of towers and three castles. The western boundary of the area is the England/Scotland Border. The north and much of the east adjoins Area 1, while the Breamish/Aln watershed forms the southern boundary. It thus encompasses most of the Till basin, all of Glendale and the eastern Cheviots, including The Cheviot.

Key Town
Wooler

L75   P475   NT992280

Wooler is the commercial and community centre for the entire area and has held this distinction for a very long time, probably since pre-Roman Britons built their forts and farming settlements on the surrounding hills. It is well sited for communications yet it was never a popular transit camp for armies which seem to have preferred more easterly routes. It was very much on the raiders' map, however, for the rich agricultural acres in Glendale and below the Cheviot massif were prime targets for them.

The town became the capital of a large barony which King Henry I granted to Robert de Musco-Campo in 1107 for a fee of four knights. Robert changed his name to Muschamp and built a motte and bailey castle in Wooler, but what he did not do was to father a son, so when he died his son-in-law, Stephen de Bulemer, inherited. To avoid any possible dispute about his holding, he changed his name to Muschamp.

Thomas Muschamp, Stephen's eldest son, inherited when his father died in about 1166, but he did not have the barony for long as he had to flee to Scotland for supporting King William, the Scottish Lion. His lands were forfeited, but in 1191, during one of King Richard's frequent absences, the king's locum restored the barony to Thomas's son, another Robert.

It was during this Robert's tenure that the family split in two. Young brother Stephen left the Wooler domicile and inaugurated the Muschamps of Barmoor, taking with him a considerable amount of land. While Robert's family only survived another generation, Stephen's descendants kept the Muschamp flag flying until the seventeenth century Civil War.

Robert died in 1208, his son, also Robert, in 1250, and then three daughters inherited equal shares of what was left of the barony. All three were married, the eldest to the Earl of Strathern, the middle girl to Adam of Wigton and Isobel, the youngest, to William de Huntercomb. Numbers one and two died during the thirteenth century, so eventually the Huntercombs became the sole holders of the title and property. William had died in 1271, but his son, Walterus, took over after him.

The Huntercombs were tenants of Chevelyingham (later Chillingham) even before that estate was transferred from the Alnwick barony to the Muschamps in about 1170. The family were prosperous farmers and built a fine stone house for themselves. This and all the tenancy became their inheritable property, of course, when Walterus became the Baron of Wooler. Unfortunately he had no sons to benefit from his good fortune; his heir was his nephew, Nicholas de Neubaud, rather a spendthrift. He changed his name to Huntercomb, but that did not improve his credit rating, and in 1326 he sold most of Wooler barony to Sir John de Lilburn. About two years later he sold Chevelyngham to Sir Thomas de Heton.

None of the Huntercombs had lived in Wooler, having a fine house just four miles away, and indeed the motte and bailey castle had not been used since Robert Muschamp died in 1250. In 1255 it was described as 'wasted'. Sir John de Lilburn and subsequent purchasers of the now defunct barony also had homes in the neighbourhood and had no need for a residence in Wooler.

Sir John, in fact, only made his purchase in order to split up the land and to sell it piecemeal at a profit. By 1360 parts were held by Sir John Coupland, Sir Peter Mousley and others, and later the Greys of Castle Heaton had a considerable interest in the area. Gradually more and more townspeople became freeholders.

Very defiant and resourceful were these people, especially in the tragic post-Bannockburn period when they had to contend with both Scottish and 'Mitford Gang' raiders without any fortifications. That they were not always successful is shown by the fact that the town was excused taxes for several years.

The sixteenth century was also very bad for Wooler, although during most of it the town did have a fortified tower. This had been provided by the Greys, now of Chillingham, and was first mentioned in 1509. It had been built on the motte of the old motte and bailey castle, and was said to hold twenty horsemen under the control of the warden of the marches. Their presence did not deter a hundred Scotsmen in 1524 who burnt five or six houses and ransacked many others, and it was the Wooler people, not the warden's men who saved the day. They grabbed a dozen prisoners and chased the others away in a manner which led one of them to boast "for one pennyworth of hurt done by them, the Scots received twenty pennyworth in return".

During this and other raids the tower was badly damaged. It was not repaired, and by 1584 it was so damaged an estimated sum of £60 would have been needed to make it serviceable. Nothing was done so it was no hindrance to Andrew Ker, the Laird of Cressford, when he led a daytime raid on Wooler in 1595. His primary target appears to have been the vicar, who lost his sheep and cattle. An appeal for reparations to the Warden's Court was fruitless, so the good churchman took matters into his own hands and led a raid into Cressford, where he took goods to the precise value of his losses. Such appalling cheek naturally provoked Ker into attacking Wooler again. He could not find the vicar, who had suddenly remembered he had an important engagement in Berwick, but he did kill two men who got in his way. One of these men was Will Storey, and his family started a blood feud with the Kers because of the murder. Such was the bitterness and futility of Border life in the sixteenth century.

Some lumps of shapeless masonry remain of the tower. They are on top of a steep little hill half way down Church Street, opposite the Police Station.

Area 2, Sub-Area A   Glendale

Humbleton

L75   P475   NT975285   2 km, 1¹/₄ miles, west of Wooler

Although so close to the Wooler barony, Humbleton was associated more closely with Lanton and Kirknewton in the Ros barony of Carham. All the places in this subsection, except one unknown, were originally in one or other of these baronies.

William of Stainsby was the first known holder, in 1242, and he was followed in 1280 by Margaret Baxter, daughter of Thomas Baxter who held part of Lanton. When Robert Ros lost his barony in 1295 the Crown sold Lanton and Kirknewton to the Corbet family. They may have bought Humbleton as well, but the Lay Subsidy Roll of 1296 showed that thirteen inhabitants were wealthy enough to pay taxes and it seems possible that they, or at least some of them, were freeholders.

The township and its hill to the south-west are called 'Humbleton' now, but the battle which took place on the hill in 1402 is known by at least three other names as well. The Ordnance Survey people call it 'The Battle of Hamildon Hill', Shakespeare in Henry IV, Part 1, called it 'The Battle of Holmedon Hill' and many modern historians prefer 'The Battle of Homildon Hill'. You can take your pick, but never confuse it with 'The Battle of Halidon Hill' which was fought in 1333 near Berwick.

The battle was really a Douglas – Hotspur Border skirmish, chiefly noteworthy because of what followed it. Archibald Douglas and his army were returning home with a large amount of booty after a successful raid as far as the Tyne when they were overtaken by Henry Hotspur Percy and the Earl of March with their army which had force-marched from Bamburgh. The Scots took up position on the hill while the English remained at its foot.

This member of the Douglas Clan and Hotspur, despite their charisma, qualified as Britain's worst ever army commanders. Hotspur was all for marching his men up the hill to batter against Douglas's unyielding wall of swords and battleaxes, but fortunately he was restrained by the wiser councils of the Earl of March, and instead volley upon volley of arrows were fired. Douglas seemed to be paralysed; he and his men just stood still, making easy targets for the archers. Eventually two knights took matters into their own hands and charged the English line, but again it was arrows which proved decisive. The scrap demonstrated the advantages of 'fighting at a distance' using the 'artillery' of bows and arrows and provided a lesson not all later commanders learnt.

A thousand Scotsmen were killed and most of the surviving leaders, including Douglas, were taken prisoner. It was customary in those days for prisoners of war to be retained by the victor and held to ransom; it was the accepted way of paying the army's wages. On this occasion a parsimonious government had kept the Percys very short of money and Hotspur was relying on ransoming Douglas and a few other prisoners to straighten the books, so he was understandably annoyed when King Henry IV ordered him to deliver his prisoners to him. Hotspur refused, and instead released them on their promise to help him teach the king a thing or two. They all rode off to Chester to join Owain Glyndior, already in open revolt against Henry. A few months later Hotspur was killed in action at the Battle of Shrewsbury.

A boulder, the Bendor Stone, stands in the middle of a field called Red Riggs (NT968294) to mark the site of the closing phases of Humbleton's battle, but it does not mark the end of warfare in the neighbourhood, for the villagers had to suffer several raids in later years. By the mid-sixteenth century some relief came in the shape of a small tower, built perhaps by an anonymous landlord or, more likely as a communal effort.

It did not have many years of usefulness. After the Union of the Crowns it was modified to improve its ventilation and access so that cattle could be housed in it, and eventually it was pulled down and its stones used for another building. Nothing remains today, although in 1878 its foundations could be traced and the site was marked by an elder bush.

Akeld

L74 & 75   P475   NT957294   4 km, 2½ miles, north-west of Wooler

Coupland

L74 & 75   P463   NT935312   6½ km, 4 miles, north-west of Wooler

Although these places are on opposite sides of the River Glen, their descents have much in common. Both were parcels in the Wooler barony and both were leased to William of Akeld, whose father had held the land before the barony was formed. William and his offspring worked the Akeld estate while Coupland was sub-let to a family called Sampson.

It is on record that a later 'Sampson de Coupland', as he styled himself, was one of the twelve English knights who, with twelve Scottish knights, drew up the first set of Border laws, the Leges Marchiarum, in 1249.

The Akeld family's progress was halted in about 1260 when four daughters inherited and the estate was split between them. Akeld and Coupland followed different routes for the next couple of centuries.

Thomas Haggerston, who was married to one of the inheritors, became the holder of Akeld. Another lucky husband was none other than John Sampson of Coupland. He became the baron's full tenant and soon changed his name to Coupland.

During the first half of the fourteenth century Akeld passed from the Haggerstons to Robert Houpyn. The Wooler barony had broken up in 1326 so this transfer was probably a sale. Across the river, John Coupland, a grandson or possibly a great-grandson of John Sampson, fought in the Battle of Neville's Cross in 1346 and managed to capture the Scottish king, David Bruce, thereby earning King Edward's gratitude and an annuity of £500 a year. This enabled him to buy his estate.

Gifts of money, whether from a king or a National Lottery, all too often induce a monetary stupefaction which renders the donee incapable of looking beyond the immediate present. John died in 1363; the annuity stopped and his wife was left penniless. She had to sell Coupland to Richard Arundel.

The Grey family, the future Earls of Tankerville, were always in the market for Glendale estates. In 1408 they bought Coupland from the Arundels, and in 1480 the Houpyn family sold Akeld to them. Thus the two estates were reunited under one owner, although farmed by different sets of tenants. A tower or strong house was built at Akeld a few years before 1541.

Unity did not suffer when the Greys sold out in about 1600, for George and Mary Wallis bought both estates. They chose to live in Coupland, where they built a strong tower; it was completed in 1619, sixteen years after the Union of the Crowns – a significant comment on the slow progress enduring peace was making.

The Wallis's also bought property at Knaresdale on the South Tyne at about the same time, and altogether they rather overstretched their purse. Their grandson, Ralph Wallis, was another worry: he married Elizabeth Ogle of the Causey Park Ogles and proved to be an unreliable spendthrift, lucky to get a menial job in Berwick. The Ogle in-laws helped the young couple financially, and when the older Wallis's retired to Knaresdale in 1713 they bought Coupland for them. They had to buy Akeld as well but quickly sold it to George Sparrow.

Ralph and Elizabeth Wallis did not stay in Coupland very long. In about 1723 John Ogle of Causey Park gave the estate to his son Chaloner who had made his father very proud by being knighted and becoming Admiral of the Fleet in 1749. Unfortunately he died without children a year later.

George Sparrow and his son retained Akeld until the estate was bought by George Culley in 1795. In 1806 brother Matthew bought Coupland, thereby uniting the two places once more. The Culleys made a famous partnership, world-renowned in the field of innovative agriculture. Perhaps their best known success was the Border Leicester breed of sheep, the result of crossing Leicesters with the hardy local breed of Tilldales.

The tower at Coupland is still in existence. It gives the viewer the impression of being in three parts although it was built as a unit. The main residential part is a large rectangle with three storeys, a vaulted ground floor chamber and a pitched roof with crenellation. In the south-east corner is a small square which has five storeys and a flat crenellated roof, and tucked between the two elements, at the back of the building, is a small but beautiful round stair turret with battlements which rise above the roofs of the other parts. Decidedly romantic, yet genuine strength is clearly evident.

Matthew Culley no doubt appreciated the elegance of the place, but not its lack of creature comforts, for he soon built a Georgian farmhouse a few yards distant from it, but in line. In 1820 he completed today's splendid mansion by joining house and tower with a linking building.

The stronghold which George Culley bought at Akeld was partly ruinous. He rebuilt it from the first floor upwards, leaving and repairing the 65 by 25 feet vaulted ground floor chamber. This chamber is now a byre and the floor above, reached by modern external stairs, is a store room.

Lanton

L74 & 75   P463   NT925312   7$^{1}/_{2}$ km, 4$^{1}/_{2}$ miles, north-west of Wooler

A hamlet, farm and manor-house about a mile upstream from Coupland. In the middle ages it was a fair-sized village some eight hundred yards to the west and boasting of two towers.

It was part of the Carham barony, least to Thomas Baxter and his family from about 1250. In 1295, when Baron Ros forfeited his land, the Crown sold Lanton with part of Kirknewton to Walter Corbet who, in his turn, lost his land because of involvement with the 'Mitford Gang'. The Baxters were still at Lanton when the property was again put up for sale, and this time David Baxter was able to buy half of it. The other half was not sold until 1360, when William Strother was the purchaser. He also bought the Kirknewton property.

Both owners built towers, Baxter in 1369 and Strother in 1415. Between these dates the Baxter family came to an end with an heiress who was married to Robert Manners of Etal, so the Baxter tower became the Manners tower – in fact a Manners residence when Robert gave it to his son John as a wedding present.

In 1496 Lanton got in the way of King James IV's invasion and one tower was razed while the other was seriously damaged. The two owners got together and decided that in future one tower jointly owned would be enough. but there is no record of the damaged tower ever being repaired, not even when Christopher Dacre suggested in 1584 that 100 Marks worth of work should be done so that a garrison of ten men under the command of Ralph Reveley could be stationed there.

The Strothers went to live in Kirknewton in or about 1500 but retained possession of their half of Lanton, which they leased to John Hall of Otterburn. The Halls held it until 1656. In 1584 the Manners part was sold to John Collingwood.

There were several owners in the eighteenth century onwards, including Sir William Davison, who was responsible for the very visible monument on top of Lanton Hill. It was erected in memory of his father, Alexander Davison of Swarland Park, and brother, John Davison. The family must have had a self-advertising chromosome in their genetic code, for father had erected an obelisk at Swarland to commemorate his friendship with Lord Nelson.

Old Yeavering

L74 & 75   P463   NT924302   7 km, 4¼ miles, west of Wooler

Ancient history must take pride of place here, but there was a medieval fortification – tower or strong house, there is no means of telling which – near a farmhouse which Ralph Grey of Chillingham built in the mid-sixteenth century. At one time the building may have been similar to the stronghold the same man built at Akeld, and, like Akeld, it was altered radically to fit it for practical use after the Border warfare ended. In this case, however, the place has been allowed to deteriorate and is now practically a wreck.

Of more interest is the nearby hill, Yeavering Bell (P463, NY924302) which has the most important Ancient British hill settlement at its summit and a survival of the primeval Caledonian Forest on its northern slopes. The site of Ad Gefrin, the Anglian King Edwin's palace, lies between the hill and the River Glen.

Kirknewton

L74 & 75   P463   NT914302   8 km, 5 miles, west of Wooler

The post-Conquest history of part of this substantial village was similar to that of Lanton's. The other part was church property from 1122 to 1538, administered from Carham by the Augustinian cell of Kirkham Priory, the founding of the first baron of Carham, Walter Espec.

The secular part of the village had a tower, probably built by William Strother when be bought the property from the Crown. Its existence is well recorded, but the records contradict themselves regarding the size of the building.

Sir Robert Bowes and Sir Ralph Ellerker described in 1541 a little tower of Strother ownership, joined to a low stone house. They told how when the house was set alight during a raid the fire nearly burnt the tower. John Warburton saw things differently in 1715. He noted that Kirknewton "Hath in it ye ruuing of a large tower with a quadrangar wall and circular towers about it, belonging to Mark Strother esq". The kindest explanation is that the tower was rebuilt at some date between 1541 and 1715.

Written complaints about damage and losses sustained as a result of Scottish incursions were filed in 1516, 1547 and 1567. In 1570, a year after the Rising of the Northern Earls, the Scots, aided by the Earl of Westmorland

and other English rebels – a total of some two thousand horsemen – pounced on Mindrum and Kirknewton with disastrous results. From Kirknewton alone they stole 400 head of cattle, sundry horses and household equipment and took over 200 prisoners "besides the hurting of divers women and the throwing of suckling children out of their clouts".

The church which gives the village the first part of its name had its origin in the eleventh century, or possibly quite a bit earlier. According to legend, King Edwin and Ethelburga were married in it by Paulinus in 625. In its graveyard lies Josephine Elizabeth Butler, the nineteenth century reformer. She was born in 1828 at Milfield, the daughter of John Grey, the Northern Estates Manager for the Greenwich Hospital, and grew up to become a most persistent and courageous activist in the cause of fallen humanity.

Hethpool

L74   P475   NT896284   9¹/₂ km, 6 miles west of Wooler

The College Burn drains the south and west sides of The Cheviot and carries the water most elegantly some eight miles to the Bowmont Water. Its contribution turns that river into the River Glen. The valley of the College Burn is peaceful now, a favourite with strong walkers seeking the delights of Northumberland's highest mountain, but in medieval times it was used by reivers from North Tynedale and Redesdale as well as by Scottish raiders from the Kale Water basin as a quick way – rough but not too difficult for their wiry hobblers – to the fruitful farms of Glendale and Tilldale. Hethpool was a check-point along this route.

There cannot have been many places more abused than Hethpool. A report of 1342 said it had been "for the most part devastated by the Scots, rebels and enemies of the king" and similar reports or letters of complaint were dated 1385, 1399 and 1429. Further raids were recorded in 1513, 1541, 1568 and 1596. This list, it will be appreciated, indicates but a fraction of the total discomfiture, for small raids were not recorded or were the subject of verbal complaints only.

It is a wonder anyone wanted to live in such a place, yet the thirteenth century population was larger than it is now. It was a Wooler barony township then, held from Baron Muschamp by Odinal de Ford. A small tower was built before 1415 when it was owned by Robert Manners, and it almost goes without saying that the Greys owned some of the estate in the sixteenth century. Roger Grey held the tower in 1541. Somewhere along the line the Blacketts had a stake in it, and it was because a daughter of that family married Admiral Lord Cuthbert Collingwood that a mansion built in 1687 became a frequently used haunt of Morpeth's favourite sea-dog when on shore leave.

The admiral was most concerned about oak tree conservation, for he feared the time might come when naval operations would be limited by the lack of suitable ships' timber. He lived between 1750 and 1810, so he could not have known that iron was soon to make oak obsolete for this purpose. He planted lots of trees on the slopes of Hethpoolbell, on his estate and within sight of his house, and he encouraged others to follow his example.

His wife tended the trees while he was at sea, but for all that they have not done very well. The soil is shallow in his wood and the trees still there have not matured as he had hoped. Chroniclers of kindly disposition credit Collingwood with the luxuriant oaks a mile upstream at Harrowbog, but in fact this is a natural wood, probably the remainder of a forest which once covered the lower slopes of Newton Tor and Hare Law.

In 1919 the seventeenth century house was replaced by a more modern mansion. The tower ruin is a feature of its garden, although at first sight it looks like a hedge separating the cabbages from the French beans. Parts of three walls are there, but are almost totally submerged in thick ivy which makes it difficult to see any masonry.

Howtel

L74   P463   NT897341   11 km, 6³/₄ miles, north-west of Wooler

A large farm lying in a pass which connects Glendale with Tilldale. At one time it was a village larger than Milfield, with a school and a smithy, and before that it was known chiefly as a convenient mustering centre for English troops or raiders intent on riding into Scotland.

In the twelfth and thirteenth centuries the township was a parcel in the Carham barony, and a good portion of it was granted by Walter Espec to his Kirkham Priory. Both the monastic and the lay administrators let their farms to a variety of people. The names of most tenants have been forgotten, but 'Burrell' is one which crops up repeatedly between 1387 and 1802, latterly as an owner.

The 1541 survey notes that there was a tower at Howtel, owned by John Burrell and damaged by Scottish King James IV in 1496. In 1584 Christopher Dacre thought it "a very small thing" but worth restoring for £50 to "defend the country and annoy the enemy". There followed a bitter argument about who should pay for the repair, the Burrells or the Queen, so nothing was done. Nevertheless quite a lot of it remains: most of the walling still stands to first floor height and it is clear there were two upper floors although no stairs are evident. The ground floor chamber had a timber ceiling, and the whole building measured some 33 by 31 feet. It is understood that English Heritage intends some day to stabilize the masonry. If this is ever done, perhaps some farmyard clutter could be removed from the vicinity at the same time so that the tower may be seen in its best light.

Kilham

L74   P463   NT884326   11½ km, 7 miles, north-west of Wooler

Another Carham barony township, held during its early years by the Archer family. They sold out in 1353 to John Coupland and, like Coupland estate, it was sold by John's widow to Richard Arundel in 1363. The acquisitive Greys got hold of it in 1408 and kept it until 1913.

Like most places on Bowmont Water, Kilham had more than its fair share of raids, most by Scots but occasionally by the reivers of North Tynedale and Redesdale as well. Sir Robert Carey, warden of the Eastern Marches, reported a pitched battle in 1597. He said that four Scots came to Kilham one night, broke down a poor man's door and took all his possessions. His neighbours chased the robbers and eventually managed to capture three of them and retrieve the stolen goods. Unfortunately the fourth escaped and raised the alarm. At daybreak a small army of Scotsmen, some on foot and about forty horsed, attacked Kilham but made little impression as the villagers were waiting for them – in fact two more prisoners were taken. "Whereon the Scots raised Tyvidale" and a hundred and sixty horse and foot descended on the village at seven o' clock that morning. Such a large force was unstoppable; all the prisoners were rescued, a man was slain, seven more were terminally wounded and many more were "hurt very sore".

As well as stout hearts, Kilham may have had a fortification to help its defence. There was not one in 1541, but Christopher Dacre marked one on his 'plat' of 1584. In itself this is not proof that one existed, but the historian Cadwallader Bates claimed in about 1890 to have seen the ruins of a strong house in the village. This has never been substantiated, and no likely site has been found.

Antechester (Thompson's Walls)

L74   P463   NT867304   12½ km, 7¾ miles, west of Wooler

'Antechester' does not appear on any modern map and its position was not known until documents dating from Queen Elizabeth I's reign were unearthed. These contain some information about "The parcel of land called Thompson's Walls or Antechester, a member of Kilham, lying between Kilham and Shotten". Thompson's Walls does appear on O.S. maps; it is a farm in a very lonely valley some two miles south-west of Kilham and slightly less due east of Shotten.

Although a "member of Kilham" in the sixteenth century, it was a separate entity in its early days, in the Wooler barony and held by William of Akeld. At that time its name was Dercestre.

When the Akeld family was derailed by four daughters in about 1260, one of the inheritors was married to a member of the Prendergist family, and

Dercestre was one of their prizes. By the fourteenth century the name had become Antrichestre. John Coupland, he with the vanishing annuity, bought it, and then, when he died, it was sold to Richard Arundel, and by him to the Greys, on the same path as Kilham.

The Greys had little use for such a remote and desolate patch but it was included in the Kilham lot. Even in 1541 it had been "waste land since before the remembrance of any man now living", and Rauffe Grey took this as a challenge. He combined it with other purchases on Cheviot's slopes to make a reasonable farm holding, and then he built a farmstead on it.

The only available evidence that a tower existed here is Christopher Dacre's 'plat' of 1584, and that would not stand up in a court of law for Dacre frequently showed strongholds he would like to see built as well as those which existed. However, it does not take much imagination to believe that the first farmer Grey installed was called Thompson, and the 'Walls' were his tower.

Downham

L74   P463   NT865339   14 km, 8¹/₂ miles, north-west of Wooler

A large farm and stables set high above Bowmont Water on the north side of Glendale, commanding fantastic views over the Cheviot massif. Originally a Carham barony township, it was large enough to contain eight husbandlands.

Its first known purchaser was that militant and libidinous priest of Ford, Sir Cuthbert Ogle, who gave it with West Lilburn to Mark, one of his four misbegotten sons, in 1530. Mark was a soldier of some renown whom King Henry VIII rewarded with a grant of arms in 1535 for his services in Scotland and for "manly and valiantly using himself". His military duties, naturally enough, were not appreciated across the Border, so a tower at Downham seemed a sensible precaution. By 1541 two floors had been completed, and a third floor, battlements and barmekyn were added before the estate was passed to Mark's brother Luke in 1568.

Its strength was tested when a band of Scottish raiders descended on it at nine o' clock one October evening in 1596. They hammered on its gate all night but failed to gain access, and it was nearly dawn when the Scots gave up and wreaked their frustration upon poor Branxton.

Ralph Carr of Ford bought the estate from the Ogles in 1600. There was no mention of a tower in the transaction but this was probably an oversight as a fortification which had performed so well in 1596 was unlikely to have disappeared just four years later. For all that, something dramatic must have happened during Carrs' ownership, or soon after the Greys bought the place in 1673, for a tower was not mentioned again, and nothing of it is left now.

Mindrum

L74   P463   NT842329   15$^1/_2$ km, 9$^1/_2$ miles, north-west of Wooler

Mindrum and Mindrummill are parts of a scattered hamlet on the left bank of Bowmont Water where it takes a sharp turn to the right. A Carham barony township, it was let to local farmers by the Crown and then sold in 1408 to the Greys, who retained it until 1913.

The case for Mindrum having a tower is based on shaky evidence. Saxton's map of 1576 shows one in the vicinity, but it may have been nearer Pawston, and Christopher Dacre's 'plat' shows one but it may have been just a recommendation. Today's inhabitants know nothing about a medieval fortification in their midst and cannot suggest any possible site where one could have stood.

Sir Robert Bowes made an impassioned plea in 1550 for "a strong tower with stabling beneath and lodging above, with a large barmekyn for cattle". He thought this necessary for two rather opposing reasons. On the one hand it would stop the villagers running for shelter in the hills whenever danger threatened and thus leaving the place unguarded, and on the other hand, if the tower was manned by the March Warden's troops it would prevent fraternisation and thus would stop "the Scots passing, as they do now, in the highe strete and waye". Sir Robert also pointed out that two watch towers existed in the hills, and signals from them to a tower could institute some resistance. Scottish raids in 1589 and 1594 suggest this plea was not heeded.

The two watch towers mentioned by Bowes were almost certainly timber structures, long since disappeared. The names of the hills on which they were sited have gone also and we can only guess their approximate positions. One was on 'Teversheughe' between Mindrum and Wark, possibly somewhere on the Camp Hill – Mindrummill Crag ridge to the north and west of the hamlet. The other was on 'Haddon Law', between Mindrum and Cheviot, ie, to the south of Mindrum. It is just conceivable that 'Harelaw' is a corruption of this name.

Pressen

L74   P463   NT836358   17$^1/_2$ km, 10$^3/_4$ miles, north-west of Wooler

An isolated farm some two miles north of Mindrum, with which it shares a common descent – Carham barony to the Greys, the latter buying it in 1398.

There is a legend which links Pressen with Wark on Tweed at the time Baron Robert Ros changed sides and declared for Scotland (1295). According to it, King Edward I was travelling north when he heard of this traitorous act; he immediately sent a thousand men to Wark to secure the castle, but they did not get that far, for Robert and his new friends came to meet them, and they succeeded in annihilating them at Pressen.

Whether or not there is any truth in the legend, Pressen's peace is known to have been shattered in 1435 or '36 when Henry Percy, Earl of Northumberland, and William Douglas, Earl of Angus, battled it out in Piper Dene, close by. Both men were accompanied by about four thousand soldiers, yet the Scots won a decisive victory.

The battle was a fairly commonplace Border encounter, made more than usually newsworthy by the size of the forces involved, the remoteness of the battlefield and the old feud between the commanders. But to many, the main interest is the weight it lends to the controversy concerning the ballad of Chevy Chase.

This was written by an anonymous Englishman, probably at the beginning of the sixteenth century, about a battle between the old rivals. A lot of people think this was the Battle of Piper Dene, while even more believe it was the Battle of Otterburn which took place in 1388. The ballad makes many statements, some of which are true about one battle but not the other, and some are simply historical inexactitudes applicable to neither battle. Neutral commentators realise from this that it was written about an imaginary battle, perhaps vaguely based on both battles, in order to highlight the futility of war. A closing couplet seems to express the writer's prayer:

"And grant, henceforth, that foul debate
'Twixt noblemen may cease".

Rather less dramatic than battling armies, but no doubt just as worrying, was the almost continuous ravaging by raiding Scotsmen, who hopped over the Border a mere mile and a half away whenever their pantries were empty. Yet there was no fortification in 1541; Bowes and Ellerker were very critical of this shortcoming and managed to stimulate landlord Grey into providing one.

It appears to have been a strong house rather than a conventional tower; a two storey, rectangular building with ground floor vault and, probably, just a single chamber on each floor. The ground floor entrance was in a long wall, while the door to the upper floor was half way up a gable wall, in a mezzanine position. The outside staircase to this door rose diagonally across the gable, but once inside the building it continued against a long wall until it reached the upper chamber.

The building has suffered radical alteration, of course – some of it quite recent – so that it could make a useful contribution to the farm. The upper floor has been removed and a new roof put on, the gable and its staircase have been replaced by full-width double doors and the vault has been reduced to just an archway. Enough remains, however, to show quite clearly the original unique design.

Its building date is rather puzzling. Contemporary surveyors put it at between 1541 and 1584 but some of the original stonework is surprisingly irregular and undressed, suggesting a much earlier date. The idea has been advanced that some use was made of the building during the Battle of Flodden in 1513, but that cannot be substantiated.

Pawston

L74   P463   NT855327   14 km, 8½ miles, west of Wooler

Pawston, or sometimes Paston, is a farm of Carham – Grey descent near Mindrum. In 1541, or just before, it was bought by Garrade Selby, and his family retained it until 1902.

The Selbys built a tower which was mentioned in dispatches only once, in 1568. The occasion was a raid by a Scottish gang which crossed the hills from Kirk Yetholme to the College Burn and there bumped into a patrolling English force. The Scots retreated in good order, steering the following English towards Yetholm where some eight hundred compatriots were camping. The English were credited with facing four charges, but eventually they had to withdraw. They retreated as far as Pawston tower, where both sides called it quits and went home.

In 1902 a large farmhouse was built around the vaulted ground floor chamber of the old tower. It is still intact, doing yeoman service as a wine cellar.

Elterton

L74 or 75   P475 or 476   NT854291

As the above vagueness would indicate, it is not known where this tower was. That it existed is beyond doubt, and there are many clues to its position, but they are contradictory. The most likely area is just south of Shotton (P463, NT842303), near the Bowmont Water. There are numerous deserted homesteads and settlements in the vicinity, even a ruined chapel at NT844293, and a tower here would have been appreciated as the Scottish raiders had only to cross the Bowmont to reach them.

It is no more than a guess, but the writer thinks the most likely site is on the northern slopes of Coldsmouth Hill, P475, NT854291. Hopefully some day archaeologists will uncover positive traces of the tower and will be able to establish its certain map reference.

Area 2, Sub-Area B   Down the Till

Doddington

L75   P463   NT998325   4½ km, 2¾ miles, north of Wooler

As are all the places in this subsection, Doddington is set a little higher than Milfield Plain, on its rim. People have chosen such positions for thousands of years, as the discovery of Neolithic celts (chisel-edged implements made of very hard stone) and a Bronze Age leather garment has proved.

The theory is that this is because Milfield Plain was once a lake. E.G. Butler, who lived at the turn of the century, speculated that before the last Ice Age the Till flowed westwards from Crookham, following roughly the line now taken by the A697 road, to join the Tweed at Cornhill. There are significant bends in both rivers which could have been the start and finish of this course. Towards the end of the glacial period ice melted and ran down the hills to the south of Crookham, bringing rock and mud debris down to block the river's passage. With no drain hole, the river became a lake and in time the whole Till valley from Wooler to Etal was covered with water. As it rose higher it began to lap over the lowest part of the rim, which happened to be near Etal. It escaped as a trickle at first; the trickle grew into a stream, and the bigger it got the more force it had with which to wear away a gorge. As the gorge grew deeper so the water was able to drain away more easily, until, after thousands of years, all the lake had gone.

This may be just a theory but there are plenty of facts to support it. The river does race through a rocky gorge near Etal and the land just west of Crookham does contain many rocks such as melting ice could have brought down. Milfield plain has a surface of sand and gravel, the normal deposit of a mountain stream which has run into a lake and below the Tankerville Arms Hotel in Wooler there is a steep bank which looks very much like the shore of a lake. As recently as the fifteenth and sixteenth centuries parts of Milfield Plain were still marshy and liable to flooding.

Doddington was part of the Alnwick barony in 1166, a reward granted by King Henry II to William de Vescy for his loyalty. What had been an Anglian settlement grew into a Norman town of some importance. In 1298 it houses thirty taxpayers and was soon to get a weekly cattle market and two mills.

Raiders, attracted by Doddington's prosperity, were a nuisance from the fourteenth century onwards. The Percy barons did not seem to care about their tenants' safety, but when the Greys bought the place some time between 1537 and 1557 – a period when the Crown was holding Alnwick barony – they soon found the money to build a strong house in the middle of the town.

The fortification frequently gets called a bastle but it was much superior to that classification. It was a three storey rectangle, 57 by 25 feet, with a projection on one side housing circular stairs. The ground floor had a wood ceiling but there was a parapet around the ridged roof.

The town remained prosperous until well into the eighteenth century, for as well as maintaining its agricultural business it developed as a craft centre, specialising in wool, leather and iron goods. There was also a considerable amount of coal mined in the area. It is reassuring to know that material wealth did not produce a counter-balancing impoverishment of religious niceties: in 1681 John Chanter was excommunicated for urinating against the church wall.

The essence of Doddington's success lay in its appeal to 'small' people – farmers with only a few acres of their own who used the common land for grazing, and craftsmen who fashioned their products slowly and skilfully by hand – and, as a consequence, the town received a double body-blow from the land enclosure acts and, later, the industrial revolution. During the nineteenth century it declined rapidly to village status, a rather unkempt village at that according to comments made by several visiting diocesan officials about the condition of the church. It seems that while the parishioners objected to a little dampness outside, they were oblivious to the wet rot inside.

One thing they were fussy about was the sanctity of their dead relatives and friends buried in the churchyard. Grave robbing was a thriving business along the Border in the nineteenth century, conducted by unsavoury villains, the 'Ressurrection Men', who sold corpses to surgeons, mainly in Edinburgh. When Archdeacon Singleton visited Doddington in 1828 he noted with amusement that the locals had built in the corner of their churchyard "a sort of blockhouse, pierced, as it would seem, for musketry, and have garrisoned it through the dark nights of two or three winters with persons determined to resist all attempts of Scotch Surgeons". He continued: "My smile has reference only to the means of security. I wish they had expended half the cost of this sepulchral guard-house on improving their chapel".

The real strong house was ruinous by this time, of course, as it had been bestowed on nature a hundred years earlier. Nature confirmed her rights one December night in 1896 by blowing down part of the south wall. Much of interest remains today; it is in a private garden but is visible from the public road.

Nesbit

L75   P463   NT983336   5¹/₂ km, 3¹/₂ miles, north of Wooler

Fenton

L75   P463   NT971339   6 km, 3³/₄ miles, north-west of Wooler

These two places, separated by three-quarters of a mile, were twin townships and shared their early history. Originally in the Wooler barony, they were granted to John Vicecomes de Babenburgh, Baron of Embleton, before the twelfth century was out. The reason for this grant is not known, but the twins remained in the Embleton barony until Henry Bolingbroke became its baron. When he was crowned King Henry IV in 1399 the twins automatically became government property and were sold to the fourth Lord Henry Percy of Alnwick.

The ever avaricious Greys bought the property and installed junior members of their family in the two places. In 1415 Radi Grey held Fenton and Thomas Grey had Nesbit. Sir Roger Grey lived at Fenton in 1541 while Nesbit was in the hands of an innominated 'Grey of Chillingham', and in 1715 it was Henry Grey's turn to hold Fenton and Neville Grey's to live in Nesbit. They remained until 1734 when the twins were sold as a single estate to Anthony Isaacson. In 1801 the current owners, the Lambton family which includes the Earls of Durham, bought it.

One of the first things Radi and Thomas did, or had done for them, was to build a tower in their respective domiciles; both were completed before 1415, probably by the same craftsmen. Nesbit's tower did not have a barmekyn and was smaller than the Fenton building which could accommodate forty men. In 1541 Bowes and Ellerker described it as "a grette towre with a barmekyn but in a sad state of repair". They strongly advocated its urgent renovation "for yt standeth in a very convenient and apte place for lyinge of an hundreth men in garrison in tyme of warre against Scotland". For once the surveyors' recommendation was acted upon, and in 1549 Sir John Forster, Warden of the Marches, was able to station a hundred footmen in the tower. After the Union of the Crowns, 1603, its services were no longer required and it was dismantled. The other tower was abandoned at about the same time.

Not a lot of enemy activity associated with the towers has been reported. Nesbit was attacked in 1402 and during the skirmish Sir Patrick Hepburn, one of the Scottish raiders, was killed. It is possible that the need to revenge this death was one reason why Earl Douglas invaded England that year, a foray which ended on Homildon Hill.

Fenton village was attacked by the Earl of Bothwell in 1558 and, inspite of the renovated tower and its garrison, he plundered and burned to his heart's content. Sir Henry Percy, brother of the seventh Earl of Northumberland, intervened eventually, but his men fled when the Scots used their newfangled muskets.

There were other buildings at Fenton, in fact the place was called 'Fenton Town' quite often. One house, now gone, was used for many years after 1541 as a dowager house for the Greys. Fenton church, also gone, was interesting as it could claim to be the mother church of Wooler. It was in a field still called Kirk Close. At the end of the twelfth century John Vicecomes gave its revenue to Alnwick Abbey for the souls of himself, his wife, heirs, father and mother. Wooler and Fenton parishes were combined before 1313, and as the former grew and the latter declined in importance, so Wooler became the main church and Fenton its dependant chapel, eventually to become redundant. There were at least two farms in the township, one of them being let to George and Matthew Culley, the famous agriculturalists, in 1767.

A mile and a half north-east of the village is Fenton House, built by the Earl of Durham for his brother, the Hon. F.W. Lambton, in 1875. It was built on virgin land; there was never a tower there. The sites of the two medieval towers have been forgotten, in fact, although remains of Nesbit's tower were said to be visible in 1715, and the foundations of Fenton were traceable up to the middle of the nineteenth century in the garden of a farmhouse, possibly East Fenton farm.

Milfield

L74 and 75,   P463   NT934338   8 km, 5 miles, north-west of Wooler

The Anglian name may have been 'Melmin' or 'Maelmin', in which case it was the new location for the royal palace of Ad Gefrin after it was moved by King Oswald from Old Yeavering. No trace of the palace has been found but some artefacts believed to have belonged to the kings of Bernicia, including bronze swords and a large urn, have been unearthed.

The human history of the area goes back a lot further than this – to the Neolithic period in fact Archaeologists are finding evidence of cultures as ancient as 4000 BC, including what they believe to be a henge which pre-dates Stonehenge. The whole 'Milfield Basin' is considered to be an archaelogical treasure house.

Milfield's 'modern' history is quite short as before the early sixteenth century its area comprised components of Lanton, Coupland and Howtel Common. In 1512 it was given a discrete identity after Sir William Bulmer ambushed Lord Home when on his way back to Scotland loaded with Northumbrian booty, and since then it has grown into a sizeable village on the A697 road between Wooler and Cornhill.

In 1541 it belonged to the widow of Michael Muschamp, and when she died it was bought by the Greys of Chillingham and used by them as another home for cadet members. There was no tower then, nor in 1584, but almost certainly one was built soon afterwards. Milfield was included in John Warburton's 'Notices of Ruined Towers' of 1715, and local historians believe they hold evidence that tower foundations lie beneath farm buildings in the village.

A lady resident has claimed that when riding her bicycle from Lanton towards Milfield one day at the beginning of World War II she very nearly fell into a wide hole in the road. Some weeks of very wet weather had caused a subsidence which revealed an old tunnel beneath the road. Being wartime, no one had an opportunity to make a proper investigation before the road was repaired, but the popular opinion was that the tunnel had connected one of the towers at Lanton to the Milfield tower.

Milfield Plain, thought to have been the bed of a post-Ice Age lake, is a prolific source of gravel these days, but two or three centuries ago parts of it were still marshy and most of the rest was covered with broom. In the 1770s George Grey, a descendant of the Milfield cadets, began the arduous task of clearing the broom and rendering the Plain suitable for agriculture. George died in 1789, leaving his widow, Mary, with the farm and John, their four year old son. She coped extremely well, and John grew up to become a keen farmer. With some guidance and encouragement from the Culley brothers, he developed into an acknowledged expert and in 1833 was appointed by the Royal Hospital for Seamen, Greenwich, as its northern manager. He moved to Dilston and took charge of the vast estates formerly owned by the Earl of Derwentwater. John Grey is remembered also as the father of Josephine Butler, the vigorous campaigner and reformer who is buried in Kirknewton churchyard.

Milfield Plain has seen other activities besides farming and gravel extraction. During much of the eighteenth century a clearing on it was used as a race course where many quite valuable meetings became a feature of local life. On 29 October 1723 a gold cup worth 60 guineas was the prize, and horses were raced here at least until 1790. An airfield was constructed on another part of the Plain during World War II and was used by both the RAF and the U.S. Air Force pilots for training. Although moved further south, there is still a gliding club there.

Ford

L74 & 75   P463   NT946377   10½ km, 6½ miles, north of Wooler

Ford castle was the first in Northumberland to be designed and constructed in the 'courtyard' or 'quadrilateral' style. King Edward I got the idea while crusading in the Holy Land and introduced it into Britain on his return in 1272, but it took sixty-six years to percolate through to the Border region. A quadrilateral castle consists essentially of a curtain wall with the usual houses of a castle – barracks, stables, bake and brew houses, chapel, etc., built against it and facing inwards onto a courtyard. There was no keep and the owner and his captain lived instead in a hall house. Not quite as strong as a Norman keep and bailey castle, but much more comfortable and adequate against raiding and marauding parties.

The castle was not the first building to occupy the Ford site. Odinal de Ford, who had been granted the land in about 1288 by Baron Muschamp, occupied a house strong enough to withstand the opportunist villain, but its shortcomings were exposed by Robert Bruce after Bannockburn.

The Herons got the property through marriage. Ordinal's daughter and heiress, Mary, took William Heron as her second husband (her first was John Cambous). William was the son of William Hairum, a constable of Bamburgh Castle with a bad reputation for avarice and repression. The couple lived in

Ford's strong house and it was not replaced by the castle until their grandson, also a William, applied successfully to King Edward III in 1338 for a licence to crenellate.

While castle building, Sir William also built a tower for his resident chaplain. It was a strong building, 33 by 20 feet externally, with vaulted ground floor and stairs in the thickness of the walls.

In 1385 Ford was attacked by a large force led by the Earls of Fife, March and Douglas. The castle fell, but was returned to Heron by the terms of a truce concluded at Billymire the following year. A band of Scots returned to Ford before the termination of the truce in 1388, killing some of Heron's men and carrying off £600 worth of cattle. Incensed by this unlawful and unsporting act, Heron retaliated strongly by grabbing 20 oxen, 1600 sheep and £100 in cash from the opposition. This seemed just requital, yet the Earl of Northumberland ordered him to return all he had taken, promising him legal compensation for his losses instead. This was the first recorded occasion when the Warden of the Marches made a genuine attempt to halt the tit of tat raiding which was fuelling Border strife.

Another quadrilateral castle was built in 1341 at Etal, less than two miles away, by Robert Manners. The neighbours were far from friendly, for reasons unclear – perhaps petty jealousies or a little boundary disputing, and in 1428 feelings ran so high that William Heron's son, another William, attempted to assault Etal castle. He wore the sheriff's chain of office so possibly his action had a veneer of legitimacy about it, but this did not prevent his death outside the castle walls at the hands of John Manners. Isabel Heron, the bereaved wife, sued the Manners for compensation; she claimed the amount her husband had been in debt – over £600 – and she won about a quarter of that sum. John also had to pay for the celebration of five hundred masses for William's soul.

In 1509 John Heron, an illegitimate black sheep member of the family, was declared an outlaw as he was wanted for the murder of Sir Robert Kerr, warden of the Scottish Middle March. John was to prove most useful to the Earl of Surrey before the Battle of Flodden, but at the time the English warden had agreed to help find him, and had allowed William Heron, his brother, to be held in Scotland as a hostage. During his absence William Selby was appointed commander of Ford castle, and forty horsemen were allocated to him. This did not stop King James IV four years later from using Ford castle as his personal billet while preparing for his battle on Flodden Hill. Elizabeth, the lady of the house, got an undesirable lodger who paid for his keep by setting fire to the place when he left.

William Heron was released after the battle and lived until 1535. He bequeathed Ford and much other property to his three year old granddaughter Elizabeth, a ward of the Crown. Widow Elizabeth married Sir George Heron of Chipchase, a close relative of William's who believed he was the natural male heir to the Ford estate, and who thus kept a close eye on things while young Elizabeth was growing up.

The castle was attacked again in 1549, this time by General d'Esse and 6000 French soldiers sent to Scotland to revive the flagging Border war in order to distract the English army in France. Sir John Ellerton, Warden of the English Middle March, was in charge of both Ford and Etal castles at the time, but it was Thomas Carr, a youngster who lived at Etal, who did most to discomfort the French. He was not able to save Ford entirely but he succeeded in defending one of the corner towers, a feat which won the heart of seventeen years old Elizabeth. By 1551 they were married and settled into the partially repaired castle.

A long and bitter dispute followed between the Carrs and the Chipchase Herons about the ownership of Ford, a dispute which entailed bloodshed before finally being settled by arbitration. The Carrs were allowed to keep the Ford estates and the Herons were given Simonburn – poor compensation as they had been using the place for years.

Four fairly peaceful generations later, in 1665, the property was inherited jointly by two ladies, one of whom was married to Francis Blake who thus got half of Ford. He had money to spare and was able to buy the other half by 1676. He bought Twizel from one of the Herons in 1685 so that he could dispense two major properties to his two daughters when he died. He did this in 1717 and the eldest daughter, Mary, married into the Delaval family, got Ford. Sarah, the younger, got Twizel.

Mary's son, Francis Delaval, inherited Ford and slightly altered the castle. When he died one of his numerous grandsons, Captain Francis Delaval of Seaton Delaval, inherited but allocated the castle in 1761 to his son, John Hussey Delaval.

As an example of medieval military architecture, Ford castle was destroyed by John. He had modern ideas, and money enough to put them into practice. The work was directed by the owner and George Raffield, a joiner at Seaton Delaval, and together they replaced nearly all the original with a 'Gothick' – mock Gothic – mansion. When Archdeacon Singleton saw the result in 1828 he described it as a "melancholy instance of the flippery and degrading taste of George II's time".

On his death in 1807, John's favourite and youngest daughter, Sarah, the Countess of Tyrconnel, inherited Ford. From her the descent was quite rapid: Susanna, her daughter, married the second Marquis of Waterford, and their son, Henry, married Louisa, daughter of Lord Stuart of Rothesay. In 1859 Henry was killed in a riding accident in Ireland, leaving his all to his widow, now Louisa Machioness of Waterford. She came to live in Ford castle.

She spent her first two years at Ford altering the place, whether for better or worse is a matter of opinion. During the following years, until her death in 1908, she threw herself whole-heartedly into local matters, improving her workers' conditions, organising the village, painting pictures on the school walls and encouraging her farm managers to innovate. After she had gone the estate was sold to Lord Joicey of Etal.

Ford castle is certainly impressive today if regarded as an elaborate Georgian mansion with Victorian modifications and not as a medieval fortification. It is still in use, as a residential educational centre. Little is left of the Parson's tower as Lady Louisa had most of it removed in 1881 because it spoilt her view from the castle.

Etal

L74 & 75   P463   NT925394   13 km, 8 miles, north-west of Wooler

Chronologically, Etal castle was Northumberland's second of the quadrilateral type. It was the smallest, it has been modified or renovated the least and is now the most ruinous – and also the most authentic.

The manor of Etal was granted by Baron Muschamp to Robert Manners in 1232. In 1341 another Robert Manners was granted a licence to crenellate by King Edward III.

The castle took a long time to build. A large residential tower was completed before 1355, but then there was a break in proceedings, probably because of financial difficulties. It was only a temporary halt as the tower was never intended to stand alone; it had stylish windows and other refinements not found on isolated towers, and it resembled a hall house built upwards rather than horizontally. When work restarted the gate tower, other corner towers and the curtain wall all conformed to the originally intended quadrilateral design. It was well into the 1360s before the whole job was completed.

Most of the Scottish unpleasantness of the fourteenth and fifteenth centuries passed by Etal. The Manners biggest headache was the aggressive-ness of their neighbours, the Herons of Ford, but generally the family was left to get on with its social climbing. In 1461 another Robert married Eleanor, a sister and co-heiress of Edmund, Lord Ros. George Manners succeeded his father in 1495 and was knighted in 1501. When his maternal grandparents died, in 1512, be became the eleventh Lord Ros. The shock killed him next year, but his son, Thomas, continued the upward drive to reach the earldom of Rutland in 1525.

Etal castle was not good enough for such grandeur and the family moved across the Till in the early sixteenth century to unfortified premises at New Etal (NT921399). They kept the castle as a bolt hole but it was empty most of the time, which was why King James IV left it alone before the Battle of Flodden in 1513, and why it was used to store captured artillery after the battle.

In 1547 the Earl of Rutland retreated from the scene, exchanging Etal and New Etal for a safer, if not so picturesque, estate in Leicestershire. From that time and for as long as it was capable of offering resistance to an enemy, Etal castle was purely a military establishment commanded by constables of the Crown's choosing. Two or three Collingwoods, Sir John Ellerker and Sir William Selby all took turns at this duty during the second half of the sixteenth century, when at least two pleas for repairs to the castle went unheeded.

After the Union of the Crowns, King James I and VI appointed George Home, Earl of Dunbar, to direct demilitarizing operations, and paid for his services with a lot of Crown-held land, including Etal. The property passed through Home's daughter to her husband, Theophilus Lord Howard de Walden, later Earl of Suffolk. He felt free to dispose of estates he did not require, and in 1636 Etal was sold to Robert Carr, the sitting tenant of New Etal. Robert is said to have been Scottish, but it would be a strange coincidence if he was not related in some way to Thomas Carr, the protector of Ford castle and the dislodger of the Herons.

Robert cleverly managed to support whichever side appeared to be winning during the Civil War, and emerged prosperous and with his estate intact. His descendant in 1746, Sir William Carr, built Etal Manor, a handsome Georgian mansion close to the castle, to replace New Etal. By the marriage of his daughter in 1762 , the estate became the property of James, Earl of Errole, and it remained an Errole possession for three generations until it was sold to James Laing of Sunderland in 1886. Lord Joicey bought both Etal and Ford in 1908.

The ruins of Etal castle are cared for by English Heritage now and are well worth a visit. The complex covers over half an acre of flat land overlooking the River Till at its most beautiful stretch. The quadrilateral outline is obvious although much of the curtain wall is missing. The main features still present are the great residential tower, 46 by 32 feet and four storeys high, the splendid gate tower, a length of wall and the remains of a corner tower. The main tower has lost all its floors and ground floor vault, but the upward view from the ground reveals a huge fireplace and two-light trasomed windows at first floor level, and further decorated windows and a second fireplace higher up. The gate tower has a vaulted entrance arch headed with the Manners' coat-of-arms, guard rooms on either side and two floors above. The remaining piece of wall is surprisingly thin, only about 3 feet, but there are traces of a walkway on top. None of the usual castle buildings remain and it is suggested that these were built of wood.

"A lylle towre which was the mansion of the parsonage" was mentioned in 1541, but there is no sign of it now. There is a chapel in the grounds of Etal

Manor but it was built in 1858; it is dedicated to St. Mary the Virgin as was a medieval church thought to have graced the river bank at one time.

Branxton

L74   P463   NT893375   13$\frac{1}{2}$ km, 8$\frac{1}{2}$ miles, north-west of Wooler

The present village marks the centre of a small estate granted in mid-twelfth century by Baron Muschamp to Gilbert of Branxton, a farmer of Anglian descent. His son Ralph built a church which he dedicated to St. Paul, and he donated its revenue to the infirmary of the monks at Durham. Later the Durham monastery owned the church land and part of the growing village. Another beneficiary was the leper hospital of St. Thomas at Bolton.

Branxton was strategically important as it lay close to the frequently used Tweed crossing at Cornhill and it waymarked an undemanding route to Glendale through the steep hills and very marshy valleys and plains which characterised this area. Thus it was visited often by Scottish raiders throughout the fourteenth, fifteenth and sixteenth centuries. A tower was built in the 1450s but it was laid low by King James IV in 1496.

In or about 1520 John Selby of Grindonrigg, a gentleman porter of Berwick, bought the part of Branxton not owned by the monastery. Lord Dacre, warden of the Marches ordered him to rebuild the tower as he wished to station ten men in it. This was done before 1541. The monastery-owned part was sold after dissolution to the Earl of Rutland, at that time still living at New Etal. Heavy raiding continued unabated, and the new tower lasted only a few years. It had been razed well before 1596, when a gang of Scotsmen, returning home after a frustrated attack on Downham, drove off 16 head of cattle and 80 sheep without appreciable hindrance.

The existing St. Paul's church stands at the western end of the village. Its chancel arch is thought to be part of the original building, the only part to have survived restoration in 1849. A few hundred yards south-west from it, atop a steep little mound called Piper Hill, is a tall Celtic cross set up by the Berwick Naturalists' Club in 1910. Inscribed on the grey granite is the simple message: "Flodden 1513. To the Brave of Both Nations".

Burradon Tower. (p487)

Digression

The Battle of Flodden

Northumberland's bloodiest battle was fought just four miles from the Border, very close to Branxton, on a wet and misty September day in 1513. The antagonists were the army of Scotland led by her king, James IV, and a force of Northern Englishmen commanded by Thomas Howard, the Earl of Surrey, King Henry VIII's lieutenant general of the north.

James IV had been crowned twenty-five years earlier; during his reign he had applied himself successfully to developing Scottish commerce, stabilizing the currency and improving the administration of justice. Wise councilling had, however, been touched occasionally by an adventurous and impulsive streak in his character. This fact asserted itself in 1496 when Perkin Warbeck, impersonating Richard Duke of York, came to him for help to unseat the 'usurper', Henry VII. James obliged by wasting seven Border towers before being stopped at Norham in 1497 by the Earl of Surrey

The ensuing Treaty of Stirling, 1499, restored peace, that relationship with England which James knew to be the most advantageous for Scotland. His marriage in 1502 to Margaret Tudor, Henry VII's eldest daughter, seemed to cement the friendship, and yet it was to last only eleven years.

In 1508 Sir Robert Kerr, warden of the Scottish East March, was slain at a wardens meeting by John Heron, the illegitimate brother of Sir William Heron, lord of Ford castle. John, a crafty man of the country who knew the Borderland intimately, made good his escape so the king demanded, and was given, Sir William to hold as hostage until John could be found and brought to trial. Fights at wardens meetings were not uncommon, but this one rankled considerably.

The English scored another black mark in 1511 when the Earl of Surrey's sons, Edward and Thomas Howard, killed Andre Barton at sea. The Scots regarded Barton as a heroic commander who, in a 'great and costly' ship James had had built for him in 1506, was clearing the Scottish coastline of Flemish pirates. To the English, however, he was himself a common pirate, fair game for His Majesty's navy. James complained bitterly to Henry VIII about the incident but failed to get even an apology – just the curt remark that "The fate of pirates was never the object of discussion between princes".

Lord Home, Warden General of the Scottish Marches, mounted a large scale raid into England in the summer of 1513, supposedly in retaliation for Sir Robert Kerr's death five years before. He succeeded in firing twelve villages and grabbing a considerable amount of booty. While returning with this across Milfield Plain he was intercepted by Sir William Bulmer, who forced him to limp ignominiously back into Scotland minus his ill-gotten gains and three hundred men.

The killing of a Border warden and a heroic sea captain, and then the humiliation of a powerful nobleman, soured James's relations with England, but they were pinpricks and not by themselves sufficient justification for scrapping his peace treaty. The main reason for his doing so was a plea for help from France.

The French had been the Scots ally ever since Balliol signed 'The Auld Alliance' in 1295. In 1512 James had reassured Louis XII he would not stand idly by if ever France was threatened. Such a situation materialised in 1513 when France found herself encircled by the Holy League and, further, was likely soon to face the additional strength of Henry VIII's army. James tried diplomacy first and pleaded for the scrapping of all invasion plans. When this approach failed, the Scottish king felt honour-bound to divert some of England's strength away from Louis and onto himself, by creating a second front in Northumberland.

And so the two armies which were to meet at Flodden assembled, the Scots in Edinburgh and the English at Pontefract.

Scotland in the early sixteenth century was still to a large degree a loose amalgam of clans, and to establish a national army James had to persuade the clan chiefs to join him. Only then would he get the men he wanted, although their loyalty was to their clans, not to Scotland. The king succeeded remarkably well and built up an army which in its early days was estimated to be at least 40,000 strong, led by the flower of Scottish aristocracy. He also had the use of a small number of French soldiers and a great array of heavy cannon, later to be pulled from Edinburgh castle by 400 oxen.

The English had long since lost their feudal ways, although landed gentry were plentiful and some of them joined Surrey with their retainers at various points along his route north. Most of the English recruits were mercenaries, however, largely from Yorkshire, Durham and Northumberland. Henry VIII had raised his army for the French campaign from the south of England in order to leave the north virtually at maximum military strength. Surrey went into battle with about 26,000 men. He had some cannon but not of the calibre of the Scottish.

On August 22 1513, James IV and his army crossed the River Tweed at Cornhill, razed Wark castle and marched downstream to Norham. The castle there resisted attack for five days, then the cannon were brought up and the garrison had no chance when the walls were breached. Etal castle was undefended and was left for possible use after the battle. His rear secure, James then positioned the bulk of his force on Flodden Hill. He chose for himself a more comfortable billet at Ford castle.

Flodden Hill was an excellent vantage point which nature might have designed specially to give James every chance of overcoming any adversary approaching it. It was accessible from the north and south, but only with care for the ways were bunkered by expanses of bog and marsh, virtually impassible for marching soldiers let alone heavy cannon, and the wet weather following a very poor summer had made even the firmer ground treacherous. The west and south-west were guarded by low but steep hills flung out by the Cheviot range, and to the east there flowed the fickle Till. With his army encamped on this natural fortress, James felt a surprise attack was out of the question and he would have plenty of warning of his enemy's approach. He was content to wait for the English to come to him.

He waited nine days, an uncharacteristically long time for this usually active king to kick his heels, and inevitably a breath of scandal filtered out from Ford castle, where Lady Elizabeth Heron was entertaining him without her husband for chaperonage. The fact was that James had no desire to penetrate any further into England. Still mindful of the proven benefits of peace, he did not want this war, and having been more or less forced into it, he did not want to queer a quick and propitious settlement when it was over. He felt he had done his duty to the 'Auld Alliance' by advancing four miles over the Border and attracting the attention of an English army which might otherwise have been available for service in France. His hope was that he could speedily discourage Surrey so that he could retire honourably back into Scotland. Indeed the French expected no more. Anne of Bretagne, Queen of France, had sent him 14,000 francs and a turquoise ring to induce him to march with his men, "if only for her sake", three steps onto English ground. Another cogent reason was that his army was not totally reliable; desertion had been rife and already his strength had been reduced to not more than 30,000 men.

Surrey, in the meantime, had moved his army from Pontefact to Newcastle and then, on 3 September, to Alnwick, where his eldest son Edward, now Lord Admiral of the Fleet, joined him with a thousand naval ratings. The English commander sent a message to James which challenged him to do battle on 9 September on Milfield Plain. The reply came two days later when Surrey was encamped near the former hospital at Bolton, a few miles to the west of Alnwick. James accepted the challenge and the date but refused to leave his advantageous position on Flodden Hill.

Surrey considered his next move. The easiest and most direct route to Flodden was via the left bank of the Till, following what is now the A697 Morpeth to Cornhill road as far as Milfield. This, however, would commit him to attack head-on a well fortified natural citadel held by superior arms and without the benefits of surprise or cover. He remembered from his 1497 campaign how treacherous was the countryside near the Border and, especially, what a difficult obstacle was the Till when in flood. But he remembered also that there was a bridge across the river at Twizel and a couple of reasonable fords near Tillmouth. He decided on attack from the rear, the Scottish side which James would least expect.

Here Surrey had a tremendous stroke of luck. John Heron, the outlaw wanted for the murder of Sir Robert Kerr, approached him and offered to guide his men along the secret ways through the bogs encircling Flodden in return for his pardon. With considerable relief, Surrey agreed to John's terms; his plan would be so much easier to follow with a guide to show the way.

On September 8 the English army set off along the line of the Till in order to give any spies who may have been watching the impression that it was heading straight for Flodden. But at Weetwood it turned right and headed due north along the line of the Devil's Causeway, hidden all the while from the west by the heights of Donnington Moor. That night it camped in woods near Barmoor.

On the fateful September 9 the English struck camp and set off at a rapid pace in a north-westerly direction. They left their baggage behind in order to travel the faster. The Lord Admiral took the vanguard and most of the artillery to Twizel Bridge while Surrey followed with the main body, crossing the Till a mile upstream from the bridge at Mill Ford, now called Heaton Ford. From the river both parties marched towards Branxton, the vanguard a little in front and to the west. The surprise element was maintained until noon.

James was with his troops on Flodden Hill, having that morning bid fairwell to his hostess at Ford by burning down her castle. All eyes were searching the south-east for the first signs of their approaching enemy when news came that the English troops had been spied to the north.

The Scots tactics had been planned on the assumption that the attack would come from the south. James realised immediately that on Flodden Hill he was vulnerable from a northerly attack, so he decided to abandon his prepared position and, with superhuman effort, his whole army, complete with cannon, moved a mile and a half north-west on to the top of Branxton Hill.

From this summit the Scots should have commanded a better view of the northern approach, but the atrocious weather closed down visibility to less than half a mile and neither side could see anything of the other. Indeed, because of this, the advance troops of the Admiral's party nearly spoilt everything; not knowing of James's move, they were beginning to climb

Branxton Hill when they suddenly realised its top was not vacant. They retired hurriedly behind Piper Hill to await their comrades.

At 4.15 in the afternoon the English were ready. Their vanguard took up battle positions on the top and western slopes of Piper Hill to face the Scottish left flank on Branxton Hill, led by Lord Home and the Earl of Huntly. They could just see each other through the mist. For some time they were content to lob cannon-balls across the valley, but eventually, when this became frustratingly unproductive, the Scots – no doubt with blood-curdling yells and soul-destroying groans from bagpipes – charged down their hill to be joined at the bottom by the Admiral's men in hand-to-hand combat. The attack was so ferocious it very nearly succeeded, and Surrey had to supply reinforcements to stop the Scots breaking through.

Thus denied a decisive victory, the Scots fell back to their previous position, and here a strange thing happened: Lord Home took himself and his men off the field. The Earl of Huntly was too weak to hold the position on his own, so he too departed. The desertion of these two contingents in the face of the enemy is hard to explain, but perhaps Home's men were getting restless, perhaps remembering their loss of 300 men on Milfield Plain just a few weeks earlier, perhaps realising they were fighting Borderers like themselves. Raiding Borderers and pinching their cattle was one thing, but a pitched battle against them was something else.

The fighting now moved to the centre of the arena where the two commanders and the main ranks of their armies faced each other. After an exchange of cannon fire it was again the Scots who took the initiative. Abandoning their dominant position, they started to charge down the hill. This time the going was not so easy: parts of the decline were steeper, the grass was more slippery and the valley at the bottom was considerably more marshy. Their progress slowed, their charge became a debacle, they became almost sitting targets for the English bows and cannon. Scots who escaped the missiles were shown the superiority of the English bills and long swords over the cumbersome Scottish pikes.

By 6.15 in the evening it was all but over. In two hours a proud army had been decimated. King James lay dead, and so too did nearly all his clan chiefs and an estimated 9000 men. The English had won the battle decisively although not without cost, for they too had lost many men, perhaps around 2000. Surrey did not bother to pursue the Scottish survivors, who were left to struggle back across the Tweed.

The last medieval battle to be fought on English soil was over. Never again were knights in armour going to stand before their personal standards to batter away with arrows and ironmongery. Soon small arms would engender a whole new ball game.

Area 2, Sub-Area C   Up The Till

Weetwood

L75   P476   NU016297   3 km, 2 miles, north-east of Wooler

Weetwood Hall is a rambling Georgian family house with four reception rooms, seven bedrooms and four attics. It replaced a Jacobean house which incorporated a tower built towards the end of the fifteenth century.

The site is on the right bank of the Till, just clear of possible swampy ground and surrounded by hills except to the west. Weetwood Moor to the south was host every Whit Monday until 1880 to a cattle, sheep and horse fair; one of its little tors commemorates this by its name, Whitsunbank Hill.

In 1595 Sir John Carey got news that a much wanted man, one of the Kerrs of Cressford, was going to the fair so he laid an ambush for him. Unfortunately for the law, Kerr's spies were as efficient as Carey's and he heard about the ambush. He went to the fair alright, but Carey never saw him.

Although so close to Baron Muschamp's land, Weetwood was a township in the Alnwick barony, held in 1242 by Hugh de Bolbec. Thomas Grey bought it in the fourteenth century, then let it to a family which took Weetwood as its surname. These people held it for two and a half centuries, and it was in this period that a tower was built. In 1541, we are told, the tower was a small one and it was in good repair. The Selbys bought it in 1608, and then the Ordes eleven years later, the latter building the still existing house round about 1715. They sold to the Dagleishes in 1719, but another branch of the Orde family bought it back in 1747 and held it for the next two centuries.

Horton

L75   P464   NU026307   4¹/₂ km, 2³/₄ miles, north-east of Wooler

A picture exists of 'Horton Castle' as it was seen by two artist brothers, Samuel and Nathaniel Buck, in 1728. It is a stylised, 'drawn with a ruler', effort but it shows clearly a very high wall with corner turrets enclosing a garden containing a high, roofless ruin. At first glance it looks rather like a quadrilateral castle, but a closer look reveals a number of features, like two-light windows and no fewer than thirteen hearths, which must down-grade it to a fortified manor-house.

It was built between 1568 and 1674 to replace a great tower with a barmekyn first mentioned in 1415 and seen as being in decay in 1541. The history of the estate goes back to 1242 when William Turnberville held it from the Baron of Alnwick. The family held it until they ran out of males in 1358 and heiress Joan passed it to her husband, David Grey, a younger brother of the mainline Greys of Castle Heaton. Horton did not belong to the mainline until the seventeenth century.

Sir John Grey, younger brother of Sir Ralph, the first to occupy Chillingham, got Horton in 1417. A soldier, he was fighting in France with King Henry V in 1419 and while his king was taking Rouen he "took by storm" the strong castle of Tanquiville in Normandy. This earned him not only the king's praise but also an earldom and an election to the Knighthood of the Garter. John chose as his title an Anglicised version of Tanquiville – he became the Earl of Tankerville.

For an unknown reason, John's son Henry lost the title in 1449. It was never abrogated, however, and was available for further use in 1695 when King William III wished to honour the Greys of Chillingham. By that time the two branches of the family had been united by the marriage of a Horton daughter to a Chillingham son.

The manor-house remained empty for several years after this union, until it was sold in 1701 to a distant cadet branch of the family, the Greys of Howick. They held what became a roofless ruin for sixty years, then it seems to have been consigned to nature. In 1808 it was demolished completely and its stone used to build West Horton farm at the foot of the knoll it once crowned.

Fowberry Tower

L75   P476   NU039293   5 km, 3 miles, north-east of Wooler

Travel from Wooler towards Belford and just before crossing the River Till on the B6349 road a large mansion will be seen on the right. This is Fowberry Tower, a most fascinating building which is not all it seems.

For starters, the face seen from the road is the back of the house, not the front as might be expected. Then the main entrance gate is on the left, not the right, of the road; the drive goes under the public road, sharing a bridge with the river, and then makes a wide circle to the front door. But by far the most unexpected and interesting secret of the house is that it completely envelopes a medieval fortified tower. Building dates range from 1400 to 1800, the newer, outside parts sitting like a cosy over a teapot, totally hiding the older parts.

Castle Hill, some six hundred yards south-west of the mansion, is the site both of a Romano-British settlement and the dwelling of the first post-Conquest farmers. The family of William de Folebyr held land hereabouts and at Coldmartin and Hazelrigg for one knight's fee from Baron Vescy of Alnwick in 1273.

Evidently the holding was too large for one family to handle as a parcel of it to the south and east of Castle Hill was passed quite soon to John de Malton for use as pasture, and then in 1327 it went to Robert de Oggil, who founded a farm on it which he called Ogleburgh. It stayed in the main Ogle family until another Robert became the first Lord Ogle, then, at a date between 1469 and 1530, it was passed to a kinsman, Cuthbert Ogle, the parson at Ford. The name 'Ogleburgh' appears on Armstrong's map of 1769, but it has been replaced by 'Newhall' on all O.S. maps (NU039286) since the mid-nineteenth century.

The principal part of the township remained in the Folebyr family for over three hundred years, during which time the name evolved through Folberry to Fowberry. A Roger Folberry built a tower close to the River Till in or about 1400, and in 1524 the owner of the day snatched two hundred Scotsmen from a powerful raiding party, an act of bravura which earned him a reprisal attack and a fire-damaged home. It was repaired before 1541.

Financially, things did not go well with the family and they had to mortgage their property to John Strother of Kirknewton. He foreclosed in 1590 and the tower became his. What happened to the Fowberrys is not recorded.

Seventy-odd years later, when there was a touch of peace in the air, the Strothers decided to make their tower more commodious: They added more rooms to each end of the old building, and they marked this enterprise by installing a sundial engraved '1666', which now graces a garden wall.

And so to 1776, when the Strothers sold to Francis Blake, the amateur architect who had inherited Twizel when a young man in 1734. His plan for Fowberry Tower was to strip off the wings the Strothers had added, and then to build a large Georgian mansion embracing the original tower, to smother it completely while taking advantage of its solid framework and sturdy vault.

Work on this scheme was well advanced when Francis died, in either 1780 or 1786 – there is documentary disagreement. His son, also Francis, did a little more work after 1790, but only got as far as installing the pediment at the centre of the front face before running out of money. His creditors sold tower and estate to Matthew Culley, one of the famous agriculturalist brothers. He completed the building work.

Although Matthew died in 1849, Fowberry remained in the Culley family until the outbreak of the Great War, when the mansion was converted for use as a convalescent home for servicemen. It is a private residence today, but should it ever come on the market it is hoped that English Heritage will consider buying it for the nation, for it is a building of exceptional interest. Quite a lot of the medieval tower's walls can be seen inside, and one length in particular, in an upstairs room, testifies to considerable strength and craftsmanship – as well as to the presence at one time of a parapet walk. The original vault is still in good shape, used now as a boiler room, fuel store and wind cellar, while above it are two large reception rooms of great merit. One has been redecorated and returned to its former glory, but the other, unfortunately, must wait awhile for financial help.

Hetton Hall

L75   P464   NU0413334   7 km, 4½ miles, north-east of Wooler

Heton, Heaton, Heddon – all have been used in the past, and all are guaranteed to cause confusion, especially with Castle Heaton which nineteenth century historians insisted on calling Hetton Castle. The modern name identifies a farmstead pleasantly, and secretly, situated near the west bank of the Hetton Burn, a tributary of the River Till.

There was a Norman township here, a parcel of Alnwick barony held in 1242 by Robert de Clifford for half a knight's fee; he paid cash to Baron Vascy in lieu of service, which was rather unusual. Little is known after this date, except from 1474 to 1779 a succession of Carrs – most with Christian name John – held the place, and one of them built a tower towards the end of the sixteenth century. Since 1918 the Cooperative Wholesale Society have been owners.

The tower, still habitable, is a medium-sized, rectangular building of three floors. The roof is not original, and several Victorian windows have been inserted, but a curious half-round projection corbelled out at first floor level and rising nearly to the eaves is authentic. This was probably a look-out; the corbels are too solid to permit of a gardrobe drain. Wings have been built on both gables, one of which is strengthened by flying buttresses and looks nearly as old as the tower.

Hazelrigg

L75   P464   NU056331   8 km, 5 miles, north-east of Wooler

A quite large township held from Baron Vascy by the Fowberry family during the twelfth century. In the thirteenth it was given to a Fowberry daughter as a wedding present when she married someone who took Hazelrigg as his surname. The couple settled down on the estate and built a home, about which all that is known is that it was on the side of a hill. There are several 'qualified' Hazelriggs – North, South, Old, Mill, Dean and Moss – but none without an adjective so the house's exact position is not known. 'Old' Hazelrigg seems the best bet as it presumably is the oldest, and it lies to the side of Dancing Green Hill.

The Hazelrigg family came to an end towards the conclusion of the fifteenth century when an heiress married Sir Thomas Haggerston. Hazelrigg was deserted while the couple lived at Haggerston, but when Sir Thomas died his widow returned to the old place and her newly acquired stepson built a tower for her protection in 1507.

It was a large fortification which housed up to twenty soldiers on occasion. The Kerrs and three hundred Scotsmen were unstoppable in 1515, however, when they pillaged the area and took thirty prisoners, eighty head of cattle, thirty horses and 'insight' – household goods and furniture. The tower was left in flames.

Some repairs were carried out before 1538, but the surveyors Bowes and Ellerker noted in 1541 that it was a low, incomplete building, what there was of it in good condition. The Scots returned in 1546 and again in 1588 and there are no further records of tower repairs. The Haggerstons retained the property, however, and in 1715 John Warburton reported that a 'good house' belonging to Edward Haggerston had been built out of the tower's ruins.

Chatton

L75   P476   NU057281   6½ km, 4 miles, east of Wooler

A pleasant village on the banks of the Till north of Chillingham. Up to the seventeenth century it sported two towers, one belonging to the parish church of the Holy Cross and the other to the Earl of Northumberland, the landlord. In a sense, both belonged to the earl, for the church had been granted to Alnwick Abbey in 1157, and remained so tied until the dissolution of the monasteries.

The village survived the plague in 1352 and grew steadily into a thriving agricultural community. By the nineteenth century it had diversified, with interests like weaving, tailoring and dressmaking, making bricks and tiles, and milling.

The vicars' tower was built near the church before 1415. It was still there in 1541, but later it was knocked down and replaced by a more comfortable, but unfortified, vicarage. In its turn, this was replaced in 1834 by a large mansion built to designs by John Dobson. During the less pious twentieth century, when one vicar could cope with four or more churches and did not need all available vicarages, the mansion was divided and sold as two homes called East and West Longstone. According to the site plan of East Longstone House, the foundations of the tower are below the lawn in its garden, which commands a beautiful view over the Till.

The Earl's tower also existed before 1415, held by Robert Forstere. During the sixteenth century it was much used by wardens of the Marches and was capable of accommodating up to eighty men. In 1541 they were commanded by Richard Fowberry of Fowberry Tower, just over a mile away. In 1616 John Collingwood was in charge, and then.....nothing! Not another word about the tower or its occupants is recorded.

One of the early surveys said the Earl's tower was built on 'common land in Chatton'. This is not very helpful as before the Land Enclosure Acts of the eighteenth century all land in Chatton township was common except a few fields around the village and Chatton Park, an area to its north-east reserved for the earl's sport. The tower may have been a shooting lodge just outside this park, or Sir Ralph Grey may have given us a better clue to the tower's whereabouts when he was accused in 1634 of surreptitiously adding a few acres of 'Chatton Common' to his Chillingham Park.

A battle, round two of the important conflict started at Brunanburgh, was fought on the banks of the Till near Chatton in 937. It was small scale but very messy, between Athelstan, the Wessex king who was trying to unite England under his flag, and some wayward Danes and Cumbrians. It is called the Battle of Wandon in history books, Wandon being a farm a mile west of Chatton (NU039281) possibly used as the headquarters of one side. The killing lasted two days, at the end of which Athelstan emerged the clear winner.

Chillingham Castle

L75   P476   NU061257   7 km, 4½ miles, east of Wooler

'Chevelyngham', the original name of this manor on the River Till, was part of the Alnwick barony until about 1170 when it was settled as a dowry on Thomas de Muschamp, Baron of Wooler, when Maud de Vescy married him. For many years, both before and after this transfer, the tenants of Chevelyngham were the Huntercomb family. Prosperous farmers, they built a fine stone manor-house early in the thirteenth century.

William Huntercomb climbed into the aristocracy by marrying Isobel Muschamp, one of three sisters who became joint inheritors of the barony when Robert, their father, died in 1250. William did rather better than he had dared hope, for the other two girls died young and he and Isobel were left in sole charge; no longer tenants, they were now the owners of Chevelyngham, with heritable rights.

Elevation meant also that the Huntercombs were on royalty's visiting list. King Henry III stayed with them in 1255 while returning from a holiday with his daughter, Scottish King Alexander III's queen, and in 1298 King Edward I called en route for less pleasant business at Falkirk.

Walterus replaced his father in 1271. He had no children so the next inheritor was a nephew, Nicholas de Neubaud in about 1300. This fellow managed to exhaust the coffers and was soon being hounded by creditors. He changed his name to Huntercomb, but that failed to mask the scent and soon he was borrowing money. The inevitable outcome was the sale of most of Wooler barony in 1326 to Sir John de Lilburn, and Chevelyngham, estate and manor-house – went to Sir Thomas de Heton in 1328. Sir Thomas moved in from Castle Heaton, which he sold to Thomas Grey.

In 1344 King Edward III granted Sir Thomas a licence to crenellate his new home, to strengthen it "with walls of stone and lime" and to convert it "into a castle or fortress". Thus encouraged, Sir Thomas knocked down most of the manor-house and built his Chillingham Castle on its site. Small parts of the old walling were incorporated in the base of the new edifice, notably in the south-west tower.

The castle was of the quadrilateral, or courtyard, type, basically similar to the castles at Ford and Etal, both of which pre-dated it by a few years. It had a strong square tower at each corner, all with vaulted ground floor rooms and with a dungeon in the north-east tower. Curtain walls connected the towers, all quite plain except the south wall which was broken by a well protected entrance. Leaning against the inside facing of the walls were the castle's essential buildings – the great hall on the east, guard room on the south and accommodation for retainers and horses on the west. There was nothing against the north wall. It seems probable, but not certain, that at this stage all the buildings were made of timber. Apparently as an afterthought, in 1348 when the work was practically completed, Sir Thomas remembered the vicar of Chillingham and added suitable quarters for him above the entrance.

Castle building seems to have been contagious in this area at this time: first Ford, then Etal, then Chillingham and now a fourth appeared at Castle Heaton, the Greys' family home. Northumbrian Borderers were making life as difficult as possible for Scottish raiders, yet they failed to eradicate the menace. In 1353 it was reported that only four of the twenty-two farms on the Chillingham estate were tenable, all the others having been wasted.

Castles are not frequently subject to swapping, but in 1398 the Greys and Ralph Neville, Earl of Westmorland, did just that. The Greys exchanged their relatively new place at Castle Heaton for the grim frontier castle at Wark-on-Tweed and the Nevilles took Castle Heaton. At the time, neighbours must have thought the Greys quite mad, but perhaps they were gifted with remarkable foresight, for within twelve months the Nevilles had decided they did not like Castle Heaton and had moved out. The Greys repossessed, and thus entered the fifteenth century holding not one but two castles. Very soon they were to add a third.

At this very crucial time there is a tantalising forty year gap in Chillingham's recorded history. It is known that Alan de Heton held Chillingham in 1415, but apart from that there is a total blackout in the records from 1400 to 1440, a period during which the Hetons lost their castle and faded out of the picture while the Greys came into sharp focus. It is a mystery why and precisely when Sir Ralph Grey (elder brother of Sir John of Horton) found himself installed in Chillingham Castle, where he died in 1443.

The Greys were a very powerful and wealthy family now. They owned Wark castle (although the Crown borrowed it occasionally) and did not let it go until 1920. They held Castle Heaton from the Durham bishops until 1559 then owned it for a further forty or fifty years. Now they owned Chillingham and retained possession until 1982. In addition, the family developed an insatiable appetite for estates in and around Glendale – Coupland, Akeld, Hethpool, Kilham, Pressen, Nesbit and Fenton, Pawston and Westwood, to name a few.

Chillingham Castle got a face-lift just before 1513, when the buildings ranged around its courtyard were replaced by larger structures in stone, providing accommodation for up to a hundred horsemen. Perhaps this is why only one attack on the castle is recorded. It happened in 1536 and came not from the Scots but from Northumbrian rebels during the Pilgrimage of Grace. They besieged the place for a short time and the walls sustained a little cannon-fire damage which was replaced before 1541.

Major changes were made to the castle during Queen Elizabeth's reign, the most significant being the demolition of the blank north wall and the building in its place a palatial entrance reached by a cascade of steps and with a fashionable long gallery above it. Other innovations were a terrace on the south side of the courtyard and, leading from it, a much larger great hall in the south range.

King James I of England and VI of Scotland came to see this 'gentleman's mansion' in 1617, and in 1623 Sir William Grey, the owner, was elevated to the peerage as Lord Grey of Wark, supposedly in recognition of his efforts to pacify the post-Union Border. Such sovereign honour did not deter the new lord from supporting Parliament during the Civil War, 1642 to 1651, however. This treachery appears to have done no harm to the family's advancement, for when King William III was bestowing honours in 1695, Lord Grey's son, who had inherited in 1674, was created the Earl of Tankerville and Viscount Glendale. The earldom had originally been given to John Grey of Horton in 1419 and had been allowed to lapse in 1449. Since then the Horton and Chillingham branches of the Grey family had merged, so it was quite proper for the title to be resurrected. It went back into hibernation when the earl died in 1701, for he had no sons, but was revived a second time for the earl's son-in-law thirteen years later. The lucky man was Charles Bennet, Lord Ossulston, and he obtained special permission in 1714 to don the earldom.

Much was done to the castle during the eighteenth and nineteenth centuries, for you cannot stop a good earl from improving his status symbol. In 1753 a portico was built in the courtyard with an arcade below and grand stone stairs leading to a balcony which gave access to a new great hall in the modified south range. Many statues were included, including a selection of William Caxton's 'Nine Worthies'. Alexander the Great, Julius Caesar and Charlemagne are there. The ground floor of the south range was converted into cellars and the outside south face was banked up with soil in order to bring the lawn right up to the hall.

In 1803 the east range was rebuilt to include a suite of state rooms. At the same time some new buildings, including a kitchen and servants' quarters, were built outside the quadrilateral on the east side. A quarter of a century later Sir Jeffrey Wyatville, fresh from his work at Windson Castle, was commissioned to lay out the gardens and decorate the great hall. Finally, in 1873, another building was added to the kitchen block.

The earl's family lived in this palatial residence until 1932, when death duties and maintenance expenses forced the eighth earl and his wife, Lady Violet Tankerville, to vacate the castle and move into a village house. They sold most of the castle's furniture and fittings but sentiment prevented their selling the building, which was left to decay. The decision finally to sell was made by the tenth earl, who lived in America, in 1982, by which time the place was virtually a ruin.

The buyer could not have been more suitable. Sir Humphrey Wakefield is an art dealer with lots of experience in restoring old buildings, and enough money to indulge in this hobby. As a bonus, his wife us a direct descendant of the Chillingham Greys. The decision to restore the castle to its former glory was acted upon immediately but will take many years to complete. By June 1986 part of the castle had been restored and the gardens had been tidied, so the public was invited to view the transformation. As work proceeds, more and more rooms are being opened.

> There are other attractions besides the castle and its gardens in or near Chillingham which are worthy of your attention:
>
> **St. Peter's Church**   Alabaster figures of Sir Ralph and Elizabeth Grey lie serenely on their decorated tomb in this beautiful old church, the nave of which is probably twelfth century. The sculptures are considered to be the finest in the Northern Counties.
>
> **Chillingham White Cattle**   Herd of wild, pure bred cattle which has been trapped in Chillingham Park since 1292. You will be escorted by a warden but it is quite safe to go to within 50 yards of these majestic beasts.
>
> **The Hurl Stone**   Ancient pillar which tradition says marks an underground passage between Cateran Hole near Eglingham and Hen Hole on Cheviot. Listen for the subterranean horsemen's cry to their horses: "Hup, Hup, and Gee again, round and round the Hurl Stone".

Hepburn

L75   P476   NU070248   8½ km, 5¼ miles, east of Wooler

An interesting ruined strong house lies on the eastern edge of Chillingham Park and can be seen from the minor road which heads towards Ros Castle, a Celtic fort and medieval signal station. It is marked on O.S. maps as a bastle, but it is much larger, more elaborate and better fortified than such a structure, and anyway it was built some two hundred years before bastles were thought of.

The house is roofless and a great cleft has appeared in one wall, but otherwise it is fairly complete. It is double gabled and has two vaulted chambers on the ground floor, one of them with an eight foot deep pit beneath, thought to have been a dungeon. Spiral stairs lead to two upper floors, the first with three rooms, the second with two low attic rooms. All the walls are at least six feet thick. The whole is commodious and the claim made in 1509 that it could accommodate twenty horsemen is quite believable.

This was the home of the Hebburn family who had held the township of Hepburn from the Baron of Wooler in the early thirteenth century, then as freehold property. They retained it until 1755, when Robert Hebburn, the last of the line, died. At first their home was probably a timber hall house, then they built this strong stone house in the fourteenth century. When it became vacant after Robert's death, the Earl of Tankerville bought it so that he could add the estate to his land. He had no use for the house and it was left alone, which is why it is still unadulterated medievalism, untouched for at least 250 years.

Little is known about the Hebburns, but there are two well authenticated stories about them. The first concerns Nicholas de Hebburn who, in 1271, gave a patch of his land to the vicar of Chillingham. The gift was matched by the villagers of Hepburn who gave honey and wax. This benevolence was intended to persuade the vicar to hold services in Hepburn's chapel of St. Mary on the three principal feasts of Our Lady.

Three centuries later the Hebburns killed John, a young member of the Story family. They freely admitted committing the act but claimed they had permission to do so by the boy's father, 'Red' Martyn Story. The victim's two brothers, unaware of their father's unnatural connivance, established a blood feud with the Hebburns, but eventually, after the death of the father in 1588, both sides submitted to arbitration. It transpired that not only had Red Martyn granted permission for the killing of his son, he also paid "such certain sums of money for the said agreement...as the Storys of that time was fully content and agree with". No reason for the death contract is known, but the feud was called off and no doubt the two families managed to coexist as the arbitrators wished, "as lovers and friends as they ought to be".   [Plate 1]

Old Bewick

L75   P476   NU065218   9½ km, 6 miles south-east of Wooler

Although best known as the place where the the Breamish becomes the Till, Old Bewick nevertheless has an intriguing history not overtly connected with the river.

It is a small village on the Chatton to Alnwick road, with a beautiful little church containing windows and a sanctuary arch dating from early Norman times. This is at the end of a narrow lane which leaves the main road at the northern end of the village. At the junction is a monument with Celtic-like decorations; it is really just an invitation to visit the church, but it also serves to mark the most likely site of a fifteenth century tower. The original village almost certainly straddled the lane, so possibly it resembled Warkworth in having its church at one end and its fortification at the other.

In medieval times there was no 'New' Bewick so the village had an unqualified name which is believed to have derived from 'Beo-wick', Old English for 'Bee Farm'. As a royal manor attached to Bamburgh, its function was to supply the royal household with honey. The monks of Bamburgh's Augustinian monastery built the first church at Bewick, so maybe they were allowed a taste of honey too.

King William II granted the manor in 1093 to Arkle Moreal, the commander of the garrison in Bamburgh's fledgling castle. It was a reward for services rendered, for it had been Moreal who killed Malcolm III, 'Ceann Mor', the King of the Scots, at Alnwick that year. His job at Bamburgh was residential and he never lived at Bewick; perhaps he never even saw the place for he lost it two years later for joining Robert de Mowbray's revolt.

Henry I, King William's successor, married the orphan daughter of Malcolm III who answered to Matilda, Maud or Edith. She resembled her mother, the saintly Queen Margaret, in her interest in religion. With singular insensitivity, in view of its recent association with her father's killer, Henry gave the manor of Bewick to his bride, who immediately rebuilt the church in elaborate Norman style. In 1107 she gave the manor to the Prior of Tynemouth as a memorial to her father who was buried at Tynemouth Priory. It remained Tynemouth's property until dissolution in 1539.

Bewick prospered under this regime. Some of the monks lived in the manor and they were joined from time to time by other churchmen desiring a restful vacation. In 1253 King Henry III granted the village the right to hold a market on Thursdays, and a market cross was erected near the church. The prior also had permission to hunt, and to take timber from the forest which at that time covered a large part of Bewick Moor.

Come the fifteenth century and the monks found that Bewick was not so peaceful after all. The prior built a tower near the end of the century and in 1509 this was occupied by Gilbert Collingwood and, during emergencies, up to forty horsemen.

After dissolution the manor reverted to the Crown and another Collingwood, Robert, was installed as bailiff. He was described at the time as "A true sharpe Borderer" who kept the tower in good condition "entirely for the defence of the inhabitants". Later bailiffs were not so public spirited; an unnamed one in 1614 was accused of holding people in the tower in order to exact illegal payment for their release. Such men allowed the tower to deteriorate and it was not long before it ceased to have any defence capability. At the end of its useful life, in the 1670s or '80s, two or three homeless people were allowed to shelter in it. Before the turn of the century the Crown had sold the manor to Ralph Williamson.

The tower ruins could be remembered by old inhabitants in 1866, but by then they were no longer visible as the main road had been laid over them. The little church had more luck: although it suffered vandalism by General Leslie's Scottish army in 1640, and its roof was blown off in 1714, it was completely restored in 1866.

Area 2, Sub-Area D   South of Wooler

Earle

L75   P475   NT987262   2 km, 1¹/₄ miles, south of Wooler

Yherdhill in the thirteenth century, Yerdehill in the fourteenth, Yerdlun in the fifteenth, Yardle in 1584, this hamlet of a couple of farms and a few houses has at last got rid of its initial letter, although the largest house in the area is still called Yearle.

From early Norman times, Earle (to use its modern name) was a township within the Alnwick barony, leased to John Viscount, Baron of Embleton from 1242 until his death in 1245 when his daughter Rameta terminated the agreement. The property went jointly to Robert Hebburn of Hepburn and Thomas de Escot. Three hundred years later the joint owners were Thomas Hebburn and Gilbert Scott – tenacious families!

The duo built some sort of strong house in or about 1500. It was marked on Christopher Dacre's plat of 1584, and it is of interest that "Here the East and Middle Marches are divided" was noted beside its position. Nothing remains of the building now. The present farmer will show you his 'pele tower', but in reality this is only a Victorian dovecot.

Middleton Hall

L75   P475   NT988254   3 km, 2 miles, south of Wooler

The present Middleton Hall is an attractive white building close to where the Harthope Burn disgorges its pure Cheviot water into Happy Valley. It was built in 1807 by the governors of the Royal Hospital for Seamen, Greenwich, for their local agent, George P. Hughes. In a meadow beyond its garden are the uncommunicative sites of two fifteenth century towers; this is historically-rich land.

Gospatric (sometimes Cospatrick), who claimed descent on the distaff side from the Bamburgh royal dynasty, was Earl of Northumberland from 1069 to 1072, during William the Conqueror's reign when county earls were county governors. He lost the job when accused of helping rebels at Durham and York and had to retire to Scotland where, a little later, King Malcolm III granted him land around Dunbar.

King Henry I, who held the English Crown from 1100 to 1135, gave Gospatric's similarly named son a position on the English side of the Border. The work has never been properly explained, but appears to have been connected with immigration. As payment, Gospatric II was granted a serjeanty of fourteen Northumbrian estates, from Longwitton in the south (NY078888) to Beanley in the north (NU081183) and including Netherwitton, Stanton, Longhorsley and Titlington. Although not actually in the serjeanty, Middleton was closely connected to it.

The township was centred on Old Middleton (NT990239). Here Gospatric made a home and, although he returned to Scotland after a short time and busied himself procreating the earls of Dunbar, he left behind a family which remained for two hundred years. The first two generations included several girls who married locals to initiate a number of important dynasties such as the Middletons of Belsay, the Merleys of Morpeth, the Fenwicks of Fenwick and Wallington and the Corbets of Stanton and Kirknewton.

Males were not so numerous and allowed the line to die out in the fourteenth century. Henry Percy acquired the township in 1335 and absorbed it into his Alnwick barony, where it was lost in obscurity until the latter part of the fifteenth century. A family called Rutherford bought it then, and some years later it was divided equally between two brothers, John and Henry Rutherford.

Each brother built a tower, close together about a mile north of the village. The 1541 survey describes them as "two stone houses or castells", so they appear to have been quite large. In 1573 John Rutherford sold his tower to Sir John Forster of Bamburgh, but Henry held on to his.

There was a rather nasty raid on Middleton in 1580 during the course of which the intruders did much damage but lost their leader, Dandye Dagleish of Limpetlaw. Time and again Border history exposes the absolute arrogance of the raiders of both sides: they seem to have expected their victims to submit placidly and were most indignant if any ventured to stand up to them. Dagleish's family was bent on vengeance, and life at Middleton was rather hectic for the next twenty years. An attempt to defuse the situation was made at a wardens' meeting in 1596, but there was another raid the following year.

Henry Rutherford's tower came out of this testing time much the worse for wear; its owner, probably Henry's grandson, decided to scrap it and build the first Middleton Hall a couple of hundred yards to its north. Forster's tower was not mentioned so presumably it was a total wreck.

The seventeenth century saw the estate split up into discrete farms. Middleton Hall itself was bought by Francis Radcliffe, the first Earl of Derwentwater and grandfather of the ill-fated Jacobite leader. In 1749 the confiscated property was granted to the Greenwich Hospital, and fifty-five years later a new mansion was built of the site of the Hall.

Tower Martin (Coldmartin)

L75   P476   NU008269   2 km, 1¼ miles, south-east of Wooler

William de Folebyr, the first post-Conquest farmer at Fowberry, held land here in 1273, and the family still held it in 1590 when the following report was written: "Cadmertoune – One tower of stone and lime of Roger Fowberry's of Fowberry gent. utterly decayed notwithstanding it hath land belonging to it able to keep two men and horsse fit for service".

Up to this time 'Cadmertoune' included all the land now assigned to Coldmartin and Tower Martin farms. The split between the two probably occurred round about 1600 as Tower Martin farmhouse and its gin-gan were built early in the seventeenth century. The original deeds still exist to prove this. Coldmartin is the more northerly of the two and the farm sits close to the top of the steep drop to Milfield Plain. This 'rim' makes the lake theory very credible.

Coldmartin as now defined, never had a tower. The only tower ruin in the area is very clearly in Tower Martin territory, and its name should reflect this. It comprises one wall only, 24 feet long and 9 to 10 feet high. The south face retains its ashlar but the other side is mainly rubble in-fill. There are no traces of the other walls. The ruin stands in the middle of a field above a small valley which marks the boundary between the farms; a shepherd's cottage was a near neighbour two centuries ago but now there is nothing, not even a tree, to keep it company.

So far as is known, only one local resident ever hit the headlines. He was called John of Coldmartin and he achieved infamy by striking a priest called John of Leicester in 1313. As a punishment he was dressed in sackcloth and beaten around Wooler church three times while a curate explained to watchers what was happening.

Lilburn

L75   P476   NU021241   5 km, 3 miles, south-east of Wooler

Sir John Lilburn was lord of both Lilburn and Shawdon in 1320. How, or why, he got there is not disclosed although it has been hinted that King Edward II had something to do with it. If the estates were as large then as they are now he was a considerable land-owner and could well afford to build a tower for his work-force in each estate before 1403.

The family preferred Shawdon as a residence, and by 1415 Lilburn tower was rented to John Carr. This lasted until 1506 when the Lilburns sold their property to William and Isabel Proctor; they lived at Shawdon while their son, Geoffrey, lived at Lilburn. Somehow Geoffrey managed to acquire another tower at Lilburn and two are noted in the 1514 and 1524 surveys.

By 1541 no Proctor was living at Lilburn but they still owned one of the towers, which was roofless. The other had been sold to Cuthbert Ogle, the parson at Ford, but was occupied by Lyonell Graye, a porter at Berwick castle and spare time farmer. Proctor's tower was probably dismantled soon after this, and neither it nor the family are mentioned again in the Lilburn context. The Ogles' tower was well maintained, however, and the Ogles were able to lease it to the Greys of Chillingham in 1596.

Enter the Collingwoods, a family of growing local importance, especially in Eslington and Ryle, during the sixteenth and seventeenth centuries. In the early part of the latter Thomas Collingwood married Anne Grey, a daughter of the lord of Chillingham. Father-in-law looked after young Thomas: before very long he owned Lilburn.

John Collingwood owned the estate in 1774 and appears to have been content to live in the cramped accommodation offered by the tower when many other property owners were building comfortable mansions. Indeed it was not until 1828 that the then owner, Henry J.W. Collingwood, called in John Dobson to design a replacement in the Tudor style.

Henry died in 1842 and his son inherited. He sold Lilburn to another part of the family, to Edward John Collingwood of Chirton, near North Shields, a nephew of Admiral Lord Collingwood. Edward added stables to the mansion and laid out the gardens; his descendants owned the place until 1995.

Interesting ruins still remain of one of the towers, which one it is impossible to say. They have been vandalised, but this was stopped by a preservation order in 1933 and the north wall still reveals its ashlar facing and the springing of the ground floor vault. The tower was built on a level rock platform above the Lil Burn and originally measured 40 by 33 feet. It probably had two floors above the vault, but there was no room for a barmekyn. Ruins of a small chapel stand close by.

Ilderton

| L75 | P476 | NU016218 | 7 km, 4¼ miles, south-east of Wooler |

Roddam

| L75 | P476 | NU025204 | 8½ km, 5¼ miles, south-east of Wooler |

Two small communities in the Cheviot foothills, just over a mile apart, with not dissimilar backgrounds. Both were home to Anglo-Saxon families who took the place names as their surnames; they share one church; both had fifteenth century fortified towers and both of these were superseded by eighteenth century mansions.

It has been suggested that the original Roddam family were cadets of the Ildertons, but the scant and rather weak evidence available does not support this, for while the Ilderstons can claim descent from Uchtred, earl of Northumberland between 1006 and 1016, the Roddams can say they were granted a charter by King Athelstan, King Alfred's grandson, when he had defeated an army of Danes and Cumbrians at the Battle of Wandon in 937.

The post-Conquest ownership of the two estates differed, but there is similarity in that, contrary to the usual practice, both families were allowed by the Normans to keep their tenancies. Ilderton was part of the Carham barony and it and the neighbouring hamlet of Roseden were held by Kirkham Priory from 1322 to dissolution in 1539. Roddam, like Middleton, was associated with Gospatric's Beanley serjeanty after 1135.

Both estates suffered greatly from raids, especially those organised by Robert Bruce after Bannockburn. The tax valuation of Ilderton, for example, dropped from £20 to less than £2 in the space of three years. Thomas de Ilderton built a tower before 1415 and one of the Roddams followed suit a few years after 1415. Both towers were ruinous in 1541 when Ranuffe Ilderton's was described as "a great tower and barmekyn but only the walls stand", and John Roddam's as "a little tower with a decayed roof and no barmekyn".

Ilderton Hall was built in 1715 by George Ilderton on the site of the tower. George's son, Thomas, achieved some fame as the joint inventor with Robert Smart of Alnwick of a crude type of threshing machine. Thomas proved to be the last of the mainline Ildertons; when he died in 1779 his house was sold.

The Roddams built their mansion in or about 1750 – it was "lately built" according to the Rev.John Wallis in 1767. Originally it was a plain five-bay building, but in 1776 Admiral Roddam added two wings. He also built a family mausoleum in the churchyard of Ilderton church, a small stone hut, surprisingly unostentatious. When he died, in 1808 at the age of 89, the direct line came to an end, but the name was assumed by a relative, William Stanhope, and the estate remained in the hands of his descendants until 1971, when Robert Holderness Roddam sold out.

A mile or so to the east of Roddam is the site of the Battle of Hedgeley Moor, a War of the Roses tussle fought between Lord Montagu for the Yorkists and Sir Ralph Percy for the Lancastrians in 1464. Percy was deserted by his friends when the fighting started and he could not contain Montagu on his own. The Battle of Hexham followed closely to complete the victory of King Edward IV. There are two momentos of Percy's heroic but vain stand near Wooperton, both accessible from the main A697 Morpeth to Wooler road. One is Percy's Cross at NU053192 and the other is Percy's Leap at NU049198. The latter is a couple of stones with an enormous gap between them which Percy's horse was supposed to have jumped during the battle.

Ingram

L81   P488   NU019163   12 km, 7$^{1}/_{2}$ miles, south of Wooler

Although on the east-flowing River Breamish and separated from the Coquet drainage area by Bloodybush Edge, one of the 2000 feet giants in the Cheviot range, Ingram, under its former name of Angerham, was one of the Ten Towns of Coquetdale, the property of the Baron of Alnwick. They were leased by William de Vescy in 1166 to Odinell de Umfraville, lord of Rededsdale, so that he could press-gang their male inhabitants into service at Harbottle castle. For this Umfraville paid two knights fee, a rent which was increased in 1242 to include a one-year old sparrow hawk each year. The arrangement lasted until 1340, when Angerham was replaced by Nether Allanton, a former part of Alwinton, in the Ten Towns.

The village we know today as Ingram existed long before Vescy or Umfraville strutted onto the stage. Its position in a fertile valley with a back-cloth of mountains would have attracted the early Anglian settlers, and it is possible they were joined by some of the Britons who, since before Roman days, had lived a safe but frugal existence on the neighbouring heights. There was an Anglian church at Ingram before 1060, the year it was restored after being damaged during a raid, and it is a measure of the village's importance that the Normans added a tower to it when they took over.

Ingram was vulnerable to raids right up to the Union of the Crowns. Like Alnham a few miles to the south, it stood at the gateway to a rough pass through the mountains, and Border raiders, mounted on their wiry little horses, could find their way through this from the Kelso and Jedburgh areas. But the villagers seemed to thrive on adversity: for example, their church was burnt down during the 1290s and by 1300 it had not only been restored but considerably enlarged. Again, when practically the whole village was wasted in 1430 a couple of years of frantic building followed, at the end of which the inhabitants had a fortified tower.

The tenure of Ingram manor went to Sir Thomas Heton in 1340, and from him to his three granddaughters in 1387, all of whom were married, one each to Sir Henry Fenwick, Sir William Swinburne and Sir Robert Ogle. All took a share of the place, but it seems to have been the Ogles who built the tower, and when in 1526 their third was transferred to the minor family of Cuthbert Ogle, the Ford parson, during the incumbency of one of his sons in Ingram parish, it gave Bowes and Ellerker cause for thinking the tower was a "mansion house of the parsonage". This was a misunderstanding, for the building was large enough to accommodate forty men, according to one report, sixty men according to another.

The 1541 survey carried a warning: "a little to the west of the tower the water of Brymyshe by rage of floode hath worne sore upon the south bank that except there be shortly made a were (weir) and defence of the same it is very likely in course of time to were (wear) away the said town of Ingram and the tower". The surveyors proved to be right about the tower: it was washed away in the 1580s and thus played no part during those traumatic years. There were two raids in 1587, lots of cattle, sheep and prisoners being taken by Liddesdale men in the first and four webs of lead from the church roof by East Teviotdale robbers in the second. Another raid occurred in 1588, and in 1598 the vicar had to flee to Berwick to escape the evil attention of Kerr of Ferniehurst.

There were some ownership changes over the years. In 1459 the Fenwick third of the manor passed by marriage to the Denton family. In 1580 Sir Cuthbert Collingwood rented the Swinburne share, and this became a purchase in 1604. In 1624 John Ogle of Eglingham, already in possession of one third, bought the Denton third, and thus created an interesting situation during the Civil War: the Ogles, committed Parliamentarians, owned two-thirds and the Collingwoods, dedicated Royalists, one third. Whether or not this caused any internecine squabbling is not recorded, but the Civil War did mark the beginning of the slow decline in the importance and size of Ingram. During the following couple of centuries it shrunk from being a modest market town to the small village which exists today.

Although nothing of the tower remains, its former position close to the river should be easy enough to locate. This would be true it we knew where the river was at the relevant time, but the Breamish is, and always has been, capricious, able to alter course without warning. A heavy rain storm in the Cheviot massif can quickly activate the little streams which feed the river, and the resultant flash flood can roar with a noise like thunder down the narrow valley onto Ingram. When the water has subsided, chances are the river is not where it used to be.

Branton

| L81 | P488 | NU046163 | 13 km, 8 miles, south of Wooler |

A small village on the south bank of the River Breamish, not to be confused with Brandon on the north side.

There was a tower here in Queen Elizabeth's day and it was marked on Christopher Dacre's plat of 1584, but there is no known record of its previous or later history. A mansion, no longer existing, was built in 1695 and the tower may have contributed to its building materials, or it may have been destroyed in a fire which engulfed most of the village in 1680. The latter possibility could give support to the story that its foundations were visible in 1864 opposite what was then a Presbyterian chapel.

Crawley

L81   P488   NU069164   14 km, 8½ miles, south-east of Wooler

Glanton Moor to the south and Hedgeley Moor to the east sweep down to form a gap at Powburn (NU062163) which since Celtic times at least has focused traffic before it crossed the River Breamish at Hedgeley Bridge (NU058171). The Ancient Britons used it, the Romans took their Devil's Causeway through it, the pre-1840 highway from Glanton to Wooler went that way, the old railway line was most grateful for it and the modern A697 road follows the old route at this point. Powburn and the bridge were thus prime targets for terrorists wishing to disrupt communications and they had to be guarded. The ideal place for the sentry-box was Crawley.

Here are earthworks believed to have been constructed some three or four thousand years ago. The Romans built a fort in one corner and John Heron of Ford built a tower in another corner, making use of a licence to crenellate issued by King Edward III in 1343. It has been altered and enlarged many times since then, and has had a farmhouse added, so it is hardly recognisable now. It is a medley in stone, one of the most curious complexes in Northumberland.

The Herons retained the property until 1683, then sold it to John Proctor of Shawdon. It is still included in the Shawdon estate and the farm buildings are still in use. A cottage made in part of the ruin was lived in until 1984, then a troop of Venture Scouts took it over for several years.

Area 3
The mid-Northumberland Coast and the Aln Basin

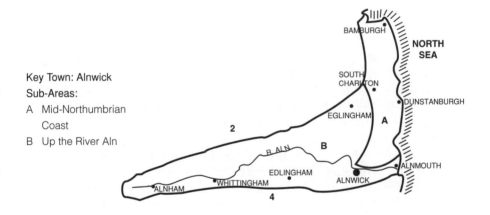

Key Town: Alnwick

Sub-Areas:

A Mid-Northumbrian
   Coast

B Up the River Aln

T wo distinct districts, both pivoting on Alnmouth and Alnwick. The coastal belt, stretching on average about five miles inland, reaches from the Aln to Budle Bay, while the tour up-river goes to Alnham via Whittingham Vale. In their different ways, the two sub-areas are very beautiful and full of history.

Key Town
Alnwick

L81   P488   NU187135

Alnwick castle stands majestically atop the steep right bank of the River Aln, at the northern end of the town. There has been a castle of some description on this site for nearly nine hundred years, but its history goes even further back for bronze instruments and Roman coins have been dug up. Claudius Ptolemy, the second century Egyptian geographer, knew of the river – he thought it was the only one between the Forth and the Wear – but the town of Alauna which he placed on its banks could have been either the infant Alnmouth or Alnwick.

According to the Alnwick Abbey Chronicle, a high-born Anglian called Bisbright Tisonne held Alnwick long before the Conquest. He was dispossessed by King William I, who gave his lands to Gilbert de Tesson or Tyson, allegedly the king's standard bearer at Hastings. The similarity of the Anglian and Norman names cannot fail to fuel speculation on the truth of the ancient records, but Gilbert Tyson was real enough and held Alnwick until 1096. He survived the bellicose attention of Malcolm Ceann Mor – King of the Scots Malcolm III – who invaded Northumberland five times before being caught and killed in 1093 on a ridge about a mile north of Alnwick. This was the work of Arkle Moreal, Earl Robert de Mowbray's commander at Bamburgh, who was rewarded with a manor at Old Bewick. Such generosity may have influenced Tyson to support Mowbray in his struggle with King William II, but it led only to the sequestration of his property.

The king selected Ivo de Vescy, a Norman nobleman, to be the next holder of the Alnwick estate. He became the first Baron of Alnwick, liable to provide twelve knights should the king ever have need of them. He built a motte and bailey castle on a mound above the river, and there he died in 1134.

Ivo's only offspring, Beatrix, married Eustace fitz (son of) John, an energetic man both as a builder and as a supporter of the Empress Matilda, King Henry I's daughter who aspired to the throne. In the former capacity he surrounded his father-in-law's earth and timber stronghold with stone walls, then levelled the mound and constructed on it an imaginative type of keep comprising several stone towers in a continuous ring round an inner courtyard. The complex occupied practically the same area as does today's castle and bits of the original exists in the curtain wall still standing. As a fighter, Eustace was not so successful, suffering defeat with his ally, Scots King David I, at the Battle of the Standard in 1138. He managed to make his peace with King Stephen soon afterwards, however, and when he died in 1157 his son William was able to inherit both the barony and the title; using his mother's name, be became known as Baron de Vescy.

Another Eustace succeeded in 1184; he was one of the twenty-five barons appointed in 1215 to enforce King John's observance of Magna Carta. When he joined a group of Northumbrian gentry who paid homage to Scots King Alexander II he suffered King John's vengeance and had his castle set alight. The damage was superficial and was soon repaired.

Two generations later, Baron John Vescy managed to forfeit the castle for fighting King Henry III in the second Barons War of 1265. It was returned to him before he died in 1288, and his brother William succeeded. He died in 1297, leaving only one son known as William de Vescy of Kildare who, because he was illegitimate, could not claim the title or property. Provision for this had been made, however; the boy was left manors in Yorkshire and Lincolnshire, and Alnwick was granted unconditionally to Anthony Bek, Bishop of Durham.

In 1309 Lord Henry Percy bought the barony from the good bishop and started the Percy-Alnwick association which has continued, with a few hiccups, to this day. Henry was a descendant of William de Percy who had come to England with the Conqueror in 1066 and had been awarded large estates in south and central England. The family originated in west Normandy, in a village called Percee, or 'forest Glade'. Henry had spent most of his early life in Yorkshire but he was no stranger to the Border, having assisted King Edward I during his tussles with William Wallace, a service which had earned him at least two large Scottish estates.

The new baron's first job was to rebuild his castle and to make of it a stronghold of fourteenth century efficiency. He kept to the original basic plan, even copying the unusual keep design by constructing seven semicircular towers round the inner courtyard, but he managed to include in it some elements designed for creature comfort, like a great Hall and kitchens. A lot of this work is still in existence.

His son, the second Lord Henry Percy, succeeded in 1315 and added the two octagonal towers which guard the entrance to the keep. Alnwick castle was now a very strong military fortification, but, inspite of the improved domestic arrangements, it was still not the acme of luxury and Henry preferred to live in Warkworth castle which the Crown added to Alnwick barony in 1332. Indeed Warkworth was the principal seat of the Percys until 1576 and Alnwick was used mainly as the march wardens' headquarters.

All the early Lord Percys were fond of a fight and gave distinguished service in the Scottish and French wars. Because of this the fourth lord, another Henry who held the barony from 1368 to 1409, was created the Earl of Northumberland. He soon managed to blot the family's copybook in two ways, by fathering a headstrong and rather foolish son who earned the sobriquet 'Hotspur' when only twelve years old, and by joining a rebellion against King Henry IV. For the former indiscretion he was given a short term of imprisonment; for the latter he had his property confiscated in 1404, and in 1409 he was killed.

The barony was granted to the king's third son, John of Lancaster who later became the Duke of Bedford. He held it for five years, until Henry V was crowned in 1414, when it was awarded to Hotspur's son, who thus became Henry Percy, the second Earl of Northumberland. He was also General Warden of the Marches so was a prime target for Scottish invaders, but Alnwick castle proved to be unassailable. Not so the town of Alnwick, unfortunately, which was burnt in 1424 and again in 1428. A licence to enclose it with a defensive wall was issued in 1433 and when eventually it was completed it sported four gates, each guarded by a tower. Clayport and Bailiffgate have disappeared, Pottersgate was replaced in 1768, but the original Bondgate and its Hotspur Tower still stand, the former controlling the traffic into the town as its southern end.

The third earl, 1455 to 1461, lost his life and all his property while fighting for the Lancastrians in the Battle of Towton. The earldom was granted to Lord Montagu, brother of the Earl of Warwick, the 'King-maker'. Alnwick castle changed hands four more times in the Wars of the Roses, but it ended up still in Yorkist hands, with Montagu still in charge. When the fighting was over, however, King Edward IV became apprehensive about the growing powers of Montagu and Warwick, so he sacked the former and re-stored Alnwick and the Northumbrian earldom to the Percy family. Yet another Henry became the fourth Percy earl in 1469, and he remained so for twenty years until murdered by a mob of tenants for imposing an unpopular tax.

The Battle of Flodden was fought during the tenure of the fifth earl, but he was otherwise engaged in France at the time and took no part in it. The castle was used as battle headquarters by the English army, however.

The sixth earl voluntarily handed his inheritance to the Crown in exchange for a life annuity. It seemed a good idea to him for he had no children, his relationship with his brothers was strained and he was always short of money. For twenty years the earldom lay dormant. The castle was used by march wardens but the Crown did little in the way of maintenance.

Towards the end of the short reign of Edward VI, the young and sickly son of King Henry VIII and Jane Seymour, John Dudley, Earl of Warwick got control of the country. Described as "a man of no principle except selfish ambition", Dudley granted himself the dukedom of Northumberland in 1552, and then persuaded the king to nominate Lady Jane Grey as heir to the throne. Poor Jane had been married against her will to Dudley's son, so had his machiavellian plan succeeded he would have achieved an invincible position. Edward died that year and Jane was duly proclaimed queen, but she reigned only nine days before Queen Mary disposed of her – and Dudley.

Queen Mary was good to the Percys who, like herself, were Roman Catholics. The earldom of Northumberland was restored to Thomas, a son of one of the rebels executed after the Pilgrimage of Grace in 1537, but he also ended up with his head on the chopping block in 1572 for supporting the Rising of the North. By then the Protestant Queen Elizabeth was on the throne and the Rising was a pro-Catholic rebellion.

The next earl took the hint and professed to being an ardent Protestant, but he failed to convince the queen so spent much time in the Tower of London; in 1589 he died there with a bullet in his heart. The next earl was well acquainted with the Tower as well because of unproven complicity in the Gun Powder Plot. When released in 1621 he was forbidden to live in the north. The power of the Percys was declining rapidly. Their position as Northumberland's leading family and largest landowners was being challenged with growing success by the Radcliffes of Dilston.

When the eleventh earl died in 1670 he left a daughter, Elizabeth, but no sons. In compliance with the laws of inheritance, Elizabeth became the Baroness of Alnwick but could not don the earldom, which became dormant. She married three times: her first two husbands died within a year of their wedding, but the third was more resilient. He was Charles Seymore, Duke of Somerset, and between them they produced a son, Algernon, who managed to revive the northern title. He was created Earl of Northumberland with the proviso that the title would pass to his son-in-law should his daughter ever provide one. This she did in 1750 when she married Hugh Smithson of Stanwick in Yorkshire. With Parliament's approval, he changed his name to Percy, so after eighty years in the wilderness there was again a Percy earl owning Alnwick – a Percy revitalized with new blood.

His refreshing enthusiasm was directed almost immediately towards overhauling and modernising the administration and methodology of the former barony, now called the Northumberland Estates, and in bringing new life to the castle, which had fallen into considerable decay since the demise of the Border wardens.

The external renovation of the castle was entrusted to Vincent Shepherd, a local architect who worked in close collaboration with the celebrated Robert Adam. The professionalism of these two was baulked to some extent by the exuberance of the owner and his wife, and consequently instead of enhancing a medieval Border stronghold they managed to produce a Gothick palace which equated with current taste but not with history. The palace theme was continued internally, where Robert Adam excelled himself. Lancelot (Capability) Brown made a good job of the river bank below the castle which, according to Canatello's painting, had previously been rock and rough pasture. John Adam, Robert's brother, designed the Lion Bridge and a Mr Johnson of Stamfordham provided the final touch of fantasy, the stone warriors standing on the battlements.

Earl Hugh Percy was Lord Lieutenant of Ireland for King George III, and for this and other services he was created the first Duke of Northumberland in 1766, twenty years before his death.

The flamboyance of the castle offended some of the later dukes, and the fourth, sixth and seventh, covering the years between 1847 and 1918, carried out extensive alterations, mainly to the designs of Anthony Salvin. A modicum of Border ferocity returned, but unfortunately at the expense of nearly all Robert Adam's internal work.   [**Plate 2**]

Area 3, Sub-Area A   The Mid-Northumberland Coast
Longhoughton

L81   P477   NU243151   6 km, 3³/₄ miles, north-east of Alnwick

King Henry I included this village in the Alnwick barony, and when Baron Eustace fitz John founded Alnwick Abbey in 1147 he endowed it with the funds and tithes of the village church of St. Peters.

It is a church of many dates and styles. It was built on the remains of its Anglian predecessor, but the oldest part still visible is its early Norman chancel arch. The lower half of the squat, square tower is late Norman. Its walls are at least four feet thick, and a survey of 1567 confirmed that it was used as a refuge for the locals when danger threatened. The upper half of the tower and the chancel were rebuilt in 1873 after a disastrous fire.

After dissolution St. Peters became the parish church. In the seventeenth and eighteenth centuries it had another use – it was a storehouse for much of the contraband brought ashore at nearby Boulmer. Its vicar between 1696 and 1719, the Rev. George Doncan, must have known about, and condoned, this illicit business, and hypocrisy must have been another of his sins, for he wrote libellous character assessments in the parish register next to his records of births, deaths and marriages. He depicted his flock in terms such as "a vile, drunken, female sinner", "a quack and warlock doctor", "a bad son of a bad father" and "a Janus tergiverse Whig". One wonders how his parishioners would have phased his obituary.

Littlehoughton

L81   P477   NU231164   5¹/₂ km, 3¹/₂ miles. north-east of Alnwick

Littlehoughton Hall stands on the site, and contains minute remains, of an early thirteenth century tower built and occupied by Gilbert de St. Clare, thought to have been a Norman knight. It passed to Peter Hering, possibly, inspite of the name, Gilbert's son. He lived in the tower until after 1314, then in about 1326 a cadet branch of the Roddam family moved in and held it until 1710.

The original building is said to have been 25 feet square, with five feet thick walls. The ground floor was vaulted and there were newel stairs in one corner. It had a massive front door locked with a four inch key which has been found recently in a rubbish pit.

The Roddam family enlarged the tower in 1686 by adding a wing to its north side and reconstructing the tower's first floor. The complex was sold by Edward Roddam to Dorothy Dawson of Newcastle in 1710, and a century later the successors built a quite large Georgian house attached, as a wing, to the south side of the tower. Earl Grey of Howick Hall bought what had become a sizeable mansion in the middle of the nineteenth century.

At the centre of today's range is some very old stonework, but whether or not this is original it is not possible to say. It has a small square window in it which would not have been incongruous in a medieval tower, and next to it is a larger window with a hood mould which could have been inserted during one of the tower's enlargements.

Howick Hall

L81   P477   NU247175   7½ km, 4½ miles, north-east of Alnwick

A beautiful mansion designed in 1782 by William Newton and considerably altered since. Only its wings are occupied now; the centre block needs urgent attention and unfortunately is getting only laggardly attention. It is surrounded by gardens which are open to the public and well worth a visit for their spring flowers and rhododendrons.

The manor of Howick, part of Alnwick barony, was held at the end of the twelfth century by Adam Ribolt or Ryband. In 1334 it passed to a kinsman, either Peter Hering, who had lived in Littlehoughton, or his son. One of these built a small tower, and it remained in the Hering family over 250 years; in 1415 the holder was Emeric Hering, the member of Parliament for Newcastle in 1421.

A member of the Morpeth cadet line of Greys, Sir Edward Grey, was the next owner. His family had held land in the vicinity since 1319 and he bought the tower and its demesne in 1597.

The tower was demolished in 1780. Its foundations may be beneath the mansion which was built on the site two years later for Sir Henry Grey, the elder brother of the first Earl Grey and uncle of Charles, the second Earl Grey who was the Whig Prime Minister from 1830 to 1834 and the navigator who steered the 1832 Reform Bill through Parliament. Charles's nephew was Edward, the first Viscount Grey of Falloden, the British Foreign Secretary when war was declared in 1914.

Rock

L75   P477   NU200202   7 km, 4¼ miles, north of Alnwick

One of the most charming of villages, but chiefly noteworthy as the place where turnips were first grown in Northumberland. John Procter in 1727 succeeded in this way to alter the course of agricultural history, for it enables farmers to winter feed their herds of cattle whereas before the arrival of the vegetable they had had to sell or slaughter each autumn all but a few beasts needed for breeding.

A manor in the Alnwick barony, Rock was granted by William de Vescy to Richard de Roc, a member of a Lucker family, in 1166, His descendants held it until 1296, then there is a gap in our information until Roger de Tuggal or Tughall took over during the latter part of the fourteenth century. A descendant of his built a tower a century later. It was quite a large one, oblong in shape.

For a few months during 1549 the tower was used to quarter Spanish mercenaries. It was not alone in this, of course, for many foreign soldiers were hired on both sides to help police the troubled sixteenth century Border. Rock's inhabitants did not enjoy their visitors and found them as badly behaved as the Scots, so they lost no time in persuading the authorities to take them away.

After the Tuggals came the Swinhoes of Scremerston, then the Lawsons who had married into the Swinhoe family, then the Salkelds. The last named built a manor house against the north side of the tower in the 1640s, and one of them, John Salkeld, greatly improved the farm. Following them was Edward Widdrington, to whom Sir Thomas Horsley willed his estates at Longhorsley and Scrainwood in 1685, John Fenwick, hanged in 1711 for the murder of Ferdinando Forster, and Thomas Procter, whose son grew the turnips. John Procter stayed until a fire in 1752 did more damage than he could afford to repair.

The last private owners were the Bosanquets. Charles restored most of the building in 1819. He left part a ruin but enlarged the rest of the complex, including the tower, making a commodious house, now called Rock Hall. The family held it to the second half of the twentieth century, when it became a Youth Hostel. More recently it became a private school run by Mrs Lalage Bosanquet

South Charlton

L75   P476   NU164202   7 km, 4$\frac{1}{4}$ miles, north-west of Alnwick

East Ditchburn

L75   P476   NU139214   9 km, 5$\frac{1}{2}$ miles, north-west of Alnwick

Two small communities in the foothills which form the western edge of the coastal plain. Both had fortified towers about which very little is known and which have long since disappeared.

South Charlton's tower was built in 1450 by the second Earl of Northumberland for the protection of his tenants. Rather unusually, it was built against the walls of an old chapel although it was never a vicarage. At a later stage it served as the village school.

The tower at East Ditchburn may have been built at about the same time as it was described as very old in 1715 when ownership was shared by the Carrs of Lesbury and the Collingwoods of 'Biker'.

Craster

L81   P477   NU251195   9 km, 5½ miles, north-east of Alnwick

The still flourishing Craster family is one of the oldest in Northumberland, although its Anglian origins are obscure. It has been suggested that the progenitors lived at Warenton, south of Belford, but evidence is lacking. We can be reasonably sure, however, that Albert held 'Crancestre', the old name for Craster, before 1168, and that there has been a steady supply of male offspring since then to maintain continuous ownership of their property or of most of it, to this day.

A tower was built in the late 1300s and was held in 1415 by Edmund Craster. It was a rectangular pile, 35 by 30 feet, with a vaulted ground floor and an entrance on the side facing the sea. It was enlarged and altered in Jacobean times, and a house in the Georgian style was built alongside it in the eighteenth century, During Victoria's reign modern windows were inserted, and the top of the building was given romantic battlements and a bit of ostentatious Gothick so popular at that time. Also, the accommodation was divided into three separate units which were occupied by three branches of the family; since then one of the units has been sold outside the family.

Dunstan Hall

L75   P477   NU248201   9½ km, 6 miles, north-east of Alnwick

Dunstan is a small hamlet of mainly modern homes about a quarter of a mile north of Craster Tower, and Dunstan Hall lies a further quarter of a mile along the road to Embleton. While the full beauty of the Hall can only be appreciated from its private garden, the restricted view from the road reveals the presence of a medieval tower tacked on to the end of a slightly less antiquated house. This is called 'Proctors Stead' on some maps but in fact a rather too obtrusive caravan site next door carries this name.

Like Craster, Dunstan was a township in the barony of Embleton. The earliest recorded tenant was Reyner of Dunstan, but his son, Michael, held only a third of the land in 1298 while Richard Wetwang held the rest. Wetwang was a Yorkshireman and it is surmised that he was employed and brought here as a steward by Thomas, the second Earl of Lancaster whose main domicile was at Pontefract but at the time was Baron of Embleton. When Michael died his son Thomas transferred his portion of Dunstan to Wetwang, who built a stone house in about 1310.

Most Northumbrian towers were built as isolated structures and frequently had a comfortable house added much later. In a few cases, as at Halton and Welton, the reverse applied, but at Dunstan house and tower appear to have been built in one operation. The house was built on the stone foundations of an earlier timber hall house, and the tower was an eastern projection on this.

The Wetwangs must have become acclimatized to the north-east and found other work to do after the Earl of Lancaster was executed in 1322, for the family occupied Dunstan Hall for the best part of four hundred years. During that period much was done to the house, although the tower remained pretty much as built. In 1385 a Scottish raid necessitated extensive repairs and the opportunity was taken to replace the thatch roof with one of lead. A major reconstruction of the house was undertaken in 1590 when larger windows were inserted.

In 1692 Henry Wetwang sold his property to Alexander Browne, who was beginning to build a lucrative business in Alnmouth as a shipper of grain. He did not stay long, for in 1705 he struck a remarkable deal with John Proctor – not a sale but a straight exchange. Proctor got Dunstan and Browne got the Shawdon estate, eleven miles inland, up the Aln valley.

The Proctors indulged in a little self-advertising by rechristening their new property 'Proctor Stead'. They also added a north wing to the house, but left the tower untouched. They sold out to neighbour Daniel Craster in 1778, and his family owned Dunstan Hall until 1937 although they never lived there. One of the family, Shafto Craster, gave the house a significant face-lift in 1831.

Currently the still habitable house has a distinct Georgian flavour. This is because in 1939 Mrs Merz, the owner then, persuaded the historian H.L. Honeyman to supervise more restoration work. The tower, now a tall ruin but still integral with the house, may have a few more windows that it had originally, but otherwise it appears to be authentic. It still carries a very public corbelled gardrobe on its second floor. The roof has gone and the top of the walls are a bit ragged, but it remains obvious that they carried a monopitch roof, rather like that of a lean-to, which is what would be expected on a projection which was slightly lower than the main part of the building.

The famous Franciscan philosopher, John Duns Scotus, who lived from 1265 to 1308, is frequently credited with a Dunstan birth. The quintessence of the belief is the following note written on the colophon of a manuscript in the library of Merton College, Oxford: "Here endeth the lecture of John Duns, who was born in a certain hamlet of the parish of Embleton called Dunstan, in the county of Northumberland, belonging to the house of the scholars of Merton Hall in Oxford".

The writer seems to have been aware that the patronage of Embleton church was given to Merton College in 1274 by Edmund, Earl of Lancaster, but his reference to Duns must have been hearsay for the manuscript which carries his note was not written until 1455, well over a hundred years after the subject's death. It may be true for all that, but it is not evidence and it failed to convince A.G. Little, author of 'Chronological Notes on the Life of Duns Scotus'. His research led him to disregard the claims of both Dunstan and another contender, Duns, the county town of Berwickshire, where there is a statue of the scholar. He had no hesitation in declaring that the birthplace was Little Dean, Maxton, near Kelso. John Duns, he asserted, was the son of Ninion Duns and nephew of Friar Elias Duns, the warden of Dumfries Convent and Vicar-General of Scotland.

Dunstanburgh Castle

L75   P477   NU256218   11½ km, 7 miles, north-east of Alnwick

The gaunt ruins on their craggy promontory between Craster and Embleton make possibly the most poignant sight in Northumberland, if not along the entire eastern seaboard of England. The stonework that remains is not abundant, but what there is is not adulterated as at Bamburgh or Alnwick, and thus is both architecturally rewarding and mentally stimulating.

Thomas, second Earl of Lancaster, High Steward of England and Baron of Embleton, commissioned Master Elias in 1313 to build him this castle. His reason for wanting it has been debated ever since. The most obvious is that he considered it expedient to have a bolt-hole into which he could crawl from the wrath of the king, with whom he was frequently at odds. Another was to guard the small haven at the southern side of the castle rock which, at that time, was capable of harbouring warships; it might have been needed as an alternative to Berwick should that port be lost to the Scots. A third reason was simply to provide protection for the inhabitants of his barony, and to house soldiers who could police the coastal route taken by Scottish invaders. In the event, none of these possibilities were ever realised, and the castle became virtually a white elephant.

When other builders were thinking about quadrilateral castles, Master Elias, one of the greatest 'engineers' of his day, remained loyal to the Norman concept of keep and bailey, although in this case he made the keep double as gatehouse. This building was an architectural triumph, for within its two drum towers were the paraphernalia of war – a fighting deck and machinery for operating a drawbridge and a portcullis – and, above, a great hall with associated rooms. The passage between the towers was vaulted and had guardrooms on both sides.

The nature of the site dictated an exceptionally large bailey, some ten or eleven acres, but the precipitous cliffs along the sea edge enabled the builder to economise on curtain wall. The north cliffs were considered adequate protection of their own, and the east wall was originally only soil faced with stone flags. The west wall was strong, but the greatest strength was given to the south wall which included two towers as well as the gatehouse.

The castle was completed in 1316 but there is no record of it ever being used by Earl Thomas. He was executed in 1323 in his main castle at Pontefract, and Dunstanburgh, after a brief experience of private enterprise, was granted to his nephew, Henry, who was elevated to the dukedom in 1351. Prominent Northumbrian gentry were hired as constables to look after the castle, and one of them, John Lilburn, built a tower in the west curtain wall. In 1351 repairs were done to the roof of the gatehouse, and some work was carried out on the defences in front of the entrance.

Earl Henry's granddaughter was married to John of Gaunt, who thus inherited Embleton barony and Dunstanburgh castle in 1362. As Gaunt was also the younger son of King Edward III he was an important figure in the government of his day. Locally he was best known as General Warden of the Marches from 1380 onwards. Dunstanburgh was useful to him, but he did not like the idea of its keep being also the first part of the castle an enemy would attack, so he blocked up the entrance and built a new one on its west side, protecting it with a new gatehouse and barbican. The twin drums became a more conventional keep, and to strengthen it further Gaunt put a robust wall in front and an inner bailey containing a tower behind it.

Gaunt's son, Henry of Bolingbroke, inherited in 1399, imprisoned King Richard II and grabbed the Crown as Henry IV, the first Lancastrian king of England. Dunstanburgh became a royal castle, unwanted but providing jobs for a succession of constables.

It did see a little action during the Wars of the Roses when King Henry VI's queen, Margaret, made threatening noises in 1462 with French and Scottish troops. The castle surrendered to the Earl of Warwick but later slipped back into Yorkist hands and had to receive further attention by Warwick in 1464. It suffered some damage to its fabric which was only partially repaired in 1470, then it was left to the tender mercies of nature and pillagers. It is alleged that Lord Dacre repaired the roof of Wark-on-Tweed castle with lead taken from Dunstanburgh's roof.

Several surveys were made of the castle during the reigns of Henry VIII and Elizabeth I, but nothing was done either to restore or dismantle it. In 1604 the Crown sold it to businessmen who, in the following year, sold it to Sir Ralph Grey of Chillingham. He and his family held it for more than 250 years yet appear to have done nothing to it. At the beginning of the twentieth century Newcastle's great benefactor, Sir Arthur Sutherland, bought it and placed it in the guardianship of the nation. At the present time it is cared for by both the National Trust and English Heritage.

The awesome appearance of the castle in its heyday was almost bound to engender stories of the 'when knights were bold' type. One such, which has come down to us in several forms, is about Sir Guy who, while sheltering by the castle walls one day during a thunder storm, was accosted by an old man who told him a beautiful maiden was in dire distress inside. Damsels in distress were Sir Guy's speciality, so he let the old man lead him into the castle, up the main stairs and into the great hall. A wondrous sight met his eyes. Centre stage stood a hundred knights beside a hundred horses, at the far end of the room were two large skeletons wearing jewelled crowns, one holding a sword, the other a horn, and between them was a coffin upon which lay a girl dressed in white and, naturally, very beautiful.

Sir Guy was told to choose either the sword or the horn, and then, whatever happened, to hold on to his choice until the girl was rescued. The sword was, of course, the fighting man's first choice, but then he thought it might be cleverer to do the unexpected so he grasped the horn, put it to his lips and blew a piercing screech. Immediately the hundred knights mounted their horses and charged down on Sir Guy. Not a pleasant thing to happen to anyone, but our hero did not turn a hair: he drew his own sword and prepared to meet the onslaught, throwing away the horn as he did so. The cavalry got closer, and yet closer...and then Sir Guy woke up.

Embleton

L75   P477   NU230224   10 km, 6¼ miles, north-east of Alnwick

Just a village, yet it was capital of an important barony of the same name. Craster, Dunstan and Dunstanburgh described above, and Warenton and Newlands covered in Area 1, were all parcels of this barony, as were two plots of land in Bamburgh and, most probably, Preston. It was created by King William II for Odard, his representative, or sheriff, or 'vicecomes' in Norman English, in the royal city of Bamburgh, and he adopted this title as his surname. In the thirteenth century it was Anglicised as 'Viscount'.

The grant was made between 1087 and 1100 because Odard needed the status which went with land ownership. He was a Norman holding an important job and he had to be the social equal of the local barons if he was to uphold the dignity and authority vested in him. The grant was confirmed on Odard's son John in c1132 for a fee of three knights.

The barony was enlarged considerably, usually by leasing. Nesbit and Fenton from Wooler barony, Earle and both Newtons from Alnwick barony and Cartington from the Ditchburn sergenty – all were included before Rameta Viscount inherited in 1242. In 1250 she married a southerner called Hereward de Marisco who had no interest in the north.

They were lucky. Simon de Montford, Earl of Leicester, wanted a presence in the north, and in 1255 he did a deal with Rameta and Hereward. Simon got Embleton barony and the couple got Chawton in Hampshire, an estate which became famous in the early nineteenth century as the final home of Jane Austen and her brother Edward.

Montford led a seditious life although married to King Henry III's sister. It ended abruptly in 1265 at Evesham when an army of rebels he was leading was defeated by Henry's eldest son, the future King Edward I.

Embleton continued its association with the élite when King Henry granted it to his second son, Edmund Earl of Lancaster, in 1269. It is doubtful whether the lucky lad ever visited Embleton, but he did give the patronage of its church to Merton College in 1274 when it moved from Merton to Oxford. The churches at Rock and Ponteland went the same way.

In 1296 Thomas succeeded as Earl of Lancaster and Baron of Embleton. His calling in life was to rid his cousin, King Edward II, of the 'court favourites' who so displeased the barons. He killed Piers Gaveston in 1313 and banished the Despensers in 1321; no wonder many people think he built Dunstanburgh Castle as a safe retreat from his enemies, although the fact is that when nemesis came in 1322 he did not try to run and hide but was content to be judged and executed in his main castle at Pontefract.

The Crown granted the barony to a wealthy Newcastle merchant who styled himself Richard of Embleton. When he realised he was expected to pay for Dunstanburgh Castle's garrison and constable he decided that after all the Lordly Strand was not for him, so Earl Thomas's brother received the grant instead. Unfortunately he died almost immediately and left everything to his son Henry, who became Duke of Lancaster in 1351.

The next effective baron was John of Gaunt, who obtained that position and the earldom of Lancaster by marrying Henry's heiress. He was the fourth son of King Edward III and became virtually the ruler of England during King Richard II's weak reign. He appears to have prized his northern estate highly and spent a lot of time, money and effort strengthening Dunstanburgh Castle in the 1380s.

When he died, in 1399, his son, Henry Bolingbroke, usurped Richard II and became King Henry IV. As Crown land, Embleton got no more barons, and, bit by bit, estates were sold to local gentry until only Dunstanburgh was left. In 1604 that too was sold, to Sir Ralph Grey of Chillingham.

So, one way or another, Embleton barony saw a lot of top echelon history and yet the village remained detached from royal intrigue and state conspiracy. Its only worry was the Scots. Their first raid, in 1385, cost the villagers dearly in lives and material. The raiders, untroubled by the close proximity of Dunstanburgh Castle, camped on Embleton Fields while they systematically plundered the surrounding countryside. They were back in 1419, and again in 1449, after which the villagers were advised to take the roofs off their dwellings and to hide the timbers in safe places to prevent the Scots burning them.

Embleton's barons never had a capital messuage, or residence, in the village and the only defence or refuge was a vicar's tower, built soon after

Bannockburn, c1316. It still exists, having been well maintained by the Church, but now it is joined to a later vicarage. The tower is strong, measures 40 by 20 feet and has a vaulted ground floor, three storeys, newel stairs and crenellations. It is reputed to also have a stream running beneath it – useful during a prolonged raid but disaster for modern furniture.

Another, very unusual, reminder of the past lies in Embleton Bay. This is the 'Vanishing Rock', so called because it is visible on very rare occasions, courtesy of the whimsical tides, then disappears from sight for several years. It was last seen in 1985, after a lapse of eleven years. Carved on it in rough capitals is the name, ANDRA BARTON who was a maritime hero to the Scots but a common pirate to the English. King James IV thought so highly of him he had a 'great and costly ship' built for him and commissioned him to sweep the Scottish coast free of Flemish pirates, so he was understandably annoyed when the Royal Navy seized his ship and killed him. James demanded satisfaction from King Henry VIII, but all he got was the disparaging remark, "The fate of pirates was never an object of discussion between princes".

Preston Tower

L75   P476   NU183254   12 km, 7½ miles, north of Alnwick

Although no proof can be found, Preston was almost certainly a township in Embleton barony. The first known holder was Robert Harbottle, and he built the tower between 1392 and 1399 before marrying Isobella, daughter of Sir Bertram Monboucher, a Breton knight who held a large tower at Horton, near Blyth. Their family held both Horton and Preston to 1572.

The Preston building was a sturdy affair rather like Langley Castle, with square turrets at each corner. These were the real strongholds, with vaulted ground floor chambers and seven feet thick walls, while the hall between them was the residential part with walls not quite so thick.

Robert's and Isobella's son, another Robert, was knighted and became sheriff in 1439. He was married to a daughter of Sir Robert Ogle and their wedding in 1417 had been rather strange because of the insistence of the bride's father "to keep and maintain his daughter and a damsel to wait on her constantly in his hostell, also his son-in-law and his valet or other servant, together with their horses when they came there" for the first two years of the marriage. The wedding present was probably worth a bit of paternal idiosyncrasy – an estate at Newstead.

John of the next generation got the job of repairing the tower. The work included this item: "To set a roofe upon the said tower and thatch the same with hather flaggs or strawe". In spite of the obvious danger of fire, a thatched roof was still common in the fifteenth century if lead was considered too expensive. John's son, Ralph, married Margaret, a daughter of Sir Ralph

Percy, the loser at the Battle of Hedgeley Moor in 1466. Their son, Guischard, was killed at Flodden in 1513, allegedly while engaged in hand to hand combat with King James IV. He left two small children, a weakly boy who died in his teens and a healthy girl, Lenna, who inherited and married Sir Thomas Percy. Their son, also Thomas, became the seventh Earl of Northumberland in 1557 so, for a short time, the Northumberland Estates were swelled by the inclusion of Preston and Horton.

It did not last long. Earl Thomas took an active part in the Roman Catholic 'Rising of the Northern Earls' and was executed on Queen Elizabeth's orders in 1572. His property was confiscated but a junior branch of the Harbottle family was permitted to lease Preston.

These Harbottles held Preston for ninety-one years, during which they halved the tower – the northern two turrets and connecting building were pulled down, leaving only the southern turrets and the curtain wall between them. A mansion, some cottages and farm buildings were built with the stones thus obtained.

The whole estate was sold to William Armorer of Ellington in 1663, and history speeds up. In 1719 the Armorers sold to Sir Thomas Wood of Barton, then in 1805 Edward Craster bought the property for his relation, Charles Atkinson. In 1861 the Baker-Cresswell family bought it, and they are still the owners.

One of them, Henry, took the half-tower in hand and reclaimed it from nature. He stabilized the ruin by building a wall along the exposed north side, improved the doorway and constructed timber stairs inside. He made use of one of the turrets by installing tanks to hold spring water for his mansion and cottages, and to enhance the attraction of the building he inserted a clock between the turrets, a 'flat bed' type similar to Big Ben.

Newstead

L75   P476   NU152272   14 km, 8½ miles, north of Alnwick

A township included in the barony of Ellingham, granted by King Henry I to Nicholas de Grenville in about 1120. A scattered barony in two detached groups, Newstead accompanying Ellingham and Doxford in the first and Cramlington, Hartley, Heaton and Jesmond forming the second.

Nicholas's daughter, who inherited before 1158, was married to Ralph de Gaugy. In due course Robert de Gaugy, Ralph's son, became baron, as did all succeeding eldest sons until the mid-fourteenth century. The Gaugy line petered out then and a junior line started by Robert's second son, Adam, who took the surname 'de Jesmond', took over. Adam had already established his family in the southern part of the barony (see Heaton, Area 10) and they or close relatives held it until the sixteenth century. The northern part of the baron, however, was sold, Newstead going to Sir John Coupland, of Coupland in Glendale, in 1346.

Sir John had been awarded a £500 annuity by King Edward III for capturing the Scottish King David II at the Battle of Neville's Cross that year, but this ended with his death in 1363. His widow was left in straitened circumstances and had to sell Coupland although Newstead remained hers until her death in 1372. She left no heirs so trustees were appointed to dispose of the estate; they sold the major part to Sir Robert Ogle, then of Lowick, who built a tower and probably went to live there in 1399 when he let a relative, John Ogle, have Lowick.

Sir Robert's daughter married Robert Harbottle, holder of Preston and Horton, in 1417 and her dowry was the Newstead estate. This descended as far as the great-great-great-grandson, the seventh Earl of Northumberland, who forfeited it in 1557 and its further history is not recorded.

The tower was in good order in 1415 but it was badly damaged during a raid by Teviotdale men in 1532 and was never repaired. Its site is not known now.

Fleetham

L75   P476   NU195283   15 km, 9½ miles, north of Alnwick

The nucleus of the old township is buried in the more recent hamlet of West Fleetham, about 2½ miles inland from Beadnell. In the eleventh century it was probably an insular estate joined legally to Warenton and Newlands and thus in the Embleton barony.

From 1272 to 1540 it belonged to the monastery at Bamburgh, a living given to the Augustinian canons of Nostell in Yorkshire by King Henry I in 1121 but which did not become active until King Edward I's reign.

There is no evidence of any canons actually living at Fleetham and the gift was probably cultivated by lay farmers, the monastery merely creaming off the profits. For many years during the fourteenth century, however, there were no profits, thanks to extensive raiding by the Scots. It is believed that a small tower was provided to help the farmers during this troubled time.

After dissolution Fleetham was granted to Sir John Forster, and its descent from then on was coupled to that of Bamburgh. The tower was not noted on any of the usual surveys, and no trace of it or its site remains today, yet W.W. Tomlinson wrote of it in 1888 using the present tense.

Beadnell

L75   P477   NU230293   16½ km, 10¼ miles, north of Alnwick

This seaside village was once famous for fishing, trading in lime and smuggling, but now its main source of income is catering for visitors. Not a lot of fishing is done, its lime kilns at the harbour are interesting relics cared for by the National Trust, and evidence of smuggling exists only in old records, such as the entry for 17 September 1762, when goods seized by excise men included 2700 gallons of brandy, 400 gallons of rum and geneva, 23 hogsheads (1250 gallons) of wine and 'some' tea.

The earliest known owners of Beadnell were Thomas Gospatric and William de Bedenhall, who shared the place during the reign of Henry III. William was a local fisherman; Thomas is rather a puzzle as 'Gospatric', as in Earl of Northumberland, was a Christian name before surnames were invented. It is theorised that he was descended from the Middleton Hall family and adopted his progenitor's name as a surname when such things became de rigueur.

Both parts of the township were sold, one part going to the Harding family of Newcastle, the other to the Craster family. This new partnership lasted until the sixteenth century when the Forsters took over. Sir Thomas Forster got the Craster share in 1520 as a wedding gift, and William Forster acquired the Harding share a bit later. Thomas was head of the family which lived only six miles away at Adderstone, and William was a member of a branch family. Between them they owned the village until well into the nineteenth century. William Reed and his wife, née Ogle, lived there around 1660 but probably they were tenants.

Towers as well as owners came in pairs in Beadnell. William Forster found one which had been built by the Hardings on his land. It dated from 1383 so it would have needed a lot of refurbishing when he added a mansion to its west end in the seventeenth century. East Hall, as it was called, contained a cupboard in the parlour and in the cupboard was a door which led into the tower. The building was partly rebuilt during the eighteenth century and the tower was sacrificed. At a later stage the mansion became the Beadnell Hall Hotel, and in 1984 it was converted into flats.

The Forsters built a second tower between 1520 and 1587. It was restored in the eighteenth century by Thomas Forster, but by 1818 it had become the back premises of the Bull Inn. Now the Craster Arms, parts of the tower can be seen still as the vaulted basement, thick walls, an original fireplace and the remains of a newel staircase.

Adderstone

L75   P465   NU141303   17 km, 10½ miles, north of Alnwick

Ranulf, who styled himself as 'The son of man', whatever that may mean, held 'Addeston' from William de Vescy, baron of Alnwick, in 1166. It is not known whether or not he was the progenitor of the Forster family, and the first authentic news of the Forsters was contained in a despatch from the Earl of Surrey immediately after the Battle of Flodden in 1513: it congratulated Sir

Thomas Forster and his sixty horsemen for giving a good account of themselves during the battle. This Sir Thomas lived at Adderstone, in a tower built about a hundred years earlier, and it was he who married a Craster girl and received part of Beadnell as a wedding present in 1520.

During the sixteenth, seventeenth and eighteenth centuries there were at least four main branches of the Forster family and usually more than one of them lived at Adderstone, making it difficult to sort them out. Two characters step out of this entanglement for brief mention here.

The first is Sir John Forster, born in 1501 and appointed Lord Warden of the English Marches in 1560 by Queen Elizabeth. He retained that position through most of the reign, inspite of almost continuous criticism. It was his responsibility to keep the peace along the Border, but the hundreds of raids made by both the English and the Scots during his stint testify to his conspicuous incompetence. It was once said of him that he 'cut a fine figure against the Scots', but if that was ever true it was just an act, for he frequently helped the enemy and favoured them when exercising his judicial duties. Inspite of making as many adversaries in England as in Scotland, he was not dismissed until 1595, at the ripe old age of 94. Eleven years before his 'retirement' he was given a second, almost nominal, job, the captaincy of Bamburgh Castle. He moved there from Adderstone and enjoyed an imposing home until his death in 1602.

Sir John's descendants kept Bamburgh until this branch of the family was declared bankrupt in 1704. Some years before then, one of them married a Forster of Adderstone, and our second character, Thomas Forster, was the son of this marriage.

Thomas was a bright lad, managed to earn enough money to build a new house at Adderstone, and was keen on politics. He had been elected a Member of Parliament a year or two before the Earl of Derwentwater brought the 1715 Jacobite rebellion into the open. The Earl persuaded Thomas to be the rebels 'general', believing that a prominent Protestant figure at their helm would add to the credibility of a mainly Roman Catholic cause. His total ignorance of military matters did not matter, and it did not mitigate his sentence after his capture at Preston. He was held in Newgate prison in London until his brave and sharp-witted sister Dorothea engineered his escape. He fled to France, where he died in 1737.

Because of Thomas's involvement in the rebellion, the Adderstone estate was forfeited to the Crown and then sold to the Bacon family. The Forsters were able to buy back their natural home in the early 1800s, but ailing finances forced them to sell before 1880.

The fifteenth century tower, the home of the Flodden hero, was incorporated in a mansion during the late sixteenth or early seventeenth century. In fact two houses were built at about this time, but both were pulled down when Thomas built his new home in the early years of the eighteenth century. This is the still existing Adderstone Hall, said to be close to the site of the tower, but thick woods inhibit visual confirmation.

Hoppen

L75   P465   NU160306   17 km, 10½ miles, north of Alnwick

About a mile and a half to the east of Adderstone, Hoppen used to be a small but discrete township but is now considered to be part of Lucker, although the railway runs between them. This is a return to pre-1288 times when the Lucker family were holders of Hoppen.

In 1288 Hoppen passed to a local family headed by Edmund de Hoppyn. The 1415 survey notes that Robert Hoppyn held a tower, but the building is not mentioned again and its site has long since been forgotten.

By 1586 Hoppen was just a lonely farmstead, owned by the Conyers family. During the Civil War Edward Conyers supported the Royalists and, later, he was ordered by Cromwell's government to pay a fine of £79 as a 'delinquent'. This he was unable to do from ready cash and he was forced to sell his farm. The Brandling family bought it, and from them it went through several hands until the Brownes of Callaly acquired it in the latter part of the nineteenth century.

Outchester

L75   P465   NU140334   20 km, 12½ miles, north of Alnwick

Another farm which used to be a village, this time two miles north of Adderstone. It adjoins the double ramparts and a wide foss of a square Roman camp.

The village had a manor-house with a tower attached to it. It was in existence in 1462, and during the sixteenth century it belonged to the Horsley family. Its last mention was in Nicholas Horsley's will in which he bequeathed all his property to his son John.

After the Union of the Crowns, when the thought of lasting peace encouraged farmers to produce more, the whole village, tower included, was cleared and one large, potentially highly profitable, farm was made of it.

North Sunderland

L75   P465   NU2123314   18 km, 11 miles, north of Alnwick

At first glance this name may seem incongruous – 'North Southland', whatever next! – but in fact 'Sunderland' means land that has been 'caste asunder' or severed from a monastic estate. The city of Sunderland was 'sundered' from

Monkwearmouth, and, similarly, North Sunderland was 'sundered' from Bamburgh Monastery's land.

Today North Sunderland is the rather dreary, inland subordinate of ebullient Seahouses, but before the harbour piers were constructed in 1886 it was the other way round – North Sunderland was the important village and 'North Sunderland Sea-Houses' was merely a "malodorous place" where fishing and fish curing were carried out.

There was a tower at North Sunderland, a two-storey building, 24 feet square, with a vaulted ground floor. It is not known when it was built, or by whom, but it was demolished in 1832 to make way for St. Paul's church. No trace of the tower remains.

John Warburton said in 1715 there was a tower in a large village called Shorston which belonged to Lord Crewe of Bamburgh. Shorston is assumed to have been half a mile north of North Sunderland, where Shoreston Hall now stands. As there is no other reference to a tower there, it is considered highly likely that Warburton's tower was actually North Sunderland's tower. It would have been an easy mistake to make if the two villages were practically linked.

Inner Farne Island

L75   P465   NU218359   22½ km, 14 miles, north-east of Alnwick

Inner Farne is the inshore island of the Farne group which is looked after by the National Trust mainly as a home for seabirds and grey seals but also as an attraction for carefully controlled human visitors during April and between 1st August and 30th September, also for a few afternoon hours in the breeding season, May, June and July. Such visitors are well advised to wear a hat as the arctic terns are adept at dive bombing.

The islands were included in the patrimony of the Lindisfarne Priory. St. Aiden and, especially, St. Cuthbert liked to retire to Inner Farne from time to time for meditation, prayer and the experience of a simplistic life. Cuthbert died on the island in 687, a few months after resigning from the bishopric of Lindisfarne.

When the Durham monks took over in Norman times Inner Farne continued to be used for spiritual battery charging. In 1255 the Prior of Lindisfarne established a tiny settlement on the island where a few peasants could scratch a living from the emaciated soil by producing barley and vegetables for the visiting monks.

The shipping lanes off the Northumberland coast, well used from the fifteenth century onwards, attracted many pirates who frequently sheltered from the weather or the law in the island cluster. If any came ashore the inhabitants were in for a rough time, so in c1500 Prior Castile (or Castell) built a refuge for them in the form of a Border tower. It had thick walls, a vaulted lower chamber and a small, round-arched entrance. Below it was a stone cistern, called St. Cuthbert's Well, where drinking water was stored. Overall, the building measured 40 by 24 feet.

Monks lived on the island until 1536. Two years later came dissolution and the Government took the tower over as a fort which collaborated with the Lindisfarne forts. Thus in 1613 William Ramsey was appointed 'Captain of the forts of Holy Island and Farne'. Later the tower was used as a lighthouse, a fire being lit on its roof each night. Now it is just a shell.

Bamburgh

L75   P4465   NU183351   21 km, 13 miles, north of Alnwick

The majestic pile which stands atop Bamburgh Rock, the precipitous outcrop of the Whin Sill between the modern village and the sea, is most people's idea of the archetypal medieval castle. It is indeed an awe inspiring sight which conjures up fantasies about knights in shining armour and beautiful damsels in distress.

The knowledge that most of what is visible today is relatively modern may disappoint the purist, but it should not be allowed to detract from the unique interest of the place. Consider the facade to be merely the latest expression of human history which started here 5000 years ago and has included a real medieval castle and just about everything else as well, from the capital city of England to a prototype welfare state.

Some of the first nomadic hunters to enter the county during the Mesolithic period about 3000BC climbed the Rock and left us their trade mark, 'pygmy' flints with which they tipped their spears. These were dug up by an archaeologically-minded rabbit while preparing its burrow. Later settlers preferred the well drained banks of rivers and inland hills to the coast, but bits of crude pottery, found at the bottom of a rubbish tip on the Rock, prove that Ancient Britons between 100BC and 100AD appreciated the advantages of the place.

Romans made use of the Rock during the later stages of their occupation when it was necessary to keep watch for seaborne invaders. They built a timber camp here and it was used by regular officers of the Roman army and collaborating Votadini Britons. Strangely, there is no evidence of a road to the camp, not even a branch from the Devil's Causeway just ten miles away.

The camp was burnt down when the Romans left, and there are no signs of the Rock being used by the Votandinis alone or by any later Britons. Legend has it that here was the castle of Joyeuse Garde, where Sir Lancelot went to die, but killjoy investigators have established that although Arthur was a real person – a noble but not a king – who led the Britons' challenge to the Anglo-Saxon invasion, his supporting cast are fictitious.

Inspite of Arthur's efforts, the Angles attacked the north-east of England with increasing success during the early years of the sixth century, and in 547 Ida felt strong enough to declare the coastline around Bamburgh to be his kingdom of the Benicas, and to claim Bamburgh Rock as his capital. He retained its old name, Dinguardi, and built a timber palace on it, adding to its natural defences by constructing a hedge – probably an entanglement of thorn branches – and, later, a stone wall.

This was the beginning of Bamburgh's most exciting phase. Ida and his descendants quickly expanded the kingdom until it covered the whole of the north, from the Humber to the Forth, what Bede was later to call 'Northumbria'. King Ethelfrith, Ida's grandson, enlarged the capital and changed its name to Bebbanburg, meaning 'fortified town on an isolated rock'. Between 617 and 670 Kings Edwin, Oswald and Oswy, because of their fighting records and personal charisma, were accepted throughout England as 'Bretwaldas', or principal kings, and for all practical purposes Bamburgh, by now a small city on the Rock, was the capital of the whole country.

After 670 Northumbria's political influence began to wane as first Mercia then Wessex achieved prominence. Bamburgh became less important because of this, and lost more authority in 759 when York achieved capital status. It remained a royal residence and fortified town, however, and became the bastion of the arts during Northumbria's greatest period of culture and learning, the guardian of Lindisfarne while its giants of religion were spreading their message through the land.

The Northumberland kings became vassals of the Wessex monarchs from about 828, and in 954 the long Anglian royal line came to an end. Oswulf was installed as the first Earl of Northumberland, and Bamburgh and York were his principal bases. Early in the eleventh century Danes succeeded in sacking Bamburgh and, although still classed by the Angles as a fortified city, it presented a dismal picture to the Norman invaders. As Reginald of Durham put it, "the city renowned formerly for the magnificent splendour of her high estate, has in these latter days been burdened with tribute and reduced to the condition of a handmaiden. She who was once the mistress of British cities has exchanged her glories for shame and desolation".

The Normans set to work improving the defences quite soon, probably when King William I took vengeance for the murder of Robert de Comines, Northumberland's first Norman earl, in 1069. Both the Conqueror and Rufus needed to demonstrate their military might in their efforts to quell the uncompromising Northerners, but it is not clear when Bamburgh was sufficiently strengthened to justify the 'castle' label. Certainly some of the town houses were squeezed off onto the drier parts of the coastal plain to make room for more garrison accommodation, but there was no keep there, even when Robert de Mowbray, the third Norman earl, defied the Crown in 1095 and sought refuge on the Rock. At that time it was being called 'the Old Castle of Northumberland' in contradistinction to the 'New Castle' on the Tyne, but it had to wait until King Henry I's reign, 1100 to 1135, before the building of a keep was started.

This is the oldest building still standing, a massive tower, second only to Norham in size. Stephen had mounted the English throne before it was finished, but it was in fighting mode when King David I of Scotland invaded Northumberland in 1138, supposedly in support of his niece, Empress Matilda. At the subsequent peace treaty, at Durham in 1139, the earldom of Northumberland, excluding Bamburgh and Newcastle castle, was granted to David's son, Prince Henry. Probably Bamburgh went his way as well because the castle's custodian at the time was Eustace fitz John, a Scottish sympathiser.

The county remained a Scottish earldom until 1157 when King Henry II cancelled the arrangement. He then tightened the defences against the Scots by building a number of stone castles near the Border and updating Bamburgh Castle. It was ready to take on William, the 'Lion King' of Scotland, when he invaded in 1174, but although Bamburgh was a target it was not tested then. William was captured before his raiding party reached it.

King Henry III's reign, 1216 to 1272, was a period of growth for Bamburgh. In 1221 a grange was built alongside the keep on the Rock. It could not stand up to the gales common to this exposed site, but when repaired and strengthened it added appreciably to the comfort of the castle's residents, for it was not a grange in the usual sense but rather a large hall house comprising a big chamber with several small rooms leading from it. The existing King's Hall may be a modern replica of the chamber. Also in this relatively peaceful period Bamburgh was provided with a port at Warenmouth to deal with its fast-growing trade with other parts of England and the Continent.

Unfortunately Henry's successor, King Edward I, managed to generate in the Scots so much hatred for the English that when he died he left a sinister legacy which his son and heir, Edward II, was quite incapable of handling. He was more concerned about his court favourites, like Piers de Gaveston whom he locked up in Bamburgh Castle in 1309 to protect him from belligerent barons. He did bestir himself sufficiently in 1314 to take up arms against Robert Bruce, but he mishandled his battle at Bannockburn so badly his army was decimated and he had to escape by boat to Bamburgh.

For a few years after Bannockburn Bamburgh, and indeed the whole of Northumberland, suffered terribly, not only from Bruce's frequent raids but also from the plundering, kidnapping and ransoming activities of Gilbert de Middleton and his Mitford Gang. The castle's constable, Robert de Horsley, did not help matters. He refused to allow the townspeople to buy a truce from Bruce for £270 unless they paid him a like amount, which put the deal beyond their means. He charged exorbitant fees for storing the inhabitants' goods in the castle, and he encouraged his porter to charge excessively for both entering and leaving the castle. He was accused, also, of seizing provisions from ships lying in Warenmouth harbour. Complaints against him were so numerous that he was sacked in 1316 and replaced by William de Felton.

One of King Edward III's first acts after being crowned in 1327 was to appoint Robert de Horncliffe as constable of Bamburgh. He surveyed the buildings and equipment with great thoroughness and reported damage and dilapidation amounting in value to £300. His report was accepted and the place was restored to a condition worthy of a royal establishment. Six years later Edward lodged his wife, Queen Philippa, in the castle while he lay siege on Berwick in the hope of drawing the Scottish army to its relief. Before swallowing the bait, Archibald Douglas and his men tried diversionary tactics by attacking Bamburgh, knowing who was inside. The castle withstood their onslaught, as the king was confident it would, and eventually they walked into the trap set for them on Halidon Hill.

Although the castle was deemed to be pretty well impregnable at this stage, the town, by now almost totally on the plain below the Rock, was decidedly vulnerable. In 1336 the inhabitants were licensed to collect money to pay for a town wall, but it was never built. Perhaps they could not raise the money, for their former prosperity had evaporated.

The Wars of the Roses put an end to Bamburgh Castle as a fighting unit. The Yorkist Earl of Warwick besieged it in 1462 and, although he had ten thousand men pitched against three hundred inside, it was not military strength but starvation which caused it to capitulate. It remained in Yorkist hands until the following spring when it was retaken by a combined Scottish and French force acting for King Henry VI and his queen, Margaret. Again Warwick came north, but this time he had insufficient men to besiege the castle so he left it alone. For the next nine months Bamburgh experienced a miniature replay of its glittering past as a royal city as King Henry held court and ruled over the surrounding few acres. In 1464 came the Lancastrian disasters of Hedgley Moor and Hexham. Henry escaped from the latter to Bywell and then to Bamburgh. He soon fled from there, leaving Sir Ralph Grey to face the force which Warwick had gathered. Grey was offered honourable surrender terms but refused. King Edward IV's great new guns were brought up – they were called 'Newe-castel' and 'London' by some, 'Newcastle' and 'Dysion' by others – and they quickly blasted holes in the castle's walls large enough for infantry to pour in. Sir Ralph and his men had no option but to surrender.

Bamburgh was the first castle in England to succumb to gunfire. It gave a clear signal to all other castles and towers that they were finished as effective fortifications. Bamburgh henceforth was a castle in name only; Sir Robert

Bowes later advocated its repair, but the Government could see no point in spending money on obsolescence.

Much of the castle's fabric had been saved by Sir Ralph Grey's prompt surrender and some residential accommodation remained, so its captaincy was quite a prize which Queen Elizabeth granted Sir John Forster of Adderstone, the aged Lord Warden of the English Marches, in 1584. This was a nominal position, intended as a reward for long service, although Sir John did not retire – or, rather, he was not dismissed – from his warden's job until 1594. Then he enjoyed his last few years in a still imposing home, dying in 1602 at the remarkable age of 101. King James I granted the deeds of the whole manor of Bamburgh, including the castle, to Sir John's grandson. Thus did a thousand years of royal ownership come to an end.

For about a hundred years the Forster family owned and used Bamburgh Castle but did nothing to maintain it. They could not afford to as they led immoderate lives and squandered the family fortune. In 1704 Sir John Forster was declared bankrupt and was ordered by the Court of Chancery to sell his estates to pay his debts. The man fell on his feet, for the purchaser was Lord Nathaniel Crewe, Bishop of Durham, his son-in-law. At the age of 67 he had married Dorothea, Sir John's daughter forty years his junior, in 1700. It is said he gave Sir John £20,000 for his estates at Bamburgh and Blanchland – Adderstone now belonged to another branch of the family so was not included – and this was sufficient to calm the creditors and produce a small income. The bishop's wife, incidentally, was the aunt of the Dorothea Forster who helped her brother to escape from a London gaol after the 1715 Jacobean rebellion.

Lord Crewe died in 1721 and left his estates in trust to charity. Five trustees were appointed to administer the bishop's will, but they did little, and in fact their only recorded expenditure was £15 to stabilise part of Bamburgh's keep which was threatening to fall. It was the second generation of trustees which really got the Lord Crewe Trust moving, and, so far as Bamburgh was concerned, most of the credit belongs to Dr John Sharp, rector of Hartburn and archdeacon of Northumberland.

He was energetic and artful, frequently getting work done before presenting the bills to his fellow trustees as a fait accompli. First he installed a much needed court room in the keep, and this served as a classroom when not wanted for judicial purposes. A proper school in the castle, to replace the village school, was his next achievement. A Mr Peacock was engaged as master at a yearly salary said to be only £6.67, and in 1776 the staff was increased to include a mistress who got £5 a year. After this John Sharp fitted out an apartment in the keep for his brother Thomas, the incumbent of Bamburgh, as there was no parsonage in the village. This work cost £300 but the trustees paid only half and Thomas paid the other half.

In 1765 John started a coastguard service. At first this was just a coastal patrol on stormy nights and free lodging for up to seven days in the castle for shipwrecked seamen, but it developed to include the storage of chains, pumps and other devices needed to help stranded ships. Later still a lighted beacon, signalling apparatus and a lifeboat were added.

Poor harvests and shortages produced by giving priority to exports made the price of corn too high for the local poor, so in 1766 John got the trustees to give him £30 so that he could buy wheat to sell in Bamburgh at a price the villagers could afford whenever its commercial price rose above 25 pence a bushel. A year later this service was put on a permanent footing and John was allowed a float of £100. The Trustees' tenants supplied the corn, it was ground free at the castle's mill and stored at John's own expense. Then he opened a shop where the poor could buy this flour as well as candles, butter, pepper, blue, pins, alum and rice, all at affordable prices.

Medical aid came next. First a chemist shop in 1772, then a surgeon was hired to give advice and perform operations every Saturday morning for half a guinea a week. This proved so popular that after three months the surgeon was occupied all day Saturday and often for parts of Friday and Sunday as well. In a year or two even this was inadequate and an infirmary was added, then a maternity wing – with clean sheets provided. All these facilities were free to the village poor.

By 1780 the school had sixty boys and sixty girls, and their education was free provided their parents earned less than £60 a year. The boys were taught writing, arithmetic, navigation, English, Latin and Greek. The girls substituted domestic subjects for navigation. By that year, also, there were two granaries in the castle and a further two in the village. There was also a slaughter house equipped with a large boiler for cooking meat and making broth. A small boarding school was added later for very poor girls.

John died in 1792 but the services he had inaugurated continued for many years. Gradually, however, interest in this miniature social welfare enterprise waned, partly because public authorities took on some of its responsibilities but also because of poor management and the financial burden of maintaining the castle in good repair. The distribution of corn ceased in 1847 and the shop closed in 1861. The day schools were transferred to council premises and shipwrecked sailors were lodged in local public houses. Only the girls boarding school, the dispensary and a large library built up by Sharp and others remained within the castle. A smell of scandal crept in when the trustees started to use the keep as rent-free residences, and this led to an enquiry in 1863 into the charity's management and its dire financial situation. A report was presented to the Attorney General, who ordered the trustees to pay rent and the school to close. The remaining charities struggled on until the early 1890s, but the decision to close the castle was inevitable.

It was put on the market and bought in 1894 by Lord Armstrong of Cragside, allegedly for £60,000. He spent a further £1 million on repairing the buildings he wished to retain, building more residential accommodation, modernising interiors, installing electric light and even putting in some central heating. The work was concluded after his death in 1900, and more repairs were necessary after the army had occupied it during the Great War. Much later, in order to spread the cost of maintenance a little, some of the accommodation was converted into self-contained apartments which were let as attractive homes. Then in 1948 certain traditional buildings, the keep and the Great Hall included, were opened to the public for a small charge.

Although Dr Sharp's and Lord Armstrong's work is very evident, there is plenty to excite the historian and the archaeologist. The gatehouse, a pair of round towers and an archway, contains some Norman work. Much of the walling which separates the three wards is original, and at the end of the inner ward are ruins of a twelfth century chapel built on the site of King Oswald's church. The great keep, although repaired by many owners from Henry II to Armstrong, is still basically Norman in concept. In the west ward, where most of the wooden houses of the Anglian city and early Norman village were sited, are mounds believed to be Anglian graves. The view from the battlements is worth a visit on its own; given a clear day, Lindisfarne, the Farnes, the Cheviots, the Lammermuir Hills, even Berwick can be seen.

Bamburgh Tower

In 1121 King Henry I decided to give the living of Bamburgh to the Augustinian cannons of Nostell in Yorkshire. The gift met such stiff opposition from Durham bishops and later kings that the canons did not get clearance to build their monastery until 1272. The chosen site was the grounds of the Norman church.

At some date before 1415 a fortified tower was added to the monastic buildings as a refuge from Scottish raiders. This tower was pulled down after dissolution, about 1540, and nothing of it that can be positively identified. It is just possible, however that some solid masonry set into one of the walls bounding the churchyard was a part of it.

Warenmouth

L75   P465   NU162354   21¹/₂ km, 13¹/₂ miles, north of Alnwick

The thirteenth century was a relatively peaceful one for the north-east of Northumberland, and Bamburgh, like Berwick further north, experienced a taste of prosperity. Its trade, especially its export of wool to other parts of England and continental Europe, developed rapidly and it soon became obvious that the town needed an easily accessible port. It was using Alnmouth, but that was eighteen miles away, a long journey for waggons.

Warenmouth, the port of Bamburgh, was constructed just a mile or so from the town, round Budle Point in Budle Bay. In 1247 King Henry III gave it his blessing and its burgesses the same 'liberties and free custom' as were then enjoyed by the merchants of Newcastle – for a small tax of course. William Heron, the constable of Bamburgh Castle and the principal advocate of the port, was so proud of his achievement he was apt to talk on the slightest provocation about "my new town", and 'Newtown' stuck as its popular name, eventually replacing Warenmouth altogether.

Looking at the sand and mud which is Budle Bay today, it seems that a port on its shore-line, even at its open sea end, could never have been feasible. It has to be remembered, of course, that sand is notoriously unstable, that river courses can change quite dramatically and that medieval ships were tiny compared to modern vessels. Conditions in the thirteenth century were undoubtedly different to those of today, and also to those prevailing in 1835 when William Andrew Chatto (non de plume 'Stephen Oliver the Younger') noted that the bay dried out at low tide except for the stream which could be waded across without getting wet above the knees. He gave the following invaluable advice to anyone contemplating such a crossing: "It is very convenient for a pedestrian tourist, or an angler, who may occasionally have to wade, to wear socks in summer, which can be taken off in a moment, while a gentleman who wears long stockings up to his very fork, and who garters above the knee, has to untruss his points and generally spends a quarter of an hour before he can uncase his legs".

The precise position of Warenmouth is not known: 'Warenmouth' is not a name which has appeared on any map since, at least, the sixteenth century. The mouth of the Waren Burn, on modern maps, would appear to be close to Waren Mill, where it runs into the southern corner of Budle Bay, but in former days the Burn was considered to run through the Bay to the open sea, so its mouth would be near Budle Point. The stream through the sand is called Budle Water now, and the Waren Burn used to do the same drainage job but probably ran closer to the south coast of the Bay. In parts an artificial channel may have been dug to ensure this. Thus the most favourable site for the harbour is the slightly sheltered spot a few hundred yards to the south-west of the Point, close to Heather Cottages.

Inspite of Heron's euphoria and King Henry's bounteousness, the port did not do as well as had been expected. By 1296 the taxpayers were pleading for reduced levies, and in 1307 King Edward II thought it prudent to exchange the unreliable revenue from rates for an assured £110 annual rent from Isobel de Beaumont, the Lord of Alnwick's widow. The aftermath of Bannockburn greatly harmed both Bamburgh and Warenmouth, and the Earl of Warwick's siege during the Wars of the Roses reduced the former to a small village and killed the latter.

Warenmouth, however, proved to be as resilient as Bamburgh; when one chapter closed another opened. During the sixteenth century a quay and a large two-storey granary were built at Heather Cottages and a port for Waren Mill was inaugurated. Grain was brought there by vessels from other parts of the country, then was taken to the mill on flat-bottomed barges at high tide. They carried flour from the mill to the port on their return journey.

The mill held a lucrative contract with the Admiralty for its flour. To protect this and its other trade, not to mention its personnel, from the Scots and pirates, a tower was built on rising ground behind Heather Cottages. The building was constructed about the end of the sixteenth century but was not mentioned until 1628, when it was called a bastle. There is no trace of it now and Newtown farm stands on its site.

Warenmouth had yet another life during the 1914 Great War. A wooden pier still exists which was used for loading ships with stone quarried from nearby Kittling Hill. Wartime necessity made this feasible, but the business could not survive the peace and the quarry has been returned to the Fulmars.

Area 3, Sub-Area B   Up the River Aln

Alnmouth

L81   P477   NU246105   7 km, 4¹/₂ miles, south-east of Alnwick

"A small sea-port famous for all kinds of wickedness" was John Wesley's enticing description of Alnmouth after spending an afternoon there in 1748. Whether he exaggerated or not, the town's history is interesting and long, reaching back to the Celtic invasion. The Angles built a church there, and it is the most likely site of Bede's Twyford where, in 684, a synod elected a reluctant Cuthbert to the bishopric. The Normans replaced the church and dedicated the new one to St. Waleric, and in about 1150 the town was granted deeds which established it as the Burgh of St. Waleric. William de Vasey, Baron of Alnwick, granted a market and a fair and set it on its feet as Alnwick's port.

Trade fluctuated over the centuries and finished, except for a little fishing, in the early years of the nineteenth because ships had grown too large for its harbour. Fortunately its natural attractions were well known and it became one of the earliest centres for holidays.

In earlier times its visitors had not been so welcome. Alnmouth was vulnerable not only to Scottish raiders but also to pirates. As late as 1779 the famous American buccaneer, John Paul Jones, fired a shot into the town, while during the fifteenth and sixteenth centuries Flemmish pirates were frequent sightings. To give warning of possible trouble, the Alnmouth people lit a beacon on the highest point of the long ridge north of the town called Bracken Hill. In 1988 The Duke of Northumberland erected a replica of a beacon cresset on the spot to commemorate the four-hundredth anniversary of the Armada.

There are several interesting old buildings in the town but neither on the ground nor in the records can any trace be found of a fortified medieval building. Perhaps the inhabitants felt safe enough with three castles – Alnwick, Warkworth and Dunstanburgh – within a seven mile radius.

Alnwick Abbey

L81   P488   NU178142   1 km, ⁵/₈ mile, north-west of Alnwick

Heiferlaw

L81   P488   NU182177   4 km, 2¹/₂ miles, north of Alnwick

The abbey was founded by Eustace fitz John, Baron of Alnwick, and his wife Beatrix, daughter of Ivo de Vescy. The living was given to Premonstratensian canons, a colony of whom later founded Dryburgh Abbey.

The Vescys and the Percys looked after their white canons, and their house was considered to be one of the finest in Northumberland. After dissolution in 1539 it was allowed to go to ruin, and now only its heavily fortified gatehouse remains above ground. This was built in the fourteenth century, perhaps two hundred years after the abbey; it is quite well preserved, with its arched entrance and four projecting corner turrets still intact.

Heiferlaw was a watch tower belonging to the abbey and having the job of warning the canons of approaching danger. It was probably built by the fourth Earl of Northumberland between 1470 and 1489.

It was a small, unpretentious, square, fortified tower, the ruin of which can be seen from the old North Road north of Alnwick. Its walls still stand full height but the roof is missing. The ground floor was not vaulted.   [**Plate 3**]

Hulne Priory

L81   P488   NU163157   3¹/₂ km, 2¹/₄ miles, north-west of Alnwick

The walled ruin of England's first Carmelite priory sits serenely on a small plateau in Hulne Park. Below it to the east is the wooded valley of the River Aln, Above it to the south is Brizlee Hill. The scene is peaceful and beautiful, the very antithesis of wild Northumberland, yet it was not immune from attack by Scottish raiders.

The priory was founded by Ralph Fresborn, a young Northumbrian soldier. While in the Holy Land, crusading with Richard, Earl of Cornwall, he had visited the monastery on Mount Carmel, in what is now north-west Israel, and had been so impressed he had taken vows and remained. He had been found there by William de Vescy, Baron of Alnwick, while on a later crusade and had been persuaded to return to England to start a sister monastery in his native land. Vescy had let him choose his site, and the resemblance which

Brizlee Hill bore to Mount Carmel is said to have influenced the lad's decision. Permission to hunt, fish and cut wood in Hulne Park was granted and he had been left to get on with it.

From Fresborn's initial work in 1242, the priory grew and prospered. Although never lavishly endowed, it became a seat of learning and scholarship, a fine example followed by Carmelite friars in other parts of the country. A library of over a hundred manuscripts on sacred subjects was built up over the years, but possessions likely to attract raiders were in short supply – yet raiders came, on several occasions. To discourage these unwanted visitors a strong wall was built round the priory, then in 1488 this was complemented by a tower, the gift of Henry Percy, the fourth Earl of Northumberland. It was a plain, strong building with ground floor vault and two rooms upstairs.

After dissolution in 1539 the priory was given rent-free to Sir Robert Ellerker for life. Thomas Percy, the seventh earl, followed until he was executed in 1572. John Forster, the Warden of the Marches, possessed it for a time, as did several other wealthy people, but it eventually returned to the Percy family when Hugh, the first Duke of Northumberland, bought it in 1755. He saw the priory as a useful annexe to Alnwick Castle; he virtually rebuilt the tower, included an oriel window and a bridge leading to a new battlemented but unfortified house he constructed on the site of the prior's residence. Both buildings were treated to the same Gothick styling he lavished on his castle.

These eighteenth century buildings are still in good order, but the original priory buildings are in various stages of decay. There is much of great interest to be seen, and permission to do so may be obtained from the ticket office near the entrance to Alnwick Castle.

Eglingham

L81   P488   NU104195   10 km, 6¼ miles, north-west of Alnwick

The name is believed to have stemmed from 'Eglys', the Ancient British word for church. This is appropriate because Eglingham was granted by King Ceolwulph to Lindisfarne monastery in 738, and in about 1110 it was transferred to Tynemouth priory. The village has had a church since Anglian times.

While in Tynemouthshire, one of the village's leaseholders, Robert Collingwood, built a rather large strong house which, in 1704, became the west wing of a mansion. This enlargement was the work of one of the Ogles, who had bought the premises in the sixteenth century and retained them until 1890.

Henry Ogle, a member of this family, lived through the Civil War and, when it was over, got the unpopular job of sequestrating the property of former royalists. Oliver Cromwell did not like him very much and it was reported that the two quarrelled after spending a night together in Eglingham. He found more favour with the common people, however, for he was instrumental in exposing and bringing to justice a so-called witch-finder whose character assassinations led to the execution during a Puritan 'trial' on Newcastle's Town Moor on 21st August 1650 of fourteen women and one man alleged to be in league with the devil.

The mansion, now called Eglingham Hall, was extended further at the end of the nineteenth century, and has been modified slightly since then. The original strong house is still there but it blends in with the rest and is difficult to detect.

Shepherds Law

L81   P488   NU087166   10½ km, 6½ miles, north-west of Alnwick

If fortified towers were to do with the prevention of crime, the building that was here had to do with the desirable consequences of crime, and thus justifies inclusion. Its name is descriptive, provided 'Law' is given a judicial and not a topographical connotation, for it was a manorial court-house.

Major A. Browne of Callaly stated unequivocally in 1987, a year before his death at the grand age of 92, that one of his forebears inaugurated the court in the 1690s, thereby breathing new life into the dying practice of maintaining order at the manorial level. The forebear in question was probably William Browne of Bolton who was High Sheriff of Northumberland in 1702 and therefore had a strong interest in the administration of justice.

The Royal Commission on Historical Manuscripts is unable to provide proof of the existence of this court; it may not have been officially recognised, but one look at the ruins of Shepherds Law must convince the most sceptic that Major Browne was right.

They stand on the north shoulder of Titlington Pike and may be reached by an unmetalled lane from the Crawley to Titlington road. They have not weathered the years very well, but much of the long front facia of the former building still stands to about first floor level to reveal a blind arcade and a grand arched entrance. Behind is an intricate pattern of foundations, broken walls and lots of loose masonry, the whole complex emphasising the domineering nature of the original.

It is believed that the manorial court did not have a long life and that later the building was used as a farmhouse for about a century. But the site is not deserted even now. Behind the ruins is a modern red-roofed house which, when visited, was occupied by a monk from Alnmouth. He lived alone in this modern hermitage and, as a relaxing hobby, he spent some time most days trying to sort out the debris in his 'garden' with a view to reassembling, jigsaw fashion, some more walls of this ancient curio. Soon he hopes to build a chapel.

Titlington

L81   P488   NU099152   8¹/₂ km, 5¹/₄ miles, north-west of Alnwick

An ancient township which was one of the fourteen estates contained in the Beanley serjeanty granted by King Henry I to Gospatric during the early part of the twelfth century. Quite soon it passed to Walter Espec, Baron of Carham and Wark, probably as a dowry for one of Gospatric's daughters.

Espec built a small motte and bailey in the township before giving it to Kirkham Priory, the institution he had founded in 1121, and there it stayed until dissolution in 1539.

Robert and Alexander Collingwood, insatiable collectors of real estate, purchased the township from the Crown in 1553. Included in the sale was a fortified tower, rather decayed and lacking a roof; apparently the prior or his tenant had flattened the motte and built this tower on it sometime after 1415.

The property was in Collingwood hands until Robert, of Eslington, sold it in 1618 to William Reade, grandson of William Reade of Fenham in Islandshire, the captain of Lindisfarne and Farne from 1559 to 1604. The Reades kept it for two generations, then another William split what was by now a farmstead into two, selling South Titlington to Henry Pearson in 1664 and North Titlington to Roger Pearson in 1675. The latter cleared the ruins of the tower and built a house on its site in 1745. At the beginning of the nineteenth century both parts of the estate were bought by William Hargrave-Pawson of Shawdon. He replaced the house with the still existing mansion in 1821.

Shawdon

L81   P488   NU092143   8¹/₂ km, 5¹/₄ miles west of Alnwick

Shawdon was one of the places Robert de Ros acquired at the end of the twelfth century to extend the barony of Carham and Wark which he had inherited from his father Piers de Ros, Walter Espec's son-in-law. The transaction was confirmed by King John in 1199.

But Robert's grandson, another Robert, lost the property in 1295 when he changed sides and joined the Scots. Sir John Lilburn held Shawdon in 1320, and it was he or his son who built a tower in or about 1350. It was large enough to be classed as a 'castrum' in the 1415 survey.

The Lilburns were landowners on the grand scale but they lived at Shawdon until 1506, when they sold to William and Isabel Proctor. They also lived there although one of their sons lived at Lilburn. Another son, Cuthbert, did some repairs to Shawdon tower which was passed as serviceable by Bowes and Ellerker in 1541.

John Proctor retained Shawdon when he sold other estates to the Ogles in 1683, then bought Crawley from the Herons to enlarge the Shawdon estate. John was involved in another property transaction in 1705 – not a purchase this time but a straight swap. He and Alexander Browne agreed to exchange their lands, John getting Dunstan Hall near Craster on the coast and Alexander getting Shawdon with Crawley. The new owner let Crawley and kept Shawdon as his home, just a mile from one of brother William's homes at Bolton (his main seat was Doxford Hall, NU185241).

In 1723 the Brownes sold to James Hargrave, a Newcastle attorney, and took over Doxford when the other branch of the family died off. James's son, William, left Shawdon to his daughter who, in 1802, married John Pawson. Their son, George, was adjudged in 1817 to be the rightful heir to the Hargrave fortune, so he changed his name to Hargrave-Pawson and he and his progeny held Shawdon until 1931.

The fourteenth century tower was demolished by William Hargrave in 1779 and an Adam-style mansion was built on the site. There are a few marked and dressed stones lying about in the garden which may have been parts of the tower.

Bolton

L81   P488   NU106137   8 km, 5 miles, west of Alnwick

Jenny's Lantern

L81   P488   NU119153   7 km, 4$\frac{1}{2}$ miles, west of Alnwick

Like Shawdon, Bolton was a twelfth century extension to Robert de Ros's barony of Carham and Wark, but, unlike Shawdon, it was granted to Kirkham Priory and a leper hospital was founded there in, or just before, 1225.

The hospital comprised two stone buildings, one for thirteen lepers, the other for the master and his three assistants. Finance was provided by the grant of Bolton township, a corn mill at Mindrum and parcels of land at Pawston, Branxton and Kilham. The master had instructions to keep a good table, dress neatly and to be hospitable to travellers. After providing "things necessary and convenient" for the efficient running of the establishment, the master had to apply any surplus money to the relief of the poor.

Some doubt exists about the exact location of the hospital. A Mr Henry Maclaughlan, a very speculative but frequently quoted local historian of the nineteenth century, suggested it was an ancient enclosure called The Guards, a quarter of a mile south of the village and close to the River Aln.

There is nothing to substantiate this idea, however, and a much more likely spot, which has the support of local inhabitants, is a low-lying meadow behind (ie, north-west) of the village street. It is claimed that stones were standing there some fifty years ago but cattle have knocked them down and now they are hidden beneath the turf.

Although the hospital was retained by Kirkham Priory until dissolution it changed its function during the early years of the fourteenth century and became solely a hospital in the original sense, a place where hospitality was extended to travellers. Not all travellers were welcome, of course, and post-Bannockburn Scots were troublesome. In 1317 Roger Purvey and two other members of Gilbert Middleton's 'Mitford Gang' captured the place and held it until they themselves were captured the following year. To avoid further unpleasantness, King Edward III issued a licence to crenellate the master's house in 1336. Either by drastic modification or reconstruction, it became a strong tower with a barmekyn, a safe haven marked as such on Gough's map of c1360.

The hospital and the surrounding area got a great many travellers on 5 September 1513 – the Earl of Surrey and his army, no less. The Earl and his senior officers took Communion in Bolton church and pledged themselves to defeat the Scots or die in the attempt. King James's herald brought a message that day to Surrey to say that the suggested date for the Battle of Flodden was acceptable but not the venue.

When the hospital closed in 1539 the Crown granted the whole area to Robert Collingwood of Eslington. His descendants held it to the 1690s, when one of them built Bolton Hall. A short length of boundary walling of this mansion contains some crossed and straight loops of the type often seen in old strongholds, and it is speculated that these were taken from the tower, which by this time was just a ruin.

William Browne bought Bolton Hall just after it was built. He was the man who inaugurated a manorial court at Shepherds Law. His grandson, Nicholas Browne, gave Bolton to his eldest daughter, Jane, in 1762 when she married into the Forster family, and the place was theirs and their heirs until 1820, when it was sold to William Burrell.

Jenny's Lantern is a ruin on top of a hill within the Bolton estate, about a mile north-east of the village. It looks like the remains of a medieval beacon tower, but it happens to be of eighteenth century vintage, although built on a Romano-British settlement. It was a shepherd's cottage, and Jenny, the shepherd's wife, was in the habit of showing a lantern at her window to guide her husband back from the local inn.

Abberwick

L81   P488   NU126131   5^1/$_2$ km, 3^1/$_2$ miles, west of Alnwick

A township originally in the Ros barony but possessed in the late thirteenth or very early fourteenth century by the Knights Hospitallers. The centre of the township was the now defunct village of Abberwick, a few yards to the west of the present village.

Not much is known about the place until the sixteenth century, but it seems probable that the Hospitallers got it as a gift from the Ros family to help their finances. There is no evidence that they ever actually used Abberwick, and they got it just about the time they started the expensive business of building their preceptory at Low Chibburn. No occupier achieved a mention on records until after the Hospitallers had left the country, about 1550, then the township was split into several estates, owned at various times by the Bellingham, Collingwood, Radcliffe and Swinburne families. During the seventeenth century this array had dwindled to just two people, Huntridge and Storey, and of these only Storey saw the century out as Huntridge was declared bankrupt in 1689.

Robert Collingwood built a tower before he was punished for taking part in the Rising of the Northern Earls in 1569. It was mentioned in deeds of 1572 and 1689, but nothing more is heard of it. Its site is not known unless you agree with the local suggestion that a stone which lies in a hollow in the area of the lost village was its doorstep.

The British Museum holds a rare tract dated 1580 which tells of a "strange and monstrous child" who lived at Abberwick. It was male and had two heads: "one ear on each head was shaped like an horse's and the other like a hog's". Unkind people may think this was only to be expected from parents called John and Elinor Urine.

Lemmington

L81   P488   NU122113   6¹⁄₂ km, 4 miles, south-west of Alnwick

Records exist about someone called Siward who lived at Lemmington in 1158, but the first occupier with unquestionable credentials was Adam de Bydnell, listed on the Edlington register in 1336.

Adam's descendants changed their surname to Bednell, then to Beadnell, but they do not appear to have had anything to do with the fishing village of that name.

Adam built a tower at Lemmington. The building date is not known but the style and workmanship are fourteenth century. It formed a rectangle 53 by 35 feet and had a small turret at the east end to accommodate the entrance and spiral stairs to two upper floors. The ground floor was vaulted and its walls were six feet thick.

In 1415 this tower belonged to William Beadnell and in 1545 it was still serviceable, owned by John Beadnell. During his innings it was commandeered for a short time as a home for a band of Hungarian mercenaries. In 1630 George Beadnell, his wife and eldest son Robert mortgaged the estate to Sir

Thomas Widdrington and John Radcliffe for £1800. A younger son, George, seems to have been a very enterprising chap: he bought brother Robert's reversionary rights in 1633, and in 1655 he redeemed the property and then bought it from his father and mother. To do this he may have borrowed from Sir James Clavering for, whether by foreclosure or purchase, Sir James became the owner of Lemmington soon after George's death in 1685.

Sir James died in 1707 and one of his two sons, William, inherited the property portfolio. When in 1716 Elizabeth, his sister, married Nicholas Fenwick, a man of substance in Newcastle, William arranged a marriage settlement which gave Lemmington to Nicholas. He was not a countryman, but eventually he got round to incorporating the tower, or the parts of it which were still usable, into a Georgian mansion designed by William Newton. It and its garden were completed by 1746, six years before Nicholas died.

They had had no children, so trustees were appointed to administer Nicholas's estate. For some unknown reason they held on to Lemmington Hall for 73 years before selling it in 1825 to William Hargrove-Pawson of Shawdon, who installed two old maiden aunts, the Misses Davidson, in it.

When they died the Hall was left empty for many years, the Hargrave-Pawsons apparently having forgotten about it. So when Sir Stephen Aitchison bought it in 1919 he had to do a lot of renovation. He managed to make a very comfortable home of it and fitted it with fine furniture and valuable pictures. The tower was given a new roof over its first floor, its second floor being beyond repair, and its first floor chamber became a billiard room. After his death the mansion became a Roman Catholic convent where mentally sub-normal girls were cared for. The billiard room became a chapel. A few years ago the nuns left, and the latest news is that the mansion is being considered for renovation and conversion into a conference centre.

Edlingham

L81   P500   NU116092   8 km, 5 miles, south-west of Alnwick

Although not included in the Beanley serjeanty granted by King Henry I to Gospatric, one of the offsprings of that prolific father somehow got hold of Edlingham and started a family bearing the place's name. In 1174 John of Edlingham was paying an annual rent to the Baron of Alnwick of one soar-hawk or six pennies. The family stayed put until the end of the thirteenth century, living in a hall house which could not be described as fortified yet was fairly substantial and had a moat, created by diverting the Edlingham Burn.

Walter of Edlington sold his estate to William de Felton in 1294. William was an up and coming officer of the Establishment, a future constable of Roxburgh castle and sheriff of Northumberland, and it is a mystery why, if he felt so attached to the place as to adopt its name, he did not live in Felton. Admittedly the straight line distance between Edlingham and Felton is only about seven miles so he could ride there quite quickly, but Felton had an important bridge on the main north-south route which was vulnerable to surprise attack yet was left undefended.

William saw to his own defences quickly enough. He started a process which was to continue through most of the fourteenth century. Strong ramparts were erected on the inner side of the moat, a gatehouse was built, the hall was strengthened and other buildings were added. It became almost as impregnable as a castle, but perhaps fortified manor-house would be a more accurate term.

The Felton tenure ended in 1396 when John de Felton died leaving his only daughter, Elizabeth, as heiress. She was married to Sir Edmund Hastings of Yorkshire, and they and their descendants held the estate to 1514.

Work on their home started immediately Sir Edmund got his hands on it, and its third and final stage was completed before 1415. He built a strong tower inside the existing compound; it had very strong walls, vaulted ground and first floor chambers and a look-out turret. He did this only partly to improve his safety; the main reasons were to get larger and more comfortable living accommodation and to flaunt his wealth. The tower was a solus, a domestic extension with a glorious fireplace, delicately ribbed vaulting and window seats, all designed for gracious living, while its ostentatious external appearance was a clear warning to the Jones.

In 1514 the Hastings leased the place to George Swinburne of Capheaton. Later he bought the property and it remained in the family until the eighteenth century. The buildings were little used and the land was let to farmers most of the time. In 1581 John Swinburne, a staunch Roman Catholic, was accused of harbouring Jesuits in the tower but a search party found nothing incriminating.

Decay had set in by 1645, and in 1660 the original parts of the complex were dismantled down to their foundations and their stone used to build a farmhouse to replace an old tower at Newtown, a neighbouring estate also owned by Swinburne.

The solus tower was retained, and perhaps this is where two yeomen brothers, John and Jacob Mills, lived when they gave their address as 'Edlingham Castle' on being sworn in as witnesses at the 1683 trial of Margaret Stothard of Edlington village. This was probably the last legal trial of a woman accused of being a witch. The judge, Henry Ogle, heard how John Mills lost his voice and his hair stood on end when Margaret appeared in his bedroom at dead of night. Jacob Mills told how Alan Nickles of Lorbottle and his wife had refused Margaret alms and their child had died unexpectedly soon after. William Collingwood claimed all was not black as Margaret had cured Jane Carr's child by transferring her illness to a calf which died, and Isobel Maine said her cheese never came out right unless Margaret cast a spell on it. We have not been told the outcome, but at least two historians have assumed she was found not guilty.

The Department of the Environment took over the Edlingham site in 1978. They stabilized the tall tower and removed a quantity of loose stones which were piled to first floor height around it to reveal two beautifully appointed chambers. The foundations of the original parts were uncovered and walk-ways were made from which the general plan of the complex could be perceived. The whole place is now in the care of English Heritage, who welcome visitors.

A view of the ruins can be obtained from the Rothbury to Alnwick road, B6341, but it is worth going down a side road to get a closer view. The ruins make a memorable picture, framed as they are by a high viaduct, a relic of the Alnwick to Cornhill railway which closed in 1935. Also there is a small church of great interest quite close to the ruins. It has a fifteenth or sixteenth century tower which was built as a fortified refuge for the villagers. It was constructed on the end of a much older nave, and the only access to the tower is through this.   [Plate 4]

Newtown

L81   P500   NU100083   10 km, 6¼ miles, south-west of Alnwick

Called 'Newton juxta Edlingham' on old documents (and very wisely, too, as there are many Newtons and Newtowns in Northumberland), it was a small village and is now just a single farm about a mile to the south-west of Edlingham. Although it enjoys good natural defences on a rocky outcrop, a tower was built in the centre of the village sometime before 1335; its builder could have been the father or grandfather of John Barker who held it in 1415.

The Manners of Etal were owners for about a century, then the Swinburnes got hold of it. They replaced the tower by a proper farmhouse in 1660. Traces of the tower were noticed in 1715, but nothing remains now.

Callaly

L81   P500   NU052098   13½ km, 8¼ miles, south-west of Alnwick

This lovely estate a couple of miles south-west of Whittingham was held by only three families from Anglian times to 1986. The first of these took the name of the place as their surname. The heads of the family were drengs, tenants of the Crown and not of any intermediary baron.

These people lived in a substantial house, probably of timber, but there is uncertainty about its location. Probably a small village called Callaly, north of the present 'castle' and down the Callaly Burn towards Callaly Mill (NU053110) is a fair guess. Where it definitely was not was the earthworks at NU052104, half a mile north of the 'castle', close to the last of the fish ponds. Henry Maclaughlan suggested that these are the remains of the first abode, and most historians since have repeated his speculation as fact. Surveyors in 1970 found that their "construction and general appearance are in the local Iron Age tradition", however, and there is no evidence of any medieval connection.

When the Normans became established in Northumberland the Callaly family were one of the few allowed to keep their estate under tenure of drengage. The Pipe Roll of 1161 records that William of Callaly paid £1.50 a year to King Henry II, and also did trunkage to the royal castle at Bamburgh. He was expected to cart a fully grown oak every other day from Whitsun to Lammas the 25 miles of roadless country to the castle. He would be thankful when this was later replaced by a £3 annual rent!

In or about 1260 Gilbert of Callaly thought it sensible to build a new home, one offering better defence against robbers and raiders than his existing house. The site he selected was on top of Castle Hill, NU060097, about half a mile to the east of the present 'castle'. He was not the first to see the advantages of this place: the Votadini people had constructed a hill camp there and had occupied it throughout the Roman era. The Roman cross-country road from High Rochester (Bremenium) to Learchild (Alauna) passed the foot of Castle Hill so the Exploratores who patrolled the road must have been friendly with these Ancient Britons and able to rely upon their neutrality, if not their cooperation.

The conical top of Castle Hill is covered with trees and ferns, yet the essential components of the camp may still be traced. Gilbert used only the eastern half of the site, separating it from the western half by cutting a forty foot wide trench through the solid rock. This not only strengthened his position, it provided him with building material. It is not clear whether his fortification was completed before the estate was sold in c1265 or whether the buyer completed the work, and, as all that remains is a couple of blocks of masonry and some foundations, we have little idea of its appearance. It is, however, classed as a tower.

The new owner was Robert fitz Roger, lord of Warkworth and holder of many estates, including Rothbury Forest and Clavering in Essex. He bought Callaly for his son Alan and did whatever was necessary to complete the Castle Hill tower for him. Alan, like the rest of the family assumed the surname Clavering in the 1300s, and lived an uneventful life on top of his hill. At least one of his descendants must have done something notable, however, as the holder of the estate in 1415 was a knight, Sir John Clavering. By that time a new tower had been built in the valley below Castle Hill, known then as Shepherds Shaw, and the hill-top tower was being called 'Kaloule vet', or Old Callaly, to distinguish it from the new. It is believed that from the beginning of the fifteenth century the family lived in the new tower but maintained the old for emergencies, and that this was so throughout the century.

An amusing story is told about the siting of the new tower. The head of the family decided to build a new home but for safety sake it still had to be high on Castle Hill. His wife preferred a more accessible site on the valley floor, but she pleaded in vain and construction started on the hill. Lady Clavering resorted to trickery: every night after the builders had left the site, she had her steward walk over to where they had been working and pull down what they had done that day. Her husband could not understand what was going on and let it be known that he proposed spending the next moonlit night on the site in the hope of finding the answer. The lady was a match for him: she dressed the steward in the skin of a wild bear and while her husband watched in terror the 'bear' danced round the site, pulling down stones while singing

> "Callaly castle built on the height
> Up in the day and down in the night.
> If ye build it on Shepherd's Shaw
> There it will stay and never fa'"

The new tower was built on the valley floor.

It still exists, if somewhat modified and no longer alone. In 1415 it was a rectangular building with seven foot thick walls, a vaulted ground floor chamber and stone spiral stairs to the living quarters. This was home to the main family while non-inheriting children lived at Duddo.

The Claverings were amongst the first families in Northumberland to recognise in the Union of the Crowns a harbinger of lasting peace, and Sir John commissioned Robert Trollope in 1619 to build a great hall next to the tower. This was the first of many extensions; other main buildings were added in 1707, 1749, 1750, 1765 and 1840 to achieve the grand complex seen today. The tower also got considerable attention during this period. In 1749 the west wall cracked and had to be replaced: a new wall was built inside the old before this was knocked down. This slight narrowing of the tower accounts for the asymmetry of the pitched roof which may be noticed when viewed from the garden. At about this time, also, the tower was given a new face, with dummy windows, so that it might fit better into the frontage of the whole mansion. The new west wall only lasted a hundred years before it too cracked and had to be replaced. At other times the vault was removed, the stone stairs were replaced by wooden ones and the overall height was reduced.

The seventeenth and eighteenth centuries were not as trouble-free for the family as the two previous centuries appear to have been. During the Civil

War Sir John Clavering and his three sons aided King Charles I and Sir John was captured by the Parliamentarians in 1644. He died in prison three years later. Callaly was confiscated but was returned in 1653 upon payment of a large fine. Then in 1715 two brothers, William and John Clavering, joined the Jacobite rebellion and were taken prisoner at Preston. They escaped the executioner only because their kinswoman, Lady Couper (née Mary Clavering) pleaded for them at their trial. The fact that Lord Couper was High Steward of England at the time may not have been an encumbrance.

The Claverings did not lose their estates on that occasion, but in 1876 they ran out of heirs to fill them. This let in the third family to own Callaly, the Brownes.

Major Alexander Henry Browne was a member of an old Vale of Whittingham family who were doing well as Alnmouth shippers, lawyers and bankers. Several of them served in the army, while others occupied the post of High Sheriff of Northumberland. Alexander's father had been the county's first Chief Constable from 1857 to 1869. They were well known in the district, having owned Shawdon from 1705 to 1723 and Bolton from 1690 to 1762, but Alexander lived at Doxford Hall, three miles inland from Embleton, until he moved to Callaly.

He made significant changes to his new home in 1893, and died in 1895. His son, another Major Alexander Browne, was High Sheriff in 1906. He handed Callaly over to his son, Major Alexander Simon Cadogen Browne, in 1925. He had to contend with ever rising maintenance costs, and in 1986, when over 90 years old, he found it necessary to sell his art treasures and have the mansion divided into fourteen apartments. He died the following year.

Whittingham

L81   P488   NU070118   12 km, 7½ miles, south-west of Alnwick

From Bolton up-stream to Alnham, where the River Aln emerges from the Cheviot massif as an adolescent stream, the valley is called Whittingham Vale. Whittingham village is the heart of this beautiful nine mile stretch, its natural centre for social, commercial and traffic intercourse since the Stone Age. Here generations of farmers met for their pints and to make their bargains; here generations of travellers between Cornhill or Scotland and the south stopped for nourishment and a night's lodging. It was important in Anglian days when King Ceolwulf gave it, with Eglingham and Warkworth, to Lindisfarne Priory in 737.

It was important enough for King Osbert to reclaim it during his reign between 850 and 855, and for succeeding kings and earls to retain it until Robert Mowbray gave it to Tynemouth Priory in c1090.

Tynemouth took the tithes and granted the land piecemeal to several farmers. A lord of the manor did not emerge until the fifteenth century, but the inhabitants managed very well without one, and during the thirteenth century they clubbed together to construct a pele for their mutual protection. This was a pele conforming to the original meaning of the word – not a tower but a timber and earth encampment surrounded by a pallisade. Legend has it that King Edward I spent a night in it on his way to Scotland in 1292. Needless to say, no trace of it remains today.

William Heron of Ford was the first man of wealth to buy land in Whittingham. He built a proper stone tower for his estate workers before 1415 and the derivative of this still stands in the centre of the village, close to the south bank of the Aln.

Another William Heron sold his Whittingham property in 1532 to Robert Collingwood. By this time there was a second tower in the village, a vicar's lodging sited a little to the west of the church on the north bank of the Aln. According to a contemporary document, this tower offered "standard accommodation for a gentleman of modest means", having a vaulted ground floor for "dead stock" such as corn and sides of salted meat, a first floor daytime living room and sleeping quarters on the second floor. Note that this document specifically stated that the ground floor vault, although "typical", was unsuitable for live animals which in times of emergency were driven to a safe place further afield.

The Collingwood family were inveterate land-grabbers and soon had assembled a large estate centred on Eslington, a couple of miles upstream from Whittingham, where they made their home. Whittingham's village tower was repaired and a more weatherproof twin pitched roof was put on to replace its flat roof.

The 1715 holder was the Hon. George Collingwood until he joined the Jacobite rebellion, was executed after Preston and had his land sequestrated. The Liddell family took over; they also lived at Eslington and had little interest in Whittingham, allowing the village tower to waste.

A century passed and Sir Thomas Liddell was elevated to the peerage as Lord Ravensworth. His wife had a lively social conscience and found a use for the tower. She dismantled all decaying parts in 1845 and rebuilt it as a charitable alms house which could accommodate four elderly couples. Not the lap of luxury, but with a £10 annual pension and free coal, it allowed a few lucky people who had given years of service to the estate to end their days in peace.

At roughly the same time the Rev. R.W. Goodenough, vicar of Whittingham from 1835 to 1880, pulled down his tower and built a more comfortable vicarage close to its site. So there remains only one tower to see in the village today. It is empty again and shows sign of weather erosion, but it is manifestly as Lady Ravensworth had made it.

Whittingham, of course, is more famous for its fair than for its tower. This annual event was not authorised by any Royal charter, it just started on

24 August 1656 in response to popular demand. Originally a cattle market, it soon developed into a lively and noisy social happening where not only farm stock and stores but also household and personal goods were bought and sold. Its heyday came during the eighteenth and early nineteenth centuries, then it gradually settled down until now it is a typical agricultural show.

Its fame is partly attributable to the publicity it got from the ballad 'Are you going to Whittingham Fair' which Northumbrians like to think is their own although other parts of the country use it with their local fair's name substituted. The old fair-opening custom also contributed to its popularity. A cavalcade of tenants would gallop round the village shouting invitations to all, and then, when throats were dry, they would stop at the Castle Inn for a drink on the lord of the manor.

The Castle Inn was a coach stop in those days, before Whittingham was by-passed. The 'Wellington' coach changed horses there on its journey in both directions between Newcastle and Edinburgh. The pub is not quite so busy now, and another famous pub, the 'Hole in the Wall' is now a private cottage. Mine host at one time was Tom Dickinson, head gamekeeper at Eslington Hall and possessor of the nickname 'Dang it', his favourite expletive. He kept a bar which must have been one of the smallest in the world – three customers at a time was a crowd and beer had to be drunk in harmony to avoid a clash of elbows. But then, if the following rhyme be true, nobody drank beer:

"If ever you go to Whittingham Fair
Be sure to call at the Hole in the Wall,
For there you will get whisky for nowt
And brandy for nothing at all".

Eslington

L81   P488   NU042120   14¹/₂ km, 8¹/₄ miles, south-west of Alnwick

The building of a tower was the first intimation that Eslington existed. Robert de Eslington was licensed to crenellate in 1335 by King Edward II, and he chose a site a few yards north of the present hall.

Thomas of Hazlerigg held the tower in 1415, and by 1532 it had been leased to Robert Collingwood. He bought it in 1540 and made it his headquarters of the large Whittingham estate. After the Collingwoods were stripped of life and property after the 1715 Jacobite revolt, it became the home of the Liddell family, later to be ennobled as the Lords Ravensworth. Before then the tower had been gutted and Eslington Hall had taken its place.

The tower had a rough ride in the sixteenth century. In 1587 the Duke of Buccleugh vent his fury on it for the execution of Mary Queen of Scots; he took many prisoners and killed at least eighteen men. Further raids, not quite so disastrous, followed in 1588 and 1589. The Collingwoods patched up the tower after these attacks.

Little Ryle

L81   P488   NU020111   16½ km, 10¼ miles, south-west of Alnwick

Great Ryle

L81   P488   NU018127   16½ km, 10¼ miles, south-west of Alnwick

Two farms about a mile apart, both components in the Collingwood empire of Whittingham in the sixteenth century.

They do not share their earlier history. Little Ryle was held by Richard of Ryle in 1295, then from 1350 by a man who kicked the fashion for surnames and preferred to be called 'Henry son of John son of Henry'. In 1429 the holder was William Swan. Great Ryle was part of the Ditchburn serjeanty, granted in mid-twelfth century by King Henry II to one of his foresters. The large Collingwood family took over in or about 1532. Alexander Collingwood held Little Ryle and Thomas Collingwood lived in Great Ryle.

Both occupiers built defences. Thomas plumped for a tower which he lost for a short time in 1549 when it was taken over for mercenaries. In 1587 it was attacked during a daytime raid by Armstrong of Liddesdale. There is no trace of it now and its site is unknown.

Alexander chose to build a strong house at Little Ryle shortly after 1541. This is still habitable, the home of a shepherd. It has been extended on the west side, but the original building is quite large anyway, about 60 by 24 feet. The whole of the ground floor is a beautifully preserved vault with very thick walls. There was a stair turret at one time.

Prendwick

L81   P488   NU002122   18 km, 11 miles, south-west of Alnwick

A large estate which, with Alnham, formed an enclave of Alnwick barony when this was held by the Vescys, and both areas were leased to farmers by 'tenure of socage'. This means that their rent consisted of service rendered by the soc, or plough – not necessarily the ploughing of the lord's demesne but rather the earning of enough money by ploughing to pay a fee. Thus William de Walays held one carucate (about 100 acres) for 10 pence, Walter de Prendwye held a similar area but paid 33 pence while both William Cocus and Gilbert de Glentedon held 30 acres each and had to use their money to buy the baron a pound of pepper.

In 1297 the last Baron Vescy died and Bishop Anthony Bek was granted the barony. He sold it in 1309 to Lord Henry Percy, but Prendwick was excluded from the sale and instead it became Crown property. King Edward III granted it to William de Emeldon for twelve years, then he gave it to John Coupland on a free lease. This reward for exemplary military service was made just two years before the same king awarded John an annuity of £500 for capturing David Bruce during the Battle of Neville's Cross.

Prendwick returned to the crown when John died in 1363 and numerous local people held short term leases until Robert Collingwood bought it in 1535. He and George Aldye, a relative of Collingwood's wife, were joint occupiers and the latter built a small tower. This building was mentioned in surveys of 1541 and 1584, but appears to have suffered terminal damage in a raid in 1587 by 500 Liddesdale men. Even its precise site is unknown now.

The Collingwood/Aldye, or Alder, connection with Prendwick continued at least to the eighteenth century, by which time the farm had become the venue for an important annual lamb sale which attracted farmers from a wide area. Local inhabitants were also attracted to Prendwick when the harvest had been collected for a celebrationary 'Kirn Supper', a social event rather like a vigorous barn dance or Northumbrian ceilidh with plenty of food and drink, dancing and dating. David Dippie Dixon's Whittingham Vale contains a most enjoyable description of this annual highlight.

Alnham

L81   P487   NT995108   19½ km, 12 miles, south-west of Alnwick

Alnham stands at the gateway between the Cheviots and Whittingham Vale, between wasteland and rich pasture, and has been guarded by British forts and Roman camps against raiders. Several tracks radiate from it, including the Salters' Road into Scotland, much used by legitimate traders and smugglers alike, and another leading to the Breamish valley.

The Barons of Alnwick have been the sole owners of Alnham since at least 1250, and neither the Vescys nor the Percys ever leased the estate as an entirety; it was always divided up into farms, and a parcel held by the Delavals until 1304, then by the Selbys of Biddlestone.

During William de Vescy's tenure two inhabitants, Adam Servaunt and William Wodester attacked a neighbour, Richard Berii, with an axe and mortally wounded him. Both fled, thus proving their guilt, and both were declared outlaws as the baron's bailiff could not find them. Adam had his chattels worth 48 pence confiscated; William owned nothing worth confiscating.

The Percys provided the villagers with a tower in mid-fourteenth century. The so-called Earl's Tower was built on a small hill above the church and it got a bad press when it capitulated to King Henry IV in 1405. Had it not done so it would have been destroyed, for the king was determined to punish Earl Henry Percy any way he could for joining Archbishop Scrope's rebellion.

By 1541 the tower was in poor repair, thanks in part to its age and to a Scottish raid in 1532 when "all the corne hay and household stuf and also a woman" were destroyed, but also to misuse, as reported later:

"The Lord hath there a faire stronge tower of ancient time built and strongly vaulted over and the gates and doors be all of great strength with iron bars and a good demesne adjoining. The house is now ruinous and in some decay by reason the farmer used to carry his sheep up the stairs and to lay them in the chambers which rotted the vaults and will in short time be the utter decay of the house if other repairs be not had."

A few years after building the Earl's tower, the Percys also built a small tower for the parson. This got its first mention in 1416 and another in 1541, but it was dilapidated by 1663 and uninhabited in 1758 when Alnham's vicar lived at Ilderton.

The foundations of the Earl's tower could be seen at the end of the nineteenth century, the last traces of a square tower and other buildings, "probably the outer offices, the dwellings of the servants and the wall of the barmekyn", but only amorphous bumps in the grass remain today. The vicar's tower fared much better. A roofless ruin in 1821, it was repaired and extended in about 1830 and became the imposing residence which still exists. As seen from the adjoining churchyard, the square tower stands to the left and proud of the later wing; the original vaulted ground floor chamber with six foot thick walls still features in the former but the windows and battlements are nineteenth century vintage. The Church sold the building in the 1930s and it became a Youth Hostel for a time, but it is a private three reception rooms, five bedrooms residence now. When put on the market in 1991 the asking price was £285,000.

Area 4
Coquetdale

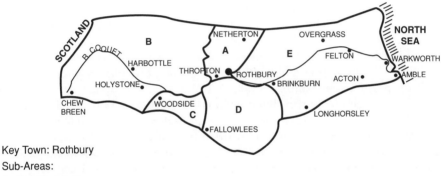

Key Town: Rothbury

Sub-Areas:

A The Wreigh Burn
B Upper Coquetdale
C The Grasslees Burn
D Rothbury Forest
E Lower Coquetdale

The Coquet, the Queen of Rivers, rises within English yards of the Border at Chew Green and, about forty miles later, splashes into the North Sea at Amble, having cut Northumberland into two. It flows through every type of country imaginable, from some of the wildest and loneliest in Britain to the agriculturally rich and well populated coast, via mountain glens, sylvan valleys and lush meadows. There is practically no industry along its banks and it washes only three communities large enough to warrant the tag 'small town'.

Key Town
Rothbury

L81   P500   NU0570

The royal house of Northumberland, Ida's descendants, held Rothbury manor and Rothbury Forest until the county earls took over in 954. They kept this great area of the chase until Robert de Mowbray upset King William Rufus in 1095 and suffered total sequestration. As Crown lands, they were administered by the king's representatives, the county sheriffs, for over a hundred years, until King John granted them to Robert fitz Roger, Baron of Warkworth, in 1205.

Robert probably hunted in Rothbury Forest quite a lot for he built some sort of shooting lodge in Rothbury. It was either a motte and bailey or an early type of tower, and it was situated on Haa Hill, a few yards south-west of the church.

The baron's descendants took the surname Clavering in the 1300s. John Clavering was the last of the mainline family, and he died in 1332, intestate and burdened with debt to the Crown. As settlement, King Edward III seized both the Rothbury and the Warkworth property and granted them to the second Lord Henry Percy of Alnwick. Apart from a few estates which have been sold, and excepting odd periods of forfeiture, the grant has remained in the Percy portfolio ever since.

The thirteenth century building was up-graded or rebuilt a few years before 1461 by the third Earl of Northumberland, another Henry Percy. Called Rothbury Hall, it was a fortified manor-house and while of only medium strength it did have massive walls and a vaulted basement which records tell us were used as the town's gaol. Sir Robert Ogle, warden of the East March, occupied the Hall for a time after the Earl lost his life and property in 1461 while fighting for the Lancastrians in the Battle of Towton.

The Hall and the church were probably the only substantial stone buildings in the town during the pre-Union era. The proletariat lived in very humble dwellings, decidedly uncomfortable and unhygenic but easily reconstructed should they be knocked down. They were manifestations of abject poverty, and as such it was hoped raiders would not be tempted to plunder them. The ploy was their major defence and it seemed to work, for Rothbury was seldom a prime target, although it did become almost a staging post for Scottish and Redesdale rievers heading down the Coquet valley to more fruitful acres.

The Union of 1603 brought only temporary peace to Rothbury, for the hills around the town became the principal arena for moss troopers. At first these outlaws were escapees from King James's massive Border clean-up operations, but during and after the Civil War their numbers were enhanced by army deserters and demobilized soldiers. They formed gangs which lived a footloose, nomadic existence in these remote areas, from which they would swoop down on defenceless people and steel their horses and cattle. During this troubled time Rothbury Hall was occupied by William Thirlwall, but he appears to have been incapable of alleviating the town's misery.

Little maintenance work was done on the Hall during the seventeenth and eighteenth centuries, but builders were at work in the town constructing better accommodation for the inhabitants – and even a few inns. The Earl of Derwentwater spent a night in one, the Three Half Moons, during October 1715 after he had made contact with Coquetdale's Jacobite supporters on Plainfield Moor, a few miles up the dale.

By the beginning of the nineteenth century the Hall was deserted and in ruins. What remained of it was cleared in 1869 when the site was required as an extension to the churchyard.

Area 4, Sub-Area A   The Wreigh Burn

Thropton

L81   P500   NU029022   3 km, 2 miles, west of Rothbury

This "considerable village" stands at the confluence of the River Coquet and one of its principal tributaries, the Wreigh (formerly Rithe) Burn. 'Tatie Toon', its satirical nickname in former days when its inhabitants won local fame as growers of potatoes, was a member of the Rothbury manor and had the same descent as Rothbury until about 1410 when at least part of it was held by William Grene, a well known character of Rothbury Forest. William built a tower before 1415.

At this time John de Cartington, who lived a mile and a half north of Thropton, was busily engaged in improving his social and financial status. Before he died in 1494 he had acquired Grene's entire Thropton holding, including the tower, and was able to bequeath it to his daughter, Anne, who was married to Edward Radcliffe.

The Radcliffes garrisoned Thropton tower as their contribution to the defence of the Border. Sir Cuthbert Radcliffe held from sixteen to twenty men there in 1541. The village and its field systems were leased to small farmers, and gradually, over the sixteenth and seventeenth centuries, these people bought their holdings so that by 1715 the entire area belonged to freeholders and there was nothing for the Crown to grab when the Radcliffes forfeited all their property. One of these freeholders built a bastle at the west end of the village; this, converted into a fashionable dwelling but still showing signs of its origin, remains with us.

The tower was extended during the eighteenth century and became Thropton Old Hall. There is uncertainty about how this was done as the whole lot was demolished in 1811 to make way for a Roman Catholic church.

Area 4A   Cartington

Snitter

L81   P500   NU025034   4 km, 2¹/₂ miles west of Rothbury

Although it contains several modern residences, Snitter is really very old and was included in the Pipe Roll of 1177. Its descent was that of Rothbury until the Radcliffe – Widdrington wedding in 1601, after which the principal owners were the Widdringtons of Cartington. The second Lord Armstrong, of Cragside and Bamburgh, bought Snitter in 1903.

The old schoolhouse at the north end of the hamlet is thought to have evolved in part from a bastle built by Roger Widdrington in the early part of the seventeenth century.

Cartington

L81   P500   NU041045   3 km, 2 miles, north-west of Rothbury

A tree trunk hollowed to form a coffin was discovered here in 1913 and has since been carbon dated. The tree was growing over 4000 years ago, clearly indicating that Neolithic Man hunted this neighbourhood.

Cartington was associated with hunting in medieval times as well. From early in the Norman era part of the manor was walled to contain animals of the chase, and this park was included with adjoining farmland in the grant made by King Henry II in 1154 to his forester, the man who had the responsibility of enforcing the Draconian hunting laws of Rothbury Forest. He was Ralph fitz Main, and his reward was the Ditchburn serjeanty, a loose collection of estates in Northumberland which included, as well as Cartington, Ditchburn near Eglingham, Great Ryle near Whittingham and Togston near Amble. His job was virtually hereditary, and Cartington was his descendants until 1320, although for most of that time it was leased to the Barons of Embleton.

This lease is interesting. It was an agreement between Roger fitz Roger (ie, Ralph's son) and John Vicecomes (later Viscount), and was tenacious enough to survive the switch from Rameta, the daughter of a later John Viscount, to Simon de Montford and all the noblemen who followed him to the Embleton barony. It also permitted the leasee to sublet.

One such tenant was William Frebern who held part of Cartington for a rent of five silver shillings. His family held it from 1168 to 1342. Another tenant, who held another part of Cartington from about 1250, was John de Cartington.

In 1320 the Lords of Ditchburn sold the whole of Cartington to Sir Henry Beaumont, brother of Lewis Beaumont, Bishop of Durham. He confirmed the old lease and agreed to their subletting to the Freberns and the Cartingtons. These two became rivals and very unfriendly neighbours, but they were unevenly matched. While the Freberns went down hill, the Cartingtons gained in stature, and by the middle of the fourteenth century they seem to have ousted the others altogether.

The Beaumonts sold out to the Earl of Northumberland in 1369. The lease survived this change, but when John of Gaunt died in 1399 and his son, Henry Bolingbroke, became King Henry IV, the Crown revoked the agreement. Earl Percy did not have the estate on his hands for long. In 1400 John Cartington bought the whole of Cartington manor from him. Their own masters at last, the family built a tower before 1415.

John was ambitious and clever. He acquired other estates, such as Thropton, and in 1428, and again in 1433, he was a Member of Parliament. His small tower was soon too small and insignificant: by 1441 it had become the south-west turret of a spacious hall house. He had intended this to be unfortified, apart from the original tower, but he changed his mind when he realised how bad were the hostilities across the Border. He applied for, and obtained, a licence to crenellate with the result that his completed home was described in the 1541 survey as "a good fortress of two towers and other strong houses"

John's son, also John, inherited about 1450 and continued the Cartington's social climb. In 1484 he married Joan Claxton who, on the death that year of her father, Sir Robert Claxton, had become the owner of Dilston, near Corbridge. This possession she did not pass on to her husband, so when John died in 1494 their daughter Anne inherited Cartington only.

Anne was the last of the family to bear the Cartington name. She married Sir Edward Radcliffe, a younger son of Thomas Radcliffe of Derwentwater in Cumberland. Their son, Cuthbert Radcliffe, inherited Cartington when his mother died, and Dilston when his grandmother Joan died in 1521. His eldest son eventually inherited Dilston, while a younger Radcliffe got Cartington.

The Coquetdale property descended through Sir Francis Radcliffe of the next generation to Mary Radcliffe who, in 1601 married Roger Widdrington, son of Edward Widdrington of Great Swinburn.

The century before this event had been traumatic. In 1512 Cartington manor had been 'wasted' by Scottish intruders, but this was nothing compared to the upheaval caused by the invasion of Margaret, the dowager Queen of Scotland, her large retinue of ladies-in-waiting and her infant daughter, born just a few days earlier in Harbottle castle. The turmoil lasted four days, then the entourage collected the nappies and baby powder and moved on to Brinkburn Priory.

There were further attacks by Scottish raiders in 1516, and in 1523 the place was inundated with Lord Dacre's troops who used it as a transit camp on their way to Scotland to try to bring some order to the post-Flodden chaos.

In 1542 Cartington became a barracks for troops equipped to rush to any part of the Middle March suffering the attentions of the Scots and their French allies.

The Radcliffe-Widdrington wedding in 1601 was an important step in the former's social climb, and to underline this the bride's father, Sir Francis Radcliffe, settled Cartington on his new son-in-law. Roger Widdrington instituted many alterations to his Hall, including the insertion of several windows with attractive Tudor hoods. In 1627 part of the manor, probably the old walled park, was leased to Thomas Ogle for twenty-one years. Mary died in 1632 and, with rather undue haste, Roger remarried, this time to Rosamond Revely, a widow from Newton Underwood. The couple lived in Cartington until 1635, when they moved to the new Harbottle 'Castle', where Roger died in 1641. His son, Sir Edward, had been assigned Cartington when his parents had moved.

The new owner was both an ardent Roman Catholic and a devoted Royalist, a dangerous mixture during the Civil War. He was on the losing side in the Battle of Marston Moor in 1644 and his property was forfeited. A local detachment of Royalists somehow managed to acquire Cartington Hall, however, and its commander, Sir Richard Tempest, made it his headquarters and arms store until Major Sanderson and a party of Parliamentarians cleared him out in 1648.

When the Monarchy returned in 1660 Cartington was handed back to Sir Edward Widdrington. The Hall was an utter wreck. He managed to restore about half of it to a habitable standard, but it never regained its former glory. On his death in 1671 his son, another Edward, inherited but he died in 1679 so the manor passed to his sister Mary, married to Sir Edward Charlton of Hesleyside, North Tynedale. They had little use for it, nor had their son-in-law, Jack Talbot, who inherited when Mary died in 1702. After him came the Alcock family in 1762, then the Beck family, and none of them did anything to stop the Hall becoming a complete ruin.

The sorry sight touched the heart of a near neighbour, Sir W.G. (later Lord) Armstrong of Cragside. He bought the property in 1883 and employed Mr C.G. Hodges to stabilize the masonry, clear out the courtyard and reveal the original plan of what he regarded as a still beautiful and interesting relic of the past, well worth preserving.

No doubt many people since have had similar thoughts, but no one has done anything about it. The grass and nettles in the courtyard have grown again, the passages through the ruin are full of rubble and the weather and cows are playing havoc with the stonework.

The ruin and the way to it are on farm land, but permission to enter can usually be obtained if a proper request is made at Cartington Farm. Visitors will see the impressive skeleton of a complex not unlike a small quadrilateral castle.

The walls of buildings on the north side stand quite high, and enough of the hall
and south-west turret (the original pre-1415 tower) remain to show some tunnel
vaulting. Much has collapsed yet there is still evidence of workmanship and
ornamentation of a standard not common in Northumberland.   [**Plate 5**]

Low Trewhitt

L81   P500   NU003047   6¼ km, 4 miles, north-west of Rothbury

King Henry I scraped together a number of estates in Cumberland,
Westmorland, Yorkshire and Northumberland and granted them as a barony
to Forne, the first Lord of Greystoke, near Penrith. Forne's son, Ivo, had a
daughter Alice who married Edgar, son of Gospatric, Earl of Dunbar, and as a
wedding present the couple was given several Coquetdale parcels of the
barony, including High and Low Trewhitt. There have been two Trewhitts
since the earliest records; 'High' appears always to have been just a farm, but
'Low' was a village as well as a farm and possessed a chapel.

Alice and Edgar had little use for Low Trewhitt but they dutifully passed
it on to their descendants, who, bit by bit, gave large tracts of land to
Brinkburn Priory. In 1280 the overlordship of most of what remained was
transferred to the Hepple barony. Farmer Hugh Trewhitt, who had bought his
farmstead, held out a while and a later Hugh built a tower at Low Trewhitt,
but eventually he was bought out by Robert Ogle, the Baron of Hepple, who,
in the fifteenth century leased all of non-monastic Trewhitt to Thomas Gallon.
His family maintained the tower, which in 1541 was reported to be "in
measurable good repar'c'on".

When Brinkburn Priory was dissolved the Gallons expanded their estate
and the whole of Trewhitt became theirs. Thomas Gallon was the residential
owner in 1568, but later members of the family got into some matrimonial
trouble involving the Widdrington, Orde and Clavering families, and after a
lengthy legal battle in 1636 Sir John Clavering was able to buy the property.
George Potts rented it, then bought it when Sir John Clavering suffered
sequestration after the Civil War in 1644.

Mary, the last of the Potts, sold Low Trewhitt to John Brown of
Cumberland in 1742. Twenty years later Hugh Boag of County Durham
bought it, and in 1871 Sir William Armstrong became the owner.

With his usual generosity, Sir William rebuilt the farmhouse at Low
Trewhitt and made many improvements to the farm, but he could do nothing
to the tower or the village as they were no longer there. Some bumps in the
field adjoining the farmhouse are thought to be caused by old foundations, but
nothing certain has been found. A small, allegedly fourteenth century window
has been inserted in an outbuilding which may have been part of the old
farmhouse, and David Dippie Dixon suggested it had been put there to

preserve a little bit of the tower. This may be true, but the present owner of the farm believes it to be a church window, not one from a tower, and certainly appearances support this view.

Burradon

L81   P499   NT981061   8½ km, 5 miles, north-west of Rothbury

As one of 'The Ten Towns of Coquetdale', Burradon was in the Alnwick barony but was leased from c1160 to the Umfravilles, Lords of the Redesdale liberty, so that they could commandeer its male inhabitants for service in Harbottle Castle. In 1166 the village was expected to supply six men for this duty.

From that time to the end of the fifteenth century the holding family was one which used Burradon as its surname. It is not known when they actually became owners, but throughout their long occupation, all members clearly had the right to bequeath the place and to pass on a good title. The most famous of them was Sir Gilbert Burradon who married Elizabeth, daughter of Robert de Umfraville when he was Earl of Angus.

The last male Burradon had two daughters to share his property when he died in 1480. One of these married Gerard Fenwick, a younger son of John Fenwick, the first of that family to own Wallington. The other took Percival Lisle as her second husband in c1510, and as they had no interest in the property – except as a source of money – they leased their half of Burradon to the Fenwicks.

A large tower at Burradon was reported as being in extreme decay in 1541. Towers did not deteriorate very quickly, even when neglected, so this one must have been built at least a hundred years earlier, by one of the Burradon family.

It is not known why or when the place was disposed of, but by 1604 it was divided between thirteen freeholders. A hundred and fifty years later the scene had changed again: the thirteen had reduced to three wealthy landowners who had each bought a third. They were Thomas Clennell of Harbottle, John Collingwood of West Lilburn and John Rutherford, a descendant of one of the earlier freeholders. This John married Anne, daughter of Thomas Forster, in 1785, and, helped by her family's fortune, they eventually came to own practically the whole estate. Round about 1825 the old house was pulled down and replaced by the mansion which is still with us. It and new farm buildings covered the tower's site so nothing of the stronghold is visible.

Netherton

L81   P499   NT988076   9 km, 5½ miles, north-west of Rothbury

Another of 'The Ten Towns of Coquetdale' leased to Robert de Umfraville, who promptly granted part of it to an old friend, Gilbert Bataille, whose grandfather had crossed the Channel with 'Robert with the Beard' in 1066. This part was

'North Side'; the other part, 'South Side' was not mentioned until 1300. Between the two halves was Netherton village, the largest in Alwinton parish.

Sometime before 1269 heiress Joan Bataille married Roger Ingoe and North Side got a new owner. It was wasted by the Scots in 1439, but the Ingoes held on until 1450. The Lords of Redesdale then leased the half township to locals until 1621 when the Widdringtons of Cartington bought it. By 1717 it had become a possession of the Selbys of nearby Biddlestone.

Netherton South Side was held by John son of Hugh when it was first heard of. His family never got round to assuming a surname, but it did not last very long as Henry, its last male, died of the Black Death in 1349 at the tender age of four years. His legal guardian had been Aunt Beatrice; she assigned the property to the parson at Ford, who dutifully passed it on to his patron, Sir William Heron. Various members of the Heron family held it until the early part of the sixteenth century, then a hundred year haze fell over its history to reveal in 1604 Robert Collingwood as the owner, with eleven tenants. This lasted to 1715.

Netherton's human interest was at its most intense in the late eighteenth and nineteenth centuries, when the village made a name for itself in the sporting world – if cockfighting and similar abhorrences can be classed as sport. There were two inns in the village, 'The Fighting Cock', later called 'The Phoenix', and 'The Star', and both seem to have done excellent business for it was said that one could get drunk in Netherton quicker than anywhere else in Coquetdale. One day a local carrier ate rather excessively of goose in Alnwick. He tried to "droon her" before he left Alnwick and he tried again at Bridge of Aln and Whittingham on his way home, but he "never gat her drooned till he gat to Netherton".

One of the houses in the village, still standing at this intemperate time although built perhaps two hundred years earlier, was thought to be a bastle. There is no sign of it now and nothing about it has been found in the records, so its bastle status can only be regarded as dubious.

Biddlestone

L81   P499   NT955083   12 km, 7½ miles. north-west of Rothbury

The village of Biddlestone was said to have been smaller than Netherton, yet as another of the 'Ten Towns of Coquetdale' it had to find fourteen men for Harbottle Castle duty whereas Netherton's commitment was only five. Never mind, its history is more complex.

This is because Robert de Biddlestone, the grandson of the village headman to whom the Umfravilles granted the township, bequeathed half his property to each of his two daughters in 1240. The two girls, Eva and Margary, commenced two different descents which did not connect until 1576.

Margary's share moved in a reasonably straight line. She married Henry Delaval and bore two sons, Eustace and Hugh. Eustace inherited the Biddlestone property and eventually passed it on to his son Robert, who died childless. Robert's cousin took over and his descendants kept hold of it.

Eva married Ralph de Feritate and her share of the property passed quite quickly through her son to her granddaughter Joan. She nearly caused the descents to unite, for she married Eustace Delaval, the man who held the other half, but he did not get her half and it passed to their daughter Margary. She married Andrew de Smytheton and when in 1311 they realised they could not have children they gave their share of the property as a wedding present to Katherine, the daughter of Eustace's brother Hugh. Katherine's bridegroom was Walter Selby and their descendants held the gift for some 600 years except for two hiccups – in 1317 when Walter had his property confiscated because of his involvement with the Mitford Gang, and in 1351 when Walter's youngest son sold it to the Delavals, who kept it a few years.

The two parts of Biddlestone finally came together when Thomas Selby bought Robert Delaval's part in 1576. The combined estate was Selby property from that date until Walter Arthur Selby, an unmarried Royal Navy lieutenant, sold it in 1914.

Walter Selby, the Mitford Gang member, who was once described as "both a robber and a warrior, alternately plundering and defending his country", met a violent death in 1346 at the hands of Scottish King David Bruce. His progeny were cast in the same mould but most of their energy was expended on policing the Border. Percival Selby, for example, attended a muster in 1538 with twenty Biddlestone men.

A tower was built at Biddlestone in the fourteenth century, and, despite other interests, the Selby family maintained it well. Also many of them were keen farmers. John bought Cote Walls in c1510 to extend this activity, and further acreage came their way at Linshields and Shillmore in 1686, Robert Collingwood's land at Ingram a year later and Scrainwood in 1829.

The first Biddlestone Hall was built soon after the Union of the Crowns. It is a common belief that this mansion, which incorporated the fortified tower as a wing, was the model upon which Sir Walter Scott based his Osbaldeston Hall featured in 'Rob Roy'. It was certainly possible for Scott to have seen Biddlestone Hall during his wanderings around the area during his youth, but by the time his book was published – 1818 – the building had been razed and a second Biddlestone Hall was being built.

The old tower was again retained and used as a wing of this new building, only this time only the ground floor vault was used, the upper floor being a Roman Catholic chapel. This unusual combination of the godly and ungodly still exists, but on its own, the mansion having been demolished in 1952. The parts of the building which formerly touched the mansion have been sealed with cement and a boiler room and chimney have been added. Encroaching vegetation, which a short time ago was life threatening, was cut back in 1996, and much needed remedial work has been carried out. Hopefully the Historic Chapels Trust will take great care of it in the future.

Apart from this curio, a nineteenth century chapel riding on the back of a fourteenth century tower vault, there are other interests at Biddlestone. There is an ice house, for example, still complete if rather dilapidated, and a little to its north is a pretty little well which bears the date 1806. Alongside the old drive to the Hall lie two large dressed stones. The Ordnance Survey maps call them the 'Biddle stones', inferring that they are the reason for the place's name, but actually they are the socket stone and a section of the pedestal of some wayside cross which have just been dumped here.

Cote Walls

L81   P499   NT973075   10 km, 6¼ miles, north-west of Rothbury

A farm of little significance which borders the Biddlestone estate. Being in Alwinton parish, it may be more than a coincidence that the parson of Alwinton church from 1316 to 1340 was Richard de Cotes, and that he was instrumental in getting the tithes of Cote Walls consigned to the nuns of Holystone.

In 1410 'Cotefeld, alias Cotewallys' – probably old forms of Cote Walls – was given by an obscure descendant of Ralph and Eva de Feritate, one time holders of half of Biddlestone, to Brinkburn Priory. The canons built a tower. They cannot have held the place for long, however, as John Selby bought it in 1500 and the seller was someone called William Chesman, not the Prior. The tower was mentioned in the deeds, and again in the 1541 survey, when it belonged to Percival Selby and was in reasonably good repair.

The Selbys wanted Cote Walls as an extension to their Biddlestone farm, but they seem also to have used the tower occasionally to house junior offspring. Thus George Selby, quite low in the pecking order, was resident there in 1628. William Selby in 1638 got the last mention but his family may still have been the owners when John Peary was included in a list of Papists as a yeoman of Cote Walls, and in 1828 when Robert Storer was a resident there. The last record, in 1715, described the place as "A vill of five houses and in it ye ruins of an old tower". There is nothing to see now.

Scrainwood

L81   P499   NT990095   10½ km, 6½ miles, north-west of Rothbury

Scrainwood, sometimes Scenwood, nestles under the Cheviot massif by the side of Scrainwood Burn, the Wreigh Burn's maiden name. Alnham and Scrainwood lie on opposite sides of the Aln-Coquet watershed, and like

Alnham, Scrainwood was a manor in William Vescy's barony until 1509. The barons leased it continuously.

The first holders were Walter Bataille and Thomas Bunte. Little is known about the latter, but the former we have met before at Netherton. William de Middleton of Belsay was the next holder, from 1289. His son John took over quite soon but he had it taken from him in 1318 because he happened to be a cousin of the notorious leader of the Mitford Gang, Sir Gilbert Middleton. All the Middletons, guilty or innocent, suffered sequestration when the gang was finally caught. Like Belsay, Scrainwood was granted to Sir John Strivelyn.

Although Strivelyn retained some interest in Scrainwood until his death in 1378, bit by bit control of the manor gradually slipped from his hands into those of the Horsley family of Longhorsley. When Roger Horsley died in 1358 he was already judged to have been 'possessed of the manor'.

One of the Horsleys built a tower towards the end of the fifteenth century, and it became an important command post and garrison in the Middle March defence. In 1509 Thomas Horsley had twenty men stationed there. In 1526 John Horsley was mentioned in despatches: "he may serve the king with thirty horsemen and is a true wise Borderer". John was praised again in 1541 for keeping his tower and barmekyn in very good repair, and these are marked on Christopher Dacre's Plat of 1584.

Thomas Horsley purchased Scrainwood from the fifth Earl of Northumberland in 1509, and the family held it as freeholders until Sir Thomas Horsley died in 1685. His will nominated his son-in-law, Edward Widdrington of Rock, as the next owner of both Scrainwood and Longhorsley. Edward had a son, another Edward, whose daughter Elizabeth Margaret married Thomas Riddell of Swinburn Castle in 1760, and when her father died two years later the Riddells became lords of Scrainwood. They retained the title until 1829 when Walter Selby bought the place to add to Biddlestone.

An old but still habitable tower was seen at Scrainwood in 1715, but there was no trace of it at the end of the nineteenth century. However, remains of something solid, perhaps a tower or a barmekyn, can still be seen in a marshy field immediately to the east of the present farmhouse.

Area 4, Sub-Area B   Upper Coquetdale

Warton

L81   P500   NU008028   5 km, 3 miles, north-west of Rothbury

An original parcel of the Hepple barony, the overlordship of which was shared by the Tailbois and Chartney families from 1259 to 1331, by the Tailbois and Ogles from 1331 to 1386, then by the Ogles alone until their tenants turned freeholders. Today Warton is a single farm, but for most of its history it was divided into several small tenements.

From its early days to the eighteenth century, Warton's premier tenants, then owners, were members of the Park family. There were others, like the Potts and the Sparks, but the Parks were the most enduring and held the largest slice of the land, possibly sub-letting some of it or allowing cadet members of the family to take over small parts.

In the sixteenth century some of these farmers built bastles for their protection against the Scots. Several still existed in 1717 when curate John Thomlinson visited Warton. Unfortunately, there seems to be no way of determining what 'several' meant as all have disappeared, their stones no doubt being reused in the buildings which still exist.

There were eleven farms in Warton in 1752, six of them owned by Gilbert Park. Lady Oxford, a descendant of the Ogles, held a couple and Edward Gallon, whose ancestors had held Low Trewhitt two centuries earlier, had bought three in 1732. Gilbert Park died in 1762 and, as his family had thinned down by then, he left his property to his nephew, another Gilbert Park, a timber merchant in London. He immediately cashed in on his inheritance by selling to John Robson, and the long Park connection was ended. By the beginning of the nineteenth century the rest of Warton had been bought by Robert Spearman, formerly of Rothley, near Cambo.

Robson and Spearman formed a working partnership and made quite an impression on the local farming community in the realm of cattle breeding. In 1842, however, both men sold their land to William Hargrave-Pawson of Shawdon. He, in his turn, sold to Sir W.G. Armstrong in 1874.

Flotterton

L81   P500   NU001024   5½ km, 3½ miles, north-west of Rothbury

One of the Greystoke townships held from the baron in the thirteenth century by a family with the local name. William son of David de Flotterton, with the baron's permission, gave 104 acres of his land to Newminster Abbey.

In 1280 the overlordship passed from the Greystoke barons to the lords of Hepple and the descent, as Hepple's, went down the Ogle line, through the Cavendishes, the Marquis of Newcastle, the lords of Oxford to the dukes of Portland. By the time this stage had been reached a lot of the barony had been sold off to sitting tenants, but what was left, including Flotterton, was sold in 1803 by the third Duke of Portland to Sir Walter Buchanan-Riddell. Very soon Flotterton alone was sold again, this time to Christopher Wealleans.

One of the many Robert Ogles who existed between 1290 and 1470 built a tower at Flotterton for the protection of his tenants. It was mentioned in the 1415 survey but never again and there is no trace of it now. Its most likely position was where Christopher Wealleans built Flotterton House.

Hepple

L81   P499   NT986006   7 km, 4¼ miles, west of Rothbury

The capital of Hepple barony, where the lords of Hepple lived during the early years, and where the Ogles, after 1386, stayed during their visits and sometimes lodged their distant relatives. We know, for example, that a certain George Ogle resided there in 1538.

Sir Robert Ogle's tower at Hepple was mentioned first in the 1415 survey but was probably built close to 1386. It had no garrison in 1514, a strange oversight as Hepple had been devastated by the Scots in 1406, 1416 and 1436. The building was so badly damaged by 1520 the baron or his locum moved home and baronial court to Great Tosson. Lord Dacre wished to station twenty men at Hepple between 1520 and 1530 and he was forced to billet them on the villagers. The 1541 survey confirmed that the tower roof had decayed.

Hepple stood like a traffic island at the centre of a three-way intersection much used during the century preceding the Union of the Crowns. From the north-west came the Scottish raiders, from the south-west came the reivers of Redesdale, and both took the eastern route down the Coquet to the rich pickings of the coastal plain. Hepple villagers feared the traffic would engulf them and, as the tower no longer offered protection, those able to do so built bastles for themselves. None remain today so we cannot tell whether of not their buildings conformed to modern ideas of bastle design, but fortifications they undoubtedly were, strong enough to resist aggressive attention until help arrived.

The walls of the tower remain still to first floor height. The *Gentleman's Magazine* reported in 1853 that workmen engaged in building new houses in the village tried to use the tower as a quarry of cut and dressed stones but had to abandon the attempt because they could not break the cement which bound the stones together.

The ruin stands in a private garden but there is a good view of it from the road, especially in winter when the trees are leafless. It is more than usually interesting because one end wall has fallen to reveal the thickness of the others – about six feet – and how they have been put together. The external measurements are roughly 38 by 29 feet and probably there were two upper floors reached by mural stairs.

The Ogle dynasty's connection with Hepple ended in 1803 when the Duke of Portland sold to Sir John Walter Buchannan-Riddell, of Riddell Water, Roxburghshire. He built a large house about a mile south of the village on the opposite side of the River Coquet; at the time it was called Whitefield House, but now it is shown on the map as Hepple Whitfield, at NY986991.

Woodhouses

L81   P499   NT965003   9 km, 5½ miles, west of Rothbury

A detached part of Dues Hill township about a mile south of Holystone and in The Harbottle manor of Redesdale liberty. Five people shared four houses, two outhouses and 82 acres of land; the male members owed service to Harbottle Castle.

William Potts, one of the five tenants after the liberty had been nationalised, built a bastle in 1602 and carved his initials and the date on its door lintel. Another tenant, John Charter, may have shared the cost of building the bastle. Two years later the Crown granted much of Redesdale, including the former liberty, to Lord Home as payment for the task of demilitarizing the Border. From him it descended to the Earl of Suffolk, and it was he who in 1617 sold Woodhouses to Roger Widdrington of Cartington, who leased it to Charters and Potts. The former progressed while the latter faded, and his interest in the place was bought by Andrew Charter in 1668. Nine years later he bought the whole estate.

The Charter descendants sold out in 1770 and Woodhouses became a frequent item on the property market. In 1889 Robert Thomas Wilkinson was the owner, then his brother and heir sold to Frank Rich, a Newcastle architect, in 1897.

Frank was rich in worldly goods as well as in name. He also bought Dues Hill Grange and made it his home. This was a small country house, probably a former farmhouse, some three or four hundred yards north of the bastle. He extended and transformed it into a Tudor-style mansion which he and his family enjoyed for many years. His son tackled the garden and enhanced it with Norman Shaw designed stone balustrades and large stone urns taken from Haggerstone Castle. The property was rechristened Beacon Grange and, later, Holystone Grange.

The bastle was in full view of the house and was not a pretty sight until the Rich's carefully restored and reroofed it in 1904. Originally it had been a typical Border stronghold, about 35 by 28 feet with two storeys, the lower one vaulted with access in a gable end with a relieving arch over the door. The upper storey had the usual type of entrance in a side wall, reached by a removable ladder. A few years after it was built, when conditions seemed more peaceful, the building was made a little more comfortable by the inclusion of inside stone stairs running through a hole cut in the south-east corner of the vault.

Unfortunately Mr Rich's roof did not last very long and by 1964 half of it had collapsed, most of the rest soon to follow. The Northumberland National Park people realised this bastle was something of a showpiece, and between 1992 and 1994 they reroofed it with stone slabs, tidied it up and provided a path through a private field to it, with a small car park by the road side.

Holystone

L81   P499   NT955026   10 km, 5¹/₂ miles, west of Rothbury

Like Woodhouses, the village of Holystone was in the Redesdale liberty and its inhabitants owed service to Harbottle Castle. Holystone was then, and is still, a compact and beautiful place with a history going back to the Britons and Romans. It had no medieval stronghold but it did boast a convent of Augustinian canonesses, founded by Robert II Umfraville during the reign of Scottish King Alexander I, 1107 to 1124, who gave it some financial support.

The convent prospered while it was able to fulfil its mission, to care for the spiritual needs of the locals and offer hospitality to travellers, many of whom used the Roman road from Bremenium (High Rochester) to Alauna (Learchild) which passed through Holystone. However, when King Edward I managed to turn the Scottish people into inexorable foes the canonesses endured front line bedlam.

In 1312 the Bishop of Durham gave them Harbottle chapel and Corsenside church, and a year later he made a public appeal, describing their plight thus: "By reason of the hostile incursions which daily and continuously increase on the March, (their house) is frequently despoiled of its goods and the nuns themselves are often attacked by marauders, harmed and pursued and put to flight and driven from their home, and constrained miserably to experience bitter suffering". The convent was granted more land, notably in Pandon, Newcastle, and in Coquetdale, but no one seems to have offered physical protection. It is a miracle it survived to 1539, when it was dissolved.

The nuns used Holystone parish church for their devotions, their house being immediately to the south of the choir – not, as the O.S. maps indicate, near the river. This is why the graveyard is to the north of the church, an unusual position. After devolution the Crown assumed ownership and leased the site of the convent to John Heron. The convent house was demolished in 1541, its stones being carted to Harbottle for use in castle repairs.

High Farnham

L81   P499   N1967026   9 km, 5¹/₂ miles, west of Rothbury

Across the Coquet from Holystone is High Farnham – 'Thirnam' until the seventeenth century – another of the 'Ten Towns of Coquetdale' in the Alnwick barony but leased to the lords of Redesdale liberty. It was held from the Umfravilles by the Hepple family, and its descent from the twelfth century to 1386 was as the Hepple barony – with one important difference: Richard

Horsley had acquired a share of it so when the Ogles took over the barony they got control of Low Farnham but High Farnham was the Horsleys.

It would seem from a comparison of their Christian names that these were not the Horsleys of Longhorsley who held Scrainwood at this time. A different family but perhaps related in some way.

The 1415 survey mentions a tower at High Farnham, belonging to Robert Horsley. It was mentioned again in 1513 and 1541, the possession on both occasions of Roger Horsley and in good condition. This Roger died in c1544, and his teenage son followed him in 1546, a month after experiencing a particularly vicious Scottish raid which did for the tower. There is a later report that its stones were used to build some local houses. Nothing of it is traceable now. The raid may have mortally wounded the lad, also, as his sister Margery was granted the estate two years later. She passed it to her husband, Cuthbert Carnaby of Aydon Hall, and it remained a Carnaby possession until they reached a distaff conclusion in the 1660s. Jane Carnaby married Sir Thomas Haggerston and High Farnham moved into that family, where it stayed until 1806 when it was sold to the Fenwick-Clennells of Harbottle.

Neither Low Farnham, five hundred yards to the south-east of 'High', nor Wreighill, another half mile in the same direction, had fortified towers. Wreighill, however, is of some interest for two reasons. First, a young lady who lived in the hamlet in 1665, a Miss Handyside, received a small package from her boyfriend in London; it was infected with the plague and virtually the whole community died. Second, George Coughron, a mathematical genius, was born here in 1752. He won numerous prizes for answering questions on 'fluxions', and when he died, at the tragically early age of twenty-one, he was working for the Astronomer Royal as his 'calculator'.

Sharperton

L81   P499   N1958040   10 km, 6¼ miles, west of Rothbury.

Another of the 'Ten Towns of Coquetdale', it was a small township which the Umfravilles rented to several people. Up to the end of the fourteenth century no resident was dominant and it is probable that most of them were retainers of the Umfravilles – Harbottle is only a mile and a half away. There was a forester, a soldier, a butler, a tanner and a vintner.

Sir Robert Ogle acquired the place before 1399, and from there on its descent was similar to Hepple's. Gradually, however, some of the tenants bought their land, and by 1744 the Earl of Oxford, an Ogle scion, owned only four of the nine homesteads. One of the earliest purchasers was a member of the Potts family. One of the last was the Rev. John Thomlinson of Rothbury who bought Charity Hall (NT967040) as an endowment for the poor of Rothbury parish.

Thomas Potts built a bastle in c1568. A descendant, Roger Potts, converted this into a larger cottage by knocking down its front and two gable walls and rebuilding against the back wall, reusing the bastle stones. This comfortable but unfortified abode was dated 1675 on its doorhead. In 1985 virtually the same thing happened again, and today it is a delightful country cottage with a bright red roof. The 4½ foot back wall of the bastle is still there.

Harbottle

L80   P499   NT932047   12½ km, 7¾ miles, north-west of Rothbury

Harbottle Castle is exactly where a medieval castle should be, on top of a steep-sided hill protected on three sides by a curvaceous river. Its position is where a tourniquet could be applied to stop the flow of intruders gushing out of the narrow Coquet valley and from the many mountain roads from Scotland and Redesdale into the wide, fertile vale of Rothbury.

The Angles knew this and had a military presence at Harbottle from time immemorial. The name stems from 'Here-bote', Old English for 'army abode'. The Normans saw immediately they took possession that this should be their advance position.

Although geographically in Coquetdale, Harbottle was included in the Anglian thanage of Redesdale. The last thane was Mildred, son of Akman, and he had the painful experience of seeing his lands grabbed by King William the Conqueror and given to Robert de Umfraville, Lord of Toures and Uian, in 1076. Robert was a close friend, perhaps a relation of the king and he got this large Border territory partly as a reward for services rendered during the conquest, and partly because England's safety required a strong presence at its junction with Scotland. The grant was a liberty, which meant that Robert and his successors had viceregal powers to govern and control the territory by his own laws, without interference from the shire's earl or sheriff. The lord of the liberty was not required to provide knights and soldiers for the king, as barons were, and the only condition imposed was that he should "keep the country free of wolves and robbers".

Robert, whose sobriquet was 'Robert with the Beard' because of his hirsute appearance, made his home at Elsdon but built a motte and bailey castle at Harbottle, manning it with conscripts taken from the 'Ten Towns of Coquetdale' which he leased from the Baron of Alnwick. His son, another Robert, took over in King Henry I's reign, and in 1133 or 4 was granted as additional territory the barony of Prudhoe on the Tyne. This was a more peaceful area and soon became the main seat of the Umfravilles.

The next in line was Odinel who was responsible for strengthening Harbottle Castle in 1157. All he did, very probably, was to face the motte and bailey with stone, but we cannot be sure as very little of this work remains. He was obeying the instructions of King Henry II who was actively refortifying the Border against the increasingly antagonistic Scots.

The work was tested and found wanting in 1174 when King William the Lion gained an entry. His success was short-lived, however, as the aggressor was captured at Alnwick and stripped of his ill-gotten gains.

Richard, of the sixth generation of Redesdale Umfravilles, like many other Northern landlords, joined in the Barons' War against king John in 1215. For this indiscretion Harbottle was confiscated and held by the Crown for six years until it was returned by King Henry III. Richard's son, Gilbert, improved the Umfravilles' social standing by marrying Maud, the Countess of Angus, in 1243. He died the next year, but their son became Earl of Angus.

This lad had a lot to contend with. He lived through the tragedy of King Edward I's attempt to gain the crown of Scotland by the manipulation of John Balliol and the Scottish people, and he experienced the repercussions. When the English king advanced into Scotland in 1296 the traitorous Robert de Ros of Wark, with the Earls of Athol and Menteith and 40,000 men, invaded Northumberland. Harbottle lay in their path and blocked their way for a time. It was besieged for two days and did not yield, the only sufferers being the deer in the castle's park which the invaders killed in their frustration. This loss was remedied later by King Edward, who had the park restocked by another Scotsman, John Comyn, who had a game reserve at Tarset in North Tynedale.

Robert de Umfraville, the next Earl of Angus, fared even worse when Robert Bruce attacked Harbottle Castle in 1318. He not only took it, he partly demolished it, and nothing could be done about it until 1328 because of a cease-fire agreement between Bruce and King Edward II.

Robert's son, another Gilbert, proved to be the last of the original mainline Umfravilles. When he died, in 1381, Redesdale liberty was settled on his half-brother, Thomas de Umfraville. Two years before he died in 1386 the old 'Leges Marchiarum' or Laws of the Marches, which had been concocted in 1249 and then pigeonholed, were brought out and given some teeth. Wardens were appointed to police the Border and Harbottle became the headquarters of the Middle March Warden. The castle was used thus until it became too decayed for anything useful in the late sixteenth century.

Two more members of the cadet branch of the Umfravilles took their turn to hold the liberty, the second one being killed in France in 1421. He left no family so his uncle, Sir Robert de Umfraville, took over. He was a larger than life character, Vice-Admiral of England and a keen cross-Border raider. The villagers of Elsdon called him 'Robin Mend-Market' because of the way he filled their market stalls with booty. During his tenure Harbottle Castle was subjected to considerable repairs and modernisation of its defences. Most of the masonry which survives today dates from this period.

As Sir Robert never married there was no close Umfraville to take over the liberty when he died in 1436. The legal heir was judged to be the progeny of Elizabeth, sister of Gilbert de Umfraville who had died in 1381. She had married Gilbert of Burradon and had had a daughter, Eleanor, who had married Henry Tailbois. Their son, William Tailbois, became the next lord of the liberty.

Two generations later, William Tailbois made the mistake of opposing King Edward IV during the Wars of the Roses. He lost his property in 1461 and his head after the Battle of Hexham in 1464. His son was repossessed in 1472 and during the intervening years the Ogles were put in charge.

A frontier fortress packed with eighty violent men is not the ideal maternity home, yet Harbottle Castle was selected by King Henry VIII as the place where his sister Margaret, widow of Scottish King James IV, should have her baby in 1515. Lord Dacre, the castle's governor, objected in vain; Scotland was not a healthy place after the Battle of Flodden, especially for an ex-queen who had married again (to Archibald Douglas), but the king considered that safety should take precedence over suitability. The new arrival was christened Margaret, and in later life she was to be the wife of the Earl of Lennex, the mother of Darnley and the grandmother of James VI and I. As soon as he could, Dacre passed mother and baby on to Cartington.

The last in the Tailbois line was Robert, who died in 1541 without issue. His sister Elizabeth inherited the liberty. She was married to Thomas Wymbysche of Lincolnshire, and they did not relish the responsibility of owning this wild northern territory, so they struck a bargain with King Henry VIII by which they got more civilized property at Brailes in Warwickshire and the king took over the Redesdale liberty. This was highly satisfactory for both parties: the Wymbysches could settle down in the peace of Middle England and the Crown could at long last terminate an archaic grant and bring state law to this Border area. The liberty became, effectively, a barony, although the Crown retained ownership for the next sixty-three years. Harbottle manor had fifteen Crown tenants, excluding the castle which remained a wardens' station until it was too ruinous to use.

After the Union of the Crowns, James VI and I commissioned George Lord Home to demilitarize the Border, to banish the reivers and moss troopers and to convert the region into his 'Middle Shires'. As payment, Lord Home was granted all the Crown lands in both Tynedale and Redesdale, including Harbottle. Later he also given the earldom of Dunbar.

When he died in 1611, his work unfinished, Lord Home left two heiresses, one of whom, Elizabeth, got Redesdale. She was married to Theophilus, Lord Howard of Walden, who was soon elevated to the Earl of Suffolk. They knew little, and cared less, about Northern England, and during their lifetime they sold off parcels of Redesdale to anyone willing to pay their price. Harbottle and some surrounding estates went in 1635 to Roger Widdrington. He assigned his Cartington possession to his son Edward and built a new house at Harbottle for himself and his wife Rosamond. He called the new place 'Harbottle Castle', which was not inappropriate as it was built very largely with stones taken from the medieval castle.

Edward took over Harbottle on his father's death in 1641 but lost it until 1660 during the Civil War. His death in 1671 brought to an end the Widdrington connection as first his daughter then his granddaughter inherited. The latter's son, Sir Edward Gascoigne, sold Harbottle to Luke Clennell in 1731. Three generations on and a union of families gave the ownership to the Fenwick-Clennells, who still reside in the area. Their seventeenth century mansion was improved by John Dobson, then converted into three separate homes in 1971.

Nature and Roger Widdrington have left only meagre remains of the ancient castle, but these are worth climbing the castle mound to see. There is a field path to it which has quite recently been opened to the public by the Countryside Commission's Stewardship Scheme. The ruin is still out of bounds but the path goes close enough for a good inspection.

The castle occupied only the western half of the mound, the eastern half being used as a barmekyn. The keep was on the original mote on the south side, overlooking a precipitous drop to the Harbottle-Alwinton road. The causeway from bailey to keep is still obvious, and bits of the keep, curtain wall and gate tower can be traced and are being stabilized. One bit of masonry has slipped down the side of the mound.

West of the castle, across the river, is the verdant estate called The Peels:
> "Harbottle Castle stands on wheels,
> If ye gied a gud kick
> It'll run to the Peels".

Places in Northumberland with names which include 'Peel' or 'Pele' are often sites of medieval towers, but neither in the records nor on the ground are there any signs of such a building here. It is suggested that, as both 'pele' and 'paling' derive from the Latin 'pelum' meaning 'stake', it was an enclosure protected by palings, perhaps the demesne land of the castle, perhaps the park which held the deer Robert de Ros slaughtered in 1296.

It also appears to have been part of Chirmundesden, the only township of the 'Ten Towns of Coquetdale' which has completely disappeared. A survey of 1604 strongly suggests this.

Alwinton

L80   P499   NT923057   14 km, 8½ miles, north-west of Rothbury

Modern Alwinton is in two parts: its church and vicarage are close to the River Coquet, about a mile upstream from Harbottle, and its few houses and a pub are half a mile further north at NT920063. The medieval village and its small fortification were close to the church.

As one of the 'Ten Towns of Coquetdale', Alwinton was effectively a parcel of the Redesdale liberty. Most of its land was leased to farmers, and some of them, over the years, bought their property. The Selbys of Biddlestone, for example, seem to have owned land close to the church, which had no glebe. The overall lordship, however, descended through the Umfravilles in exactly the same manner as has been described for Harbottle – right down the line to Sir Edward Widdrington, who died in 1671. Whereas he left Harbottle to his daughter, he left Alwinton to his sister, Lady Mary Charlton. It stayed in her family until 1740.

The church is a mixture of dates, little bits of it late eleventh or early twelfth century, although the earliest record is dated 1233 when its rector was Thomas of Rule. It appears to have had a rector or vicar fairly continuously throughout its existence, but the vicarage is not mentioned until 1541 when it was described as a 'bastle house' in poor repair. That this was a tower was confirmed in 1635 when it was recorded that the vicar had lost "the old pele tower rectory house". The poor clerics had to find their own accommodation until the parishioners built a new vicarage during the ministry of Thomas Moses, 1758 to 1798.

It is believed that this vicarage, and its 1844 replacement, were built on the site of the original tower. Nothing more is known about Thomas Rule's little place, and there are no remains.

Clennell

L80   P499   NT928071   14 km, 8½ miles, north-west of Rothbury

The River Alwin, a tributary of the Coquet, drains Kidland Forest, most of which lay within the Redesdale liberty. Clennell is the gateway to this vast wilderness and, as one of the 'Ten Towns of Coquetdale' was included in the liberty only by agreement.

Records of Clennell township go back to 1181 when the second Odinel de Umfraville was laying down the limits of Kidland prior to granting it to Newminster Abbey. The monks had to pass through Clennell to reach Kidland, and Thomas of Clennell, the first known occupier, reached an agreement about wayleave in 1228. The payment was the promise of burial in Newminster Abbey.

The Clennells were a durable family, with sufficient males on hand to last until the eighteenth century. The distaff side took over in 1720, and within two generations the Fenwick-Clennells were the owners and Harbottle Castle had become their home. First the Wilkinsons then the Drew-Wilkinsons took Clennell into the twentieth century.

The township did not get a tower until the sixteenth century although it must have needed one much earlier. Kidland was held by monks but it was well used by the ungodly coming from and going to Scotland, and Clennell stood in their way. Percival Clennell added battlements to his tower soon after it was built, and he declared his intention to add a barmekyn when funds permitted. An Elizabethan two-storey wing was added in 1568, and a third storey was added to this in the 1690s along with a few windows and a stone fireplace. This composite hall-house and a farm was all that was left of the township by now. The former was further added to in 1895, the result being the pleasant mansion to be seen today. It is a holiday centre now and when last visited the tower vault was being used as a games room.

Barrow

L80   P499   NT912061   15 km, 9½ miles, north-west of Rothbury

Farms above Alwinton are few and far between. Barrow is one which has been a farm for a very long time. Most of the others were 'shielings' originally, shelters where lived the shepherds who brought lowland flocks up to feed on Cheviot grass for a few summer months.

   Although very isolated, Barrow was on the military map and in 1522 the Warden of the Middle March ordered the stationing there of twenty soldiers, an attempt to block the Coquet corridor.

   John Barrow, the holder in 1522, appears to have paid his rent directly to the lords of Redesdale liberty and to have enjoyed full hereditable control over his land. His son Gerald was in charge when a band of Scotsmen out-manoeuvred the garrison and destroyed the tower his father had built. The Warden should have rebuilt it, but did not, and the Barrows did not have the money to do it, so only traces of the tower could be seen during the nineteenth century, and nothing positively identifiable remains now.

   The Barrow family lasted until 1663 then faded out. George Potts bought the farm in 1668 when Andrew Charter eased him out of Woodhouses, but by 1717 the Selbys of Biddlestone were the owners.

Linbriggs

L80   P499   NT892063   17km, 10½ miles, north-west of Rothbury

Another ancient farm about a mile and a half upstream from Barrow. It had a tower, but the first mention of it was in 1541 after it had been 'caste down' some years before. The owner then was Roger Horsley of High Farnham, and David Dippie Dixon has suggested that he collected the stones from the tower ruin and dumped them in a field on rising ground called Ducket Knowe with the intention of building a new tower in a more defensible position. This is very doubtful as 'Ducket' meant 'dovecote' so the pile of stones were more likely to have been the remains of a pigeon loft. So there is no clue as to the original position of the tower, or of its size.

Across the river is another farm, Linshiels, which, as its name suggests, was once a shieling. For a long time it was part of the Cartington estate, and when in 1632 Roger Widdrington and his bride-to-be travelled to Scotland in order to be married by a Roman Catholic priest, they stopped here to pick up a couple of witnesses.

In 1840 both Linbriggs and Linshiels were worked as one farm by the Dunn family, but they were separated in the 1930s when Thomas Hedley held the latter. He had a manager working the farm while he lived in the former Red Lion Inn in Alwinton, by then the village shop and post office. He owned a very high Ford truck, ideal for wading the many fords up the valley, there being only one road bridge then above Alwinton. Every Tuesday he would load up this truck with groceries and other necessities and take them to all the farms up to and including Carlcroft. Payment was made partly in money, but mainly in eggs, which Thomas would box and take to Rothbury on Thursdays. A great character, he was very nearly as wide as he was tall, yet he was the leader of the local Boy Scouts troop.

Chew Green

L80   P498   NT788084   28 km, 17 miles, north-west of Rothbury

Within yards of the source of the Coquet and just inside the Border is an array of grass-covered Roman remains of marching camps, a labour camp, a compound for relay horses and a fortlet which had acted as a police post. It is one of the most distinct, significant and dramatic Roman earthworks in Britain.

Old historians frequently called Chew Green camps 'ad Fines', but this name was concocted by Richard of Cirencester and has no validity. If the Romans had an official name it has been lost, and the name the legionnaires gave such a wild and inaccessible place is probably unprintable.

Dere Street, a continuation of Watling Street, was the Romans' main road into Scotland. It passed from Corbridge up the North Tyne, through the main stations at Habitancum at Woodburn and Bremenium at High Rochester to Chew Green, then on to Newstead on Tweed, near Melrose. Road-making became a lost art after the Romans left, and their roads were the best there were, with few exceptions, until the eighteenth century. Dere Street was a main route, with Chew Green a useful service station, throughout the Middle Ages. Even the route from Newcastle via Ponteland, Belsay, Cambo and Elsdon went over the Border at Chew Green, while the apparently easier way via Otterburn and Carter Bar was merely a drovers track until 1779.

The safer route into Scotland was along the coast, and it was a motley crowd which frequented the tavern built in medieval times at Chew Green. It had a plentiful supply of illicit whisky, distilled in hidden corners of the Cheviots, and this was its best protection against crime. The service station was too much appreciated by all travellers to destroy, and a fortified tower was neither necessary nor built.

Area 4, Sub-Area C   The Grasslees Burn

Harehaugh

L81   P510   NY973998   8½ km, 5¼ miles, west of Rothbury

A farm beside the Elsdon to Holystone road, close to where the Grasslees Burn runs into the River Coquet. It lies in Holystone township.

It was reported in 1541 that Rog' Hangingshawes had started to build a strong tower at his own expense but had been unable to finish it because his money had dried up.

Although the Hangingshawes – later simplified to Handyside – retained Harehaugh until it was sold to Matthew Forster in 1776, the family never finished their tower. It was left to Forster to make a small house of it. This is a ruin in the farmyard now; one of its walls appears to be bastle material.

Grasslees

L81   P510   NY9551976   11 km, 6¾ miles, west of Rothbury

A small farm bestriding the Elsdon road, 250 yards above Grasslees Burn. The farmhouse is set into the steep hillside on the west side of the road. Its main interest is its plinth; the building stones are cemented onto a single course of large boulders which can be seen all round the house.

Plinths such as this are often the only clue that the site held a bastle at one time. Not all bastles were built on them, but plinths with sides roughly in the proportion 35 to 25 feet are pretty reliable indicators of previous bastles. Sixteenth and seventeenth century builders were not too clever about foundations, but if the ground was marshy or liable to flooding they often laid a bed of large boulders and built on that. In this case the trouble was flood water which can pour down the hillside, and a plinth was laid in the hope of bringing the floor of the bastle above the anticipated flood level.

The bastle was demolished in the eighteenth century and the present house was built on the old plinth. Originally it had no back door; because of this the house got excessively hot in summer, so a back door was inserted. The plinth proved to be not high enough, and there were occasions after very heavy rain when the flood water rushed through the house, in at the back and out at the front. The present occupier can remember this happening as a child.

The remedy, of course was to protect the back door with a lean-to extension and to shape the back garden so that water would flow round the house rather than straight at it. This work was done this century.

The Raw

L80   P510   NY942980   11¹/₂ km, 7 miles, west of Rothbury

This is the first of four bastles in Woodside, an isolated manor of Harbottle within the Redesdale liberty. The others are High Shaw, Iron House and Craig. Unlike these, The Raw is not in the Otterburn Training Area and thus may be visited at any time.

The bastle still stands but is no longer the farmhouse: a more commodius replacement was built near it in the late eighteenth century. It is still in use, however, as a farm building. Its roof has been replaced but its vault and outside staircase are still serviceable. A small upstairs window remains in the southern gable which has stone jambs decorated with curious carvings – they could be a human head and a rosette, a figure and a clock or a couple of flowers, they are too weather-worn to be sure.

The old name of the bastle was 'Haws Pele'. Probably it was always a farmer's residence, but Woodside was quite a large community in the seventeenth and eighteenth centuries and some of the local people worked in small coal mines which dotted the area.

During the latter part of the eighteenth century a Mr Crozier lived in the bastle, and when he died his widow, Margaret, opened a drapers shop in it. On August 29th 1791 she was murdered in her bastle and her stock-in-trade was stolen. The crime, which caused much neighbourly distress, was quickly pinned onto a pedlar called William Winter and his two companions, Jane and Eleanor Clark, on the evidence of a sharp-eyed shepherd boy. The day before the killing this lad had met the three travellers resting against a hedge, and had noticed how the nails in Winter's boots were arranged in an unusual pattern. His description of this matched exactly the footprints outside the bastle, so the three were arrested and subsequently hanged at the Westgate of Newcastle. Winter's body was gibbeted later on gallows erected at Steng Cross, a wayside marker at the highest point on the Elsdon to Rothley road, much frequented by travellers of all descriptions. There is a sequel to this which will be told under Fallowlees.

When the hanging body had decayed to the point when it was no longer a visible warning, it was replaced by a wooden head, a target for vandals on several occasions. Sir Charles Travelyn had a tale to tell about this gruesome message. Tramps passing the Cross were frequently intrigued by it and would ask Mr Potts, the farmer at Harwood Head, half a mile along the road, what it meant. When told about Winter and the murder, English and Scottish tramps always said of Winter, "serves him right", but Irish tramps invariably said, "poor fellow".

High Shaw

L80   P510   NY935982   12 km, 7$\frac{1}{2}$ miles, west of Rothbury

Iron House

L80   P510   NY933983   12 km, 7$\frac{1}{2}$ miles, west of Rothbury

Two isolated bastle ruins in Woodside, but also in the Otterburn Training Area so cannot be visited without permission. Both ruins are surrounded by grass-covered foundations of farm buildings, signifying that they are examples of early agricultural settlements.

It would appear that both were considered to be still worth somebody's money in about 1800 when the following notice was displayed on the door of the Presbyterian Meeting House in Harbottle

> "This is to give Notice that Highshaw and Ironhouse in the parish of Elsdon is to be Lett, Either together or Separate. Who Ever Inclines to take the Same may apply to Mr John Gallon who will Treat with them about the Same."

Whether or not the advertisement was successful is not known, but by 1840 High Shaw was owned by the Maughan family. By that time, however, the farmstead had probably been moved to its present site, about half a mile away from the bastle and just above The Raw.

The ground floor vault of High Shaw bastle is still in use as a farm store, and its walls are sound up to about twelve feet. All round the top of these walls is a chamfered string course, or projecting 'curb' which is believed to be unique. The ground floor walls are thick for a bastle – over five feet – and it seems probable that the upper floor walls were thinner and that the switch from thick to thin was protected by the 'curb'.

The building measures about 40 by 24 feet and has some near-derelict lean-to shanties against its south wall. The entrance to the vault, on the east wall, has a relieving arch over the lintel stone and holes for drawbars.

Iron House, half a mile to the north-west, has had other names during its long history – 'Highshaw Iron House', 'Herne House' and just 'The pele near Watt's Sike'. There is no modern farm near it and it would appear that the place was allowed to die with the last tenant. It is a roofless ruin now and the wooden ceiling of the ground floor has rotted away, but the gable walls still stand about twenty feet high and the side walls are between six and eight feet high.

Positive dating of either of these bastles is not possible, but both conform to the general design of Border bastles built between 1550 and 1600.

Craig

L80   P510   NY937998   12 km, 7¹/₂ miles, west of Rothbury

This is a working farm at the northern extremity of Woodside manor and a good mile into the Otterburn Training Area. It is surrounded by a few fields which are out of bounds to the army – and, hopefully, to its shells.

'The Crage', as it was known then, was surveyed in 1604, so we have some idea of its age. The only known occupants were the Burton family in 1840.

The bastle has been stabilized and adjoins the farmhouse. Its ground floor vault is almost complete although a modern entrance has been inserted in the south wall to facilitate its use as a store. The west wall is nearly full height but the other walls go little higher that the vault. The lower steps of a very narrow mural staircase in the south-west corner exist but have been blocked off as part of the stabilising process; it is most unusual to find bastles with internal stairs and almost certainly they were installed a few years after the initial construction. This happened at Woodhouses, where a hole was made through the vault; here the vault was left intact and some infill rubble was removed from the wall to accommodate the stairs.

Darden Lough and High Rigg

L81   P510   Around NY972956

10 km, 6¹/₄ miles, south-west of Rothbury

High Rigg is an eminence in the rough uphill ground on the south side of the Grasslees Burn, quite close to Harwood Forest. Darden Lough is a small lake half a mile to its south and between it and Darden Pike. The area has never been populated but it affords a fine view northwards and westwards over the hills behind Woodside so it is an ideal location for watch towers. No band of raiders could gallop across what is now the Otterburn Training Area without being spotted by a guard stationed here who could signal an advance warning of approaching trouble.

Both Darden Lough and High Rigg have been noted on old documents as the sites of fortified watch towers, but the available evidence is so scant it is impossible to say whether there were two or just one with two names. There are stones lying on the ground near the Lough which could be from a tower, and ground markings on High Rigg could be grassed-over foundations, but both clues could also be illusory.

There is one thing about Darden Lough that is fairly certain: the medicos of yore caught their leeches here.

Area 4, Sub-Section D   Rothbury Forest

Whitton

L81   P500   NU058011   1 km, ⁵/₈ mile, south of Rothbury

Whitton township stands high up the southern bank of the River Coquet at Rothbury. Originally part of Rothbury Forest, it has belonged to the Rothbury rectors since 1201, granted as part of their salary – it contained arable and pastoral land and a few leased houses, all capable of swelling the rectors' coffers. Not surprisingly, the rectory was built here, in the form of a strong tower, during the fourteenth century.

It measured 46 by 33 feet externally and had walls eleven feet thick in places. Its original height is unknown as Alexander Cooke, rector between 1433 and 1474, increased this dimension while making other alterations and some repairs. His weather-beaten coat of arms still enhances his work.

Further repairs, alterations and extensions were made in the seventeenth and eighteenth centuries, and a mansion was added by the Rev. C.G. Vernon Harcourt between 1822 and 1871. While doing this he renewed practically everything and incorporated the ground floor of the tower as a wing. In 1934 the Church Commissioners sold the building to Angus Watson of Newcastle who, with the cooperation of the Newcastle City Council, founded a children's convalescent home there as a useful memorial to his wife Ethel. This lasted until 1986, when it was put on the market.

The Rev. Thomas Sharp, Rothbury rector from 1720 to 1758, was one of the trustees appointed in 1737 to administer Lord Crewe's charity trust in Bamburgh. He was interested also in the 'occult science of astrology', which in those days had a touch of basic astronomy in it. To give work to Rothbury masons, and quite coincidentally to advance his hobby, he had a tall round observation tower built near his home. This 'Sharp's Folly' still exists. His son, John, was in his time rector of Hartburn, Archdeacon of Northumberland and, from 1758 to his death in 1792, the most active of all the Bamburgh trustees.

Newtown

L81   P500   NU035005   2¹/₂ km, 1¹/₂ miles, south-west of Rothbury

Sandwiched between Whitton and Great Tosson, Newtown, as its name suggests, is not quite such an old settlement as many in the neighbourhood. It is believed to have been created a little before 1240 by John fitz Robert, Baron of Warkworth, son of the original recipient of Rothbury. Employees were given small pieces of land in Newtown for which they paid peppercorn rents. Although these rents increased, Newtown remained a collection of leased small holdings until the eighteenth century.

It is guesswork that it was the Earl of Northumberland, the then owner of Rothbury Forest, who built a bastle in or soon after 1586 to try to avoid a repetition of a disastrous raid that year by the Scots. The area in which David Dippie Dixon claimed to have seen the ruined walls of the bastle, on rising ground a few hundred yards south of East Newtown farm, is a blanket of thistles now, but numerous half-covered walls and grassed-over foundations are evident. These are probably the remains of small holders' cottages and field walls, and no bastle shapes have been found.

By the beginning of the nineteenth century the numerous plots of land had amalgamated into three farms, East Newtown, West Newtown and Carterside. The Duke of Northumberland sold East and West Newtown to Sir W.G. Armstrong in 1883 but retained Carterside.

Great Tosson

L81   P500   NU029004   3 km, 2 miles, south-west of Rothbury

Tosson was mentioned in the twelfth century, and even then it was divided into Great Tosson, or Tosson Magna, and Little Tosson, once 'The Other Place' or Alter Tosse. There is a fine tower at Great Tosson; nothing fortified is at Little Tosson, about two miles to its west.

About half a mile uphill from Newtown, the tower is still a landmark, in a field roughly opposite a large house which in the eighteenth and nineteenth centuries was the Royal George Inn. Much of the ashlar has been removed from the walls of the tower, but the rubble infill is so firmly cemented together there is no danger of them falling. External dimensions are 42 by 36 feet and the walls are about nine feet thick. Inside, the springing of the ground floor vault remains, also traces of stairs in the north-east corner and a first floor mural chamber. The whole stands about 20 feet high and would benefit from some English Heritage attention.

Ownership descent to the nineteenth century was very similar to that of Hepple. Both Tossons were in Greystoke barony but were granted to the Hepple barons in 1204. The Ogles took over in the fourteenth century and built the tower in the fifteenth. In 1520 they moved to Tossen from Hepple after a disastrous raid. The Duke of Portland sold to Sir John Buchanan-Riddell in 1803, and from him the property went first to William Orde of Nunnykirk in 1805 and then to Sir W.G. Armstrong in 1883.

Real peace, meaning freedom from moss troopers and other horse thieves, did not reach Great Tosson until the eighteenth century, and then the district started to attract farmers from outside the area. One of these was Samuel Donkin, who came with his bride in 1720. Thirty years later their son William married Eleanor Shotton from the same village, and Sam used the occasion to treat all his friends and relations – 550 of them – to a memorable meal in Rothbury. It is reliably recorded that they did justice to 120 quarters of lamb, 44 quarters of veal, a 'great quantity' of beef, 12 hams and 'a suitable number of chickens, etc'. All this was swilled with 8 half ankers (an anker is believed to have been about eight gallons) of brandy made into punch, 12 half ankers of cider, a 'great many gallons' of wine and 90 bushels of malt brewed into beer. The record goes no further (perhaps the recorder was one of the guests) so we do not know how, or if, they all got home that night. The feast did Sam no lasting harm, however, for he lived to see his 102nd birthday.

Bickerton

L81   P499   NT995002   6 km, 3³/₄ miles, south-west of Rothbury

A township in the Hepple barony held from about 1170 to 1369 by a family which took Bickerton as its name and who lived from about 1272 in a fortified farmhouse. As with modern newspaper reporters, the old chroniclers found black sheep much more interesting to write about than their cleaner brethren, so a story concerning Thomas Bickerton, living in the middle of the thirteenth century, has come down to us when much pleasanter stories have been lost.

Thomas, it seems, had brutal and oppressive streaks in him. On one occasion he incarcerated three local women in his damp and dingy cell from Sunday to Wednesday without food or drink. They were Emma, who had a baby with her, Edith and Christiana. On the Wednesday he sent them to Newcastle gaol, where they were charged with stealing a bushel of Thomas's malt. Christiana and the baby died in gaol, so only Emma and Edith stood trial at the assizes. Fortunately the jury were able to demonstrate the humane side of the law: they conveniently put the responsibility of the theft on dead Christiana, so that the other two could be found not guilty and released. They got some recompense by bringing a counter-action against Thomas, who was fined sixty shillings.

Bickerton township was an Ogles possession until 1628, when it was sold to Percival Snawdon. His family was prolific, and by 1663 they owned five houses in the village. Gradually they died out and today there is only one farm. Its farmhouse is said to incorporate a small part of one of the Snawdon houses, while the others are green mounds in an adjoining field.

Butterknowes

L81   P511   NZ091991   4¹/₂ km, 2³/₄ miles, south-east of Rothbury

Mackenzie, in his *View of Northumberland (1825)*, informs us "The whole of (Rothbury Forest) is now dotted over with solitary farmsteads, from a quarter of a mile to a mile distant from one another. These houses, or rather strongholds, are very old and are usually called Peels". However many there were in the historian's day, only a handful are known now, most of them farmhouses which have derived from or have replaced bastles or towers.

Butterknowes is one of them. It and Brockley Hall and The Lees are evenly spaced along the Forest Burn, a lovely stream which rises on Simonside and empties into the River Coquet at Pauperhaugh. There is a lot of bastle left in Butterknowes farmhouse. The south-east wall has been rebuilt but the other three, about four feet thick, still exist although now they are interior walls, extensions having been built against them.

The bastle was built by the Earl of Northumberland before 1586, when the occupier, James Wetherborne, complained that, despite his new fortification, he had lost to Scottish raiders "22 Kyne and Oxen, 1 naig and 20 shepe to the value of xxxl".

Brockley Hall

L81   P511   NZ086987   4 km, 2½ miles, south-east of Rothbury

Nothing remains of the original bastle, save perhaps some of the stones, but two artefacts of the rather pretentious replacement have been saved. One is a stone mantle shelf, richly carved and inscribed "Thomas Wharton 1666", has been inserted, rather profanely, in the gable end of a farm building. The other remains in its original position above the main door; it is a decorated lintel stone on which has been carved an armorial shield containing the letter 'M' surrounded by the date 1666. What the 'M' stands for is not known – perhaps Thomas's wife.

The house is not particularly pretentious now, apart from its doorway, and obviously many alterations have been made since it was built. The Whartons vacated the place before 1844, in which year John Redhead of that address was charged £6.20 by the rector of Rothbury in lieu of tithe.

The Lee

L81   P511   NZ080979   4½ km, 2¾ miles, south of Rothbury

The present name is a corruption of 'Elyburne' which was listed as a strong house in the 1541 survey. Today's farmhouse, neatly tucked into the deep glen of the Forest Burn, is the non-fortified replacement for the tower, of which nothing remains.

Bog Hall

L81   P511   NZ073978   4 km, 2½ miles, south of Rothbury

The last of the Rothbury Forest fortifications to be demolished, but the job was done thoroughly for all that; there is nothing but a patch of nettles to see now. It does not appear to have been replaced as the nearest dwelling is 400 yards away and has a different name. The site, about half a mile west of The Lees, is shown on an old map entitled 'Plan of Lee Ward in Parish of Rothbury, 1847', but it is marked 'Bog Cottage'. Obviously the place has grown in stature since its demise. 'Cottage' seems more appropriate than 'hall', however, for its 1844 occupant, Thomas Bell, was charged only 15p in lieu of tithe by the rector of Rothbury. Compared to John Redhead's charge, this very small amount would indicate a delicate financial position.

Morrelhirst

L81   P511   NZ058960   5¹/₂ km, 3¹/₂ miles, south of Rothbury

This isolated farm, half a mile west of Forestburn gate, carried no hint of its former state, yet old records state that it was a tower a few years after 1541. It was not new then so it must have been built well before bastles were thought of.

'Hirst' is an abbreviation still used locally, but in the sixteenth century the short and long forms of the name seem to have carried equal weight. Thus the Warden of the Middle March and the Earl of Northumberland both called it 'Moryslehirst, or sometimes 'Moreslehirst', while in 1569 Thomas Potts the occupier, laid a claim for £9 for "The spoyle of the Towere at the Herst".

Fallowlees

L81   P511   NZ020943   8 km, 5 miles, south-west of Rothbury

Fallowlees and the two sites to its east, Newbiggin and Ritton White House, lie on the southern base line of Rothbury Forest, and thus are included in this section even though their waters drain into the River Font and not into the Coquet. Fallowlees, at the west end of this line, is reached by traversing miles of rough road through Harwood Forest, and has thick coniferous woodland on all sides save for a corridor of meadow affording a generous view down to the Fallowlees Burn and across to the Greenleighton Moor to the south-east.

Although separated from its 'capital' by the Simonside Hills, Fallowlees was a member of the Hepple barony and shared its descent through the Chartney, Tailbois and Ogle families until Robert, the fourth Lord Ogle, sold it in 1530. Being on the sunny, southern slopes of the Simonsides, Fallowlees township was much sought after as prime pasture, until the Forestry Commission planted the trees, and as such was documented as early as 1331. In 1436 there was enough cattle in its fields to attract the undivided attention of Scottish raiders. Its name was a true description.

It was for this pasture that John Hall of Otterburn first leased then bought Fallowlees in 1530, and why a small community of stockmen became established in permanent wooden houses around Fallowlees. A junior member of the Hall family came to live there and, at some time between 1541 and

1581, built a bastle. His descendant, Edward Hall, became estranged from the main family and he and Anthony Radcliffe of Thropton were pardoned for the manslaughter of William Hall of Otterburn in 1615. They appear to have made it up after that, for John Hall of Otterburn and Charles Hall of Fallowlees jointly took out a mortgage on the latter's property in 1669.

The need for a mortgage appears to have been just a temporary aberration or, at worst, the very early systems of trouble, for the Halls continued to own Fallowlees until 1705. It was a fair-sized hamlet by this time with two farms and at least one other stone house, called Dod House. The present farmer, while ploughing one of his fields, recently discovered a quantity of broken clay pipes of 1600 vintage. Such a find is usually indicative of peaceful village life.

In 1671 William Veitch, the Scottish evangelist, came to live in Fallowlees and to farm a few acres of Charles Hall's land. Veitch had been a leader of the Scottish Covenanters opposed to a revival of episcopacy. He had been outlawed by the bishops after the abortive Pentland Rising of 1666, but had continued preaching along the Border until persuaded to find refuge for himself and his family on the English side. He stayed at Fallowlees until 1677, then moved to Stanton Hall.

Edward Hall sold Fallowlees in 1705 to Sir William Blackett, owner of the adjoining Wallington estate. His sole interest in the place was its shooting, and he built Blackcock Hall as a shooting box rather more than a mile north of Fallowlees (NZ021962). He allowed the hamlet to decline until only one farm and the bastle remained.

The Blacketts died off in 1777 and Sir John Trevelyan took over at Wallington. In 1812, when Sir John was well over eighty, Blackcock Hall was burnt to the ground. The cause of the fire was never discovered, but local people were sure it was the work of gypsies and a sequel to the murder of Margaret Crozier at The Raw in 1791. William Winter and his two accomplices, who were hung for that crime, had been members of a guild of gypsies who frequently squatted in some cottages at Swindon, near Hepple. In 1792 magistrates, in empathy with public opinion, turned out the squatters and set fire to the cottages. One of those magistrates was Walter Trevelyan of Netherwitton, Sir John's younger brother. No charge of arson was ever laid against the gypsies, but no one had any doubt that after twenty years they had taken their revenge. Possibly this story gave Sir Walter Scott some ideas for his 1815 novel, *Guy Mannering*. A few interrupted courses of stone are all that is left of Blackcock Hall now.

Close to Fallowlees are two knolls, one at the forest edge and the other, called the Comb, a little to the north. The former was thought to be a tumulus until the Forestry Commission dug some of it away and found nothing. Now both are classed as 'eskers', natural ridges of sand and gravel laid down during the last glacial period.

The Hall's sixteenth century bastle is still an evocative sight. One wall and a good part of another stand about six feet high and reveal lower courses and quoins of boulders so large it is a mystery how they were ever put in place. Air shafts penetrate these walls. The rest of the building has disappeared or is reduced to its foundations. There are traces of a later stone extension attached to the south-west end.

Newbiggin

L81   P511   NZ036940   8 km. 5 miles, south of Rothbury

This farm was in existence at least a hundred and fifty years before Rothbury Forest began to be subjected to enclosure acts, for the farmhouse is a bastle derivative.

The building is a mixture of dates and there is nothing external to suggest if was ever fortified, but inside there is a thick bastle wall, a partition between the original and an extension.

Ritton White House

L81   P511   N055944   7 km, 4¹/₂ miles, south of Rothbury

It is a fair bet that any place called 'White House' once belonged to monks who wore white habits. Ritton White House belonged to the Cistercian monks of Newminster Abbey, who were never happier than when soiling their white robes at one of their farms, for they were keen and innovative agriculturists.

The farmstead was given to them in 1250 by Robert fitz Roger, Lord of Warkworth. John Birtley, Abbot of Newminster from 1467, built fortifications at Rothley and Nunnykirk for certain, and most probably here and at Greenleighton at the same time. All were completed before 1500.

The monastery was dissolved round about 1537, and all its land was grabbed by the Crown. In 1541 a tower and barmekyn were reported as being in poor condition, and they were never renovated in spite of being recommended as potentially important for defense in 1584.

There is no sign of the tower today, not even the smallest clue. This is rather ironical as it is one of the few medieval monuments marked on the O.S. Pathfinder map – admittedly as a bastle, which it never was.

Area 4, Sub-Area E   Lower Coquetdale

Hope Farm

L81   P500   NU097015   4 km, 2¹/₂ miles, east of Rothbury

When Brinkburn Priory was founded in c1133, William Bertram granted the Augustinian canons the secluded riverside site for their monastery and a fair strip of land along the northern side of the Coquet to go with it. This extended from the Black Burn in the west to Weldon in the east, and included at the western end the grassy slopes which were, much later, to become Brinkburn Hope, now just Hope Farm. For four hundred years canonic sheep nibbled away at its lush sward before the first lay farmer staked his claim to the land after the Priory was dissolved in 1536. He built a bastle at the end of that century and some evidence of it still exists.

The modern farm was enlarged in 1979 when a brick extension was added to the north side, but the older stone building is of bastle proportions and, in fact, is built on the plinth of the original bastle. A single course of large boulders is very obvious, and the west wall is probably original. There are signs in it of a blocked up waggon entrance, as if the bastle owner, when he considered it safe to do so, had wished to garage his cart inside.

Brinkburn Priory

L81   P511   NZ116983   6¹/₂ km, 4 miles, south-east of Rothbury

While Lindisfarne Monastery and Hulne Priory had fortified refuges, Newminster Abbey and Brinkburn Priory had nothing purpose-built for emergencies. The latter, founded between 1130 and 1135 by William Bertram, Baron of Mitford, as a house for Augustinian canons, had the protection offered by a very secluded position on a well-wooded bend of the River Coquet, yet it had many unwelcome visitations and should have been better equipped for defence.

Brinkburn Priory was never a rich establishment, but, like most monasteries, it did manage to acquire a certain amount of liquid assets which attracted villains. A gold chalice was practically as good as ready cash. In 1322 the Prior had to ask King Edward II for financial assistance because of losses sustained during the Scottish War of Independence. He got some help, and more came in 1333 and 1334, but he was still complaining of poverty in 1391. In 1419 the canons were relieved of their books, vestments, ornaments and charters, and the Bishop of Durham threatened the evil doers with excommunication unless they restored the goods within twenty days.

There is no doubt the reverent gentlemen suffered considerably, but either they were not entirely honest or thieves on one occasion panicked and dumped their booty, for a large hoard of gold coins dating from the reigns of Edward III and Richard II were found by workmen doing repairs in 1834.

Although it had no tower, the priory did have some strongly made buildings which may have been used as refuges. The church is the only complete building on the site today, but fragments of a charter house remain which seem to indicated a most robust structure, and the adjoining manor house has a cellar which is believed to have been the canons' refectory and looks pretty strong too.

After dissolution in 1536 the convent buildings passed through many secular hands, including those of the Fenwicks, who built the manor-house, and the Hodgsons, who rebuilt it in the 1830s. In 1965 the whole site was given to the nation and is looked after now by English Heritage.

Brinkheugh

L81   P511   NZ121984   7¹/₂ km, 4¹/₂ miles, south-east of Rothbury

Brinkburn Priory's original endowment of local land was on the northern side of the River Coquet and included Hope Farm. No documentary evidence can be found to connect property on the south side of the river with the Priory, and it is significant that the known history of the township of Brinkburn, which adjoined the Priory, does not start until a few years after dissolution.

The township comprised the three farms of Thistleyhaugh, Westerheugh and Brinkheugh. The joint owners in 1568 were Roger Thornton and Cuthbert Horsley, the latter of Longhorsley. It is understood that throughout Queen Elizabeth's reign Brinkheugh was a favourite residence of the Horsleys, who found it less draughty than their tower at Longhorsley. Later purchasers were James Bilton in 1660, John Fenwick of Morpeth in 1746 and C.H. Cadogan in 1856.

Brinkheugh farmhouse today is a pleasant two-gabled building. The front half is late seventeenth century, and the rear is a bastle which still exhibits several original features. The long north wall has been heavily daubed with cement but the outline of the upstairs blocked-in entrance can be seen still. The ground floor doorway has been hidden by low extensions. High up on the west gable is a small square window with vertical iron bars. The walls are four feet thick.

Longhorsley

L81   P511   NZ146946   11¹/₂ km, 7 miles, south-east of Rothbury

A manor in the Beanley serjeanty granted by King Henry I to Gospatric, son of the 1069 to 1072 Earl of Northumberland. One of his daughters, Juliana, married Randulf de Merley, Baron of Morpeth, and Longhorsley, with Stanton and Netherwitton, went to him as a dowry. One of their daughters married William Lord Greystoke in 1271 and they got Longhorsley, and held on to it for a long time. During the fifteenth century the manor was divided into two estates and the Lindon part was conveyed to the Dacre family of Naworth Castle, then on to the Howards, who eventually became the Earls of Carlisle. In 1765 this estate was sold to C.W. Bigge. The other part of Longhorsley went to the Horsley family sometime before 1358.

Like the manor, the Horsley family was also in two parts, and it was the High Farnham part which got the first mention: in 1244 Roger de Horsley was one of the jurors at the inquest of Gilbert de Umfraville. The other, more enduring, Horsley family was not chronicled until 1320 when Roger de Horsley was appointed one of the keepers of a truce arranged between the English and the Scots. In 1337 he was constable of Bamburgh Castle for a year, and when he died, in 1358, he was assessed as holding Scrainwood and land at Longhorsley.

Come the seventeenth century and this property was still in Horsley hands. Sir Thomas Horsley left it to his only child, Dorethy, who married twice. Her first husband was 65 year old Robert Lisle of Felton, and when he died in 1659 Dorethy carried Scrainwood, Longhorsley and Felton to her second husband, Captain Edward Widdrington of Rock.

The head of the next generation, another Edward, built a mansion at Felton in 1732. He styled himself 'Edward Horsley Widdrington' to acknowledge the benevolence of his ancestors, and his main claim to fame was his generosity to the Duke of Cumberland's army as it passed through Felton on its way to Culloden in 1746. It is said that he caused "the contents of his well-stocked cellar to be carted to the village street where he regaled the different corps as they advanced with bread, beef and beer". This gesture was not entirely philanthropic: an earlier Widdrington had marched with the 1715 Jacobites so he felt it advisable to demonstrate his loyalty to King George II.

When Edward died in 1760 all his property joined the Swinburn Castle empire as his daughter was married to Thomas Riddell. Since that time there has been some selling in Longhorsley and Felton, while Scrainwood was sold to Walter Selby of Biddlestone in 1828.

There is still a very fine, inhabited tower in the Horsley part of Longhorsley. It was probably built during the sixteenth century by one of the Horsleys. A tall, rectangular building measuring 42 by 30 feet, it has a vaulted ground floor, three upper storeys and a flag turret. Windows have been replaced, but little else has been done externally, while the interior has been well maintained to a high standard. Now it is a luxury home with two bathrooms, five bedrooms and two dungeons (very useful for grandchildren), the whole assessed in 1992 at £400,000. For many years at the beginning of the twentieth century it was used as a presbytery, and there is a small Roman Catholic chapel next door. To its north is a walled enclosure which was once a deer park; when Sir Walter Blackett of Wallington wished to stock his Rothley Park he got his deer from here.

The situation today is that the Lindon part of Longhorsley is dominated by the Lindon Hall Hotel and the remaining village is mostly owned by freeholders.

Swarland Old Hall

L81   P500   NU159019   10½ km, 6½ miles, east of Rothbury

Old Swarland was a parcel of the Bertrams' Mitford barony in the twelfth century. It was let to several tenants, then in 1270 it was sold to Thomas de Carliolo, a burgess of Newcastle whose descendants dropped the final 'o' and became wealthy merchants. Newcastle landmarks such as Carliol Square and Carliol House commemorate them.

Peter Graper, a wool merchant, married a Carliolo heiress in 1334 and acquired Old Swarland. By a similar marriage contract it went to the Hazlerigg family in 1389, various branches of which held it until 1735. The last of one branch, bachelor Robert Hazlerigg, built Swarland Old Hall for himself and bought the neighbouring estate of Overgrass for his cousin, all in 1640.

Mackenzie described the mansion as being "in the worst style of architectural bad taste", but it was redeemed in his eyes "by incorporating the gable of an old keep". To modern, less critical eyes it seems quite a pleasant house. It is not very big – inside it is really quite small as so much of the front part is wasted in hall and stairway – with just four bays and two storeys plus attic. The windows have semicircular pediments which look rather like arched eyebrows. What is decidedly strange about the place is its east gable, a wall considerably higher than the house, topped with battlements and containing three arch-shaped depressions resembling blocked-up windows. This curio could not be older than the house, and is more likely to be a younger addition; it certainly is not the gable of an old keep.

The present owner of the house, who recently had extensive repairs and modernisation done, suggests that one of the Hazleriggs – perhaps Robert or one of the later members – had this gable built to kid passers-by he lived in a castle. Not very convincing but it is difficult to think of a better reason for such a pretentious absurdity. There is nothing in the vicinity older than the house, and no mention of a medieval fortification can be found in the records, so it rather looks as if Mackenzie was fooled by the curious end wall.

In 1735 the Old Hall was sold to Richard Grieve of Alnwick. Thirty years later a new Swarland Hall was built in beautiful parkland about a mile to the east. The builder was Alexander Davison, an army clothing contractor, who claimed to be a friend of Lord Nelson. In 1807 he erected an obelisk at the side of what was then the Great North Road (NU174029); it was inscribed "Not to commemorate the Public Virtue and Heroic Achievements of Nelson, which is the duty of England, but to the memory of Private Friendship, this Erection is dedicated by Alexander Davison". A year later Davison was fined and imprisoned for fraudulently accepting Government commission on the sale of private stock. The mansion was demolished in the 1950s but the obelisk is still there, although not so prominent as its companion on Lanton Hill in Glendale.

Overgrass and Newmoor

L81   P500   NU144033   9 km, 5$^1/_2$ miles, north-east of Rothbury

Overgrass tower, in its heyday, strongly defended its owner and the local peasants, but now, in its decadence, it itself is defended by massive weeds and a muddy approach. Definitely a place to visit in wellington time, when the nettles and thistles are resting.

For all that, the ruin is beautifully situated on a haugh made by the Swarland Burn, a lively little tributary of the Coquet. The ground floor vault is still intact with walls over six feet thick.

It demonstrates very clearly how in their original state such places would have been quite unsuitable for housing cattle or sheep. The lower steps of a newel staircase are supposed to be visible, but they are only to those with vivid imagination. Much of the ashlar remains outside, and a lot of stonework still stands around the tower, parts of a barmekyn and bits of houses of the old village that used to be here.

The replacement, but still old, village is up the stream's right bank, close to Newmoor Hall. This three hundred year old mansion, once owned by the Manners of Etal Castle, is, or was when last seen, in urgent need of repair, yet it is still a delight, especially its Doric pilasters around the main entrance. The village is a collection of largely derelict houses, one of which is a bastle.

Overgrass and Newmoor were separate estates until 1874, although originally both were in the Mitford barony. Overgrass was occupied by Ralph de Herle from about 1256; he was probably a younger brother of Hugh de Herle of Little Harle. In 1355 a descendant, Sir Robert Herle, passed the property to his sister who was married to Sir Ralph de Hastings. One of the Forsters of Adderstone was the owner in mid-sixteenth century, then in 1640 Robert Hazlerigg, living in the adjoining estate of Swarland, bought it for his cousin of Sleekburn, another Robert Hazlerigg.

This branch of the family remained static much longer than did the Swarland people, but in 1874 they sold Overgrass to W.J. Robinson of Newmoor Hall. The two estates have been worked as one farm ever since by Mr Robinson's descendants.

Newton Green

L81   P500   NU160040   11 km, 6$^3/_4$ miles, north-east of Rothbury

A farm about half a mile west of the village of Newton-on-the-Moor and was included in the estate Rameta Viscount acquired from the Alnwick barony in

1256. Descent was as Embleton's, via Simon de Montford et al. Owners after 1600 included the Strothers, Widdringtons and Lisles. A Widdrington family, incidentally, still lives in nearby Newton Hall.

The farmhouse is basically a bastle with thick walls, traces of a blocked-up upper doorway and a slit vent near ground level. It looks like a comfortable Tudor house now, thanks to extensive alterations in 1661 – commemorated by an inscription 'PM 1661' over the door – and 1889.

Shilbottle

L81   P500   NU195087   15½ km, 9½ miles, north-east of Rothbury

An ancient village, thought to have been at one time the 'abode of Shiplinge', an Anglian nobleman. Its church, rebuilt in 1885 but containing elements of its Norman predecessor, has a pre-1415 fortified tower at one side of its graveyard. Until recently this was used as the vicarage, but it would appear that it was not built for this purpose because in 1526 it was let by the owner, the Earl of Northumberland, to Charles Watson, a layman, for six pence a year.

The ground floor of this tower is the original vault, but the upper floor and the adjoining house were built in 1863. The whole has been modernised and maintained as an attractive dwelling.

A short distance south-west of Shilbottle is a house called High Whittle and a farm called Low Whittle (NU183066) where once there was a hamlet which, on one October night in 1522, became the target for a Scottish raid. Mark Ker of Cessford had a feud with Henry, the fifth Earl of Northumberland, and, just to show him he could do what he liked on the English side of the Border, Mark let it be known that he intended to come within three miles of the Earl's house to "give him a light to dress by at midnight". It matters not which house he meant, for he came to Whittle which is about three country miles from both Alnwick and Warkworth. He came with thirty horsemen, and not one of them had thought to bring flint and tinder. Not a fire was burning in the hamlet, and no means of starting one could be found. Frustrated, Mark killed a pregnant woman then returned home, leaving the Duke to dress in the dark.

Acton

L81   P500   NU184024   13 km, 8 miles, east of Rothbury

Originally in the Mitford barony, Acton found its way into the Percy empire during the sixteenth century. A report of a survey of the Alnwick barony dated 1584 mentions the existence of a ruined 'bastle house', in modern parlance probably a tower or a strong house. Nothing now to see.

Felton

L81   P500   NU185003   12¹/₂ km, 7³/₄ miles, east of Rothbury

Where the Great North Road crosses the Tyne there is Newcastle's castle, at the Wansbeck crossing there is Morpeth castle, at the Aln there is Alnwick castle and at the Tweed there is Berwick castle, but where the road crosses the Coquet there is nothing – and, so far as can be ascertained, there never has been any sort of fortification there. Very unusual.

Perhaps it is understandable, though, as Felton was owned by no less than eight different families in three hundred years, and they were all absent landlords with seats elsewhere.

The Bertrams, Barons of Mitford, were the first known owners; they had Felton from early twelfth century to 1265. A member of the Balliol family, Barons of Bywell, possessed it from 1265 to 1278, and then it was passed to his widow who took Robert de Stuteville as her second husband.

The Stutevilles, father and son held it to 1314, during which period we hear of William of Felton, but he bought Edlingham in 1294 and was not a major landlord in Felton. The next owner was Aymer de Valence, Earl of Pembroke, who bought the place in 1314. In 1323 a niece of Aymer's wife, married to David Strathbolgi, Earl of Athol, got the property and passed it on to her son in 1330, who held it until 1375. David's uncle, Sir Aymer de Athol, owned it from 1375 to 1403, when it went to his son-in-law, Sir Ralph de Eure. The last in this glissade was Ralph's brother-in-law, Sir Robert de Lisle, who took charge in 1421.

Sir Robert and his descendants held Felton until 1659, except for a few years of forfeiture during the sixteenth century. Their main seat was at Newton Hall near Bywell in Tynedale, but they sold that in 1537 and it is not known where they lived after that, or, indeed, if they lived at all after 1659. The other Newton Hall, two miles from Felton, was not built until 1772.

The rest of Felton's descent has been recounted already under Longhorsley. Edward Horsley Widdrington built a mansion there in 1732, and in 1760 it went by marriage to the Riddells.

The pantechnicons were so busy in Felton during the thirteenth and fourteenth centuries it hardly had room for anything else, yet in 1215 it was host to King Alexander II of Scotland and a large gathering of northern magnates. The latter were so dissatisfied with their lawful monarch, King John, that they preferred to throw in their lot with the Scottish king, and they assembled at Felton to do homage to him. When King John heard of this he very quickly and decisively dealt with the dissidents.

While Humphrey de Lisle was the proprietor, in 1557, Felton had a hostile visit from Lord Home. Fortunately Sir Henry Percy was on hand to chase him away, but there was more serious trouble the following year when General d'Oysel brought a Franco-Scottish force of over a thousand horsemen to the village. Again Percy foiled the enemy's plans, but not before Felton was virtually destroyed. It could have done with a castle or tower then.

Eshott

L81   P512   NZ200985   15 km, 9½ miles, south-east of Rothbury

A very explicit earthwork disturbs the tranquillity of a flat grass field near the confluence of the Eshott and Longdike Burns, about a half mile north of Eshott Hall (NZ220978). No stones are visible above the grass, yet here at one time stood an impressive stone fortification.

Eshott was a manor in the Mitford barony in the twelfth century. When Baron William Bertram died in 1199 he left an under-aged son who had as a guardian William Briewere, Lord of Horsley, near Belper in Derbyshire. Briewere's bailiff, a very ambitious and resourceful man called Godfrey Mauduit, managed, in ways it is perhaps best not to delve into, to persuade King John to confirm the estates of both Eshott and Bockenfield, its neighbour, on him. This happened in 1200.

Godfrey's grandson, Robert, applied successfully in 1310 to King Edward II for a licence to crenellate, and he built what was officially called a castle. In 1358 a confirmation of the grant covered "the castle, town and manor" of Eshott. So on two occasions the Crown called the Mauduit fortification a castle, yet quite obviously it was too small to contain all the essential ingredients of a true castle, and it was more likely to have been a tower, rather like the 'camera' at Tarset in North Tynedale. In support of this contention is the fact that the ground around the building is quite flat and thus would be difficult to defend, also that the Mauduits were never wealthy enough to build or run a castle.

In 1377 the estate was sold to Sir John Heron of Ford and his descendants held it for nearly two hundred years, probably using it as a centre for field sports. Names like Bockenfield, The Brocks, Kennel Wood and The Pheasantry seem to suggest that this went on in the neighbourhood.

When the Herons lost Ford to the Carrs in the sixteenth century the latter got Eshott as well, and held it until William Carr dismantled the stronghold and had Trollope build Eshott Hall with its stones. One of the nineteenth century owners, the present owner's great-great-grandfather, was E.M. Bainbridge, founder of the world's first department store. The building got a face-lift in the eighteenth century and another, inside and out, was started in 1996.

Butlesdon House, Low Buston

L81   P501   NU224074   18 km, 11 miles, north-east of Rothbury

Butlesdon is thought to be the name of the original, now deserted, village which lay a little lower down the Tyelaw Burn and belonged, extraordinarily, to the barons of Wark-on-Tweed and Carham,. It was granted to Walter Espec by King Henry I and descended through the Ros family. The Greys of Wark and Castle Heaton had it from about 1400, and it was not until 1623 that it got a local owner, one of the Forsters of Adderstone. It was probably this family who built what eventually became Low Buston Hall, renamed the village and moved it to be near the Hall.

Butlesdon House beat them to it. It was built in 1601 and thus is the oldest building in the village. Seen from its garden on its south side, it still looks like a bastle, but all detail has been hidden by extensions against its west and north walls, while one of Low Buston Hall's out-buildings blocks the view from the west. Thick walls are a feature of the original house.

Warkworth

L81   P501   NU247057   20 km, 12½ miles, north-east of Rothbury

Nature has given Warkworth the ideal defensive site which has been used as such by all settlers since the Stone Age. The mischievous River Coquet plays its last trick here before running into the sea; by describing a sharp bend around a rocky obstruction, it provides a tongue large enough to accommodate a village at the closed end and a castle mound at the open end.

Here was a Votadini hill fort before and during the Roman occupation. Here, also, the Bernician kings founded a settlement and a stronghold to guard it. According to legend, the illegitimate descendants of King Ida lived here. Later, Ceolwulf, King of Northumbria from 731, founded a church in the settlement then gave it and the stronghold to the monks of Lindisfarne when he abdicated in 737 to embrace a monastic life. In taking this step he probably was influenced by his great friend and mentor, Bede of Jarrow monastery, who dedicated his *Ecclesiastical History* to him.

King Osbert sacrilegiously revoked Ceolwulf's grant and grabbed Warkworth for his own use. His death in battle in 855 was regarded as just retribution, but it meant that no one was in command to save Warkworth from the Vikings when they sailed up the Coquet in 875. They effectively closed down historic records for the next two hundred years.

It was the custom in the eleventh century to award land recovered from the Vikings to the county earl. Thus it could have been any one of half a dozen post-Conquest earls, but most likely either Gospatric or Waltheof, who was responsible for constructing a motte and bailey castle, the new-fangled type of fortification introduced by King William I, on Warkworth's mound. Under its protection the settlement became established as a village, and its tithes were a much appreciated gift which Earl Robert de Mowbray presented to the monks of his recently founded priory at Tynemouth between 1087 and 1095.

The unexpected decision of King Stephen's, after his victory over Scottish King David I at the Battle of the Standard in 1138, to grant the whole of Northumberland, except his old and new castles at Bamburgh and Newcastle, to David's son, Prince Henry, to hold as an earldom, was said to have been suggested by the Pope as an appeasement to the Scots. As such it worked very well and Northumberland enjoyed a period of peace. Prince Henry worked diligently for fourteen years to improve the welfare of his 'subjects'. He insisted on living on the job and he built a suitable residence and headquarters, protected from local dissidents by a stone curtain wall, on Warkworth's mound.

Prince Henry died in 1152 and William, his son, took over, but King Henry II cancelled the earldom and reinstated Northumberland as an English shire in 1158. Warkworth was granted to Roger fitz Richard for one knight fee, a low price which reflected the king's gratitude for past brave deeds. Although a soldier, Roger soon found that owning a Border castle was no sinecure. In 1162 William, the displaced earl and now the king of Scotland, tried to recover Northumberland by force, and in 1173 he got round to attacking Warkworth. He easily captured Roger's castle, but it proved to be a short term victory for William was taken prisoner at Alnwick the following year.

Roger died in 1177 and was succeeded by Robert fitz Roger, a child who lived in Norfolk. He moved to Warkworth when King John confirmed the grant on him in 1199, and, realising what he had been missing, he became very interested in Northumberland and Northern affairs. He was the county sheriff in 1203, and two years later his friend, King John, granted him more land, including Corbridge and Rothbury. This made him a wealthy man and enabled him to rebuild Warkworth castle.

His first priority was to add considerably to the strength of the place. This he did by making the north and east sides of the mound and bailey much steeper, and by digging a wide moat across the south side, which was adjacent to flat fields. The west side drops steeply to the river and needed no strengthening. Behind the moat he built a massive curtain wall with a tower at its west end – he called it the Carrickfergus tower after his Irish estate – and a gatehouse at its centre. This, with guardrooms either side and a long vaulted entry, still exists although it was heightened during Edward I's reign. Creature comfort and domestic efficiency also got attention, and Prince Henry's residence was extended and a solus added, making it an attractive hall house. In the bailey he built a chapel and other houses for his entourage, Finally, he built a structure of some military importance on top of the mound, but as nothing remains of it it is not known what it was. It could have been a keep, or perhaps just a watch tower.

The lords of Warkworth dwelt here with apparent contentment throughout the thirteenth century. In 1310 the owner was John fitz Robert who at last made a concession to fashion and adopted a surname; he chose Clavering, the name of his estate in Essex. Relations with Scotland were extremely tense during his tenure and the castle's garrison was enlarged, his own troop of twelve men at arms being supplemented by four men at arms and eight light horsemen, or hobelars, provided by King Edward II. In 1323 the king ordered John to provision the castle generously, to guard it diligently and to be ready at any time for an attack. A couple of attacks were experienced in 1327, but they were half-hearted affairs, easily quelled.

Perhaps John was rather too generous, for when he died in 1332 he was so far in debt the Crown felt it necessary to seize his Warkworth and Rothbury properties in settlement. Fortunately for his brother, Alan Clavering, Callaly was not involved, and it was fortunate, too, that John had no family to disappoint. The Crown granted Warkworth and other Northumbrian estates to Henry, the second Lord Percy of Alnwick.

Warkworth Castle became the favourite northern home of the powerful Percy family until the sixteenth century – inspite of its damning description by Shakespeare in Henry IV Part 2 as "this worm-eaten hold of ragged stone". Perhaps the Bard was not aware that the place had been improved considerably in the early fourteenth century. The gatehouse had been repaired, the curtain walls strengthened, the Grey Mare's Tail tower had been built into the east wall and the structure on top of the mound had become, either by amendment of rebuilding, a true keep, a small part of which is to seen in the present keep.

Ambitious plans were made by the first Earl of Northumberland, but his premature death on Bramham Moor in 1409 prevented him from proceeding. His only memento was the damage done by seven discharges from King Henry IV's cannon in 1405 when he was being punished for treacherous behaviour. The plans were put in hand by Hotspur's son: they included a new front to the hall house and a completely new keep, the massive structure which still dominates the scene today.

It is a complex building which, although immensely strong, also panders to the human desire for comfort: it is more like a tower house than a keep. It is a square with about 65 feet sides, flattened corners and large bays projecting at the centre of each wall. The first floor has an entrance lobby and is vaulted throughout; it is given over very largely to military requirements and includes a guardroom, with a punishment pit below it on the ground floor. It is interesting to note how the many chambers and the staircase are arranged so that an enemy gaining admission would find it difficult to find his way. The upper floors are devoted almost entirely to domesticity, with a great hall, solus, chapel and large kitchens. Running from top to bottom in the centre of the building is a square shaft called the lantern which lets in light and rain water, the latter to flush the garderobe outlets.

Another item on the first earl's plan, and only partly carried out by the second earl, was to found a college for secular canons within the bailey. The idea was to use some of the existing buildings and to build a collegiate church across the width of the bailey. The foundations for the church were laid and are still evident, but the scheme was soon scrapped.

The third earl, another Henry, was killed in 1461 while fighting for the Lancastrians in the Wars of the Roses Battle of Towton. The Yorkists took over Warkworth next year and the Earl of Warwick used the castle as his headquarters while laying siege to Bamburgh, Alnwick and Dunstanburgh castles. The Percys did not get their home back until 1469, and the third earl's son was not styled Earl of Northumberland until 1471. He was murdered by his tenants when he tried to levy an unpopular tax.

His son, 'The Magnificent', brought Warkworth to its pinnacle of grandeur, although he lived mainly in the south and came north only occasionally. He added elegance and style to the hall house, built the Lion tower as a porch to this, repaired the other buildings in the bailey and made the keep more comfortable. He and his successor also repaired or rebuilt some of the curtain wall.

After this it was downhill all the way for the castle. The sixth earl gave his property to the Crown in exchange for a life annuity, and for twenty years Warkworth was used only by Border wardens. When returned to the Percys in 1557 the hall house needed reroofing, but the seventh earl had no time to repair it before he was captured and beheaded for joining the Rising of the North. The castle was never again the home of earls; the eighth and ninth spent much of their lives in the Tower of London, and when they were free they were forbidden to live in the north.

In or about 1604 the 'manor house or castle called Warkworth Castle' was leased to Sir Ralph Grey of Chillingham. He never lived there and did nothing to stop the rot. A survey taken in 1608 said that all the buildings in the bailey except the keep were ruinous and the place was being used as a cattle fold, its gates left open day and night. By 1618 the keep was being used as a grain store, while during the Civil War it was commandeered on two occasions as barracks, in 1644 for the Scottish army and in 1648 for Cromwell's soldiers. The coup de grace came in 1672, administered, rather ironically, by a Percy. The widow of the eleventh earl gave her estate auditor, John Clarke, permission to use the castle as a quarry. He is said to have taken 272 cartloads of lead, timber and stones to Chirton, near North Shields, where he was building a manor-house.

He left the castle a picturesque ruin. The fourth Duke of Northumberland did repair the keep and made its top storey habitable, but the eighth duke in 1922 placed the castle under the guardianship of the then Ministry of Works. Now it is an English Heritage property.

The main street of Warkworth village runs gently downhill from the castle to the river. Although it was the castle's moat, essential to its defence, the Coquet nevertheless had to be crossed here, if only for the convenience of the villagers. A bridge was built during the last quarter of the fourteenth century, and to ensure only people with legitimate business used it, it was provided with a small fortified tower.

A bridge tower is unique in Northumberland and rare in the country, and this one is a fine example. It is a square building on the south side of the river. It has a rounded archway through it and its upper parts are ruinous. When no longer needed for its designed purpose, it became the local gaol, a duty it performed until the nineteenth century. A modern bridge, built alongside, carries the vehicular traffic today, but the old one is still used by pedestrians.

Coquet Island

L81   P501   NU293045   24 km, 15 miles, east of Rothbury

This 16 acre, flat, wind-swept island lies about a mile off Amble and the mouth of the River Coquet. St. Cuthbert knew of it and legend has it that Elfledo, Abbess of Whitby, met him there in 684 and tried in vain to persuade him to accept the bishopric of Hexham. Bede talked of it as a "concourse of monks" so possibly the early Tynemouth church had an interest there. They certainly had later, in the 1090s, for the Priory established a Benedictine cell and maintained it until dissolution. One of the earliest inhabitants was a Dane, styled St. Henry of Coquet, who went there with Tynemouth's permission to escape an unsavoury marriage. Sometime before 1415 the Prior of Tynemouth built a small tower on the island to protect the monks from pirates.

After the cell was disbanded in 1539 the island was granted to the Earl of Warwick, who had a temporary hold on the Northumberland estates. He was executed in 1553 and the island was granted to the Widdrington family who owned much of the adjoining mainland. They seemed to have ignored the gift for it acquired an evil reputation as a thieves hide-out. In 1567 it became known as "a place of secretness for coiners". Just as well the counterfeiters produced such poor coins they were soon put out of business.

The Civil War touched the island slightly in 1644. King Charles stationed two hundred men on it with orders to let the Scottish army pass then to come ashore and attack it in its rear. General Leslie got to hear of the plan and did a quick cleansing job as he marched towards Newcastle.

In 1753 'Cockett Island' joined the Northumberland estates. By arrangement with the third duke, Trinity House erected a lighthouse in 1839 and as solid foundations for it the ground floor vault of the fifteenth century tower was made use of. Forty years later the Warkworth Harbour Commission had the idea of using the island as a prison and joining it to the mainland with breakwaters. This proposal did not get very far.

Today the island is a bird sanctuary belonging to the RSPB. It is one of the most important sites in Europe for the endangered roseate tern. Humans are not allowed to land, so the best view of the lighthouse on a tower is obtained from the mainland coast between Amble and Hauxley. Alternatively, there is a lovely framed view from a window in Warkworth Castle.

Gatehouse, North Bastle, showing the stairs which were added when the danger of attacks had receded. (p296)

Area 5
Wansbeck and Blyth

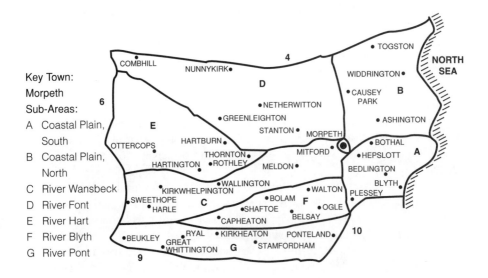

Key Town:
Morpeth
Sub-Areas:
A Coastal Plain, South
B Coastal Plain, North
C River Wansbeck
D River Font
E River Hart
F River Blyth
G River Pont

A large area drained, in the main, by two rivers and their many tributaries. The land generally is fertile except, formerly, in the coastal plain where there was much heavy clay until field drainage was introduced in the mid-nineteenth century. Coal was a compensation. Wilder scenery exists in the north-west, although there is nothing over 1000 feet, and the south-east borders on, and is slightly tainted by, industrial Tyneside.

Key Town
Morpeth
L81   P523/4   NZ200855

Not long after the Norman Conquest, William de Merley was granted Morpeth Barony, a reward for helping his king to establish a presence in

213

Northumberland. de Merley built a motte and bailey castle on top of Ha' Hill, well positioned to overlook a crossing of the River Wansbeck and a settlement in a loop of the river.

When the Conqueror died, in 1087, the de Merleys were one of the many families who thought Robert Curthose should inherit the throne of England and not his younger brother, William Rufus. They joined the rebellion initiated by Robert de Mowbray, Earl of Northumberland, and for their trouble had their home destroyed when King William II came north in 1095 to settle his score with Mowbray. A rather smaller replacement castle, which may have included some stonework, was built on the same site.

The settlement at Morpeth grew in size and importance, and in 1138, when Randulf de Merley was the baron, it was classified as a burgh. It was Randulf and his wife, Juliana, a daughter of Gospatric, who that year founded the Cistercian abbey of Newminster, less than a mile to the west of Morpeth. Juliana, incidentally, brought Netherton, Stanton and Longhorsley into the barony as her dowry.

The de Merleys of early thirteenth century virtually re-enacted the mistake of their eleventh century ancestors. Roger, who held the barony from 1212, joined several other local gentry in paying homage to Scottish King Alexander II at Felton in 1215, thereby registering a vote of no confidence in the English king, John. Vengeance was quick and decisive; Morpeth castle was reduced to a ruin.

In spite of this, Roger continued to live in Morpeth until he died in 1271. Four daughters, no sons, were his beneficiaries, but Mary, married to William de Greystoke, got most of the barony. The part including Netherwitton went to Isobel, wife of Robert de Somerville.

The Greystokes were lords of a very scattered barony centred on Penrith in Cumberland. They held some estates in Coquetdale, but in 1271 they were in the process of giving these away so that they could concentrate on their lands further south. William de Greystoke appeared to be grateful for his wife's inheritance, nevertheless, and he and his successors held most of it for two hundred years. In the early part of the fourteenth century one of them built a keep and bailey stone castle on a hill just to the east of Ha' Hill. It was listed in the 1415 survey when the owner was an unspecified Baron of Greystoke.

The Dacre family superseded the Greystokes in the latter part of the fifteenth century. The name 'Dacre' crops up frequently in the history of the marches and, because it is a long way from their home in Naworth Castle near Brampton, they may have used Morpeth while working in the east.

Being the lord of Morpeth was no sinecure. A well known cattle market was held weekly in the town and, despite all the restrictions on cross-Border travel, many Scottish farmers attended it. Their presence was enough to endanger peace, but throw in some Redesdale reivers as well and it is no wonder that one of the Dacres found it necessary to build a fortified tower in Bridge Street (NZ199859) for the protection of the townspeople.

George Dacre was the last of the line, and he was killed in a riding accident in 1569. He was an adventurous child and his horse was wooden and rocked. His mother Elizabeth had recently discarded her widow' weeds to marry Lord William Howard. There was a very long legal battle between him and the Dacre uncles about the ownership of the Dacre estates, and in 1603, just before she died, Queen Elizabeth herself intervened; she found in favour of Howard, so Morpeth became his. In 1661 Charles Howard became the first Earl of Carlisle and either he or a descendant renovated the castle's gatehouse and installed his agent in it.

The rest of the castle was not touched, probably being considered beyond repair. When General Leslie marched down from Scotland towards Newcastle and Marston Moor in January 1644 to help the Parliamentarians win the Civil War, he had left a troop of his men there and their commanding officer, Lt.Col. Somerville, had described his quarters as "This ruinous hole, not tenable by nature and far less by art". It was still strong. however, and it took the Marquis of Montrose and his Royalist troops twenty days and six cannon to regain the place.

Nothing more happened to the castle until the gatehouse was once more made habitable in the nineteenth century. The tower in Bridge Street outlived its original purpose and was converted in 1704 into a gaol. It served in this capacity until the purpose-built prison, designed by John Dobson, was opened in 1829. This is the castellated building on the main road into the town, opposite Carlisle Park; it is often mistaken for the castle, but in fact it is not fortified.

Of the three medieval strongholds of which Morpeth can boast, the oldest, the motte and bailey, is lost without trace although Ha' Hill, its site, has a flattened top which looks as if manpower has been employed in shaping it. Dacre's tower has been modified out of recognition but its bones are still in situ, now housing the Department of Social Security, which somehow seems appropriate. When it was converted into a gaol large buildings were added to its back, and these were used in the nineteenth century as workshops and a brewery.

The gatehouse of the Greystokes fourteenth century castle has once again been renovated and is let as holiday accommodation. Behind it a fair amount of curtain wall remains but at the time of writing the bailey was a jungle. It may have been tidied up by now.

Morpeth can boast, also, of several famous sons. They include, in chronological order, Dr William Turner 1608 – 1568, Dr John Horsley 1686 – 1732, Admiral Cuthbert Collingwood 1750 – 1810, and Robert Morrison 1782 – 1834. Turner was the first man in England to study plants scientifically; his classic work, *The New Herbal*, was published in sections between 1551 and 1568. Horsley was a local historian and author of *Britannia Romana*; he is called sometimes 'the father of British archaeology. Collingwood, whose house still stands in Outgate, near the Clock Tower, was Nelson's second-in-command at the Battle of Traffalgar and took command when Nelson was killed. Morrison, probably the least well known of the quartet, was a missionary in China and translated the whole Bible into Chinese. He also wrote a Chinese grammar and dictionary.

Area 5, Sub-Area A   The Coastal Plain – South
Bothal

L81   P524   NZ240865   4 km, 2¹/₂ miles, east of Morpeth

The name is derived from the Old English 'Bottell', meaning 'abode' (as Harbottle = army abode), but the earliest documented evidence about Bothal was dated in William II's reign. This was a contract confirming the grant of the tithes – one tenth of its annual product – from Robert de Mowbray to the Prior of Tynemouth.

When in 1095 Mowbray rebelled against his king and had his property sequestrated, Bothal was granted by the Crown to Guy de Balliol to add to Bywell barony, given to him by the same king a couple of years earlier. This was most convenient as Guy's daughter Hawise was about to marry William Bertram, the Baron of Mitford, and Bothal, just four miles down stream from Mitford, made a most appropriate dowry for the bride to bring to her groom.

Ungrateful soul that he was, William passed Bothal on to his younger brother Richard. There was no castle there then, just a hall house, probably of timber, but it served the cadet branch of the family a lot longer than Mitford served the seniors.

Six generations of male Bertrams passed down from Richard in an orderly, unremarkable fashion, then the seventh, Sir Robert Bertram, showed some initiative. He became high sheriff and, during his term of office, in 1343, he applied successfully for a licence to crenellate his house. He started to build his castle at Bothal and had it habitable three years later when he had to dash over to Durham to help stop David Bruce at Neville's Cross. King Edward III made a special point of thanking Sir Robert for this service, but a few months later Edward was reprimanding him for allowing the Earl of Wigton, a prisoner taken at the battle, to escape.

Sir Robert had no sons; his daughter, Helan married Sir Robert Ogle, so Bothal joined the Ogle estates when Helen inherited in 1362 or '64. Their son, another Sir Robert Ogle, fought at Otterburn in 1388 and died in 1409, leaving Ogle to his elder son, yet another Sir Robert, and Bothal to his younger son, Sir John.

This arrangement may seem to be a fairly reasonable way to provide for two sons, but the elder did not think so. Indeed he felt so upset about not being left his father's total wealth that he took up arms against brother John. Bothal Castle was besieged for four days before Robert got possession. But justice will out: John appealed to the courts and the aggressor was forced to quit. This show of fraternal discord so sickened John he changed his surname from Ogle to Bertram, his grandmother's maiden name.

The new Bertrams lasted two generations, then died out and Bothal went to the then next of kin, Ewyn, the second Lord Ogle, during his tenure of Ogle Castle, 1461 to 1486. He and several of his successors preferred Bothal to Ogle and used it as their principal seat.

The Ogle family kept tight hold of both Ogle and Bothal although, because of distaff links, names such as Shrewsbury, Cavenish, Newcastle, Oxford and Portland appear on the list of owners.

Somewhere along the line, probably in the sixteenth century, a son of the house married a Carnaby heiress. Before the wedding the bride's father, Cuthbert Carnaby, visited Bothal to inspect his daughter's future home. His thoughts about the castle are lost, but his enthusiasm for the garden is on record still: "Where-in grows all kinds of herbs and flowers, and fine apples, plums of all kinds, and pears, damsons, nuts, wardens (a cooking pear), black and red cherries, walnuts. also licorices, very fine".

What he might have said about the castle was that it was a noble complex caught, with its beautiful village, in a tree-lines dene at the apex of one of the Wansbeck's attempts to draw an inverted 'V'. He would have noticed, had he taken his eyes off the fruit, that its layout was typically Norman, inspite of its late building date and except that the keep was also the gatehouse. This fine building would have appealed to his status-seeking instincts; it was, and still is, a 40 by 30 feet rectangle with two semi-octagonal turrets at each side of a vaulted passage, above which are two stone figures and a series of armorial shields. These decorations are said to be genuine, not Gothick floss as at Alnwick. The figures depict a horn blower and a man about to throw a heavy weight onto the heads of intruders below. The shields are those of influential friends and relations who could be expected to lend their support should the castle be attacked.

The keep has been well maintained and modernised internally, and is still habitable. At the present time it is used as a hospitality suite by a local electronics company and thus is not open to the public. The great hall occupies the whole of the first floor, while other domestic and military offices were in separate buildings in the bailey, unfortunately no longer standing. The curtain wall remains, intact in most places. A good view of the front of the castle can be obtained from the village and the curtain wall is visible from the roads from Pegswood and Hepscott.

Hepscott

L81   P524   NZ223841   3 km, 2 miles, south-east of Morpeth

This little community has always been closely associated with Morpeth and now can almost be described as a suburb of that town. Most of its houses are highly desirable, modern residences, but one, Hepscott Hall, is rather old, having been built in the thirteenth century.

It was built as a tower by Roger de Merley, Baron of Morpeth, during the reign of Henry III, perhaps as a hide-away after King John had destroyed his castle. He kept it until his death then it went to daughter Mary, married to William de Greystoke.

Thereafter descent was as Morpeth until the end of the sixteenth century when records show that the owner was Widow Thompson. It is not known who she was, but she built two wings to the tower in 1603 then sold the place to the Howards.

The original tower was 21 feet square with 4 feet thick walls. It has been modified and enlarged several times, not only by Widow Thompson, and quite recently it has been completely revamped in order to compete with its modern neighbours. It was offered for sale in 1985 for £139,000.

Choppington

L81   P524   NZ256842   6½ km, 4 miles, south-east of Morpeth

Within the Durham Bishops' palatinate of Bedlingtonshire and, later, part of North Durham, Choppington was not a legal or administrative part of Northumberland until 1844. Choppington is one of the two places within this area – Bedlington is the other – which can claim to have had a fortified building. Raiders were not drawn here as the land in medieval times was rather unproductive.

The bishops seldom sold their property but leased it to a number of people, many of whom had their eyes on the possibility of coal mining. One of these was Garven Ogle, the son of the first Baron Ogle's second son William. He built a tower in 1503 and lived in it the rest of his life. In 1578 Bishop Barnes allowed Cuthbert Ogle to take over provided he paid £5.40 annual rent, put down £100 key money and undertook to repair the building. This was not the only repair job done, for the Ogles continued to live there until 1710, when George Bulman, a Newcastle merchant, bought the place.

What the tower looked like is not known because its site is not known and there are no obvious traces in the area. The Rev. John Hodgson suggested that it occupied the space now taken by Glebe Farm, NZ254830, or perhaps the name of the southern part of Choppington, Scotland Gate, is a clue.

Bedlington

L81   P524   NZ257819   7 km, 4½ miles, south-east of Morpeth

Bedlington until 1844 was the administrative centre of Bedlingtonshire, one of the unattached parcels of land which collectively became known as North Durham after the Durham bishops lost it. Blyth, Cambois, East and West Sleekburn, Choppington and Netherton as well as Bedlington were included in this irregular shape lying between the Rivers Blyth and Wansbeck.

There was a church at Bedlington in 1069, for the monks of Durham spent a night here during their flight to Lindisfarne. In fact it had been built in about 900 and was dedicated to St. Cuthbert. It is still in the town and, although much renovated and extended, it is still noteworthy, if only for this laconic legend on one of its tombstones:

"Poems and epitaphs are but stuff;
here lies Robert Barras, that's enough."

A fortified tower was built during the sixteenth century, by whom is not known. There were numerous small holders in Bedlington at this time, any one of which might have been the builder. Much later the tower was used as the nucleus of Bedlington Hall which was divided into apartments and let to deserving poor during the second half of the nineteenth century. It was demolished in 1959 to make room for council offices.

Bedlington has a long history of coal mining. In 1368 Thomas Hatfield, Bishop of Durham, appointed a mines supervisor in the town, and until recently coal has been the lifeblood of the area, attracting many a poor farmer from the barren hills, and no doubt not a few reivers with them. From the mid-eighteenth century a favourite recreation in the town has been the breeding of Bedlington terriers, a hobby they shared, it is believed, with Walter Calverley Blackett of Wallington.

Bebside

L81   P524   NZ271809   9 km, 5½ miles, south-east of Morpeth

A manor in the Tynemouth Priory's domain from Edward I's reign to the sixteenth century. The monks had a manorial hall, grange and farm here, the hall being their local office for Cowpen and Hartford as well as Bebside. It was not a fortified building but it was encircled by a moat, vague traces of which can still be detected at Bebside North Farm.

After the dissolution of Tynemouth in 1539, the Crown leased its land to local farmers until 1565 when Bebside was bought by John Ogle of Newsham. He or his successor replaced the building with a new hundred feet long hall incorporating a 30 by 20 feet tower. This remained in the Ogle family until 1702 when it was bought for £2200 by John Johnson, a Newcastle hostman.

The hall and tower were demolished in 1853 and there are no signs of them now.

Horton

L88   P536   NZ280796   10 km, 6¼ miles, south-east of Morpeth

When this was a manor in the Whalton barony it was called 'Horton iuxtra Mare' to distinguish it from Horton in Glendale. The original fortification and village was close to Low Horton Farm, and the manor included Stickley Farm and Hartford.

The original barons soon ran out of descendants and the barony returned to the Crown at the end of the twelfth century. In 1205 King John granted it to his friend Robert fitz Roger, Lord of Warkworth, who, in his turn, granted it to Walram Viscount, a grandson of Odard of Bamburgh and second son of the Baron of Embleton. He assumed the title Sir Walram of Horton, and died in 1257.

His only offspring, Isabella, inherited. She went through two husbands in ten years, then got stuck with a third, Sir Guischard de Charron, in 1269. Third time lucky, for Sir Guischard had been sineschal, or steward, of the Honour of Richmond from 1261 to 1268, and when he married Isabella, his second wife, he was sheriff of Northumberland. He built a large, unfortified hall house at Horton but preferred not to live there, so in 1279, eighteen years before his death, he settled the place on his son by his first wife, another Sir Guischard de Charron.

King Edward I broke his journey at Horton in 1292 while travelling south from Berwick where he had seen John Balliol crowned king of Scotland. Guischard was shrewd enough to see that this investiture would lead to trouble of the sort he was ill-equipped to deal with, so he requested, and was given, the King's licence to crenellate his house. In fact he built a completely new tower which the 1415 surveyors thought was large enough to call a fortalice. It became known as Horton Castle.

The king evidently approved of the new building for he called again in 1301 when Guischard's son, a third Guischard, did the honours. In 1304 Edward brought his queen, Margaret, to stay a week before moving on to Tynemouth Priory.

The Battle of Bannockburn claimed the life of this Guischard, and his death brought the Charron line to an end. His daughter Joan married Sir Bertram de Monboucher, a Breton knight, and they held Horton for the rest of their lives, although they did not reside there all the time. On one occasion when they were not at home the tower was invaded by squatters – Sir Walter Selby and one or two other fugitives from the liquidated Mitford Gang who were lying low for a few weeks after December 1317.

William de Whitchester, whose mother was a Delaval, leased the tower in 1415 for a short time, and in 1425 it got a new owner. Isobella Monboucher, an heiress, had married Robert Harbottle of Preston, near Embleton, and their son, also Robert, became lord of both Preston and Horton.

For the next 147 years Preston and Horton were jointly owned. Robert Harbottle married a daughter of Sir Robert Ogle and was sheriff of Northumberland in 1439. He was succeeded by son John, then the next in line was Ralph who married Margaret, daughter of Sir Ralph Percy, he who fought a one-sided battle on Hedgeley Moor in 1464. The old Christian name of Guischard was revived for their son, who was killed at Flodden in 1513. He had sired a weakly boy, who died in this teens, and a healthy girl Lenna, who in 1528 married Sir Thomas Percy.

This Percy was executed in 1537 for participating in the Pilgrimage of Grace, and his son, another Thomas, inherited. Inspite of his father's disgrace he was allowed to keep Horton and Preston, and eventually Queen Mary gave him the earldom of Northumberland. Like father, like son: Thomas lost everything, including his life, when he joined in the Rising of the Northern Earls in 1572.

A cadet branch of the Harbottles was permitted to take over Preston in that year, but it is not known whether this concession included Horton. Indeed nothing more is known about Horton until 1595 when it was sold for £1200 to Robert Delaval. Robert's branch of this large family held it until 1718 when his kinsman, Admiral George Delaval, bought it and installed his two maiden sisters in it. They were the last to live in the tower.

There is nothing left of it now. At the beginning of the twentieth century one of its moats was visible, but that had gone before the present farmer's memory had begun to function. Apparently there had been double ramparts and moats enclosing an area of nearly an acre. Of the tower itself, nothing is known save that it was large.

Plessey

L88   P536   NZ228790   7½ km, 4½ miles, south of Morpeth

The Plessey manor, part of the Merley's barony of Morpeth, was physically and historically divided into two parts by the River Blyth. The northern part had no fortifications and its descent until 1890 was exactly as Morpeth's. The southern part had a career of its own.

From about 1170 South Plessey, which included Shotton, North Weetslade and Blagdon, was held from Roger de Merley by Adam de Plessey for two knights fee. Adam's successors continued to hold the land until Richard Plessey and his wife Margaret ran into money troubles in 1346 and were forced to obtain a mortgage from Roger de Widdrington, the heir apparent to the

Widdrington estate. It is a pity modern building societies cannot take Roger as their archetype, for when Richard died, in 1349, and Margaret was unable to continue the repayments, he was very generous and helpful to the widow. He foreclosed, certainly, but not only did he not turn Margaret out, he actually built a small hall house for her and gave her a pension.

Another Roger Widdrington, about a hundred years later, married Elizabeth, youngest daughter of Sir Ralph Grey of Chillingham, and indulged in a large family, several of whom became responsible for inaugurating Widdrington cadet branches. One of their sons, Robert, took South Plessey and there produced an only daughter, Anne. When she inherited she was married to Charles Brandling, an honest Newcastle businessman, but he died and in 1667 she married Sir Richard Neille who was quite the reverse. He mismanaged the estate to such a degree it had to be sold when he died.

The buyer in 1669 was Sir Thomas Radcliffe, uncle of the charismatic leader of the 1715 Jacobite rebels. After their annihilation at Preston, South Plessey, along with all Redcliffe property, was confiscated by the Crown, but, unusually, it was not granted to Greenwich Hospital. Instead it was sold to Sir Matthew White in 1723. He, almost immediately, built Blagdon Hall, NZ215770, and went to live there. Another example of his industry, less sophisticated but still visible, is a strange straight-sided windmill which he built on an elevated site near Plessey Checks (NZ238788).

Sir Matthew had no family of his own, so when he died, in 1755, the estate was bequeathed to his brother-in-law, Matthew Ridley. His ancestral home was in the Ridley territory of South Tynedale – Nicholas Ridley of Hardriding was one of his forebears – but he had been living since about 1713 in Heaton Hall, Newcastle. To acknowledge their debt to their benefactor, Matthew and his descendants adopted the surname White-Ridley.

A few generations later, in 1890, Sir Matthew White-Ridley bought land on the north side of the River Blyth, thus uniting the two parts of Plessey. Much later, in 1973, the north side of the river running through Plessey Woods was bought by the Northumberland County Council and became a Country Park.

Sir Matthew became the first Viscount Ridley of Blagdon in 1901 on his retirement from the office of Home Secretary. His home is too modern to have been fortified of course, but the small hall house which Roger Widdrington built in 1349 for Margaret Plessey was fortified when it was enlarged after the lady's death. With a moat and wall it achieved the status of a fortified manor house, and as such it served the Widdringtons and the Brandlings. It was demolished by the imprudent Sir Richard Neille, who replaced it with a farmhouse he could ill afford in 1680. This unfortified building remains, and so do very distinct earthworks in a field between it and the river which are considered to be all that is left of the medieval building.

Area 5, Sub-Area B   The Coastal Plain – North

Hirst

L81   P524   NZ280880   8½ km, 5¼ miles, north-east of Morpeth

Hirst lies in the parish of Woodhorn at the north-east extremity of Ashington. Part of the Bothal estate, it was held by Richard Bertram from 1166 to 1177, and then by seven male descendants until Sir Robert Bertram died in 1364. His heiress married Sir John Ogle who changed his name to Bertram, but in 1461 Lord Ogle held the estate under his own name.

The land was leased to several people, including various members of the Widdrington family and, from 1536 for some years, to a cadet Ogle called George. A tower was built for him that year by the owner, Lord Robert Ogle, and in 1549 George was held responsible for lighting a beacon on its roof when marauders were about. In 1585 Thomas Widdrington was the holder, and it appears he became the owner at some date after that. Ogle descendants, however, regained ownership of at least part of the property in the eighteenth century.

According to John Warburton's Notices of Ruined Towers, which he compiled in 1715, there had been two 'piles' at Hirst, "Ye one belonging to ye Duchess of Newcastle, and ye other one Johnson, both formerly possest by ye Widdringtons". Nothing is known about Johnson, but the duchess was an Ogle descendant. The ninth Lord Ogle had been made Duke of Newcastle by King Charles II in 1665, and this lady was his son's widow.

Warburton's duality has been accepted by some modern historians, yet only one tower was mentioned in the 1536 contract, and John Hodgson could see only one in 1827. By that time the tower had been incorporated into a farmhouse, the roof of the former elevated slightly above the roof of the latter. It was demolished in 1910 so there is nothing to see now. Indeed there is uncertainty about the exact site of the tower Hodgson saw but probably it is where a garage now stands.

Cockle Park

L81   P512   NZ201910   5 km, 3 miles, north of Morpeth

Another part of the Bothal estate, held first by the Bertram family and then, from the fifteenth century, by the Ogles and their descendants, the Cavendishes, the Dukes of Newcastle and the Dukes of Portland. The tower, which still exits, has a large armorial panel carved on one wall which shows the arms, crest and support of Lord Ogle, so it must have been built after his ennoblement in 1465.

The only recorded use of the tower by the Ogles was as a dower house for Adda, the widow of the fourth Lord Robert Ogle, who died in 1589. For many years after that it was a farmhouse, glorying in the lovely name 'Bubbleymire'. Now it is a farm store within the Newcastle University's Experimental Farm.

The building is a large oblong, beautifully made with rounded turrets projecting at each front corner, a vaulted ground floor and three storeys. It has been modified on at least two occasions and, although it needs the support of timber buttresses today, it still gives the impression of great strength.

Tritlington

L81   P512   NZ206925   6¹/₂ km, 4 miles, north of Morpeth

A small hamlet about a mile north of Cockle Park and two miles west of Ulgham. Yet another parcel of the Bertram-Ogle estate of Bothal, but this time the ownership descent is rather more complex, Odenell Heyrun (possibly connected to the Heron family of Ford) paid tax of £6.95 for Tritlington, and a little later the Lisles of Woodburn held it. The Ogles recovered the property in the fourteenth or fifteenth century and held it to the seventeenth century when the Middletons bought it. Sir John Middleton was the owner in 1710, but by 1895 it was back in the Ogle family.

Tritlington Old Hall is an eighteen century development of a medieval tower and a slightly less old wing. Part of a newel staircase from the former survives in a rear turret, as does a vault on the ground floor.

Causey Park

L81   P511   NZ178949   9 km, 5¹/₂ miles, north-west of Morpeth

Ralph, the third Lord Ogle, acquired this former parcel of Mitford barony, probably as a dowry when he married Margaret Gascoyne. When he died in 1513 he passed it to his second son William, who thus became owner of a fairly venerable tower built, it is believed, by the second Earl of Northumberland while he held the barony after 1416, and an attached, very sturdy, cowshed with upstairs accommodation for the cowherd.

William Ogle, who was knighted in 1526, never lived here, but his son James made it his main seat and called himself 'James Ogle of Causey Park'. He inherited in 1546 and it took him forty years to get round to improving the accommodation. He converted the cowshed into an extension to the tower in such a way that the whole resembled a spacious Elizabethan manor-house, the basis of the present farmhouse.

James's grandson, also James, died in 1664 so heavily in debt that two creditors, John Clarke, the Earl of Northumberland's auditor, and William Armorer of Middleton Hall (who was also to die in debt), took the estate as a guarantee of eventual repayment. This was not done until 1674 when James's son, William, retrieved the estate. He also fathered six children, one of whom was Elizabeth who married Ralph Wallis of Coupland in Glendale, a man who, according to Hodgson, wasted his money "in riot and extravagance" and was lucky to have a job as the store-keeper of Berwick garrison. The Ogles helped the couple financially, and bought Coupland for them when Ralph's parents retired to Knaresdale.

During the next two generations the Ogles themselves suffered financial worries and eventually they had to sacrifice Causey Park to pay outstanding debts. The tower survived under the care of a local farmer; the grandfather of the present owner-occupier renovated what by his day had become a rather dilapidated farmhouse. He inserted more windows and made other improvements, but he found the basic structure to be sound. More recently the walls have been rendered with cement to keep out the damp, and two spiral stairs, one in the tower and one in the former cowshed, have been removed. When digging the ground outside the tower to examine the foundations, it was discovered there weren't any! The building relies solely on its great weight, the width of its walls and the reciprocal support of adjoining walls to keep it standing.

There is a curious sundial in the garden which bears the Ogle family arms and the date 1705. It is surrounded by a globe and a veritable almanac of information about the sun and the moon. It would seem that this was a gift from the Ogles as The Wallis couple, who occupied the place in 1705, would not have been able to afford such a luxuriant ornament.

Cresswell

L81   P512   NZ293933   12 km, 7½ miles, north-east of Morpeth

The seat of the Cresswell family at least since the early part of King John's reign, and perhaps, if legend is to be believed, since the age of the Vikings. A tower was built here in the thirteenth or fourteenth centuries, and a manorhouse followed soon after. Both appear to have weathered the harsh North Sea gales remarkably well, for the house was not replaced until the middle of the eighteenth century, and the tower got its first major overhaul at the same time.

The new house did not last so long. It was replaced after a hundred years by a rather grand hall, built adjoining the tower by A. J. Baker-Cresswell, a member of the original family who had assumed the double-barrelled name when he succeeded to some property formerly owned by his wife's cousin, John Baker.

In 1861 Mr Baker-Cresswell bought Preston Tower and Cresswell Hall was demolished, leaving the tower standing alone. A noble ruin now, it can be seen to advantage from the Ellington or Lynemouth roads, close to Cresswell village. It has two floors above the vaulted ground floor chamber, and, although the top floor lacks its timber, the stone walls stand full height. The crenellated parapet is intact, and so is a small square turret in the north-west corner. There are spiral stairs inside, and the top room has the convenience of a gardrobe in the thickness of the wall.

A tragic legend is told about Cresswell. A young Viking walked out of the sea and into the heart of a daughter of the house one day in the Dark Ages. When he and his companions had finished raiding the area they sailed away, the youth promising the girl he would return for her. And return he did; the girl, who had kept daily watch for him, dressed always in white and ready to be carried away, saw him walking towards her from the beach, but so also did her three brothers. They thought he was bent on doing mischief so they killed him. The lady was so heart-broken she never touched food again and soon died of starvation.

True or false, this story is not so well authenticated as the following, which concerns a village girl, not an inhabitant of the tower.

On a bitterly cold, stormy night in January over a hundred years ago the Swedish steamer 'Gustav' floundered on the rocks off Cresswell. The ship broke up and the crew could be seen clinging to rocks and spars, but the spectators on shore were powerless to help. There was no lifeboat at Cresswell and all the able-bodied men were at sea, fishing. Peggy Brown, a girl of unknown age, was one spectator who decided that something ought to be done. The nearest lifeboat station was at Newbiggin, a good four miles away as the crow flies and almost double that distance by the coast. Peggy picked up her skirt and ran all the way, soaked to the skin and half blinded by the storm. She stumbled along the links, scrambled over the rocks, waded waist-high through the freezing water of River Lyne and staggered round the edge of Newbiggin Moor, eventually reaching the station with just enough breath left to alert the coxswain. His boat reached the wreck just in time to save all but one of the Swedish crew.

Some people suggest that Peggy Brown was as much a heroine as Grace Darling.

Widdrington

L81   P512   NZ255957   11½ km, 7 miles, north of Morpeth

The Widdringtons were one of Northumberland's great families and some of their many exploits are described under Little and Great Swinburn, Haughton, Plessey, Cartington and Harbottle. The base camp and ancestral home from 1162 to 1715, however, was Widdrington, a small village near Druridge Bay.

The first known member of the family was Bertram de Woderington, a knight to whom his liege lord, Baron Walter fitz William of Whalton, granted the vil of Widdrington and half of Burradon in perpetuity. The later was quickly disposed of, but a manor-house was built at Widdrington which served Bertram's descendants until 1341.

In that year Sir Gerard de Widdrington obtained a licence to crenellatee from King Edward III and built a tower. Although this no longer exists, its site is still marked by a low mound in a field behind the church. Leading to it from the village is an avenue of lime trees; originally there were twelve and were called 'The Twelve Apostles', but there are more now. The only description of the tower is a contemporary one: "Splendid, with lofty battlements".

The head of the family in 1593 was Edward Widdrington, but he was denied access to the tower for several years because his predecessor's widow held on to it even when she remarried. Thus her new husband, Sir Robert Carey, was able briefly to call Widdrington his, and this explains why he stopped there on his momentous sixty hour dash from London to Edinburgh in 1603 to tell King James VI of Scotland that Queen Elizabeth was dead and he was King James I of England. The tower was also used by the king as an overnight stop on his journey to London to receive his new crown.

Edward's grandson, William, 1611 to 1648, was a soldier whose contribution to the Royalists cause in the Civil War earned him a peerage. He took the title 'Lord William of Blankney', a tribute to his wife who came from Blankney in Lincolnshire. He was killed at Wigan.

Lord William's great grandsons, William, Charles and Peregrine, rode with the Earl of Derwentwater in the 1715 Jacobite uprising, and Widdrington was confiscated by the Crown.

By all accounts, William, the eldest and the fourth Lord Blankney, did not acquit himself very well at Preston. As a peer he was expected to be a natural leader, but he was never seen at the barricades and the only occasion he led from the front was to offer his surrender. He was imprisoned in London and, in January 1716, he was tried for high treason in the House of Lords. He pleaded guilty but claimed in mitigation that joining the rebels had been an unpremeditated, foolish act committed suddenly when he heard of the rising just the night before it happened. His fellow peers accepted his story and treated him with supreme clemency, for not only did they spare his life, they gave him his freedom and, in 1723, he was awarded £12,000 from the sale of his property.

Widdrington tower and manor passed through the hands of a few speculators before being bought by Sir George Borlase Warren. This man considered the old building to be too dilapidated to accept the modern improvements he wanted, so in 1775 he had it demolished and a replacement was started. This was gutted by fire before it was completed, but in 1777 Sir George tried again on a different site. This time he succeeded in building a shooting box which contemporaries thought was "a slight, fantastical, insulated building possessing neither grandeur nor convenience". It was demolished in 1862, except for an octagonal tower which was allowed to stand alone for a few more years. No trace remains now, and the site has been forgotten.

Low Chibburn

L81   P512   NZ266965   12½ km, 7¾ miles, north-east of Morpeth

A preceptory of the Knights Hospitallers was built in the small manor of Chibburn, part of the Walton barony, in the early years of the fourteenth century. The Widdrington family had held the lease since King Henry II's reign, after a possession dispute between Bertram de Woderington and William Tascha was settled by a duel of champions at which Tascha's failed to present himself.

The Knights had the place on free loan and got it in full working order by 1313. They were dedicated to caring for travellers and had chosen this site for their preceptory because it was roughly half way between the monasteries of Durham and Lindisfarne, a journey undertaken frequently by pilgrims. They had built a house, chapel, stables and servants quarters as a hollow square, and here they could give material and spiritual succour to the pilgrims. Of this original complex only the ruins of the chapel have survived and there is nothing to suggest the place was fortified.

For well over two hundred years this philanthropic work continued without serious interruption, but the Knights found their lives growing increasingly difficult after the Act of Supremacy was passed and monasteries were dissolved; the preceptory was closed and vacated by 1550. In 1554 Sir John Widdrington retrieved the site and leased Chibburn manor and its buildings to farmers.

They soon found that as a farmhouse the old preceptory held little attraction, so Sir John pulled down the house and built a new one. The ruins of this still exist, and it is clear it was designed to keep raiders away – it was, in fact a strong house. Its walls are only about three feet thick, but they are solid stone with no rubble in-filling. Some of the upstairs windows project a little way on corbels, presumably to make it easier to deal with undesireables below. As an added defence there was a moat, filled with water in troubled times by diverting a stream which flows passed the house.

This suited a succession of farmers, but occasionally the house was used as a home for Widdrington dowager ladies. It was considered to be part of the Widdrington estate and as such it was confiscated in 1715 and sold to Sir George Borlase Warren, who had no need for it and allowed it to deteriorate.

Opencast coal extraction turned most of Chibburn manor into a sea of mud in the 1970s, but the house and chapel were spared, left on a tiny island without even a moat. The ruins today are still interesting, and at the time of writing there are signs that English Heritage are going to tidy them up. A visitor attraction here would enhance the Druridge Bay area, already a haven dedicated to wildlife peace and human recreation.

Togston Hall

L81   P501   NU252025   16 km, 10 miles, north of Morpeth

The main part of Togston today is linked with Broomhill, about three miles north of Widdrington, and North Togston, the smaller part, is rather less than a mile further on. This division is of very long standing, for in the twelfth century the township, probably uniquely, was held from the king as two serjeanties. De Toggesdene held the smaller part for his service as carrier of King's Writs and keeper of cattle held by the Crown for unpaid debts. Ralph fitz Main held the larger part for his service as the king's forester in Rothbury – it was a little bit of his Ditchburn serjeanty which included Great Ryle near Whittingham and Cartington in Coquetdale.

The descent of Togston is not known in detail but ownership of the two parts appears to have been sewn together fairly quickly. There was a succession of absentee landlords, amongst whom the Carnabys, Fenwicks and Haggerstones can be named.

Togston Hall, in North Togston, started off as a tower with thick walls and slit windows; a datestone of 1546 may indicated the building date, or perhaps an alteration. In 1685 a stair wing was added and other changes were made to improve comfort. William Smith bought it in 1812, then found the old place was too small and dark so he built a new hall in 1820. The tower was retained as a rear outbuilding, but there is little to see of it or of contemporary bake and brew houses now.

Digression

The Christian Knighthoods in Northumberland

The Knights Templar was a militant Christian Order founded in the Holy Land in 1119 by a French nobleman, Hugues de Payens of Champagne, to protect Crusaders from the Saracens. All members took vows of poverty, chastity and obedience, and wore white robes decorated with red crosses. They were very active during the Crusades of the twelfth and thirteenth centuries.

To promote their activities, recruit new knights and bolster fund-raising, the Templars opened offices and temples in all Christian countries, including England. There were Templar churches at Dover and Bristol and at a few other places such as Hartburn in Northumberland. There they took over the village church in about 1250, with the consent of the owner, the Abbot of St. Albans monastery, and converted it to their own requirements. When it was judged to be of the right standard they engraved two daggers above a Maltese Cross by the entrance as a sign that it was a Knights Templar temple and could be used for the induction of young squires into the knighthood.

The Knights appear to have led a quiet but satisfying life at Hartburn for about sixty years, but internationally they were too successful at raising money and grew too powerful for their own good. Affluence helped them to forget their vows while it created jealousies in several European countries. King Philip IV of France, particularly envious of their wealth, had all the Templars in his country thrown into prison and tortured until they confessed to a trumped up charge of heresy. With so many confessions he was able to persuade Pope Clement V to abolish the Order in 1312.

Acting on instructions issued by the Pope, King Edward II had the English Knights arrested and divested of all their property. Where practicable, this was to be returned to the original owners, and in other cases it had to be sold. These instructions were amended next year.

At about the time the Templars were on their way out a new Order was on its way into Northumberland. This was the Order of the Hospital of Saint John of Jerusalem, members of which were known generally as Knights Hospitallers. They were not so bellicose as the Templars and, although founded in the Holy Land for the welfare of the Crusaders, they extended their activities to caring for all travellers in all Christian countries. They built a preceptory – a hospice where both body and soul were given sustenance – at Low Chibburn and their black habits and eight-pointed cross soon became a welcome sight, especially to pilgrims journeying between Durham and Lindisfarne.

Building their house and chapel had been an expensive business, so they were relieved when the Pope changed his instructions in 1313 for the disposal of Templar property; it was all to be handed to them. Some of the property had been disposed of by this time, and Hartburn was not available as it was never owned by the Templars, but both Temple Thornton and Temple Healey (now Healey, near Slaley) were gratefully received as revenue producing estates. So were rents from Abberwick, given to them by Baron Ros of Carham, and Throckrington, the gift of the Archbishop of York.

The Hospitallers have never been disbanded, but they have had to move their international headquarters several times. After the fall of Acre in 1291 they established themselves in Cyprus, and then moved to Rhodes in 1309. They were expelled from there by the Ottomans in 1522, but eight years later Emperor Charles V took pity on them and gave them Malta, where they stayed until Napoleon dislodged them in 1708. Now their headquarters are in Rome. There were none of them in England after 1559, and in fact they did not survive for long as an active force after the Act of Supremacy and the dissolution of the monasteries. They vacated Low Chibburn about 1550.

Area 5, Sub-Area C   River Wansbeck
Newminster Abbey

L81   P523   NZ189858   1 km, ³/₄ mile west of Morpeth

Between 1467 and 1500 Abbot John Birtley built fortified houses for his
monks at Carrycoats, Filton White House, Ritton White House, Nunnykirk,
Rothley and Greenleighton, but neither he nor anyone else seems to have
bothered about providing any sort of refuge at the Abbey. Strange, considering
that it suffered a nasty Scottish raid even before it was completed.

The abbey was founded as a Cistercian establishment in 1137 by
Ranulph and Juliana de Merley of Morpeth barony. They installed eight
monks under Abbot Robert of Whitby, on land about a mile from their castle.
The inspiration was said to have been Yorkshire's Fountains Abbey which had
been founded a few years earlier and which the Merleys had visited.
Newminster can claim to be the 'eldest daughter of Fountains'; in its turn,
Newminster 'mothered' Roche Abbey near Maltby in Yorkshire, Pipewell
Abbey in Northamptonshire and Sawley Abbey in Lancashire.

Many Northumbrian landowners gave land to the abbey and the monks
became large scale and efficient farmers. The Abbot kept a good table and
many princes and nobles took advantage of his hospitality. In many ways the
abbey was an asset to the county, yet it failed to find popularity amongst the
proletariat of Morpeth and, in or about 1537, when the monks resisted its
dissolution, the locals not only helped the commissioners close the place
down, they actually attacked its fabric and took away a large amount of stone
which eventually was used to build town houses.

Largely because of this desecration, the abbey is deficient now in the sort
of romantic ruins which attract the attention of heritage conservationists.
There are a couple of fine arches and a section of cloister on the site, but these
have been reassembled from stones lying on the ground and are not all that
impressive. Some excavation work has been carried out on three or four
occasions and interesting artifacts have been found, but the bumpy nature of
the ground seems to tell of much more to be discovered. The area is privately
owned but access can be requested; cows are the most common visitors,
however, and neither they nor the annual invasion of nettles and shrubs are
doing the place any good.

Mitford

L81   P523   NZ170854   3 km, 2 miles, west of Morpeth

The Mitford family held land west of Morpeth in Anglian times. At the
Conquest the head of the family was Robert, and when he died he left all to
his only child, Sibella. She was ordered by King William I to marry Sir Robert

Bertram, one of his knights. It was a convenient way of granting him a barony. Although Sibella was the last of the mainstream Mitfords, there must have been cadet branches to carry on the name for it crops up again nearly four hundred years later.

Ponteland, High Callerton, Callerton Derreyne (now Darras Hall) and Kirkley were among the more distant parts of the barony, but it is not known whether they were in from the beginning or were added by the Conqueror.

In about 1095 Sir Robert and Sibella Bertram's son, William, married Hawise, a daughter of Guy de Balliol, Baron of Bywell. Their domestic arrangements during their first twenty years of married life are a mystery, but they must have had somewhere pleasant to call home as Robert gave Hawise's dowry, the Bothal estate, to his young brother. By 1115, however, the couple were ensconced in a motte and bailey built on a steep hill at Mitford, close to the junction of the Wansbeck and Font rivers. Before they claimed the site, the hill had been like a small burgh where the villagers lived; they were moved to the valley below and, as some compensation, the Bertrams built a church, parts of which can still be seen although the present church is mainly 1875 work. A little later, between 1130 and 1135, William founded Brinkburn Priory.

Roger Bertram was the baron in 1166; he replaced some of the motte and bailey's timber with stone, paying special attention to the curtain wall. His son, also Roger, built the stone keep, quarrying one side of the castle's hill to get his material. It was an unusual building with five sides, possibly the only one in Britain at the time. The strengthening work was completed by Roger's son, William, so that the Bertrams had a finished stone castle before 1215. This was a fateful year for many Northumbrian castles, but not for Mitford, and indeed it is rumoured that King John stayed there awhile when he returned from his blitzkrieg of vengeance against those noblemen who had payed homage to Scottish King Alexander II.

Criticism of the autocratic Crown did not end with Magna Carta nor with King John's death, but simmered on through Henry III's reign and was eventually brought to the boil by Simon de Montford, Earl of Leicester and a friend of Roger, William Bertram's son. The lad joined the Earl's revolutionary force in 1264, but two years before, perhaps acting on a premonition, he sold part of Ponteland and his Callerton estates to William de Valence, Earl of Pembroke, a half-brother of the king. An astute move, for after Montford's defeat at Evesham in 1265 the Bertrams were stripped of their remaining property. Roger escaped with his life but he left the pages of history, a broken man.

The Crown sold Kirkley and Newton Underwood to Sir Hugh de Eure in 1267. All the remainder, including Mitford, was granted to the Earl of Pembroke, to add to the property he had bought. He did not have it long: he got married and during a tournament organised to celebrate the wedding he was killed. His successor was Aymer de Valence, the second earl, who had no use for Mitford Castle and allowed it to stand empty. Sir John de Eure, a former escheater of the Northern Counties with property at Kirkley, had no difficulty in persuading the Crown that it should play a more important role in the defence of the marches. He was permitted to garrison it with twenty men-at-arms and forty troopers in 1315. These soldiers were Eure's men and became part of the muscle of the 'Mitford Gang' which brought mayhem to Northumberland, already traumatized by Robert Bruce's post-Bannockburn attentions.

The story of the county's period of self-inflicted misery is not one of which Northumbrians can be proud. The initiator was probably Thomas, Earl of Lancaster, an ambitious and unscrupulous member of the ruling clique who may have thought more civil unrest on the Border would further highlight his king's inability to govern, Eure, a friend of the Duke, was certainly the master planner and behind the scenes supremo, while the leader in the field, the man most closely associated with the nefarious events was Sir Gilbert de Middleton of Cramlington and Hartley, brother of John de Middleton of Swinburn Castle and cousin of Sir John de Middleton, lord of Belsay. He was assisted by brother John and Walter Selby and had the active backing of several property owners.

The Gang's usual modus operandi was to call on any farmer or squire with fields still in cultivation or who appeared to have some money. The hapless victims were given the opportunity to join the Gang, but a refusal or any show of resistance was dealt with summarily. Their fields would be wasted, their stock either killed or led away to the farm of the nearest supporter. Often their families were killed or left to starve, but they themselves were taken captive and put into the dungeons of Mitford Castle, there to remain until they produced the required ransom money.

A variation to this routine was played out in 1317 at Rushyford in County Durham. Gilbert and Walter, with a small armed band, waylaid a party of Church dignitaries, including the Bishop of Durham elect on his way to Durham Cathedral for his consecration. This man, Lewis de Beaumont, and his brother Sir Henry Beaumont, were captured and taken to Mitford to await the payment of a huge ransom.

Exploits such as these came to a welcome end when Mitford Castle was taken by a trick and most of the Gang was captured in December 1317. Gilbert and John de Middleton were sent to the Tower of London and next month they were hung, drawn and quartered, but Walter Selby escaped and hid for a time in Horton Tower before flying to Scotland.

"So ended", wrote a monastic chronicler, "a year that was barren of every crop but misery, when Northumberland, wasted by the Scots and reduced to poverty by its own outlaws. lay between the hammer and the anvil". In fact it was not quite the end of the story, for Robert Bruce, in the business of keeping Northumberland miserable, took Mitford Castle and, no doubt relishing the irony of it, put Walter Selby in charge of it. The English authorities were unconcerned; Selby by rights should have been in gaol but he was virtually a prisoner anyway in his castle so they were prepared merely to watch and wait. In 1321 he had had enough and surrendered himself and the castle to the sheriff of Northumberland. This probably saved his life. He was incarcerated in the Tower of London until 1327, then freed to live an adventurous life until David Bruce executed him in 1346.

As a fortress, Mitford Castle was now a back number, but the barony remained a good investment. In 1323 Aymer de Valence, the second earl, died of apoplexy while in France. He had no offspring of his own and the heiress to his estates was judged to be his niece, Joan. She was a well connected lady, being a sister of John Comyn who had been killed at Bannockburn and, more importantly, the wife of David Strathbolgi, Earl of Athol. He got control of the whole of Mitford barony (still excluding Kirkley), but he allowed his younger brother, Sir Aymer de Athol, to take Ponteland, a grant which remained good until Earl Douglas burnt his tower on his way to Otterburn in 1388.

David Strathbolgi died in 1380 and was succeeded by his son, another David. When he died in 1375 the property was divided between two heiresses, both of whom were married to younger sons of Henry Percy, the first Earl of Northumberland. The entire Percy family lost property and honour between 1404 and 1414 for rebelling against King Henry IV, but when Henry V was crowned they were returned to Hotspur's son, Henry, the second earl. Thus did the 1415 survey list Mitford as belonging to Henry Percy. The land remained within the earldom of Alnwick for over two hundred years.

In 1441 descendants of the long forgotten Mitford family turned up, at Seghill which they bought that year from the Delavals, and which they kept until Michael Mitford sold it in 1723 to the Allgoods. Then, as if their reincarnation was not enough, the Mitfords actually returned to Mitford! They built Mitford Manor House in 1637, 86 years before Seghill was sold so either the family was rich enough to run two mansions or two branches were involved. The new house was built on the valley floor; a ruin now but part of its embattled porch tower remains. A replacement, Mitford Hall, was built with Dobson's help in 1823 and it was occupied by Mitfords until it was sold in 1992.

Nobody has replaced the castle. It remains a striking ruin, seen to advantage from the church gates.

Newton Underwood

L81　　　　P523　　　NZ149861　　　5 km, 3 miles, west of Morpeth

A small parcel of Bertrams' Mitford barony which was sold by the Crown with Kirkley to Sir Hugh de Eure in 1267. He installed a cadet branch of the family in it, and John and Agnes de Eure were reported to be occupiers in 1326.

At some date during the fourteenth century one of the Eures built a tower. Newton Underwood today is a cluster of two farms and a house, and in its midst is all that remains of this tower, an arch which once was part of a vault over a ground floor chamber. A thick pile of rubble lies above the arch, and around it is a jungle of nettles and wild roses.

The third Lord Eure sold the estate in 1613 to an enterprising farmer from Ancroft, George Revely. The purchase carried bad luck, for George died the next year, and his only son, Bertram died a few years later, leaving George's widow, Rosamond, alone. She married Roger Widdrington in 1632 and as they had Cartington in Coquetdale to live in they sold Newton Underwood.

Roger had the curious habit of carrying three watches about his person. Inspite of this, his time was up in 1641.

Meldon

L81   P523   NZ120837   8 km, 5 miles, west of Morpeth

A manor of Mitford barony leased in 1166 to John son of Seman. Like most of the barony, it was acquired by William Valence, Earl of Pembroke, in 1265, yet by 1325 one third of the manor was owned by Sir William Heron and the other two-thirds was the property of Sir John Fenwick of Fenwick.

The Heron part was passed to cadet family members and in 1405 Nicholas Heron enlarged the holding by leasing some of Temple Thornton, Meldon's western neighbour, from the Knights Hospitallers. He also built a fortified tower at Meldon. The other part remained in Fenwick's hands and in 1622 the Heron third joined it when Sir William Fenwick foreclosed on a debt owed by Alexander Heron.

Sir William Fenwick was married twice. The eldest son by his first wife, formerly Grace Forster, inherited Wallington and the leadership of the family. The eldest son by his second wife, née Margaret Selby, was called William like his father, and he took all the Meldon property. He was knighted by King James I.

There are several versions of Meldon's history during the seventeenth and eighteenth centuries, some quite incredible. The following is offered as a logical scenario which is consistent with the few safe factors known.

One of Sir William's daughters married the son of Edmund Lawson of Scremerston, near Berwick, and William bought the freehold of the place from Lord Walden, Earl of Suffolk and presented it to the couple as a wedding present. Two children, a boy and a girl, were born there and brought up in a happy environment, but life at Meldon was not so idyllic. The Fenwicks were committed Royalists and the Commonwealth government confiscated Sir William's property in 1650. He died two years later in stricken circumstances.

When Edmund Lawson died, in 1655, Scremerston was divided between the two children. In 1660 the girl, Catherine, married Sir Francis Radcliffe of Dilston, the future first Earl of Derwentwater. He bought Meldon manor from King Charles II's government and gave it to his bride; a nice thought this, for he would know Catherine held fond memories of her grandfather who lived there, and it suited him as well as he was building up his property portfolio.

That portfolio was torn to shreds after the 1715 Jacobite fiasco. In 1735 Meldon was granted to Greenwich Hospital, and seven years later it was sold to Isaac Cookson, whose descendants still own much property in the area.

Meldon Park, which runs alongside the Dyke Neuk to Hartburn road, was enclosed before 1670 as a deer park, and the Dobson-designed house there (NZ107855) was built in 1832 by Isaac Cookson. Nicholas Heron's tower was in Meldon village, on the Dyke Neuk to Whalton road. Hodgson, writing in 1839, enthused about the ruins which lay 150 yards south-east of Meldon church. He claimed to have seen the walls of vaults, a covered sewer and the remains of a barmekyn. In 1888 Tomlinson said that "only the slightest vestiges remain". The disappearing act seems to have been completed now.

North Middleton

L81   P523   NZ059850   14 km, 8$^{1}/_{2}$ miles, west of Morpeth

Bit of a problem here: there is no such place as North Middleton in the Wansbeck valley! There was a South Middleton, a medieval village on the river bank, and there was an East Middleton, now Middleton Bank Top farm. There still is a Middleton village, while Hall, Burn, Bridge and Mill are still to be found appended to the name – but no North Middleton. And yet the 1415 survey states very clearly that a tower existed at North Middleton.

The full name appears again on two later documents, but nothing can be found which gives the precise location. Local people seem to be unaware of the mystery.

The explanation is likely to be that the original settlement, the no longer existing medieval village by the river, started life as plain Middleton. Later, when buildings appeared on the hill to the north, they were grouped together and called North Middleton. Over the years this group grew in importance while the original declined, so eventually 'North' became superfluous and 'South' was added to the older place, just to avoid confusion. All this means that Middleton Hall in the modern village of Middleton is the most probably site of the tower, in fact it is believed to be a tower derivative, although architectural proof is not obvious.

The whole Middleton district was part of a detached manor of Styford barony which, in 1166, Walter de Bolbec had leased to local worthies. The river bank was one of several estates which went to Gilbert de Burum of

Bolam, but the higher ground to the north appears to have been separated and let to John Morell for a one-third knight fee. A further name complication here: for the short time he held it, Morell called his plot 'Middleton Morell'! John was probably the grandson of Arkle Moreal (Morell, Moreal, Morel, the name appears in several forms) who was awarded Old Berwick in 1093 for killing Malcolm III at Alnwick.

By the beginning of the fourteenth century 'North' Middleton was held by Sir Robert Ogle who had been given it as a dowry when he married Margaret, the heiress of a local landowner called Sir Hugh Gubium. Sir Robert lived to 1368 and is the most likely builder of the tower, although he gave the estate to his son in 1329. The descent from him runs through the Ogle family to 1797 when the Duke of Portland sold out for, allegedly, £14,300. Such a high price suggests that the tower had been converted into the Hall by then.

Wallington

L81   P523   NZ028842   17 km, 10½ miles, west of Morpeth

Like Middleton, Shafto, Cambo and several other places in the neighbourhood, Wallington was included in Bolbec's Styford barony, and in 1166, when landlords had to make returns to the Government, it was leased to Hugh de Grandene, an unknown character probably related to the Greys who succeeded to the property in the early years of the fourteenth century.

John Grey incorporated Wallington in his title and built a tower before 1326. A few years after this he was granted half of Little Harle estate, but he continued to live at Wallington until he felt his days were numbered. In 1352 he sold to John Strother and moved to Little Harle, where he died just a few months later.

There was another Strother family in the north of the county at this time; they may have been related but not close enough for inheriting purposes. John's family ended in the fifteenth century with co-heiresses. The eldest, Mary, inherited Wallington and married John Fenwick.

John was in the junior line of Fenwicks, a grandson of Sir John Fenwick who built Fenwick Tower in 1378. He had to wait a long time before he could claim the family seat, but even then he and his descendants remained at Wallington.

Eight generations of Fenwicks held Wallington, the third one adding a comfortable Tudor manor-house to the tower. The last one was the most interesting, not because of any military achievements but because he led a fulfilling life and died a convicted traitor. He was Sir John Fenwick, the third baronet, born in 1647.

An interest in horses probably came from his grandfather, the first baronet, who was one of the founders of the Pitman's Derby and was responsible in 1621 for presenting the Plate. The interest developed in Sir John, who became one of the most successful horse breeders the county has ever known and Master of Horse to King Charles II. He is credited with breeding the first pure-bred pedigree English racehorse, Dodsworth, a recognised milestone in the history of the turf. He also travelled overseas on the king's behalf to buy Oriental bloodstock. When the king died in 1685 he bought Dodsworth's mother for forty guineas.

Bloodstock had held Sir John and King Charles in close friendship, so the Fenwicks were not keen supporters of the Glorious Revolution of 1688 which brought William and Mary to the throne. Sir John remained loyal to the Stuarts and became an active Jacobite. In the eyes of the Government, he went too far, and in 1697 he was arrested and accused of planning regicide. His trial was a travesty of justice. The prosecution could produce only one, most unreliable, witness, and when it seemed certain that the case would be dismissed, King William got Parliament to pass an Act of Attainer which ensured that Sir John was legally murdered in January 1698. Even in those days this was unpopular barbarism, and the Act of Attainer weapon was never used again.

William III was also enthusiastic about the sport of kings and personally confiscated the Wallington horses, including Sir John's favourite mare, White Sorrel. He was riding this horse one day in March 1702 in Hampton Court Park when it tripped on a molehill and fell, sending the king crashing to the ground with fatal consequences. The eighteenth century Jacobites bestowed great honour on White Sorrel, and at their meetings they were want to toast the builder of the fateful molehill, the 'Gentleman in Black Velvet'.

Sir John Fenwick seems to have had some foreknowledge of his fate, for in 1684, thirteen years before his arrest, he sold nearly all his Northumbrian property to Sir William Blackett. Wallington went for £4000 and an annuity on Sir John's and Lady Mary's lives.

Sir William was a coal mining and shipping magnate, one of Newcastle's commercial princes. Wallington estate made a pleasant weekend retreat and a great place in which to entertain his business associates and those whose support he craved for his election to Parliament. The Tudor house and the older tower were too cramped and uncomfortable for his requirements, however, and in 1688 he demolished both and build instead the lovely Hall which stands today.

That is the end of the tower's story. The Hall occupies its site and possibly uses its foundations to supplement its own; on one occasion this century while excavating below the ground floor some unexplained masonry was found which may have been a fragment of one of the early buildings. There is certainly nothing of the old places to see.

In 1705 Sir William died and his son, another William, inherited at the tender age of sixteen. He developed into a tycoon like his father and built up the Newcastle business still further. After his majority and until his early death at the age of thirty-nine he spent much time representing Newcastle in Parliament. While thus engaged he developed a sympathy for the Jacobite cause and the sheriff kept his eyes on him. He allowed the Earl of Derwentwater to believe that when the uprising occurred he would join them with his keel men from the Tyne, but in the event he did nothing. He claimed his homes, Anderson House in the city and Wallington Hall, were being watched too closely for him to steel away. So the 1715 excitement came and went and the Blacketts retained their property.

The next in line was Sir Walter Calverley Blackett, a son of Sir William's sister Julia. He reigned from 1728 to 1777, and much of what makes Wallington special was inspired and put in hand by him. He remodelled some of the rooms in the Hall and built the grand staircase. The entrance and clock tower were his. The woods and gardens near the Hall were planned by him. Most of the farms in the estate were built or improved on his orders, and decent roads and bridges were constructed.

Just as Sir Walter had done, the next owner inherited Wallington from his uncle. Sir John Trevelyan was a member of a Somerset family who had married Julia, Sir Walter's sister; understandably, he was loath to leave the civilized warmth of his southern home for the unknown wilderness of the Border, and both he and his son were absentee landlords. His grandson, however, Sir Walter Calverley Trevelyan, did travel north in 1846 and he liked what he found so much he stayed in Wallington to his death in 1879. His wife, Pauline, was very artistic and entertained several eminent painters and poets. She was responsible, also, for roofing the central courtyard and making it a large lounge. Some time later one of her guests, William Scott Bell, painted eight scenes from Northumberland history, and these, with some simpler paintings by Pauline herself, still decorate the lounge wall.

The next two Wallington Trevelyans took the Hall into the twentieth century. Sir Charles Edward Trevelyan married Hannah, Lord Macauley's sister. Sir George Otto Trevelyan is best remembered as the father of George Macauley Trevelyan, the famous historian.

The last of the line was Sir Charles Philip Trevelyan, who inherited in 1928. Having sired two daughters only, he decided to leave Wallington to the nation rather than to sons-in-law, so in 1941 he consigned the estate to the National Trust.

Cambo

L81   P523   NZ026856   17 km, 10½ miles, west of Morpeth

Although less than a mile north of Wallington Hall, Cambo was a separate estate leased by Baron Gilbert de Burum from the Styford barony and sub-let to Sir Robert de Camhoe, thrice sheriff of Northumberland. That was in the thirteenth century, long after it had contained a Bronze Age 'factory' making metal objects such as celts and rings, and a century before John Grey bought it. Descent from him, via Strothers, Fenwicks, Blacketts, Trevelyans and The National Trust, was as Wallington.

Cambo village was created during the Strother era in the fifteenth century on a site slightly east of its present position, down hill near Saugh House (NZ033858) where John Wesley preached in 1782 on his seventieth birthday. It had a small chapel on a prominence still called Chapel Hill.

The bastle was built by the Fenwicks, probably Sir William between 1571 and 1613. The site chosen was a few hundred yards from the village but it had the advantage of height and long views.

It stood alone until 1714, then William Blackett, the second to occupy Wallington Hall, built an inn bordering the road from Newcastle to Elsdon and Scotland. With a businessman's eye, he knew it would become a coaching inn, and, later, the 'Chevy Chase' changed horses there. The inn's name was 'The Two Queens' or locally, it is alleged, 'The Rival Queens', the queens in question being Elizabeth I and Mary Queen of Scots. Sir Walter Trevelyan, a nineteenth century teetotaller, converted it into a temperance hotel and then, when that did not pay, he used it to house his agent.

Sir Walter Calverley Blackett was responsible for moving the village up hill to join the bastle. He built a row of single storey cottages, mainly for use by his Wallington Hall staff. He also built a school in or just after 1728; Lancelot 'Capability' Brown of Kirkharle must have been one of its first pupils, for he left in 1732.

The early Trevelyans improved and expanded the village and, in 1842, built the church. The bastle was radically altered by raising the roof to squeeze in an extra floor, replacing the thatch with stone tiles, blanking off the gable door and inserting new windows. The internal stairs were probably added at this time. The church tower had to wait until 1883; Sir Charles Edward Trevelyan was responsible for this, and also for bending the main road so that Cambo was bypassed.

The village at this time was a thriving community. It could boast of a blacksmith and farrier, a butcher, a joiner, a baker and a grocer. The bastle housed a general store on the ground floor and a tailor on the first. The store was run by a man called Handyside, a Rip Van Winkle figure with a long beard and tousled hair, wearing a smock and broad-brimmed hat. He was reputed to be a warlock so had no problems about debt collecting. The tailor was called Wales and worked sitting cross-legged on a wooden dias; it was a descendant of his who took over the whole building in 1920, improved its internal appearance and opened a post office on the ground floor. It is there still.

Fawns

L81   P523   NZ007853   19 km, 11³/₄ miles, west of Morpeth

A farmhouse west of Cambo, a parcel of the Wallington estate through the ages, although it does not appear to be National Trust property now. A little tower was mentioned only once, in 1541, as belonging to Sir John Fenwick, and there is nothing to see now.

Kirkwhelpington

L81   P522   NY996844   20 km, 12¹/₂ miles, west of Morpeth

Part of the Prudhoe barony from the twelfth to the fifteenth century. The first baron, Richard Umfraville, knew the village well during King John's reign and once assembled his entire entourage there to witness the granting of some of his property to the monks of Kelso. It was probably the same man who built the church, the 'kirk' at Whelpington, which was consecrated in the thirteenth century.

The church tower is low, square and robustly buttressed and, while not overtly a fortification it is believed to have been used as a refuge. The vicar got his own strong tower which was used continuously as the vicarage until 1983. Wings were added to it in 1760 by Rev. Nathaniel Ellison at his own expense, and in 1771 the ground floor chamber was converted into a kitchen and other alterations were made "towards which Sir Walter Blackett, bart, out of his own generosity and of his own accord, gave me the sum of £110".

There was also a bastle in the village, although no one seems to know where. Called Bolt House, it was standing in the Rev. John Hodgson's day and he published an engraving of it in his History, most of which was written while he was vicar of Kirkwhelpington. It looks like a typical two-storey, thatched bastle with outside stairs and farm buildings attached to one gable.

Kirkharle

L81   P523   NZ013824   19 km, 11³/₄ miles, south-west of Morpeth

This old village was in the Styford barony but leased to the Baron of Warkworth. From the death of Styford's baron, Hugh de Bolbec, in 1266 to 1355 when the barony was granted to the Nevilles of Raby, John of Lancaster or his heiress held half the barony, the part containing Kirkharle. The daughter married Sir William de Herle so he was lord of the manor when King Edward III took over Warkworth in 1332 and terminated the lease of Kirkharle.

Herle was considered to be the owner after this and he was able to lease Kirkharle to John de Strother, he who was to buy Wallington in 1352. His family held it until two daughters inherited in 1455. The eldest, Mary, got

Wallington and the younger, Johanna, got Kirkharle and passed it to her husband, William Loraine.

The Loraines made Kirkharle their home and their vocation for close on four hundred years. William and Johanna's grandson, Robert, was a conscientious law enforcement officer and because he knew he must be on the reivers' hit list, he built at tower to give him and his family some protection. It did not: he was murdered while walking home from church one Sunday morning in 1483.

In 1718 Sir William Loraine (his father had been made a baronet for his public benefactions) started to improve his estate. He started with the garden and this necessitated moving the villagers to new and better houses a little to the west of the old site. When he got this to his satisfaction, in 1722, he tackled the house, making a mansion of it, attached to the repaired fortified tower.

One family living in Kirkharle village had a son in 1716 whom they called Lancelot Brown. In later life he was to be better known as 'Capability Brown', the landscape gardener. He left Cambo school when sixteen years old, in 1732, and for seven years was employed by Sir William Loraine as an apprentice gardener. This was ten years after Sir William had created his garden, and Lancelot had been only six at the time, so he cannot take any credit for that, yet a plan accredited to him has been discovered. It bears no date so may have been drawn either as an academic exercise during his apprenticeship or during one of his visits to the area in later life. Either way, there is no evidence that the plan was acted upon, but the present owner has been reported as saying he wishes to lay out a garden conforming to the plan to see just what a Capability landscape was like when new.

The Loraine era came to an end in 1836 and Thomas Anderson of Little Harle bought Kirkharle. Living so close, Mr Anderson had no use for another mansion, so he demolished most of it, including the tower, unfortunately, leaving only the east wing to serve as a farmhouse.

Little Harle

L81   P523   NZ014834   18¹/₂ km, 11¹/₂ miles, west of Morpeth

West Harle

L81   P522   NY990820   21 km, 13 miles, south-west of Morpeth

Little Harle was called East Harle originally. East and West estates had much in common: both were in Kirkwhelpington parish, both were parcels of Umfravilles' Prudhoe barony and, for two periods, they were held by the same families. Physically they are about two miles apart and Kirkharle, in a different parish and barony, lies between them.

In 1240 Gilbert Umfraville granted East and West Harle to the Herle family. This, in descending age order, consisted of Hugh, John, Arthur who had died and is represented by his widow, and Ralph. Hugh got East Harle, while his son, Sir William, got Kirkharle by marrying John of Lancaster's daughter. John and Arthur's widow got West Harle and Ralph was left out for some years but eventually was granted Overgrass from Roger Bertram, Baron of Mitford. This situation continued through descendants for two or three generations. When the West Harle occupants fell foul of the law by joining the Mitford Gang, their connection with the Prudhoe barony was ended, but happily Sir William's son, Sir Robert, was a rich man and was able to buy their property to ensure a move was not necessary.

East Harle was granted to John Grey of Wallington in 1330. His descendants held it until the seventeenth century, just as the Herle line held West Harle. Both estates acquired a tower in the fifteenth century. In 1624 the Herle family ran out of heirs and sold their property to a partnership of Fenwicks and Widdringtons, who, in their turn, sold to Charles Aynsley in 1629. He immediately extended his tower to form a commodious farmhouse. The Grey family lasted to 1650, when an heiress married Randall Fenwick, a member of a very junior branch of the Fenwick family which had no connection with Wallington. Randall bit off more than he could chew and had to mortgage Little Harle with a relative of his wife, Edward Grey, who foreclosed and sold the estate to Gawen Aynesley, Charles Aynesley's son, in 1669.

From that date to 1833 Little and West Harle were united under the Aynesley flag with Little Harle the main seat. In about 1745 the tower was modernised internally with some parts decorated with Italian plasterwork. In 1833 Thomas Anderson bought both estates, and three years later he added Kirkharle to his possessions. The family still own the three places, with Little Harle still dominant. A picturesque mansion was added to its tower there in 1861.

The tower at West Harle was described in 1722 as "a stone vaulted room used as a kitchen" – in other words, it was completely enveloped by the farmhouse Charles Aynsley built and nothing of it was, or is, visible from the outside.

West Whelpington

L81   P522   NY973837   22¹/₂ km, 14 miles, west of Morpeth

This was a medieval village, well placed for defence on a whinstone outcrop providing a precipitous drop to the diminutive River Wansbeck. The parish register at Kirkwhelpington records the births, marriages and deaths of the villagers up to 1715 but nothing after that; the place has been deserted for nearly three hundred years. In that period natural and human elements have eliminated most of the signs of civilisation.

The Rev. John Hodgson could see in c1830 that the village had consisted of two rows of houses and a large green with a cockpit at its centre and, nearby, a 'pele' with tower-like dimensions of 23¹/₂ by 21¹/₂ feet and a small barmekyn in front. Observers in 1857 said some walls were standing, but now there is nothing so obvious – indeed half the site is not there at all, it has been quarried.

West Whelpington and Ray, a mile or so to the north, together formed a manor within the liberty of Redesdale held from the immediate post-Conquest years to 1432 by the Umfraville family. It was leased in about 1240 to the holders of Chipchase, the Lisles, to 1340 and then the Herons. The latter became owners in the fifteenth century and sold the manor in 1697 to the Milbanks of Yorkshire.

As absent landowners, they put their trust in a single tenant, Thomas Stott, from 1700 to 1749. He was given a free hand in West Whelpington and also got control of Cornhills and Ferneyrigg farms, but it appears he had nothing to do with Ray. Ambitious, efficient and ruthless, Stott soon made his land more productive and less labour intensive by enclosing easily manageable fields and growing more corn, for which there was an expanding market and an export bounty (from 1689 to 1766). By investing in modern methods and machinery, he took away the livelihood of the men of West Whelpington. The village died as families moved away in search of work, several finding it in the coal mining areas of south-east Northumberland.

There was a noticeable drop in the village's Lay Subsidy between the thirteenth and sixteenth centuries which is attributable to the frequent raids made by local and Scottish reivers. As there is no way of knowing when the 'pele' was built, it is debatable whether or not it played any part in these troubles.

Ray

L81   P522   NY969857   23 km, 14¹/₄ miles, west of Morpeth

Ray was coupled with West Whelpington as a manor in the Umfraville liberty of Redesdale and so shared in the latter's descent until the Herons sold it to the Milbanks in 1697.

There was some habitation at Ray during that time, but not enough to make a village. The only building known of was a bastle, the low walls of which still exist as if to mark out its conventional plan of about 35 by 25 feet.

No records have been found to cover the period from the Milbank purchase to the nineteenth century when Sir Charles Parson bought the estate and built a mansion in it. The steam turbine and optical glass virtuoso was attracted to Ray by the beautiful views it offered of the Wanney moors, and also by the presence of the single-track Scots Gap to Redesmouth railway which passed the foot of his garden. There cannot have been many people who could boast of having his own halt at his retirement sanctuary.

Unfortunately, neither mansion nor railway exists today. The line, constructed in 1862, failed to see its hundredth birthday. The house was neglected after Sir Charles died in 1931 and was demolished when the estate was taken over by the Forestry Commission after the second World War. A few cottages and stables are all that remains to keep the bastle ruin company.

Hawick

L81 P522 NY962825 24 km, 15 miles, south-west of Morpeth

Sweethope

L81 P522 NY956819 $25^1/_2$ km, $15^{13}/_4$ miles, south-west of Morpeth

Two ancient settlements, now lonely farmsteads, close to the juvenile Wansbeck, downstream from Sweethope Lough. Both were bought by the Strothers of Wallington and Kirkharle, Sweethope by John in 1359 and Hawick by son Alan in 1378, and thereafter both descended down the Wallington line as far as the Blacketts, being let to farmers all the time.

There was no common factor in their earlier history, however. Hawick was one of the many places the Baron of Bolam leased from the Baron of Styford in the twelfth century, and then was awarded to the Reymes family of Shortflatt. Sweethope was an Umfraville possession, held by a family which adopted the place name. Warin de Sweethope held East Bitchfield in 1311 and was the Archbishop of York's bailiff of Hexham in 1318, but his son displeased King Edward III and his lands were transferred to John Darrayns.

The 1541 survey records the presence of 'Bastell Houses' at both places. Both buildings were in good repair at that date but were not new, so they may have been built around 1500 by the tenant, '...Bellyngiam' in the case of Hawick and by Sir John Fenwick at Sweethope. 'Bastell Houses' in the nomenclature of that time were almost certainly 'Strong Houses' in today's terminology – house-shaped buildings nearly as strongly fortified as towers but providing more accommodation and comfort. Nothing remains of either building and their precise sites are not known.

Area 5, Sub-Area D   River Font

Stanton Hall

L81 P523 NZ131895 $7^1/_2$ km, $4^1/_2$ miles, north-west of Morpeth

Stanton was one of several estates included in the Beanley serjeanty granted by King Henry I to Gospatric, son of a former earl of Northumberland, in about 1135, for services of a non-military nature. Many daughters were sired by son Gospatric; one of them, Juliana, married Randulf de Merley, Baron of Morpeth, and her dowry included Stanton. After that the property passed by marriage to the Greystokes and then to the Corbet family, who held on to it until the sixteenth century. John Corbet built a tower before 1415, and this was mentioned again during King Henry VI's reign (1422-61).

During the first few years of the sixteenth century the Corbets sold to Sir Ralph Fenwick, a grandson of the first John Fenwick to hold Wallington, and his second wife, the former Elizabeth Widdrington. Sir Ralph was high sheriff of Northumberland for a time, and it was in this capacity that he tried in vain to capture the alleged murderers of his predecessor, Albany Featherstonehaugh, at Tarset Castle in 1524, and again a year later.

The Fenwick family held Stanton throughout the reigns of King Henry VIII and Queen Elizabeth. Soon after the queen's accession they extended their living quarters by building a house against the south-west face of the tower. Further extensions and new windows were added during the following years to what was now Stanton Hall.

When the Fenwicks left the building stood empty for about fifty years, which did not do the house much good although the tower, made of stronger stuff, remained habitable. The Covenanter William Veitch moved into it in 1677 from Fallowlees. Two years later he gave temporary shelter to another rebel opposed to the restoration of episcopacy in Scotland, the Earl of Argyll.

During the eighteenth and nineteenth centuries the house part of Stanton Hall was a roofless ruin, while the tower was degraded to a very sleazy existence. In turn, it was a poor law workhouse, the home of a blacksmith, then a gardener, a grain store and a shop. It had to wait until the 1980s before the renovation of the whole Hall was started.

Witton Shields

L81   P511   NZ122904   9 km, 5¹/₂ miles, north-west of Morpeth

A cleverly renovated strong house standing close to a farm between Stanton and Netherwitton. The initials 'NT' and the year '1608' are carved on one of its walls, suggesting that the builder was Nicholas Thornton, a direct descendant of Roger Thornton of Netherwitton. Nicholas had married Jane Radcliffe of Dilston, thus uniting two staunch Roman Catholic families, and a possible reason why it was considered necessary to build a fortified house so late in the day was that it offered protection from anti-Catholic elements.

The house had four storeys originally but the top floor was removed during its 1914 restoration. It is a sturdy, rectangular building with a projection containing the entrance and spiral stairs. When built, one of the upstairs rooms was a chapel.

Netherwitton

L81   P511   NZ102904   10¹/₂ km, 6¹/₂ miles, north-west of Morpeth

Originally an estate in the Beanley serjeanty, Netherwitton, or 'Witton by the Water' as it was then, was given by Gospatric to his son-in-law, Baron Ranulph de Merley of Morpeth in 1135. A descendant, Roger de Merley, left it to a daughter, Isobel, when he died in 1271. She was married to a Staffordshire man, Robert de Somerville, and they soon sold this northern property to a Welsh knight, Thomas Ap Griffiths. He and his successors farmed the land until 1405, then sold it to Roger Thornton.

Roger is something of a local legend. He was born in the 1360s but his early days are shrouded in mystery. Leland thought he came from a well-to-do family not necessarily connected with Netherwitton, but the popular belief is that he was a bond man tied to a Netherwitton farm. He went to Newcastle in 1382, either as a free agent or as an escapee; an old ditty seems to support the latter:

"At the West Gate came Thornton in,
With hap, a halfpenny and a lamb's skin."

He stayed in town with his uncle for about a year, but soon made his own way to fame and fortune. He was an astute operator, buying and selling wool, timber. coal and wine. He bought lead mines in Weardale and a fleet of ships to carry the metal overseas. He quickly became a Midas, but was generous with his money. Elected a Member of Parliament in 1400 and, being instrumental in divorcing Newcastle from Northumberland, he was several times made mayor until 1419.

He bought his 'place in the country', Netherwitton, in 1405. Desirous of a peaceful life, he built Witton Castle, a medium-sized fortified tower, on the outskirts of the village, and this became his principal seat after his retirement and until his death in 1430. A long line of descendants, none of whom appear to have inherited his flair for commerce, have lived in it ever since; even the present occupier, although called Trevelyan, is related through a distaff link.

Considerable restoration work, amounting almost to rebuilding, was carried out on the tower in 1483, and it was incorporated into a mansion in 1677. This was designed by Robert Trollop, who had been responsible for Capheaton Hall a few years earlier. The front of the house is topped with a balustrade and has twenty windows, each with a different style of open pediment. At the back of the house there is considerable evidence of the old tower, and, interestingly, the beams supporting the roof of this part of the house are the original roughly trimmed tree trunks, some still with bark on them.

The tower and its grounds received two notable visitors in the seventeenth century. In 1640 General Alexander Leslie and his 30,000-strong army camped there one night on their way to Newburn and their meeting with Lord Conway and his 3000 stalwarts. Ten years later Oliver Cromwell briefly harboured his force there during its march to Berwick and Dunbar. It was rather crowded, for Cromwell was accompanied by two mounted regiments with 2450 horses, a regiment of foot and a select body he called the Lifeguards. They used a large quantity of hay, burnt down a barn, destroyed some oats and peas and killed a sheep, but Lady Ann Thornton, who held the estate at that time, received £95.27 as compensation. She also received letters of protection guaranteeing her safety, a magnanimous gesture considering Cromwell's feelings about Royalists and Roman Catholics, but they failed to prevent Cromwell's government sequestrating the estate in 1652. The family were allowed to buy it back later, however.

In 1715 John Thornton rode with the Earl of Derwentwater and was taken prisoner at Preston. He was reprieved on the forfeiture of his property, but, again, the family was allowed to buy it back later. The price was £13,520, a very high figure for that age which reflected the grandeur of the 1677 Hall.

A game larder, a small square structure where meat was hung, adorns the green behind the house. Some historians have indicated the presence of a second tower in the area, possibly on or near the Roman road, the Devil's Causeway. Supporting evidence cannot be found, however; there are no suitable ruins and the people at the Hall know nothing about it.

South Healey

L81   P511   NZ085917   13 km, 8 miles, north-west of Morpeth

A farmhouse which is a bastle derivative. It stands at the end of a long lane in a delightful garden and looks too bright and cheerful to be a medieval fortification, but its thick walls give the truth away. The reclamation has included extension, new windows and front door and new slate roof, all done with great sympathy.

There were two other houses in the area at one time, both now ruins. North Healey, about a half mile to the north-west, definitely was unfortified, but Healey, three hundred yards to the north, could have been another bastle. It is too much of a wreck to be sure, but there are bastle-like elements present. The whole vil was almost certainly part of the Morpeth barony but its occupants have always been anonymous farmers.

Nunnykirk

L81   P511   NZ082926   13 km, 8 miles, north-west of Morpeth

Ranulph and Juliana de Merlay gave this parcel of their Morpeth barony to Abbot Robert and his eight Cistercian monks when they installed them in Newminster Abbey in 1138. The monks built a grange upon it, and in this they collected the fruits of their labours and the contributions of farmers in the neighbourhood.

At least one monk was permanently on duty at the grange to receive and guard the contents. Security proved to be inadequate in the fifteenth century, however, when reivers from both sides of the Border realised that the grange contained pre-packed plunder waiting to be collected by them. Abbot John Birtley tried to solve the problem, which was common to five other granges as well as Nunnykirk, by building a tower between 1467 and 1500. No remains are visible now, so we can only guess that it was quite small – just large enough for a single man of frugal habits to live in – and attached to the barn of the grange.

The Crown took over when Newminster was dissolved in 1537, and it was leased to Roger Fenwick, then sold in 1610 to Sir Ralph Grey of Chillingham. A son of his, Edward, held both Nunnykirk and Ulgham Grange in 1675.

The Greys sold to Edward Ward of Morpeth in 1716. In due course Edward's granddaughter, Anne, inherited. She was married to William Orde, a wealthy businessman, but Nunnykirk remained Ann's to bequeath to her second son, another William. He was a barrister with chambers in Lincoln's Inn, but he was as well known on race courses as in the courts. At one time he owned the celebrated mare 'Beeswing' which won fifty-one races and earned the title 'The Pride of the North'. It earned William quite a lot of money, too, and with some of it he bought Great Tosson in 1805, which his family held until 1883.

Anne's eldest son inherited his father's property, but William and his family kept the Orde name connected with Nunnykirk until the middle of the nineteenth century. In 1825 the grange and tower were demolished and replaced by a gracious mansion designed by Dobson. During later modifications, the foundations of the tower were seen below those of the new building. A Captain Noble owned the mansion towards the end of the nineteenth century, but today it is a residential home and preparatory school run by the Dyslexia Institute.

That Nunnykirk has a very much longer history than is recounted here was demonstrated some years ago by the discovery there of an Anglo-Saxon cross dating from about AD900. The lower part of its shaft, depicting an unusual design of birds and animals waiting expectantly with their mouths open for grapes, may be seen in the Museum of Antiquities in Newcastle University. It is regarded as one of Northumberland's most important Dark Ages find.

Combhill

L81   P511   NZ065928   15 km, 9¼ miles, north-west of Morpeth

A lonely farm which was at one time part of Gospatric's Beanley serjeanty then, later, was coupled with Netherwitton. The present farmhouse has been derived from an orthodox bastle. A chimney stack has been added to the west gable so the ground floor entrance has had to be move to the long south side, the windows are modern and the roof is new. Otherwise the conversion has involved few basic changes.

The site is close to an old River Font crossing much used by reivers and moss troopers when they ventured out of Rothbury Forest. Hence the need for a bastle.

Greenleighton

L81   P511   NZ027920   18 km, 11 miles, north-west of Morpeth

First heard of as a detached manor of the Bolbecs' Styford barony, it was leased to Gilbert de Burham of Bolam in 1166 together with Cambo, South Middleton, East and West Shafto, Hartington, Rothley and Harnham, all for two and a half knights fee.

The descent of Bolam barony was split by two co-heiresses in 1206, the two parts eventually being based on Aydon Hall and Shortflatt. Greenleighton appears to have been shared, although its management was probably Shortflatt's responsibility. In 1247, however, both the owners, Sir Richard de Gosbeck and James de Cauz, agreed to grant about 16 acres from each share to Newminister Abbey, and from that time until 1663 there were effectively two Greenleightons, a secular one and a monastic or, after dissolution, a Crown-owned one.

The secular portion grew to become a village of some seventy people, all tenant farmers with their families and labourers. They prospered sufficiently to attract the attention of the Fenwick family, who in 1412 purchased a foothold. Their patch grew significantly after Wallington was acquired in about 1460.

The Abbey's land was also farmed, probably by the monks themselves for they were enthusiastic agriculturalists. Soon after 1467 Abbot John Birtley built a fortification for them; at the time it was described as a 'strong stone house with barmekyn', so perhaps it should be classified as a strong house rather than as a tower.

In 1568 the situation was that the Crown owned the former Abbey's part and had leased it to Richard Stritham, John Fenwick owned the other part and the strong house was a ruin. A century later the whole manor became part of the Wallington estate, and it remains so to this day.

During Sir William Blackett's innings at Wallington much of Greenleighton was enclosed and many small farms were grouped to make larger, more efficient, units. The village was run down and only one farmhouse was left.

Greenleighton Hill, less than half a mile north-east of this farm, was used as a beacon during the dark days of the Anglo-Scottish wars, its warning of approaching danger being visible from as far away as Fallowlees and Fairnley. The beacon's cresset, or fire-pan, has been preserved and may be seen at Wallington. It is the only relic of that time and place: no remains of the strong house are to be seen.

Area 5, Sub-Area E   River Hart

L81   P523 Grid – see text   About 10 km, 6 miles, west of Morpeth

There were three Thorntons, all contained in a square mile based on the Dyke Neuk to Hartburn road (B6343). Most important in medieval times was West Thornton, NZ098866, formerly a sizeable village and now a farm called Thornton House. Across the fields and over Prop Hill was East Thornton, never more than a couple of farmsteads, only one of which remains with the new and strange name of Needless Hall, NZ111864. This, incidentally, should not be confused with the East Thornton at NZ116873, a stabling establishment which should perhaps be called Thistlecock. Lastly, there was and still is Temple Thornton, a small complex of buildings by the roadside near Meldon Park, NZ103856.

'Thornton' is not an uncommon name is Northumberland. This study deals with two others, one near Berwick and the other at Newbrough. The Rev. John Hodgson said 'Thorn' is a derivative of the Saxon word 'Donj', as in 'Donjon' meaning a fortification. A later vicar of Hartburn agreed that 'Thorn' is Saxon but believed that it has entered our language without changing its meaning – thus Thornton was a homestead near thorns. Officially it is just coincidental that from the fourteenth to the eighteenth centuries the principal family in the district was also called Thornton, but the possibility that Roger Thornton of Netherwitton adopted the local name in preference to a bondman's tag cannot be ruled out altogether.

During the reign of King Henry II (1154 – 89) Thornton was a manor within Bolbec's Styford barony and was held for one knight fee by Otwell de Lisle of Woodburn. The Lisles never lived here, so far as is known, and sublet the land to farmers. After 1250 they gave a hundred acres to the Knights Templar of Hartburn in return for a chaplain for their chapel at West Thornton. This plot of land became known much later as Temple Thornton.

All change in the fourteenth century. The Knights Hospitallers were handed the Knights Templar's land at Temple Thornton when the former were disbanded, and St. Albans Abbey, represented locally by their cell at Tynemouth, purchased the Lisles' major portion of Thornton. Both the new owners were just after money and let their estates to farmers.

St. Albans, and Tynemouth, were dissolved in 1539 and their property was taken by the Crown, which sold to local gentry. The same happened to Temple Thornton when the Hospitallers departed in about 1550.

In 1568 Lawrence Thornton of Netherwitton held roughly half the whole manor, and Robert Hall of Monkridge had a sizeable share as well. By 1590, however, the Thornton's share had reduced to West Thornton only and the other names had disappeared while Alexander Heron of the neighbouring estate of Meldon owned the lion's share. Thirty-two years later Alexander was in dire money trouble and Sir William Fenwick took over his share when he foreclosed on a debt. He did not last much longer, for his property was confiscated in 1650 by the Commonwealth Government, and ten years later Sir Francis Radcliffe, grandfather of the Jacobite rebel, bought the property.

The county rates returns for Thornton for 1663 are interesting. They showed that Sir Francis was assessed at £80 for East Thornton, John Thornton, the current member of the family which still had West Thornton, was assessed at £60, and an unknown, John Smith, paid on £6.65 for Temple Thornton, which, presumably, he had bought from the Radcliffes. The Smiths built a house on their plot and held it for three further generations before selling it back to the then owners of Meldon.

After the rout of the 1715 Jacobites, East Thornton was confiscated and eventually, in 1735, it was given, with Meldon, to the Greenwich Hospital: Temple Thorton joined them by purchase. Isaac Cookson, a Newcastle Alderman, bought the whole district in 1742, and his family still owns Meldon and much of the Thorntons.

East Thornton contracted from two to one farm during the Radcliffe tenure, but, so far as is known, there never was a fortified tower there. Its new name of Needless Hall is explained by the Rev. A.F. Donnelly of Hartburn as a fun sobriquet applied because the ground there was so good hard work was needless. Nickname it may have been, but it did not become the proper appellation until relatively recently as East Thornton appears regularly in Hartburn Church's Vestry Book until 1821.

West Thornton village occupied the field to the east of Thornton House farm. Only grass-covered foundations and the clear outline of the village pond remain today. There is little doubt that one of its buildings was a tower, and it was probably sited where the farmhouse stands now. It had a barmekyn – Hodgson could see its remains – and it was built, it is thought, by or for Brother Leonard, an unknown ecclesiastic, in 1338. Some of the farm land is now used for fruit cultivation.

Temple Thornton became a workshop for the Meldon estate and Smith's house was extended with similar houses on one end and a dovecote on the other, making a small hamlet of tied cottages. A tower here is just a non-proven possibility. The Knights Templar may have built one as a camera, a quiet and safe retreat, between 1250 and1307, but there is no mention of it in the specification drawn up when they left. A couple of nineteenth century historians claimed to have seen likely remains, but their descriptions are so vague they may have been writing about West Thornton. The dovecot may be mistaken for a tower when seen from a distance; at close range it looks more like a church tower, but in reality it was a purpose-built store for very fresh pigeon and certainly was not fortified. Today its ground floor is a tool shed and above are bedrooms joined to the house next door.

Angerton Hall

L81   P523   NZ095851   10¹/₂ km, 6¹/₂ miles, west of Morpeth

Access to this site was denied to the writer – one of the very few – but it has been reliably reported that there is a ruined bastle within the grounds of the Hall. It is said to feature a round arched ground floor entrance in its west gable.

This report conflicts with the Rev. John Hodgson's claim that neither High nor Low Angerton had any trace of a fortified building. The reverend historian, of course, did not take much notice of bastles, and in any case he was thinking of something much grander. Apparently Hugh de Bolbec's widow, the Baroness Theophania, and her daughter Maud, lived at Angerton, and he would have expected there to be signs of some dwelling befitting their rank.

After the Bolbecs, the Howard family got possession in King Henry II's reign, and it somehow escaped the sale board and confiscation until the Earl of Carlisle conveyed it to Ralph Atkinson of Newcastle in the nineteenth century. Probably he built the present Hall, which is a nineteenth century structure.

Hartburn

L81   P523   NZ089860   10¹/₂ km, 6¹/₂ miles, west of Morpeth

Visually and historically, the church dominates this peaceful village, which was part of Earl Waltheof's extensive estate before and just after the Norman Conquest.

During his short term of county duty, from 1072 to 1076, Waltheof managed to persuade the Bishop of Durham to allow monks from Jarrow Monastery to visit Tynemouth Priory. To help his infant progeny, he endowed it with some of his land, Hartburn included. Robert de Mowbray, earl between 1087 and 1095, confirmed this grant although he severed Tynemouth's connection with Jarrow and Durham and instead made the priory a cell of St. Albans Abbey, Hertfordshire. As a sign of their gratitude, the new monks of Tynemouth built and consecrated the church at Hartburn.

The Prior of Tynemouth, responding to orders from St. Albans, took his responsibilities seriously and maintained a supply of monks at Hartburn to care for the spiritual needs of the locals and to supervise the collection and storage of tithes. These men soon felt the need of material protection against thieves and raiders, and a fortified tower was built in the early years of the twelfth century. Originally it was free-standing, but after a year or two the church was extended to join onto it. The tower had a vaulted ground floor chamber in which the tithe corn was stored and an upper floor where the monks lived.

In 1966, during extensive restoration work on the existing church, human skeletons were found in shallow graves within the tower. Scientists carbon-dated the bones as between 800 and 1000 years old. Could it be that the monks found their tower was not quite so impenetrable as they had hoped?

The Knights Templar took the church over in about 1250, with the consent of the Abbot of St. Albans. Tynemouth Priory withdrew its monks and, in 1255, it also lost the tithes as King Henry III issued instructions to send them to St. Albans in order to provide the monks there and their guests with an adequate supply of bread and ale.

The Templars liked the church's location but the building was not to their required standard. They virtually rebuilt the nave on a larger scale, and the nucleus of what remains today dates from this time. The tower was renovated and allowed to remain, but a new vicarage was built a hundred yards distant from the church; this too was a fortified tower with a vaulted ground floor. When all was to their liking, the Templars engraved two daggers above a cross by the church entrance as a sign it was a Knights Templar temple and could be used for the induction of young squires into the knighthood.

There are no available reports of misbehaviour by the Templars during the next sixty years, so perhaps they refrained from justifying their bellicose reputation. Their leaders, at least, appear to have coalesced with their neighbours and probably enjoyed the occasional off-duty relaxation at Temple Thornton, which had been given to them by the Lisle family. For all that, the Pope thought fit to ban them in 1312, and Hartburn church and vicarage were returned to St. Albans Abbey, with Tynemouth Priory in charge. Temple Thornton went to the Knights Hospitaller of Low Chibburn.

St. Albans bought more local land from the Lisles, and kept this until it was dissolved in 1539.

The church has always been kept in good repair, and the vicarage, by extensions in the reigns of Edward VI and George II, has been converted into a mansion, now privately owned. Of the many vicars who have served in the former and lived in the latter were two notable characters: Dr. John Sharp, best known for his imaginative work for Lord Crewe's Charity at Bamburgh, and John Hodgson, who completed his *History of Northumberland* here.

Rothley

L81   P523   NZ043880   15^1/$_2$ km, 9^1/$_2$ miles, west of Morpeth

Rothley was a possession of Newminster Abbey, and Abbot John Birtley built a tower to protect his monks in 1467. It was still serviceable in 1541 but was allowed to deteriorate afterwards. A little of its masonry was noticed close to the road into the village in 1922, but since then the stones have been used to patch a drystone wall.

After dissolution the Crown sold Rothley and Rothley Moor to Sir John Fenwick of Wallington, and they have descended from there as part of the Wallington estate.

Man of commerce Sir Walter Calverley Blackett, who held the estate between 1728 and 1777, established a deer park on Rothley Crags for his own and his business associates recreation. Its containing walls still exist. To add a bit of romance to this he commissioned David Garrett, an architect who had built some farms on Wallington land, to build an authentic-looking ruined castle in a prominent position on the moor. This folly also exists and, since 1992, is accessible to the public.

When Garrett had finished this job he was asked to build another, slightly more practicable, building on the same moor but about a mile north of the folly. In July 1745 Sir Walter got news that Charles Edward Stuart, the Young Pretender, had landed on the west coast of Scotland and was forming an army of Highlanders with which to march to London. Sir Walter figured that the Bonny Prince had the choice of several routes across the Border into England, and that one of them, the old Salters' Way, went through his estate, following more or less the line now taken by the B6342 road between Rothbury and Scots' Gap. Mindful that his predecessor had been a Jacobite suspect in 1715, Sir Walter thought it expedient to demonstrate his loyalty to the Hanoverian dynasty, so he got Garrett to build a gun platform on a prominence commanding a length of the road. Six cannon were bought from the Master of Ordinance at Chatham Dockyard and installed on the platform, using the specially strengthened mounting points Garrett had provided. A tower behind the platform was planned for the storage of ammunition, but this was never built because, presumably, the danger had evaporated before work on it could be started. The platform was christened 'Codger Fort' for some unknown reason and travellers still pass within a few yards of it. In the event the Border was crossed near Carlisle, so the cannon were never fired in anger, but they were in celebration, it is alleged, when the Highlanders were defeated at Culloden in 1746. Nevertheless the platform was not a total waste of money for Capability Brown was able to use it as a garden folly when he landscaped Rothley Lakes in 1769. This, incidentally, was the only job Brown did in the estate; he was serving his apprenticeship at Kirkharle Hall when Wallington desmesne was landscaped.

Hartington Hall

L81   P523   NZ022880   17¹/₂ km, 10³/₄ miles, west of Morpeth

A medieval strong house derivative, originally built by the Fenwick family of Wallington and first mentioned in 1541 as owned by Sir John Fenwyke. Thereafter it was used for many years as a dower house.

Plate 1   Hepburn stronghouse. Claimed in 1509 to have room for 20 horsemen. (p104-5)

Plate 2   Hotspur Gate, built shortly after 1433, the only one left of four through Alnwick's town wall. (p115-9)

Plate 3   Alnwick Abbey Gatehouse. Built in the 14th century, 200 years after the Premonstratensian abbey it protected. (p145)

Plate 4   Edlingham Church. The strong tower was a refuge when danger threatened. (p152-4)

Plate 5 Cartington: all that remains of a spacious hall house. (p166-9)

Plate 6   Tarset 'Castle', a stronghold in wild North Tyne country. Its 'platform' still dominates the landscape. (p292-4)

Plate 7   Bog Head bastle, home of Corby Jack, an inveterate reiver. (p300-1)

Plate 8   High Cleugh bastle. The end wall on the left has been rebuilt recently. (p321)

Plate 9   Haughton, a fortified 'Gentleman's residence' near the North Tyne river. (p362-4)

Plate 12   Newcastle: Heber Tower and part of the town's west wall. (p465-471)

One of the widows who used the place was the former Margaret Selby, Sir William Fenwick's second wife. Her son, another Sir William, lived at Meldon and she visited him frequently, travelling there by underground coachway – or so legend tells us.

A lot of strange things were told about 'Meg O' Meldon', her sobriquet. Her clothing and demeanour, and especially her meanness, convinced the locals she was a witch. She struck terror in the hearts of all who knew her, both before and after her death in 1652.

The Hall has been sympathetically restored and is still habitable, on a long lease from the National Trust. Some traces of the original have been retained, notably the beamed ceiling of the ground floor.

Fairnley

L81   P523 NZ004889   19½ km, 12 miles, west of Morpeth

A farm at the end of a mile-long lane, west of the Cambo to Harwood road. It has been part of the Wallington manor since Hugh de Grandene acquired the lease from Baron Bolbec in the twelfth century.

The first occupier to be recorded was Robert de Farneylaw who was alive in 1286. In 1344 John de Fernelaw – note the spelling development – married a Swinburne girl, but nothing further is known about the family.

A good-sized tower once stood in the farmyard behind the farmhouse. It is said to have been a strong building with a vault and a long view both north and south. Its site is bare now; nothing remains to provide a hint of its building date.

Fairnley is called High Fairnley sometimes to distinguish the farm from Low Fairnley, a country cottage half way along the farm lane (NZ009887). This is an enlarged and mainly rebuilt bastle, the changes made in 1713 and further improvements in the 1970s or '80s.

The outline of the present building is the original, but the bastle had an extra floor, with two rooms on each floor. Its walls were only three feet thick and their stones were held in clay, not lime, so it was not of any great strength. It had no vault but the first floor did have a hearth carried on corbells. A spy hole was a special feature, and one can imagine that if an enemy was seen through it the occupants would decide that perhaps after all the tower belonging to the farmer was a safer bet than their bastle.

Catcherside

L81   P522   NY992876   20½ km, 12¾ miles, west of Morpeth

Another farm in the Wallington manor. According to one old surveyor, there was a tower in 1584, but whether this was fact or wishful thinking is impossible to say. There is no evidence of one now.

There is an obvious bastle derivative in the farmstead, however. This is Catcherside Cottage, the home of one of the farm workers. It looks a comfortable dwelling now, with a porch, windows, new roof and chimneys, but the conventional bastle shape remains, the walls are very thick and there is a blocked-up ground floor entrance with rounded arch in the east gable.

Ottercops

L81   P522   NY956889   24 km, 15 miles, west of Morpeth

A farm drained by one of the two burns which when united make the River Hart; originally it was in the Umfravilles' Redesdale liberty.

From the fifteenth to the seventeenth centuries there was a farmstead a few hundred yards to the north-east of the present place, belonging, it is believed, to a cadet branch of the Halls, the dominant family in Redesdale. The first building to be erected on the present site was a bastle: this in 1560, give or take a few years. It was joined by a second bastle in 1604, when 'Attercops' was rented by Gabarial Hall for one penny a year.

'Joined' is used literally here, for the two bastles were actually attached. The eastern house, the older of the two, was slightly shortened when the western house was built, and, some years later, both were provided with outside stone stairs.

In 1628 Thomas Hall was a freeholder in Ottercops. It is theorized that he and his family lived in the farmhouse while farmworkers, or perhaps married sons, lived in the bastles which we know were occupied long after the need for protection had passed. Until recently there was even a kitchen range in the first floor chamber of the older bastle. This room is used occasionally now as a lecture room for farmers and students who take advantage of the Demonstration Farms Project sponsored by the Countryside Commission.

Area 5, Sub-Area F   River Blyth

Kirkley

L88   P535   NZ150772   10 km, 6¼ miles, south-west of Morpeth

Part of the Mitford barony until Baron Roger Bertram forfeited his lands in 1264 for participating in Simon de Montford's abortive attempt to unseat King Henry III. The Crown sold Kirkley – also Newton Underwood – in 1267 to Sir Hugh, the third son of John fitz Roger, the lord of Warkworth. As father had no surname, sons were free to choose whatever they fancied: 'Clavering' became the favourite, but as Hugh inherited much property from his mother he selected the name of one of her estates in Essex. It was 'Iver' at first, then it became 'Ever' and finally 'Eure'.

Sir John de Eure, Sir Hugh's son, inherited during the last few years of the thirteenth century and fairly soon became involved in political intrigue. He may well have been on friendly terms with Earl Thomas of Lancaster, the big stirrer of the day, and this plus his personal disgust of the post-Bannockburn chaos in Northumberland persuaded him to take a back-seat driver's part in the nefarious exploits of the Mitford Gang. He was the organising shadow who let Sir Gilbert Middleton take all the credit – and the blame. Sir John was imprisoned after the kidnapping of Lewis de Beaumont, the bishop-elect, in 1317, but nothing could be pinned on him, apart from the fact that the deed was done on his land at Rushyford, and he had to be released. Nevertheless, the Crown continued to hold him in deep suspicion and during the Battle of Boroughbridge, Earl Thomas's last engagement against authority in 1322, he was quietly put to death, no questions asked.

Sir John's descendants were more conventional and useful members of society, holding such positions between the 1380s and 1540s as sheriff of Northumberland, sheriff of Yorkshire, governor of Newcastle's castle and captain of Berwick. One Sir William Eure was elevated to the peerage for his good work in 1544, four years before he died.

With homes in Yorkshire and Durham, the family's mansion at Kirkley was frequently empty, so John Ogle, a younger brother of the fourth Lord Ogle, was appointed as resident stewart to keep the place aired. The position developed and for a time Kirkley became the rented home of minor Ogles, and in 1580 two brothers, Henry and John, held the farms on the estate. In 1612 the third Lord Eure sold the place to Jane Ogles's husband, soon to become Lord Shrewsbury, and, although ownership changed round a bit within the family, it remained Ogle property until 1922.

A tower was built at Kirkley a few years before 1415 by Sir William Eure, and a manor-house was added to it later. These two buildings were totally demolished by Cuthbert Ogle, who replaced them with Kirkley Hall.

When the main line Ogles got derailed by heiresses it was left to cadet branches to carry on the family name. One of the most notable of these was Newton Ogle, Dean of Winchester, who was very fond of his Northumbrian seat and extended the estate. It was he who erected the still standing obelisk in 1788 to commemorate the centenary of the Glorious Revolution, the deposing of the Catholic King James II. He improved the Hall, but it still failed to satisfy his successor, John Saville Ogle, who did a complete rebuilding job in 1832. In 1922 John Francis Ogle sold all the estate except the demesne to local farmers, and the Hall went to Sir William Joseph Noble, a Newcastle shipper. Today the whole estate, including a much expanded Hall, is an agricultural college.

Ogle

L88   P535   NZ140790   9 km, 5¹/₂ miles, south-west of Morpeth

The locale of the Ogle family's genesis, the centre of the manor of Ogle held in

1150 by Umfrid de Hoggell, a knight who owed allegiance and feudal service to Walter fitz William, Baron of Whalton. By 1158 Umfrid possessed his own mill and was beginning to make his name known in the county.

The family grew in size and importance, partly because the spear descent was uninterrupted for four hundred years, and partly because of advantageous marriages. In its heyday there were at least fifteen important cadet branches and all these, as well as the main line, held substantial estates. Every generation produced more junior sons, cousins and nephews to take root not only in Northumberland but in Lancashire, Lincolnshire, Yorkshire, Staffordshire, Scotland, Ireland and America as well. And the spark which caused this explosion was ignited here, in Ogle.

The Hoggells lived in a fortified home mentioned as early as 1180. It was a timber building surrounded by a palisade and, possibly, a moat, and it served many generations until Robert Ogle, the second of that name, replaced it by a large, rectangular, barrack-like tower with corner turrets for which King Edward III issued a licence in 1341. This was given the courtesy title of Ogle Castle.

During the fourteenth century the barony and castle of Bothal was added to the Ogle portfolio and Ewyn, the second Lord Ogle, chose to live there – a choice with which all his descendants concurred inspite of the fact that the first Lord had added a comfortable manor-house to the east of the tower at Ogle. Nevertheless this was maintained in good condition for a further two centuries, probably as a residence for a cadet branch.

If anyone was living there in February 1644 they must have been ejected without ceremony when General Leslie came a second time to Newcastle with a large Scottish army. Some of his soldiers were billeted in the manor-house and tower, the large first floor hall in the latter making a most convenient barrack-room. According to contemporary reports, 'Ogle Castle' was in a sad state when it was derequisitioned; it was not repaired, was in decay in 1675 and little was left in 1776.

These reports proved to be incorrect, for when the fourth Duke of Portland, an Ogle descendant, built the still standing, very beautiful mansion in 1827 for a cadet family plenty of the original buildings were found to include in it. Thus the west wall of the tower, complete with corbelled gardrobe, forms most of the west wall of the mansion, there are several original fireplaces from the manor-house, including a magnificent kitchen range now in the entrance lounge, some ceilings exhibit their original beams and a large upstairs room is so like the room the Scottish soldiers occupied it is called 'the Barrack-room'. Outside, the moats are still traceable, and the site of the dependant village, destroyed in the seventeenth century, may be picked out by aerial photography.

As a Border fortification, 'Ogle Castle' had a relatively uneventful existence, but the family which owned it was arguably the most remarkable of all those which have graced the pages of Northumberland's history. As the name 'Ogle' crops up so frequently in this study, it is perhaps helpful to append here a table showing the main line of descent. This does not, of course, include all those cadet branches met with elsewhere, but it may explain the many name changes which complicate events from the middle of the sixteenth century.

Ogle Heads of Family

1.	Umfried de Hoggell	One of Baron of Whalton's knights
2.	Gilbert, eldest son	Held manor in 1165
3.	Richard, eldest son	
4.	Sir Thomas, eldest son	Married a Tyson heiress
5.	Sir John Oggell, eldest son	Succeeded c1240; married Annabella Selby
6.	Sir Robert Ogle, eldest son	Alive 1297; married Margaret Gubium
7.	Sir Robert II, eldest son	Married Joan Chartney, heiress,of Hepple baron, in 1331
8.	Sir Robert III, eldest son	Married Helen Bertram of Bothal in 1362
9.	Sir Robert IV, eldest son	Married into the Heton family, died 1410
10.	Sir Robert V, eldest son	Tried unsuccessfully to annex Bothal; died 1437
11.	Robert, Ist Lord Ogle, eldest son	Ennobled 1461; married a Lancashire lass
12.	Ewyn, 2nd Lord, eldest son	Succeeded 1469, died 1494
13.	Ralph, 3rd Lord, eldest son	Married Margaret Gascoyne
14.	Robert, 4th Lord, eldest son	Died 1539
15.	Robert, 5th Lord, eldest son	Died 1546
16.	Robert, 6th Lord, eldest son	Died 1562 without issue.
17.	Cuthbert, 7th Lord, younger brother	Married Carnaby heiress, died 1597
18.	Jane Ogle, eldest daughter	Married Edward Talbot who became Earl of Shrewsbury in 1615
19.	Catherine Talbot, eldest daughter	Married Sir Charles Cavendish; made Baroness Ogle in 1628 and died next year
20.	Sir William Cavendish, eldest son	Created Baron Ogle and Viscount Mansfield in 1620, Baron Cavendish and Earl of Newcastle in 1628, Baron Bertram and Marquis of Newcastle in 1643, Earl Ogle and Duke of Newcastle in 1664. Died 1676

21. Earl Henry of Ogle, eldest son — Married Elizabeth, heiress of Earl of Northumberland

22. Lady Margaret Cavendish, sister — Married John Holles, Earl of Clare; died 1711

23. Henrietta Cavendish Holles, eldest daughter — Married Edward Harley, Earl of Oxford and Mortimer in 1713; died 1741

24. Margaret Cavendish Harley, eldest daughter — Married William Bentinck, second Duke of Portland

25. William Henry Cavendish Bentinck, Duke of Portland III, eldest son — Home Secretary under Pitt the Younger, Prime Minister 1807-9. Married a daughter of Duke of Devonshire

26. William Henry Cavendish Bentinck, Duke of Portland IV, eldest son — His titles include Marquis of Titchfield, Viscount Woodstock, Baron of Cirencester and Lord of the Barony of Bothal. Built Ogle mansion 1827.

Whalton

L81   P523   NZ131813   8 km, 5 miles, south-west of Morpeth

Whalton was the capital of one of our oldest Norman baronies, granted during the lifetime of King William I. The first baron for whom there are records was Walter fitz William, who was alive in 1166 and held his property for three knights fee. Two of his knights were the progenitors of the Ogle and Widdrington families.

Walter had no sons and only one daughter, Constance, who married Ralph de Crammavill. They had one son, Robert, an only child who died without issue, so the barony reverted to the Crown. In 1205 it was granted by King John to his great friend, Robert fitz Roger, lord of Warkworth, part of a bouquet of bounties which included Newburn and Rothbury.

Whalton continued as a manor of Warkworth barony until it was inherited by John de Clavering in 1310. He was desperately short of both heirs and money, and in 1312 he sold Whalton to Geoffrey Le Scope, who in 1335 became the chief Justice of the King's Bench. He died in 1340, but he was followed by further Lords Le Scope for the next two hundred years.

Lord Henry Le Scope, head of the family in the early years of the sixteenth century, married Margaret, daughter of Thomas Lord Dacre. Father-in-law did not believe in dowries so instead made a deal with Henry: Whalton was transferred to Leonard Dacre, Thomas's brother, and the Le Scopes got an equivalent estate in the Dacre empire, which extended into Cumberland and Durham. But Leonard did not have Whalton long for in 1569 he got involved in the pro-Catholic rebellion, the Rising of the North, and found it expedient to flee to Holland, where he died in 1581.

The Crown took Whalton again, and kept it until after the Union of 1603, when it was sold piecemeal to sitting tenants and local gentry.

All baronies should have had a castle, or at least an imposing tower, in their capital, but Whalton does not appear to have anything of that sort. The original barons may have had something, now long disappeared and forgotten, but later holders had large estates elsewhere and ruled from afar.

The ordinary residents did better than their landlords. According to W.W. Tomlinson (1897), "The old castle-houses, of which the village was formerly composed, have all disappeared". If by 'castle-house' he meant some type of defensible stone-built house, these villagers were unusual – most families of the soil lived in hovels which they hoped were too mean to attract the attention of raiders – but not unique as both Hepple and Chesterwood are said to have consisted of bastles as one time. The village parson did best of all: his rectory was a strong tower built, probably, in the fourteenth century when extensive work was done on the church. It was much extended at a later date but it still contains two vaulted ground floor rooms, one of them with the remains of a spiral stair.

Bolam

L81   P523   NZ086823   11¹/₂ km, 7 miles, south-west of Morpeth

King Henry I, shortly after his enthronement in 1100, granted a small, irregularly-shaped barony centred on Bolam to James de Burum. The grant was neither generous nor well thought out for it comprised only Bolam vill, Bradford and Belsay with much local and desirable land omitted.

James's son, Gilbert, improved the situation appreciably by reaching an advantageous agreement with Walter de Bolbec, Baron of Styford. By negotiating a long lease, which turned out to be virtually a purchase, he gained for Bolam in 1166 the vills and manors of Cambo, East and West Shaftoe, Greenleighton, Harnham, Hartington, Harwick, Rothley and South Middleton. King John confirmed the transfers in 1204 and added Aydon, near Corbridge, and some small estates on the banks of the River Tyne. When Gilbert's son, Walter, died in 1206 he was holding a barony which, in feudal terms, was worth the services of five and a half knights.

Walter and his predecessors had lived in a tower on top of the 'bol' or hill at Bolam. This had been a strong 40 by 30 feet fortification built inside an ancient British camp and making use of its double vallum and ditch on three sides, but when Walter's widow Emma decided to remarry she and her new husband, Peter de Vaux, thought it was too dilapidated to live in. They built and moved into a timber manor-house on a piece of Harnham's land which they called Shortflatt. Bolam lost its role as barony capital.

Emma had two daughters by her first husband, and they were joint beneficiaries, The sisters. Aline and Alice were married to two brothers, John and James Cauz – two 'As' with two 'Js'. Neither couple exercised much influence over the barony, for John and Aline Cauz were both dead by 1234, and James and Alice died just eight years after the decease of Peter and Emma Vaux, in 1248. Both, however, spawned a single daughter – John and Aline had Margery and James and Alice had Mary (two 'Ms'!) – and these two girls married holders of land outside Northumberland who became absent controllers of Bolam barony.

The ensuing history of the barony evolved around its principal estates and is told under Shortflatt (below) and Aydon (Area 9). The vill of Bolam was considered as just one of the parcels included in the Aydon section, but, whether by judicious management or intuitive flair is not known, it flourished during the next two hundred years. It was granted a market and fair by King Edward I in 1305, and gradually grew into a small town with some two hundred houses set around its green. In the sixteenth century over five hundred people lived there, but eventually it withered until little was left.

During the eighteenth century Robert Horsley bought the whole parcel, then Lord Decies got it by marrying Horsley's daughter. Decies built Bolam House, using as much of the old tower as he could find, and he created Bolam Lake to give employment to local people during the two disastrous winters of 1816 and 1817.

Shortflatt

L81   P523   NZ079810   13 km, 8 miles, south-west of Morpeth

A timber manor-house was built in 1206 in a corner of Harnham estate held by the Barons of Bolam. It was the home of Emma, the baroness, and her second husband Peter Vaux. The name is said to be a synonymic expression for 'furlong', the length of a farrow in a common field, now 220 yards, but if this was intended to be a dimension of their land it is rather misleading as a furlong square is only ten acres whereas we are told they annexed a hundred acres from Harnham.

The barony eventually descended to two female cousins, each of whom held half. Mary, married to Thomas de Bickering, held Aydon and Bolam vill but lived with her husband in Lincolnshire. Margery inherited the Shortflatt part of the barony and married William de Bretun, a nephew of the Archbishop of York.

William died in 1246 without spawning any heirs. Margery married a second time, to a Suffolk knight called Sir Richard de Gosbeck. It was alleged that she was the willing victim of abduction and was married without a licence, an offence for which the couple were fined. Sir Richard died in 1281 and Margery in 1284, but they did manage to leave a son and heir, Hugh. While his father and mother had not bothered about their northern possession, Hugh did a little better by letting Shortflatt to William de Middleton, the rector of Bolam, who is believed to have been a very caring custodian.

When the rector died in 1293, Hugh got rid of his unwanted responsibility by transferring Shortflatt to his family's life-long friend, wealthy Ipswich trader Hugh de Reymes of Wherstead in Suffolk. There was a minor hiccup in the conveyance as neither Hugh had remembered to obtain Crown permission; the estates were confiscated for a few months, then released on payment of a £60 fine. By this time, however, Hugh de Reymes had died and his son, Robert, found himself the owner of half Bolam and, at the Aydon people's request, agent for the other half.

This suited him admirably, for Robert was a soldier and welcomed the opportunity to plant roots in the Border region where, it seemed quite obvious, King Edward I was about to stir up lots of action. He took up residence in Shortflatt – then had to move out rather quickly when the timber house caught fire. He started to build a stone house at Aydon, and work on this was continuing while he was with his king at Stirling Bridge in 1297 and Falkirk in 1298, but it was interrupted twice by enemy incursions.

These raids decided Robert to apply for licences to crenellate both Aydon and Shortflatt. They were granted by the ailing king in 1305. The fire debris at Shortflatt was cleared away and a large tower was built on its site. It was a fine building, warranting the classification 'fortalice' in some old histories, yet the Scottish raiders got the better of it in 1311, 1312 and 1314 and major repairs were the order of the day. When completed, the tower measured 34 by 20 feet internally and had walls at least six feet thick. It had three storeys below a pitched roof which had a parapet walk all round. The ground floor was barrel vaulted and a small wing containing a solar was attached to its east side.

Robert died in 1323, leaving the property to his son, Robert II. He held it for twenty-six years then died of the Black Death. Robert III, his son, took over until 1360 then, because he died without issue, his brother Hugh became the lord of Shortflatt. He lasted only a couple of months, and because he also died childless, descent took another sideways step to another brother, Nicholas. He was the family's black sheep and was languishing in gaol for harbouring murderers so he could not take possession until 1376. That was the year the agency of Aydon became the ownership of Aydon; ever since the mid-thirteenth century the Bickerings had allowed first the Gosebecks then the Reymes to look after their Northumbrian lands, but now Shortflatt and Aydon were united under one owner.

Nicholas died in 1394 and then followed a succession of seven Roberts, all eldest sons, who filled the fifteenth and sixteenth centuries almost exactly. It was a hazardous time for Northumberland property and Shortflatt tower and estate were frequent targets for Scottish virulence,as a consequence of which their value for tax purposes dropped to zero in 1450, and had improved to only £1.44 by 1490. The Reymes' coffers emptied: there was not enough money even to maintain the tower, and Roberts VIII and IX lived in a smaller house. The estate was sold bit by bit and Shortflatt tower was let to anyone able to pay the small rent required. One such was Thomas Fenwick, a member of a gang of freebooters – another black sheep who suffered the ultimate penalty in 1528.

John, the tenth Robert's son, had only Shortflatt to receive from his father, and it was'nt a very welcome inheritance: rather shabbily he passed the liability on to his son, Henry, who in turn got rid of it as quickly as he could. By 1607 William Selby was the owner.

William, believed to be from the Biddlestone stock, had enough money to save Shortflatt tower. He was able to restore it to its former splendour, and to so stabilize it that it still exists in this condition today. He also cleared away the small east wing and built instead a comfortable manor-house. A later Selby added a north wing.

Harnham

L81   P523   NZ074804   13½ km, 8¼ miles, south-west of Morpeth

What was left of Harnham manor after Shortflatt's hundred acres were purloined went to Robert Swinburne of Capheaton in 1412. A tower was built during the next three years.

This tower sits on top of a north-west facing precipice, a precarious perch which must have presented the masons with some tricky problems. There is a sheer drop to the field below except for a short section where room was found for a small terrace with positions in its wall for shooting at an approaching enemy. This front remains much as it must have been in the fifteenth century, except that its windows are seventeenth century replacements.

In about 1500 part of the tower's south wall was pulled down and replaced by a manor-house. The approach to this side is gradual and is used by the lane from the Belsay – Otterburn road; from it the manor-house appears to be quite unexceptional, the last building in a line of houses which comprise the hamlet of Harnham.

Major Philip Babington, a Cromwellian officer and one-time governor of Berwick Castle, bought the manor-house cum tower in 1660. Both he and his wife Catherine were devout Puritans who had been in their element during the Commonwealth and now were strongly antagonistic to King Charles II and the return of the Church of England. Catherine, or 'Kate', had the right background, being the daughter of Sir Arthur Haselrigg and widow of Colonel

George Fenwick, both prominent characters in Cromwell's era. Small wonder that Harnham became a haven for Puritan sympathizers and non-conformists persecuted by the Crown.

Kate was also a celebrated beauty. According to one story, the magistrates of Durham City issued an order obliging her to eat in a back room when she went for lunch as if she could be seen from the street such large crowds gathered that the traffic was held up. She was also a lady with spirit and fervour. When the Reverent Forster resumed his living at Bolam church in 1661 she had him pulled out of his pulpit. For this she was excommunicated but escaped imprisonment on the understanding she would be confined to a room in the tower.

Major Babington improved the manor-house; the ceiling of the living room proves this as his crest, a dragon, is imbossed in the plaster. It is doubtful, however, whether Kate ever saw the result as she stayed a prisoner in her room in the tower until she died in 1670. To while away the time she wrote poetry and occasionally scratched messages on the window glass with a diamond ring: 'Omnia Vanitas' (all is vanity), was one such message. She was refused burial in consecrated ground and her coffin was laid in a vault cut into the rock in the garden below her home.

East Shaftoe

L81   P523   NZ059817   14¹/₂ km, 9 miles, south-west of Morpeth

East and West Shaftoe were two more estates the barony of Bolam obtained from the barony of Styford in 1166; they were the responsibility of the owners of Shortflatt until 1568.

In 1296 there were twelve people paying subsidy (tax) in the two parts of Shaftoe, and prominent amongst them was a family which assumed the name of the place and lived at East Shaftoe, allegedly in a tower. Four years after this William de Schaftowe married Isobel Bataille de Bavington, an heiress who in 1306 inherited most of her father's estate. The couple made their home at Little Bavington, in what was later to develop into Bavington Hall.

By 1377 only six families were paying tax, but tax evasion is not a new phenomenon and in reality there were enough people to populate a village at East Shaftoe – a village large enough to have a chapel and, from 1378, a chantry and resident priest.

Presumably these people prospered, but records are missing until 1568, when William Aynsley bought a tower (a 'capital messuage') at East Shaftoe. He did not build it but it was fairly new and certainly was not one William de Schaftowe might have had. Recent architectural surveys of the still existing building have assessed its oldest datable component, a pointed arched doorway, as fifteenth century work.

At first the Aynesley family owned a vill at West Shaftoe as well as East Shaftoe, but by 1633 John Aynsley was making do with the former only and Dalston Shafto was holding East Shaftoe. Note that he and his descendants dropped the final 'e' in their name, although it is retained for the place. Dalston was the younger son of William, the lord of Little Bavington; he was fifty-seven years old at the time and a captain in the Commonwealth army. He and John Aynsley ran a coal mine near Shaftoe Crags.

East Shaftoe was inherited by Dalston's son, then by his grandson who adopted his grandmother's maiden name of Vaughan to avoid any possible confusion with his uncle, an active Jacobite. He sold his property to Sir William Blackett, who held Wallington from 1705 to 1728, but he continued to live at East Shaftoe as a tenant.

The next Wallington owner, Sir Walter Calverley Blackett, was an energetic innovator who improved the efficiency of his farms with robust enthusiasm. Perhaps it was this which caused the decline of East Shaftoe village. In 1734 seven families lived there, but Armstrong's 1769 map shows only the tower, presumably with the elegant dwelling house which by now stood next to it, and one other building. The village houses and the chapel had gone.

Robert Horsley bought East Shaftoe towards the end of the eighteenth century. In 1810 his heiress and her husband, Lord Decies, who built and lived in Bolam House, expanded the property by adding West Shaftoe. It is strange that after two and a half centuries of 'freedom', the two Shaftoes should return to 'subjugation' by Bolam. In 1821 Lord Decies built the present farm at West Shaftoe and at least one farm building at East Shaftoe. One wall of this includes a large grave-cover stone bearing the Aynsley arms which Lady Decies had unearthed near the foundations of the old chapel.

The fifteenth century tower still exists although it is necessary to enter it to appreciate this, for it was incorporated into the house during the eighteenth century. It is still obvious, however, that the tower was rectangular and had a stair turret at one corner to provide access to the upper floors and, probably, a crenellated walkway. The single ground floor chamber was barrel vaulted and its eight supporting square ribs still spring from the floor. The pointed arch doorway is in the east wall and now connects tower to house. A couple of slits provide the only ventilation downstairs, but the upper chambers will have had small windows.

The modern house has a beautiful garden, but of course its greatest distinction is the splendour of the heather-covered moors and rugged cliffs of Shaftoe Crags. Above the boulder-strewn face seen from the main road are two early British camps, a tumulus and a standing stone; there were two of the latter until Sir Walter Blackett pinched one for Wallington. The Devil's Causeway, the Roman road which traverses the county, crosses the area, and another track, not quite so old, climbs Salters' Nick, a small cutting in the crags. This was the Salters' Way, used by smugglers taking salt from the south-east coast to trade in Scotland.

At the highest point of the crags is a huge boulder balanced on the cliff edge. Its pock-marked surfaces have engendered many possible explanations, from weather-beaten cup and rings to witches symbols. But the largest hole, smoother than the rest, appears to be reasonably understandable: it must have been a hiding place for salt when the customs officers got too close to the smugglers. Not so! In fact it was a natural hole which was greatly enlarged to take several gallons of liquor provided at a party the Vaughans held in honour of their landlord, Sir William Blackett, on the occasion of his marriage to Lady Barbara Villiers in 1725. Thomas Whittell, "a queer fellow who never stayed long at one thing" and who is said to have entered Cambo on the back of a ram, was proud of the way he had chiselled the stone to make the punch bowl. Actually he was quite a skilled carver of stone and made all the sundials in the neighbourhood; he was a creditable poet and painter as well. He died at Hartburn in 1736.

Capheaton

L81   P523   NZ038805   17 km, 10¹/₂ miles, south-west of Morpeth

Thomas Fenwick, head of the third generation of Fenwicks of Fenwick, held Ingoe, Stamfordham and Great Heton as well as his main seat. He sold Great Heton to Alan de Swinburne, second son of John de Swinburne of Great Swinburn, in 1274. Thereafter the place was known as Capheaton. Alan was rector of Whitfield in 1264; he never married so in 1284 he transferred Capheaton to his nephew, Alexander de Swinburne, son of his younger brother William. Alexander initiated a line of Swinburnes which stretches to the present day.

It is alleged that Alan bought a tower, not just a plot of land, but no fortification is mentioned until 1415. The building then surveyed was inhabited until 1668, and was equipped with a moat and drawbridge. A beacon was lit on its flat roof as a warning of raiders in the area, and local gentry frequently rendezvoused in it when retaliatory sorties were organised. This was probably why the Charltons of North Tynedale led the Croziers of Liddesdale to Capheaton in 1543: they left the tower and village in flames, but the damage was repairable.

A remarkable story is told of John Swinburne who was orphaned when his father and mother were killed during the Civil War, 1642-51. He was packed off to a monastery in France for his protection and education, and there he remained the rest of the war and the following interregnum, forgotten by his family and friends. Quite by chance, the Loraines of Kirkharle visited the monastery while on a grand tour of France in 1660, and they thought they recognised John. To prove his identity, John correctly answered two questions, the inscription on a punch bowl at Capheaton and the colour of his cat, so the Loraines brought him back home to assume his inheritance. King Charles II bestowed a baronetcy on him in recognition of his father's service and his own suffering. It was this Sir John who commissioned Robert Trollop in 1668 to build Capheaton Hall to replace the old tower.

The Swinburne family were ardent supporters of Roman Catholicism and during the period when the 'old faith' was proscribed many clandescent services were held in Capheaton Hall, and there were more than one secret cache in the building where the priest could hide should the law decide to interfere. The family also supported the Jacobites, but when the call came for action in 1715 the then head of the family hedged his bets. Deciding that his property and his line of descent were more important that the cause, he did not join the rebels and refused to allow his eldest son and heir to join, but he sent two younger sons.

In about 1800 William Newton was engaged to renovate and expand Capheaton Hall. He added a north face and two large wings, destroying some of Trollop's decoration while doing so. He found no trace of the original tower, the exact site of which is not known.

Bradford

L87   P535   NZ068795   14½ km, 9 miles, south-west of Morpeth

A barn in the farmyard of Bradford South Farm is a good example of a house built in the style of a Border bastle but with relatively thin walls and thus not a stronghold. It demonstrates very clearly how conservative were the sixteenth century designers of vernacular buildings, who appear to have considered it quite unnecessary to change a house plan of proven success merely because it did not have to be strong enough to resist raiders.

The barn in question was built for Gabriel Ogle, son of Matthew Ogle of Saltwick, in 1567. It has an iron roof now, and the windows are replacements, but the fireplace, inscribed 'G.O.1567', is original, as is the shell of the building, two stones thick without any rubble infilling.

But, for all its lack of protection, Bradford was a place of some importance. It was one of the few estates which were part of the original barony of Bolam. In about 1246 it became a possession of Sir Richard de Gosbeck of Shortflatt and Suffolk, who gave it as a dowry when his daughter Alice married Robert de Bradford, the son of the sitting tenant. The young couple and their descendants held it for over three hundred years, until the Ogles bought it.

As early as 1296 it was home to ten tax payers who paid on an assessment of £17.66 – more even than was collected at Hepple or Newburn – and right up to the nineteenth century Bradford was larger than Belsay and Ponteland.

Its attraction was its central position in a locally important traffic system. Belsay, in its original position close to the tower (NZ086785), had good access to the south and was only a mile away, and there were direct routes from Bradford to Harnham, Bolam, Capheaton and Cambo. It lost these advantages when Belsay was moved to the east and the main road from Newcastle to Otterburn was turned to go through it and to connect with the 'New Line' (1830s) which bypassed Bradford. It lost even its cattle droving business when the Morpeth to Scots Gap railway was opened in 1862. The effect was immediate: Bradford dwindled to two farms and a couple of cottages.

Belsay

L88   P535   NZ084785 $13^1/_2$ km, $8^1/_4$ miles, south-west of Morpeth

Like Bradford, Belsay was an original estate in the Bolam barony as bestowed by King Henry I on James de Burum. Before 1166 Robert de Bellesse had been granted the heritable rights of Belsay, and in 1171 he passed these to his son who, for some unknown reason, preferred to be called William le Scott. The usual feudal arrangement of providing service for land was changed during his tenure to socage – he paid rent in money. From then on the ties between tenant and baron grew more and more tenuous.

Two daughters succeeded when William died in 1242. They were married to two brothers, John and Richard Middleton, descendants of Gospatric of Middleton Hall near Wooler. Richard was the brighter of the two and soon bought John out and thus became the founder of the very enduring Middletons of Belsay line.

Richard was ambitious and successful in public life. He became secretary and chancellor to King Henry III and was knighted for his efforts. In 1270 he was granted the signal honour of free warren in his demesne lands, something the king normally held tenaciously for himself.

He had three sons. The first died young so number two, William, inherited Belsay, as did his son Sir John after him. The youngest, Gilbert, inherited some of his father's property at Cramlington and Hartley. He married Juliana Swinburne of Great Swinburne in 1279 so when he died, in 1310, both their sons inherited considerable wealth, Gilbert his father's estates and John his mother's. Young Gilbert became the Mitford Gang's field commander and his brother one of his lieutenants; both lost everything, including their lives, in 1318. Cousin Sir John may or may not have had anything to do with the rebels but his close relationship with Gilbert engendered sufficient doubt to cause the Crown to confiscate Belsay.

John de Strivelyn, who had been a victim of the Mitford Gang, bought Belsay on advantageous terms designed to compensate in some measure the distress and hardship a Middleton had caused him. His wife, Barnaba

Swinburne, also regained her inheritance, Little Swinburn, which had been confiscated a few years earlier when her father, Alan, had fallen foul of the law.

Sir John Middleton made sure that his Belsay would return to him eventually by the simple expedient of marrying the Strivelyn daughter and heiress, Christiana. He had to wait until about 1370 before his father-in-law died, but when he did the reward was not only Belsay but Little Swinburn as well. The former was destined to remain in the family until the present century, the latter to the end of the seventeenth century.

The fourteenth, or perhaps the late thirteenth, century saw the construction of Belsay 'castle', a large tower, probably discrete and obviously designed for Border defence yet containing all the home comforts required by a medieval lord of the manor and his entourage. There was a ground floor vaulted kitchen, a very commodious great hall on the first floor and sleeping quarters on the third. Small chambers, one possibly a chapel, were packed beneath a high turret at the south-west corner. All the main chambers had gardrobes en suite. Sir John Middleton's son, another John, is on record as having lived in "his turris at Belshowe" in about 1390, and also in 1415.

Just the presence of this mighty bulwark seems to have been enough to keep the worst excesses of Border warfare away from Belsay for the next two hundred years. Even Earl James Douglas, on route from Newcastle to Otterburn in 1388, gave the area a wide berth. Members of the Middleton family frequently exposed themselves to the ungodly as wardens of the marches, justices of the peace and Members of Parliment, so they would have expected some attention.

In 1614 Thomas and Dorothy Middleton extended the tower by building a manor-house against its west wall. When completed, this did not seem to be large enough so a further extension was added to its west face. The complex was ready in 1629, about the time when King Charles I was getting into some difficulty and a civil war was looking ominous. Thomas was a Protestant without any strong political leanings and was able to assist both this monarch and Cromwell, but his son supported King Charles II, who awarded him a baronetcy in 1662.

The eighteenth century witnessed a minor altercation in family relations. When George Middleton died his widow, Cecily, remarried rather hastily against the wishes of her children. The new husband was John Heron, son of Sir Harry, the last Heron to own Chipchase. He was penniless and expected his bride to exercise her widow's rights so they could live at Belsay. But George had left an heir and he objected to this take-over bid, an objection upheld in the Court of Chancery. John and Cecily went to live in Bowlby in North Yorkshire, where they had one son. He added his mother's name to his – Thomas Heron Middleton – in the hope of swinging the succession pendulum his way, but he died childless in 1780, the last of the male Heron line.

Sir Charles Middleton, Cecily and George's grandson, inherited Belsay when he came of age in 1801. He also inherited considerable wealth and an estate at Caenby in Lincolnshire from his mother's parents, whose will contained the wish that Charles should adopt their name. Thus it was Sir Charles Monck who married his cousin, Louisa Cooke, in 1804 and set off for a two year honeymoon in Greece and Sicily. Sir Charles, who had studied art and the classics at university, became hooked on Greek architecture to such a degree he became determined to bring a little bit of it back to Belsay. As soon as he got home he set about building a new house on a prominent spot overlooking Belsay Park. He provided the general ideas while John Dobson rolled them into a professional design, and the result is a Graeco-Roman structure, a perfect square with hundred feet sides and complete with pillars and embellishments said to be similar to those found in an ancient Greek temple. This, the new Belsay Hall, was completed in 1815 to the accompaniment of criticism both good and bad. Is it an example of Greek Doric purity which can stand comparison with anything in the country, or is it a tasteless misfit in the Northumbrian ambience?

The manor-house, a quarter of a mile from the Hall, was renovated and became the residence of the estate steward. Its extension was partly dismantled as being surplus to requirements. Belsay village was a little to the east of the tower – not really in the way but it had to go because the road to it interfered with the Hall's view and the privacy of the gardens. It was moved about a mile further east and the main Newcastle road was bent in order to run through it. The 'New Line' turnpike was started from its northern end.

When Sir Charles' grandson inherited the family's wealth the family's name of Middleton returned. But interest in Belsay was on the wane: the Hall was occupied only spasmodically and the gardens and manor-house were neglected. At the beginning of the Second World War the place was empty and, in 1980, Sir Stephen Middleton placed the estate in the care of the Department of the Environment. It is an English Heritage showpiece now, attracting crowds to see the Hall and the magnificent gardens.

Bitchfield

L88   P535   NZ090770   14 km, 8½ miles, south-west of Morpeth

A manor in Bywell barony which Guy Balliol gave, with Bothal, to his daughter Hawise when she married William Bertram, Baron of Mitford, in c1095. In 1264 Roger Bertram sold West Bitchfield to Sir Richard Middleton of nearby Belsay, and from then to 1503 it was treated as an extension to the Belsay estate.

During the fifteenth century the Middletons built a tower at West Bitchfield. It was not a very large one but it had a vaulted ground floor, mural stairs to one upper floor and a corbelled turret, a moat and a barmekyn.

There were several owners after 1503. John and Alice Harbottle (not the Preston family) were the first; they bought the manor to pass to their daughter Margery when she married John Fenwick, son of Sir John Fenwick of Fenwick. The bridegroom already had a tower at Ryal so Bitchfield was passed on to younger brother Roger. His descendants kept it until 1630, adding an attractive manor-house just before selling it to Edward Grey of Howick The manor-house was built alongside the tower's eastern wall and it carried the inscription 'R.F.', which presumably stood for the occupier at that time, Robert Fenwick. In about 1680 Sir James Clavering of Calally bought the place, then at the beginning of the nineteenth century Bitchfield returned to the Belsay estate.

It is not know why Sir Charles Monck (Middleton) wanted this near neighbour for he did nothing to it. House and tower were left to decay and were practically ruinous when finally sold in 1930. Fortunately the purchaser had enough money to restore them and today the double building is an attractive, modernised dwelling. It seems rather strange to find a w.c. in a fifteenth century stronghold, but it fits neatly into the former gardrobe and the plumbing runs out of sight down the old chute.

Area 5, Sub-Area G   River Pont

Ponteland

L88   P535   NZ165729   13^1/$_2$ km, 8^1/$_4$ miles, south of Morpeth

The Pont joins the River Blyth roughly two miles east of Kirkley Hall. From its source near Dere Street its course is generally easterly to Ponteland, then for its last four miles it runs northerly through low-lying ground which used to be wet marsh. 'Pont-eland' was an island in this fen country – plus marks for its defence capability. Adequate drainage was not achieved until mid-nineteenth century.

From early Norman times to 1264 Ponteland was a manor in the Bertrams' barony of Mitford, and during the latter part of this period the place may have made history as a meeting place of kings. Considerable work was done both in England and Scotland on establishing a mutually acceptable Border line, and the treaty of York, signed in 1237, was supposed to settle the question. King Alexander II of Scotland remained unhappy about some elements of the agreement, however, and his cavilling so annoyed the English king, Henry III, that he mustered an army of five thousand horse in Newcastle, intending to establish the Border by force. Alexander collected a thousand horse and came to meet him, but realised just in time that the odds were heavily stacked against him. Instead of fighting, the two kings met and discussed their grievances, and there is an apocryphal report that this meeting took place in Ponteland in 1244. The historian Cadwallader Bates did not agree; he maintained the meeting took place two years earlier in "the standing corn of the Newcastle Nuns", presumably Nuns Moor on the edge of Newcastle.

William de Valence, Earl of Pembroke, bought Ponteland in 1264 and built a tower opposite the church. He and his family settled there until Aymer de Valence, the second earl and King Edward II's lieutenant in Scotland, died of apoplexy in France in 1323. His death created a succession problem – he died childless – which the Crown settled in 1325 by awarding the manor to Aymer's niece, Joan, the wife of David Strathbolgi, Earl of Athol. David let his younger brother, Sir Aymer de Athol, occupy Ponteland tower and he was still there, or more likely his son of the same name was still there, when Earl James Douglas called on his way from the walls of Newcastle to Otterburn in 1388. Sir Aymer was captured and his home was burnt down.

Ponteland tower seems to have been left a ruin for two hundred years, until Mark Errington bought it and restored it to habitable condition in 1580. Mark's family had considerable property in the greater Hexham area; this purchase was most likely to provide a son with a home of his own. A Jacobean manor-house which incorporated the tower was built about a century later, and lived in until 1788. It is not known when it became a public house or why it was called the Blackbird.

There is a second tower in Ponteland, a vicarage built about 1400. As seen from the Belsay road it is quite impressive, but a closer look is very depressing. It was repaired in a very clumsy fashion during the eighteenth century when anything to hand, even bricks, were used, and another attempt in 1971 did nothing to improve it. It's more like a firemen's practice tower.

High Callerton

L88   P535   NZ161705   15¹/₂ km, 9¹/₂ miles, south-west of Morpeth

Formerly Great Callerton or Callerton Valence, this little hamlet and neighbouring Darris Hall, Callerton Darreyne as was, were part of Ponteland manor until the mid-sixteenth century and shared its Bertram, Valence, Strathbolgi descent.

In 1558 Sir Robert Brandling bought part of High Callerton, and Giles Gofton the other part. The Goftons were a local family whose memorial stone is to be seen in Ponteland church. Brandling was a wealthy Newcastle family and Sir Robert liked to make a little extra by buying and selling property. In this case the buyer was William Shafto of Little Bavington.

The Goftons' part was sold quite quickly, and the new owner built a bastle round about 1600. It is most unusual to find such a building so far from the Border and so close to a large conurbation; obviously someone felt very frightened but could not afford anything better. It came in useful in 1649 as a secret hide-out for a small group of rebels. This was the year King Charles I was executed and it is assumed that the rebels were Royalists who took a dim view of Cromwell. The bastle became known as Rebellion House, and it still exists under that name as a modernised residence retaining its rafters of rough-hewn trunks and huge stone fireplace.

The Rev. Robert Bonner came to live in High Callerton in 1663 and built Callerton Hall a few years later. Descendants took the name Warwick in 1792 and held the Hall to at least 1924, when the occupier was Robert Maddison Warwick. It is a rest home now.

Stamfordham

L88   P535   NZ076720   18¹/₂ km, 11¹/₂ miles, south-west of Morpeth

An old village on the north bank of the Pont which in the distant past was subservient to Heugh, a mile to its north. Stamfordham developed into a market town, however, while Heugh stood still and today is still just a small cluster of houses.

Guy de Balliol claimed Stamfordham and district as part of his Bywell barony granted to him by King William II in 1093. It was held by someone called Wieland in 1121, and his son, who took the name Ralph de Stamfordham, passed it on to his son-in-law, Hugh de Normanville, in 1201. The Fenwicks became owners in 1245, but the Normanvilles remained the occupiers until 1351 when it was forfeited to the Crown for too much fraternisation with the Scots. The Swinburnes of Capheaton, already tenants in a small way, began to buy extensively during the second half of the fourteenth century until, in 1399, they were the chief landowners in the village.

There are today two public houses in Stamfordham, the Bay Horse and the Red Lion, but three hundred years ago there was a third, Cross House, two doors away from the Red Lion. Here gentry with leanings towards the Jacobite cause – people like the Derwentwaters, Swinburnes, Collingwoods and Widdringtons – used to meet regularly to play bowls overtly and to plan rebellion surreptitiously.

The Swinburnes built a tower before 1460, almost certainly for the vicar. The present vicarage is a Tudor building with eighteenth century modifications and much older vaulted cellars. It is probable that these are the last remains of the tower, but there is just the possibility that the church tower was originally the vicar's fortified lodgings. It is strong and massive enough to be a refuge, and the facts that it has no outside door and the land falls steeply from it encourages this thinking.

Fenwick

87   P535   NZ057728   19¹/₂ km, 12 miles, south-west of Morpeth

The great Fenwick family, like many other successes, sprang from Gospatric stock at Middleton Hall near Wooler. Robert, the first recorded member, was granted Bolbec land to the west of Stamfordham. They had a heritable right to this and eventually they became the owners when the strength of the feudal system declined. They called it 'Fenwyke' because that was what it was, a dwelling by a fen or swamp.

Early family members lived in a timber manor-house, considered at the time to be adequately defended by the nature of the land. They prospered and expanded. Thomas, Robert's grandson, was knighted in 1245 and awarded more land at Capheaton, Stamfordham and Ingoe. More honours and wealth came their way during the following century, then Sir John was granted a licence to build Fenwick tower in 1378. This date can be seen still, roughly scratched on a stone in one wall, but this may be later vandalism.

In 1388 John and Alan Fenwick, two of Sir John's sons, were taken prisoner during the Battle of Otterburn. When he heard this news, father rode off to pay ransom for his sons, this being the normal way of obtaining the release of war captives in those days. He probably took a bag of money with him, but not all he had, not wishing to give the impression of wealth. What he left behind he hid below the floor of the tower. William Cooke, engaged in 1775 to repair the tower, unearthed this treasure while removing flagstones, and, very honestly, handed it over to the authorities. It contained 226 broad pieces in mint condition and dated from Edward III's to Richard II's reigns.

John, one of these sons, also took part in King Henry V's French wars, and was knighted for doing so. His eldest son, yet another John, married twice, the first time to Mary Strother, heiress to Wallington. In 1459 he inherited Fenwick, but he seemed to prefer to live at Wallington and Wallington it was which became the Fenwick's main seat for over two hundred years. Fenwick tower was retained for use by junior members, and so were a large number of other properties throughout Northumberland. John had six children, three by Mary and another three by his second wife Elizabeth, née Widdrington, and his portfolio of property was so full they all received sizeable chunks of real estate.

In 1697 Fenwick tower, and now farm as well, were sold to Sir William Blackett, the recent purchaser of Wallington and most of the other property. This was just eight years before the then head of the family, Sir John Fenwick, was executed for alleged high treason.

The Blacketts improved the efficiency of Fenwick farm but did nothing to preserve the tower. Writing in 1715, John Warburton noted that in Fenwick "is ye ruins of a noble tower", but about a century later its upper deck was dismantled and its ground floor was being used as a farm store. This rump remains today, closely surrounded by more modern buildings.

The execution of Sir John Fenwick was by no means the end of the clan. There were Fenwicks at Brinkburn until 1792, for example, and the descendants of a Fenwick – Clennell union in 1766 still live in the Harbottle area. Perhaps the biggest post-seventeenth century splash was made by Nicholas Fenwick, many times mayor and MP of Newcastle, who married Elizabeth Lady Clavering in 1716 and lived in what was until a few years ago the Liberal Club at the foot of Pilgrim Street in Newcastle. He died in 1750.

Kirkheaton

L87   P535   NZ019774   20 km, 12¹/₂ miles, south-west of Morpeth

When Northumberland was carved up into baronies the royal advisers must have been jigsaw puzzle freaks. Although surrounded by parcels of Bywell and Styford baronies, Kirkheaton was a manor of the Prudhoe barony!

Baron Odinel de Umfraville halved this property and gave one portion to Hexham Priory in 1298 – hence the 'Kirk' in the name; before this it was called Little Heton. The Priory held the land until dissolution, leasing plots to farmers and, in the later stages, mining the coal. The secular part was held by the Middletons of Belsay until 1530, except between 1318 and 1371. In the 1530s the whole manor was put on the market, and there seems to have been an unseemly scramble for bits of it. Those successful included Cuthbert Heron of Chipchase, John Atkinson who had held a farm from the Priory, and Charles Shafto of Little Bavington. The coal mines were bought by the Fenwicks of Wallington, and they went with the estate to the Blacketts, who worked them to 1880.

During the Civil War Kirkheaton was a northern command post during Cromwell's campaign. It is alleged that the commander stayed one night in the village.

A small, square tower was built at the end of the village during the sixteenth century. It was not included in the survey of 1541 so is unlikely to have been the work of the Hexham canons, and the most likely builder was Cuthbert Heron. A manor-house was built against the tower's west wall late in the seventeenth century, then a few years later the tower was replaced by a square building, taller than the house, which has fine Georgian windows. This was built on the tower's foundations and contains the original spiral staircase.

Ryal

L87   P535   NZ014742   22 km, 13¹/₄ miles, south-west of Morpeth

A small township in the Bywell barony which came by a circuitous route to Robert Musgrove in 1333. A later member of that family, Thomas, left his property to his daughter, Joan, when he died in 1482, and so it got into Fenwicks' hands as she was married to William of that ilk.

The next in line, John Fenwick, was given Ryal as a wedding present, and it is this marriage contract that contains the only mention of a tower in the place. The property descended through the Blacketts and Travelyans in Wallington style, but never again was there a hint about Ryal's defences. There is nothing on the ground or on paper to prove its existence.

Great Whittington

L87   P535   NZ005707   24¹/₂ Km, 15¹/₄ miles, south-west of Morpeth

This was where Oswulf, King of Northumbria, was murdered in 758 by officers of his household, allegedly encouraged and paid to do so by Ethelwald Moll, who grabbed the crown in 759.

In slightly more recent times, but still before the Norman Conquest, Great Whittington became a possession of the Anglian family of Halton, of the neighbouring manor of that name. The Norman kings allowed them to keep their lands, which were held in capite. Until the late seventeenth century, with the exception of a few years in the fourteenth, Great Whittington had the same owners as had Halton. Since then the place has filled up with freeholders.

There are no authentic records of a medieval fortification here, and the only reason for its inclusion in this study is to scotch a rumour put about in 1990 by an estate agent who suggested the house in the village he was offering for sale had a 'pele tower'. The house does have a round stair turret but this is relatively modern.

Beukley

L87   P534   NY983708   26 km, 16 miles, south-west of Morpeth

John Warburton claimed in 1715 that there was an ancient tower at Beukley, but unfortunately he was not precise about its location. It may have been in the farmstead which now has the tall Stagshaw radio mast as its neighbour, or it could have been in the more naturally defensible area of Redhousecrag, a mile to the west. There is nothing to see now.

Beukley, sometimes spelt 'Bewclay' and formerly 'Boclive' was a parcel of land in Cocklaw township. Its earliest record, dated 1250, is of its grant by Adam Bertram, a junior member of the Mitford family, to Archbishop Grey of York, but, apart from this, the place appears to have been owned consistently by the Erringtons of, first, Errington Hall, then Cocklaw tower and, finally, Beaufront.

Prudhoe Castle c1880. (p461)

Tynedale
An Introduction to Areas 6 and 7

To our medieval administrators, Tynedale included both the North and South Tyne basins but not the combined River Tyne. This was a huge district stretching from the Scottish Border in the Cheviots down to the Alston Moors, practically the whole of the western side of the county. This study covers it in two 'areas', with Redesdale included in Area 6 and omitting Alston from Area 7, the town being a mile and a half inside Cumbria.

The history of Tynedale differs radically from general Northumbrian history during the Middle Ages because for much of the time the State laws did not apply within its bounds and the sheriff and his men could not enter. For many years Scottish kings had more authority in it than had the English kings.

Before 1031 the region belonged to the ancestors of Earl Waltheof, the most powerful family in pre-Norman Northumberland, but his influence in its west was greatly diluted by the close proximity of Duncan, at that time king of the Scottish dependant state of Strathclyde and regulus of Cumberland. In 1031 Duncan married a sister or niece of Siward, then Danish earl of Northumberland, and as a wedding settlement he was given twelve townships in Tynedale. His authority for doing so is dubious, but King Canute allowed him to keep the gift, so when Duncan became king of all Scotland, the twelve townships were regarded as Scottish territory.

Ten of the twelve townships were to get strongholds later so are included in this study, nine of them in Area 7 and one in Area 8. The complete list is as follows:

Haltwhistle	Area 7 Key Town
Thirlwall	Area 7A
Walltown	7A
Knarsdale	7B
Kirkhaugh	7B

Melkridge   7C
Thorngrafton   7C
Plenmellor   7D
Ridley   7D
Whitfield   8C
Elrington   NY861634, 1 mile SE of Haydon Bridge
Ouston   NY776529, ¹/₂ mile SW of Ninebanks

In those days the word 'township' meant more than just a collection of houses, it was virtually synonymous with 'manor' so, as the named places were probably the most important and influential in Tynedale, it meant that Duncan's gift gave him practical control of the whole district.

Duncan was killed by Macbeth in 1040 and history is silent about the fate of the twelve towns until 1092 when Scottish King Malcolm III undertook to pay homage to the English Crown for the lease of Lothian and was rewarded by English King William Rufus with confirmation that Duncan's gift was still valid.

King Stephen made a strange decision after winning the Battle of the Standard in 1139: he awarded the whole of Northumberland (except Newcastle and Bamburgh) to Scotland's Prince Henry, to hold as a dukedom. This generosity was revoked by King Henry II in 1157 but, as some compensation, he granted the Scottish monarchy Tynedale as a liberty, a 'feoff' held from the Kings of England for homage only.

For nearly 140 years the whole of Tynedale was Scottish for all practical purposes. It was ruled from Wark-on-Tyne by representatives of the Scottish kings and English law did not apply, a much more disciplined arrangement that the twelve townships gift had been. It lasted until King Edward I started hammering the Scots after King Alexander III's death, then was restored in 1293 for John Balliol but was finally withdrawn in 1296 when the Scottish Council concluded the 'Auld Alliance' with France.

Tynedale continued to be a liberty for nearly two hundred more years under the lordship of several English Crown nominees – except for a few years after Bannockburn when an euphoric Robert Bruce reclaimed it. Bishop Bek, Piers Gaveston, King Edward II's favourite, Thomas Featherstonehaugh, John Darcy, Queen Philippa, Edward III's wife, the Duke of York, the Earl of Cambridge and Thomas Grey, they all had a turn before the Crown ended it all in 1484. In 1496 Tynedale was brought into the county by Act of Parliament and, theoretically at least, the laws of the land applied.

But not everybody in Tynedale relished the idea of having a sheriff checking up on their activities. Reiving on a large scale was getting into its stride and the 'surname' system seemed a good enough way of running the district, especially the far northern part. Consequently right up to the Union of the Crowns the law men were complaining of their lack of real authority.

Area 6
North Tynedale and Redesdale

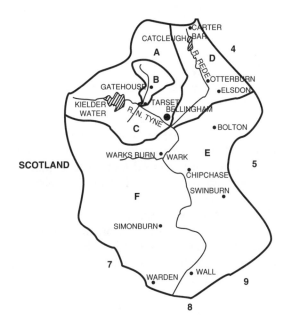

Key Town: Bellingham

Sub-Areas:

A Upper North Tyne,
    North Side

B Tarset Burn

C Upper North Tyne,
    South Side

D Redesdale

E Lower North Tyne,
    East Side

F Lower North Tyne,
    West Side

This area, stretching from the Border in the north to the River Tyne in the south, includes the most lawless territory in Northumberland, the home of reivers, the sheriff's no-go zone.

One hundred and eighteen strongholds are listed, the greatest concentration in the Tarset and Rede valleys where raiding was the normal way of life and the population relied on mutual assistance and protection afforded by the 'Grayne' or 'Surname' system.

The region considered is bounded by the watersheds which confine the North Tyne and its tributaries, and thus some places quite a distance from the rivers are included. This is specially noticeable on the east side where the distinct topographical division between this area and Areas 4 and 5 leaves a wide drainage system.

Key Town
Bellingham

L80   P522   NY840833

Situated just a mile and a half above the Rede – North Tyne confluence, Bellingham is a delightful little market town which, since the sixteenth century, has been the social and commercial hub for a widespread community. Sir Robert Bowes wrote in 1541, "In all the country of Tynedale there is not any other town or place of common resort where vyttalles is to be sold for money but only at Bellingham".

And yet it probably did not even exist before King Henry II allowed the Scottish kings in 1157 to hold Tynedale (ie, both the North and South Tyne valleys) as a liberty. The Scots soon saw that its position made it a natural as a community centre, and in about 1180 enough people lived there to justify a church, while in 1250 it became a manorial capital.

The church deserves consideration. Now a parish church, the premier one in Bellingham Deanery, until 1814 it was merely a chapel of ease in the huge Simonburn parish. When consecrated it was the only stone building in the neighbourhood, and it remained the strongest until after the Union of the Crowns, so it was natural for the Bellingham people to flock to it not only to pray but also to seek shelter from enemies. As a consequence it was a viable target and was damaged on at least two occasions, the last being in 1597 when the Duke of Buccleugh fired cannon at it. The walls were breached, the wood and thatch roof was burnt and many people were killed. By 1603 repairs had been completed and the church once more stood resplendent, but now with a roof of stone slabs – so heavy many supporting buttresses had to be built during the following years. A thorough refurnishing was carried out in 1763, but the stone roof remains, the only one on a church in England.

In or about 1250 Scottish King Alexander III granted most of Bellingham manor to his forester, who then styled himself rather grandly as 'Bellyngiam of Bellyngiam'. The all-important mill lay outside his grant and he had to pay the king the exorbitant annual fee of £10 for its use; no doubt he passed on this expense to his farmers. He lived in a motte and bailey castle, the only purpose-built stronghold Bellingham ever had, and unfortunately it is only a featureless mound now at the junction of the Redesmouth and Woodburn roads.

The forester's appointment was confirmed in 1263 and again in 1279, but Sir William de Bellingham lost it at the end of that century when King Edward I withdrew the liberty from the Scottish kings. Out of a job and with his wooden home no doubt succumbing to wet rot, he move into a stone house built, not in Bellingham, but some sixty miles away in Burniside, near Kendal, in what used to be Westmorland. His English overlords allowed him to retain his property in Bellingham, which he controlled in absentia.

Just before his departure, Bellingham and Ealingham, a former village now just a farm a mile and a half to the south, were jointly fined by the liberty's coroner for beheading a thief without getting prior permission. This indicates that there was some semblance of law and order at least in this small area.

There was a change of ownership in 1531, scarcely noticeable by the inhabitants. The Burniside family sold the manor to cousin Alan Bellingham, a deputy warden of the marches who no doubt wished to live on the job – although there is no record of a suitable house in the town at that time. For some reason Alan also leased a 'bastill house' at Hawick, near the head of the River Wansbeck. Sir James Bellingham is credited with owning Bellingham manor in 1604, and a descendant of his had most of the manor in 1715 although he lived at Levens, six miles south of Burniside. Another part owner of the manor was Sir Frances Radcliffe of Dilston, who acquired a few houses when he bought Wark-on-Tyne, five miles to the south, in 1665.

Although they did not live in the town, the Charlton families greatly influenced life in Bellingham, as indeed they did throughout the region. One of them got into trouble in 1711 for engaging in the last recorded sword fight in the area. William Charlton 'of the Bower' – although he lived at Redesmouth – fought a fair fight with Henry Widdrington of Buteland over a dubious result of a horse race on the Dodd Heaps, just outside Bellingham. Henry was killed; William was taken prisoner but was released without trial. That was the family's influence working! Henry's widow charged William with having "wilfully and with malice aforethought assaulted and murdered her husband". Again the case was dismissed, and in 1713 William received a royal pardon from Queen Anne. This document and the Queen's seal are still to be seen at Hesleyside. In the hope of getting some revenge, Mrs Widdrington had her husband's body exhumed and reburied in Bellingham church by the door to the Charlton' pew as a constant conscience troubler, but even this did not succeed as William stopped going to church.

When William Bellingham died in 1731 his Bellingham estates passed to his daughter who was married to George Gibson. A descendant, another George, sold to Greenwich Hospital in 1817. This transaction brought the whole manor together as Greenwich property, for the Radcliffe portion, sequestered after the 1715 Jacobite rebellion, was granted by the Government to the Hospital in 1775.

Life was never easy in Bellingham, yet throughout its history there has run a thread of social awareness. Highlights were its weekly market and its biannual fair, the latter taking place on the Wednesday before Easter and the first Wednesday after 15 September. The autumn fair was the forerunner of 'Cuddy's Fair', the still popular North Tyne Agricultural Show held on the last Saturday in August. Its sobriquet is a reminder of the many legends connecting

St. Cuthbert with the area. And do not get the impression that all males in Bellingham were reivers: some followed the lucrative and honest occupation of fishing for salmon. They used a special boat called a 'trow', really two narrow boads joined by spars at each end but with clear water between them. The fish were speared with a lethal-looking weapon called a 'leister', which was thrust into the water between or on either side of the hulls by the fisherman standing astride, with a foot in each boat.

Area 6, Sub-Area A   Upper North Tyne, North Side
The Riding
L80   P522   NY826841   1¹/₂ km, 1 mile, north-west of Bellingham

A pleasant farmhouse, the left half of the south range of which is a bastle with five feet thick walls made of large, irregularly-shaped stones set in irregular courses. It was extended in the eighteenth century by continuing the front to the right, then by building what amounts to a new house on the back, making the whole a two-gable building. It has been occupied by working farmers throughout its existence.

Longheughshields
L80   P522   NY820847   2 km, 1¹/₂ miles, north-west of Bellingham

Although only a half mile from the Bellingham to Kielder road, this is a most isolated spot. There is a 'drive' to it from The Riding, but as this looks as if it will be waterlogged even during a drought, the best approach is by the old railway line to Riding Wood, then by pleasant meadow up hill.

There is one habitable cottage here, used occasionally by civilisation escapists, and several ruined dwellings. A century ago Longheughshields was a hamlet occupied by the men who worked the stone quarries which have pock-marked Longhaughshiel Crag to the north-east. The domestic site was chosen because there is a little reasonably level ground and a plentiful supply of water there, no doubt the same reasons why a summering shepherd built a bastle there in the sixteenth century. None of the ruins nor the cottage are bastles, but bastle-like stones are to be seen incorporated in many of them. It appears that the old place was used as a supply of suitable building material when the quarrymen's homes were erected.

Charlton
L80   P522   NY808850   3¹/₂ km, 2¹/₄ miles, north-west of Bellingham

This was the home of the senior line of the Charlton family from the reign of King Richard I (1189-1199) to that of King Edward II (1307-1327). It was called Little Charlton in those days and was held in fee from the Comyns, the lords of Tarset manor.

A tower was built in the early years of the fourteenth century, either just before or just after the family moved across the river to Hesleyside, so no doubt it was to accommodate the junior branch which replaced it.

Charlton tower changed hands sometime before 1531, when there was an exchange of prisoners at a wardens meeting and a man called Beaumont was handed over by the Scots, given a new velvet coat as compensation and sent home – to Charlton.

The Hesleyside Charltons bought Charlton tower back in about 1717, but held it only until 1730 when they sold it to Archibald Reed of Bellingham. According to a traveller in 1799, the tower showed its age but still wore "an aristocratic expression as if it was the seat of a Border landowner".

Nothing is left of it today; Charlton is a large farm and a group of cottages just off the Bellingham to Kielder road.

Boweshill

L80   P522   NY805856   4 km, 2½ miles, north-west of Bellingham

A small farm perched on top of a hill above Charlton. Neither the farmhouse not its barn show any sign of having been a bastle, but large bastle-type stones and a slit vent are built into a field wall on the north side of the buildings.

This suggests that the farmhouse replaced a bastle, but of course the tell-tale stones could have been brought from somewhere else.

Oldhall Farm

L80   P521   NY763863   8 km, 5 miles, north-west of Bellingham

A farmstead, very neat and tidy, with a two-storey farmhouse which has been extended at its back and one side. The shape of the original part, its walls, which are nearly four feet thick, and some internal features seem to confirm the belief that it is a bastle derivative.

Camp Cottage

L80   P521   NY754861   9 km, 5½ miles, north-west of Bellingham

In the twelfth century this was part of the Donkleywood hunting forest where King William the Lion enjoyed the chase. The name relates to an Ancient British camp which lies in one of the farm's fields.

The farmhouse is quite old but looks spic and span after major surgery in the 1980s. The bastle ruin is forty yards to its east. Most of its masonry is practically at ground level, but one wall still stands, untidy but erect, to a height of about five feet. A miniature arboretum grows within its walls, while the whole is guarded very effectively by high weeds.

Donkleywood

L80   P521   NY746863   10 km, 6¹/₄ miles, north-west of Bellingham

A small hamlet of three or four houses, some farm buildings and a ruined bastle. Two walls of the latter stand shoulder height at the side of the road; they are jammed between other buildings, making a small space which, when last seen, was full of weeds and debris. Hopefully these have been cleared by now.

The old name for the area was Dunsliveshalch and it was a hunting ground when Tynedale was a Scottish liberty. King William I, 'The Lion' (1165 – 1214) used it when he was not chasing human game. Unlike his later imitators at Tarset and Dally, who built towers, William appears to have been content with a timber hunting lodge, of which nothing remains. By 1279 Donkleywood was a permanent settlement with arable fields, a rare sight so high up the North Tyne valley. The bastle was built some three hundred years later still, as a farmer's shelter.

In 1279, according to a court record which still exists, the inhabitants of Donkleywood, with those of Thorneyburne and Tarsethope, were fined one pound at Wark for executing a thief without first informing the coroner.

Falstone

L80   P521   NY724874   12¹/₂ km, 8¹/₄ miles, north-west of Bellingham

The name probably derives from the Anglo-Saxon 'Fausten', meaning a stronghold, and indicates that even in those far-off days the area was disputed and fought over, its people needing protection.

Evidence of Falstone's importance to the early Anglian settlers was discovered over a century ago: a fragment of a cross bearing an inscription which translates as "Ecomaer set this up for his uncle Hroethbert – pray for his soul". The find is important for two reasons. First, the epitaph was inscribed in Roman uncial letters on one side and in Anglo-Saxon runes on the other, suggesting that Romanic Christian influences were still fighting the old pagan cultures when the stone was carved, estimated to have been the early part of the seventh century. Second, the uncle's name could be the forerunner of Robert, Robertson and Robson, names still to conjure with in the valley head.

Ever since the reign of King Canute Tynedale had had strong Scottish connections, as an official Scottish liberty from 1157 to 1296 and as an unofficial one created by Robert Bruce after Bannockburn. During this latter period, in 1317 or '18, Bruce conferred Falstone on Sir Philip Moubray, the former commander of Stirling Castle for King Edward II who changed sides after the English defeat and accepted the Scottish peerage of Dalmeny. Moubray is on record as having built a fortified stronghold in Falstone, but probably it was an earth and timber affair as no sign of it remains.

Falstone, in common with the rest of the Border zone, had to contend with raids, both perpetrated and suffered, and blood feuds. Often raids and feuds merged, as when the Robsons of Falstone tried to settle their feud with the Grahams of Liddesdale by raiding the latter's domain and driving off some of their sheep. They put the stolen animals with their own flock, which soon developed scab, a nasty skin disease with which the Scotties were infected. Greatly aggravated, the Robsons returned to Liddesdale where they hanged the first seven Graham men they saw, then left a warning that "the niest tyme gentlemen cam to tak schepe they war no to be scabbit".

Bastle building, when the sixteenth century ran into the seventeenth, was the harbinger of a reasonable standard of civilisation in the Falstone area, although it took the North Tyne railway, which reached it in 1861, to complete the transformation from aggressiveness to harmony. There were three bastles in or close to the village at one time, but only one remains to be seen today.

This is Falstone Farm, between river and church. It has been extended on it east end, and a door and porch have been added to the south long wall, but the original still has many attributes of a genuine bastle. Its windows, added in the late seventeenth century, are rather randomly placed, possibly to take advantage of earlier openings. The ground floor is vaulted, and the doorway leading into it, originally from outside but now from the extension, has a lintel which is inscribed with a line of letters and odd ciphers. This gobbledegook has puzzled many experts and remains a mystery, but the end ciphers are commonly read as the date, 1604. To this writer they look more like 1060-1.

Hawkhope

L80   P521   NY714881   13½ km, 8¼ miles, north-west of Bellingham

Half a mile upstream from Falstone is a range of buildings dwarfed by its backcloth of the Kielder Water dam. This is Hawkhead, a former farmhouse set between farm buildings to its south and a small house to its north.

The Forestry Commission, the present owners, converted the farmhouse into a modern home in 1987. This was not its first alteration, and originally it was built as a stronghouse. Its front, facing downstream, has three floors, but because it is built on a slope its back has only two floors.

In all other respects the building conforms to the usual Border bastle specification – rectangular plan, large quoins, central first floor entrance (now reduced to a window) and thick walls. It did not have a vault, and the ground floor gable entrance is hidden by the adjoining building.

Kielder Water – Belling and Starsley

L80   P521   NY7088   15 km, 9¹/₂ miles, north-west of Bellingham

Bastles at Belling and Starsley were dismantled before the valley was flooded in 1980 to create the Kielder Water reservoir. Nothing is left to indicate their exact position, but both were close to the northern shore of the lake between the small peninsular called The Belling and the dam.

In the sixteenth century Belling was a small farm. During that and the following century it was worked by a succession of enterprising farmers who gradually took advantage of improving conditions and incorporated the neighbouring farms of The Law, Woodhouse, The Kennel and Starsley. Their own farm was improved as well, and the original farmhouse became a barn. It was later identified as a bastle.

The Duke of Northumberland bought this farming complex in 1828. He wanted the land only for shooting over and the buildings were let at peppercorn rents to people in non-farming occupations – mine workers, probably, or railway workers after 1850.

The barn at Belling survived until 1980. It had walls five feet thick, but no other details are known.

Starsley farm was one of those taken over by the Belling farmers. Known locally as Stone House, the farmhouse was a roughly constructed bastle with walls, between four and a half and six feet thick, comprising large boulders and rubble bonded with clay. It was abandoned when its land was taken, but the Duke had it repaired so that he could let it to a railway worker and his family called Rafferty.

Wainhope

L80   P509   NY670925   19 km, 11³/₄ miles, north-west of Bellingham

According to a document dated 1279, a lady called Emma lived at 'Waynhoppe'. Fifty years later there was a "chief massuage, park and assarts" there. The place was mentioned last in 1330. No more is heard of it until a farm called 'Wainhope' appeared in the nineteenth century.

Only the names suggest that the old and new places occupied the same site. The modern farm lies in the heart of Kielder Forest, formerly wild moorland only five miles from the Border, hardly the ideal place for a gentleman's principal seat, even if it was a tower and used only as a shooting lodge. The nineteenth century farm did have a sixteenth century precursor – but just a humble bastle. There is no trace of this now and its precise site is not known.

Kielder Head

L80   P509   N666980   22km, 13½ miles, north-west of Bellingham

Another little farm in the sticks, four miles up the Kielder Burn at the junction of the Scaup Burn and the White Kielder Burn, north-east of Kielder village. The occupier built a bastle here, probably at the end of the sixteenth century, and vague traces of it may still be found in the farm buildings.

A further half-mile up the White Kielder Burn is a deserted medieval village called Caller (or Colour) Cleugh (N675984). It may be the same site as some modern historians are calling White Kielder village, but there are several such deserted villages in the Kielder region, around the source of the North Tyne. There are two possible explanations for this. One is that junior members of large families living in the lower, more hospitable valleys may have been forced to find new land from which to scratch a living because the ancient custom of 'gravelkind' made it necessary for all sons to get equal shares when their father died, and such shares may sometimes have been too small to support anybody. The other possibility is that these settlements were occupied by Scottish people. This was part of the 'debatable land' until James I drew a clear-cut line between the two countries, and some of the thieves of Liddesdale are thought to have encroached across it in order to get a base nearer their Northumbrian targets. As Lord Eure said in a letter to Lord Burghley in 1596, "They take our habitable grounds and chaise us further into the land, making their entry easier".

Kershope Castle

L80   P509   NY614959   25 km, 15½ miles, north-west of Bellingham

Where the Kielder Burn joins the North Tyne stands the pleasant forestry village of Kielder. There is nothing very ancient here – even the majestic-looking Kielder Castle is really just a shooting box built by the Percys of Northumberland in 1772 – but there are a number of deserted medieval villages in the vicinity. One of these, at Bells, close to Kerseycleugh Bridge (NY613949) was the original Kielder village, the home of Sir Richard Knout, one time county sheriff who died about 1290. He was associated in legend with the 'Cout O' Kielder, a giant with magic chain-mail who drowned in the Hermitage Water and is buried in Hermitage chapel graveyard in Liddesdale.

Higher up the North Tyne valley is Kershope Castle, now deep in the forest and not easily approached. If this did not belong to a Liddesdale reiver it must have been the home of someone in league with the Croziers or Armstrongs, as otherwise he could not have survived five minutes in such an exposed position. He must also have been a braggard to have called his place a castle. There are just some grass mounds left now, difficult to tell what they hide but most likely a tower. Ruins of a longhouse, contemporary with the tower, if that is what it was, stand about 200 yards to the east, suggesting that a bit of farming was done.

There is a persistent legend about this area. When the Catholic revolt against Queen Elizabeth, the Rising of the Northern Earls, was crushed in 1569, Earl Percy and his wife, Lady Elizabeth fled to what they believed to be a safe retreat over the Border, and the legend says that they stopped a night on the way at Kielder Castle. So far as we know, there was no such place at the time, so perhaps the royal couple B and B'ed with Sir Richard Knout's descendants. Or perhaps they stayed at Kershope Castle.

Area 6, Sub-Area B   Tarset Burn

Tarset Castle

L80   P521   NY788854   5¹/₂ km, 3¹/₂ miles, north-west of Bellingham

During the period when Tynedale was held as a liberty by the kings of Scotland from the kings of England, Tarset manor was granted by the former to the Comyn (sometimes Cuming) family of Badenock, a property on the fringe of the Highlands. The man was influential in Scottish political circles and had to be treated generously, but why anyone with the freedom of the Cairngorms and Rothiemurchus Forest should want to chase deer here is beyond understanding.

The manor extended from the North Tyne to Greenhaugh on the Tarset Burn. John 'Black' Comyn warmed to the place and built a 'camera' there, after getting the necessary licence from King Henry III in 1267. A 'camera' was a secret place, no doubt a good description of Comyn's building, but architecturally it was a tower, albeit a very strong one built of stone on a natural eminence with steep banks down to the Tarset Burn and the North Tyne on three sides and a moat on the fourth. It was long and narrow as dictated by the shape of the mound, and it had a high wall around it and its bailey with small rectangular turrets at each corner. In effect, it was an economical castle-substitute which made full use of what nature had provided, of the type favoured in the thirteenth century.

A small village sprang up below the tower. It had its own mill and its inhabitants were able to indulge in a little trading with travellers following two pre-Roman routes which crossed near them; one connected the Haltwhistle area of South Tynedale to the Border near Chew Green, and the other joined Hexham to the Border above Kielder. Most of the inhabitants, however, were servants at the tower, or gamekeepers in the deer park which was enclosed during the early years of the fourteenth century.

Red succeeded Black. John 'Red' Comyn was a political opportunist and, supposedly, a friend of Robert Bruce. After the great Competition for the Scottish crown in 1290-92 he settled down as a loyal subject of the English King Edward I, probably to see what he could salvage when the inevitable happened. Edward saw only good in him, however, and rewarded him with the heritable rights of Tarset Castle and manor, so it remained his even after the Scottish kings lost the liberty. Robert Bruce began to see his friend as a potential thorn in his flesh while he was angling for the Scottish throne, so he murdered him in 1306 in front of the high altar in the Greyfriars Church at Dumfries.

John's son, another John but without a colour, remained loyal to the English and was killed at Bannockburn. He left an heiress who was married to Sir John Bromwich, and in due course Tarset became his to sell, which he did in 1373, to the fourth Lord Percy of Alnwick.

The purchase was given to his son, Henry 'Hotspur' Percy, who was nine years old at the time and preferred playing with soldiers to stalking deer. Tarset was not forgotten altogether, however, as it is on record that Lord Percy obtained pardons for three members of the Dodds grayne of Tarsetdale in 1397. The property was confiscated by the Crown when Hotspur rebelled in 1403, and thereafter ownership followed the vicissitudes of the Northumberland Estates.

Tarset Castle appears to have remained empty, or perhaps on short lets, until it was destroyed. It was certainly empty at Easter in 1524 when Hector Charlton of the Bower reacted to an interdict placed on the 'Evil Country' by taking Sacramental wine and breads from Bellingham church to the castle and then persuading a Scottish friar of dubious qualifications to give the dalesmen their communion "after a fashion".

By this time Tynedale had ceased to be a liberty and theoretically was open to the county sheriff. Just how open it really was was demonstrated later that year, 1525. Word got through to the law officers that Nicholas Ridley of Unthank, Hugh Ridley of Harden and one or two others, all wanted for questioning in connection with the murder of Albany Featherstonehaugh while he was High Sheriff of Northumberland, were hiding in Tarset Castle. Albany's successor, Sir Ralph Fenwick of Stanton Hall, set off to investigate, accompanied by a posse of eighty men. The North Tynedale men knew little about what was happening outside their own secret world, but they did realise that Fenwick represented law and order and had to be opposed. Two hundred of them, under their leader William Charlton, chase the intruders not only out of Tarset but out of Tynedale as well.

The match was replayed the following year, with both sides reinforced. Fenwick had a hundred men with him, and Charlton brought in his sometimes friends, sometimes enemies, the Croziers from over the Border. Tarset Castle was taken and set on fire. The law retreated in some disarray, but it managed to retain one long arm. Seven years later, William Charlton and two members of his family were seen at Colwell by Lord Dacre, warden of the middle march. He and his bodyguard, helped by the surprise element, easily caught the wanted men and hanged them from the nearest tree.

Tarset Castle was never refurbished after the fire, and was used as a quarry. Reenes farmhouse, half a mile north-west of Bellingham, is said to incorporate some of its stones. Fragmentary excavations have been undertaken, and one by W.L.S.Charlton in 1888 revealed an underground passage which caused great excitement, especially when a bronze key was found in it. There is an ancient legend about a tunnel connecting Tarset with Dally Castle along which ran carriages drawn by headless horses.

The plan of Tarset Castle can be seen with reasonable clarity today although most of it is grass covered. Some small bits of masonry and foundations show, and the moat is very distinct. The old railway line cut through part of the south side of the mound. The view from the site is terrific and well worth a visit for this alone, as also is a view of the site from the Burnmouth to Redheugh road higher up the valley. [**Plate 6**]

Boughthill

L80   P521   NY788872   6½ km, 4 miles, north-west of Bellingham

Boughthill farm is close to the right bank of Tarset Burn, not very far above Tarset Castle, but the bastle ruins of that name are a further half mile up the burn, roughly half way between the farm and Thorneyburn Church. There is not a lot to see – a few stones and grass mounds, little else.

Most, if not all, the bastles in the Tarset valley were built during the last thirty years of the sixteenth century, and this one is no exception. It was mentioned in a letter to Queen Elizabeth which Sir John Carey wrote in 1595. He told Her Majesty that the Duke of Buccleugh had visited 'Bowght Hill' and there had found and killed "4 of the Charltons, very able and sufficient men". Reason? The Duke's family, the Scotts, were in deadly feud with the Charltons.

Burnbank

L80   P521   NY782875   6½ km, 4 miles, north-west of Bellingham

During the reiving days of the sixteenth and seventeenth centuries Charlton was the head surname in this district, and Dodds and Milburne were second equal on the ladder of command. They controlled a band of villains which, to the outside world and especially to their victims, seemed to personify absolute obedience where dissension of any sort would be impossible. It is surprising, therefore, to find some discord within the Dodds (Dode, Dodd or Dodde) surname, whose chief home was this bastle.

Rose Dode and her son Henry presented a petition in chancery in 1593 which pleaded for ownership of Burnbank for Henry. She claimed the property should have passed to him, according to custom, when her husband died as he and his ancestors since "time out of mind" had held it. But instead John and Katherine Dodd had somehow got hold of the evidence of possession and had taken over; they had lived there eight years and had even boasted about dispossessing Henry.

Rose did not win her argument. According to the minutes of the Earl of Northumberland's baronial court of 1605, a jury found that George Dodds had been the previous owner and his son and heir was John Dodds, who was thus entitled to the property. It is assumed that, inspite of the spelling, this John was Katherine's husband.

The disputed bastle is no more. It was inhabited until the end of the seventeenth century when the existing West Burnbank farm was built and the occupier moved into greater comfort. Neither the farmer who lives there now nor his neighbour at Burnbank farm know anything about a bastle ruin or earthworks, but an old historian claimed the site was on a small plateau between the Tarset and Tarret Burns. Such a place has not been found by this John Dodds.

Burnmouth

L80   P521   NY792880   7 km, 4¼ miles, north-west of Bellingham

No doubt about where this bastle was, for one of its long walls still exists and is used as a farmyard boundary. It is about six feet high and three feet wide, and from its west side there is a sharp drop into the dene where the Tarret Burn joins the Tarset Burn. The wall is visible from the road.

Redheugh

L80   P521   NY784884   7½ km, 4½ miles, north-west of Bellingham

A pleasant, very isolated bastle derivative, now a farmhouse. It retains its thick walls, but was greatly improved in 1732 and its doors and windows are twentieth century additions.

There is a date stone in the front wall which reads "W.C.1732". The date is that of the renovation, the initials are those of William Charlton, nicknamed 'Run Away Will' because he is said to have run away from his debts. He was the head of the main Charlton family of Hesleyside, the man who ordered the reconstruction of Hesleyside Hall in 1713. Perhaps it was because he could not pay the builder that he prepared Redheugh as a hideaway. The house is still a Charlton possession.

Gatehouse

L80   P521   NY788889   7¹/₂ km, 4¹/₂ miles, north-west of Bellingham

There are, or has been, at least four bastles at Gatehouse so it classifies as a bastle hamlet. Its name explains why its inhabitants felt the need for so much protection.

'Gate', formerly 'Yet' or 'Yate' and pronounced 'Get' in this context, means a 'way through' or 'clear the way', so plainly Gatehouse was the point raiding parties from Scotland and Redesdale had to pass when en route for the more prosperous parts of the Tarset valley, and similarly where the dalesmen could congregate before embarking on raids to the north and east. It was the lodge at the end of the drive. Although there were more bastles up-stream, Gatehouse was chosen because it was at the head of the Charlton-controlled part of the valley, the home ground of many sixteenth century reivers.

When used by outgoing parties Gatehouse had a passive role to play, indeed it would not be surprising if one of the bastles doubled as a pub to serve stirrup cups. But in its defensive mode, the hamlet needed sufficient strength to hold out against the raiders long enough for a message to be carried or signalled down the valley to warn the men there that trouble was on its way. No matter that the inhabitants of Gatehouse were probably reivers themselves, they were fair game to the Scots, and also they had to be prepared for violent retribution by past victims.

Who the bastle occupiers were is virtually impossible to tell, but they appear to have belonged to several different families, one of which was probably Milburn. There were sales of property in Gatehouse involving Milburnes in 1624 and 1662, and it seems likely they occupied the property fifty years earlier. Edward Charlton had property in the hamlet in 1680 which he included in his daughter's wedding contract. In 1754 George Ridley died leaving his house and land in Gatehouse to Bellingham Free School – was it an ancestor of his who carved 'T.R.' inside one of the bastles? An Adam Thompson of this area was executed in Bellingham in 1293; a Thompson was living in Gatehouse in 1938, and his father and grandfather had also lived there, so could there be a link stretching across the centuries?

Of the four known bastles, two still stand, one on either side of the road. Two others are little more than foundations now, in Gatehouse Farm. A fifth may have stood at the west end of the hamlet, close to a cattle grid, but its existence cannot be authenticated.

Gatehouse North bastle is the most complete and interesting, not only in the hamlet but arguably in the whole county. It was 'preserved' by the Ministry of the Environment in 1974, not in its original condition but as it was when last inhabited during the seventeenth century, after some improvements had been made when raiding became less of a menace. In this way the radical changes made when the building was relegated to farm use have been eradicated. The building is on private land, but access is usually possible, while most of the outside is visible from the road, just a few yards away.

The original doorway to the ground floor chamber still exists in the north gable. It is only 27 inches wide (just wide enough for one man to enter at a time), is outlined by stone uprights and lintel and has a relieving arch above. The opening widens slightly inside to accommodate two doors, or more likely a door and a grill, one behind the other; horizontal tunnels in the thickness of the adjacent walls house draw bars with which to bolt the doors, bars which were themselves locked in position by a vertical bar.

The chamber is dark and originally was very poorly ventilated by only two slit vents. This and the narrow door are two of several reasons why it could never have been the builder's intention to house live cows or sheep here. During its more peaceful stage, one or two horses were stabled and some stone flags have been laid on the ground at the south end for the horses to stand on. A second doorway has also been inserted at that end to make it easier to get the horses in and to improve the air flow. These changes were made, probably, in the middle of the seventeenth century. The chamber was not vaulted and had a wooden ceiling supported on axe-hewn beams resting on corbels. A few of the beams remain, but most of them, and the ceiling, are replacements. The original ceiling would have had a trapdoor in it through which the man who bolted the doors could climb to his living quarters above.

The upstairs chamber has two small, original, barred windows and a door in its east-facing long wall. The external stone stairs to the latter are most interesting as they reveal very clearly how the occupiers improved convenience as they grew less frightened of attack. As built, there was a sheer drop from the door sill to the ground and access was made – with difficulty by the very old and very young – by a removable ladder. Next came a stone stage or platform outside the door which made it a little easier to get on and off the ladder. Finally, the ladder was discarded and stone stairs were built from the stage to the ground. The stairs and the stage are not keyed into each other, and neither are keyed to the house, proving that they were afterthoughts. This is further demonstrated by the presence of a shaft through the stairs to a slit vent in the bastle wall which would otherwise have been blocked.

The small dais and fire hearth in the upper chamber are modern replacements for originals which required the support of extra strong corbelling below them. Part of the west long wall had been pushed out by a nineteenth century farmer so that he could more easily load the grain and feed he stored here onto his wagon; this damage has been repaired, using the original stones found lying on the ground outside. At the hearth end of the room there is evidence that once there was a loft or half-floor above, for sleeping or storage; it is believed that the bastle as built was at least two courses higher and had a more steeply pitched roof than it has now. The replacement roof is slated, but the original was probably just heather thatch, for no stone slabs have been found.

The bastle has one further surprise. The outside walls are made of roughly shaped stones set in irregular courses, and thus quite deep crevices occur between them. Most unusually, this building had been 'harled' to keep driving rain out of these crevices, and also to prevent an agile attacker from using them as toe-holes to climb to the roof. Harling is still done on some cottages along the north-west coast of Scotland; it means simply that exposed walls are rough-cast with lime and small gravel, and this, looking like a yellow stucco, still adheres in patches to the west wall of the bastle.

Gatehouse South bastle is probably contemporary with North bastle, but has suffered more at the hands of eighteenth and nineteenth century farmers. For many years it stood roofless, stairless and with one long wall partly removed so that farm machines could be lodged in it. In 1991 the walls were made safe and a roof was laid over the building, but there does not appear to be any plans to do a proper preservation job on it.

All that remains of the third Gatehouse bastle is its plinth upon which the nineteenth century farmhouse of Gatehouse Farm has been built. The plinth shows best at the back of the house, its large boulders standing several inches above ground level.

A single storey building adjoins the farmhouse, and this too is built upon a plinth; it has been used as a stable – several horseshoes, some of unusual design, still lie about inside it – and was built about the same time as the house. There is nothing to indicate what the plinth supported originally.

Across a small farmyard, to the south of the house, is another line of plinth boulders linking up to a perimeter wall which contains ample evidence that once it was the wall of a fourth bastle. There are large quoin stones and a slit vent built into it, the whole coursed irregularly like a bastle.

Tarset Head

L80   P509 $8^{1}/_{2}$ to 12 km, 5 to $7^{1}/_{2}$ miles,
                          north-west of Bellingham

Hill House (Woodhouse) NY771897
Waterhead NY767901
Highfields NY739912
Shilla Hill (Starr Head) NY763904
Bog Head (Corby's Castle, Barty's Pele) NY761910
Comb (Combe, Keyme) NY767904
Black Middens (Black Middings) NY767904 Also P521

These seven bastles, in varying states of disrepair, are clustered together in a two-mile diameter circle within the upper reaches of the Tarset Burn. Their occupiers in the reiving years were tough, self-reliant, independent, ungovernable highlanders who shared a rough and dangerous life and derived from it a binding camaraderie which demands group treatment.

Five of the seven bastles are within the Kielder Forest Park where the motor car is not welcome, so a very rewarding way of seeing the majority, while at the same time enjoying their remarkable environment, is to walk the 'Reivers Trail', an undemanding three mile trek prepared and waymarked by the Forestry Commission which starts at a car park at Sidwood (NY779889). Leaflets describing the route are available at all visitor centres in the neighbourhood.

One reason why the bastles were set so close together was to facilitate the visual communication of warnings of raids. If one was attacked the occupiers of the others would soon know about it and would rush to help. This mutual aid system was well known to Kinmont Willie Armstrong of Morton Rigg, a Scottish master raider who commanded a large 'army' of would-be reivers. One day in 1583 he successfully neutralized the strategy by dividing his force into small groups which attacked all the bastles simultaneously. The result was so devastating the victims took the unprecedented and uncharacteristic course of complaining to the warden of the middle march. Bertram Mylburne of Comb wrote about the attack on his bastle, while Jenkin Hunter of Waterhead did the same for the other six bastle-holders.

Part of Hunter's missive is reproduced here, with a few parenthetic explanations. If his spelling seems rather strange it should be remembered it was written seventy-two years before Samuel Johnson tried to introduce a standard, and anyway it was very clever of him to be able to write at all – so extraordinary, in fact, that perhaps he got a parson to write for him. He describes how the Armstrongs and their accomplices "in warlyke maner" ran an open foray in daylight to...

"...Black Myddynes, Hill Howse, The Water Head, The Starr Head, The Bog Head, The High Feeldee, and there raysed fyer and bruntee the most parte of them (set alight and burnt most of them),and drove away fowre hundrethe kyen and oxen (400 cattle and oxen), fowre hundrethe sheip and goate, xxx horses and mears (mares) and the spoylw, the insyght of the howses (inside and outside domestic and farm equipment) to the walewe (value) of towe hundrethe pounds, and slewe and murdered crewellie six parsons (persons) and maymed and hurt ellevin parsons, and tooke and led away xxx presoners, and then do deteign and keip in warlyke maner myndinge to ranson them (having their ransom in mind) contrarie the vertewe of trwews (contrary to Truce agreements [England and Scotland were not at war at the time]) and lawes of the marches".

Hill House, as its name implies, stands on a small hill from which a glorious view across the valley to Black Middens is obtained. It is a small building which has retained all four stone walls to a height of a few feet, but, rather weirdly, they cannot be seen as soil and grass have covered them completely. Walking along the wall top is rather like tramping through strips of meadow framing a pit of nettles.

Waterhead was the home of the letter writer, Jenkin Hunter. The building is known to have been in existence in 1552, and was inhabited until 1851, yet very little remains today. Allowing that some of its stones have been reused in the field walls, it remains difficult to understand why there is not more to see. There is a cottage close by which has been inhabited until quite recently for it has electricity laid on.

Highfield Bastle is not on the Reivers' Trail but about a mile and a half to its north-west. The O.S. map marks the site as close to Highfield farm but nothing has been found there. The bastle ruins are further up the forest road, at Highfield Hope.

It was mentioned in a Border survey of 1604, and its ground floor vault was still to be seen in 1804. Now there is a not very revealing jumble of stones lying in such a way as to indicate roughly the outline of a typical bastle. Soon even this evidence will be hidden, for the ground is marshy and nature is very active.

Shilla Hill is back on the Reivers' Trail, at the summit of a rounded hill. In 1988 this was impenetrable forest and the bastle could neither be seen nor approached, but the trees have been harvested since then and the well made path leads right up to it. The path also offers magnificent views down the valley.

One gable of the bastle stands about six feet high, but its other walls have only a few courses left. The building measures 24 by 48 feet externally and the walls have been at least four feet thick. The land around the bastle has built up considerably over the years, or perhaps the walls have sunk, for the gable entrance is only some three feet high. What can be seen of the door arch is in good condition, however, and its jambs show clearly how two doors were fitted and locked with drawbars. The whole has rather a strange appearance as a large tree has grown inside, at one corner. It has been cut to wall height but young branches are shooting up from it.

Bog Head is now a substantial ruin on haugh land near the Tarset Burn. It was the home of Hodge Corby, or Corby Jack, and consequently it has been known for centuries as 'Corby's Castle'. Unfortunately it has acquired another nickname, 'Barty's Pele', which is confusing as Barty Milburn, Corby Jack's friend, lived a little lower down the valley at Comb.

The strongly constructed building still stands full height except on the north side where some walling collapsed when the ground floor vault fell in. The gable entrance is intact although the relieving arch above it has some stones missing. External dimensions are 22½ by 13½ feet, so it was a small bastle compared to most on the Border. It was documented in 1604 but was occupied some fifty years earlier.

Close to the bastle are the remains of two cottages, built at a later date. Also, if the grass and reeds are not too high, some enclosures may be seen near by. Corby Jack may have used these to grow hay or as in-bye fields during lambing time.   [**Plate 7**]

Comb, originally The Keyme, is a quarter mile off the Reivers' Trail and hardly warrants a diversion, for this is the only bastle of the seven to have disappeared without positive trace. Comb farm may have been built on its site, or it may be the cause of some rough and stoney ground in a field opposite.

This was the home of Barty Milburn, whose exploits have been recorded by Dr Edward Charlton in his *Memorials of North Tyne*. Barty may well have been the Bertram Mylburne of the Keyme who complained about the Armstrong's raid in 1583, although it is hard to think of him as a man of letters.

There is a story about Barty and his friend, Corby Jack, which has been told so many times some people are beginning to believe it. The gist of it is as follows:

Barty woke one morning to find some of his sheep missing. Instinctively blaming Scottish reivers, he collected his friend and together they set off to find the missing animals. Spoor led them a little west of north, through Redesmire to somewhere close to Letham in Scotland, where they lost the scent. Unwilling to return empty handed, they stole some Scottish sheep, then started their return journey.

To make good their loss in this way seemed perfectly normal and justifiable to Barty and Corby, but the sheep's rightful owner could not agree. He and a friend came after them and caught them up at Chattlehope Spout, above Catcleugh. A terrific fight followed in which Corby Jack was killed and Barty was wounded in the thigh. There is nothing like a spot of blood-letting to raise the hackles; Barty was furious and swung his sword with added strength, neatly decapitating one of his adversaries. As he recalled with relish many times later, "Garred, his hied sprang alang the heather like an inion".

The other Scot was terrorised and began to run, but Barty soon caught him and cut him to pieces. He then calmly staunched his wound, picked up the swords of the deceased, threw his friend's body over his shoulder, rounded up the sheep and strode off for home, a mere seven or eight miles across the hills. He dropped Corby at the door of Bog Head, then penned the sheep and went home to bed.

Black Middens is the last bastle in the group and is the most complete, although it has lost both roof and floor. English Heritage looks after it, having stabilized it and made it suitable for visitors by providing a viewing gallery, information plaques and a car park. It is outside the Forest Park.

The walls are full height. The ground floor gable door has been blocked but its jambs remain and they still show signs of having been much used as sharpening stones. There are stone stairs to the upper door, the headstone of which appears to have been made from an old window lintel as sockets for three iron stancheons are visible. Two ground floor doors are later additions, inserted, no doubt, when an eighteenth century farmer wished to convert the building into a byer.

Next to the bastle are the ruins of a long and narrow eighteenth century cottage which stands on much older foundations. The original building here probably was contemporary with, or perhaps it even pre-dated, the bastle, although some experts believe it was also a bastle.

Area 6, Sub-Area C   Upper North Tyne, South Side
                                          including Chirdon Burn

Hesleyside

L80   P522   NY815837   2½ km, 1½ miles, north-west of Bellingham

The Charlton family can trace their lineage back to the reign of Richard I, 1157 to 1199. At first they lived north of the river at Charlton (then called Little Charlton), but from their inception they held land on the south side as well, a district called Hesleyside which included South Charlton, Scele (now Old Man's Sheel) and the future site of Hesleyside Mill.

In 1293, while the district was still in a Scottish liberty, Alexander Lindsay tried to appropriate Hesleyside and add it to his estate centred on Dally Castle. Adam Charlton challenged his right to do this at the court of the Scottish justices itinerant at Wark-on-Tyne, and it was established that the Charltons had a legal right to the land as it had been held by Adam's great-grandfather, William. Soon after this Lindsay had to vacate Dally Castle when King Edward I terminated the liberty status of Tynedale.

The Charltons built a tower at South Charlton and moved in during the early years of the fourteenth century, leaving their northern property to a junior branch of the family. They called their new place Hesleyside Tower to avoid confusion with Charlton. Edward Charlton, Adam's son, was the first recorded resident of Hesleyside Tower, in 1343; he liked its extra comfort and convenience, and felt just as safe there as the tower was built on swampy land and the river defended him from attack from the north.

During the fifteenth century, although no records appear to have been kept, the Charltons must have been busy expanding in numbers, property and stature, for they emerged into the sixteenth century the undisputed leaders of all the reiving surnames in the North Tyne system, at least between Bellingham and Falstone. They were the chief reivers, the organisers, the commanders of operations and the family most feared and yet most wanted in all Northumberland.

Naturally enough, such megastars had plenty of enemies, but they were well prepared for trouble. In 1525, for example, Hesleyside Tower was attacked by a large band of Scottish raiders but they were quickly seen off by the Charltons' resident garrison of fifty men. Their biggest worry was their blood feud with the Scott clan, the Duke of Baccleugh's men. "The quarrell is said to be this", explained Sir John Carey in 1595, "the Scottes long since made a great rode upon Tynedale and Resdale and took up the whole country and did very neare begger them for ever. The Charltons retrieved not only their own goods but they also heartened and persuaded their neighbours to take theirs and not be afraid – this has ever since stuck in Buccleugh's stomach. Mary, he makes another quarrell and caused the Tyndale men to go to Buccleugh's country when they took Buccleugh's grandfather and killed several of his countrymen and they took away his grandfather's sword and would never let him have it since. This is the quarrell".

Grandfather's sword, an impressive weapon with a basket hilt made by Andrea Ferrara, is held to this day in Hesleyside Hall. Other treasures kept there are the silver spur which the lady of the house was wont to serve her lord when the larder was nearly empty and it was time he did some more reiving, and Queen Anne's pardon and seal given to William Charlton of the Bower in 1713 after he had killed Henry Widdrington.

Although their deeds were scandalous and rightly condemned by all Church leaders, the Charltons yet maintained a touching faith in their Roman Catholic religion. Thus, at the request of John Heron of Chipchase, the keeper of Tynedale, William Charlton raised an army of his men to march towards Hexham during the Pilgrimage of Grace in 1536. Their intervention was not required on that occasion, but later, in 1540, when Heron had lost his position to Sir Reynold Carnaby, a man less tractable than Heron, they kidnapped the new keeper and allowed Heron to 'rescue' him. His apparent ability to act so efficiently, coupled with his generosity in helping an old enemy, so impressed the authorities that Heron was given back his keepership – and the Charltons were happy.

The tower had been extended by this time and was being described as a massive square building with a collection of dwellings at its foot. This did not satisfy Edward Charlton in 1631, who built unfortified wings to the north and east of the tower. This was the start of Hesleyside Hall. Between 1713 and 1719 William Charlton added a third floor to these wings and re-faced the south front. William's nickname was 'Run Away Will' because of his skill in avoiding paying his bills, but so far as is known it was not an irate creditor who caused a devastating fire in the Hall in 1738. Repairs were completed before 1770, when a stone tower was built to house a clock made by Hindley, the man responsible for York Minster's clock. At about the same time Capability Brown was given a free hand in the gardens; he drained the marsh into the Hesley Burn.

William Newton was commissioned in 1796 to redesign the east wing, and a few years later the west range was built by Ignatius Bonomi, better known in Northumberland as a restorer of churches; he was a friend and distant relation of the Charltons and a friend of Newton. The medieval tower was demolished in this exercise and a small square building erected on its foundations. A few more minor alterations were made during the remainder of the nineteenth century before the Hall came to look as it does today.

As their house evolved, so did the character of the Charltons. They remained leaders of their society, but upright and charitable leaders, a far cry from the former reiver kings. Amongst many other things, the workhouse in Bellingham was a gift from the Charltons to the local authority, as was Bellingham bridge over the river. William Henry Charlton, the present owner's great-grandfather, was instrumental in bringing the railway to the North Tyne valley. Since Wellington's day, several generations of Charltons have served with distinction in the armed forces.

Snabdaugh

L80   P521   NY786846   5¹/₂ km, 3¹/₂ miles, west of Bellingham

This farm is near the North Tyne – Chirdon Burn confluence and, although on the Bellingham to Keilder road , it was considered to be in Chirdon manor, the early history of which is recounted under Dally Castle. We first hear of a small settlement called Snabothalgh during the middle part of the thirteenth century. The word 'bothal' will be noticed in this old name, and the remainder of it, 'Snagh', is perhaps a corruption of an Old English word meaning land or clearing, so in total it means 'an abode in a clearing'.

The first owner was David de Lindsay, the justiciary of Lothian, but he had to relinquish this property in 1296 when King Edward I terminated the Tynedale liberty. The Crown granted part of Chirdon manor, including Snabdaugh, to Robert Swinburne of Gunnerton and Little Swinburn, and from his niece it passed by marriage to Sir Roger Heron of Ford. The Herons held on to Snabdaugh to 1696, when they sold it to Sir Lancelot Allgood, the man who was to build Nunwich Hall near Simonburn in 1760. The farm is owned and run by an Allgood to this day.

The Herons, around 1600, decided they needed a fortified farmhouse at Snabddaugh – something slightly better than a bastle but not so grand or strong as a tower. The resultant strong house, which still stands, is believed to be unique in England.

Viewed from the road, and ignoring the various appendages added later, the farmhouse looks much like scores of others in Northumberland, the only slightly unusual feature being an 'off-set' or ledge along the front face at first floor window level. The building's secret lies inside and discovered – 'rediscovered' is more correct, presumably – only a few years ago when electricity was being installed. The electrician needed to run cable above the first floor rooms and, finding no trapdoor into the loft, cut a hole in the ceiling. Climbing through this he found a barrel-shaped stone vault!

An upstairs vault is common enough in castles and large towers but is decidedly odd in domestic buildings, and archaeologists, architects and historians came running to see it. They discovered that the vaulting was not restricted to the top of the house but actually sprang from ground level. The whole place is a stone tent, deceptively concealed beneath prosaic walls and slate roof. The curve of the vault is not noticeable at ground and first floor level, yet is sufficiently pronounced to permit the outer wall to take a foot-wide step inwards at first floor window level – hence the ledge seen from outside. Above the first floor rooms the curve is very obvious and swings in a tight radius beneath the ridge of the roof. The flooring of the first floor is supported on corbels, while the ceiling appears to be a later refinement.

Dally Castle

L80   P521   NY775843   6½ km, 4 miles, west of Bellingham

The grandiose name of a medium-sized tower, the earliest building in Chirdon manor. The Chirdon Burn rises in the extreme west of Wark Forest, but all its known strongholds are in the last four miles before it joins the North Tyne. The valley and about a mile of moorland on each side was a manor, a parcel of the superior manor of Wark-on-Tyne and of the Tynedale liberty held by Scottish kings until King Edward I's revocation in 1296. Very roughly, it would fit in the modern parish of Greystead.

From 1214 to 1249 it was the turn of King Alexander II to hold the liberty, but he passed it to his youngest sister, Margery, in 1230, retaining only the feudal services of the Comyns of Tarset and the Ros family of Haltwhistle. Margery almost immediately leased Chirdon manor to David de Lindsay, an influential landowner and law lord. This was new hunting ground to him and he commissioned men from Bellingham to enlarge and heighten a small hill near the entrance to the valley, prior to building Dalley Castle as a hunting lodge.

News of the building work soon reached Hugh de Bolbec, then sheriff of Northumberland, who saw it as a potential threat to England's defences.

In 1237 he asked King Henry III what he should do about it , and while awaiting a reply he put a temporary stop to it. Eventually Lindsay was given the all clear to proceed. Between 1246 and 1249 he was one of the twelve Scottish knights who, with twelve from England, tackled the vexed question of the position of the Border, so obviously the king thought him trustworthy.

During the late thirteenth century the moorland around the valley began to attract lowland farmers requiring land for summer grazing. They paid very small rents for this privilege, but collectively they swelled Lindsay's coffers considerably, and he wanted more. He tried in 1293 to extend his property into Hesleyside to increase his letting area, but the law put a stop to this move. Three years later, Lindsay was forced to leave.

The tower he vacated measured 70 and 50 feet and it had a turret at one corner and a small wing at the south end. Although it had an upper floor, reached, it is believed, by an outside wooden staircase, its main defensive positions were on the ground floor where loops were provided for bowmen to shoot through.

The Crown placed much of Chirdon manor under its own Wark-on-Tyne wing, but Dally was amongst the estates which were granted to Robert Swinburne as a reward for army service. Having no children of his own, he willed this grant to his brother's daughter, Elizabeth, who was married to Roger Heron of Ford.

The change of ownership occurred in 1326, at which time Chirdon was in a deeply depressed state. After Bannockburn Robert Bruce had assumed control of Tynedale illegally and had used it as a launching pad for his sorties into the Northumberland heartland. He had left hardly a house standing in North Tynedale; Chirdon's inhabitants, both all-the-year-rounders and summer visitors, had either fled or had been killed, and rents fell to nearly zero. Heron held on, and after Bruce's death in 1329, determined to give his property a safer future, he drastically modified Dally Castle. He transferred its main defences from the ground floor to roof level, blocking the low-level loops and strengthening and crenellating the upper part of the building.

Having this strong 'gate' at its entrance, the sheltered Chirdon valley was seen as an ideal secret corral for stolen cattle, sheep and horses taken by the fifteenth and sixteenth century North Tyne reivers. A farm had sprung up at Dally, held by a Dod, a reiving surname, and it was his job both to man the defences and to warn the valley inhabitants of approaching danger. Those inhabitants were mostly members of the Charlton family.

In 1593 a long-simmering row about the ownership of Chirdon manor boiled up, and then was settled amicably. It was agreed that Dally, Birks (also held by Dods, NY781848), Chirdon farm and The Bower were Crown tenements, while the Herons could keep all the other settlements.

The Crown held a lot of land in the northern dales at this time, and all of it was given to George, Lord Home, when he was elevated to Earl of Dunbar and entrusted with the demilitarization of the Border in 1605. It descended by the Earl's daughter to Lord Howard of Waldon in 1611, and in 1644 he sold the Dally estate to the Charltons of Hesleyside.

The farm and its fields were the attractions which the Charltons wanted and they had no need to refurbish Dally Castle. Indeed they hastened its ruination by removing much of its stone and using it to build a mill on the banks of the Chirdon Burn. When the Rev.John Hodgson visited it in 1830 all he could see were grass covered bumps on top of a mound. He never saw the treat which Mr W.L.S. Charlton revealed by excavation in 1888.

The whole rectangular plan of the tower is visible now, marked by walls from two to five feet high. The turret and wing are there, also the blocked loops. The most surprising aspect is the high quality of the stonework and the obvious skill with which all surviving parts have been carved and put together. No trace of a staircase has been found, however, and it can only be assumed that the original outside wooden affair was replaced by one inside and that this has been dismantled. In 1998 plans were announced to turn Dally Castle into a tourist attraction, after the completion of some remedial work – mostly repointing – by the National Park and English Heritage.

Chirdon Farm

L80   P521   NY761830   8 km, 5 miles, west of Bellingham

Probably a rebuilt bastle, but it could have been a tower. John Warburton described it in 1715 as "an ancient pile", which usually means a tower, and Hodgson in 1830 called it a "peel with a vault", which could mean either. What is on view today is a small one-up-one-down, very dilapidated cottage with eighteen inch walls and the remains of a wooden ground floor ceiling. It has one interesting feature: in the south-west wall there is a patch of rougher masonry in the shape of an arch. It could have been the end of a vault.

The cottage is called Old Chirdon and is actually on Whitchester farmland. The replacement Chirdon farm, New Chirdon, is close to the Chirdon Burn and only a few yards from The Bower.

Both (Old) Chirdon and The Bower were in that part of Chirdon manor which became Crown property in 1593 and eventually passed via Lord Home to Lord Howard of Waldon. From at least 1500 the Charltons leased both properties, but The Bower was the more important while Chirdon was kept for married sons or some other close relatives. It seems most likely that the Charltons built the strongholds at both places.

The Bower

L80   P521   NY757832   8½ km, 5¼ miles, west of Bellingham

The 'Bowrie Charltons' were always the younger elements of the family, the sons who just missed inheriting Hesleyside and the responsibilities of leading the surname. As a consequence they were the audacious, reckless men who caused the greatest havoc.

They lived by reiving during the late fifteenth and throughout the sixteenth centuries, and The Bower was built by them as a safe retreat, a home which sheltered them when their many enemies became too attentive. It was a small but strong tower constructed near the Chirdon Burn to stop intruders from the south entering their part of the dene where the fruits of their escapades were kept, just as Dally Castle closed the northern entrance.

Although reiving was technically dead by the early 1600s, the Bowries continued to steal horses and cattle through most of that century inspite of strenuous efforts to stop them. Two of them, John and Thomas Charlton, were caught and hanged in 1629, but this was no more than a minor hiccup. Early in the eighteenth century they moved to Redesdale but retained The Bower for a time for 'business purposes'. Even the more civilized ambience of their new home failed to quench their thirst for adventure, and in 1715 William Charlton joined the Earl of Derwentwater in the Jacobite rebellion. He escaped from Preston and in 1736 he succeeded his brother and moved to Hesleyside. By the end of the eighteenth century the Bowrie spirit had at last been subdued by respectability. The tower was pulled down and the still existing farm built in its place. Nothing to remind the visitor of its past was left visible. ˎ

Ridley Stokoe

L80   P521   NY743854   10 km, 6¼ miles, north-west of Bellingham

Smalesmouth

L80   P521   NY731857   11 km, 6¾ miles, north-west of Bellingham

Two adjacent farms on the high right bank of the North Tyne, Ridley Stokoe nearly opposite two other Stokoes, High and Low, on the left bank. The meaning of 'Stokoe' is obscure and there are no features common to all three which could help to explain the name.

Ridley Stokoe's farmstead is roughly equidistant from two bastles. To the east, at NY752855, is a string of ruined buildings above Stokoe Crags, once called Crag Cottages for this reason. The main building measures about 33 by 20 feet and still has some thick walling, as high as 8 feet in places. This undoubtedly was a bastle, but the building attached to its east end is more puzzling for it measures only 15 feet wide. Its length of 40 feet makes it more like a 'long house' medieval farm building, yet there is a partly blocked gun loop in its gable wall, and its construction is very bastle-like. Fragments of more buildings lie in line towards the east.

West Ridley Stokoe, at NY739854, is another ruin, distinctly bastle-shaped, with one wall 6 feet high and most of the others mainly fallen masonry. It is rather unusual in that the ground floor chamber had a window, and its doorway was at the end of a long wall, not in the gable.

This bastle is really on Smalesmouth land but is always regarded as a Ridley Stokoe possession. There was another bastle at Smalesmouth proper but only the boulders of its plinth remain. These are at the east end of the farmhouse, a completely reconstructed building.

Ridge End

L80   P521   NY728858   11½ km, 7 miles, north-west of Bellingham

Another South Bank farm, some 300 yards north-west of Smalesmouth, across the Smales Burn. The farmhouse is an excellent example of a bastle derivative. The original thick walls still stand, but were heightened a little about 1700 to accommodate an attic. At the same time a new roof was constructed with a gentler pitch. A little later windows and a porched door were inserted and the house was extended westwards a short way. The outline of the upstairs door still shows.

The field beyond the house drops sharply to a boggy area, and on this decline is a two foot deep stone step set into the ground, rather like a miniature ha-ha. This step and the just discernible foundations of three walls together form the outline of what most likely was a second bastle. It has been quite a large building, just as old as, or perhaps even older than, the farmhouse bastle.

An interesting small, unfortified building ruin lies half hidden in Smale Dene, a hundred yards downhill from the farm. It had two rooms only, without a communicating door and with a fire hearth in each. It could have been a pair of semi-detached one-room cottages, but local opinion favours the idea that it was a smithy. Perhaps this was where the packhorses which carried North Tyne coal over the Border in the eighteenth century were shod.

Stannersburn

L80   P521   NY721865   12½ km, 7¾ miles, north-west of Bellingham

A small hamlet bypassed by the Bellingham to Kielder road, close to its junction with the road to Falstone. Old records say there was a bastle here, but both traces and memories of it have gone.

A resident has a very old picture of the hamlet which shows ruins of a building on a bank at its west end. This could have been the bastle, but there is no way of making sure as the ruins were removed round about 1900.

Yarrow

K80   P521   NY717871   13 km, 8 miles, north-west of Bellingham

Another clearly recorded bastle which has been lost. One authority claims it was near the river a few yards north-east of Low Yarrow farm. Another advocates the corner made by the Bellingham – Kielder road and the Yarrow lane, and supports this by saying the bastle's name was originally Shilling Pot Bastle, Shilling Pot being a neighbouring area. The most promising suggestion, however, came from a very old lady who lives at Yarrow. She said that as a child she played amongst the ruins of the bastle, which were close to where a thorn tree grows now, on the north side of the main road some 400 yards north-west of the Falstone road. The ground thereabouts is very rough and rocky but no obviously used stones can be seen. The old lady said they were covered by heather a long time ago, so if she is right about the location she is right about this too.

Kielder Water – Shilburn Haugh

L80   P521   NY693871   15 km, 9¹⁄₄ miles, north-west of Bellingham

We know precisely where this medieval pile was sited, but it is still beyond our reach, for it is under water in the Kielder Water reservoir. Pre-flood maps show Shilburn Haugh farm about 350 yards to the west of Tower Knowe promontory.

John Warburton in 1715 noted it as "an old pile belonging to one Robson". This argues strongly that the building was a tower, for Warburton was not concerned with anything less. Admittedly Sir Robert Bowes stated categorically in 1541 that there were no fortifications higher up the North Tyne valley than Tarset Castle, but this was probably because he had not ventured any further – and who could blame him.

Kielder Water – Leapish

L80   P521   NY660880   18 km, 11 miles, north-west of Bellingham

The former Leapish farm is on dry land, close to the shore of Kielder Water and currently being used as part of the sporting facilities offered around and on the man-made lake. There is no trace of there ever having been a fortified building here, however, and it is believed that, as at Ridley Stokoe, the bastle was a few hundred yards from the farmhouse – and is now under water.

An official complaint was lodged in 1611 – eight years after the Union of the Crowns – that Robert Elliot of Redheugh, near Hermitage Castle (not the Redheugh in the Tarset valley), had crossed the Deadwater hills with fifty supporters and had killed Lionel Robson and several others at Leapish. They had also broken down Lionel's house with axes. There is nothing to connect this incident with the bastle, of course, which was built of stone and not vulnerable to attack by axes, but it does show how far behind the mood of the times were these places at the head of the North Tyne and on the Border.

Hexham Prison – designed to keep criminals in and would-be rescuers out. (p408)

Digression

Border Laws and Lawless Borderers

Before the Anglo-Scottish wars the native population of the English Border country were no less law-abiding than any other folk, but unfortunately the natives were not alone. The Northumbrian section of the Border was practically all liberty land, owned and governed by viceroy-like magnates who suffered very little interference from the monarchy and worked to their own set of laws, administered by their own judiciary. Because the county sheriff had no power in these lands and the 'King's Writ did not run', wrongdoers of all descriptions sought sanctuary in them – and often continued with their evil ways. The Scottish side of the Border at that time was in much the same predicament because of the power of the local clans.

Alexander II, King of the Scots, recognised the need for special treatment in this zone between his country and England. He also needed to know precisely where the Border was, for in 1237 he had signed the Treaty of York to renounce his claim to Northumberland. The Tweed, Cheviots and Solway Firth line had been drawn roughly in 1018 at Carham, but when you have promised to keep to one side of it you must know exactly were the line runs. Accordingly, in 1246, he commissioned twelve Scottish and twelve English knights to deliberate under the supervision of the sheriffs of Berwick and Northumberland and to produce, first a detailed map of the frontier, and, second, a set of rules which could be applied to both the English and Scottish sides of the Border.

The commissioners' findings were published in 1249, the year King Alexander II died and was succeeded by his son, Alexander III. The Border question was resolved reasonably satisfactorily although some 'Debatable Lands' remained, while the set of rules the knights produced was a significant breakthrough. These 'Leges Marchinrum' were to form the bases for a developing social and military system which operated until the Union of the Crowns.

Initially these Laws covered fourteen subjects, including homicide, duels, methods of recovering fugitives, bondmen, debts and stolen goods, the calculation of sureties and safe conduct for malefactors. They set out practical rules – bondsmen, for example, could be recovered by their masters within forty days, or longer if a King's Writ was obtained – but they said little about the administration of justice, only that disputes had to be settle by single combat.

Punishments for the various crimes were prescribed. Strangely, murder was not a capital offence and was punished by the imposition of a fine of twenty-nine cows and a heifer. Although duelling was proscribed, by far the most popular punishment was just that – man-to-man duelling with any weapons they chose. This was seen as a way of determining guilt and inflicting punishment at one and the same time.

It appears to have been left to the landlords of the Border territories to administer these laws and dispense punishment, and no sort of constabulary was appointed until 1296, when English King Edward I commissioned a few 'Captains and Keepers of Our Peace' to guard the Border. In 1309 these people were called wardens, but by this time the Border had deteriorated into a battlefield.

King Edward, by his tyrannical treatment of John Balliol and the Scottish people, managed to engender an intense enmity throughout that country towards the English. First William Wallace from 1297 to 1303 then Robert Bruce from 1307 to 1329 indulged in continuous raiding and plundering across the Border in an attempt to persuade the Edwardian kings to recognise Scottish independence. As well as the immediate hardship and danger these raids and their inevitable counter-raids created, they had two most distressing long term effects. First, the Scots sought aid from France, and the 'Auld Alliance' was the cause of Border warfare long after the independence question was settled, for on a number of occasions, notably before Nevilles Cross in 1346 and Flodden in 1513, the French required the Scots to engage the English in diversionary attacks. Second, so much fighting and thieving had a psychological affect on the Borderers of both nations; taking up arms in order to grab other people's property became a natural way of life, something that was perfectly acceptable, and it took a very long time to eradicate this unfortunate concept.

The then existing Border Laws were quite inadequate in these new circumstances, and they were revised and enlarged many times over the next three hundred years. There is uncertainty about the dates of the changes, but the net result was that by the time King Henry VIII reached the throne in 1509 both sides of the Border had been divided into three marches. The East March stretched from Berwick to the Hanging Stone on Cheviot and included all the River Tweed section of the Border. The Middle March included the rest of

Northumberland and the Border Region of Scotland. The West March covered
Cumbria and what used to be Dumfries-shire. At first there was only one
warden for each side of the Border, but soon one was appointed for each
march, and gradually they gathered the support of deputy wardens, keepers,
land sergeants and bailiffs, the English team controlled, in theory at least, by a
Government-appointed Council of the North. A further step was the appointment of a General Warden with overall responsibility for law interpretation
and enforcement. The English General Wardens were often members of the
Percy or Neville families, while the other officers were usually local peers and
knights.

The new laws extended the old both in scope and severity. On pain of
death, for example, it was forbidden to marry anyone from across the Border
or to sell horses on the other side. The concept of 'Hot Trod' was introduced:
the victim of a robbery by a thief from across the Border was allowed to try to
track him down in the thief's country, provided this was done within six days
of the robbery and he went with 'hue and cry, with hound and horn' and
carried a burning peat on the end of his lance.

The wardens were both policemen and judges. They held courts to try
offenders and to untangle disputes, and they did their best of defend the
Border. At the same time they had an aggressive role to play: they were
responsible for raising raiding parties and leading them across the Border,
sometimes as reprisals but sometimes to initiate trouble, for when England
and Scotland were at war it was considered desirable to harness the war-like
populations living along the Border to 'annoy' the other side.

Very little seems to have been done during the fourteenth and fifteenth
centuries to bring tit for tat hostilities to an end, but one attempt to do this is
on record. When Ford Castle was raided in 1388 during a period of truce
some men were killed and £600 worth of cattle were driven off. Sir William
Heron, the owner, retaliated in the usual way, by grabbing oxen, sheep and
cash from the Scots, but the Earl of Northumberland, then General Warden,
ordered Heron to return his booty, promising him legal compensation for his
losses instead. It was not a popular move and was seldom, if ever, repeated.

The Church tried occasionally to introduce some control. In 1313 the
Bishop of Durham had a few men arrested who had been excommunicated
because of their bad behaviour yet continued taking communion. In 1498
Bishop Fox issued a 'Monition Against the Notorious Thieves of Tynedale and
Redesdale', accusing them not only of continually robbing their neighbours
but also of boasting about their crimes and bringing up their children to
regard stealing as an acceptable art. Yet churchmen were not above using the
Borderers to do their dirty work. Bishop Bek engaged a hundred Tynedale men
to assault the Priory of Durham in 1300, and much later the Prior of
Tynemouth commissioned a small army to commit mayhem in Newcastle.

Whilst the large raids organised by the state or influential landlords and involving several hundred men tailed off during the sixteenth century and virtually ceased when the Auld Alliance was terminated in 1560, petty thieving by small gangs presented a new problem for the wardens throughout the century.

These gangs were made up of 'reivers', a mutation of 'riders' which related to the men's use of 'hobby' or 'hobler' horses to get to and from their victims. The gangs were organised, very largely, on a 'surname' basis, or a 'clan' basis in Scotland. At first their cross-Border activities were actually encouraged as an annoyance to the enemy, but in Queen Elizabeth's reign they became a dangerous hazard to be stopped and punished. The big trouble with reiver gangs of both sides was they did not confine their activities to the enemy country but were just as likely to raid their neighbours or fellow countrymen in other dales.

A typical reiver was a farmer who supplemented his income by nefarious means. A lot of romantic excuses have been offered for his behaviour, and indeed charitable readers may consider him to stand a step above a common thief because, firstly, generations of experience of taking other people's property had numbed his conscience, and, secondly, he did not have enough land on which to grew his family's needs. His home territory was over-crowded: in Tudor times the population of the North Tyne and Rede valleys was 200% greater than at the end of the nineteenth century, and 'gravelkind', the ancient custom of dividing the father's land equally amongst all his sons when he died, added to the problem. He preferred to live in penury rather than move out of his district, and the task of converting the outlying moors from summerings to all-year-round farms was still too difficult and dangerous for most to try. The famous picture in Wallington Hall of a spur being served at the dinner table as a hint it was time the menfolk went reiving to replenish the larder is very pertinent.

On the English side of the Border, the men of North Tynedale and Redesdale were by far the worst culprits. It was said they did more harm to Northumberland that did the Scots. Coquetdale men were not so unruly; a Royal Commissioners' Report of 1541 said they were "the truest and best sort of any that do inhabit endlong all the frontier or border of the Middle Marches", but in fairness it should be added that they were noted for the skill with which they could twist a cow's horn or disguise a horse so their owners could not recognise them. The Scots were "alike in their plundering propen-sities, knowing no measure of law but the length of their swords". Liddesdale could rival Tynedale in this respect. Strangely, no criticism, good or bad, of the men of either side of the River Tweed can be found although it is known that the area around Duns in Scotland and the Glen and Till valleys in England suffered considerably from raids.

Reiving to settle a feud could be done at any time of the year, but if food was the main objective, as it usually was, the favourite period was the autumn when the nights were long enough to shroud the approach and getaway in darkness, when horses were strong after summer feeding and cattle and sheep were well fattened. Before John Procter of Rock introduced turnips in 1727, the only winter feeding for farm animals was straw and a little hay, so it was common practice in late autumn to retain only enough cattle and sheep, etc., to ensure adequate herds and flocks next year, and to either kill or sell the rest. Those killed were butchered, salted and stored in the ground floor chamber of the farmer's bastle; the survivors were kept in in-bye fields, perhaps even in barmekyns, where they could be guarded. Reivers "sought the beeves that made their broth" when they were roaming free on the hillsides and not when corralled or lying in salt – when they were "on the hoof, not the hook".

Scottish reivers had an additional objective when they went raiding – timber. Leland, King Henry VIII's Royal Antiquary, reported in 1538 that Cheviot Forest, "one time greatest in Northumberland, is spoilt now and only crooked old trees and scrub remain". A few years later the surveyors Bowes and Ellerker explained that this was because the Scots had stolen the trees "which is to them great profit for the maintenance of their homes and buildings". In 1598 Sir Robert Carey said "their (the Scots) custom is to bring a hundred men to cut and carry away wood".

The march wardens soon realised that more Draconian laws were needed to cope with reiving, and those found guilty of murder, maiming, fire-raising and deadly feud could expect severe punishment. To cope with the cross-Border raiding, a new type of Wardens Court was set up.

These were convened at suitable points actually on the Border. Their date and location were proclaimed in market towns and the appointed day was marked by some pageantry and a twenty-four hours truce. They were attended by the wardens of each country, accompanied by an assortment of lords, knights and gentry, with an armed escort not exceeding a hundred men. A jury of six Scots and six Englishmen was selected by the opposing wardens and it was the duty of these twelve true men to consider each complaint. Upon conviction, the guilty party had to be handed over to his country's warden, or, if this was not possible, sureties had to be provided. Penalties were inflicted on the spot; for stealing a man found guilty would have to pay 'double and sawfie' – double the value of the stolen goods plus another sum, usually also the value of the goods, to cover the cost of collection.

These and their national courts, and the organisation of reprisal raids when considered necessary, kept the wardens busy while their assistants were more concerned with supervising preventative measures. The revised Border Laws stipulated how and by whom watches were to be maintained, by day from hills commanding views of the tracks likely to be used by reivers, by night at the fords and passes. Each township was held responsible for a certain stretch of the Border and had to provide the required number of watchers. 'Searchers' were appointed to post the watchers and to ensure they stayed awake. Sleugh hounds were often used, and beacons were provided on certain hills or towers to give warning of approaching trouble.

Until Queen Elizabeth got her teeth into the problem, the English wardens were enlisted from local landlords. They were given a small salary from the Government and provisions and forage for their personal guards. Their headquarters were provided rent-free. They were entitled to retain half the booty they brought back from punitive raids they organised, and half the fines imposed on wrongdoers. They benefited also from the unofficial forays carried out with their connivance. On the debit side, they were expected to pay their assistants and servants.

The vigilant queen soon saw the flaws in using local men as wardens, and replaced them with gentry of known worth living in other parts of the country, men unlikely to have personal interests which could militate with their duty. An exception was Sir John Forster of Adderstone. He was appointed warden of the middle march in 1560 and soon appeared to "cut a fine figure against the Scots". He was considered to be Enemy No.1 to both English and Scottish thieves, yet he also managed to gain the disrespect of many Northumbrian gentry who accused him of being in league with some of the leading Scottish reivers and of being incompetent and neglectful in fulfilling his judicial duties. When Sir Robert Carey complained officially that there had been no redress for any Scottish outrage for six or seven years Sir John was dismissed – only to be reinstated within a few months because his successor did no better. He was finally retired in 1595 at the ripe old age of 94.

The field duties of the wardening staff were considerably eased by a statute called 'The following of the fray'. All men living in the Border zone were obliged to keep their steel caps, jacks and arms ready to hand at all times of the day or night so that they could pursue raiders on horse or foot immediately the alarm was given.

There were plenty of cards stacked against them, yet the reivers enjoyed a long run. They continued to pillage and destroy and the only way to escape their felonious attention seemed to be to pay 'saufey' or blackmail which brought some immunity. The evil reputation they gained throughout North England and South Scotland did not seem to worry them; they paid no heed to decrees such as that the Merchant Adventurers' Company of Newcastle issued in 1554: "No fre brother of this Fellysshype shall, from hensfourthe, take non appretice, to serve in this Fellysshype of non suche as is or shal be borne or brought up in Tynedale, Ryddisdale or anye other suche lycke places, in payne of £20".

The reivers' success owed much to their surname backing. Victims knew only too well that if they took any raider to court and he was sentenced to be hanged then his surname would start a deadly feud and would seek terrible revenge.

But gradually Queen Elizabeth's new and improved wardens gained the upper hand. In this they had some assistance from King James VI who was anxious to please the English queen because of his ambition to succeed her. By about 1580 the sting had gone from the reivers.

The story of the Border ended when the Border disappeared. England and Scotland did not unite as one kingdom until 1707, but when the two crowns came together in 1603 and both countries were ruled by one king there ceased to be any reason for a line between the two. To emphasize this, King James proclaimed the former Border zone to be his Middle Shire. He demilitarized the fortresses and appointed George Home his chief adviser on matters affecting the area. In 1606 Home, now Earl of Dunbar, was put in charge of law enforcement, and he virtually eliminated the reivers and outlaws in both countries by execution and deportment. The March Laws were repealed in 1607.

Unfortunately, this was not quite the end of violence in Northumberland, for those who escaped from the Earl's clutches became moss troopers. Gangs of unruly, nomadic ruffians haunted the wilder parts of the Cheviots and periodically swooped down on isolated farms to steal horses and cattle which they sold surreptitiously in Scotland. There were loners, too, who worked up large businesses stealing farm animals, hiding them for a time in secret places then selling them in distant markets, sometimes as far as London and Aberdeen.

This type of crime lingered on through most of the seventeenth century, and indeed the moss troopers received some stimulus when they were joined by demobilised Civil War soldiers. The law enforcement officers did not get rid of them completely until after the 1715 Jacobite rebellion.

Area 6, Sub-Area D   Redesdale

Hole

L80   P522   NY866846   3 km, 2 miles, north-east of Bellingham

The bastle at this farm must be the most conspicuous in Northumberland, for it stands on a knoll by the side of the Bellingham to Woodburn road, a dark, foreboding building with a high, steeply pitched roof, one small window upstairs and a grilled opening near ground level.

A more revealing view is available to those with wellingtons and the courage to tread the gooey-manured floor of the stockyard on the other side. Here is seen the original long-wall door and its stone external stairs, a couple of original windows and two larger and later windows. The building measures about 35 by 32 feet with 4½ feet thick walls. The ground floor is vaulted and its door was in the east gable but has been blocked by another farm building. A new door in the side wall and all the extra ventilation necessary for a home for cattle was added, it is estimated, about two hundred and fifty years ago. Cattle still use the place – they seem to wander in and out at will – while fodder is kept upstairs. The bastle is in fair condition, considering its age and current usage, but a little stabilising would not come amiss; the stairs, a fine example worth preserving, needs urgent attention especially.

Being in Redesdale, the farmstead was in the Umfraville liberty, but there appears to be no record of its holders. Like so many who lived in these off the beaten track places, they were most likely either hard working, honest farmers who did nothing to earn the attention of the chroniclers or they were reivers who never got onto the courts' register.

Low Leam

L80   P522   NY876861   5 km, 3 miles, north-east of Bellingham

This and the next two entries are situated on the gently rising moors to the north-west of the Rede between Hole and West Woodburn. Having well drained land which catches the midday sun, they have been important food providers since the early settlers, and undoubtedly the soldiers holding the Roman fort of Habitancum, on the other side of the river, relied on them for much of their victuals.

Low Leam is on the road side. It has a bastle in its farmyard, much changed for use as a byre and hay loft but still sporting some original stonework. It has a door at each end now, and at first floor level there is gap in the exposed long wall where the entrance to the living quarters has been.

In 1240 this farm was held from Gilbert de Umfraville by Walter de Swethope for the princely annual rent of six pennies. Anonymous farmers held it after him, until 1663 when Sir Edward Charlton bought it for the shooting.

Low Cleughs

L80   P522   NY877867   5½ km, 3¼ miles, north-east of Bellingham

Despite its name, this lonely bastle is high above Low Leam, on a shelf of nearly level ground in the hillside. Some years ago it made a forlorn picture, its west gable propped up by wooden buttresses. Eventually buttresses and wall fell down and it looked even more abandoned, but in 1997 the Northumberland National Park people came to its rescue and, as well as rebuilding the gable, they cleaned up and made safe the whole building.

The work was worth doing, for it is an unadulterated ruin of great interest. It is larger than most bastles and still exhibits features which indicate it was owned by a wealthy family who were able to abandon it and move to a more comfortable abode as soon as five feet thick walls became unnecessary – before even outside stone stairs were considered. The remains of a fire hearth can be seen in the upstairs living room, which has three windows and, another unusual feature, both upper and lower doorways are in a long wall, one above the other.   **[Plate 8]**

High Leam

L80   P522   NY880872   6 km, 3¾ miles, north-east of Bellingham

A large farm with exceptional views over the river and far beyond. Documents tell us that at least one, perhaps two, bastles were here, but there is no sign of them now. The farmhouse is a lovely Georgian building dated 1850 with a little bit of an earlier building forming an eastern wing, but there is nothing to suggest the former presence of a bastle.

The estate, with Hudspeth near Elsdon, were given by Richard de Umfraville to Hugh de Morwick when he married Richard's daughter, Sibilla, in 1221. The couple lived in the bridegroom's property near Warkworth and High Leam was rented to farmers, Nicholas de Aketon being the first. Hugh died in 1237 and in 1242 the widow gave Hudspeth to Newminister Abbey, but we do not know what she did with High Leam. Its later descent is not recorded until John Hall of Otterburn bought it in or before 1663.

Hall Yards

L80   P522   NY902867   7½ km, 4½ miles, north-east of Bellingham

This East Woodburn property was the original Northumberland home of the Lisle family who are believed to have migrated from the Isle of Wight during the eleventh century. 'Lisle' was and is the popular name, but the family were known also as 'insula' on Latin documents and 'L'Isle' on French documents.

The Lisles had a knack of acquiring property. Otwell de Lisle, of the second known generation, leased Newton Hall near Corbridge from Baron Balliol. A generation later Peter de Lisle obtained a grant of Chipchase and a small piece of land at Whittle from the Umfravilles for a third of a knight fee. Sir Robert Lisle was bequeathed Felton when his brother-in-law, Sir Ralph de Eure, died in 1421. Robert's grandson had land in South Gosforth during the sixteenth century, and when Sir Humphrey Lisle died in 1576 he was holding Bywell manor.

The mainline family lived at Hall Yards until the middle of the thirteenth century, when they moved to Newton Hall; the Woodburn property was retained until 1661 for cadet branches, however. It was a rich and influential family but, although Sir Robert de Lisle was sheriff in 1264, it never achieved the acme of importance. In 1513 Sir Humphrey fought with distinction at Flodden, but his son, Sir William, rather blotted the copy-book when in 1527 he raided Newcastle's gaol and released nine prisoners whom he used to attack Sir William Elleker and to rob him of forty head of cattle. For this and other indiscretions he was hanged, drawn and quartered in 1529.

A fine tower was built by Otwell de Lisle in the early part of the thirteenth century and it was occupied continuously for 450 years. It was built on top of a rocky knoll close to the road from West to East Woodburn, just a few yards above the River Rede. It was either knocked down or fell down when the Lisles vacated it, but the Rev. John Hodson claimed in 1827 that he could see "extensive masses of prostrate ruins" on the site. This report probably gave rise to the erroneous belief that there was once a bastle there. At the end of the nineteenth century a vicarage was built in exactly the same place, perhaps using some of the old tower's stones and foundations. All Saints church was built to its west, and when it was consecrated in 1907 it replaced the twelfth century church at Corsenside. On the other side of the vicarage (now the former vicarage, the vicar having moved to a new house behind the church) are the very well defined outlines of fish ponds, the only survivors from the Lisle era. There are two large rectangular, dried out ponds connected by a small cutting through the common embankment. There is no mistaking their purpose, but how they filled with water and how fish got into them, are complete mysteries for they are near the foot of a hill so small it could never have supplied more than a trickle of water, and the river is at least ten yards below.

Townhead (East Woodburn)

L80   P522   NY909866   8 km, 5 miles, north-east of Bellingham

There are two farmhouses here and the more easterly one contains a fragment of a bastle in its walls. It does not look at all like a bastle now as there are extensions at its back and one end, the windows are relatively new and the doors and roof have been changed.

Harewalls

L80   P522   NY925867   9½ km, 6 miles, north-east of Bellingham

A small farm close to a large one called Blakelaw, some two miles east of East Woodburn, on the banks of the Lisle Burn.

The still inhabited farmhouse is thought to be a bastle derivative, but, although obviously very old, the farm building attached to its west end seems to be a safer bet for bastle honours. It has been much altered and ground floor doors have been inserted in both long walls. There are stone stairs against the north wall which lead to the upstair door; this is not far off the ground as the building stands on a steep slope, high at the front and low at the back.

Cherry Tree

L80   P522   NY896871   6½ km, 4 miles, north-east of Bellingham

As West Woodburn village is mostly on the north side of the River Rede, and East Woodburn is totally on the south side, buildings like Cherry Tree on the north bank are thought of as belonging to West Woodburn, even though some distance from the village.

Cherry Tree is an inhabited house, much altered but still unmistakably a bastle. It has four feet thick walls and the doorway is original although a modern lintel has been inserted under the relieving arch. The windows are modern and an extension has been added to one side.

The house lies close to an old road which connects the Woodburn communities with Corsenside and Otterburn Old Town. It is also near an old embankment which carried a temporary narrow gauge railway line laid in 1894 to carry materials from Woodburn station to Catcleugh while the reservoir there was being constructed.

Townhead (West Woodburn)

L80   P522   NY901870   7 km, 4½ miles, north-east of Bellingham

Pity the poor postman – two farms with the same name and just the river between them! This Townhead, on the north side, stands like a pivot-post around which the Rede swings from south to west. It is a very beautiful part of the dale.

The farmhouse is probably a bastle derivative. There is no positive evidence to be seen and records are hazy, but parts of the building date from bastle building times and its construction suggests that it was a fortification.

Corsenside

L80   P522   NY890892   7½ km, 4½ miles, north-east of Bellingham

This is the name of a large division of Redesdale, from Woodburn northwards and consisting mainly of the open moorland of Corsenside Common, and also of a nearly deserted village, of which only a church and one house remain.

Legend has it that the village was one of the resting places of the Lindisfarne monks during their flight with St. Cuthbert's body from the Vikings in 875, so inevitably when the church was consecrated in 1120 it was dedicated to St. Cuthbert. It is an interesting little building, basically Norman but with later windows and furnishings, in which one service is still held each year. In 1311 it was granted by the Bishop of Durham to the nuns of Holystone, to help their finances in a meagre way. About a hundred years after 1539, the date of the convent's dissolution, the church needed financial help itself and John Hall of Otterburn came to its rescue as its lay patron. From 1617 for forty-eight years the vicar was John Graham, a "sordid and scandalous fellow" who received a stipend of £6.65. In 1665 a sailor returned home with the plague and the entire community was wiped out.

Only the church survived, but a new three storey house was built in 1685, perhaps as a vicarage. It was not a fortified building, nor, so far as is known, were any of the original village houses. The new house never attracted neighbours and the replacement village was built further south, on the banks of the Rede. It was named West Woodburn.

Coldtown

L80   P522   NY892885   7 km, 4½ miles, north-east of Bellingham

A large Corsenside farm half a mile south of the ancient village. It has a fairly complete bastle, a former farmhouse now used as a store. A door and windows have been inserted and the roof renewed, but otherwise it is in good shape.

A Roman milestone was found earlier this century on the farm, which is bordered by Dere Street. The stone has been re-erected at the point marked 'Tumulus' on O.S. maps, NY889877.

The Brigg

L80   P522   NY891897   8 km, 5 miles, north-east of Bellingham

Another Corsenside farm, this time to the north of the ancient village, Its bastle is not a pretty sight for it has been given a metal roof, several windows and a door in its long side. It is used as a stable.

Monkridge Hall

L80   P510   NY901923   11 km, 6³/₄ miles, north-east of Bellingham

A farmstead with a rather fine farmhouse built in 1774 for Gabriel Hall while he was the keeper of Redesdale. The complex is by the side of the Belsay to Otterburn road (A696) – so close to it, in fact, that the 'New Line' had to make a sharp turn to miss it. This house probably had a predecessor, also owned by the Halls, but the original dwellings in the area were two bastles which belonged to cadet members of the Lisle family.

These are close together to the west of the Hall, down a steep bank and across the Heatherwick Burn, a small tributary of the Rede. The site of one bastle is clearly marked by loose stones and some short sections of wall two or three courses high. A few yards to the east is a similar site, slightly less clearly defined but nevertheless showing every sign of having been a bastle.

Although only a hundred yards from the busy road, the bastle area is secluded. Terraced hillsides and many interesting-looking bumps in the ground suggest the Ancient Britains were here.

Elsdon

L80   P510   NY937933   14 km, 8¹/₂ miles, north-east of Bellingham

This is the village of history par excellence! No other place in Northumberland has quite such a store of medieval interest, both visible and documented. It lies where the Whiskershiel Burn runs into the Elsdon Burn, some three miles due east of Otterburn on the B6341 road which links Redesdale and Coquetdale.

The Bronze Age people probably began the human story of Elsdon, or at least its surrounding hills, and the Romans almost certainly used the tranquil valley floor as a burial ground; excavation has produced a Roman altar with relevance to this usage. It was the Angles, however, who gave Elsdon prestige by making it the capital of Redesdale. They probably invented the name, Ellysden, derived, perhaps, either from 'Elles-dene, meaning 'Valley of Waters', or 'Ellers-dene', the 'Valley of Alders'. On the other hand, of course, legend claims the name commemorates Ella, a Danish giant who resided in the valley and created terror in the district, and legend is much better at etymology than are modern experts.

An Anglian capital had to have a mote or moot, a place of assembly where the elders could meet in council and administer the law. A natural spur which rises sharply from the valley floor at the north end of what is now Elsdon village was used for this purpose, and, inspite of a later change of usage, the spur is still called Mote Hill.

The last thane of Redesdale was Mildred, son of Akman. The generally accepted course of events, although now disputed, is that William I dispossessed him in or about 1076 and his territory was given to the Conqueror's friend, Robert de Umfraville, or 'Robert with the Beard'. He, a knight and lord of Tours and Vian, was charged with defending the county for ever from wolves and the king's enemies, and Redesdale was made his liberty so that he could carry out these instructions without interference from the State's government or law lords. He was the absolute master of all he perceived.

Robert took over Elsdon as his residence and capital, and did two things to it rather quickly: he built a small church and he forced the locals to shape the Mote Hill into a motte and bailey castle.

The church was replaced later so all that is known about it is that it was dedicated to St. Cuthbert because legend had it that in 875 the Lindisfarne monks had rested on the spot it was built on. The motte and bailey is still with us – devoid, of course, of its timber buildings and palisading but still displaying with great clarity how the hill was fashioned.

This is the most perfectly preserved motte and bailey in the county, perhaps in the country, as it has not been built on or ploughed. It is seen best from the air, which is difficult, or from a little way up the Cambo road out of the village. The highest part of the earthworks is the round motte, flat topped, edged with earth bulwarks and surrounded by a deep moat; here the owner and his garrison commander lived in a large timber house built above a pit where prisoners were kept. The bulwarks and moat were considered necessary protection against possible rebellious soldiery below. A removable ladder or ramp connected this command post with the bailey, where stood all the huts required by the fighting men – sleeping quarters, cookhouse, brewery, stables, smithy and perhaps a chapel. The main defences around the bailey were earth bulwarks, a pallisade and a moat, the latter perhaps filled with water but more likely with quickthorn. The single entrance had the special protection of small towers on either side. Defence was the castle's keynote; it was not designed for aggression – the soldiers went outside and attacked their enemies in the open.

The Umfravilles fulfilled their obligations so well that in 1133 or 4 King Henry I granted Robert's son, another Robert, the barony based on Prudhoe on the far bank of the River Tyne, twenty-two miles to the south. In due time the family moved there after a fine castle was built. King Henry II ordered more building work for the Umfravilles to do – their other property at Harbottle on the Coquet had to be strengthened to take its place in the defensive line the king desired.

Harbottle was very much a military outpost, and in fact much later, in 1384, when march wardens were appointed, it became the headquarters of the Middle March. The Umfravilles never lived there, but Elsdon motte and bailey was abandoned in about 1157 in favour of Prudhoe.

The lords of Redesdale did not forget Elsdon, however. They appear to have rehoused the villagers in cottages à la mode, set around a huge village green, and in 1281 William de Umfraville successfully prevailed upon King Edward I to grant the village a charter authorising a weekly market on Thursdays and a three-day annual fair on the eve, day and morrow of St. Bartholomew, the 23rd, 24th and 25th of August.

At some time towards the end of the fourteenth century the Umfravilles rebuilt the old Norman church. It has been modified many times since then, but much of this building still stands like an island in the village green; a tiny part of it, two pilasters and two small round-headed windows, came from the older church. Elsdon Tower, built as a vicarage about the same time, stands on higher ground overlooking the church.

As a vicarage, the tower must have looked reassuringly strong, and indeed there is no record of it ever having succumbed to enemy action. But a succession of incumbents complained bitterly about its cold draughts and lack of comfort. Some, like the Rev. Thomas Singleton, rector from 1812 to1842, who build the attached house, tried their best to improve matters, but others just grumbled. The most humorous of these was the Rev Charles Dodgson, great grandfather of Charles Lutwidge Dodgson who, as Lewis Carroll, wrote 'Alice in Wonderland'. The good rector stuck his living conditions for three years, from 1762 to 1765, during which he slept "in the parlour between two beds, to keep me from being frozen to death, for as we keep open house, the winds enter from every quarter and are apt to creep into bed with one". He would hardly recognise the building now, for during the first half of the 1990s the lay owner, with assistance from (but not always with the total agreement of) the Northumberland National Park Authority, undertook a thorough overhaul. Whilst painstakingly restoring the fabric, inside and out, previously unsuspected stone arched windows, fireplaces and a Murder-hole were revealed.

Just before he died, in 1381, Gilbert de Umfraville, now Earl of Angus as well as the Baron of Prudhoe, but also the last of the direct-line family, granted Redesdale to his half-brother, Thomas de Umfraville, and he and his son Robert held the liberty for fifty-five years.

The Battle of Otterburn in 1388 made little impact on Elsdon except that the church ground appears to have been used for the burial of some of the victims of that skirmish. Two large batches of tightly packed skeletons of young and middle-aged men were unearthed in the nineteenth century, and the Battle appears to be the only cause of so much killing.

Most of the lawlessness both initiated and suffered by the men of Redesdale and upper North Tynedale belongs to the late fifteenth and sixteenth centuries, but raiding was far from unknown in Elsdon in the fourteenth century. When Robert Umfraville held the lordship he was nicknamed 'Robert Mend-Market' because he stole so much food during raids into Scotland and then sold it at bargain prices in Elsdon market. This man must have been very attached to Elsdon and the wild frontier for he made frequent long journeys to the area from London and the south coast, where he was stationed as Vice-Admiral of England. He died childless in 1436 and was succeeded by William Tailbois, his nearest relative and son of Elizabeth, Gilbert de Umfraville's sister.

This family held Redesdale until William's grandson was beheaded in 1464 after the Wars of the Roses' Battle of Hexham. The Ogles were made wardens of the liberty for eleven years, then the Tailbois were repossessed and a youngster called Robert Tailbois took over. When he died in 1541 his sister Elizabeth succeeded; she was married to Thomas Wybysche, a southerner who had no stomach for the rigors of the north, so they arranged with King Henry VIII to exchange the liberty for Crown lands at Bailes in Warwickshire. The king took the opportunity in 1547 to terminate the liberty and to bring Redesdale into Northumberland and, technically at least, within the jurisdiction of the county sheriff.

This did not worry the local population unduly. They were in the midst of an epidemic of raids, counter-raids, blood feuds, corrupt wardens and inept keepers, and neither state nor march laws had much practical relevance. The surnames were the only masters, and usually they were the chief villains. The following extract from *A Book of the Losses in the Middle Marches by the Scottes Thefes* is most revealing:

> "Elsdon the chief town of Ridesdale was burnt by 500 of Lidsdale and iiij men murdered in their houses, 100 beasts carried away and in pursuit thearof wear a C men taken prisoners and 7 slain and 60 horse loss, divers rannsomed and payed their rannsome in Sir John Fosters (Warden of the Middle March) garden at Alnwicke in the 26th of her m. reign (1584) and no recovery had. Since which time the chief dooers thearof vz Martin Ellwood and Robin Ellwood of Lidsdale and their friends ar agreed with Sir John Foster and his friends and have daily recourse to his house at Alnwicke, and Ridsdale dare not fynd fault with them".

While such raids were taking place it is to be hoped that the rector opened his tower to the villagers, but one family, living at the south-west end of the village, decided to look after their safety themselves. The house called Townfoot is a bastle derivative dating from the end of the sixteenth century; there is fragmentary but unmistakable bastle masonry in its walls.

Things quietened down a little when King James VI and I appointed George. Lord Home, to supervise the transition from Border to Middle Shires. George was elevated to Earl of Dunbar in 1605 and was granted all the Crown lands in Redesdale and Tynedale, including Elsdon. He died in 1611, leaving his Northumbrian property to his daughter Elizabeth, married to Theophilus, Lord Howard de Walden. The Howards, soon to become the Earl and Countess of Suffolk, were the holders until their death, but their descendants were forced by financial inadequacies to sell to the Earl of Northumberland in 1750. The Earl became the Duke of Northumberland in 1766 and the current holder of that title still owns much of the northern dales. Some parts in the north-east belong to Lord Redesdale, however; Sir John Mitford was given this title in 1902 and the present holder, Clement Napier Bertram Mitford, a cousin of Nancy and Unity Mitford, is a considerable landowner in the area.

When most of the reivers had been rounded up and hanged or deported, there still remained a few moss troopers and cattle thieves, but the most common visitors to Elsdon were drovers and smugglers. This traffic, which had started in early medieval times and had been interrupted by the reivers during the sixteenth century, restarted in the seventeenth and many of the popular paths across the Cheviots led to Elsdon, where there was drink and free parking on the village green. The drovers led cattle over the Border for the English markets and sometimes returned with Redesdale coal and lime slung over their horses. Smugglers carried many different duty-frees, perhaps the most profitable being whisky brought from the illicit stills hidden in the mountains.

The Roman Dere Street, which crossed the Border at Chew Green then made a nearly straight line to Corbridge, was the only hard surface road in the region until well into the eighteenth century. Others barely deserved to be compared with modern bridlepaths, yet they were used extensively by pack horses and strong carts. Elsdon was an important service station on one of the busiest routes, from Newcastle to Scotland via Ponteland, Belsay, Bolam and Cambo. At Elsdon it headed north-west over the hills to join Dere Street about four miles short of Chew Green. It did not touch Otterburn, just a tiny hamlet, nor Carter Bar which did not exist then.

In 1749 the Newcastle to Elsdon road was vastly improved and surfaced with Whitstone by local landowners who were permitted to retrieve the cost by levying tolls. The road was extended from Elsdon to Otterburn, and from Otterburn to the Border, in 1779. Carter Bar was one of its toll booths. The better surface and the avoidance of the difficult country above Elsdon meant that coaches such as John Croall's 'Chevy Chase' could make regular runs between Newcastle and the Scottish towns, as far up as Edinburgh. The drovers, however, avoided the toll roads as much as they could; most cut out Elsdon and came straight over the hills to join, or cross, the Cambo to Elsdon road at a point about a mile east of Steng Cross. Here was a smithy's shop – the site is still marked by four trees called 'Shop Trees' – where farriers were kept busy shoeing not only the drovers horses but their cattle too! Their tender hooves had to be protected from the gritty roads which lay ahead.

This was a blow to Elsdon's economy, but much worse came in 1833 when the 'New Line' from Belsay to Otterburn was opened. This bypassed

Elsdon and the travellers' trade was transferred to Otterburn. Even the few drovers who still sought refreshment at Elsdon disappeared after the railways took away their trade in the 1850s and '60s. Elsdon could only relax into the peaceful backwater it is today.

The huge village green, the heart of Elsdon, has seen it all – the drunken brawls, the excitement of the fair (which lasted to 1870), the round-up of stray sheep into the pinfold which is still there, the cock fights, the punishment of wrongdoers on gallows and pillory, and the Midsummer bonfire through which the cattle were driven to ward off the influence of the Evil Eye. During the first quarter of the eighteenth century new stone buildings began to appear around the green, and three of these were inns. Only the Bird in Bush remains licensed, the other two, the Bacchus (still sporting a statue of Bacchus on a barrel) and the Crown are private houses now.

Whitlees

L81   P510   NY960926   15 km, 9¼ miles, north-east of Bellingham

A farm two miles to the east of Elsdon, up the Whiskershiel Burn, a pleasant pasture and forest valley with an important nature reserve up one of its feeder burns, a limestone flush which supports an array of spring and summer flowers like Thyme, Rock Rose and Fragrant Orchids.

No doubt Whitlees began life as a herdsman's shieling, like its larger neighbour, Whiskershiel Farm, but someone, name unknown, converted it into an all-year-round farm, probably in the late seventeenth century. At the same time, the sixteenth century bastle would have been converted into a useful farm building – that is, if it really had been a bastle. It is a very low building, which means it was either a bastle which had its upper floor removed, and a blocked doorway and relieving arch in its north-eastern gable suggests that it was, or it was just a very small, single storey strong house, and a small grilled window suggests that this was the case. Whatever it was, it had stout walls and a bastle-type plan. The long wall facing the farmhouse has been rebuilt and a double door wide enough for carts has been inserted.

Bowershield

L80   P510   NY940948   15½ km, 9¾ miles, north-east of Bellingham

Another former shieling on the moors, this time about a mile north of Elsdon, just below the Rede-Coquet watershed.

The inhabited farmhouse was called Low Bowershield formerly, but the adjective has been discarded as unnecessary as High Bowershield is now just a jungle of broken walls, used only as a sheep shelter. Amongst this mess is a clearly defined bastle with some walling up to five feet in height and exhibiting three slit vents. Near it are other fragments which could be the remains of a second bastle.

Girsonsfield

L80   P510   NY890936   11½ km, 7 miles, north-east of Bellingham

A trim, whitewashed farmhouse, standing half way up the steep bank of a tributary of the Otter Burn, is the successor to a small tower, the foundations of which are nearly lost in the grass a few hundred yards further into the hills. There is barely enough of the tower left to date, but almost certainly it was a fifteenth century building.

It was a Halls' strongholds, and is believed to have been the home of the 'Fause-hearted Ha's' who in the second half of the sixteenth century played the dirty trick on Parcy Reed which is described below under Troughend.

Otterburn

L80   P510   NY887931   11 km, 6¾ miles, north-east of Bellingham

Modern Otterburn could challenge Elsdon with some justification for the title of Redesdale's capital, but up to the mid-nineteenth century it was just a small hamlet, insignificant compared to Elsdon.

Its first mention is in the report of the inquest which followed Gilbert de Umfraville's death in 1245. Then it comprised ten cottages and land for bondsmen, a few freemen's cottages, a brew house and, probably, Otterburn Tower. The latter was not listed but it is known that the tower was built in the middle of the thirteenth century, and it seems feasible that Gilbert was responsible rather than his son who was an infant when he inherited.

This small hamlet – it did not have a church until Dobson built one in 1858 – was in a very isolated position. The main route into Scotland went from Elsdon over the hills to Chew Green, missing Otterburn by three miles, and the old Roman road, Dere Street, also bypassed it to the west. Only locals and a few itinerants used the apparently easier route up the River Rede, so Otterburn had no incentive to grow, although a corn mill was built beside the Otter Burn in 1330.

Jean Froissart, the French secretary to Queen Philippa, King Edward III's wife, who toured Scotland and north England, recorded in his journal that Otterburn Tower was "tolerably strong". This judgement was tested and found to be correct in 1388 when Earl James Douglas, fearing his troops might get bored while waiting for Hotspur to show up for the Battle of Otterburn, staged a day-long assault upon it. They failed to gain admittance, but, never mind, they won the battle.

The Umfravilles held the tower throughout their lordship of Redesdale, but when the Tailbois inherited in 1436 it was leased or sold to the Halls. John Hall held it in 1530, as had his forebears before him.

The Halls were the most powerful surname in Redesdale during the sixteenth century, and possibly the most prolific: many settlements in the dale were occupied by branch families. As leaders, they were responsible for most of the raids across the Border or area boundaries and fought the most duels, but frequently they professed support for the law by accepting the office of Redesdale Keeper. They lived in a crazy world.

After the Union of the Crowns there was a time of reckoning when the chronically criminal were beheaded or deported and the more astute became shamelessly virtuous. A spark of rebellion was never far below the surface, however, as when Judge Hall, better known as Mad Jack Ha', heard that the Jacobites were on the march in 1715. It is said that he was sitting on the bench of the Alnwick Quarter Sessions when the news reached him, and that he ran out of the courthouse so fast he forgot his hat. Nine months later he had no need of a hat.

Mad Jack had lived in Otterburn Tower: he lost that as well as his head, but the Crown allowed another member of the family, Gabriel Hall of Catcleugh, to buy the building. It passed to his son, Reginald, who added a square wing before he died in 1745. Robert Ellison, a close relative who lived in Newcastle, inherited, but it was passed to his son Henry within a few years, and in the 1780s it was sold to a Mr Storey, a North Shields shipbuilder.

There was a fair estate attached to the tower in those days, and when Mr Storey died the property was divided into two lots: John Davidson, a Newcastle attorney, bought the land to the west of the Otter Burn, and James Ellis, another attorney of Newcastle and Hexham, bought the tower and the land east of the burn.

When Mr Ellis died, in 1830, his property was sold to Thomas James of Tynedale. He reckoned the tower was beyond repair – it was about 600 years old by then – so he had most of it and the newer wing pulled down and a mansion in the castellated style popular at that time was built in its place.

The next owner was Howard Pease, a distinguished writer about the countryside and collector of folklore and legend. He extended the rear of the house and built the stable block in 1904.

Since 1944 the tower has been a pleasant hotel. There is nothing of the original immediately visible in it, but fragments of a thick wall at the back of the entrance hall seem to be a lot older that the rest of the place. Also there is a well, kept covered by a trapdoor, which was once the tower's water supply.

Meanwhile, whilst the tower was advancing into modern life, the village was also developing in its own way. When the reiving menace was brought under control, drovers began to use the riverside route from the Border to the cattle markets, and the needs of these thirsty men were satisfied in a small inn by the bridge over the Otter Burn. At roughly the same time the Beighatt family started a small textile mill. The most momentous event, however, was the construction of toll roads connecting Otterburn to Elsdon and the Border in 1779, developments which put the village on the travellers map. The inn was enlarged to cope with increased business, and it was given the name 'The Percy Arms' as a compliment to the lord of the manor. After 1820 coaches such as the Blucher, which ran between Newcastle and Jedburgh, and the Chevy Chase, which went on to Edinburgh, stopped there for fresh sandwiches and horses. Business improved still further when the 'New Line', a direct road from Belsay, was opened in 1833.

The Beighatt mill lasted sixty years. In 1821 William Waddell from Jedburgh bought the premises and started a small enterprise. At first he supplemented and organised the local cottage wool industry, then gradually he concentrated more and more on production in the mill. His speciality was hard wearing rugs, often in the natural sheep colours, and their name 'Otterburn' became world famous. Production was moved to another mill in 1977, but Otterburn Mill remains in the village as a shop and display unit.

In 1870 the Percy Arms was taken over by Lord James Murray, who changed its name to The Murray Arms. He also built Otterburn Hall, just outside the village. The coach business did not survive the coming of the railways, but Murray kept his inn until 1920. The new owner reverted to the original name of The Percy Arms.

The famous Battle of Otterburn was fought in 1388 a mile or two north of the village. It was a Border fight between two keen rivals, Hotspur (Sir Henry Percy, eldest son of the Earl of Northumberland) and James, Earl of Douglas. This was no deadly feud, more the outcome of a love – hate relationship, so when Douglas taunted Hotspur by filching his pennant outside the walls of Newcastle, a scrap was inevitable.

Douglas, with his army variously estimated as comprising from 3000 to 7000 men, reached his carefully chosen battle site a day before Hotspur learnt where he was. As soon as he got the intelligence he marched his army of roughly similar size the thirty-two miles to Otterburn. They arrived just before dusk, and immediately an attack was launched.

Tired and hungry though his soldiers must have been, Hotspur led them straight towards Douglas's camp, probably hoping that a night-time onslaught would create panic. A detachment commanded by Sir Thomas Umfraville was ordered to make a wide detour and attack Douglas's rear, but these men got lost and played no decisive part in the battle.

Instead it was Douglas who bypassed his advancing opponents and attacked them in their rear. Night time is not conducive to orderly tactics and the battle became a melée inwhich many heads were lost, both English and

Scottish. Several hours passed before Hotspur was captured and conceded defeat. The Scots were clear victors, but their leader lay dead.

The battle was given undeserved publicity by the ballad *Chevy Chase* which many people believe is about the Otterburn affair. There are indeed lines in it which are relevant, but equally there are other lines which could apply to the Battle of Piper Dene in 1435 or 6, so the only realistic conclusion is that the work is about no particular battle, just Border warfare in general, and how utterly futile it was.

Troughend

L80   P510   NY866923   9½ km, 6 miles, north-east of Bellingham

The Reed family closely rivalled the Halls as the most influential in Redesdale. Soon after 1415 the head of the family acquired Troughend Tower, which had been built during the previous century by William Butecom. It served the Reeds well during the traumatic period of raids and counter-raids, then was replaced by a more commodious hall house by Elrington Reed in about 1716. It is said to have been built in front of a much older brewhouse and kitchen which were kept in use. Unfortunately all these have gone now and the present farmer lives in a modern house. It was built when he was a young boy over thirty years ago, and he remembers the hall which was then a ruin, having been hastened into that condition by fire in 1952. The precise site of the tower is not known, but a small wood by the roadside is suspected of covering its foundations.

The most noteworthy member of the family was undoubtedly Parcy Reed who lived at Troughend (pronounced 'Troffen') during the second half of the sixteenth century. At the time the following story was enacted he was the Keeper of Redesdale, a post subordinate to the warden of the Middle March with special responsibilities in his area. In this capacity he arrested and sent for trial a young reiver belonging to the notorious Crozier clan, which reigned supreme in Liddesdale. The lad's father did not think much of Parcy's action and declared a blood feud.

Poor Parcy was the target of another feud at the same time. Three Hall brothers, who probably lived across the valley at Girsonsfield, were very upset that one of their family had not got the Keeper's job; it frequently did go their way, but this time they had missed out, and that was enough for them to wish Parcy harm.

A rogues' meeting between these Halls and father Crozier was arranged and a simple but effective plan was agreed. Parcy was invited to spend a day with the Halls hunting up the Bateinghope Burn, a small and lonely tributary of the Rede close to the Border. A keen huntsman, Parcy readily accepted the invitation, and on the appointed day set off with his hosts and his dogs. They hunted all day, only stopping for a rest when the sun was setting. Parcy fell asleep. When he woke up the Halls had vanished, his horse was bridleless, his gun lay in a pool of water, his sword had been jammed into its scabbard, his dogs were missing...and a party of Croziers were bearing down on him. By the time they were finished with him he was handless and feetless and there were thirty-three wounds in his very dead body.

The Halls were never punished for their part in this brutal murder, but great indignation was felt in the dale, not only about the untimely end of a respected member of the community but also about the manner in which it was perpetrated. The three brothers thereafter were always referred to as the 'Fause-hearted Ha's'.

Dargues

L80   P510   NY863937   11 km, 6³/₄ miles, north-east of Bellingham

The O.S. Pathfinder map marks a 'Peel (remains of)' near Dargues Bridge, but confirmatory evidence has not been found.

Some not very convincing large stones exist in a high wall overlooking the Dargues Burn, on the boundary of the Dunns Cottage property. These may have been taken from a bastle.

Shittleheugh

L80   P510   NY869950   12 km, 7¹/₂ miles, north of Bellingham

A conspicuous ruined bastle standing high on the side of Blakeman's Law, overlooking the Otterburn – Carter Bar road. It was occupied by a branch of the Reed family during the sixteenth and seventeenth centuries, and probably was built by one of them around about 1560.

The two gable walls remain almost full height, but both long walls are broken, leaving only sufficient to see that the ground floor chamber had been vaulted and that the doorway into it had been made from just three great stones, two uprights and a lintel. A long wall entrance is rather unusual, although there is another one not far away at Low Cleughs. Foundations of two small buildings lie close to the bastle.

There is a local legend that the door to the bastle was one large rock which was rolled open or closed in true Arabian Nights fashion. Not true, unfortunately: probably a shepherd started the story by using the ruin as a sheep pen and blocking the entrance with a rock.

Rattenraw

L80   P510   NY850952   12 km, 7¹/₂ miles, north of Bellingham

Two miles north-west of Otterburn, at the junction of the A68 and A696 roads, is a farm called Elishaw which once was a hamlet sporting a 'hospital' –

ie, a place where hospitality was extended to travellers. It was founded as a charity by one of the Umfravilles, probably in the thirteenth century, and for at least two hundred years it was well patronized by horsemen using the Roman Dere Street and by gypsies of all kinds – faws, tinkers, muggers, pedlars and other itinerants.

Close to the present farm, but on the west side of the River Rede, is a gate guarding a farm lane. Two further gates up this lane is another farm, Rattenraw; the name is supposed to mean a row of houses, so perhaps this too was a hamlet at one time. A field separates the farmhouse from the river, and in this is a wall containing a stretch of about 30 feet where the stones are larger and the construction stronger than the rest. This is believed to be a still intact wall of a bastle. A few yards away is a collection of large stones loosely piled up to form a wind-break; no doubt this is where the rest of the bastle ended up.

Horsley

L80   P510   NY844968   13½ km, 8¼ miles, north of Bellingham

The wayside inn here, the Redesdale Arms, started life as a bastle and was converted to an inn after the Otterburn – Carter Bar route was made a toll road fit for carriages in 1779. Older readers may remember when it displayed two signs; one facing north read 'The first inn in England', the other facing south read 'The last inn in England'. Before the 1939 war it was run by a rather cantankerous but interesting ancient codger called Ben Prior who, when fuelled with sufficient whisky, could tell a riveting tale about nothing in particular.

Unfortunately the building suffered major fire damage in August 1993. It was thought that intruders may have overturned gas cylinders which leaked into the cellar where sparks from a freezer thermostat caused the conflagration. Only some stark walls remained, mainly at the northern end which was the original bastle; the nineteenth century southern end and its twentieth century glass porch were reduced to rubble. The owner, Lord Redesdale, pledged to rebuild the inn, and in July 1995 this work was completed most satisfactorily. The northern bastle walls and the visible plinth of boulders upon which they stand have been saved and the rest of the building has been renewed sympathetically.

Stobbs

L80   P510   NY837971   14 km, 8½ miles, north of Bellingham

Evistones

L80   P510   NY830967   13½ km, 8¼ miles, north of Bellingham

Both these places are reached by a narrow lane signposted 'Redesdale E.H. Farm' which leaves the Carter Bar road about half a mile beyond Horsley.

Stobbs is the first stop; it is a farm near the left bank of the River Rede. The farmhouse has walls containing large, roughly dressed stones and its walls are some 40 inches thick, so it can be assumed with safety to be a bastle derivative.

The lane continues across the river, up-stream a little way then starts to climb before turning south and running across a hill. At one point on this stretch it runs about 80 yards below the deserted medieval village of Evistones.

This is now a wide area of largely fragmented masonry which takes an expert or someone with a vivid imagination to decipher. One authority claims that all surviving parts of buildings show signs of having been bastles, and that there were six or seven of them. This may be a slight exaggeration, but three bastles at least can be distinguished with a fair degree of confidence. These include one where a sizeable chunk of its vault remains; one end of it disappears into the hillside while the other has been walled up with a door inserted, presumably to make a store or shelter. Another recognisable structure is a strong curtain wall which once surrounded the entire village. The inhabitants must have been very frightened of being attacked.

Local records show that two graynes lived here, the Hedleys and the Fletchers, but that only the latter survived to see the seventeenth century. The community had a bad reputation for thieving, and the expectation of just vengeance probably accounted for the unusually strong defences. Three Fletchers were tenants in 1604; they were probably executed or deported during the Border clean-up as records end then.

The Redesdale E.H. Farm, signposted at the main road, is a little further along the lane. The letters stand for 'Experimental Husbandry' and the farm does empirical studies designed to improve the efficiency of hill farmers. One matter it is alleged to have applied its best brains to has caused many a chuckle in Otterburn. It appears that sheep, like humans, can suffer tooth decay when they get old, and this condition prevents them eating properly and becoming ready for the market. To restore their youthful appetite, some have been fitted with stainless steel false teeth! So do be warned, should you visit Evistons, some of those sheep which graze so peacefully around the bastle ruins pack a mighty strong bite!

High Rochester

L80   P510   NY832985   15½ km, 9¼ miles, north of Bellingham

This village is of special interest to Roman archaeologists for it is contained within the perimeter of the frontier fort of Bremenium, much used, first by Agricola in 80AD, then by Quintus Lollius Orbicus in 139AD when they tried, unsuccessfully, to conquer Scotland, and again in the third and fourth centuries when 'Exploratores' policed the Cheviot outposts. There is not a great deal of Roman memorabilia left above ground now – the west gate is a glorious exception – and indeed the medieval village is not what it was either. The place still possesses the ambience of hallowed antiquity for all that.

There are two bastles here. One, much disguised. lies in the centre of a row of three cottages; the other, externally very little changed, stands in splendid isolation. Both are still inhabited. The owner of the isolated bastle was trying desperately when we went to press to obtain permission from the National Park Authority to make some much needed alterations.

Two roads connected Bremenium with the outside world and, as they were much used in the Middle Ages, are mentioned frequently in this study. One was Dere Street, the main route from England into Scotland, and the other was an unnamed cross-country road which joined the Devil's Causeway at Alauna, now Learchild, not far from Wooler.

Branshaw

| L80 | P510 | NY880996 | 17 km, 10½ miles, north-east of Bellingham |

Sills

| L80 | P499 | NT826004 | 17½ km, 10¾ miles, north of Bellingham |

Both these places are in the Otterburn Training Area and may be visited only with the Army's permission.

Branshaw is a very dilapidated ruin close to the Roman cross-country road and several hill tracks made by reivers and smugglers. A bastle with a vaulted ground floor is little more than a heap of stones now. It became a farming settlement after the Union; the Sanderson family owned it in 1840.

Sills is still a working farm close to Dere Street. A well-documented small tower was here but there is no sign of it now. Neither the present farmer nor his father have found any trace of it. In 1840 the farm was run by a family called Ellison.

Catcleugh

| L80 | P498 | NT745032 | 20 km, 12½ miles, north-west of Bellingham |

The head of the Rede was desolate summer shieling country until a branch of the Hall family enclosed a large tract near Catcleugh and started all-year-round farming in 1682. The settlers built a fine house for themselves; a 'peel' mentioned in a deed of 1658 was somewhere close to this but as there is no trace of it now it is impossible to pinpoint its exact site. The popular belief is that it stood on the valley floor and is covered by the water of Catcleugh reservoir, which was constructed between 1894 and 1905.

The Border is a couple of miles north-west of the reservoir, on the watershed called Redeswire which provides the lactation for the River Rede running southwards and the Jed Water running northwards. It was the setting in 1575 for the celebrated affray called the 'Raid of the Redeswire', the result of mistrust and worn tempers during a wardens meeting. A path had crossed the Border at this point for many centuries, used by reivers, smugglers, gypsies and cattle drovers, but it was not until a road was built between Otterburn and Jedburgh in 1799 that it became a main link between the two countries. It was a toll road, and Carter Bar was one of its toll booths.

Between the reservoir and the Border is a farm called Whitelee. It became an inn fifty or so years before the road was made and it enjoyed a healthy trade until 1890 when the reservoir builders closed it because it was producing too much sewerage.

Area 6, Sub-Area E   Lower North Tyne, East Side

Birtley

L87   P534   NY880781   7 km, 4½ miles, south-east of Bellingham

An old township in Prudhoe barony, belonging to the Umfravilles until the end of the fourteenth century and then to the Percy earls. Neither family ever lived here and it was retained simply as a letting property.

No tenants names have been recorded until 1533 so it is not known who held the 'chief messuage' at Birtley in 1307. The term usually means a fortified main seat, often a tower, and the holder is generally a knight or a gentleman important enough for a mention, but in this case there is nothing either about the abode or its occupier.

John Heron of Chipchase leased land at Caryhowes, said to adjoin Birtley Wood to the west of the village, in 1533, and his descendants were still there in 1606 when the lease was renewed for twenty-one years at an annual rental of £20. One of them is believed to have built a bastle, but if true the site has been lost. There is a derelict farmstead at High Carry House (NY865790) which is partly roofless and partly good enough for the Birtley Shields farmer to use as a store, but it has thin walls and has never been a fortified building. The O.S. Pathfinder map has "Peel (rems of)" marked at NY865792, but there is nothing there either. A university student recently spent two days in the area looking for clues and found nothing, not even a likely-looking stone.

In 1552 the Herons installed a junior member of the family in Birtley village, and in 1611 a small tower was built for him or his son. The ivy-covered ruins of this still stand some twenty courses high in a corner of the garden of Birtley Hall, which is opposite the church and was the vicarage at one time. It is an interesting ruin with indications of corner turrets and rather rough stonework. It is alleged that some damage was done to it in 1961 by a sonic boom. Its date stone is inscribed '1611, J.H.': the builder was John Heron and it is the opinion of experts that 1611 – very late for a tower – is the original building date and not that of some repair or alteration.

John Heron of Birtley may have been a junior in the Heron conglomerate, but he probably had more money in 1611 than had his seniors, for all their flamboyancy. Not only could he build his tower, he also was able to buy a large property at Shield Hall in Hexhamshire. Some of his descendants settled there, including a great-great-grandson who purchased Ninebanks tower and manor house in 1770. The family held their Birtley property until 1805.

In 1711 Birtley manor was sold by the Percys to George Allgood, the Newcastle merchant who had already bought several possessions of the money-strapped main Heron family. He enclosed the common land around Birtley in 1750 and all his tenants received a share.

Tone

L80   P522   NY902802   7¹/₂ km, 4¹/₂ miles, south-east of Bellingham

Tolland, its former name, was granted with Filton Moor by Odinel de Umfraville to Newminster Abbey c1180. The monks used the ground for summer grazing, and later built a grange there.

After the abbey was dissolved in 1537, the Crown sold the estate to one of the Widdringtons. John Widdrington of Widdrington, known to have been interested in this part of the country as in 1567 he bought part of Haughton, may have been the builder of a strong house at Tone, but it could have been built before he was born by John Birtley, the energetic abbot of Newminster from 1467 to c1500.

Some generations later, William, the fourth Lord Widdrington of Blankney, sold Tone to Allan Swinburne, the tenth child of William Swinburne of Capheaton. His daughter and heiress, Mary, married Phillip Hodgshon, a name later pruned to Hodgson. Tone became theirs.

Their children were very active in the Jacobite rebellion. Alan, their son, was incarcerated in Morpeth's gaol on suspicion of treason, and he was left there until he died. One of their daughters is said to have disguised herself as a gingerbread wench to follow the Duke of Cumberland's army as a spy, while another daughter, Mary, delivered messages from 'General' Forster to his 'troops'. She got to know Forster quite well and thought he was a "pig-headed fool" who, nevertheless, could manage his magnificent black charger well.

The strong house, a short distance west of the Tone Inn on Dere Street, was converted into the existing pleasant dwelling in about 1800. The front was renewed then, but the gables were left, and the eastern one still shows a blocked ground floor entrance. The old walls are four feet thick.

Carrycoats Hall

L87   P534   NY924799   9¹/₂ km, 6 miles, south-east of Bellingham

Filton White House

L80   P522   NY929808   10¹/₂ km, 6¹/₂ miles, south-east of Bellingham

Both places were in the Filton Moor estate which Odinel de Umfraville granted, with Tone, to the Newminister Abbey before 1182. The estate was to the east of Dere Street, near Tone Inn.

The monks used the estate for summer grazing until dissolution in 1537. The Crown did not sell immediately but instead leased it in four lots. Two went to the Shaftos at Bavington Hall and they built strong houses which they called Felton White House and Carrycoats. The first name suggests that the monks were the builders; perhaps the Shaftos just modified a shieling. The third part went to John Heron, the fourth to Roger Widdrington, and all four parts were used for summer grazing. Roger build a shieling on his part, a building which later developed into Colt Farm (NY929784).

This arrangement lasted for more than a century, then the Crown decided to sell the estate to the Widdringtons. In 1661 they, in their turn, sold Filton White House and Carrycoats to the sitting tenant, Charles Shafto, the current holder of Bavington Hall.

In due course a farm replaced Filton White House, the stones of the old strong house being used to build the farm buildings, leaving only a grass-covered outline. Carrycoats strong house was retained until the 1830s, although much modified during the eighteenth century. Eventually it was replaced by Carrycoats Hall, a pleasant mansion with a Tudor-style frontage. Parts of the strong house can be traced to its rear, and a wide staircase dating from the eighteenth century modifications is incorporated.

This hall has a place in history as a frequently used retreat of Lord William Henry Beveridge, author of the 1942 Beveridge Report about the welfare state. He paid many visits during the last years of his life, the hall's owners being his step-daughter and her husband, Colonel Burn. When he died he was buried in the churchyard of Thockrington church, some four miles to the south.

Thockrington

L87   P534   NY958790   13 km, 8 miles, south-east of Bellingham

This parish was yet another possession of the Umfraville family, but only until 1226, inwhich year it was seized by the Archbishop of York as compensation after Richard de Umfraville had "violated the liberty and peace of the priory of Hexham and inflicted injury upon the Archbishop's land". In 1313 the

Knights Hospitallers were allowed free tenure of the church, probably a way of legalising their collection of the tithes. There was a small village set around the church then, housing eighteen tax payers.

Hexhamshire became Crown property in 1545. This was just about the time the Knights Hospitallers were packing their bags, so it was convenient to sell Thockrington to a very eager buyer, one of the Shaftos of Bavington Hall in the neighbouring estate. The bargain included the farms of Hetchester, North Heugh and Quarry House, as well as the village.

One of the Shaftos – probably William who was born in 1576 and later became a captain in the Commonwealth army – built a fortified house of some sort on the northern side of the village, most likely as a safe retreat for the villagers in times of strife. There were still eleven houses in the village at that time.

Another William Shafto had his property sequestrated for helping the 1715 Jacobite rebels. William's brother Edward bought the Little Bavington estate from the Crown in 1716, but the fate of Thockrington is not known. The villagers paid rent for their land, but to whom is not recorded.

Today there are only two cottages, a farm and the church in Thockrington. Earthworks surround these buildings, the foundations of the strong house being entangled with cottage remains. One set of grass-covered mounds is still called the 'night folds', supposedly where cattle and sheep were held for overnight safety. No doubt this happened although the mounds look like old foundation coverings.

The church is interesting. Basically Norman, it retains only a little of the original as it has been repaired and practically rebuilt on several occasions, but a couple of windows and the chancel arch are survivors. The tunnel-vaulted chancel and the seventeenth century double bell-cot are unusual. In its yard is the grave of Lord Beveridge, who died in 1963.

Bavington Hall   Little Bavington

L87   P534   NY992787   16½ km, 10¼ miles, south-east of Bellingham

The present mansion started life as a tower listed in the 1415 survey. There is no trace of this today, although a two-storey library wing may mark its site. Its history, however, goes back to pre-1066 times when Bavington was an Anglian settlement of a family called Bavingas. The Umfravilles included it in their Prudhoe barony in c1134 and, for letting purposes, they divided the manor into Great and Little Bavington, or 'Babington' as it is sometimes spelt in old history books. The feudal tenants of Little Bavington were called Bataille.

Nothing changed until the fourteenth century, when Isobel Bataille inherited and married William de Schaftowe of East Shaftoe. They made their home at Little Bavington and eventually got round to building a tower.

Eventually, also, they found time to simplifying their name to Shafto – never, strangely, using the final 'e' found on East and West Shaftoe.

Just to complicate the tower's descent, records show that Robert Langwath lived there in part of the fifteenth century, and John Delaval, a relative, made it his home in 1608 and 1609. It was always Shafto property, however, and William Shafto was both owner and occupier in 1715, by which time the tower had been enlarged and modified, justifying John Warburton's description, "a well situated and graceful building incompass'd with a grove; good garden". But in that year William lost it all for helping the Jacobites.

William's brother, Edward, bought Bavington Hall and lived there with his wife Mary. The mainline Shaftos moved to Whitworth, near Spennymoor in County Durham. Here lived the hero of the famous song, Bobby Shafto, who was a member of Parliament in 1761 and a well liked, generous and cheerful landlord. Another branch of the family lived at Beamish.

It soon became apparent to Edward and Mary that buying Bavington Hall had been a mistake. It was in urgent need of expensive repairs, and they had no money. They were very lucky for Mary's brother came to their rescue. In c1720 Admiral George Delaval, newly arrived at Seaton Delaval after a lifetime at sea, had enough money to build a new place for himself at the coast and to virtually rebuild his sister's place, to create the existing Bavington Hall.

George Shafto, Edward and Mary's son, inherited the rejuvenated building, and his descendants were the owners, but infrequent occupiers, until well into the twentieth century. Most of the time they let it, and eventually they sold it. In the 1960s Mr and Mrs Robert Shafto sold their home at Beamish – it became an open air museum – and bought Bavington Hall. It was theirs until the 1990s.

Little Swinburn

L87   P534   NY949778   13 km, 5 miles, south-east of Bellingham

It seems to be the fashion these days to spell both the geographical and the family name as 'Swinburne', but it is suggested that neither Little nor Great Swinburn need the terminal 'e' as both their names are derived from the Swin Burn, which never saw an 'e' in its life. The family name is a different matter; the original was 'Swyneburne' so it makes some sort of sense to perpetuate the final 'e' (while forgetting about the middle one). In this study, therefore, 'Swinburne' is animal and 'Swinburn' is vegetable and mineral.

The earliest known holder of Little (sometime East) Swinburn was Ulfehill de Swyneburne, whose liege lord during the final years of the twelfth century was Ralph de Gunnerton. Both Little Swinburn and Gunnerton were in the Bywell barony held by the Balliols. During the next hundred years the Swyneburne and Gunnerton fortunes changed dramatically, and in 1296 Ulfehill's great-grandson, John de Swyneburne, acquired Gunnerton from

Ralph's great-great-grandson, Nicholas de Gunnerton. He obtained property at Haughton and Humshaugh as well.

John and his wife, Avicia, had two sons and when their father died, in 1313, the elder, Robert, inherited Gunnerton while young Adam got Little Swinburn and the other property.

Robert was a soldier who, for services rendered, had been granted Chirdon manor in 1296, and Knarsdale in the South Tyne valley was granted to him in 1315. When he retired from the army in 1324 he was a very sick man who sought peace and quiet in a new environment. He bought Little Horkesley, an estate in Essex, and lived his last two years there. His son, Thomas, moved to East Mersy, also in Essex; his other inherited properties were held in absentia for many years by him and his progeny, except Chirdon, which went to Robert's favourite niece, Elizabeth.

Adam, lord of Little Swinburn, was a political animal, a free thinker in matters connected with the law. In 1297 he demonstrated his distaste for King Edward I's Scottish policy by leading "the hordes of Athol and Monkieth" to Hexham where they did much damage. He served a short term in prison for this, and the experience did wonders for his rectitude: he emerged the very model of an ambitious local dignitary. By 1315 he was sheriff of Northumberland and had bought a house in Thirlwall and some small estates along the Roman Wall. A spark of the old fire remained, however, and he used his position to publicise his opinion of King Edward II's handling – or bungling – of the post-Bannockburn crisis in Northumberland, when three years of ruined harvests and the attentions of Robert Bruce had reduced the county to a moan for succour. His strictures were so close to the bone the Government put him back in prison, to shut him up in two senses. His friend, Sir Gilbert de Middleton, thought this treatment most unfair, and it may well have been the trigger which fired the nefarious exploits of the Mitford Gang. Adam died in prison in 1318 and his property was confiscated.

Adam had been married twice and left one boy and three girls. The boy, Henry, and Barnaba, the eldest girl theoretically inherited Little Swinburn jointly, but the confiscation prevented this. When he was old enough, in 1323, Henry petitioned for the return of the property. The petition was listened to sympathetically and Little Swinburn was returned – but to Barnaba alone and not to Henry. She got one or two of the Roman Wall estates as well, but these she kindly gave to her half-brother as some compensation. Christiana, Barnaba's full sister, got the Haughton property, while Elizabeth, Henry's full sister, got Sewingshields and also Simonburn from her mother and Chirdon from her Uncle Robert.

Give a medieval girl property and say goodbye to it, for when she married it went either to her husband or to their offspring. Barnaba married Sir John Strivelyn, he who had bought Belsay from the Crown when the

Middletons suffered sequestration after the capture of the Mitford Gang in 1318, so Little Swinburn left the Swinburnes and became a parcel of the Belsay empire. Their daughter, Christiana, their heiress, married Sir John Middleton, so there was no change until the end of the seventeenth century.

It seems probable that there was no tower at Little Swinburn when the Middletons took possession, and that Sir John Middleton or his son made good this deficiency. The 1541 survey lists "a little tower at Little Swinburn of Thomas Middleton of Belsay, with roof decay". Assuming that the final phrase refers to the tower and not the man, it is rather surprising the building had not been mentioned in 1415; if it had not been completed then, it must surely have been soon after. Its vital statistics were 40 by 27 feet externally, with 5 feet thick walls and a vaulted ground floor.

By a strange coincidence, ownership of Little Swinburn returned to the Swinburnes in about 1690 when Edward Swinburne bought it from the Middletons. But Edward was not related to the original owners for he was the youngest member of the Capheaton family, who could trace their ancestry back to the thirteenth century holders of Great Swinburn. Like all his family, Edward was a zealous Roman Catholic and Jacobite supporter. He marched with the Earl of Derwentwater in 1715, was captured at Preston and died in prison in 1718 of spotted fever.

Little Swinburn was confiscated and sold by the Crown in 1719 to Sir William Loraine of Kirkharle, who, with his son, held it until 1826. A farmhouse was built close to the tower in 1808 but nothing was done to the tower which, consequently, is now a ruin. It can be seen quite clearly from the narrow lane which connects Colt Crag and Hallington reservoirs; it stands to nearly roof height at two corners and includes part of a doorway and the lower few steps of a mural staircase.

Great Swinburn

L87   P324   NY934753   13 km, 8 miles, south-east of Bellingham

In spite of their similar names, Great and Little Swinburn had little in common until 1826. Indeed, in Norman times they belonged to different baronies, the latter to Bywell and Great Swinburn to the little known and well scattered barony of Hadston, a distinction it shared with neighbouring Colwell.

King Henry I granted Hadston barony to Ansketel de Wirecestre. It comprised, as well as Great Swinburn and Colwell, a bit of Benton and West Chirton in what is now North Tyneside, and Hadston, a hamlet on the coast below Amble. Not a very generous grant, valued at only one knight fee.

By the 1160s the barony had descended to two brothers, Radulf who held the eastern part and Pagan who got Great Swinburn and Colwell. Radulf's share passed in due course to his heiress's husband, Jordan Hairan, and their descendants did very well for themselves after they changed their surname to Heron. Pagan's share was inherited by his son John, who also changed his name – to Swinburne – and enlarged his possessions by purchasing Chollerton.

John Swinburne had three sons, Nicholas, Alan and William. Alan was rector of Whitfield in 1264, and in 1274 he purchased Capheaton from Thomas de Fenwick. As he never married, Alan transferred his holdings to his nephew Alexander, son of his younger brother William, when he felt his end was nigh, and Alexander initiated the line of Swinburnes who are lords of Capheaton to this day.

William inherited Chollerton from his father and acquired a little bit of Haughton from Reginald Pratt. Nicholas, the senior son, got the family seat at Great Swinburn but failed to establish a long line of descendants for he sired only girls. Juliana, the eldest, was married in 1279 to Gilbert de Middleton, youngest son of Sir Richard Middleton of Belsay and owner of property at Cramlington and Hartley. Gilbert and Juliana had two sons and when their father died, in 1310, Gilbert, the elder, inherited his estates and John, his brother, got his mother's land at Great Swinburn. He held it only eight years; John joined his brother in the Mitford Gang, and was executed with him in 1318. The Crown became owner of Great Swinburn.

The property proved difficult to sell and it was let on short leases until c1345 when Roger Widdrington, a younger brother of Sir Gerard Widdrington of Widdrington, bought it. He also took possession of Plessey in 1349, and in 1362 he became head of the family when Gerard died without issue.

The accommodation at Great Swinburn – a manor-house of unknown description – was not good enough for Roger, and in 1346 he applied and received a licence to crenellate. He built a large tower on the site of the manor-house, and this served many generations of a cadet branch of the Widdringtons, as the surveys of 1415 and 1541 testify. Little is know about it except that it had two vaults, rather unusually set in line, not side by side, and that it was called Swinburn Castle.

In 1593 Sir Henry, head of the Widdrington family, died without heirs, so Edward of Great Swinburn, the next in seniority, stepped up a place. He had two sons, one to carry the line forward, the younger, Roger, to start another cadet branch at Cartington in Coquetdale. Edward's senior grandson, William, became head of family in the 1630s and in 1643 he was elevated to the peerage for his exploits during the Civil War. He chose the title Lord William Widdrington of Blankney. Before that, in about 1640, he built a new manor-house next to the tower, which by this time had become ruinous. It was a handsome building which featured a massive chimneystack, but the builder did not enjoy it for long as he was killed in 1648 at the Battle of Wigan.

After three hundred and thirty years at Great Swinburn, the Widdringtons finally severed connections with the place in 1678. William's grandson, the third Lord Widdrington of Blankney, found the financial burden too great and sold it to Thomas Riddell, a successful merchant of Fenham. The transaction included the manor-house, the whole park, the tied village to its north and Colwell.

Life in the country must have suited this town emigrant and his family for their descendants are still there. The manor-house, however did not suit Thomas's grandson – who, incidentally, married a girl from one of the Widdrington cadet branches – and in c1760 he built another alongside it, actually on the site of the old tower, which was cleared except for the two vaults. The earlier house was modified for use as a service wing of the new, and stabling and an orangery were added.

In 1826 the two Swinburns were united. Ralph Riddell bought Little Swinburn from the Loraines.

The eighteenth century mansion was demolished in the 1980s, and with it went the two vaults, relics of the original tower. The 1640 manor-house is still there, an L-shaped building which not so long ago contained the mansion's kitchens, treasury and butchery but which is now used by a stabling establishment. There is a finely worked stone coat of arms on one gable. The eighteenth century stabling block remains, part still stables and part estate offices. Also still there are the archway into this part of the complex and the old laundry next to it. The orangery, which at some time was converted into a billiards room and was decorated externally with Tuscan columns and a frieze saved from the earlier mansion, is still there although looking rather sad. There is much to see still, but there is no replacement for the habitable building.

Swinburn Park, nowadays, is a thriving farm. The owner occupies a large house at the southern end of the estate, and between it and the old buildings are some reminders of the very distant past – a tumulus, an exceptionally fine monolith and a set of well formed cultivation terraces. Great Swinburn village is a single street of houses and a small church at the north end of the Park, and behind is an isolated building called the Tithe Barn. There is some doubt about whether it was ever a store house for the vicar's dues as it was built, in Gothick style, in the eighteenth century when tithe collecting, although not unlawful until 1836, aroused public opposition and was not often practiced. It has several blocked windows with rounded arches and could be mistaken for a Welsh chapel.

Gunnerton

L87   P534   NY904750   11½ km, 7 miles, south-east of Bellingham

Like Little Swinburn, Gunnerton was granted by Baron Balliol to Ralph de Gunnerton (or Gunwarton) in 1093. Gunnerton was the star attraction and Little Swinburn was sub-let by Ralph to Ulfehill de Swyneburne.

Ralph must have been a man of some standing for he built a motte and bailey castle on a spur between the Gunnerton and Coal Burns, NY907756. The site, incidentally, is on Money Hill, so called because legend has it that treasure lies buried there, guarded by a dragon. King Henry I probably encouraged Ralph to build his castle as he desired a line of defences between Hexham and Bellingham to contain and control the wild men of the west. In the event he got motte and baileys at Gunnerton, Wark-on-Tyne and Bellingham only, hardly enough for his purpose.

Sir John de Gunnerton was the holder of the grant in 1279. When he died, in the 1290s, his son Nicholas expected to inherit, but there was some doubt about his legitimacy so, rather than wade through lengthy and expensive litigation, it was decided to sell. Thus the heritable rights of both Gunnerton and Little Swinburn were bought in 1296 by the Gunnertons' tenants, John and Avicia Swinburne.

This couple separated the two estates and John's will of 1313 gave Gunnerton alone to his eldest son, Robert. He moved to Essex in 1324, but Gunnerton was retained by him and his descendants for over a hundred years. In 1425 they sold to John Fenwick, recently installed in Wallington. Although John preferred to live in Wallington, Gunnerton was always considered a prime property by his descendants and one of them, another Sir John Fenwick, built a tower and stone house there before 1541.

In 1689 yet another Sir John Fenwick sold Gunnerton to Sir William Blackett, who already had Wallington. Most of the other Fenwick estates went the same way.

The Blacketts wanted only the land, and Gunnerton's tower was never used by them. In fact it was probably dismantled as nothing of it remains today. Its site is known with a fair degree of certainty, for two reasons. First, a farm on the north side of Gunnerton Burn, slightly to the west of the village, is called The Demesne, and land kept for the lord's own use, the demesne land, is usually around his home. Second, the tower was said to be near a well, and The Lady's Well is close by.

It is inevitable that Gunnerton should be compared with Elsdon, for both claim a motte and bailey and a tower. And, like Elsdon, Gunnerton also has a bastle derivative. It is Close House in the village street, and it dates from about 1600. It is basically a two-storey building with four feet thick walls, but it has a later single-storey building at one end and three doors with Tudor-style lintels have been inserted. Elsdon, however, must take the prize for, for one thing, its tower is still in existence, and, for another, the earthworks of its motte and bailey are not only in good shape but are clearly seen. Gunnerton's earthworks are reasonably complete and very interesting, but a shroud of trees precludes a comprehensive view from a distance, either from the ground or the air.

Not to be totally outdone, Gunnerton can offer two good stories about its villagers. The first concerns the brothers Edward and William Shafto who, in May 1689, went walking on Gunnerton Fell and came across a man lying in a pool of blood, still able to talk but obviously dying. The victim told the brothers he had been staying with Mr Errington at the Linnells and had decided to ride out to the 'high lands' with Roger, one of Errington's servants. They had stopped for a rest and, while dismounted, Roger had shot him in the back and had disappeared with "two guineas, one silver watch, one crown piece of silver, three or four shillings, his velvet cap, his spurs, his crivitt (cravat?) and sleeves". At the inquest held the following day it was learnt that the dead man was William Breaecliffe of Yorkshire, and that Roger the servant was nowhere to be found. So far as is known, he never was.

What brings a special twist to this tale is its similarity with an old legend. The identity of the victim is different – he was a Scotsman in the legend – but the circumstances of the murder are much the same. Roger the servant was caught in this version; he was executed and hung in chains from a gibbet on rising ground still called Roger's Hill. One wonders if the brothers had heard this legend and had hatched some Machiavellian plot!

The second story is about Mr and Mrs Cook. One evening in 1739 a candle set fire to straw in Mr Cook's byer in Gunnerton village. Mrs Cook was alone at the time; she ran to the byer and managed to untie their nine cows, two oxen and a bull. The bull was the most frightened and the most affected by the smoke; it got to the byer door first, and there it collapsed, blocking the only exit. Poor Mrs Cook and all the animals were burnt to ashes by the time Mr Cook returned.

Gunnerton seems a happy place today, inspite of these stories. It is worth visiting, and the motte and bailey is a must for anyone interested in early Norman defences.

Chipchase

L87   P534   NY882757   9½ km, 6 miles, south-east of Bellingham

Chipchase Park was a parcel in the barony of Prudhoe, granted by King Henry I to the Umfravilles as a rather more civilized extension to their Redesdale liberty. It was good hunting ground then, hence the 'chase' in the name. It also contained a village, originated in Anglian times, in which was held a regular market, and this explains the 'Chip' part which derives from 'Chepan', the Anglo-Saxon verb meaning to buy and sell. A score of other places in England, like Chipping Sodbury and Cheapside, can thank their old markets for their names.

During the thirteenth century the Lisles, a virile family based in East Woodburn, were having difficulty housing all their offspring. Peter de L'Isle, to use the style common in those days, solved this problem by leasing Chipchase and Whittle, near Ovingham, for the feudal services of a quarter of a knight. It is believed he built a small tower in or close to Chipchase – W.W. Tomlinson claimed in 1888 that foundations could be traced in the southern part of the park, but nothing remains now to verify this.

Junior members of the Lisle family occupied Chipchase for about a century and then ran out of male heirs. Sir Robert, the holder in 1348, had outlived his only son and his only granddaughter, Cecily, was his heiress. As her guardian, he had to ensure she continued to enjoy the delights of Chipchase in the company of someone of suitable rank, so he made a deal with William Heron of Ford: if one of his sons married Cecily he could have Chipchase straight away. It was Walter, William's third son, who volunteered – or was volunteered – and he and Cecily settled down in Chipchase to start a new Heron branch. They built the grand tower which still excites today's visitor, also a small adjoining manor-house.

A later William Heron was similarly deficient of male heirs and had to leave Ford castle and most of his property to his granddaughter Elizabeth in 1535. She chose her husband herself, a local lad called Thomas Carr, and, naturally enough, they claimed all that Ford stood for. George Heron of Chipchase married William's widow and, equally naturally, they also claimed all that Ford stood for. A feud developed between the two houses, and things got so nasty that the Herons even tried to take Ford by force, and one of their supporters, Robert Barrowe, mayor of Berwick, was killed. Then in 1558 Thomas Carr was murdered. The culprit was never found – obviously the Herons were suspects – but the crime was sufficiently dramatic to bring the contestants to their senses. The question was put to arbitration in 1559 and the Carrs' dependants won. The inheritance laws proved stronger that the widow's rights. The Herons were allowed to keep Simonburn – poor compensation as they owned the place anyhow.

So Chipchase tower and house became the principal seat of the Herons, who continued to prosper inspite of this setback. Several sixteenth century males became keepers of Tynedale and it was suggested by the envious that much of their wealth came to them as hush money from the Charltons of Upper North Tyne. John Heron was involved in the dissolution of Hexham Priory and the Pilgrimage of Grace (as told under Hexham), and one of his brothers was killed at a Wardens Meeting at Redesmire, near Carter Bar. The latter misfortune evoked some Scottish humour: they sent a gift of several live falcons to Chipchase with a note saying the English were being treated nobly as they were being given live hawks for one dead heron.

When John's son, George, died in 1593 he bequeathed Chipchase to a grandson, Cuthbert, bypassing his own sons, presumably because they were comfortably ensconced in other property. Cuthbert was under-age when he inherited, but he soon made a name for himself. In 1621 he built a beautiful Jacobean mansion and linked it to the tower and the old manor-house, much spruced up for the job. Throughout the Civil War he remained solidly but discreetly pro-Stuart, and was rewarded with a barony by King Charles II in 1662.

From this high the Herons could go only one way – downwards, beneath a growing weight of financial difficulties. Making adequate provision for the family's widows and marriageable daughters were reasons offered to explain the slide, but it is just possible that extravagances thought to be in keeping with their elevated social station had something to do with it. When Bockenfield Manor, near Eshott, was bought, for example, perhaps it was not absolutely necessary to commission the most expensive architect available, Robert Trollope, to practically rebuild it. The dreary business of mortgages and foreclosures on their estates began in 1677 and ended fifty years later when Sir Harry Heron sold Chipchase to George or Robert Allgood.

John Heron, Sir Harry's son, tried to retrieve the situation by marrying Cecily, widow of George Middleton of Belsay. John was penniless but harboured hopes of getting Belsay through his bride. The experience of his sixteenth century forebears should have warned him: George had had the good sense to provide a male heir and, once again, the laws of inheritance prevailed. Cecily was left with just enough money to buy a little place at Bowlby in North Yorkshire. When their son, Thomas, was born they included Middleton in his surname, as if to keep alive his link with Belsay, but in 1780 he died without heirs, and the main Heron line died with him.

Chipchase Castle – really a tower – is a lasting memorial to this engaging family. It is not usually open to the public, but adjoining gardens are and good views can be obtained from them. The building measures 53 by 38 feet and has a vaulted ground floor and three storeys above. The main area of each floor is a single chamber, but several smaller rooms, a couple of corbelled-out gardrobes and a chapel lead from them. The roof is not crenellated but does have a projecting parapet and four circular turrets supported on corbels, one at each corner.

Barrasford

L87   P534   NY915732   13¹/₂ km, 8¹/₄ miles, south-east of Bellingham

Like Birtley, four miles away, Barrasford was originally in the Prudhoe barony. Since the seventeenth century it has been owned by, in chronological order, the Widdringtons, the Shaftos, the Crown and the Percys, but before then the area around the village was farmed by a collection of leaseholders supervised by a 'Head Man' who has not been identified. After 1307 a market was held in the village every Wednesday and a fair every Martinmas, 11th November. The village also contained a 'head house', the home of the 'Head Man'; it had been burnt down by the Scots before 1289 and replaced by some form of fortified building, perhaps a small manor-house. This was extended and updated by the Herons in the sixteenth century, and after the Union of the Crowns a wing was added. It was still standing in 1897, but soon after it was replaced by the existing mansion, the east wing of which suggests that some stones and roofing slabs for the original have been used again.

Cocklaw

| L87 | P534 | NY939712 | 16 km, 10 miles, south-east of Bellingham |

Errington

| L87 | P534 | NY959716 | $17^1/_2$ km, $10^3/_4$ miles, south-east of Bellingham |

The ancient Hexhamshire family of Errington held Cocklaw township in 1225 and lived within its bounds at Errington Hall, where now stands the hamlet of Errington. The Hall appears to have been a substantial strong house, but evidently it was not considered strong enough, or perhaps not sufficiently impressive, and the family built and moved into a tower a mile of so to the west, at East Cocklaw, during the second half of the fourteenth century. The original Errington Hall disappeared a long time ago and its replacement, the existing Hall, has no fourteenth century work visible.

Cocklaw tower, the family's home to the sixteenth century, is a tall ruin of considerable interest. It has resisted the depredations of six hundred years remarkably well considering there is no evidence of major repairs, and it would have done even better had not the men of Galloway forced an entry in 1408 and set fire to it in 1423.

Its external dimensions are about 50 by 35 feet; it has a vaulted ground floor with two floors above, and a mural chamber on the first floor was also vaulted. This small room seems to have been used as a solus and there are still a few patches of decoration on its walls. The stairs are to the right of the entrance, and to the left was a gruesome type of prison cell. Its side wall has been broken down, but originally its only access was a trapdoor on the first floor. Prisoners were dropped through this into the 8 by 5 feet cell which had no door or window. It is an example of a 'bottle-neck dungeon', or 'oubliette', not often seen in England. The roof of the tower has perished, but there are signs of a parapet and a turret at its southern end.

In 1586 the Erringtons moved again, to Beaufront between Hexham and Corbridge, and there they remained until 1827. Cocklaw tower appears to have been consigned to nature and the hazards of a farmyard.

Wall

L87   P547   NY917690   20 km, 12$^1/_2$ miles, south-east of Bellingham

Drivers going between Chollerford and Hexham pass through Wall but do not see the proper Wall village. It is set round a large green just to the east of the main road, and is well worth the diversion. Those with sufficient energy can leave their car on the village green and walk a little way up the scrub-covered hill further to the east (there is a well-made path with steps). From this vantage point it will be seen that the village has been an enclosed one, all its houses but one forming a perimeter wall protecting the cattle, sheep and people within.

To strengthen the defences, many of the old houses around the green, and one which stands with the church in the centre, exhibit evidence of bastle origin. There are blocked-up doorways and slit windows, large quoins and the distinctive irregular masonry to be seen in profusion, especially on the north and east sides. These clues set the date of the village as about 1600, and, as if to confirm this, two date stones relating to refurbishing work show 1631 and 1642 respectively.

A thousand years before the village was built, Wall had an even greater importance, for, according to Bede, it was a royal settlement belonging to the Northumbrian King Oswiu. Here Sigberht and his East Saxon supporters were baptized by Bishop Finan of Lindisfarne. Here also Peada, son of Penda the pagan king of Mercia, was married in 653 to King Oswiu's daughter and was baptized at the same time.

Area 6, Sub-Area F   Lower North Tyne, West side, including Warks Burn

West Ealingham

L80   P522   NY843807   2$^1/_2$ km, 1$^1/_2$ miles, south of Bellingham

West Ealingham farm is marked as just 'Ealingham' on some maps, a perfectly reasonable abridgement since the village of that name is no more and there is no East Ealingham. The farmhouse has been built on the site of a bastle which was one of four spaced evenly along the 180 metre contour of the south facing slope of Ealingham Rigg. The Houxty Burn runs along the foot of the slope and the River North Tyne is a mile to the east.

The bastle replaced by the farmhouse is the only one of the four devoid of ground evidence. The regular spacing of this and the others is unusual and difficult to explain as their occupiers had nothing to do with army discipline and were ordinary farmers seeking the security of stout walls and the ability to hail friends when help was needed.

The village of Ealingham was probably close to the river. The only surviving record concerning the villagers says that they and Bellingham's inhabitants were fined for beheading a thief without getting prior permission from the coroner. This was in the thirteenth century; the village had disappeared before the bastles were built.

The most westerly of the bastles was close to a former hamlet called Stobby Lea, of which only the ruins of the schoolhouse remain. The bastle ruin, at NY838807, and still known locally as Stobby Lea bastle, stands from five to ten feet high. It is a plain rectangle about 34 by 21 feet, and its walls are four feet thick. The doorway in the north gable has been blocked, but the relieving arch above it is still quite clear. A little remedial work has been done to part of the ruin which, with a small walled compound added to its south end, is used now as a sheep dip by the West Ealingham farmer.

Working east, the next in line is the farm, and then another bastle ruin stands a few fields away at NY846808. This also has been adapted for agricultural use: three of its four to four-and-a-half feet thick walls stand nearly to roof height, but the fourth has been knocked down for the convenience of cattle which use the place as a wind-break and winter feeding post. It was another plain rectangle with outside dimensions of 36 by 24 feet.

A patch of rough grass, which can be seen from the main road, draws attention to the most easterly of the four bastles, at NY850809. All its stones, save one loose door jamb, have gone and its foundations are practically hidden. It appears to have been about the same size and shape as the cattle-sheltering bastle.

Lee Hall

L87   P534   NY861797   5 km, 3 miles, south-east of Bellingham

A pleasant early eighteenth century house standing close to the River North Tyne between its confluences with the River Rede and Houxty Burn. It is the result of a radical transformation carried out in the seventeenth century on a strong house, bits of which are still evident at the back of the building. In 1620 this was termed a 'capital messuage'; the earlier structure had housed people since at least the thirteenth century.

Up to the fourteenth century the site was called Evelingham. It was granted in about 1250 with Bellingham to King Alexander III's forester, but in 1279 it was transferred to Jedburgh Abbey, It was church property only seventeen years, until King Edward I terminated the Scottish king' hold on Tynedale liberty. It lay waste for many years, then King Edward III granted it to his grandson, the Earl of Cambridge, who held it until 1415, when it returned to the Crown.

Relevant records are missing from that date until 1604, when William Charlton managed to convince the courts that he had the right of possession of Lee Hall because his forebears had held it since 1537 at least. William was head of an important branch family – second only to the Hesleyside Charltons – which has held the Hall ever since.

Between the 1660s and 1716 another William Charlton held the Hall. Although the main family had by this time become highly respectable and greatly esteemed, William hid behind his lawful facade – he was keeper of North Tynedale – a close connection with the criminal classses. With schizo-phrenic zeal he directed a gang of horse thieves. He was a turbulent and arrogant character who, presumably when acting in his official capacity, drove one of the Halls from Monkridge Hall and, on another occasion, captured Lowes of Willimotswick and chained him to his kitchen range with just enough movement to allow him to reach the servants table – an indignity from which Lowes was rescued by Frank Stokoe of Chesterwood, a man of gigantic stature.

Forster Charlton succeeded in 1716, and it was during his tenure that the drama of the 'Long Pack' is said to have unfolded. The story has been repeated many times with variations and different locales – even Mrs Gaskill offered one in 'Cranford' – but a gravestone in Bellingham churchyard shaped like a long pack gives Lee Hall some merit points for originality.

The bare plot of the story is that a pedlar called at Lee Hall one winter afternoon when the family was away and Alice, a maid, was in charge, assisted by two male servants. The pedlar requested a night's lodgings, and when this was refused he begged permission to leave his heavy pack in the house until the following morning. This request was granted and the pack was stood in the entrance hall. During the evening the thing was seen to move slightly so one of the servants fired a shot into it. The movement stopped and blood gushed out. When opened, the pack was found to contain a man, now dead, who had a whistle hanging round his neck. Alice realised he had been planted in the house so that during the night he could open the door and blow a 'come and get it' signal to his accomplices outside. The resourceful girl collected a few local worthies and at midnight she blew the whistle. As anticipated, several horsemen approached, to be met by a barrage of gunfire. Survivors carried their dead away, but the long pack man was left for the Charltons to bury.

Another story associated with Lee Hall was found written on the manuscript of John Warburton's 'Notes of Ruined Towers' (1715), but it is not in his handwriting so its origin is a mystery. The subject of the story is a spring in the grounds of Lee Hall; this is how it was written:

> "An exclent spring, ye vertue is such yt if ye lady of ye Hall dip aney children yt have ye rickets or any other over-groone distemper, it is either speedy cure or death. The maner and form is as followeth:- The days or dipping are on Whitsunday Even, on Midsumer Even, on Saint Peeter's Even. They must bee dipt in ye well before the sun rise, and in ye River Tine after sun dee set: then the shift taken from ye child and thrown into ye river and if it swim...child liveth, but if it sink sure dyeth."

It is difficult to imagine any mother willingly submitting to this test – the child would probably die of cold anyway.

Wark-on-Tyne

L87   P534   NY860770   8 km, 5 miles, south of Bellingham

When dealing with Wark-on-Tweed it was suggested that the name meant 'work' in the local dialect and reflected the immense amount of labour which had been needed to construct the castle there. At Wark-on-Tyne nature had done most of the castle site preparation, so historians have promoted the idea that 'Wark' is derived from 'Weorc', Old English for fortification.

As at Elsdon, the Anglian Mote Hill was chosen for the twelfth century castle. The ancestors of Earl Waltheof had held their council meetings and had administered justice on this steep rise near the river bank, south of the village, and Scottish King William I, 'The Lion', decided it was the ideal spot for his liberty capital when he inherited the feoff of Tynedale in 1165. The top of the hill needed a minimum of levelling before a motte and bailey was constructed.

The Scottish kings held Tynedale liberty for homage only until 1295, when English King Edward I started getting tough with Scotland. In quick succession, the lordship was given to Bishop Bek, Piers Gaveston, Thomas Featherstonehaugh, John Darcy, Queen Philippa, Edmund Earl of Cambridge, Edward Duke of York and Thomas Grey. Intruding into this list is Robert Bruce, who took the title by force after Bannockburn and held it for two or three years. All these liberty lords used Wark as their administrative and judicial centre, even though people in the western parts complained about the long distance they had to travel to pay their taxes. The Crown took possession in the early part of the fifteenth century, and in 1495 the liberty status was revoked, Tynedale at last becoming subject to the laws of the state.

The original motte and bailey could not stand such courtly wear and tear for long and was replaced by a stone tower. This was not reported until 1399, but it is thought it must have been built at least a century earlier. By 1541 it was practically a ruin and was rebuilt in an unfortified style.

Wark manor was part of a large consignment of land given to Lord George Home in 1605 to encourage him to bring peace to the Border zone. It descended to the Earl of Suffolk, whose son James sold it to Sir Frances Radcliffe in 1665. Sir Frances' famous grandson, the Earl of Derwentwater, lost it after the 1715 Jacobite fiasco and it was granted to Greenwich Hospital. The Duke of Northumberland bought it in 1835.

Sometime during the late seventeenth or early eighteenth centuries the top of the Mote Hill was cleared of all buildings and completely levelled except for a short dyke which may be the remains of the motte and bailey's defences. Here the farmhouse and farm buildings were erected which still exist; the former has a Tudor door-head which probably had been saved from the 1541 mansion. The Battlesteads Hotel, at the foot of the hill, is thought to be where the court officials left their horses.

Lowstead

L87   P534   NY815783   6 km, 3³/₄ miles, south-west of Bellingham

A small farm about a mile north of Warks Burn, standing on top of the steep bank of the Blacks Burn, which becomes the Houxty Burn further downstream. The farmhouse is a bastle derivative and the byre attached to its east gable is also like a bastle. A pair of semi-detached bastles is a possibility, but more likely the farmer-builder thought his cattle needed as much protection as he and his family did.

The house has been extended to the west and north, and its roof has been raised at some time, but there remains visible evidence of a first floor doorway.

Mortley

L87   P534   NY824773   7 km, 4¹/₄ miles, south of Bellingham

A farm above the north (left) bank of Warks Burn, approached rather muddily from the valley road by a field track through Barmoor farm. The reward for venturing so far is a heap of weed-infested rubble contained in walls near the farmhouse. The walls are seven feet high in places and four feet thick; they belong to what has been a 30 by 19 feet bastle which had a vaulted ground floor chamber. Its gable door is still evident although partly blocked, and very noticeable are its large quoins.

Horneystead

L87   P534   NY814772   7¹/₂ km, 4¹/₂ miles, south-west of Bellingham

The name is spelt without the 'y' sometimes. It is a small nineteenth century farm standing on a hill with a bastle ruin set behind the farmhouse. During the sixteenth and seventeenth centuries the area was owned by the Ridleys of Willimoteswick.

This is an example of a very early bastle, built in mid-sixteenth century before bastle plans began conforming almost to a standard, for it is practically a square. Three of its walls are now averaging only about four feet in height, but its west wall stands to about fifteen feet and contains a doorway with a single stone lintel and a relieving arch above. There is no roof and the interior is so filled with debris and weeds it is not possible to see any detail, but a suspicion of a vault is there.

Roses Bower

L87   P533   NY799768   8¹⁄₂ km, 5¹⁄₄ miles, south-west of Bellingham

A lovely name and a lovely place! The farmstead, a recently renovated line of farmhouse, cottage and workshop, stands near the edge of a precipitous drop to the Warks Burn, offering wide-ranging views over Wark Forest. The former bastle is not here, however – not quite, it is a short walk downhill to the east, at NY800769 on Pathfinder map 534.

There is a derelict building at this lower point which used to be called Low Rose's Bower. Its tumble-down condition may have been accelerated by the last family to occupy the place – there were eleven children! In its day it was a small eighteenth century farmhouse built on the foundations and, on its south side, the first few courses of a bastle. It literally hangs on the edge of a steep bank above the Warks Burn, "daringly constructed right on the edge of the rocks", as one chronicler has put it. To see what is left of the bastle it is necessary to scramble some way down the bank and then to look up at the south wall of the building. It will be seen that the lower courses are of rougher stones and contain a couple of ventilating slits.

Close to the house, and actually corbelled out over the precipice, is a 'long-drop loo'. Some preservation work was done to this in 1995, so hopefully it will not fall over the edge as it threatened to do before. It is reputed to be the longest drop in England and one can only wonder how the eleven children family stayed intact.

The land hereabouts was owned by the Ridleys of Willimoteswick during the sixteenth century and until the Commonwealth Government ordered its sale in 1652 because of Musgrave Ridley's support of King Charles I. Musgrave was the son of John Ridley of Walltown who married Anne, daughter of Edward Charlton of Hesleyside. Francis Neville of Wakefield was the buyer in 1652, and in 1658 his tenant was Edward Charlton. Sir Edward Blackett of Matfin became the landlord before 1680, and he sold various properties in the Warks Burn valley, one by one, to sitting tenants. It is not known whether the Charltons were buyers.

Somewhere in this descent, the Rose's Bower estate was occupied, almost certainly illegally, by Anthony Milburn, a cattle thief of the seventeenth century. He lived in the bastle – in fact he may have built it – and he kept his live booty on a haugh made by a bend in the stream immediately below. A very steep path lies to the east of the house, and Anthony would drive the castle down it to rest awhile in the secret haugh until it was safe to take them to market. It was an ideal situation for someone in his profession.

Low Moralee

L97   P534   NY848761   8 km, 5 miles, south of Bellingham

The only Warks Burn bastle on the south or right side of the burn. It is of no great interest, being a farmhouse which was a bastle originally but which has been lengthened and partly rebuilt, leaving only the thickness of its walls to indicate its previous defensive quality.

Simonburn

L87   P534   NY870736   11 km, 6³/₄ miles, south-east of Bellingham

North Tynedale shared its duties: Wark was the administrative and legislative capital, Bellingham the main market town and community centre, and Simonburn was the spiritual metropolis. It contained the parish church, the hub of the largest parish in England – extending from the Scottish Border to the Roman Wall – until it was split up in 1814. There are traces here of an Anglian church of the ninth century, but the church which dominates the present village was built in the thirteenth century. It is dedicated to the sixth century Glaswegian bishop and missionary, St. Mungo.

It is not known what the Anglian community called their village. If it was 'Simonburn' or something like that then the name probably honoured Sigmund, son of Volsung and a famous Teutonic warrior, but if the name is medieval then the following sequence of events may suggest a reason for it.

Waltheof, Earl of Northumberland from 1072 to 1075, owned much of Tynedale, including this area, and when he was executed his daughter, Maud, inherited. She married twice, the first time to Simon de Senlis, Earl of Northampton, by whom she had a son, also called Simon. Her second marriage, in 1114, was to David, a son of the Scottish King Malcolm III. She had another son by him: Prince Henry. Simon was the senior of the two half-brothers, but he knew full well that if it ever came to a dispensation of honours Henry would be the favourite because of his royal father. And so it came to be. David's two elder brothers both died without issue so David was crowned King of the Scots in 1124. In 1138 he invaded England and was stopped at the Battle of the Standard, the strange outcome of which was that Northumberland was granted as an earldom to David's son – to Prince Henry, not to Simon. It can be quite alarming when one is cast aside like that, and Simon thought he ought to prepare for the worst: he built a motte and bailey castle which he called Simonburn, after himself.

This thought process is only conjecture, but there could have been a motte and bailey at Simonburn in the twelfth century. The mound upon which the later tower was built looks as if it could have supported one, but actual proof is lacking.

English King Henry II regained Northumberland in 1157 but as some compensation for their loss he gave the Scottish kings the liberty of Tynedale. In their turn, the Scottish kings granted parcels of Tynedale to their friends. Simonburn was so granted to Henry Graham, believed to have been the son of Sir John Graham, a soldier of distinction who later fell at the Battle of Falkirk. The date of this grant is not known, but by 1291 Henry Graham had completed Simonburn tower.

He chose a site about half a mile west of the present village, at NY863738, which has the natural defence of two converging streams. It was a strong building of four storeys with a vaulted ground floor chamber. Local opinion has it that it was square in plan with walls about 36 feet long and with a small turret projecting from one side.

When Henry died he left his tower to his daughter, Idonea, the second wife of Adam Swinburne of Little Swinburn. They had a boy called Henry and a girl called Elizabeth, and it was the latter who inherited her mother's property. In 1330 she married Roger Heron and thus Simonburn became the property of the lords of Ford, later of Chipchase.

Several junior members of the Heron family lived in Simonburn, but after 1550 they preferred a strong house called Hall Barnes which they built for their greater comfort. There is still a Hall Barnes at the same place, NY873733, but it contains no old fabric. Also in 1550, or thereabouts, a small tower for the vicar was built next to the church. There is nothing of this remaining, the present vicarage being mostly 1725 vintage.

The tower was quite ruinous when the Herons slipped into pecuniary misery in the 1670s and had to sell the whole Simonburn estate. For the best part of a century the place had ineffective, absent landlords and the villagers took advantage of this lack of supervision to vandalize the tower. Someone had put it about that there was treasure hidden there, and hardly a stone was left unturned in a vain search for it.

In 1760 Sir Lancelot Allgood, grandson of Robert the Snabdaugh, Upper North Tyne, purchaser, bought a lovely estate between Simonburn and the River North Tyne and built a gracious retirement home which he called Nunwick Hall. He planted many beech trees in his grounds, but before they grew tall he could see the ruins of Simonburn tower, a mile to the west. He decided to improve this view so he bought Simonburn estate and, in 1766, he rebuilt part of the old ruin, purely as a folly.

Some of this restoration work fell down in the 1940s but no one noticed as the beech trees had long since grown tall enough to block the view, and the ruin was also surrounded by trees, hiding it even from the farm road which passes within a few feet of it. A close inspection reveals some walling three or four feet high and a lovely pointed arched doorway.

Tecket

L87   P534   NY865729   11³/₄ km, 7¹/₂ miles, south of Bellingham

Tecket is a farm about a mile south-west of Simonburn. The farmhouse and buildings stand alone in a wide expanse of country which could be described as generally undulating but which carries a deep dene behind the farm, an unsuspected feature but one which, once discovered, should be explored. Here the Crook Burn pushes water collected in Haughton and Simonburn Commons over a series of little waterfalls and through a tree-lined, rock-bound vale of exceptional beauty. Here, also, is a shallow cave, locally called 'The Summer House', where the Reverend John Wallis, one time curate of Simonburn, wrote much of his masterpiece, "The Natural History and Antiquities of Northumberland", which was published in two volumes in 1769.

The property-doting Ridley family claimed this area of common land in the fifteenth century and started to farm it. Because of its close proximity to criminal-infested wastes to the west, they wisely built a small tower to use as their farmhouse.

William Ridley was the owner in 1541, but the tower appears to have been sold during the following century because when Robert Smith bought Haughton in 1642 he described himself as being 'of Tecket'. It probably remained empty until shortly after 1684, in which year Giles Heron of Hall Barnes dies and left all his money in trust for the poor of the parish and to pay the salary of a schoolmaster for Wark school. The trustees invested some of the bequest in real estate and bought Tecket. Considerable alterations and extensions were made to the tower in the seventeenth century, whether by Smith or the trust is not known, and the farm was rented to farmer tenants.

The farmhouse was heightened and reroofed in the eighteenth century. When finished, the building consisted of an old tower on its south side, an extension on its north side, a raised first floor ceiling, and all, except a small lean-to on the north wall, under one integral slate roof. From the garden on the south side, the house looked like a reasonably conventional seventeenth century farmhouse offering no hint of the tower inside.

When the present tenants took over in the early 1980s they found much to do as the house had been neglected for several years. When decorating a ground floor room in the 'modern' part they found that beneath the plaster on the wall separating it from the tower part were three arches. This wall had been an outside wall, so what three arches were doing in it beggars the imagination. They got another surprise when they attempted to insert a window in a tower chamber. The wall is at least five feet thick but it is not solid stone; like most medieval strong buildings, it consists of outer and inner 'skins', each about a foot in width of good size stones, with an inner cavity filled with rubble. When they made a hole through the inside skin this rubble poured out in a most disconcerting way. Never mind, they have the consolation of knowing that their rent still goes to the Giles Heron Trust, and still helps to finance schemes to help the needy.

Haughton (With Humshaugh)

L87   P534   NY918729   14 km, 8½ miles, south-east of Bellingham

Below Barrasford the River North Tyne decides it has flowed in a south-easterly direction far enough and should turn due south in order to meet the River South Tyne at Warden. In its efforts to change course, it makes a large bulge, leaving a haugh, or area of flat land, on its western side, and in this area two townships have grown up. Both have taken their name from the haugh – Haughton and Humshaugh. Of these, Haughton is the most important in the context of this study.

Like Simonburn, this part of Tynedale was the personal property of Waltheof and his family from before the Norman invasion until the twelfth century, when one of them, Randulf, assumed the surname 'de Haughton' as a concessionary gesture to the Normans. He sired a girl and a boy, both of who inherited the estate in due course, the girl one third of it and the boy, Randulf II, two thirds. This division proved to be enduring, and the two parts of Haughton did not unite until 1567.

The girl married Reginald Pratt in 1177 and her one-third share of Haughton was transferred to his name as the wedding settlement. In the same year her husband was appointed by King William the Lion of Scotland to be his forester at Knarsdale in South Tynedale, which even then was Scottish land, having been one of the twelve towns granted to Duncan in 1034 and confirmed by King William Rufus in 1092. Mr and Mrs Pratt moved to Knarsdale but retained their part of Haughton and passed it to son Reginald II. In 1256 it was taken from him by William Swinburne of Great Swinburn; the transfer was probably a straight sale but a rumour was circulated that it was in lieu of repayment of a loan made five years earlier. This is unlikely to be true as the debt was only three marks.

Meanwhile the larger share of Haughton stayed in the de Haughton family for a further generation, until Randulf III proved to be too generous, or careless, with his property. As an old man in 1275 he gave his mill at Humshaugh to John de Swinburne of Little Swinburn. The reason for this gift is not disclosed, nor are we told why John was not content with it and demanded the whole of Randulf's inheritance – which he got eventually by what is euphemistically described as 'a complicated legal manoeuvre'.

Thus at the beginning of the fourteenth century we have the strange situation of a still divided Haughton being owned by two people called

Swinburne but of entirely different families, one of Little Swinburn and the other of Great Swinburn.

William's (Great Swinburn) one-third share travelled down a fairly straight path through the Capheaton Swinburnes which his son started. John's (Little Swinburn) two-thirds share had a slightly more torturous journey. John and his wife Avicia had two sons and the younger one, Adam, inherited this property, then passed it on to his daughter, Christina, who married John Widdrington in 1327. The Widdrington family held it for over two hundred years.

A manor-house was in this part of Haughton – it had been in existence when John and Christina took over having been built, it is believed, soon after 1256 by the last Randulf de Haughton as an unfortified 'gentleman's residence'. Built of stone, it was a most attractive 92 by 32 feet rectangle with turrets at each corner, five arch-buttresses projecting six feet from the side walls, two storeys and a high-pitched roof. Sir Gerard Widdrington, John's son, fortified this around about 1340, and it is said his workmen did the job with the greatest care and did not spoil the pleasant appearance. They built a strong curtain wall and gateway and enclosed the buttresses with thick walls. The house walls were strengthened, heightened and crenellated and a new flat roof was constructed. The turrets were raised to above the level of the new roof, and one of them was further heightened for use as a watch tower. An official report of 1373 confirmed that the manor-house had been transformed into a tower which henceforth was known as Haughton Castle.

From 1345 the Widdringtons also owned Great Swinburn so had little use for another house so close to it, be it ever so strong. The Capheaton Swinburnes, still holding a third of Haughton, happened to be short of living space for junior sons, so the Widdringtons leased Haughton Castle to them. Sir Thomas Swinburne, a warden of the Middle March, was living there during King Henry VIII's reign – he and his line liked to be called the Lords of Chollerford, incidentally, Chollerford being within their part of the estate.

A story is told about Sir Thomas which suggests that on occasion these hard men of the Border could reveal a tinge of humanity. The good knight had captured Archie Armstrong, a leading Scottish raider, a few days before setting off for London. He had thrown his prisoner into his under-ground dungeon and had forgotten to tell anyone he was there. It was not until he had arrived at York that he remembered what he had done, and realised Armstrong would be starving. He turned his horse round and raced for home, his London mission abandoned. He arrived too late, but at least he had tried.

This cut no ice with the men of Liddesdale who could only see that Sir Thomas had killed their head man. By way of revenge, they attacked

Haughton, stealing nine horses and £40 and damaging the building so badly that the 1541 survey described it as in great decay.

The Swinburnes had had enough of Haughton. In 1567 they sold their share to John Widdrington, thereby at last giving the Widdringtons the combined estate. John repaired part of the tower, just enough to provide some reasonable accommodation, then let it to a succession of short-term tenants. One of these was Thomas Errington, a junior member of the Beaufront family and kinsman of the Carnabys; he paid an annual rent of forty marks.

John's son, Sir Henry Widdrington, died in 1593 without issue, so the most senior of the remaining family, Edward of Great Swinburn, took over as lord of all their property. Money was beginning to get rather short, however, and by the time Edward's grandson assumed power it was felt that something had to give. In 1642 he sold the whole of Haughton to the Smith brothers for £2500.

Robert Smith from Tecket and Walter Smith from Warden moved with their families into the habitable part of the tower, but they allowed the rest of the building to become even more ruinous.

Money was very short for the first century of the Smith occupancy, then William Smith arrived on the scene and brought some prosperity. He lived from 1751 to 1825; his early manhood was spent at sea, then in the 1780s he retired to Haughton and opened a paper mill on the banks of the river close by. By 1793 the venture was doing great business, largely because of a lucrative contract for specially watermarked paper, vast consignments of which were dispatched weekly by mail coach to London. Apparently it was used to produce forgeries of the French Revolutionary Government's currency, called 'Assignates', and these were put into circulation as a Whitehall-inspired dirty trick to devalue the real currency. The scheme appears to have worked as Parliament was told in 1794 that the value of Assignates had dropped by a quarter. The mill completed the contract in 1795, but it got plenty of other orders and continued to function until 1888.

By 1812 William Smith had amassed enough money to repair his home, but a proper job was not done until 1845, when John Dobson was commissioned. He returned the building to its original mode, a gentleman's residence, although managing to retain the fortification features. In this condition it was sold by the Smiths in 1862 to a Mr Crawshay, who added a rather unsympathetic west wing by Anthony Salvin in 1876. A few years later the Cruddas family took possession, and they have kept the place well maintained ever since.

By comparison with Haughton, the neighbouring village of Humshaugh is almost a nonentity Yet it contains traces of four bastles, set in pairs. One pair was built into Linden House, the other pair into Dale House and its attached cottage. The reconstruction of the latter was done in 1664.   [**Plate 9**]

Walwick Grange

L87   P547   NY907692   16¹/₂ km, 10¹/₄ miles,
                                             south-east of Bellingham

Walwick Manor was a gift to Richard and Hextilda Comyn from King David I of Scotland while his son, Prince Henry, was Earl of Northumberland between 1139 and 1152. The use of the word 'Grange' to identify one estate in the manor rather suggests a monastic relationship, and it is just possible the Comyns allowed Hexham Priory to use it, as had happened at Carraw, but there is no confirmation of this.

The Comyn line finished at Bannockburn when John Comyn was killed in 1315. His heirs were two sisters, Joan, wife of David Strathbolgi, Earl of Athol, and Elizabeth, married to Richard Talbot of Herefordshire. They agreed to take half the manor each, and the Talbots got the Grange land next to the River North Tyne.

The Strathbolgi part – the area sitting on the Roman Wall – descended in 1375 to two more heiresses, and they were married to the two younger sons of Lord Henry Percy. His eldest son, Hotspur, somehow acquired the Talbots part so the whole manor became Percy property.

They lost it temporarily when father, by now the first Earl of Northumberland, and Hotspur committed lese-majesty, but it was restored in 1413 when King Henry V created Hotspur's son the second Earl of Northumberland.

The Wall part of the manor was granted to William, Lord Burgh, as a marriage settlement, but Walwick Grange was retained as a leasable property by the Percys. Nine generations of the Errington family rented first a tower then a tower and manor-house combination from the Percys.

The tower was built in, or just before, 1505 by either William Errington or his landlord. The manor-house was attached early in the seventeenth century. Both were well maintained until 1737 when the last Errington, Edward, replaced them with the three-storey, five-bay mansion which exists today. This was built on the tower site and includes a little of the tower's masonry.

Unfortunately for Edward, he died the year after his new home was completed. His widow moved to Hartburn where she married the Rev. Richard Werge, the vicar there, so Walwick Grange became a vacant possession. It is presumed that the Percys had helped to pay for the new building, for now they had no compunction in reletting it – and its furniture. They advertised in the *Newcastle Courant*, 'handsome new house very well furnished'. They did not sell the property until 1766.

Alterations were done during the nineteenth century and the tower's remains are noticeable now only as a few stretches of extra thick walls. The tower's fish ponds can still be seen in a nearby field, however.

Warden

L87   P547   NY912665   20 km, 12½ miles, south-east of Bellingham

O.S. maps show a 'Motte' on the ridge above this village. This is a new meaning of the word, for there never was a motte and bailey castle here. It is simply a trench, a look-out post used, occasionally perhaps, as a front line defence.

It was probably from this vantage point that a Scottish army was first sighted in 1138, enabling a message to be sent to Hexham to prepare for an attack. Thanks to this intelligence, Hexham was able to raise a scratch army of young men who, with surprise of their side, routed the invaders.

Warden's church is very interesting. It was founded by St. Wilfred in AD704; the nave was rebuilt in 1764 and considerable repairs were carried out in the nineteenth century, but the bottom three-quarters of the tower are unadulterated Anglo-Saxon. The base, probably the oldest masonry in the county, is extremely strong with thick walls and a few narrow slit windows. Whether or not intended as a refuge, the villagers used it for that purpose, and it is still called locally the 'pele tower'.

The manor of Warden was given by Adam de Tindale to the Prior and convent of Hexham in 1298, and was held by them until the priory was dissolved in 1536. A family called Leadbitter provided the main occupants of the village from 1613 to the middle of the nineteenth century.

Area 7
South Tynedale and The Wall Country

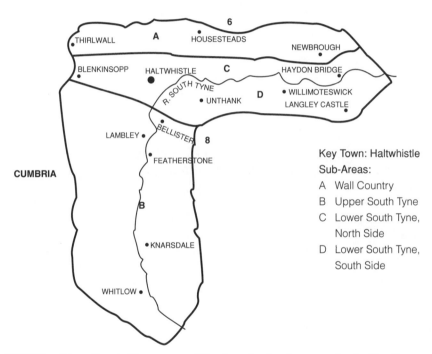

THIRLWALL · 6 HOUSESTEADS · A

NEWBROUGH ·

BLENKINSOPP · HALTWHISTLE · C HAYDON BRIDGE ·

R. SOUTH TYNE · D · WILLIMOTESWICK
· UNTHANK LANGLEY CASTLE ·

LAMBLEY · BELLISTER 8
· FEATHERSTONE

CUMBRIA

B

· KNARSDALE

WHITLOW ·

Key Town: Haltwhistle
Sub-Areas:
A Wall Country
B Upper South Tyne
C Lower South Tyne,
    North Side
D Lower South Tyne,
    South Side

The River South Tyne enters Northumberland one and a half miles north of Alston. It flows in a northerly direction until it reaches Haltwhistle, then turns eastwards, maintaining this general direction until it unites with the River North Tyne at Warden, just west of Hexham, to form the River Tyne. The area thus covers a long river valley which grows agriculturally richer as it descends. Additionally, the area covers the Great Whin Sill, from Thirlwall in the west to Newbrough in the east. This is predominantly Roman country, containing the best of Hadrian's Wall, the military zone and Agricola's Stanegate, but medieval man knew it also and there are a dozen places where attempts were made to hinder his enemies.

Key Town
Haltwhistle

L86, 87   P546   NY705640

A pleasant market town bypassed by the A69, 14 miles west of Hexham. It existed before Tynedale became a Scottish held liberty, as witness its inclusion on Duncan's wedding present list, but its first real claim to fame came in 1178, when its church was built, and in 1191 when it, with Bellister and Plenmeller on the other side of the river, was awarded by the Scottish Lion, King William I, to Baron Robert de Ros of Wark-on-Tweed. There must have been something romantic about the place as this, also, was a wedding present: Robert was marrying the King's daughter, Isobel.

There was a motte and bailey on Castle Hill (NY711641) in Haltwhistle which Robert may have built although it is more likely to have been the work of some unnamed predecessor as by 1191 most castles were being built in stone. Apart from some evidence of human landscaping, there is nothing left on Castle hill to see now.

The town appears to have prospered under the Ros family's patronage. In 1207 King John granted another Robert Ros the right to hold a market, and King Edward I, nearly a hundred years later allowed it to hold a biannual fair. They were still being held in the mid-eighteenth century, on the 14th May and 22nd November, and each was preceeded by a few days of merry-making when farm labourers offered themselves for hire. These occasions were called 'The Hoppings', a name still connected with Newcastle's annual Race Week Temperance Festival.

During the troubled year of 1296, when King Edward I cancelled Scotland's hold on Tynedale liberty, the mainline Ros turned traitor, so the King issued a decree in 1307 – one of his last – transferring the grant to William Ros, a younger brother.

William had no use for Haltwhistle and sold it straight away to Sir William Musgrave, whose family were absent landlords for nearly three centuries. They appointed a succession of bailiffs with local responsibilities, and as they became prime targets for raiders they were given the protection of a tower, the 'Turris de Hawtwissel', before 1415.

There were frequent raids on the town, and they became more numerous as the years went by. Some were politically motivated, but most were vicious dashes for plunder by the outlaws who gathered in the 'Debatable Lands', an area to the north-west which neither country wanted because of its evil reputation. Even when the Borderline was finally agreed, in 1553, practical control was not possible for many years, so when in 1575 Sir Simon Musgrave sold the town to Sir Richard Lowther the new owner found the place still very defensive conscious.

In 1598 there was a sequence of raids such as to make the balladeers sing – and this forty-five years after the outlaws were supposed to have been disposed of. The Armstrongs of Liddesdale entered Haltwhistle in daylight, as they had done many time before, and rode through the streets, killing or capturing all the inhabitants they could see, driving off cattle and setting fire to the houses. They were about to turn and go when Alec Ridley, hiding in one of the unmolested houses, fired his musket and hit Wat Armstrong in the head, killing him outright. The gang vowed to return to take vengeance for this crime.

This incident, and the threat of more to come, persuaded Sir Robert Carey to act. He was the warden of the English Middle March, a man of unusual ability who had suffered "great annoyances" from the outlaws. His appeal for help to his opposite number in Scotland was fruitless, but King James VI, while admitting he could do nothing himself, suggested that Carey might like to tackle the outlaws personally. If he did this without harming any of his honest subjects it would make him "very glad".

So a reprisal raid was launched and Carey rode at the head of two hundred horsemen into Liddesdale. They killed only one Armstrong, the others wisely remaining in their strongholds, but they took away a lot of booty. The outlaws retaliated with another raid on Haltwhistle, during which yet another member of the gang was killed. The Armstrongs vowed that before the year was out they would lay the whole Border waste.

Carey took this threat seriously and rode again into Liddesdale where he and his men built a strong, semi-permanent defence post in which they could reside in safety and from which they could make rapid sorties to catch the outlaws one at a time. The Armstrongs thought this a great joke and stole a cow from the town which they offered to Carey in case he desired some English beef while he waited. The stratagem worked, however, and in time all the Armstrongs were killed or captured and their gang was broken for ever.

Haltwhistle remained a dangerous place, nevertheless, and many new buildings incorporated a degree of protection. Also a strong house was constructed in the main street, a few doors east of the tower. It carried a 1607 date stone.

This was the year Sir Richard Lowther died and bequeathed Haltwhistle to his great-grandson, Albany Featherstonehaugh, a young son of the ancient family living at Featherstone. Albany and his wife decided to reside in Haltwhistle and built for themselves another strong house on the north-east flank of Castle Hill, overlooking the Haltwhistle Burn. It was completed and occupied in 1611 and they and their family used it for three generations although Albany sold the rest of the town to Lord William Howard quite soon. His son inherited it in 1640 but forfeited it to Cromwell nine or ten years later. In 1663 the Government sold it to George Pearson, who held it until 1714.

During the first half of the eighteenth century a three storey wing was built onto the three hundred year old, still habitable, tower near the market Several repairs and alterations were done to it then and in 1880 when the wing was refaced so that it could merge as a single building with the tower. It was opened as the Red Lion Hotel.

The hotel operated for more than a hundred years. A bit of the tower's parapet could just be seen by the inquisitive, and there were some interesting water-spouts protruding from one side, but little else of fifteenth century vintage was evident. In 1996 work started on a major renovation programme and many hitherto hidden features were revealed, including the entrance to a tunnel. Although carefully blocked up, there is evidence that it once connected the tower to the vicarage, some 200 yards away, and formed a convenient escape route whenever the vicar felt threatened by raiders. When the work was completed, the building was opened as 'The Centre of Britain Hotel' – a rather cheeky move, this, as Allendale Town has a better claim to being the geographical centre of Great Britain.

Nothing remains today of the two strong houses. The 1607 building, no doubt constructed by Sir Richard Lowther, was demolished in 1969. It had been a two-storey house, 31 by 20 feet, with internal stairs and other refinements, most of which had suffered at the hands of renovators before it was razed. The Featherstonehaugh's 1611 building was quite small originally, only 26 by 21 feet, but with three floors. Its walls varied between 3 and 5 feet in thickness. A twisting staircase connected the ground floor with the living room which had a large fireplace supported on corbels. The next floor was reached by ladder; this was the bedroom, but also it was the main defensive position and was equipped with a small turret with loops commanding extensive views east, south and west. The family soon found this house too small for their needs and added a wing to its eastern gable. Still more accommodation was obtained by modifications carried out in 1680 when, amongst other things, the groundfloor store was converted into a kitchen. In 1870 it became necessary to reroof the whole building and when the original stone flags were removed it was found that they had been laid on solid oak beams and fastened by sheep shank bones. Demolition came in 1963.

Area 7, Sub-Area A   Wall Country
Thirlwall

L86   P546   NY659661   5 km, 3 miles, north-west of Haltwhistle

The spectacular ruin of Thirlwall 'castle', standing high above the Tipalt Burn, is about all that is left of the ancient town of that name, the centre of a barony created by Scottish King Malcolm IV between 1153 and 1165. The elected baron, a local magnate who assumed the surname Thirlwall, lived in a manor-house made originally of timber and later rebuilt in stone.

The baron's first recorded action was to complain in 1279 to King Alexander III's justiciar at Wark-on-Tyne's assizes that the prioress of Lambley Convent had pastured some of her cattle on his land without permission. The spirited lady denied the charge and challenged the baron to single combat, a common way of settling disputes in those days. She was not offering herself as the first female all-in wrestler, for each side was allowed to nominate a gladiator to do the actual fighting. Her man turned out to be so much smaller than the baron's man she decided she was guilty after all and paid the fine of £10.

The 'castle' – really a single building and thus a tower – was first mentioned in 1360. It was designed for defensive strength with very few concessions to comfort, and it is unlikely that any member of the Thirlwall family lived in such a gloomy place. King Edward I stayed the night of 20th September 1306 in the town; he may have been accommodated in the tower – it could have been built by then – but more likely he enjoyed the homely comfort of the manor-house. As the historian Hutchinson said, "Thirlwall Castle was the stronghold rather than the seat of the Thirlwalls".

The town boasted other desirable residences as well as the manor-house. A man with the joyless name of Bricius Cokeman owned one which he sold before 1315 to Adam Swinburne of Little Swinburn. "Land in the Heiside on the south side of the Wall, in the township of Thirlwall" went with the house, and, at the same time, Adam purchased other small properties along the line of the Wall.

The Crown confiscated all Adam's property and put him in gaol for political incorrectness. He died there in 1318, but it was 1323 before the property was returned, and then it was given not to the heir but to his sister Barnaba. She was a fair-minded girl, however, and gave her brother the Thirlwall and Wall property as some compensation.

The tower was kept garrisoned and maintained with such efficiency that, if records are to be believed, it was never attacked by Scottish raiders. During the Civil War, 1642 to 1645, the building was still in good enough condition to be commandeered by Scottish troops helping the Parliamentarians for use as a supply depot. They damaged its fabric so much that it was not considered worth repairing when they had gone; the need for such a place had passed by then, of course.

In about 1660 John Thirlwall moved from Thirlwall to Newbiggin, south of Hexham (NY943608). His family retained the tower until Eleanora inherited it from William Thirlwall in 1710 and sold it to the fourth Earl of Carlisle in 1748. It was a remarkable coincidence, incidentally, that in 1735

Eleanora married a Swinburne. He was of the Capheaton variety, however, and his ancestors had not held a house in Thirlwall.

Some renovation was attempted in 1759, but this did not stop nature taking a hand in the descent of the tower. In 1831 the east wall slipped and fell into the Tipalt Burn.

The walls which survive, made entirely of Roman stones filched from the Wall, are from eight to ten feet thick and stand to almost roof height. Where they have fractured it is possible to see their cross-section and to discover several small chambers within their thickness. The building has been a rectangular three storey block some 47 by 19 feet internally, with the entrance in the north-east corner and a turret at its south end. Windows appear to have been strictly rationed and very small; the stairs were in the thickness of the north wall. The Northumberland National Park Authority was granted funds from the National Lottery and the European Union Regional Development Fund in 1997 to stabilize the masonry and do what is necessary to create a tourist attraction.

Low Old Shield

L86   P546   NY668668   4½ km, 2¾ miles, north-west of Haltwhistle

A lonely farm on the edge of Thirlwall Common, north of the Wall. As its name suggests, there was a shieling here originally, probably a wood and mud hut where herdsmen could shelter while their cattle worked the surrounding moor during summer.

During the latter part of the sixteenth century the hut was replaced by a bastle, while in the eighteenth century farm buildings were added to convert the establishment into an all-the-year-round farm.

The present farmhouse is little more than a renovated bastle with a porch and windows added. A drain spout, originally connected to a sink in the bastle's living quarters, protrudes above the porch. A good length of plinth shows along the west wall, although some of it has had to be strengthened with concrete. Some of the farm land was drained in the nineteenth century so today's farmer can concentrate on rearing sheep whereas his predecessors were cattle farmers as the ground was too boggy for sheep.

Walltown

L86, 87   P546   NY678665   3½ km, 2¼ miles, north-west of Haltwhistle

A former township with only a farm remaining, built in the 1670s with stone taken from a fifteenth century tower. The Rev. John Hodgson claimed that a fragment of this tower remained in 1769 and that even in his day – 1839 – the site was "shown by the bare craggy masses of the heart of its walls on the bright blue limestone which covers the whin rock behind the present farmhouse". Today there is no blue limestone visible, let alone any craggy masses, but there is an outline in the grass north-west of the farm which could be that of the tower. It is not possible to be sure as there is so much of Roman origin in the area.

The tower was built in the fifteenth century, after 1415. In 1541 it belonged to John Ridley, the "well-beloved brother" of Bishop Nicholas Ridley who was to be martyred at the stake in 1555 on Queen Mary's orders. John was married to Elizabeth, daughter of Christopher Ridley, another of the bishop's brothers; the union would appear to have been incestuous but it did not offend the bishop. John and Elizabeth had only one child, a girl also called Elizabeth, and she also married a close relative, so it was just as well their grandson, Musgrave, introduced some new blood by marrying Anne Charlton of Hesleyside.

The Ridleys remained at Walltown until the 1670s, then they sold the property to Thomas Marshall, who dismantled the tower and built the farmhouse.

Peel Crag

L86, 87   P546   NY752675   6 km, 3³/₄ miles, north-east of Haltwhistle

There is a trace of a medieval tower here which has been discovered by archaeological survey and not from a study of old documents. Indeed, so far as is known, there are no relevant documents to study; not a single mention of it has been found.

The square outline of the tower and the run of its interior walls can be seen quite clearly amongst the reeds and coarse grasses by the south side of the Roman Wall about two hundred yards east of Steel Rigg car park, on the gentle slope leading down to Peel Gap. The Wall has been used as the tower's northern wall, and a few stones from its other walls are scattered around, not all of them of the Roman shape. Running southwards down the hill to the lane at Peel Cottage, then on to the Military Road and beyond, is a double line of low banks which probably mark the run of a medieval drove road. This may be a clue to the purpose of the tower, although why this particular route should have the protection of a tower when so many others had nothing is a mystery.

The tower site has not been excavated and is never likely to be as the medieval era comes a poor second to the Roman period in this area. During the 1980s a lot of work was done in Peel Gap, where an unexpected Roman turret was found and an interesting stretch of Wall was uncovered, the latter revealing how the foundations were prepared for a wider wall than was built. The whole length of Wall between Steel Rigg and Housesteads is deservedly popular, for here John Clayton renovated, in parts rebuilt, the Wall in the nineteenth century with stones he found lying about.

Bradley Hall (With Easter Bradley)

L86, 87   P546   NY779877   8 km, 5 miles, north-east of Haltwhistle

The Bradley Burn flows out of Crag Lough (NY769689) and takes an erratic south-easterly course through a break in the Whin Sill, across the Military Road at one of those ferocious dips and into the Bradley fields where it turns south-east to form the boundary between Bradley Farm and Bradley Hall Farm. The farmhouse at Bradley Hall and the triangular field to the north of the burn, the site of the deserted hamlet of Easter Bradley, are of special interest to bastle hounds.

First, Bradley Hall. To be pedantic, it is not the existing farmhouse – although it may be a bastle derivative – but what was there before it that is of interest, the 'hall' after which the farm is named. We know from Bowes and Ellerker's detailed survey of 1541 that there was a stone house there then, and we suspect it or its predecessor was there in 1306.

In that year King Edward I was sixty-seven years old and feeling his age. He had just completed an exhausting few years upsetting the Scottish people, and he felt he deserved a restful retirement when Robert Bruce got himself crowned and began stirring up the Scottish fever of independence to such an extent that Edward had to postpone his rest to deal with him. He and his court journeyed north in short stages from Lanchester to Newbrough, north of Haydon Bridge. Here the king had to rest for six weeks before continuing his journey in September along Stanegate. He reached Bradley Hall in the evening of Monday 5th September, 1306. The entourage spent that night there, then next day covered the short distance to Henshaw, where they rested for the remainder of the week. On Sunday 11th September they went on to Haltwhistle for a night, then, for some unknown reason, they back-tracked to Bradley Hall for one further night's rest. After that they stopped at Melkridge, Thirlwall and Lanercost, and eventually they reached Burgh-on-Sands, within sight of Scotland, in the late spring of 1307. Edward's illness took a serious turn there and he died on 7th July that year.

The royal wardrobe account confirms that 'Bradele in Tyndale' accommodated king and court on the two nights of 5th and 12th September, and the fact that a 'prest' – payment for board and lodging – was paid proves that they slept under a roof and did not bivouac. There must have been a large house at Bradley in 1306, and presumably it was Bradley Hall.

Adam de Swinburne of Little Swinburn bought Bradley before 1315, along with property in Thirlwall, but the bill of sale covered land only and makes no mention of a building. In 1425 the Ridleys of Willimoteswick became lords of Thorngrafton and are said to have leased Bradley Hall. In 1541 it was held by Nicholas Carrow and in 1568 Henry de Bradley was assessed for tax on Bradley Hall. None of this information provides a description of a hall, which must remain an enigma.

It is a relief to find stone evidence in the triangular field to the north of Bradley Hall farm. An earthwork survey carried out during the summer of 1988 by the National Trust located several traces of cottages, a corn kiln, a drainage system and at least one bastle. The latter's foundations are still evident, and a door pillar lies on the grass nearby. There is another possible bastle in the field but its remains are too sparse for positive identification.

It is theorized that the bastle was, or the bastles were, built during the second half of the sixteenth century while Henry Bradley or his father Richard occupied Bradley Hall. No doubt the whole hamlet was built at the same time to house the staff and farm hands employed by the Bradleys. Certainly Bradley Hall and Easter Bradley were coupled together as one property when it formed part of a marriage settlement in 1615 when Margaret, daughter of Nicholas Crane of Crawhill married Ralph Clavering of Bowsden, a junior member of the Callaly family.

After it leaves the Bradley estate, the Bradley Burn turns to flow in a south-westerly direction, negotiating many scenic bumps in the ground while doing so, and eventually flows through the Roman settlement of Vindolanda, a must for everyone interested in the Roman era.

Grandy's Knowe

L86, 87   P546   NY781673   8^1/$_2$ km, 5^1/$_4$ miles, north-east of Haltwhistle
                (Shown as 'The Knowe')

A deserted and ruinous farmstead – its former land has been devoured by West Crindledikes farm – which includes an eighteenth century farmhouse with a bastle attached to its southern gable. The latter is little more than a heap of masonry.

It is not known who built the bastle, but it is known that during the second half of the seventeenth century it was owned – or, at least, occupied – by a gang of horse thieves led by the Armstrong brothers. The bosses lived in a bastle at Housesteads but this was their headquarters and where some of the gang lived.

The bastle is perched on top of a steep-sided knoll overlooking the many ravines which scratch the surface of Bradley Hall's land to the west. It is quite possible that the gang hid their stolen animals in these ravines until they found buyers for them; they could watch from the bastle to see that no unsporting farmer attempted to recover his property.

Housesteads

L86, 87   P546   NY789687   10 km, 6¼ miles, north-east of Haltwhistle

Many thousands of people come here each year to look at Rome's fading glory, but Vercovicium, as the Romans may have called it, has not been a tourists' attraction for very long. Our interest has been aroused during the past century or so by such people as Dr. Bruce, John Clayton, the Rev. John Hodgson and the Birleys, but before them the place and the district were very isolated and lonely – and dangerous.

The Roman army vacated Housesteads fort in the 380s and its dependent vicus quickly withered, leaving the way open for the Picts to pass freely from Scotland into England. Throughout the Dark Ages this frontier land was waste, fit for commuting armies and outlaws but not for respectable settlers, and it was probably well into the sixteenth century before some brave soul started to recultivate the terraced slopes which once had provided food for the cohortes.

This pioneer farmer may well have made his home amongst the ruins of the fort. Its fragmented walls offered him a little protection from reivers and bandits, but he soon found it desirable to build a small bastle by the south gate into which he could retreat when danger threatened. It kept him and his progeny out of harms way until after the Civil War, by which time the reivers had been replaced by vicious itinerant villains, the moss troopers, and equally nasty horse and cattle thieves. The fort was ideal for their purpose as animals could be hidden from sight amongst the ruins. Our hero had the choice: go or be killed. Until 1757, when the Military Road (B6318) between Newcastle and Carlisle was completed and civilizing influences could reach the area, no honest person dare travel between Newbrough and Haltwhistle, never mind live there.

The Nixons were probably the first horse thieves to use Housesteads, but the most notorious were the Armstrong brothers, the heads of a large gang which operated on a Mafia-like scale, selling their ill-gotten gains anywhere between Aberdeen and London. The gang's headquarters were at Grandy's Knowe, a mile to the south-west, but the brothers lived at Housesteads and almost certainly made use of the bastle.

When at last effective law and order reached the Wall country the farmers returned. One made use of Housesteads, perhaps not as a home but certainly as a cattle shelter. He built a long barn just inside the fort, and also he constructed a corn drying kiln in the old guard chamber by the south gate, making an entrance to it from the bastle.

This usage continued while Housesteads was owned by Thomas Gibson and his descendants, from 1703 to well into the nineteenth century. Then John Clayton of The Chesters bought Housesteads and began to indulge in his absorbing passion for Roman archaeology.

The little bastle, built against the south-facing wall of the fort, has had its other walls stabilized at about five feet. Its ground floor entrance is on the west long wall, while the first few steps of its external stairway are against its east wall. It is built largely of Roman stones, but some bigger and rougher slabs of rock are included. It is featureless inside, except for the opening in the north wall to the kiln.

Sewingshields

L86, 87   P534   NY811705   12½ km, 7¾ miles, north-east of Haltwhistle

This is a farm which sits on the line of the Wall, on top of one of the bumps in the Great Whin Sill. On the northern side of the ridge the land drops down to a wide expanse of level ground called Fogy Moss, a rather dreary, marshy waste which in the Middle Ages was no doubt a bog impenetrable to all save those with knowledge of its secret paths. In its midst there is an island of firm ground where stood a fourteenth or fifteenth century tower. It was first mentioned in 1415, and by 1541 it was in "great decay", so it had only a short, and probably a rather useless, life, for it protected nothing of value. There are no remains now, its stones have been removed and the site ploughed over, but some earthworks remain which could have been a fish pond.

The fourth Sir Robert Ogle is on record as being the owner of the tower in 1415 – why beggars belief, and in fact he got rid of it in 1437 by willing it to a clerk, William Thimilby. Before then both Sir John Halton, from 1266, and Adam de Swinburne, from 1315, owned the manor, but neither of them was the tower builder. Adam's daughter Elizabeth inherited and passed the land to her husband, Roger Heron of Ford, in 1330, and again no building was included in the transaction.

The Herons again held Sewingshields in the sixteenth century and the Erringtons bought it from them in 1695. This may have been an act of charity for the property was still waste land and the Herons were desperately short of money. Only after the Military Road was constructed were honest farmers attracted to the area.

The name 'Sewingshields' has had many people guessing. The second part of the word obviously indicates a summer lodging for a herdsman while tending his cattle grazing on the ridge, but the first part could mean a lot of different things: a subject of litigation, proximity to a 'seugh' or fosse, a reference to the ditch in front of the Wall, a place where corn was sowed – these are some of the suggestions. Trust Sir Walter Scott to come up with a romantic answer: he called it the 'Castle of the Seven Shields' in *Harold the Dauntless*. This has at least the merit of blending into the legend about 'King' Arthur's fate.

The story has many variations and different locales but it loses nothing by such blatant plagiarism. It seems that King Arthur was staying in a castle here with his queen, his court of lords and ladies and his pack of hounds. One day while resting in a great hall below the castle they were frozen into immobility. One minute they were sitting or standing around the room talking to each other, the next they were silent statues. As such they were condemned to remain until someone found them and broke the spell by drawing a sword from its scabbard, cutting a garter with it then blowing a bugle, these props lying on a table near them.

Years passed, then a young shepherd found the entrance to the hall and entered. He drew the sword and cut the garter, and the statues began to stir in expectation. This movement frightened the lad so much he ran away without blowing the bugle. As he ran he heard a voice booming behind him:

> "O woe betide that evil day
> On which the witless wight was born,
> Who drew the sword, the garter cut,
> But never blew the bugle horn."

There are several Arthurian associations in the Wall country – King Arthur's Chair on Sewingshields Crag and King Arthur's Well at NY680667, for example, and there are at least two other legends. One is about Arthur and Queen Guenevere, who, one day, were each sitting on top of a crag some seven or eight hundred yards from each other. He wished to talk to his wife but she was too busy combing her hair to be sociable. Playfully, Arthur tossed a twenty ton rock at her to attract her attention. With practiced dexterity, she caught the rock in her comb and volleyed it back in his direction, but, not being quite as strong as her husband, it did not travel the whole distance but fell to the ground roughly half way between the two crags. This explains the existence of King's Crag at NY796712 and Queen's Crag at NY795705, and a large rock with one scored side between the two.

Another legend gives Arthur two sons and explains the existence of an old parish boundary marker stone on Haughton Common called Comyns Cross, some two miles north of Sewingshields (NY799736). Comyn was a wise old chieftain who once visited Arthur at Sewingshields on a peace mission. Arthur received him courteously and gave him a gold cup as a token of friendship. This was seen as an act of weakness by Arthur's two sons, who set off in pursuit of Comyn. The cross was erected on the spot where they caught up with him and killed him.

A place bereft of real romance needs legends like these and it is a pity they are only legends. Modern scholars believe Arthur was a real person, a sixth century soldier, aristocratic but not royal, who devoted his life to helping the Britons oppose the Anglo-Saxon menace, but all the supporting cast – Queen Guenevere, the Knights of the Round Table and Merlin the magician – were just the figments of story-tellers like Layamon, Malory and Tennyson. Yet arguments persist about Arthur's twelve battles. Did he really fight the

Saxon pagans at the mouth of the River Glen, at Trewhit near Rothbury and at Bremenium, the Roman station at High Rochester? Sewingshields is not a candidate for this sort of speculation, but legends and local names frequently hide a spark of truth so perhaps this area was not entirely unknown to the great warrior.

Carraw

L86, 87   P534   NY849711   16 km, 10 miles, north-east of Haltwhistle

While the Scottish Prince Henry held Northumberland as an earldom between 1139 and 1152, his father, King David I, granted a large parcel of land between the Wall and the South Tyne to Richard Comyn and his wife Hextilda. Both were descendants of King Duncan. Carraw appears to have been the capital of the area.

The Comyns passed their gift on to Hexham Priory who received it with mixed feelings for it was mostly waste land and tithes must have been very small or non-existent. The Augustinian canon tried to make something of it in the fourteenth century and built a small tower to give a farmer some security. They added a stone house to the tower in 1406 which the Prior used occasionally as a summer retreat. Both tower and house were uninhabited and decayed when Hexham Priory was dissolved in 1536.

Carraw was Crown property until 1601 when John Forster bought it for his grandson, John Fenwick, the son of Sir William Fenwick of Wallington. The grant was for life only, and it returned to the Forsters after John died. They held it until Henry Forster died in 1699, then the property was willed to a distant relation, John Bacon of Staward Manor. He sold it in 1706 to a Newcastle clerk called Robert Tomlinson, and from his family it passed to Christopher Soulsby of Hallington. Michael Dodds of Pitland Hill bought it in 1815.

Nothing remains of tower or house today, and even their sites are lost. If, as seems quite likely, they were built actually on the line of the Roman Wall then the Military Road will cover them. The contractors who built that Newcastle to Carlisle connection were more than happy to use existing foundations.

Settlingstones

L87   P547   NY845682   14$\frac{1}{2}$ km, 9 miles, north-east of Haltwhistle

This place and the next, Newbrough, are some distance from the Wall but are considered to still be in the Roman frontier zone as they lie on Stanegate, the road constructed by Julius Agricula in AD78 to link his early forts between Corbridge and Carlisle.

The name, Settlingstones, is thought to be a corruption of 'saddling-stones', an old name for mounting blocks. Perhaps this was where the gentry transferred from carriage to horse before setting off to hunt in the western wilderness.

There is a farm here now, and in Tudor times it was one of several small estates in South Tynedale bought by Sir Reynold Carnaby of Halton. He granted it in or about 1434 to William Carnaby, a close relative for whom he felt some responsibility. It is not known who built a tower which, in 1541 was said to be in good condition. There is no trace of it now.

Newbrough

L87   P547   NY874683   17½ km, 10¾ miles, east of Haltwhistle

A very pleasant village on the Roman road Stanegate. In 1930 a small Roman fort was discovered in the churchyard here; like all Stanegate forts, it was built some forty years before Emperor Hadrian authorized the building of the Wall, and it is thought it was a staging post, being roughly half way between Corbridge and Vindolanda.

The Romans were not the first to appreciate this area, for it was well known to Stone and Bronze Age tribes. A rich deposit of their artefacts has been discovered in a cist at Allerwash, half a mile to the south of Newbrough.

In post-Conquest Northumberland the area was known at Thornton, a name now applied only to the medieval tower. The land was granted, with Carrow, Henshaw and Walwick, to Richard and Hextilda Comyn by King of the Scots David I while his son, Prince Henry, held the earldom of the county between 1139 and 1152. The Comyns did not pass this grant on to Hexham Priory as they had done on other occasions, and indeed they and their descendants appear to have treasured it for in 1221 they obtained a charter legalizing a weekly market, and then, a little later, they extended the inhabited part of Thornton by creating a 'new burgh' which, most unimaginatively, they called Newburgh.

The tower is first mentioned in the 1541 survey: in good condition, owned by Lord Burrowe. No doubt it existed long before then and might even have been King Edward I's rest home during the summer of 1306.

In 1692 Thornton Tower belonged to John Armstrong, thought to have been a respectable gentleman not related to the horse thieves of Housesteads. He held it until his death in 1715, the year that saw the Earl of Derwentwater in hiding in Newbrough. The Jacobite leader was a wanted man who had to outwit the bailiffs until he and his friends were ready to declare openly for James III and to start their ill-fated ride to Preston.

What remains today of Thornton Tower is in a farmyard just north of the village street. Three of its walls are only head high but the lime holding the stones together is in wonderful condition. The fourth wall is about twenty feet high and forms one of the walls of a farm building, once the threshing shed and now a grain store. The area enclosed by these walls is roughly 42 by 33 feet and full of very aggressive-looking nettles.

Area 7, Sub-Area B   Upper South Tyne
Bellister

L86, 87   P546   NY700629   1 km, ½ mile, south-west of Haltwhistle

Like neighbouring Haltwhistle and Plenmeller, Bellister was owned by Robert de Ros and his descendants from 1191 to 1295, then by William Ross for a short time. Robert de Bures took possession by marrying the right girl in 1307 and it is believed he built the tower which kept him and his heirs safe for 163 years.

Gerrard de Blenkinsopp moved in from Blenkinsopp Castle in 1470, and his family remained until 1697, building a comfortable house adjacent to the tower in 1669.

The tower is a ruined shell now, but a tall one with a few interesting features. The house was virtually rebuilt by John Dobson in 1826 with a castellated top. It was badly damaged by fire in 1901 but was expertly repaired and is still inhabited. Both tower and house stand on a little mound, partly man-made, which also has room for a very old and gnarled sycamore, once used as a gallows.

There is room for a ghost as well, the 'Grey Man of Bellister', allegedly to be seen amongst the ruins at twilight. He was a wandering minstrel who was mauled to death by sleuth hounds set free by the master of the house without any proof that the man was doing any harm.

House, tower and grounds belong to the National Trust, but admission is restricted and a written application is required. A good view of the estate is available from the Haltwhistle to Park Village road, however.

Featherstone

L86, 87   P546   NY673609   4½ km, 2¾ miles, south-west of Haltwhistle

A hotchpotch of crenellated towers, some round, some rectangular, all connected to each other around a courtyard but looking very solid when seen from the river to the west. Fans of the Palladian style of architecture should stay away, yet this prime example of asymmetry, because it lies in sympathetic surroundings, is gratifying and intriguing.

It is, of course, the final product of several different builders, working in several different eras from the thirteenth to the nineteenth century. The first part was a fairly humble hall house built by Helias de Featherstonehaugh, the earliest known member of a remarkable family which produced sufficient males to retain the property until the eighteenth century, with just one short intermission.

Helias's grandson, Thomas, became keeper of Tynedale in the 1320s and built a tower next to the hall house because of the danger this job entailed. This tower has grown over the years and is now a four storey building arranged like a letter L but with rectangular projections at three of its four corners. The parapet is crenellated and held off the building on corbels.

Thomas became big-headed about his building capabilities and decided to tender for a job King Edward II wanted doing – the building of a castle, no less, at Staward Pele. He offered to do this in four months for £100, a tender the king could not resist, and work started in April 1326. By June of that year Thomas had to admit he was out of his depth and could not possibly keep to his bargain, so he petitioned the king for more money and time. It appears that he got what he asked for, for the castle was completed, and Thomas kept his post of keeper for another year or two.

The Featherstonehaughs continued to serve king and country with largely unchronicled distinction for many generations. Early in the sixteenth century Sir Albany Featherstonehaugh was high sheriff of Northumberland and was killed in 1524 while trying to carry out his duties. Nicholas Ridley of Unthank and Hugh Ridley of Harden were wanted for questioning in connection with the crime, but they sought asylum in Tarset Castle, where the Charltons of North Tynedale prevented their capture.

Richard Featherstonehaugh was a younger son of Sir Albany who entered the Church and became chaplain to Catherine of Aragon, Henry VIII's first wife. In 1532 she lost her place to Ann Boleyn and was kept virtually a prisoner until she died in 1536. During all this trauma she had Richard both to console her and to fight her cause; he became such a rebel that he was executed in 1540.

Timothy Featherstonehaugh was a supporter of King Charles I in the Civil War and raised a troop of horse for him at his own expense. For this he was knighted by the Cavaliers and beheaded by the Roundheads. Featherstone was confiscated by the Commonwealth government and granted to the Earl of Carlisle, from whom Matthew Featherstonehaugh retrieved it in 1711. Matthew lived to see his hundredth birthday in 1762, but his mental facilities were impaired several years before then and his son, also Matthew, was able lawfully to sell Featherstone in 1747.

The purchaser was James Wallace, a London barrister who believed he had roots in South Tynedale and wished to end his days there. In 1769 he bought Knarsdale and moved there, leaving Featherstone with his son Thomas. Even though his house and tower had been improved and fitted with more windows during the previous century, Thomas developed a passion for domestic improvements, and when he could afford to do so, in the early 1820s, he set to work on the old place and transformed it. He added towers, connecting pieces, a completely new range of buildings next to the courtyard, and a porch at the eastern entrance, the whole in an ornate, castellated style. In 1828, after he had inherited his father's property, Thomas became the Baron of Knarsdale.

Lambley Farm

L86, 87   P559 NY674593   5 km, 3 miles, south-west of Haltwhistle

A small nunnery, probably of the Benedictine Order, stood near the western bank of the River South Tyne from the twelfth to the sixteenth century. It was founded by Adam de Tindale, who died in 1190, and his wife, variously called Helwise or Heloise. They built a church and endowed it with 2600 acres of not very fertile 'pannage' and common pasture on both river banks. This appears to have been all the help the nuns ever got.

The gift was confirmed by King John in 1201. In 1279 the prioress was fined £10 for pasturing her cattle on Baron Thirlwell's land, and in 1296 her buildings were burnt by invading Scots. Nothing more is known about the nunnery until it was dissolved in 1538, at which time it had six nuns and its gross annual income was less than £6. The Holystone convent in Coquetdale was considered to be impoverished yet its income was twice that amount.

The Crown sold the nunnery and its land to Richard Carnaby, who sold the estate to one of the Featherstonehaughs in 1553. The buildings were replaced by a large farmstead.

In the early eighteenth century the Allwoods of Nunwick took the place. They remodelled the farmhouse and for more than a century it was a favourite hideaway for that family.

Fragments of the original nunnery remain in the farmhouse and these include some thick walling, suggesting that the nuns had some solid protection. Other fragments can be seen in the farm buildings, some of which look as if they were build as bastles.

Two miles to the west of Lambley is a farm called Halton Lea (NY651581) about which little information can be found except that the farmhouse was a strong house before it was renovated in the nineteenth century. It sits very close to the Northumberland – Cumberland border so it no doubt had a rough time in the bad old days.

Lingy Close

L86, 87   P559   NY686576   7 km, 4¹/₂ miles, south of Haltwhistle

A ruin in a corner of a field between Rowfoot and Eals. Most of its side walls are down but the northern gable is almost roof high and contains the ground floor doorway. The southern gable is only half that height but also has a doorway which led into an extension, now almost wholly rubble. The standing walls are thick, leaving no doubt this was once a bastle.

No history is known. The views from it are extensive – miles of the most beautiful part of South Tynedale, including the impressive Lambley Viaduct.

Knarsdale Hall

L86, 87   P559   NY679546   10 km, 6¼ miles, south of Haltwhistle

1177 was the most memorable year in Reginald Pratt's whole life, for then it was he married Randulf de Haughton's daughter and received her inheritance of one-third of Haughton on the North Tyne, and also he was appointed by King of the Scots William I to be his forester in his Knarsdale Forest.

A strong tower in Knarsdale was a perquisite of this job for the forester was expected to apply the Draconian laws of royal forests with utmost ruthlessness, and thus was not the most popular chap in the area. Nothing is known about this tower except that it stood on the site of Knarsdale Hall, on the left bank of the River South Tyne, about a mile north of Knarsdale village.

The Scottish king held the forest because it was part of Tynedale Liberty, granted by King Henry II in 1157. By the same token, it ceased to be his land when King Edward I cancelled the liberty agreement in 1296. Reginald Pratt, his son and his grandson had all held the practically inheritable position of forester until this date, then the last of them had to go.

Knarsdale became Crown property and was without a local lord until 1315, when a grateful King Edward II granted it to Robert Swinburne, of Little Swinburn, as an award for his military services. Both Robert and his son Thomas chose to live in Essex and, so far as is known, neither they nor later members of the family ever visited Knarsdale, although they appear to have clung onto it to the beginning of the seventeenth century. Then it was that George and Mary Wallis of Coupland in Glendale bought the tower, demolished it and built instead the still existing Knarsdale Hall.

In 1730 the Wallis's sold out to John Stephenson, a prosperous Newcastle merchant and owner of Coxlodge colliery. He paid £2,600 for it, and thirty-nine years later, after his death, his son sold it for £5,000. His dad would have been proud of him.

London barrister, James Wallace, was the 1769 purchaser. In 1747 he had bought Featherstone, which he gave to his son Thomas when he moved up-river to Knarsdale. It has been suggested that his desire to foresake London for the South Tyne was motivated by some former family connection with the area, so perhaps the similarity of his name and Wallis, the seventeenth century owners, is not entirely coincidental.

The Hall stands above a trench which almost certainly was the moad of the former tower. The building was never fortified but it was strongly made, with walls supported by stone buttresses. Originally it was a five bay house, but it was extended by the Wallaces and more windows were inserted. Its stone roof has gaping holes in it now, and the building looks altogether in terminal distress.

Kirkhaugh

L86, 87   P569   NY694499   14 km, 8½ miles, south of Haltwhistle

Temple House

L86, 87   P569   NY693499   14 km, 8½ miles, south of Haltwhistle

Two farms down a gated field track off the A689 Alston road. Kirkhaugh is the lower and larger of the two, and claims a quite remarkable ownership history.

Scots King William I granted the estate to William de Veteriponte, and as the grant was confirmed by King John in 1209 the Veteriponte family were allowed to keep the property after the Scottish influence had been removed. In 1258 they leased their land to the Tindale family for one mark a year, and eventually tenants became owners. It descended step by distaff step through the Tindale kinship until in 1526 it reached the Hilton family, relatives of a family called Vepont, the name a lax corruption of Veteriponte. So, after nearly three hundred years, Kirkhaugh had gone full circle! The eighteenth century owners appear to have joined the Jacobite rebellion, for the farm became the property of Greenwich Hospital.

Kirkhaugh and Temple House are so close a family link could be expected, yet nothing of that sort is on record. A name including 'Temple' is often the former property of the Christian knighthoods, but this was the exception. There is a small church across the river which may have been the owner at one time, however.

Two definite and one possible bastles can be traced at Kirkhaugh, very altered and roughly maintained as farm buildings. A barn at Temple House is quite a good example of a bastle.

Underbank

L86, 87   P569   NY699493   15 km, 9½ miles, south of Haltwhistle

About half a mile south of Kirkhaugh, on the left bank of the river, stands a fairly modern church, a replacement for a medieval one. The existing building has been modelled on one in the Black Forest, and is the only one in England to bear the dedication 'Paraclete' – the Holy Spirit as advocate or councillor. Its parish contains no village and only about forty people, so a visit would be most welcome!

A few yards south of this is a farmstead called Underbank, a very descriptive name. There is a bastle derivative in the farmyard.

Whitlow

L86, 87   P569   NY697483   16 km, 10 miles, south of Haltwhistle

White Lea

L86, 87   P569   NY724497   15 km, 9½ miles, south of Haltwhistle

Two farms on opposite sides of the river, but both within yards of the Northumberland – Cumbria boundary. Whitlow is also close to the Roman fort of Whitley Castle on the Maiden Way. It has not yet been turned into a tourist attraction so is worth a visit.

The farmstead of Whitlow contains nothing medieval, but in a field to its west is the ruin of a bastle. Only a short length of wall five courses high and a door pillar remain standing, the rest is a heap of rubble.

The farm house at White Lea was a bastle until it was practically rebuilt in 1682.

Digression

Feudalism

Feudalism was not William the Conqueror's brain-child. Anglo-Saxon ealdormen had practiced a limited form in their shires as early as the ninth century, and probably it was known in Continental Europe at about the same time. But William must shoulder the responsibility for introducing it into England on a nation-wide scale, and two of the system's key ingredients, the knight and his castle, were certainly Norman innovations.

In essence, feudalism was a rank-orientated, rather despotic system of land tenure and army recruitment. The Conqueror declared, on behalf of himself and his successors, that the king owned the whole of England. He retained many royal castles and estates, kept control of vast areas as royal forests and granted the remainder to favoured subjects who became his 'tenants in chief'.

There were a few types of grant at the monarch's disposal, the most common being the barony. The Norman kings created many of these – there were twenty-two in Northumberland alone – for the benefit of the aristocracy, who thus became barons. They held their land 'in capite', or direct from the king. As payment, the king demanded homage and service from each baron.

The service required was usually of the military kind, measured in units called 'knights fees'. When making a grant, the king calculated how many knights the barony could sustain, and when he required an army he would order the baron to supply this number of knights and their posses of armed retainers. The logic of the calculations is not always obvious, thus, for example, Mitford barony was worth 6½ knights fees (reduced to 5 in 1204), Wooler was worth 4, Callerton 2, Warkworth 2, Bywell 5, Prudhoe 2½ and Alnwick 12. The fractions referred to knights with fewer than normal retainers.

Within each barony the baron kept some land as his 'demesne' – for his own use – and divided the rest into manors, one of which he granted to each of his knights, for fidelity and service, the latter military and often farming and domestic as well.

In their turn the knights – and sometimes the baron direct – granted estates to squires and farmers on a 'freehold' basis, and they too were expected to shoulder some of the burden of service. 'Copyhold' was another form of tenure, very like freehold except that the beneficiaries were given copies of the record of their holdings on the manorial roll as added security. If there were villages or townships within a knight's manor he was expected to provide common fields on which the 'villeins' or peasants sowed, reaped or kept cattle for their living in return for their labour on certain days on the manorial farm or in the knight's fighting troop. At the very bottom of the social ladder, in a position very difficult to climb out of, were the 'bondmen', virtually slaves tied to the manor and holding no land of their own.

The shires were headed by earls in the early part of the Norman era, as they had been in Anglo-Saxon days. In Northumberland these earls held the land below the Tweed which had formerly belonged to the Bamburgh kings. They were nominated by the king, and represented him in his dealings with the barons. Hugh Pudsey, Bishop of Durham 1190 to 1194, was the last Northumbrian governing earl; after him legislation and administrative matters were the responsibility of sheriffs and 'earl' became little more than a rank in the peerage.

The common law, the law of the land, applied in baronies and the sheriff was free to enter them when chasing criminals. In civil matters such as disputes over service and the recovery of debts the baronies had their own courts called 'courts Baron'. Similarly, manors often had their 'manorial courts', but the punishment they could dispense was strictly limited. Manors might also be authorised by royal charter to hold 'courts Leet' annually to inspect the manor's residents and to punish misdemeanours.

Two developments affected baronies and manors quite early in their history. One was the substitution of a money fee for physical service, the other was agreement that holdings could become heritable.

The money fee – 'socage' – was offered as a choice at first but soon became mandatory. It helped both the king and his tenants, enabling the former to hire foreign mercenaries to fight his many wars in France, Wales and Scotland without upsetting the economy of his kingdom, the latter to spend their full time working their land and thus increasing their efficiency which absence on military duty had so badly affected. This at least was the theory of the change; in practice quite a lot of military and servile conscription continued.

Heritable land meant that its holder became virtually its owner, and father could will it to his son or sons as he wished. Unless the property had an 'in tail' restriction, his daughter or daughters could also inherit, although the sons, even the youngest, always took precedence. If the girls married their inherited property did not automatically go to their husbands, but frequently the bride's father would convey it to the bridegroom as his dowry. One of the pleasant things readers of this study may have notices is that daughters were nearly always well looked after., There certainly was no sex equality, but fathers usually went to some pains to make sure their girls continued to enjoy the sort of lifestyle they were used to.

Other types of royal grants of land included liberties, church lands, serjeanties and the tenure of drengage.

A liberty was almost a separate state, ruled by a lord who had viceroy powers. The county sheriff could not enter it and the common law did not apply. The lord had his own chancellor, sheriffs and coroners, made his own laws, held his own courts and imprisoned and executed in his own name; within his boundaries he could do everything normally expected of a king except formulate foreign policy, raise large offensive armies and issue licences to crenellate – ie, to build fortresses. The king granted liberties sparingly and only if he considered the safety of his realm depended on having a man in a danger zone who could act when necessary on his own initiative without recourse to the distant seat of government. Northumberland had two liberties, Redesdale and Tynedale, which covered most of the Border. The lords of liberties paid for their privileges by doing homage to the king and promising to keep the peace.

The Church received a lot of land from the king, some of it simple grants, some, like Durham, Tynemouth and Hexhamshire like liberties. A lot of monastic out-by land were free grants given by lay landowners who wished to ensure their safe passage to heaven when they died; if these were given to monasteries holding liberty status then they became part of the liberty.

Serjeanties were similar to baronies but the service demanded as payment was jurisdictional or authoritative and not military. Thus Nafferton was held as a serjeanty by Phillip de Ulcotes because he was a coroner. Byker was held by a man who guarded the pledges given to honour debts. Holders of serjeanties were usually not so affluent as barons and their estates were smaller, although Gospatric's Beanley serjeanty was a very notable exception.

When the Normans conquered the country most of the land-owning Anglians or Saxon thanes were sent packing and Norman aristocrats took their place. There were some exceptions, however; thanes who readily submitted to the Normans and appeared to be trustworthy were allowed to keep their property under tenure of drengage. These men were not trusted to the extent of paying their fee by military service, but instead had to do more menial duties. The Callalys, for example, paid for their land near Whittingham partly by carting a tree trunk to Bamburgh for the king's hearth every other day between Whitsuntide and Lammas. Others paid monetary rent direct to the king.

By its very nature, the feudal system could not survive very long against the growing strength and influence of the proletariat and the improved social conscience of, at least, the emerging middle classes. By the thirteenth century it was in decline, by the fifteenth only a few diehards like the Northumbrian Percys were keeping it alive, and it was abolished by Act if Parliament in 1660. All land-holders became either legal owners or tenants paying rent. 'Baron' became merely an order of nobility, unconnected with land tenure.

Area 7, Sub-Area C   Lower South Tyne, North Bank
Blenkinsopp Castle

L86   P546   NY664644   4 km, 2½ miles, west of Haltwhistle

The area south of the Tipalt Burn used to be a very wild part of the northern
Pennines until the Haltwhistle to Carlisle road was redirected along the valley
in 1818. There were no claimants for it when the Normans were sharing out
their conquered land, so the sitting owner, an Anglian called Blencan, was
allowed to keep it. By 1340 his descendant, Thomas, had come to realise that
if you can't beat 'em you might as well join 'em, so he changed his surname to
Blenkinsopp and applied successfully for a licence to crenellate.

He used Roman stones taken from the Wall near Thirlwall to build a
fairly large, square tower. It had a vaulted ground floor, a high curtain wall all
round and a moat round the southern half of its perimeter; the northern half
was protected naturally by steep banks down to the Tipalt. Here the family
lived for 130 years, part of the time in the company of a ghost.

Somewhere along the line was a Bryan de Blenkinsopp who married a
very rich foreign lady. She arrived at the matrimonial home bearing a chest full
of gold and jewellery, her dowry and, according to local gossip, the reason
why Bryan had married her. The lady heard the gossip and decided to test its
accuracy: she hid the chest, and Bryan walked out. Too late she realised she
loved her husband, be he ever so mercenary, and she scoured the country
looking for him, to no avail. He never returned, but she did eventually, as a
white lady ghost still seen occasionally gliding round the tower ruins.

In 1415 John de Blenkinsopp owned the tower. He died without male
heirs but a cadet branch took over and held the place until 1470 when
Gerrard de Blenkinsopp moved to Bellister, nine miles to the south-east. He
did this to avoid expensive repairs to the near-ruinous tower, but the condition
of the building did not deter Henry Percy, Earl of Northumberland and
warden of the middle march. He bought it to house a Border garrison. This
usage did not last long, and the tower was left to deteriorate further. By the
late eighteenth century there was practically nothing left but some curtain
walling. The local parish council bought it then and built a small house within
these walls inwhich to accommodate some destitute people.

A mine owner bought the property in 1832. He owned a small but
profitable coal mine situated directly below the tower site and he wanted a
handy place for his mine manager. The small house was replaced by a larger
one, built with castellations in an attempt to blend it into the medieval
surroundings. By 1870 it had acquired a strange ornament, a large chimney-
like tower which was really a ventilating shaft connected to the mine below. A
few years later the whole estate, above and below ground, was bought by
Edward Joicey, the business man who was to become Lord Joicey of Etal.

Between 1877 and 1880 he virtually rebuilt the house in Gothic style and restored some parts of the old tower. The house was used as mine offices as well as a home.

A fire gutted the place in 1954. The Gothic house was ruined completely, but the east wall of the renovated tower and a few other parts survived, and remain today as interesting skeletons., A new complex of buildings sprang up on the west side of the tower, and today these serve a caravan park as club house and restaurant.

Melkridge

L86, 87   P546   NY738639   3 km, 2 miles, east of Haltwhistle

As one of the twelve towns given to Duncan in 1031, this place must have had an importance then which escapes it now. It was part of the Ridley empire from about 1500, and in 1652 the Commonwealth government sequestrated it and sold it to a cadet branch of the Neville family of Chevat, near Wakefield. Before 1680 the Blacketts of Matfin were in possession.

The village contained an interesting strong house until 1955, when it was pulled down. It was a rectangular building like a bastle but with three storeys and a look-out turret corbelled out from the top of its east gable. Its design was similar to that of the strong house on Haltwhistle's Castle Hill, and was probably the work of the same builder at about the same date, between 1607 and 1611.

Henshaw

L86, 87   P546   NY763645   6 km, 3³/₄ miles, east of Haltwhistle

Like Carraw, Henshaw was granted by King David I to Richard and Hextilda Comyn at some date between 1139 and 1152. However, unlike Carraw, which was given away totally, Henshaw was divided into two parts and only the smaller went to Hexham Priory and the larger was retained for hunting. The Priory kept their share until dissolution, but the Comyn part changed hands early in the fourteenth century when their surname ended with two married daughters.

Just before then, in 1306, the last of the male Comyns entertained King Edward I for four nights during his slow progress to the Solway. As at Bradley Hall, it is a mystery where the court lodged as there is no record of a large house in the area at that time.

From the sixteenth century Henshaw travelled the same line of descent as Melkridge – Ridleys, Nevilles and Blacketts. Until about 1713 the Ridleys also held Hardriding Hall, near Henshaw. Nicholas Ridley of Hardriding was an ancestor of the present Viscount Ridley of Blagdon Hall.

A retired schoolteacher who lives in Henshaw village possesses a photograph of 'The Old Bastle of Henshaw'. She does not know when it was taken but it is in colour so it cannot be very old. The picture shows a detached building in the centre of the village which clearly was a bastle derivative. Unfortunately its site is occupied now by a pair of semi-detached houses.

Tow House

L86, 87   P546   NY767643   6 km, 3³/₄ miles, east of Haltwhistle

A hamlet close to the river, more or less contiguous with Redburn and a mile west of Bardon Mill. There used to be a ford at this point – hence the existence of a bastle; fords were dangerous things.

The bastle has been modernised and refashioned sufficiently to make it a comfortable country cottage, fallaciously called Tower House, but it retains the essentials of a sixteenth century Border stronghold. It has a plinth and quoints of large boulders, walls 4¹/₂ feet thick, a door to the ground floor chamber in the west gable and heavy beams supporting the first floor. An internal newel staircase was added after it was built.

The builder was one of the Ridley family, so prolific in this part of the world. It was sold in 1747 in order to raise money to pay the expenses incurred by Richard Ridley when he contested a Parliamentary election. The Martin family bought it, and here in 1772 William Martin was born. He never achieved the fame accorded to his artist brother, John, who was born in Haydon Bridge seventeen years later, but he did make a useful contribution to society – he invented the spring balance with circular index.

Also in the hamlet is a recently restored heather-thatched barn, the roof of which is supported by four crucks, or curved beams, which spring from ground level.

Bardon Mill

L86, 87   P546   NY781645   7¹/₂ km, 4¹/₂ miles, east of Haltwhistle

Bit of a contradiction here, for the village's name is said to refer to a woollen mill established as recently as 1800, yet there is at least one bastle, and possibly as many as five, established about two hundred years earlier. Seems to be an old centre of habitation with a new name.

The certainty is now a garage in the grounds of a pleasant nineteenth century house falled The Grange, formerly Millhouse Grange. Much of its south facing side has been replaced by garage doors, but there is a Tudor arch around a blocked-up doorway above them, and the roof supports are original.

Across the road is a terrace of cottages which the experts say originated as three attached bastles. Who knows, they may be right, but the evidence is very slim. Near them is a workshop which is of the right shape but in such a mess any bastle clues remain hidden.

Thorngrafton

L86, 87   P546   NY781653   8 km, 5 miles, east of Haltwhistle

An old village half a mile uphill from Bardon Mill which may well have had several bastles at one time although documentary and ground evidence has been found for only two.

One of these is at the entrance to West End Town farm. It is a two-storey derelict building, roofless and with unbastle-like windows, but with unmistakeably bastle walls. It was subjected to extensive alterations in the eighteenth century so no doubt the windows were inserted then.

The other no longer looks like a bastle, it has been changed so much, but one of its gable walls remains more or less as built and gives the game away. It is inhabited and bears the refurbishing date of 1884. It is called The Hott and stands on the side of the road from Bardon Mill.

The village was part of Thorngrafton township, a large expanse of country which spread from Wall to river. In 1425 the Ridleys of Willimoteswick became lords of Thorngrafton, but as they leased most of it to several farmers it is not known who was responsible for building the bastles. The lordship remained in the Ridley family until 1652 when it was sequestrated with most of their property and sold to Francis Neville. He sold to John Lowes, whose descendants held it until 1812.

Birkshaw

L86, 87   P546   NY775656   7½ km, 4½ miles, north-east of Haltwhistle

Whitshield

L86, 87   P546   NY796652   9½ km, 6 miles, east of Haltwhistle

Two farming estates within the Thorngrafton township.

Birkshaw was held by leaseholders from the fifteenth to the nineteenth centuries. Hugh Crawhawe of Crawhall (Crow Hall on some maps, NY795647) had it in 1568 and was the most likely builder of its bastle. Nicholas Crane, also of Crawhall, held it at the beginning of the seventeenth century, and, as part of of Margaret Crane's dowry, he transferred the lease in 1615 to the bridegroom, Ralph Clavering of Bowsden. Ralph did rather well, for the dowry also included Bradley Hall and Easter Bradley. There is virtually nothing to see of the bastle.

Whitshield's bastle has been converted into the farmhouse and extended by the addition of a wing set at right angles to the original part. It is thought to be contemporary with Birkshaw's bastle. A member of the Lowes family,

John, went to live in it towards the end of the seventeenth century when his brother, William, was acting as the family's bailiff in the township.

Rattenraw

L86, 87   P547   NY830643   12¹/₂ km, 7³/₄ miles, east of Haltwhistle

It is strange that there should be two places in Northumberland with such an unusual name. The Rev. John Hodgson said it was derived from 'Row-town-row', or a row of houses, which may have been an accurate description of both places at one time but is no longer. 'Rotten Row' in London's Hyde Park has a quite different derivation, being a corruption of 'Route de Roi'.

South Tynedale's Rattenraw was in the Langley barony and is said to have contained a 'Cluster of old Bastles' at one time. There is only one farm there now, called West Rattenraw, and it exhibits no bastle features.

Chesterwood

L86, 87   P547   NY830651   12¹/₂ km, 7³/₄ miles, east of Haltwhistle

Half a mile north of Rattenraw, Chesterwood also is said to have had a 'cluster of old bastles', and in this case some of them are still detectable. The local newspaper claimed in 1987 that there had been thirteen in the hamlet originally; in 1970 the Royal Commission on Historical Monuments could count five, but the present writer can safely identify only three. Even this number was probably surplus to requirements for records indicate that Chesterwood was not much troubled by raiders.

The hamlet was mentioned first in 1365 as a parcel in Langley barony. From the Lucy family it descended through the Prudhoe barony to the Percy family, who lost it to the Crown in 1405. It remained Crown property for about fifty years, then the Ridleys of Willimoteswick bought it. It was sequestrated in 1652 and sold to Francis Neville, then to Sir Edward Blackett.

The history of Chesterwood is brightly illuminated by stories of one of its inhabitants who lived at the end of the seventeenth century and beginning of the eighteenth. Frank Stokoe was a man "of gigantic stature, a bold and determined character"; here are three proofs:

> Frank, who lived alone in a bastle, was awakened one night by men trying to force his first floor door. He climbed down to the ground floor chamber through the trap door, opened the gable door and caught four or five men red-handed. "you damned treacherous rascals", he is alleged to have yelled at them, "I'll make the starlight shine through some of you". He fired his musket at them, killing at least one and dispersing the others rather quickly, then he returned to his bed as if nothing had happened.

In or about 1710, when Frank was in his early twenties, he managed to rescue one of the Lowes of Willimoteswick, a county law lord. William Charlton of Lee Hall near Bellingham, a poacher-cum-bailiff type of keeper of North Tynedale, had captured him and had chained him to the kitchen range at Lee Hall with just enough movement to enable him to reach food on the servants' table. A most unsatisfactory story, this, as we are not told how Frank got into a strong house and broke the captive's chains.

Frank joined the Earl of Derwentwater when the Jacobites rose in 1715, and fought vigorously by his side at Preston. Unlike the Earl, he escaped capture by making his horse jump a high wall, an act he afterwards though to be disloyal. He atoned for this by managing, with great daring and cunning, to purloin the Earl's body and take it back to Dilston in secret for internment in the family's chapel.

The first of the recognisable bastles in the hamlet is used as a farm store now. The upper floor has been removed and a door and two windows have been inserted into a long side. Some of its large quoins are beginning to work loose. The second is an inhabited house with external stone stairs leading to a first floor main door. The stairs may be original but have been carefully repaired and fitted with a side wall. Windows have been inserted in the house, which looks very comfortable. Within living memory it was a club house serving a local golf club. The third bastle is the end house of a terrace of three; it should be classed as a derivative as it clearly comes from bastle stock. There are other houses in the hamlet which may be bastles but do not exhibit enough clues to make identification certain.

Haydon Bridge

L86, 87   P547   NY843642   13½ km, 8¼ miles, east of Haltwhistle

The original settlement was at Haydon, nearly a mile north of the river. Haydon Bridge overtook its parent partly because it was a river crossing and partly because the Baron of Langley established his court and prison there. Possibly because of these facts, but also because it had no structural defences, Haydon Bridge had to suffer greatly from enemy attacks.

Raiders from Liddesdale and North Tynedale were only too frequent visitors, and occasionally the villagers had to contend with heavier opposition. Thus in 1327 Earls Douglas and Murrey brought a large army into England, crossed the South Tyne at Haydon Bridge then ravaged southern Northumberland and County Durham. King Edward III made a valiant effort to catch these marauders but was saddled with some false intelligence. He was told the Scots had broken camp at Stanhope and were heading for home, so he force-marched to Haydon Bridge, expecting to catch them as they re-crossed the river. For a week Edward waited with his troops in constant rain and with the pangs of hunger growing ever more persistent, then news came that their enemy was still at Stanhope. When camp was broken the return to Scotland was made by a different route so Edward never had a chance to stop them.

The sixteenth century was a particularly bad time for Border reiving and Haydon Bridge suffered from many raids. The one which occurred in 1587 is of special significance to historians as it showed up the rottenness of the Border's official defences. The village was attacked in daylight in October by four hundred horsemen from Liddesdale led by William Armstrong of Morton Rigg, better known as Kinmont Willie. Their approach was not opposed and, although they met some resistance later and there were casualties on both sides, they were able to do much damage. Sir Robert Hunsdon, newly appointed warden of the middle March, filed a report afterwards which condemned Heron of Chipchase and Ridley of Willimoteswick for failing to assist the villagers. Both had had advance warning of the raid, Heron because a young shepherd had seen the horses and had run to Chipchase to give the news, and Ridley because he himself had seen them from his vantage point across the South Tyne – yet neither had lifted a finger to help. Suspecting some collusion with the Scots, Hunsdon took the matter further. He was able to gather enough damning evidence to take Heron and Ridley to court, but records of the trial were conveniently lost so we do not know the outcome. If they were judged to be guilty it is unlikely that their punishment was anything more than a small fine.

Inspite of the obvious need, no tower or bastle was ever built in Haydon Bridge. No doubt the Langley prison was a strong building, but its aim was to keep people in rather than out, and it would have offered no refuge to the villagers. It was built on the site of the Anchor Inn, on the south side of the river near the old bridge. During recent alterations to the inn a search was made for signs of old masonry, but nothing was found.

Langley Castle is less than two miles from Haydon Bridge so there was a strong affinity between the two. One of the barons, Anthony de Lucy, 1308 to 1343, procured a charter for the villagers in 1323 which allowed them to hold a market each Thursday and a fair each year 'on the eve, day and morrow of the Feast of St. Mary Magdaline' (21 July).

Alton Side

L87   P547   NY855651   15 km, 9$\frac{1}{2}$ miles, east of Haltwhistle

A mile or so down river from Haydon Bridge is this small farmstead. One can imagine it being larger and more important in the late seventeen century, for the farmer not only had money enough to extend his bastle and turn it into a comfortable farmhouse, he could also indulge in a little one-upmanship by providing an elaborately decorated frame to the upstairs entrance.

Area 7, Sub-Area D   Lower South Tyne, South Bank
Plenmeller

L86, 87   P546   NY714631   1 km, ³/₄ mile, south-east of Haltwhistle

Unthank Hall

L86, 87   P546   NY730630   2¹/₂ km, 1¹/₂ miles, south-east of Haltwhistle

Plenmeller, which included Unthank in olden days, was granted with Haltwhistle and Bellister by King of the Scots William I to Robert de Ros when he married his daughter Isobel in 1191. The family held these estates for just over a hundred years, then another Robert de Ros displeased King Edward I by holding his castle at Wark-on-Tweed for the Scots. He was divested of all his property in England, and while Haltwhistle and Bellister were passed on to Robert's brother William, who had remained loyal to Edward, the Plenmeller estate was retained by the Crown.

Not much is known about Plenmeller during the next three hundred years, but as it definitely belonged to the Crown in 1524, 1568 and 1605 it is generally assumed to have been Crown land all that time, and that its occupants were Crown tenants. Somewhere along the line Unthank came to be regarded as a separate estate.

These tenants appear to have been members of the large Ridley family for most of the time, or at least in the sixteenth century. For example, Hugh Ridley held Plenmeller in 1599, while in 1555 Unthank was the martyr bishop Nicholas Ridley's sister' home, and possibly his also when he could get away from his London duties. In 1568 William Ridley had taken over Unthank and paid an annual rent of twenty shillings.

In 1605 King James VI and I gave both estates, as well as all Crown land in Tynedale and Redesdale, to George Home, Earl of Dunbar, as payment for bringing law and order to the former Border. In 1611 the Earl's daughter and her husband, Theophilus Lord Howard of Walden, inherited. Their descendants gradually sold off the land and Plenmeller and Unthank were amongst the first to go. Kinsman Lord William Howard of Naworth, near Brampton, bought them and continued to lease them until a Mr Dixon bought them in 1835.

Plenmeller is now an agricultural estate with four farmhouses in it. The interesting one is West Plenmeller which is a bastle reconstructed in or about 1800. A barn, added to the rear fifty years earlier, and the original gable doorway, now blocked, may still be seen.

Unthank is also a small complex of buildings today, but Unthank Hall dominates. It started life as a bastle and, although John Dobson remodelled it in 1815 and again in 1865, and others made further alterations in 1900 and 1955, there is still a length of four feet thick wall to prove it.

'Unthank' is a very strange name, yet there are at least two more in Northumberland, near Alnham and Tweedmouth. It is thought to mean just what it seem to mean, the opposite to 'thank', and could have been a sardonic expression of disgust made by farmers when given land so unproductive it did not warrant a 'thank you'.

Black Cleugh

L86, 87   P546   NY751622   5 km, 3 miles, south-east of Haltwhistle

A ruined bastle two miles south-east of Unthank, in a lonely part of Plenmeller Common. Isolated now, without even a path to it, but when in use it had neighbours in the adjoining valleys.

For all that if raiders attacked the occupants had to rely pretty well on their own resources. It is interesting to note, therefore, that the bastle had a circular gun loop in a gable wall. The ground floor doorway is in one of the long walls because of this. Enough of the ruin remains to make a visit worth while.

Willimoteswick

L86, 87   P546   NY770636   6½ km, 4 miles, east of Haltwhistle

This was the original and main base of the Ridley family, the hub of a circle of South Tynedale kinsfolk. There were 'Rydeleys' here in 1306, and the modern spelling has been used since 1424. Before them there was a Udard de Willimotswyke here in 1233, and a Nicholas de Willimotswick in 1299. 'Nicholas' has been a popular family name over the years so the latter man may have been a Rydeley, but where that surname came from nobody knows. Hodgson suggested it originated in Ridley in Cheshire but he was unable to back the idea with convincing evidence.

The importance of the early members of the family may be judged by the fortified complex they started to build at Willimoteswick in the fourteenth century, and added to repeatedly during the next century. The plan was to produce something rather grander than a tower, more like a small castle, and what was achieved can be classified now as a fortified manor-house.

Two elements have survived. The first is a couple of small towers which stand at either end of a sixteenth century replacement of the original hall house. The towers are rectangular and narrow, with a pronounced batter or slope at their base. The second is a well preserved gatehouse with a vaulted arch giving access to what used to be the bailey or courtyard and is now the farmyard. The gatehouse has two upper floors and corbelled-out battlements; some mullioned windows are seventeenth century additions. The modern farmhouse is at the far end of the yard, at right angles to the towers; it is of 1900 vintage, Tudor in style and makes use of two moulded doorways taken from the original.

The high point of the Ridley family came in the sixteenth century. According to local documents, in 1599 James and Oswald lived at Walltown, Hugh at Plenmeller, Christopher at Unthank, Thomas at Melkridge, John at Henshaw and Nicholas at Hardriding. There were others, for example the occupiers of Tow House, Chesterwood and Ridley, whose names have been lost. Another Nicholas lived at Willimoteswick: he was a cousin of the greatest of them all, Bishop Nicholas Ridley who was executed in 1555.

Very briefly, the Bishop was born in 1500 and ordained in or about 1526. He became chaplain to Archbishop Cranmer, and in 1547 was made Bishop of Rochester. He assisted Cranmer to draw up the Thirty-Nine Articles of the English Church and the Book of Common Prayer, and when he was made Bishop of London he seemed to represent the more extreme Protestant view popular in Edward VI's reign. When Catholic Queen Mary came to the throne in 1553 he, his friend Bishop Latimer and Cranmore lost their jobs and were arrested as 'obstinate heretics'. In 1555 Ridley and Latimer were taken to Oxford and there were burnt at the stake for heresy. A similar fate befell Cranmer five months later. As the faggots were being lit around the two ex-bishops, Latimer turned to his friend and said, "Be of good comfort, master Ridley, and play the man; we shall this day light such a candle, by God's Grace, in England as I trust shall never be put out".

The martyr appears to have owned Willimoteswick at the time of his execution but his brother William lived there and assumed ownership so that he could will it to his son, another William. This chap got out of his depth financially and landed up in a debtors' prison, so cousin Nicholas took over the family home before the end of the century.

By the middle of the seventeenth century Musgrave Ridley, husband of Anne, née Charlton of Hesleyside, had possession of Willimoteswick. This was Civil War time, and Musgrave was an ardent supporter of the king. In 1652 the Commonwealth government sequestrated all the property in Musgrave's name, including, besides Willimoteswick, his estates at Ridley, Melkridge, Thorngrafton, Henshaw and Chesterwood and his farming investments in the Warks Burn valley. All were sold to Francis Neville of Chevat, near Wakefield. Some of the property was retained by him then sold to the Blacketts in or just before 1680, but Willimoteswick, Ridley and the Thorngrafton township were sold almost immediately to John Lowes, whose family retained them until 1812.

Beltingham

L86, 87   P546   NY789639 $8^{1}/_{2}$ km, $5^{1}/_{4}$ miles, east of Haltwhistle

Ridley

L86, 87   P546   NY793638   9 km, $5^{1}/_{2}$ miles, east of Haltwhistle

Beltingham is the principal village within the Ridley estate, the property contiguous with Willimoteswick. There was once a village of a dozen or so houses at Ridley but now there is only a farm, a bastle and Ridley Hall. Beltingham village is one of the most beautiful in Northumberland; it comprises several cottages, a bastle, a substantial vicarage, a large house and a fine church.

The estate was acquired by the Ridleys of Willimoteswick in the sixteenth century; the church is the only building of that age remaining, so possibly they just wanted more farm land. In 1652 Musgrave Ridley lost his property to the Commonwealth government, who sold it to Francis Neville. Next year John Lowes bought Ridley from him.

John was the great grandson of Robert Lowes of Thorngrafton, the first of the family to get a mention, in 1552. It is said he took his surname from the 'lowes' or 'loughs', the many small lakes which enhance the Roman Wall scenery.

William Lowes, John's grandson, built the first Ridley Hall in 1743, then followed this by building a farmhouse and barns near Beltingham church, which his father is believed to have renovated in 1691. The family used the Ridley building until another John Lowes died without issue in 1812, when it went to a cousin, John Davidson. His family kept it for about seventy years, then sold it to the Bowes-Lyons, a junior branch of the Ancient Scottish line whose chief was the Earl of Strathmore and Kinghorne. In recent times, the fourteenth Earl, who died in 1944, was the father of Queen Elizabeth the Queen Mother.

The Bowes-Lyons renovated Beltingham church, which they used as their chapel, and built a new Ridley Hall in 1891. Designed by Horatio Adamson in the neo-Tudor style, it replaced all of the old building except the stable wing. In 1903 they dramatically improved the farmhouse in Beltingham, converting it into a luxury mansion which they either let or used as a dowager house. At the same time they converted the farm buildings into cottages for their retired servants. In this way they virtually created the modern village, set around or close to the village green – no bigger than a turning circle – which was once the duck pond.

At the beginning of the first World War the army requisitioned Ridley Hall and the proprietor at the time, the Hon. Francis Bowes-Lyon, moved into Beltingham House, which is still held by the family. When that war was over Ridley Hall became a private school, then the County Council bought it for use, first as a teachers training college then as a boarding wing of Haydon Bridge School.

Of the two bastles in the estate, that at Ridley is the most conspicuous as the road very nearly bumps into it. The farmer who lives on the opposite side of the road can remember when it was used as a byre, but it has been renovated twice during the last forty or so years and now is a charming country cottage owned by a professional couple. Gone is its thatched roof, but most of the rough-hewn timber roof frame and the ground floor door remain, together with a pair of small corbels which once supported a chimney stack and a built-up upper door. History books called it Ivy Cottage, but its modern name is simply Ridley Bastle.

The other bastle is White Heather Cottage in Beltingham. This also has been renovated more than once, and an extension containing a new entrance has been tacked onto its eastern end. Otherwise the building's exterior has not been altered much, and it still features a boulder plinth and large, roughly shaped stones. The roof is very old, if not original, and is a good example of a 'wrestler' roof, a rare type in Northumberland. It has stone slabs which are shaped and interlocked at the ridge, giving this a saw-like appearance. The house is a private residence now but once was used as the village school with classroom on the ground floor and teacher's living room upstairs.

Another attraction of this village is a group of three giant yew trees in the churchyard. One of them is believed to be 900 years old. Beltingham is definitely a place to visit.

Langley Castle

L86, 87   P547   NY834624   13 km, 8 miles, east of Haltwhistle

About two miles out of Haydon Bridge on the A686 Alston road, this most impressive 600+ year old tower on its elevated clearing midst the trees of Langley Wood demands attention. Big, strong and very complete – so complete, in fact, it is now a luxury hotel – it is arguably the best example in Northumberland of near-pristine military medievalism.

The known history of Langley pre-dates the tower by two hundred years, however, for it was the centre of a barony granted by King Henry II between 1157 and 1165 to Adam de Tindale for one knight's fee or one mark. The main part of the barony extended northwards across the South Tyne to Stanegate and southwards to Allendale Common, and included Staward on the River Allen; it also included some isolated pockets of land both east and west of the core.

The Tindale family ended with Philippa who married Nicholas de Bolteby of Ravensthorp, near Thirsk in Yorkshire. A tax return dated 1235 confirms that Nicholas was then the Baron of Langley. His family held the place for about fifty years, then Isabelle passed it on to her husband, Thomas de Multon, whose parental home was near Spalding in Lincolnshire. The difficulties of travelling in those days never seemed to deter the young ones from searching far and wide for their spouses! Perhaps it was because they had no trains, buses or travel agents and had to rely on their own ingenuity. Thomas did not like his surname – too similar to the Norman-introduced word for sheep meat – so he changed it to his mother's maiden name of Lucy.

In 1308 Anthony de Lucy inherited the barony, and it remained his for thirty-five years. Like his forebears, he lived at Langley in an unfortified hall house, a risky thing to do while the Scottish War of Independence was getting into top gear. He felt reasonably safe, however, because he maintained a garrison of fifteen men-at-arms and forty hobilars (light horsemen) at Staward, a couple of miles to the west. There he had converted a derelict Anglian refuge on a virtually impregnable site into a 'pele', a timber blockhouse surrounded by a stout palisade. He felt this forward line of defence would prevent even a small army from reaching Langley, and indeed it did until King Edward II put a spoke in his wheel. Using his power of compulsory purchase, he annexed the River Allen part of the barony in 1326 and commissioned Thomas Featherstonehaugh to build a castle for him at Staward Pele. Anthony had to withdraw his garrison.

Anthony's son, Sir Thomas de Lucy, inherited in 1343, and three years later his hall house was destroyed by King David Bruce, who had invaded at a time when he believed all Englishmen except "Sutlers, skinners and merchants" were across the Channel fighting the French. He found he was mistaken when he reached Neville's Cross, near Durham, for there he met an English army large enough to defeat his soldiers and to take him prisoner. Sir Thomas was one of the commanders of the English force so he had the double satisfaction of discomfiting his king's enemy and taking vengeance for the loss of his home.

Faced in any case with the need to build a new home, Sir Thomas decided against a direct replacement but instead to go for something really strong and capable of keeping out all intruders. He had plenty of money for as a professional soldier he had seen service in France and had brought back much plunder, and also he received compensation from the Royal Exchequer for the damage to his property.

The original plan appears to have been for a tower of three storeys shaped like a capital H, with the centre part measuring 82 by 25 feet, and with four square towers at the corners forming the 'legs' of the letter. It is permissible, perhaps, to theorise that Sir Thomas was fighting for his king in Scotland or France when building started and that his first view of the nearly completed shell was when he got home on his annual furlough. He would have seen immediately that all was not as it should have been: the building was not tall enough for a start, and just look at that door – completely unguarded and giving access straight into the ground floor chamber! The disappointed soldier would have summoned his engineer and told him in no uncertain terms to add a fourth storey and to construct a fifth tower against the eastern wall to accommodate a secure entrance, complete with portcullis, guard chambers and stairs to all floors. This hypothesis could explain why the entrance tower is not keyed to the main structure, it having been built after the completion of the other, and why the fourth storey is built with stones a shade lighter in colour, the mason having to buy extra supplies from a different quarry. The corrections made, the building was completed in 1365.

Sir Thomas enjoyed his new residence for a couple of years then died, leaving everything to Maud, who could have been his sister but probably was his daughter. She was married to Gilbert, Earl of Angus, and the last Baron Umfraville of Prudhoe. She was widowed in 1381 and, rather hastily, she married Henry Percy, recently elevated to the earldom of Northumberland. When Maud died in 1398 Percy collected both Prudhoe and Langley baronies and added them to the 'Northumberland Estates'.

This should have satisfied the most covetous of men, but Percy remained discontented and joined Archbishop Scrope's revolt against King Henry IV in 1405. It never really got off the ground, yet it caused the king to march into Northumberland seeking vengeance. Percy escaped but all his property was confiscated. Langley was granted to Sir Robert Umfraville of a cadet branch of the old family, but, hard luck for him, the beautiful new tower was gutted by fire.

What started the fire is not known. It may have been an accident or a raider's mischief, but most likely it was ignited on purpose by a detachment of the King's army, rather over anxious to complete Percy's downfall.

The Earl was killed at Bramham Moor in 1409, and then followed more than two hundred years of domestic confusion, during which the Percy family ran in and out of trouble and Langley oscillated between public and private ownership. Some stability seemed to be in sight when John Murray, Earl of Annandale, bought the barony in 1625 as this marked the end of the Percy connection, but Murray's steadying influence only lasted seven years as the property was sold to Sir Edward Radcliffe in 1632.

Sir Edward was baron of Dilston, a man of considerable wealth and ambition. Since his inheritance in 1622 he had busied himself buying up properties, including the lucrative lead mines around Alston, so that he could claim the mantle of top Northumbrian aristocrat which the Percys seemed bent on fraying. His grand plan went a bit astray when he backed the loser of the Civil War, but his son, Sir Francis, put matters right, and in 1687 was awarded the Earldom of Derwentwater together with the viscountcy of Radcliffe and Langley and the barony of Tynedale.

Neither he nor his son had any interest in Langley, nor, it seems, had vandals or stone thieves, for the tower remained virtually as the 1405 fire had left it. His grandson James, who inherited the honours and property in 1705, left the place alone also; he had other things on his mind. Ten years later he set out on that fateful ride to Preston, imprisonment and execution.

The only people to benefit from the Jacobite revolt were the governors of the Royal Hospital for Seamen at Greenwich. In 1749 they were granted all the estates the Radcliffes had owned and which the Government had confiscated. This, of course, included Langley, but the Hospital was more interested in the smelting mills there than the tower, for they produced considerable income by processing the lead brought down from the Alston mines. So for a hundred and thirty years – then the bottom fell out of the British lead market and the Hospital was willing to sell.

Cadwallader Bates saw his chance and bought the whole estate. He saw in the stark ruins of the tower a unique opportunity to restore its fourteenth century grandeur, for, as he said, "Thanks to its destruction by fire soon after its erection, paradoxical though it may sound, the castle of Sir Thomas Lucy retains in an almost, if not quite, unique manner the essential outlines of a fortress house in the great days of Crecy and Poitiers. Had it continued to be inhabited it would sure to have been subjected to all sorts of Perpendicular, Tudor, Elizabethan, Jacobean, Queen Anne, Georgian and Strawberry Hill Gothic alterations and accretions, at the cost of architectural purity".

Although Bates was careful not to change the ambience of the tower, he did deviated from absolute purity in the matter of windows and door, and he had to guess and use his knowledge of medieval fortifications when rebuilding the battlements, for there was nothing to copy there. Internally he felt no misgivings about modernising the style and constructing what he thought would be a comfortable home for himself and his wife. He reduced the floors to three, each with higher ceilings than had the four storey rooms, and this is why the landings on the staircase in the little entrance tower do not line up exactly with the floors of the chambers. He constructed a very handsome wooden staircase in the south-west tower, which formerly had been devoted entirely to gardrobes. He divided the central space into conveniently sized rooms, and he added a kitchen and all the facilities in vogue in his day.

Unfortunately Bates died in 1902 so did not see the completion of his daunting task. His wife finished it off, and added a little chapel to his memory. Since her death the tower has been a girls' school, a theme restaurant, a private home for a Hexham business man (who installed a lift) and an hotel. The latter gives remarkable relevance to the Rev. John Hodgson's comment in 1839:

> ...while I gaze on it, even at a great distance, it seems to bid a stern defiance to the attack of time, as if determined once again to resume its roof, and hang out over its battlements its blue flag and pillared canopy of morning smoke, as emblems that joy and high-minded hospitality have returned to reside in it.

Cocklaw Tower. (p352)

Area 8
Hexhamshire and River Derwent

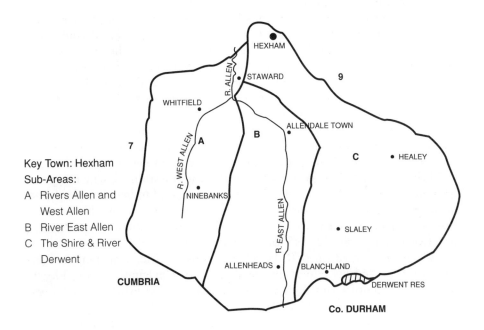

Key Town: Hexham

Sub-Areas:

A Rivers Allen and West Allen

B River East Allen

C The Shire & River Derwent

(Map labels: HEXHAM, STAWARD, 9, WHITFIELD, R. ALLEN, ALLENDALE TOWN, 7, R. WEST ALLEN, A, B, C, HEALEY, NINEBANKS, R. EAST ALLEN, SLALEY, ALLENHEADS, BLANCHLAND, CUMBRIA, DERWENT RES, Co. DURHAM)

The major part of the ancient ecclesiastic liberty of Hexhamshire, which lies to the south of the Rivers Tyne and South Tyne, is covered in this Area section. Allendale was a very wild district in the Middle Ages and had lots of bastles to prove it: only those for which ground or documentary evidence has been found are included – there probably were lots more – and many of these are devoid of recorded history so qualify for short notices only. What is nowadays often called 'The Shire', the area beyond the bounds of Hexham and in the Devil's Water valley, is included although Dilston is considered a Tyne Valley site and is described in Area 9. The River Derwent here forms the boundary between Northumberland and County Durham, so only the few places on or near the left bank are covered.

Key Town
Hexham

L87   P547   NY935641

Oswald, a prince of the Bamburgh royal family, returned to Northumberland in 634 from Iona, his exile home and Christian Alma Mater, and at Hefenfeld (or Hefenfelth, now usually Heavenfield) he defeated Cadwallon, king of Gwynedd, later killing him after a chase up the Devil's Water. His victory enabled him to unite Bernicia and Deira as the Kingdom of Northumbria, of which he became king and chief Christian revivalist.

With Oswald in this momentous battle was Oswy, his younger brother, whose help and support was rewarded by a gift of a large tract of land which later was called Hexhamshire. Its precise boundaries at that time are not known, but almost certainly Chollerford and Wall north of the River Tyne were included, as well as Hexham, Allendale and the Devil's Water basin south of the river. It was largely virgin territory then; these settlements had not arrived and there was only a scattering of farms.

In 642 Oswald was killed and Oswy took his brother's place as king of Bernicia. He got Deira a little later by committing murder, but inspite of this political misdemeanour, he proved to be a worthy monarch who advanced the Christian cause. It was his lot to settle the question of which type of Christianity, Celtic or Roman, should predominate, and to help him do this he held a synod at Whitby in 663. The most eloquent speaker at this meeting, whose powerful argument for Roman Catholicism eventually won the day, was a twenty-nine year old cleric of Ripon called Wilfrid.

When Oswy died, in 670, he left two sons. Egfrid, who inherited the Bernicia throne and his father's personal estate of Hexhamshire, and Elfwin, who became king of Deira. Egfrid married a lady called Etheldryd, who was given Hexhamshire as a wedding present.

Inspite of this generosity, the marriage was not a success. Etheldryd wished to untie the knot, and she asked Wilfred, by now bishop of Northumbria with headquarters at York, how she could do this. He advised her to enter a convent, for by Canon Law all marriages were rendered void by this act. She took his advice and because a nun has no need of property, she gave Hexhamshire to Wilfrid in 672 or 3. He wasted no time in building a Benedictine abbey at Hexham, complete with a church said to have been the most splendid this side of the Alps.

Whether it was in response to a plea by the Archbishop of Canterbury or a petulant act of revenge for the help Wilfred had given his queen is not known, but in 677 King Egfrid divided the Northumbrian diocese into two parts, creating the see of Lindisfarne from the Forth to the Aln and the see of Hexham from the Aln to the Tees. Wilfred was offered the Hexham part but was far too proud a man to take demotion lightly; he declined and went to Rome to appeal to the Pope. Eventually he did relent, and in 707 he returned to his Hexham creation for a few years.

The cleavage of the Northumbrian ministry worked well enough for two centuries, but there was re-unification when Lindisfarne Bishop Earwulf left his island ahead of Viking invaders in 875 and settled seven years later in Chester-le-Street. He still hankered after a slice of Northumberland, however, and cast covetous eyes towards Hexhamshire. Just before he died, in 900, the wily old cleric took advantage of a temporarily vacant bishop's throne and grabbed part of the Hexham see. For the next 171 years Hexhamshire and Hexham Abbey were under the auspice of Eardwulf's successors.

In its heyday Hexham had been a seat of learning and a highly respected centre of Christian missionary life. A town had grown up around the Abbey and it too had known prosperity. But after the Chester-le-Street bishops took over both went into decline. This trend may have been helped by a jingoistic army of Norwegians from Ireland in 914, but in the main it was simply the result of lack of interest. The patrons appear to have appointed a succession of provosts to lead the Christian community in Hexham and then to have washed their hands of any further responsibilities.

The ex-Lindisfarne convent moved from Chester-le-Street to Durham City in 1018, where the monks gained an increasingly bad reputation for secular behaviour. Hexham Abbey got less and less attention, and appeals to Bishop Aethelwine in Durham produced only prevarication. In 1071 Uhtred, the Hexham provost at that time, got so fed up with the situation he took matters into his own hands and invited Archbishop Thomas I of York to take over. His invitation was well received and immediately acted upon, for after all, it had been a bishop of York who had founded Hexham Abbey four hundred years earlier. Bishop Flambard tried later to get the transfer rescinded, but King Henry I, who rather enjoyed frustrating this bumptious priest, did not heed his pleas and instead confirmed Hexhamshire as a liberty belonging to the Archbishop of York. So it remained until 1545.

In 1113 Archbishop Thomas II of York began the task of reincarnating Hexham's monastic life. He posted two of his Augustinian canons there, and soon followed this start with many more: when the number reached two dozen they and their prior started to rebuild the old abbey and its church. Thomas II and his successor, Archbishop Thurstan, were most generous with finance and practical aid, and by mid-century there was a well housed, well managed, highly efficient Augustinian priory in Hexham.

Whereas Wilfrid's Benedictine monks had led secluded lives of prayer and study, the Augustinian canons could move outside their priory to help and teach the populous and to farm the many gifts of land which came their way. In all humanitarian and spiritual matters they represented the archbishop in

Hexhamshire, while more mundane issues like rent collecting, keeping the peace and administering the liberty's laws were left to a bailiff appointed by the archbishop.

This official was kept busy. The big trouble with liberties was that, because the county sheriff had no powers in them, all the villains who had committed crimes in neighbouring areas and were on the run came into them for sanctuary. While thus sheltering from justice they were liable to continue their felonious ways and to encourage others to follow their example. Policing a liberty was thus a dangerous and time-consuming occupation, but even more onerous was the bailiff's job of protecting his people and their land from Scottish raiders. The 1138 bailiff did this rather well when word reached him from Warden that a Scottish army was approaching: he was able to raise a scratch army of young Hexham men who surprised the invaders and routed them.

For a century and a half the canons in their fine church and priory and a succession of bailiffs in their hall across the market place watched contentedly as Hexham prospered, becoming the undisputed capital of Tynedale. Then King Edward I upset the apple-cart by raising Scottish hackles: the next three centuries were to be as hellish for Hexham as for the rest of the county.

In 1296 the Scots poured over the Border to make the first strike for independence. Next year, with William Wallace providing some direction to their efforts, the 'hordes of Athol and Monkieth' descended on Hexham and the Tyne valley, having been helped by the treachery of Adam Swinburne of Little Swinburn. As well as doing a vast amount of damage to all parts of the town, they totally destroyed the nave of the church, and this was not rebuilt until 1908. The story told by a Lanercost monk, that they locked up a crowd of boys in Hexham school and set fire to it, is not confirmed by any other chronicler, but no doubt many atrocities were perpetrated. Wallace made Hexham his headquarters for a few months and ravaged wide areas of Cumberland, County Durham and the lower Tyne from this central position.

After Wallace came Robert Bruce, a frequent visitor who brought nothing but misery and degradation. The destruction of cattle and crops forced the bailiff to waive rents in Hexhamshire for a time, while starvation added to the death-roll. Bannockburn seemed to settle nothing, and although King Edward III gave the Scots their independence in 1328, it was not until Bruce's son, David, was captured at Neville's Cross in 1346 that Hexham could breath relatively freely. Even then Border strife, the endemic raiding and, not least, the Black Death, remained as obstacles to progress.

During all this turmoil the men of Hexham tried to give as well as to take punishment, and they were not without some success in taking prisoners. It was probably this, plus an increase in civilian crime committed by the inevitable exploiters of other people's misfortunes, which led the Archbishop of York to order the building of a prison in 1330.

He had it built as a strong tower close to the bailiff's hall, forcasting correctly that frequent attempts to storm it would be made to free prisoners. In 1332 it was opened for business, equipped with chains, manacles and 'other necessities', and John the Barber was appointed jailer at two pennies a day. It was the first purpose-made prison in England, and it remained a prison until the liberty was terminated.

It was not too long before the archbishop was again on a building spree, this time with his bailiff's protection in mind. The old bailiff's hall was unfortified and decrepit; a new lodging, incorporating a council chamber and a court of law in a gatehouse and tower, would not only benefit everyone in the town but would also further safeguard the prison and other buildings, notably the bake and brew houses, in that area. Work on this enterprise started in 1355 on the eastern edge of the market place.

The entrance through this gatehouse had three pairs of gates, and a ground floor vaulted room measuring 20 by 30 feet was for the guards. Above were single chambers measuring 20 by 40 feet on each of two floors; the first was the moot hall and court room, the second the bailiff's home. The whole was an immensely strong tower.

The Wars of the Roses impacted on Hexham on two occasions. The first was a small battle in 1463 between a French and Scottish force led by Queen Margaret for the Lancastrians and a Yorkist force gathered on the right bank of Devil's Water. The Lancastrians were soon in full flight and, according to legend, the queen was left to wander with her infant son in Dipton Wood, where she was found and cared for by an outlaw. This story is hardly credible, but there is still a natural shelter called the Queen's Cave at NY905616.

The second involvement was preceded by a a serious encounter which took place on 25th April 1464 on Hedgeley Moor, near the road to Wooler. It was a battle between the Yorkists led by Lord Montagu and Sir Ralph Percy with 5000 men for the Lancastrians. Most of Percy's troops deserted him when the going got tough, leaving their leader to be killed. Duke Henry Beaufort of Somerset rounded up what was left and took them to Hexham Levels (probably Tyne Green) to re-form. Montagu gave them no time to do this: he followed them to Hexham and launched a surprise attack on 5th May. The tattered army had no chance and was quickly destroyed. Henry VI, who happened to be in Hexham at the time, escaped to Bywell Castle, and Somerset was beheaded in Hexham market place.

The sixteenth century saw the worst of the reiving menace, but Hexham and the Shire had an even more pressing problem: the liberty's collection of criminals were getting out of control. Stealing, blackmail and murder were becoming so rife the Bishop of Carlisle felt compelled to complain to Cardinal Wolsay in 1522 that thieves were robbing both rich and poor as they travelled to Hexham market. Wolsay's answer was to engage a man of strength to be

Hexham's bailiff – Thomas, Lord Dacre, warden of the western march, no less. He showed the trouble-makers no mercy, filling the prison with them and burning the homes of those who managed to escape.

Such harsh measures curbed, but failed to cure, the trouble, but the archbishop did not have to worry about it for much longer. Thomas Cromwell became King Henry VIII's principal secretary in 1531 and reformation was in the air.

A break with Rome, and all that that could lead to, was not regarded with much enthusiasm in Northumberland. Naturally the Church and monastic leaders were utterly opposed to it, but many of the landed gentry were equally hostile to the idea. Reynold Carnaby was an exception, for he stood to gain considerably from the upheavals Cromwell was planning. He had been one of the Earl of Northumberland's Gentlemen of the Chamber, and in this capacity had managed to procure a lot of land from the earl – some, like Corbridge manor and the demesne of Langley on 99 year leases and others, notably a valuable estate in Kent, as a gift. He had managed to sell the Kent land to Thomas Cromwell on favourable terms and with the prospect of future patronage. By 1535 he was the King's chief steward in Hexhamshire and commissioner in North Tynedale.

Hexham Priory was chosen to be amongst the first monastic establishments to be dissolved, but when Carnaby arrived with two commissioners in 1536 to take the place over in the King's name they met unyielding opposition from the canons, the local landlords and the townspeople. The commissioners retired to Corbridge to await reinforcements. Three weeks later they were still waiting there, the atmosphere in Hexham was becoming more and more explosive...but the canons' resolve was weakening. Sir John Heron of Chipchase stopped them from capitulating by concocting a tale about Carnaby intending to send four heads of canons, four of townspeople and four of men of the Shire to the king, as proof that he had carried out instructions. He stressed the importance of their continuing opposition to dissolution and suggested they enlisted the help of the men of North Tynedale. The prior was loath to involve such notoriously ungodly reprobates and turned down the idea, but Heron, who was keeper of North Tynedale, went ahead and instructed William Charlton to raise his 'army'.

Heron's next trick involved the kidnapping of Carnaby. He told him the reivers were coming for him and that his only chance of survival was to ride with him to the safety of Chipchase Tower. The two rode off in the direction of Heron's home, but on the way Carnaby realised he was being led into a trap, so he slipped away and found sanctuary in his Langley estate. Where he stayed there is not known – certainly not in the tower for that was a ruin – but it served him well enough until the trouble was over.

Heron was the ringleader in this 'support the canons' campaign, but this was only one aspect of a much larger revolt against King Henry and his government. Many of the north's nobles and gentry, led by Sir Thomas Percy, brother of the earl, were fearful of losing their feudal rights, their tenants were bitter about rent increases and farmers and their workers were concerned about the enclosure of common land. The whole cauldron of complaints had bubbled up as the Pilgrimage of Grace, a rumbustious movement which had started in Lincolnshire and had found ready support in Northumberland. It was enough to cause Secretary Cromwell to take stern suppressive measures.

By February 1537 the Crown's authority had been restored. Hexham Priory was dissolved without further trouble, Sir Thomas Percy was hanged and Sir John Heron lost his keeper's job. Reynold Carnaby emerged from hiding in victorious mood. The priory church in Hexham became the parish church in the diocese of Durham and the priory buildings were taken as a private residence by a new secular administrator, Reynold Carnaby. The Archbishop of York retained his liberty of Hexhamshire – without the use of his buildings in Hexham – until the Crown took it over in 1545. In 1572 its separate jurisdiction was abolished by Act of Parliament and it became part of Northumberland, subject to the laws of the state as administered by the county sheriff.

The Crown sold the Shire first to Sir John Forster, Lord Warden of the middle march, then Sir John Fenwick acquired 'the manor of Hexham' in the early years of the seventeenth century. The town prospered as the market place for a wide agricultural area and as a centre for tanning. Later a cottage industry in glove making grew quite famous. The Civil War, 1643 – 49, appears to have left Hexham untouched.

Sir John Fenwick's grandson, the third baronet, sold nearly all his property, including Hexham, to Sir William Blackett in 1684, and five years later Hexham manor went by marriage to the Beaumont family, who were associated very closely with lead mining in Allendale and Tynedale. Hexham benefited indirectly by this connection and became the supplier of food, leather footwear and harness, ropes and metal castings.

The Jacobite rising in 1715 aroused a lot of sympathy for the Earl of Derwentwater, whose seat at Dilston was less than three miles from Hexham, but no active support was recorded. The 1745 rising produced a similar passive reaction, although on this occasion Hexham did get a mention in army dispatches. When the Young Pretender took the west road from Edinburgh into England instead of the east coast route as had been expected, General Wade, who had been waiting for him in Newcastle, had to move swiftly to catch the rebels in Carlisle or Penrith. He did not make it. The road out of Newcastle, the 'Auld Heeway' was shocking at the best of times, and autumn rain and snow had made it well-nigh impassable. He managed to get as far as

Hexham, where he camped by the river, but further progress proved to be impossible. This experience led to the construction of the Military Road, which bypasses Hexham north of the river.

The final violent episode in Hexham's long history occurred in 1761 when the Government decreed that recruits for the army should be selected by ballot. The method was bitterly opposed in Northumberland, and in Morpeth and Whittingham large gatherings of protesting villagers and farm workers had succeeded in getting the ballot stopped. Men and women in Tynedale tried to do the same in Hexham and assembled in large numbers in the market place when the magistrates were due to pick names out of the hat. Trouble had been foreseen, however, and two battalions of soldiers were drafted into the town to keep order. There was stalemate for some hours, then a hothead in the crowd shot a soldier, and the soldiers retaliated by firing into the mob. By the end of the day some fifty country folk were dead.

Both the gatehouse tower and the prison remain with us today, both having been repaired in 1550 and kept well maintained since. The former was used as a court room until 1838; more recently it housed the Brough library and now is used as a picture gallery. The old prison became the manor office when the liberty was cancelled. Part of it is now a tourist information bureau and part a museum concerned with the history of the middle marches.

Area 8, Sub-Area A   Rivers Allen and West Allen
Staward Pele

L87   P546   NY799607   14½ km, 9 miles, south-west of Hexham

Meagre ruins stand on perhaps the most impregnable site in Northumberland. To its west and south is a precipitous drop of 200 feet to a small haugh made where the River Allen takes a turn. A similar drop to the Harsondale Burn defends the north. Only the narrow south-east neck of the site was slightly vulnerable; a moat has been dug, but beyond it is a large field which was probably marshy in bygone days and access through it was by a narrow causeway.

Always mindful of surprise attack, the Romans chose this safe place to build a temple. A complete altar dedicated to Jupiter was found there, and it is believed the situation reminded the centurions and their men of the hills of Rome.

What the Britons did with the site during the Dark Ages is not known, but the Angles almost certainly used it to protect their farm stock from their enemies. They coined the name 'Staward', 'Sta' in their language meaning a fenced enclosure and 'ward' meaning yard. No doubt they used the temple stones and some of the wood which is in abundant supply locally to fashion a kind of shelter.

Staward was included in the Langley barony by King Henry II so it came under Adam de Tindale's rule in c1160. By 1308 the barony had descended to Anthony de Lucy of Langley, and in 1316 he replaced the Anglian refuge with a timber blockhouse and palisade – a 'pele' in its original and only true sense. It became known as Staward-le-Pele, a name which stuck right up to the early part of the twentieth century when the 'le' was dropped. Lucy stationed fifteen men-at-arms and forty hobilars, or light cavalry, in this defensive position, mainly to guard his back door at Langley but also, possibly, to keep watch for intruders heading for Tynedale.

So for ten years, then King Edward II annexed the western fringe of Lucy's barony, including Staward. His estranged queen Isabel, and her paramour, Roger de Mortimer, were making things difficult for him and he felt he could do with a well hidden, easily defendable bolt hole. Staward Pele seemed to be just the place, and he called for tenders for the dismantling of the existing pele and the building of something suitable for a monarch. Thomas de Featherstonehaugh, keeper of Tynedale, flushed with the success of his one and only building operation, a tower at Featherstone, offer to do the job for £100 in four months, provided he could have all the timber he needed free. The offer was accepted and work started on the same day the property became legally the king's – 24th April 1326. Anthony de Lucy moved his troops out.

Poor Thomas soon realised he had under-estimated his costs and his construction time. His letter to the king – which is still available for study – requested more of both and contained enough detail to indicate that he was engaged in the building of a full scale castle. The king's reply is not on record, but it would seem that Thomas got what he wanted, for the castle was completed and he kept his job as keeper.

The king's plan was never put into practice for in the same year as his new castle was ready for him – 1327 – he was deposed and died, probably murdered in Berkeley Castle, Gloucestershire. His son, Edward III, had no use for Staward, but his wife, Queen Philippa, discovered the secret place, liked it and was given it in 1337, For reasons which she alone could understand, she had bought North Tynedale from John Darcy the year before and this was the best and newest property in the neighbourhood which she could use when visiting her purchase, or for housing her steward. Her enthusiasm for the north did not last long, however, and she took up having children instead. She was very good at this, producing eleven; one of them, Edmund Langley, born 1341, was granted the land and castle.

To have been able to say that this lad got his name from Staward's neighbour would have made a colourful codicil, but regretfully it must be admitted that the Langley in question was some two miles south of Hemel Hempstead in Hertfordshire, and is now called Kings Langley.

Edmund became an important person. He had to wait his turn, for he was number 3 son of Edward III and Philippa, coming after Edward the Black Prince and John of Gaunt, but in 1385 he became the first Duke of York, the progenitor of the Yorkists, the victors of the Wars of the Roses. The year he became a duke was the year he leased Staward to the canons of Hexham Priory for an annual rental of five marks. They kept their rented castle until dissolution in 1537 when the Crown took over and held it until George Home, Earl of Dunbar, got it after the Union of the Crowns, along with all the other Crown lands in Northumberland.

Staward Pele was not used legitimately again, but its illegal use makes rather a good story. It is about a cattle thief called Dicky of Kingswood, who made his headquarters amongst the fast deteriorating castle buildings, probably harbouring his prizes in the haugh below. It seems that one day he stole a couple of fat oxen from a farm at Denton Burn and drove them to Lanacost without being detected. He sold them to a farmer there who, being a kindly soul, allowed Dicky to stay the night under his roof. Next morning Dicky had disappeared, and so had the farmer's most valuable mare.

On his way home to Staward, Dicky met the Denton Burn farmer. "Have you seen a couple of fat oxen?" asked the farmer. "Yes" replied Dicky, struggling to be truthful for once in his life, "I saw them at Lanacost". The farmer thanked Dicky and was about to go on his way when Dicky said "I tell you what: I havn't far to go – you can buy my mare if you wish. It is better to ride than to walk". The mare and a purse of gold changed hands, then the men parted company. We are left to imagine what happened when the Denton Burn and Lanacost farmers met.

This story has been told so often there may be an element of truth in it. although Dicky's ability to drive a couple of beasts over fifty miles from the outskirts of Newcastle to Cumberland seems hardly credible. But – just a thought – are we thinking of the right Denton? There are several quite close to Brampton, within easy walking distance of Lanacost.

Staward Pele was a fairly substantial ruin in the eighteenth century, but since then nature and stone thieves have worked with a will and now only the remains of a few walls are left. This paucity of visual evidence has led inevitably to arguments about the true classification of the 1327 complex. So far as is known, it was never called a castle on ancient documents, yet there seems to be at least three good reasons why it should be classed as one. First, the original contract and Thomas de Featherstonehaugh's letter requesting more money and time make it abundantly clear that the enterprise was very considerable; much more in the way of defensive walling, guarded entrances and enclosed buildings was required than would be appropriate for anything less than a castle. Second, a king specified it and a queen owned it; towers were for knights and squires, but royalty demanded castles. And third, a plan exists dated 1759 which shows what was left at that time; a study of it reveals a gatehouse with adjoining substantial walls enclosing a bailey with a building in it which looks like a keep.

On top of this evidence, there are still existing bits of wall to consider. Nearest to the neck of the promontory is a bit of masonry which has been identified as the north-east corner of a gatehouse. The stones used are the roughly dressed type often kept for outer defences. Near the far edge of the site are bits of wall made of beautifully dressed stones such as the Romans used for their temples and later builders would reserve for the most important structures. There seems little doubt that, despite its name, Staward Pele was a true castle.

Staward Manor

L87	P547	NY811603	13 km, 8 miles, south-west of Hexham

Formerly called Low Staward, this pleasant residence started as two bastles, built while the whole Staward estate was held by the Crown. After the Union of the Crowns it went the way of all Crown lands in this part of the world.

In 1635 John Sanderson rented one or both bastles and moved there from his previous residence at Healey. A few years later his son, William, bought the property, but his son, in 1664, sold it to George Bacon who had made his pile in the lead mines of Allendale. He knocked the two bastles together and blocked up an upstairs doorway with a stone engraved 1668. The senior descendants of the family stayed at Staward to about 1836, but John Bacon, one of George's younger grandsons, bought Styford from the Forsters of Adderstone in 1708. He lived there until 1752, then died taking a cure at Bath.

The Styford transaction was the cause of deep friendship between the Bacon and Forster families. When 'General' Thomas Forster lost his property as a result of the Jacobean fiasco, the Bacons bought Adderstone from the Crown then sold it back to the Forsters when all their troubles were behind them.

The Loraines bought Staward Manor when they moved out of Kirkharle in 1836, and kept it until it was sold to the present owner in 1954. They were responsible for considerable renovations to the two bastles. As seen today, the eastern bastle has been extended and re-windowed and has lost its bastle look altogether. The western bastle retains its identity but has acquired two sets of stone mullion windows, both with beautifully designed pediments partly set below older lintels. Staward Pele's Roman alter dedicated to Jupiter stands in the garden.

Asheybank

L87	P559	NY787576	15^1/$_2$ km, 9^1/$_2$ miles, south-west of Hexham

Burnlaw

L87	P559	NY791575	15^1/$_2$ km, 9^1/$_2$ miles, south-west of Hexham

Asheybank is an old farmhouse reached with some difficulty by a rough lane from Burnlaw. It is just a possible bastle; the original part of the building looks like one but positive clues have been hidden by more than one rounds of extensions and alterations.

Burnlaw can be more positively identified as a bastle of fairly standard design, built in 1602. It has been joined to a small two-storey unfortified house with mullioned windows built by Thomas Sharp in 1662.

Allendale West Side

L87   P599   NY790573   16 km, 10 miles, south-west of Hexham

A good example of a bastle built during the early years of the seventeenth century when the prospect of Border peace had tempted the builder to economise a little on wall thickness and to think more about creature comfort.

Because of this it had a much longer life as a dwelling than was usual for a bastle. Repairs were carried out periodically, of course, but no radical alterations were made and the building was inhabited continuously until a replacement farmhouse was constructed in the nineteenth century.

The old place still stands and is used as a farm store. It measures about 38 by 21 feet, has doorways to groundfloor and upstairs on the long side facing onto the farmyard, and sports some stone-framed windows.

Hunter Oak

L87   P559   NY795572   15½ km, 9½ miles, south-west of Hexham

It was rumoured that there was a bastle on the premises, and the house is old enough to have have had one, but proof is missing. It is a charming house, nevertheless, with two foot thick walls, seven bedrooms and a wonderful view. It is believed to have been a hunting lodge belonging to the Prince Bishops of Durham – after the withdrawal of the Archbishops of York from Hexhamshire in 1545.

Hollybush

L87   P560   NY803566   16 km, 10 miles, south-west of Hexham

A farmhouse although occupied by a builder. It was once a bastle but has been dramatically altered in the late seventeenth century and again in the eighteenth. Thick walls and a ground floor doorway are still evident, and a rough stone spout remains at first floor level, used by the bastle dwellers to take waste water from their slope-stone.

South Hayleazes

L87   P560   NY805558   16 km, 10 miles, south-west of Hexham

A bastle derivative which has been much enlarged and is now about 36 feet long.

Whitfield Old Town

L87   P559   NY784585   15¹/₂ km, 9¹/₂ miles, south-west of Hexham

The village of Whitfield, on the road between Bearsbridge and the South Tyne valley, is dominated by St. John's church (NY778583), the so-called 'old' church. It is not really old, but it is older than the 'new' church which has replaced it as the parish headquarters. It was built in 1813 and has been partly dismantled, leaving it with only a chancel and a bit of nave. There has been a church hereabouts since 1180, and Alan Swinburne of Great Swinburn was rector in 1264. The 'new' church, dedicated in 1860 to the Holy Trinity, can be seen from the main Alston road (NY779568) and is as beautiful inside as it is outside. It was built by the Reverend and Mrs J.A. Blacket-Ord in memory of William Ord, the grandson of the 1750 purchaser of Whitfield Hall.

The Church Burn passes the old church and flows eastwards through a verdant plateau before dropping down to the River West Allen at Burnmouth. The few houses near the church are called Town Green, and a farm three-quarters of a mile along the plateau is called Old Town, so it seems that the ancient village lay between the two.

Tradition has it that there were 'several old peles' at or near these two places, but no evidence can be seen. About 500 yards west of Old Town, however, there does appear to be the remains of a bastle. It is a very dilapidated ruin which has the shape of a bastle although many of its stones have been reused in two converging field boundary walls and others lie scattered on the grass or buried beneath mounds of soil. The local name for the site is Thacky.

Whitfield Hall

L87   P559   NY778564   17¹/₂ km, 10¹/₂ miles, south-west of Hexham

To be precise, the west bank of the River West Allen was in Tynedale, not Allendale, so we are taking a diabolical liberty in dealing with Whitfield Hall and village here. Both Whitfield and Monk, across the river, were in Whitfield parish, however, so diabolical, Hexhamshire or Tynedale liberty – it does not matter, they should not be separated.

In c1160 the Archbishop of York and Countess Ada, Scottish King David's queen, agreed to grant part of Whitfield parish – the part containing Whitfield and Monk – to Hexham Priory. The Countess (she liked to be so called although really a queen) went further and granted the manor upon which Whitfield Hall was to be built later to her chaplain, Robert, for the annual payment of one soar hawk. Robert's son, Matthew, assumed the surname Whitfield and leased the rest of the Priory's part of the parish.

The Whitfield family successfully outmanoeuvred all forfeiture and heiress problems to draw a straight line of descent over six centuries. At first they lived in a manor-house, then they built a tower which was mentioned in the 1415 survey. At that stage the lord of the manor was Sir Matthew Whitfield, son-in-law of Sir Robert Ogle (the man who tried to oust his brother John from Bothal) and prospective sheriff of Northumberland.

In 1537 Hexham Priory was dissolved and the Crown sold to the Whitfields the land they formerly rented. All went well until 1744 when another Matthew needed to raise £5,500 and mortgaged his estate with William Whalton to get it. He could not keep to the conditions of the mortgage and Whalton foreclosed in 1750. He sold to William Ord of Fenham, whose descendants, now Blackett-Ords, still own the estate.

The fourteenth century tower was replaced before 1750, for the house William Ord bought was large, square and 'of no great antiquity'. This was not allowed to get antiquated either, for William razed it in 1785 and built in its place the nucleus of the present Whitfield Hall, designed by William Newton. Perhaps some stones of the tower were reused to build the rear of the Hall, but there is nothing obvious. Some alterations were made,and a storey was added, in 1856.

Monk

L87   P559   NY783565   17 km, 10½ miles, south-west of Hexham

Monk farm sits on a shelf which interrupts an otherwise regular slope down to the east bank of the River West Allen, practically opposite Whitfield Hall. The farmhouse and working part of the farmstead are nineteenth century, but the original buildings to their west form an interesting range over a hundred feet long of four attached fortified buildings.

The oldest building is at the southern end of the range. It is nearly square – 22 by 20½ feet – and its corners are strengthened by massive quoins, some a yard long. Although, like the rest of the range, it has been extensively altered during and after the eighteenth century, there are some original features which suggest this building is older than a bastle could be – perhaps it is a small, rather crudely made tower of the fifteenth or sixteenth century. The ground floor doorway, now blocked, is not a bastle-type doorway, and the slit windows are wrong for a bastle also. There are no signs of external stairs, but the north wall has been thinned down internally, and this may have been done as part of the process of removing internal stairs. It is possible, also, that the ground floor chamber had a vaulted ceiling and the removal of it and its springing could partly account for the wall thinning as well.

The rest of the range is clearly of the bastle era. The second building has been altered and about the only interesting original feature is a blocked ground floor doorway with a semicircular head made out of a single stone. The third and fourth buildings are not so high as the others and now have one floor only. The north face of the end building has a centrally positioned door, now blocked, and above it is a square stone dovecot which appears to have been made by altering a chimney.

As part of Whitfield parish, Monk was granted to Hexham Priory in about 1160, and the canons held it until dissolution in 1537, leasing it all the time to the Whitfields of Whitfield Hall – although there is an unconfirmed report which says the Priory used Monk as a 'house of correction'. If true, this usage could account for the building of a tower.

After dissolution the Crown sold the estate to the Whitfields who, in their turn, leased Monk to John Falaker for an annual rent of 62½p. It is believed the tenant added the bastles to the range and developed Monk into a profitable farm.

A short distance south of the old buildings is a small stone structure thought to have been a tithe barn. Experts have dated it as of the eighteenth or early nineteenth century, so it rather looks as if Whitburn parish church had claimed its dues when Hexham Priory was out of the way.

Ninebanks

L87   P559   NY782532   18½ km, 11¼ miles, south-west of Hexham

A small tower stands by the roadside in Ninebanks village, attached to the post office at the end of a terrace of houses. Although now an empty shell, it is still in good condition up to roof height and it can be seen that originally it housed a staircase which reached three storeys at first then was extended to four storeys of a much larger building no longer in existence. This building would seem to have been a quite complex tower but it was described in the eighteenth century as a manor-house.

A weathered heraldic device above the second floor window has been deciphered as the arms of Sir Thomas Dacre, the Archbishop of York's Hexhamshire bailiff from 1515 to 1526. That fixes the date of the building, although it was one of Dacre's local lieutenants, a man called Bee, who first occupied it. Bee seems to have been a man of means, a lord of the manor, who grew even richer when he was granted a licence to build and run the only corn mill in West Allendale.

Most lucrative jobs were hereditary in those days, and the Bees were the local lords until 1613. The family ran out of males then, and two sisters inherited and split the property between them.

Anne, the elder, married Robert Eden of West Auckland and they got the part of Ninebanks which contained the old manor-house. Their descendants held it until mid-eighteenth century, when Sir John Eden developed a financial affliction and had to borrow money from John Heron of Shield Hall, using his property as collateral. Heron foreclosed in 1770.

Jane married William Swinburne of Capheaton and she left the part of Ninebanks she had inherited to live with her husband elsewhere. Their son sold the surplus property in 1678 to a local man called Edward Robson. He built a house in the village which, much later, became an inn; it was knocked down in the nineteenth century. Edward died in 1700, his son died in 1729, and his son, George, married a girl called Elizabeth in 1748 – who just happened to be the daughter of John Heron of Shield Hall, the man who became the owner of the other half of Ninebanks twenty-two years later!

Furnace House

L87   P559   NY773515   20 km, 12½ miles, south-west of Hexham

This tumbledown ruin is a mile and a quarter south-south-west of Ninebanks, up the Mohope Burn, a busy place in lead mining days. It was clearly a bastle, although altered in 1639, the date engraved on its ground floor lintel, and partly reconstructed during the nineteenth century. It would have accommodated a mining family, perhaps that of the furnace stoker.

Whiteley Shield

L87   P570   NY802480   20½ km, 12¾ miles, south-west of Hexham

Hartleycleugh

L87   P570   NY805484   20 km, 12½ miles, south-west of Hexham

The house and small holding at Whitley Shield is close to the head of West Allendale, wild country which in the past was used for summer pasturing only, as the name implies.

A few yards south of the house is a range of ruins which represent three building periods. The most easterly part was a bastle; its free gable still stands nearly to roof height and contains a perfectly formed ground floor doorway, now blocked. Its other walls are only about four feet high and have some ventilation slots.

The middle building in the range is the most ruinous, its walls being little more than two or three feet high mounds of stone, grass and weeds. It too is of bastle shape and probably was the first part to be built.

The western end is square and, although its walls are only five or six feet high, their appearance suggests that they were built after the other parts of the range, although probably still in the seventeenth century. A slit ventilator and a small square window can be seen here.

A rather better preserved bastle is at Hartleycleugh, some five hundred yards to the north-east of Whiteley Shield.

Area 8, Sub-Area B   River East Allen

Low Bishopside

L87   P560   NY807581   14 km, 8¹/₂ miles, south-west of Hexham

Hindley Hill

L87   P560   NY802577   14¹/₂ km, 8³/₄ miles, south-west of Hexham

A couple of ruined bastles. That at Low Bishopside had been extended to about 30 feet in 1657 for use as a farmhouse, but now it is a practically derelict barn.

The Hindley Hill bastle was once the home of the Wilson family, about which nothing is known. It is used as a farm building now; its southern gable adjoins an eighteenth century range and this hides its ground floor doorway.

Allendale Old Town

L87   P560   NY818582   13 km, 8 miles, south-west of Hexham

The nineteenth century farmhouse has a bastle attached at both ends. They have been partly rebuilt and are still serviceable as farm buildings.

The eastern bastle has three original walls standing to a height of thirteen feet. The old walls of the western bastle stand to first floor level and are made of enormous stones. Both had a gable door leading to the ground floor chamber, that in the eastern building has been enlarged while the other has been blocked up, although its triangular head and chamfered jambs are still in position.

Fairly close to the farm is a mound and ditch earthwork which many believe to be the remains of medieval defences. This is believable as protection for Catton and Allendale Town from raiders from the north would have made sense. But others, led in 1715 by John Warburton, dispute this and suggest instead that the earthwork was part of a Roman camp.

Wester Old Town

L87   P560   NY814579   12¹/₂ km, 7³/₄ miles, south-west of Hexham

Most modern maps, if they show this and the previous farm at all, call them both 'Old Town'. Local people, of necessity, have to differentiate between them, and do so in the manner shown. Wester Old Town is a quarter of a mile due south of Allendale Old Town, a quarter mile further down the right bank of the River East Allen.

The greater part of Wester's farmstead is nineteenth century, but one byre and grain store is a converted bastle. Strangely, this is the newest looking building in the yard, and why this is so makes an encouraging story.

For many years before 1984 the byre was in a dangerously dilapidated condition; its front wall was bulging, and the weight of old stone roofing slabs was adding to its distress. As a Grade Two listed building, the local council's authorisation was necessary before any remedial work could be started, and the farmer considered some financial help should be offered as well. Repeated requests were made to the council, but nothing happened. Then during one wild night in the winter of 1984 the front wall finally gave way: it crashed to the ground, closely followed by the roof and parts of the other walls. The farmer was very lucky in being able to save all his cattle in the byre, but the building was a write-off.

A replacement was an urgent necessity. A modern prefabricated structure would have been the quickest and easiest answer, but the farmer and his son decided to rebuild the bastle, to conserve as far as possible a worthwhile ancient building and to restore the old-world charm of their farmyard. They cleaned and stacked all the fallen stones and made sure that everything still standing was sound. Then they rebuilt the place, and such was their interest in its history, they made it almost exactly as it was in 1767, when it had been converted from the original. Only the roof defeated them; the stone slabs had broken into small pieces when they fell, and the cost of new flags was quite beyond their means.

So, thanks to the concern and enterprise of these farmers, Wester Old Town has once again a bastle derivative, completely genuine except for its corrugated roof and its clean condition.

Oakpool

L87   P560   NY808576   14 km, 8½ miles, south-west of Hexham

First a bastle – a very long one, over 41 feet, and nearly qualifying for strong house status – then a farmhouse, and now a most delectable home for a retired couple. The building has been much altered over the years, of course, but bastle features still remain, notably a blocked ground floor entrance in a gable and a small upstairs window, still with its iron bars, in the same gable.

Oakpool is in a very secluded position in the sylvan dene through which the River East Allen flows. It may be approached from either north or south by a narrow lane which crosses the river close to the house by a picturesque stone bridge donated by Mr Christopher Wilkinson. He was founder and first principal of the Free School of East Allendale at Bridge Hill, probably near Bridge End (NY834557). Educationalists were not rich in those days, but Mr Wilkinson managed to leave £10 in his will of 1700 "to be employed towards the erection and building a bridge over the East Allen Water within three years of my decease".

Curtain House, Catton

L87   P560   NY828576   12 km, 7¹/₂ miles, south-west of Hexham

Catton is a pleasant village not at all intimidated by its close and much larger neighbour, Allendale Town. It existed in 1295, when it was called 'Catteden', which some would have us believe meant 'Wildcat Valley'. It suffered a very damaging raid in 1589. A mile north of the village is Catton Beacon (NY822592) which still sported a pole and cresset in 1755; it was part of the Borders communication network and linked with another beacon on Whitfield Fell.

A former bastle is tucked away in a corner of the village green. The building was converted and extended to make a pleasant home in the eighteenth century and, rather curiously, the extension is set at a slight angle to the bastle in order to avoid protruding onto a public path at its rear.

An upstairs window of the bastle may disguise the original doorway leading to the living quarters.

Low Broadwood and Broadwood Hall

L87   P560   NY833556   13 km, 8 miles, south-west of Hexham

Two names but really a single farming complex shaped like a letter 'L'. Part of the short arm was helped to fall down shortly after 1901 to make room for a garage, but a painting remains of it and this shows clearly that it was a bastle. A short length of its rear wall was left standing and this contains a window, still with iron bars across it, and its skilfully chamfered frame. These are not bastle material, but they could have been inserted during a major refurbishment in 1669. Also of interest are some stone steps of a spiral staircase taken from the old place and left lying amongst the grass near the farmyard.

The long arm of the 'L' consists of three buildings. The first is an old farmhouse, not fortified although probably contemporary with the bastle. Next to it is another inhabited building of uncertain vintage, and finally there is a barn with a low extension tacked on to it. The barn has been subjected to much structural alteration, including a roof replacement and the insertion of an extra door, but a boulder plinth is still visible to suggest its bastle origination.

Wooley

L87   P560   NY828545   14¹/₂ km, 9 miles, south-west of Hexham

This is very special – a whole farmstead built to resist raiders. All its buildings are arranged round a small triangular farmyard, doors on the inner side, with only a narrow, easily blocked entrance.

The building on the east side of the triangle was built before bastles were thought of, probably early in the sixteenth century. It is a true 'long-house' –

cattle at one end, humans at the other – and it has not been altered too drastically. On the north side is a long range of lovely old buildings, now made into three homes. They have stone roofs and thick walls, and were constructed like bastles during the bastle-building period towards the end of the sixteenth century. They have windows in them now, and are well kept, but whether or not they are true bastle derivatives it is not possible to say.

Finally, the west side of the triangle contains the only 'modern' interloper, a house built in the middle of the eighteenth century. As if to compensate for this indiscretion, there is a ruin right next to it. It has no roof, and one wall has broken down, but it has most of the hallmarks of a bastle save that it has been built to a practically square plan.

Low Swinhope Shield

L87   P570   NY845492   17¹/₄ km, 10³/₄ miles, south-west of Hexham

Here there is a range of buildings representing four different dates. The farmhouse near the middle is a bastle derivative with windows added on either side of the front door. Its original length is marked by large quoin stones, but on the northern side the house extends beyond this, adding a further set of windows. The wall between the living room (original) and the kitchen (extension) is over three feet thick and provides clear internal evidence that the house has been lengthened.

Next in the range is a slightly lower building with only one small upstairs window; this was added in the nineteenth century and is used as a farm store. On the other side of the farmhouse there used to stand another bastle until 1990. It was in ruins and of little use to the farmer so it was demolished that year and a completely new house was built on its foundations in 1991. It is a stone building with windows which match those of the farmhouse, and when the weather has rubbed some of the newness off it will look totally in keeping with the rest of the range.

Peasmeadows Cottages

L87   P570   NY850471   18km, 11 miles, south-west of Hexham

An angled range of buildings which look contemporary with the ark. It lies by the riverside below Peasmeadows House, and appears to have been part of a hamlet at one time although now it is a working farm.

The farmhouse is a converted bastle, still with a ground floor doorway in its south gable. Next to it is a small gap with old foundations showing – possibly of an extension to the bastle. Further on there is a farm building with a back wall of bastle origin which stands roof high. Finally come two derelict houses, similar to bastles but with walls that are not thick enough to qualify. Altogether a mysterious sort of place, very secret yet in a beautiful setting.

Shorngate

L87   P570   NY866451   19½ km, 12 miles, south-west of Hexham

Little more than a heap of rubble which experts claim to have been a bastle, although its external dimensions were only 22 by 21 feet. It is in wild moorland east of Allenheads.

The main interest here is its alleged connection with the story, referred to elsewhere, about a Scottish army under Earls Douglas and Murrey hoodwinking England's King Edward III in 1327 by returning to Scotland from Stanhope by an unexpected route and not by Haydon Bridge. The path they took is believed to have passed through Shorngate.

Other Bastles in the East Allen Drainage Area

All between 12 and 20 km, 7½ and 12½ miles, south-west of Hexham, maps L87, P560, 570.

Cross House   NY820564
A bastle derivative, now a pleasant house with new windows. Both bastle doors have been blocked but in each case a shallow recess has been left for decoration. A slightly narrower extension and a barn are attached.

Haggburngate   NY826535
An altered and patched up bastle, now a farm building attached to a nineteenth century farmhouse. It has windows and a corrugated roof now, and a new but correctly positioned upstairs door. It is possible to see where the external stairs were. The free gable end partly collapsed some years ago and has been repaired with bricks. A plinth is visible.

Hayrake   NY851523
A small hill farm known to have been occupied before its bastles were built. Thomas Williamson lived here in 1547, and in 1686 Alexander, a descendant of his, was incarcerated in Hexham prison for not paying his tithes.

There are two bastles in the farmyard. The first is a ruin, featureless save for its northern gable which remains high enough to include a doorway with a single stone triangular head. The second is an extension to the first and is still standing – just – and is used as a store.

High Oustley   NY815560
Nineteenth century farmhouse, extended at various times but originally a

427

rebuilt bastle. Large quoins at its northern end are used-again parts of the bastle. The adjacent barn looks older that the house, and as it contains fireplaces was probably the original farmhouse. It is not a bastle, however.

Hollin Close   N829529
The case of the missing bastle! In 1984 an expert field archaeologist saw a 'truncated bastle' in this farmstead, but five years later it had gone. The farmer claimed that the oldest building on his land was his eighteenth century farmhouse.

Hope Head   NY830473
A well preserved bastle which was extended in the 1690s – not length-wise as was usually the case but upwards; an attic was added. Much later, in the nineteenth century, a house was built onto one end of the bastle.

Housty   NY836571
A nineteenth century farmstead stands at the edge of the site of a former village. It commands a fantastic view across the East Allen valley. At the west side of the village site is a ruined bastle, still with a gable wall high enough to contain the ground floor doorway. This is unusual: it has a flat stone head on the outside and a half-round head on the inside. A sheep shelter is attached to the other gable. There are many stones and bits of foundations on the site, and by the southern fringe is a very sparse ruin thought to have been another bastle. An old kitchen range lies amongst the debris.

Knockburn   NY839508
A bastle which was converted into a charming farmhouse in the eighteenth century. The alterations were drastic, even providing the ground floor with bay windows, and little bastle evidence remains apart from thick walls. There are old farm buildings on either side of the house, and the whole range is painted white.

Low Hayrake   NY836479
Another bastle derivative, the first conversion done in the eighteenth century and a further extensive modernisation completed quite recently.

Low Sinderhope, or Sinderhope Shield   NY848520
The farmer here does not seem to worry about the name of his place – he will accept either, and so will his postman. His farmhouse and main farm buildings make a terrace and most of it comprises what may have been bastles at one time. One short length sandwiched between the farmhouse and a barn has not been altered much and is still an obvious bastle, however. It is of unusually

strong construction and is unusual also in that its first floor door is reached by a rough stone staircase which is not against the bastle wall but projects from it. The doorway so served has a flat head, but a ground floor door adjacent to the stairs has a well preserved half-round head.

Moor House   NY850565
A bastle which has been extended during the latter part of the seventeenth century, and then had a house attached to it in the nineteenth century. The free end of the bastle has a half-round arched ground floor doorway.

Nine Dargue   NY829539
A 'Dargue' was a day's work done by a tenant for his landlord in lieu of rent, so the farmer who held this place presumably did nine days labour. For all that, his home was not kept in good condition and now is an isolated ruin. Only one wall stands high enough to include a half-rounded doorway.

Riding Hill   NY828565
A bastle ruin with gable walls still standing to first floor height. The jambs of the ground floor door and corbels for the support of the first floor hearth remain.

Rowantree Stob   NY839512
A ruined farmhouse derived at the end of the seventeenth century from a bastle, reputed to have been one of the first to be built in Allendale. It lies on a steep slope near the bottom of a valley so the first floor doorway could be entered from the hillside and there was no need for stairs. The walls remain to roof height in places, and a gable end exhibits a half-round headed ground level doorway.

The Steel   NY833540
A luxurious house practically 70 feet long which, almost unbelievably, started life as a small building resembling a bastle and built, it is claimed, in 1547. Close inspection reveals some masonry, doors and quoins of the type associated with bastles; the oldest walls are only about $2\frac{1}{2}$ feet thick, but perhaps this was considered sufficient in the very early bastle-building days.

Area 8, Sub-Area C   The Shire and River Derwent
West Wharmley
L87   P547   NY881667   6 km, $3\frac{3}{4}$ miles, north-west of Hexham

This farm is well sited for defence from the north for the River South Tyne makes an effective moat, but was vulnerable to attack from the south, and this was the side many invaders passed along on their way from the Haydon Bridge river crossing. Although standing on a small hillock, it was still considered necessary to build the farmhouse as a bastle or strong house and to set the farm buildings around a farmyard to form a defensible complex.

The present farmhouse is a nineteenth century replacement, but the farm buildings are sixteenth century originals and they exhibit several bastle-type walls and blocked doorways.

Low Ardley

L87   P560   NY908587   6 km, 3³/₄ miles, south-west of Hexham

The drainage basin of the Devil's Water, still well wooded, was a thick forest in the bad old days and offered plenty of natural protection from raiders and cover for the lawless fraternity which frequented the Hexhamshire liberty. As a consequence, not many man-made defences were needed or built in this area, but Low Ardley was an exception.

It is a pleasant house, three miles north-west of Whitley Chapel, which developed from a tower or strong house – probably the former but there is not enough of the original left to be absolutely sure. What can be seen is practically a square of walls up to six feet thick and with exceptionally large quoins.

High Holms

L87   P560   NY9205573   7 km, 4¹/₄ miles, south of Hexham

An out-building here is a well preserved bastle, a classic in its way except that both ground floor and first floor doorways are in a long wall. The estate is a half mile south-east of Whitley Chapel.

White Hall

L87   P560   NY916545   9¹/₂ km, 6 miles, south of Hexham

Hesleywell

L87   P560   NY918527   11¹/₂ km, 7 miles, south of Hexham

Two more bastle derivatives south of Whitley Chapel. At White Hall it is the farmhouse which, according to the date stone above the door, was renovated in 1755. The Hesleywell bastle is a farm building now so has not been so thoroughly disguised. The ground floor doorway has a single stone lintel, and there are some slit windows.

Shield Hall

L87   P560   NY953586   5$^1/_2$ km, 3$^1/_2$ miles, south of Hexham

A tower, believed to be of thirteenth century vintage, appears to have been built into a range of farm buildings as original equipment here. Its first documentation was in 1569 when it was owned by the Earl of Westmorland. The Nevilles and the Percys were great rivals, and neither took much heed of the boundary between the two earldoms. In that year, 1569, Neville lost Shield Hall to the Crown for participating in the Rising of the Northern Earls. The Percys did not cheer much; they had similar troubles of their own.

The king frequently took his time in disposing of his impounded property, and it was 1607 before Shield Hall became the property of John Eldred and George Whitmore. They held it for only four years before selling it to John Heron.

John was an entrepreneurial son of the Birtley branch of the Heron family. He was followed by two sons, George who held the estate to his death in 1669, then John held it until 1686. The descendants were lords of Shield Hall until 1853, but only another John, the great-great-grandson of the original, was of any significance. His eighteen year old daughter, Elizabeth, married George Robson in 1748 and lived in George's half of Ninebanks, on the River West Allen. The other half of Ninebanks, containing the tower, was owned by Sir John Eden, and when he got into financial difficulties John Heron was conveniently to hand to lend him money, taking his property as collateral. When no repayments materialised, John foreclosed in 1770, thereby becoming owner of one half and the father-in-law of the owner of the other half of Ninebanks.

The tower at Shield Hall protrudes from the old farm buildings. It is in a good state of preservation and must have been meticulously maintained over the centuries. It has a vaulted ground floor and mural stairs to a stone-flagged upper chamber. Its roof is fairly modern. Unfortunately the visual appeal has been somewhat impaired by an electric power gantry which has been mounted on the prominent gable of the tower.

Blanchland

L87   P560   NY966503   14 km, 8$^1/_2$ miles, south-west of Hexham

One of the best places to take a Northumberland sceptic is this beautiful village set in beautiful countryside, for it cannot fail to seduce the most stubborn philistine. Blanchland was once an abbey, and although its buildings have been replaced or altered for secular convenience, it retains still an ambience of peace and tranquillity. True, on some days in midsummer its plaza (the old abbey's courtyard) fills with sightseers, but even then the magic of the place is triumphant: noise and ice cream are no match for omnipresent composure.

Walter de Bolbec, Baron of Styford, gave some 5000 acres of his land on the north bank of the River Derwent at Wulwardshope to the Premonstratensian Order, and twelve canons came from Croxton in Leicestershire to establish an abbey in this very lonely, inaccessible spot in 1165. The Order had been founded in 1120 by St. Norbert at Premonstre Abbey in the Forest of Coucy in Northern France; their first English abbey was at Newhouse in Lincolnshire which started in 1143 and, four years later, another abbey at Alnwick was founded. St. Norbert had laid down strict rules for his abbots and canons to follow, but these did allow incumbents to preach and work amongst the people, and in fact their discipline was intended to produce capable and learned parish priests. They wore a white cassock beneath a surplice and a white cloak and cap; it is tempting to reason that the abbey at Wulwardshope was called Blanchland because of their habit, but in fact the name was taken from its affiliated abbey at Blanchelande (meaning white wasteland) near Cherbourg.

The canons built their first church and accommodation of wood, but replacement in stone seems to have got underway in the thirteenth century and continued intermittently during the next four hundred years. The church contains the oldest fragments of masonry, and a guest-house was an early building, for one of the duties of all monasteries was to cater for the needs of travellers. The abbot's living quarters were constructed between the church and the guest-house, and beyond the latter were sited the kitchen and refectory. The canons' cells were built round an L-shaped courtyard, probably with some workshops on the far side of this. Finally, cloisters and the abbey garden were constructed on the east of the main buildings. The whole complex was subject to frequent change over the centuries; the need for repairs often led to expansions or new designs, and many times destruction caused by Scottish raiders made rebuilding necessary.

Small groups of reivers did not bother Blanchland very much – they were more interested in readily accessible valleys – but larger bands of robbers and invading armies from Scotland became a menace, partly because abbeys were always potential sources of expensive portable booty and partly because Blanchland happened to be on a route to the south. There is a famous apocryphal story, told about Brinkburn Priory as well as here, of Scottish marauders being lost on the hills above the abbey in thick mist until the sound of church bells directed them to their target. The canons are supposed to have rung them when they thought the danger had passed, to celebrate their deliverance.

A well documented incursion came in 1327. An army of 20,000 men under the Earls of Murrey and Douglas crossed the South Tyne at Haydon Bridge and ravaged a large area of south Northumberland and County

Durham. Blanchland felt the full force of this thrust and much damage was done to crops and buildings, the abbey church amongst them. The army camped at Stanhope, and King Edward III, who just happened to be in Durham City with an army said to number 60,000 men, set off up the River Wear to catch them while they rested. On the way a scout brought news that the Scots had broken camp, so the king immediately changed course and force-marched to Haydon Bridge, believing, rather naively, that his enemies would make for home the way they had come. For a whole week the English force, cold, wet and hungry, waited in vain on the South Tyne, then intelligence reached Edward that the Scots were still at Stanhope. He moved south in the hope of meeting them, staying a night as a guest of the abbot in Blanchland on the way, but this move, too, was unproductive as the Scots, laden with plunder after a trouble-free week of pillaging, were marching back to the Border by the Rookhope and Allenheads route, not by Blanchland.

Experiences of this nature persuaded the abbot that he and his abbey needed some physical protection, and so he rebuilt his quarters as a fortified tower, and he closed the north end of the abbey courtyard with a strong gatehouse. These two buildings are still with us, but if ever there was a second gatehouse to the southern end of the courtyard it has disappeared.

Blanchland Abbey was never a rich establishment. The original allocation of land was extended slightly in 1214 and again during the 1490s, but it had no granges or grants of distant land such as were bestowed on Newminster Abbey, and after the de Bolbec family died off it had no philanthropic patron. It was given three parishes to look after, at Bywell St. Andrew, Heddon-on-the-Wall and Kirkharle, but these were negative financial aids for the canons became their resident priests and felt responsible for building maintenance. When Bishop Redman inspected the abbey in 1506 he found nothing wrong with its work or the conduct of the canons – except that one young novice was unsure about taking his vows and there was rather too much interest in hunting – but he was very worried about a debt of ten marks and the fact that there was no money for a barber or washerwoman. The Crown closed the abbey in 1536, relented and allowed it to continue from 1537 before finally shutting it in 1539. At that time the abbey's personnel consisted of one abbot, one sub-abbot, five canons and two novices; all received state pensions.

As often happened after dissolution, the monastic property was sold quickly to local people, or to people claiming a close connection with the place. Thus William Greeve, the Earl of Northumberland's receiver and an officer of the Court of Augmentations, got Blanchland Abbey's buildings, and neighbouring farmers John Bellow and John Broxham shared the land. Soon, however,the powerful Radcliffe family of Dilston had acquired both buildings and land, and in 1623 they passed this estate to the Forsters of Bamburgh and Adderston as a wedding gift.

The church was ruinous by this time, and the other ex-abbey buildings were little better. The Radcliffes did the minimum necessary to convert the canons' cells into dwelling houses, and the abbot's lodgings, guest house and kitchen into a hunting lodge. They did enough to last a further hundred years.

In 1704 Sir John Forster, the owner then, was declared a bankrupt and was ordered to sell Bamburgh and Blanchland to pay his debts. Enter fairy godfather Lord Nathaniel Crewe, John's sister Dorothea's husband: he bought both properties and saved the day – but not John's life, for he was assassinated in Newcastle by one of his creditors. It should be explained that the Adderston Forsters were not implicated in this bankruptcy and purchase; Thomas of that branch, Member of Parliament and soon to become the 'general' of the Jacobite rebels, was Dorothea's nephew, although, just to complicate matters, he had a sister called Dorothy. It was she, not the older lady, who engineered Thomas's release from prison after his days of glory had ended at Preston in 1715.

Lord Crewe died in 1721 and left a fortune to charities, to be administered by trustees. They were a bit slow off the mark, but when Dr John Sharp joined them things began to happen. They virtually made the Blanchland village we can see today.

The Lord Crewe Trust, as they became known, found the village in a dilapidated condition. In the 1740s the descendants of the lay workers of the old abbey who were still living there were joined by hundreds of lead miners and their families, so for a short time the place was grossly over-populated. When John Wesley preached to them in 1747 he noted in his diary that the old abbey was "little more than a heap of ruins". The Trust's first job, therefore, was to rebuild the houses round the plaza and to make the place look respectable. What was left of the church – the choir, north transept and tower – was refurbished, and in 1752 Blanchland was made a separate parish and this became the parish church. Radcliffes' hunting lodge was partly rebuilt in exuberant Gothick style, but the old fortified tower and the gatehouse were left virtually untouched. A wider opening for traffic was made at the side of the latter.

Further work was done between 1880 and 1900, and continuous surveillance was, and is still, kept by the Trust to ensure nothing is done to disfigure the place. At some date before 1850 the old guest-house, the kitchen and the abbot's fortified apartment became the Lord Crewe Arms hotel. Since the end of World War II this has become a first class hotel – no significant changes have been made to its exterior, but inside modern requirements have been blended into the old fabric in a pleasing way. The first floor of the tower is now a sitting room called 'The Dorothy Forster Room', while the vaulted ground floor is an emotive bar.   **[Plate 10]**

Healey Hall

L87   P561   NZ003578   9 km, 5^1/$_2$ miles, south-east of Hexham

John Balliol, Baron of Bywell, gave the Healey district to the Knights Templars in c1260, but neither they nor their successors, the Knights Hospitallers, did anything to it other than accept its rents. The Crown took over in 1550 and leased it as two estates. Sir Cuthbert Radcliffe paid £2.67 annual rent for the larger part, and John Ord held the smaller part for £1.34 per year. Three years later both estates were bought by Sir John Widdrington, who gave it to a kinsman with the same name.

Later, Sir John built a strong house about three-quarters of a mile from the church. A drawing of it exists which shows it was a tall building with a crenellated turret at one end. By 1570 the owner was a gentleman who must surely have taken his name from his purchase – Robert W. Healey! He passed it on to a grandson, John Lawson, before 1608, and he sold it to John Sanderson after just a few years. The Sandersons moved to Staward Manor in 1635.

By 1815 most of the agricultural land in the combined estate had been sold to farmers, while the house and its grounds were the property of Robert Ormston. A wing had been added by then, but this did not please the owner who demolished the whole building and built the present mansion on the vacated site. It is just possible that part of the wing is incorporated in the stable block behind the mansion. A new wing was added to the new house in 1882, when the property was willed to a cousin, William Aldam of Frickley, near Doncaster. His descendants, now called Warde Aldam, are still the owners.

Hole Row

L88   P561   NZ075507   19 km, 11^3/$_4$ miles, south-east of Hexham

A pleasantly situated estate about half a mile above the River Derwent and the Northumberland – Durham boundary at Allensford. It was in the Styford barony and was granted by Baron Walter de Bolbec to Walter de Huntercomb while he, Huntercomb, was holding Chevelyngham – later, Chillingham – from Baron Vescy of Alnwick. Allusion to these two barons puts the date of the grant as after 1100 and before 1170.

In the middle of the thirteenth century the Huntercombs sold, or otherwise transferred, Hole Row to William de Middleton. Although small parts of the estate were sold or given away as marriage settlements, the greatest part was retained by the Middleton family until 1848, an incredible six centuries.

The nineteenth century historian, E. Mackenzie, said in his 'View of the County of Northumberland' that there was a tower at Hole Row. No other historian mentions even the possibility, no known survey includes it and, most significantly, a thorough search of the deeds of the estate – and they go back to the thirteenth century – has failed to reveal any reference to a fortified building here. And yet there are markings in the grass on the south side of the estate which strongly suggest that Mackenzie was right. A veteran who lives on a farm in the neighbourhood says that although there was never any stonework on the spot during his lifetime, locals believe there was once a small tower which was knocked down so that its stones could be used to build a barn.

The deeds, incidentally, expose an extraordinarily long list of names by which Hole Row has been known through the ages. They include Holes, Hole-Raive, Whole Row, The Raw, North and South Holerow, Holrain, Little Haw and Hollorain.

There is an eighteenth century farmhouse here and a few other fairly old buildings, but most buildings are very new, for the estate is now an hotel and holiday complex.

Woodhead

L88   P561   NZ089579   16 km, 10 miles, south-east of Hexham

An old farmstead, probably all basically seventeenth century, with a farmhouse which shows several indications of being derived from a bastle. It is about a mile south-east of Hedley-on-the-Hill and a little further north-east of Whittonstall. It is a rather picturesque building, with some quaint windows.

Area 9
Tyne Valley

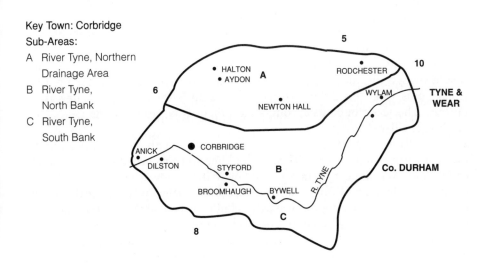

Key Town: Corbridge

Sub-Areas:

A River Tyne, Northern
   Drainage Area

B River Tyne,
   North Bank

C River Tyne,
   South Bank

H exham is a town which can wear two hats – it is the indisputable
capital of Hexhamshire and the acknowledged capital of Tynedale.
The former fits rather better than the latter in a medieval context, so
Hexham is considered in Section 8 and the small and ancient town of
Corbridge has been chosen as this section's key town.

As well as the strongholds to be found near both banks of the Tyne,
from the union of the North and South rivers to the Newcastle and Gateshead
boundaries, those on land between the duel carriageway A69 and the Military
Road B6818 are included as Sub-Section A.

Key Town
Corbridge
L87   P547   NY991643

Corbridge has two fortified towers but both were built for the protection of privileged individuals against Border raiders and had little effect on the history of the area, which goes back to the first century AD at least.

The Roman era was probably Corbridge's busiest. When the Brigantes were finally subdued, Roman governor Agricola pushed northwards in AD79 and established a string of forts along the Tyne Valley, the most easterly of which became the coupling between his two roads, Dere Street running north and south and Stanegate running west. The site of this small fort was uncovered in 1974 while the A69 bypass was being surveyed (NY984653).

Corstopitum (NY982648) was one of the great Roman stations, built during the early part of the second century AD to service these Stanegate forts. Its importance increased when the Wall was built, and it became probably the most used supply depot on the northern frontier.

It had its trials – in 197 it was sacked by anonymous 'barbarians' and rebuilt by Severus, and in 290 it succumbed to the Picts and was repaired by Constantius – but this did not stop civilian camp followers from settling at its portals. The vicus built to accommodate them was probably the genesis of Corbridge village.

The Romans departed in 385 and little is known about Corbridge during the next three hundred years. The first building to be recorded was the Church of St. Andrews, almost certainly built by Wilfred when he built the Abbey Church at Hexham. Roman stones were used extensively but little of the original remains, it having been partly rebuilt in the eighth century when the settlement the Anglians called Et Corabridge grew around it.

In 796 King Ethelred of Northumbria was murdered in Corbridge by his disgruntled noblemen. Inspite of this, Corbridge continued to be a favourite alternative residence for the Northumbrian kings and it had the distinction until 1204 of being a royal town, the home of a royal representative, or sheriff. It is credited by some as having been the capital of Northumbria for a short time, but there is no real evidence to support this and almost certainly the seat of government was transferred directly from Bamburgh to York in 759.

Throughout its medieval history, Corbridge remained an open settlement, with no castle or any sort of fortification which could have defended all its inhabitants. As a consequence it suffered greatly at the hands of Regnald the Dane in 914 and of King David I in 1138. King John visited the area three times to look vainly for hidden treasure amongst the ruins of Corstopitum, which he believed had once been a prosperous town suddenly destroyed by an earthquake.

There were innumerable small raids during the thirteenth century but they failed to stop Corbridge becoming a fairly affluent town. King John had revoked its royal status in 1204 and the manor had been granted to the lords of Warkworth. It went from them to the Percys of Alnwick in 1332, but no matter who was the owner, the inhabitants did quite well for themselves, trading mainly in iron taken from local ironstone deposits.

In stark contrast, the fourteenth and fifteenth centuries were catastrophic and saw the town plunge to the status of a slovenly village. King Edward I's provocation of the Scots was largely to blame for this. William Wallace attacked in 1297, and Robert Bruce made unwelcome visits in 1311, 1312 and 1314. Then, taking advantage of the resulting melancholy, the Mitford Gang played havoc in 1317, riding daily from their local headquarters at Aydon.

After 1323 the storm eased a little and the people of Corbridge set about rebuilding their lives. The famous Stagshaw Fairs, held six times a year on Stagshaw Bank Common, about two miles north of the town, no doubt brought in many visitors with money to spend. But in 1346 tragedy returned in the shape of King David II, Robert Bruce's son, who was intend on invading England while King Edward II was otherwise engaged in France. He used Corbridge as a supply base, and the town's fabric and food stocks suffered as a consequence. The inhabitants did not object at all when eventually he marched off to his defeat at Neville's Cross.

It was not long after this when an even more terrifying visitor descended on them – the Black Death. Many people in 1349 camped out in the surrounding fields, but the disease took a heavy toll nevertheless and left Corbridge a miserable village once more.

Its recovery took centuries to complete. Even the building of its bridge over the Tyne in 1674 brought little relief, and as recently as 1830 the Rev. John Hodgson said this about Corbridge: "Its streets are filthy with middens and pigsties, its people looking half fed, the women sallow, thin armed and the men flabby, pot-bellied and tender-footed." The pastor-historian was not displaying much Christian charity, however, as there are several fine houses in the village which were built before his time, and W.W. Tomlinson, writing just fifty years later, was able to enthuse about "one of the most picturesque and interesting of Northumbrian villages, as it is one of the most considerable". He told us also that "Corbridge has become one of the most popular health resorts in the county".

Of the two medieval fortified homes the town boasts of, the most frequently noticed is the vicar's tower, built in the churchyard in 1318. Corbridge belonged to the lords of Warkworth at that time, so they probably helped to finance its construction. It is very small but immensely sturdy, with walls of Roman stones, a vaulted ground floor and mural stairs to two upper floors. There is still an overhanging parapet and the door, possibly original, is of oak boards bolted onto an iron grille.

The other tower, Low Hall, is at the east end of Main Street, opposite Monksholme, an elegant seventeenth century house. The tower is attached to a house which may be even older than this, although not so old as the tower itself, a fifteenth century building. It was built by a member of the Baxter family, most likely Thomas Baxter who was named as a freeholder in 1500.

Lancelot Baxter sold the property in 1625 to George Prinne of London, who settled it on his illegitimate daughter, Abigaile, wife of John Nichol of Alderham in Hertfordshire. It seems rather like father sweeping his mistake under the carpet, yet the Nichols thrived in the rough northern ambience for they stayed nearly fifty years. The next buyer was Sir Francis Radcliffe, who bought it for his friend, Richard Gibson of Hexham. It passed down the Gibson line, one of them renovating both hall and tower, inserting refinements like mullioned windows in each and mounting a sundial dated 1700, until Richard Gibson had the property confiscated for joining the 1715 Jacobite rebellion. He died in prison and Low Hall was sold to John Aynsley.

The tower is a well preserved rectangle with a vaulted ground floor, a staircase which is in the thickness of the wall for part of the way then converts to a newel type, a pitched roof and a parapet walk all around. The combined tower and house is probably the most interesting building in Corbridge, yet few people stop to look at it. It was put on the market in 1993 with an asking price of £375,000, and in 1995 the new owner obtained planning permission to make a few minor alterations.

Area 9, Sub-Area A   River Tyne, Northern Drainage Area
Portgate

L87   P547   NY987686   4 km, 2¹/₂ miles, north of Corbridge

This was where the Roman Dere Street cut through the Roman Wall, 2¹/₂ miles north of Corstopitum. Nowadays there is a pub and a garage at the junction of the A68 Corbridge to Jedburgh road and the B6318 Military Road, but no sign of a medieval fortification either here or at Portgate Farm, a few yards to the west. We are assured by John Warburton such a building did exist in 1715, and he is probably correct as the area has been held by wealthy people since 1335.

Thomas Shawes of York and his descendants leased the land from that date to 1537 from the Archbishop of York, who owned it as it was in the parish of St. John Lee, a part of Hexhamshire. When Hexham Priory was dissolved Sir Reynold Carnaby assumed ownership, and his family retained it until Sir Edward Radcliffe bought it is 1613. The Radcliffes were squirrels regarding property, but for some unknown reason they got rid of Portgate after only forty years to Richard Errington of Beukley. Some years later it was passed to Richard's grandson, Edward Widdrington.

Portgate probably never attracted many visitors – not peaceful ones, anyway – but Stagshaw Bank Common, on its southern boundary, was a great magnet six times a year when the Stagshaw Fairs were held. The really big fair took place on 4th July, those on 6th May, Whitson Eve and 26th September were nearly as important, while smaller 'Wiste' fairs were held on 5th August and 24th October. All were essentially cattle, sheep and horse markets and attracted farmers and dealers from all over northern England and southern Scotland, but they were also great social gatherings and crowds thronged to them to buy and sell "all things moveable" from the side stalls. The main fair started in 1204 and continued until 1927 – over seven hundred years of bargaining!

Halton Tower

L87   P547   NY997678 $3^1/_2$ km, $2^1/_4$ miles, north of Corbridge

The Halton family were Anglians and had held this thanage for centuries before the Normans came. It was probably part of the royal township of Corbridge which the Norman kings were content to leave alone, but later it was a separate entity, for when King John revoked the regal status and awarded Corbridge manor to the lords of Warkworth, Halton was not included and the resident family continued to hold their land on 'drengage' tenure, paying their rent directly to the king, not to any baron.

William de Halton died in 1212 possessing Clarewood (NZ019700) and Great Whittington (NZ005707) as well as Halton. Sewingshields (NY811705) was added between 1266 and 1315. William's son, another William, managed to lose Halton temporarily in 1218 when the litigious Simon of Rudchester put forward a claim to it which the court thought had some merit and ordered the matter to be settled by personal combat, which Simon won. It returned to the Halton fold in 1233 when William's son John bought it back.

John was knighted as a reward for holding several royal appointments, including sheriff in 1266. For all that, he did not have much respect for the law for on at least one occasion he lifted some cattle from Wark and hid them at Sewingshields. He was arrested thirteen years later but bought himself out of trouble. When he died in 1287 it was found he had added more land to the family's portfolio – an estate in Hartburn parish.

Just before John's son, William, died, in 1297, William Wallace and his Scottish guerrillas set fire to the timber home at Halton, and a stone replacement was put in hand. Very little of this building remains – just a doorway and some masonry – as it was practically rebuilt in the late fifteenth century.

Another Sir John, William's son, was head of the family at the time of Bannockburn and, to protect his family, he made an illegal deal with Robert Bruce, perhaps with Gilbert de Middleton as well. When news of this leaked out Sir John was arrested on a charge of 'treasonable complicity'; he escaped imprisonment and forfeiture, but a fine was imposed which he could pay only by selling all his property. He was lucky: his two daughters had married wealth in the shape of brothers Robert and Thomas Lowther, and these husbands were able to buy Halton, Great Whittington and Clarewood for their father-in-law.

This generous act made everyone happy until Sir John died. Then the division of the property led to altercation, for Thomas had died by then and his widow had married William Carnaby, who disputed Robert's right to take the whole property. The argument rolled on until Robert died in 1383, when the court declared for the Carnabys.

Just before he died, round about 1380, Robert built a tower adjoining his house at Halton. This still exists, in a well preserved state. It was built with Roman stones, it has bartizans sticking out on corbels at each corner, a ground floor vault, a flat roof and stairs which are spiral to the first floor then mural to the second and third floors. William Carnaby II got the benefit of this when the court allowed him to take over, but it did not save him and many of his servants from capture when the Scots attacked in 1385. They had to pay ransom for their freedom.

The Carnaby descent through the fifteenth and first half of the sixteenth centuries was unremarkable. Then in 1528 Sir Reynold and his brother Thomas ingratiated themselves with Henry Percy, Earl of Northumberland, and this led to the rather unsavoury performance connected with the dissolution of Hexham Priory, from which Sir Reynold emerged in victorious mood in 1537. It is satisfying to report, however, that his beaten adversary in this affair, Sir John Heron of Chipchase, did have the last little chuckle. One of Carnaby's prizes was Heron's job as keeper of Tynedale, an appointment as unwelcome to William Charlton, leader of the notorious North Tynedalers, as it was to Heron himself. Charlton and Heron had a long established secret and mutually advantageous 'understanding' which enabled them to play a little charade now. The reivers kidnapped Carnaby and held him prisoner, then Heron came along and rescued him. This apparently courageous act, so generously and efficiently carried out to help an old foe, impressed the authorities enormously and Heron was given his job back.

In 1540 Sir Reynold bought Aydon Hall for Cuthbert, the youngest of his brothers, but he continued to live at Halton until he died in 1543. The estate remained intact, and for a further hundred years the Carnabys prospered. Sir William Carnaby was Member of Parliament for Morpeth in 1623 and again in 1640, but his Royalist sympathies barred him from the

House in 1642. He remained loyal to the king throughout the Civil War and fought on Marston Moor in 1644, making it necessary for him to live abroad during the interregnum. The family lost much of their wealth during this period; Aydon Hall was the first property to be sold, and the last was Halton itself, in 1695. The buyer, who paid the princely sum of £4600, was generous enough to allow William to remain in the property until he died in 1700. He was John Douglas, Newcastle's town clerk. During those five years of waiting he had an elegant two-storey house built against the walls of the tower. This, the tower and the fifteenth century house still stand and make a delightful group framed by a pleasant garden.

John Douglas bought Aydon Hall in 1702, and in 1715 he settled both properties on his son Oley when he got married. Eventually Oley's daughter inherited, and when she married in 1751 Halton and Aydon passed to her husband, Sir Edward Blackett of Matfin. Halton is still a Blackett home.

There is a small chapel in the grounds of Halton Tower, built by John Douglas in 1706 to replace a much older building. He incorporated parts of the old, notably some Roman stones, some fourteenth century detail and an early Norman chancel arch. The old building had replaced an even older church of the Anglian era: according to the Anglo-Saxon Chronicles, it had been erected in memory of Aelfwold (sometimes Alfward), who was king of Northumbria from 779 to his murder in the vicinity in 788. He was slain "by Sicga on September 23BC 788, and a heavenly light was often seen there where he was killed; he was buried at Hexham in the church". [**Plate 11**]

Aydon Hall

L87   P548   NZ001662   2 km, 1¼ miles, north-east of Corbridge

Aydon was granted to Walter de Burum, Baron of Bolam, by King John in 1204, and thus it and Shortflatt, the two principal properties which developed from that barony, are closely bound together.

When Walter died in 1206 his widow Emma married Peter de Vaux and they lived in a timber house at Shortflatt. Emma's two daughters by her first marriage married two brothers: Aline took John Cauz and inherited Shortflatt, and Alice took James Cauz and got Aydon – two As married two Js! Both couples died before 1250, but both produced one daughter before doing so. Aline and John's Margery married William de Bretum and held Shortflatt, and Alice and James's Mary (two M's!) married Thomas de Bickering and held Aydon, but because they lived in Lincolnshire they arranged for the other couple to act as their agents.

The Shortflatt descend passed from Bretums through Gosbecks to Reymes, all acting as agents for Aydon. Robert de Reymes was the first to take an active interest in Aydon: he lived at Shortflatt until his house there was burnt down by enemy action in c1296, so he moved to Aydon and started to build a stone house there. The work was badly interrupted on two occasions by William Wallace's guerrilla-type incursions, experiences which convinced Robert he needed a fortification. He obtained a licence to crenellate in 1305, and, armed with this, he completed a superior, very strong fortified manor-house, Aydon Hall.

The Hall did well to rebuff the enemy without – Robert Bruce tried three time to force an entry without success – but no amount of armour can deter the enemy within. While Reymes was fighting at Bannockburn in 1314 Hugh de Gales, the custodian of the Hall, opened the door to a party of plunderers who did much damage to fabric and furniture and stole goods valued at £300. When he returned, Robert petitioned King Edward II for compensation and received not one penny.

Gales must have had a very smooth tongue, for he kept his job as custodian although he remained a traitor to his employer. In 1317, while the owner was again absent, he allowed three members of Gilbert Middleton's Mitford Gang to take up temporary residence and to use the place as a base from which to terrorize Corbridge and the surrounding countryside.

Poor Robert lost practically everything, for his house and estate at Shortflatt were wasted as well, and he was left with an income of only 73 pence a year. He did his best to recover, and even succeeded in becoming a Member of Parliament in 1322, but he died a broken man the next year.

His son, another Robert, had no better luck. In 1346 Scottish King David captured Aydon Hall and lodged in it while his troops occupied Corbridge. Then in 1349 he died, a victim of the Black Death.

He left three sons, the eldest two of whom died young to leave the youngest, Nicholas, to inherit. He was the family's black sheep and was in gaol for harbouring murderers at the time so could not take possession until 1376. That was the year the Bickerings' descendants decided the agency agreements should end and Aydon should belong to the Reymes. Thus Shortflatt and Aydon were united under one owner.

Nicholas died in 1394 and his son married Margaret Ogle. Then followed a straight line of descent through the fifteenth and sixteenth centuries – all eldest sons and all called Robert – until it reached Robert X who broke the tradition and christened his first born John. But by then the family had lost Aydon: it was sold to Sir Reynold Carnaby of nearby Halton Tower in 1540.

Cuthbert Carnaby inherited Aydon from his elder brother in 1543. He put in a lot of much needed work on the Hall, restoring its former strength and adding to its comfort. It stayed in the family until financial troubles necessitated its sale in 1653. Captain William Collinson of Tynemouth bought it for £653, made some minor improvements and his son sold it in 1702 for £2350.

The Collinsons proved to be the last owner-occupiers; the next owner, John Douglas, Newcastle's town clerk, put in a farmer, and it continued to be used as a farmhouse until Sir Edward Blackett of Matfin acquired it by marrying John Douglas's granddaughter, Ann. The Blacketts passed it to the Ministry of Works in 1966.

English Heritage, the present custodians, have carefully and sympathetically restored the old place to its medieval splendour. It is roughly diamond shaped, three sides of which sit atop the steep, wooded banks of the Cor Burn. The house occupies the southern side and walls surround the other sides, a D-shaped tower gracing their northern angle. Within their confines, besides the house, there is a large outer courtyard, two inner courtyards, an orchard and the site of employees' lodgings. The main rooms of the house are at first floor level, reached by an outside staircase, and include a hall, a solar and a kitchen. Below the hall is the original kitchen complete with fireplace, the chimney of which runs up the outer face of the wall and ends below the eaves, surely a rather smokey arrangement.

It was opened to the public in 1986 and visitors are welcome during the summer. The Hall is a happy place, often besieged by children who are brought here from schools all over northern England for a few hours of medieval life. They dress and act the parts of their ancestors, preparing and eating appropriate food, brewing ale, growing herbs, spinning wool and dancing and singing to the music of long ago, all under the knowledgeable eye of a leader provided by English Heritage. Visitors will not find the children distracting – they are far too interested in what they are doing to run wild – and the 'hands-on' experience they are gaining seems so worthwhile; what better way could there be to show them what life was like before television and computers, how better could they be introduced to the joys of history?

Newton Hall

L87   P548   NZ039650   4¹/₂ km, 2³/₄ miles, north-east of Corbridge

Here is an unhappy example of planning law failure. In the *County History Volume VI*, published in 1902, is a detailed description and dimensioned plan of a fourteenth century tower at Newton Hall, but alas, it is no more. It was scheduled as a listed building in 1939, but somehow it has missed later recordings, so when the Hunday Tractor Museum was being constructed out of the Hall's old stables in 1979-80 there was nothing to stop the tower's stones being reused in the village and its site being occupied by the museum's entrance and shop. The well in the tower became a wishing well. The museum has closed now, but there is no way of restoring our bit of heritage.

The tower described in 1902 and which existed at least to 1939 equalled in size to Chipchase and Cocklaw towers but differed from them in having huge buttresses at each corner, set diagonally across the angle made by the walls. The buttress in one corner had contained a gardrobe, the bottom of its shaft being still visible. A good amount of walling remained, standing from six to eight feet high and with ashlar in good condition. They were nine or ten feet thick. The entrance was missing but a jamb stone and step had been found. Inside the tower had been a draw well said to be thirty feet deep.

The name 'Newton Hall' applied to a whole manor within the Balliol's barony of Bywell, and not just to a hall and tower. There is a village with the same name and it has a rather special church which has been described as a miniature cathedral.

Baron Bernard de Balliol granted this manor to Otwell de Lisle of East Woodburn in the mid-twelfth century for a quarter of a knight's fee. It was assessed for lay subsidy in 1250 at £7.70, and in 1296 at £9.78. The mainline Lisles made it their principal seat, leaving Hall Yards to a cadet family.

The Lisles held many public appointments and became rich as a result. They acquired several estates – the best investment in those days – including, in 1421, one in Felton formerly belonging to Sir Robert de Lisle's brother-in-law, Sir Ralph de Eure. The family held it until 1659.

Sir Humphrey Lisle gave Newton Hall to his sister Elizabeth in 1505 when she married William Hayning, but he repossessed when the couple died childless and when he died in 1516 his son Sir William inherited.

This lad developed an alarming criminal talent in 1527 and was hung, drawn and quartered in 1529. Both Newton Hall and Felton were confiscated by the Crown, but were returned to Sir William's son, another Humphrey, in 1536. He preferred to live in Felton and sold Newton Hall in 1537 to Sir Reginald Carnaby, a brother of Sir Reynold of Halton, who in due course split Newton Hall three ways between his three daughters. Complications are best resolved by tabulations:-

Part 1	Part 2	Part 3
Catherine	*Ursula*	*Mabel*
married	married	married
Cuthbert, Lord Ogle	Edward Widdrington	George Lawson
	had son	had son
	Roger Widdrington	Edward Lawson
	who married	who sold in 1613
	Mary Radcliffe	to
Short break during	and gave to	Cuthbert Radcliffe
Commonwealth	Sir Francis Radcliffe	son of Sir Francis

Part 1	Part 2 & Part 3
	Radcliffe Family
	Confiscated by Crown in 1715 and granted to
	Greenwich Hospital
Ogles sold 1789 to	who leased,
Robert Jobling	later sold
inherited by	to
Sir John Cresswell Jobling	William Jobling

1843: whole manor united and owned by Jobling family

Unfortunately, the responsibility of all three parts, plus some imprudent speculation in lead mining, were too much for the Jobling purse and in 1850 they had to sell Newton Hall to Captain C.E. Blackett. He sold to Colonel John Joicey in 1869, then, c1900, it was bought by a trust and the hall was converted into Mowden Hall preparatory school.

Nafferton

L88   P548   NZ073657   8½ km, 5¼ miles, north-east of Corbridge

Guy Tisun was appointed by King Henry II in 1155 to be the coroner for Northumberland south of the River Aln, and as remuneration he was granted a serjeanty comprising a small part of Newcastle, West Matfin and Nafferton. The post does not appear to have been heritable for the next coroner was Sewal son of Henry, and after him, in 1210, Philip de Ulcotes.

Ulcotes was a most unsuitable candidate for a law office, but he got the job because he was a friend of King John. By all accounts he was an unsavoury villain who blackmailed and stole from the neighbouring gentry. This made him a lot of enemies, but he felt safe from them while he had the protection of the king. When the king died, in 1217, he had to resort to more conventional protection and started to build a tower at Nafferton. He failed to get the necessary permission to do this, so the building did not get very far.

Fortifications built without a licence to crenellate issued by the king were 'adulterous' and could be objected to. Richard de Umfraville reckoned Ulcotes' building would be an "offence to Prudhoe Castle", his home less than four miles away. He managed to get a writ issued to stop work at Nafferton, and to make sure this was obeyed the sheriff of Newcastle confiscated all Ulcotes' building timber.

What was left after 1221 was very endurable and either reasonably waterproof or capable of being made so, for it was made use of in the sixteenth or seventeenth century by another villain – Long Lonkin. His criminal activities earned him notoriety in his lifetime, but in death ballad and folklore have elevated him still higher on the scale of wickedness. His fame is such that even modern Ordinance Survey maps call Nafferton tower 'Lonkin's Hall'.

Only a short length of masonry is left of this building. It used to be seen from Whittle Dene lay-by on the A69 Hexham to Newcastle road, but growing trees have hidden it now.

Welton

L87   P548   NZ065675   8 km, 5 miles, north-east of Corbridge

Welton Hall and Slate House, 300 yards to its west, are the only remains of the medieval village of Waltheden, part of Prudhoe barony and a gift the Umfravilles gave to the Prior of Tynemouth. He leased it in 1189 to a local man called Simon of Welton, but soon it became a collection of smallholders. It boasted a fine church dedicated to St. Michael, but this disappeared from the records after a couple of centuries, inspite of a growing population which in 1538 provided no fewer than forty-one men – fifteen mounted – for watch duty on the Border.

Simon of Welton's descendants dominated the scene until the seventeenth century and lived in the manor-house now called Welton Hall. It became desireable to fortify this during the fifteenth century so a strong tower was built against its west wall. Quite small, only 24 by 20 feet with 5 feet thick walls, it was built with Roman stones which, it has been suggested, were third-hand; there is a trefoiled window in the tower which has an ecclesiastical air about it, smelling a little like church plunder. There were two upper floors reached by internal stairs.

The manor-house was virtually rebuilt in 1614, without disturbing the tower which was retained for emergencies. The owner at this time was William 'Long Will' Welton. Legend has it that he slept in the kitchen, the largest room in the house, with his head against one wall and his feet touching the wall opposite.

Another legend concerns another tall man, Long Lonkin of Nafferton. He is supposed to have called at Welton Hall one evening in the seventeenth century when the master was absent. Orange, a maid and possibly a partner in crime, was downstairs nursing a baby, while the mistress was upstairs. Orange was told to prick the baby, whose resultant screams brought the lady rushing downstairs – to be killed by Larkin. He then ransacked the building without fear of interruption.

The whole village, Hall and tower included, was sold in 1694 by Long Will's son, Michael, to Sir William Blackett of Wallington. He was agriculture's new broom and quickly brushed away the village and all its smallholdings to make a large and efficient farm. He installed his farmer in Welton Hall, adding farm buildings to it.

The Hall is still inhabited, while the adjoining tower remains as a tall ruin. They may be seen from the road to their north, but their southern faces are more interesting. The residential part is particularly pleasing, exhibiting a two-storey bay window of fine proportions and a large chimney-stack; the farmer's permission is necessary before these can be seen.

Rudchester

L88   P548   NZ112673   12 km, 7½ miles, north-east of Corbridge

The eastern section of the Newcastle to Carlisle Military Road is constructed on top of the Roman Wall, and thus goes right through the middle of this Roman station, built by Emperor Hadrian. He called it Vindovala according to the Ravenna list, Vindobala according to the Notitia, and it was used by foreign auxiliaries until the Romans retired from Northumberland. On one occasion it was put out of action by fire which reddened some of its stones which were used much later to build nearby houses, and this is said to be why the English name is Rudchester. Although parts of the station were excavated in 1924 and 1962 the soil was returned and only some bumps in the ground can be seen now; so far it has escaped the tourist industry.

To the south of the station is Rudchester Hall, a charming eighteenth century mansion incorporating a medieval fortified tower. This is not obvious from the outside, but inside the wall thickness and the top of the tower beneath the rafters give the game away.

This was Umfraville country in the twelfth century, part of Prudhoe barony. Odinel II Umfraville, who lived until 1181, granted Rudchester to his steward, Eilaf, son of Roger, and Eilaf's cousin, Simon, inherited both the job and the land during the tenure of Richard Umfraville, from 1195 to 1226. This Simon, who styled himself Simon of Rudchester, was quite a character: he was a litigious freak. Going to court to make wild accusations or improbable claims was his hobby, and, while usually the only harm done was to his purse, on one occasion he actually tasted success. His claim to be the rightful owner of Halton was judged to have some merit and had to be settled by single combat. Simon's champion won the duel so Halton became his – until the Halton family bought it back in 1233.

Another Simon built Rudchester tower in 1285 and his descendants lived in it until the fifteenth century, until a daughter inherited it and passed it to William Rutherford, her husband. They and their descendants were staunch Roman Catholics who did much to uphold their faith when it was proscribed. A pursuivant called Fenwick attempted to serve a sixteenth century Rutherford with a warrant for his arrest on the charge of harbouring a priest. Rutherford managed to escape, but he left his wife and daughter hiding in a secret priest's hole in the tower. Fenwick settled down in the tower to wait; all was quiet for two days, but on the third Rutherford returned and gave himself up, having realised that any further delay would have killed his family, who had no food in their hiding place.

Being Catholics, they supported the Royalists during the Civil War so had their property forfeited to the Commonwealth government. King Charles II returned it, but soon afterwards, in 1667, the Rutherfords sold their tower to Thomas Riddell of Fenham.

There has been a succession of owners since then, but the Riddells stayed long enough to build the present mansion. There was still enough of the old tower to make it worth while incorporating it into the new building, and in fact its entire southern wall is original, although now punctured with Georgian windows.

As well as further evidence of thirteenth century fortifications, the house contains two surprises. One is a fireplace of Roman stone which included a Roman Cohort and Centurial Stone taken from the Wall. The other is a recently uncovered window in the eastern wall. It is very small and quite useless, obviously taken from some other building, perhaps for sentimental reasons. It looks extremely old, but perhaps not quite as old as Saxon, as the present owner suggests.

Area 9, Sub-Section B   River Tyne, North Bank
Anick

L87   P547   NY955655   4 km, 2½ miles, north-west of Corbridge

Anick is pronounced 'A-nick' to distinguish it from the Duke of Northumberland's town. It is a small collection of prestigious houses and a pub called 'The Rat' set high on the northern bank of the Tyne with gorgeous views across the river and into Dilston Park. One of the houses started life as a bastle, and adjoining houses may well have been converted from its farm buildings.

Except that it was in Hexhamshire and owned by the Archbishop of York from 1071 to 1545, there is little to tell about Anick. Sir William Fenwick owned it in 1663 when it had seven tenants, all apparently law-abiding and avoiding the records. The bastle was remodelled as a conventional farmhouse circa 1700, but the thick walls and the surrounds of both ground and first floor doors remain. The south front has had five windows and a door inserted, and an extension has been built onto the north face.

Beaufront

L87   P547   NY963659   5 km, 3 miles, north-west of Corbridge

The beautiful, south-facing ediface seen from all the three roads which join Corbridge to Hexham is an 1841 John Dobson creation lacking the slightest trace of medieval masonry. Nevertheless, its site is an historic one for which records exist which go back to 1225. It was part of Hexhamshire and was leased by the Archbishop of York in that year to Peter de Vaux, a direct descendant of Robert de Vallibus who founded Lanacost Priory in 1169.

Peter had two wives, the second the widow of Walter de Burum of Bolam. It was a daughter of the first marriage, however, who inherited the Beaufront lease. She married John de Errington, a younger son of the Erringtons of Cocklaw, and it is generally assumed that it was he who built a tower on the site in c1380.

The Erringtons were related by marriage to the Carnabys of Halton, and John assisted Robert and William II Carnaby in their struggle to ease the Halton property out of the hands of Robert Lowther. The bond between the two families must have been very strong as between 1380 and 1572 junior branches of the two took turns in occupying Beaufront tower.

In 1572 Hexhamshire became Crown land and was sold en bloc to Sir John Forster, who immediately transferred the deeds of Beaufront to Regnold Carnaby. The mainline Erringtons bought it from him in 1586 and moved there from Cocklaw tower. Very soon they built a large barrack-like mansion which incorporated some of the tower it replaced. It was surrounded by a castellated wall adorned with stone figures of heathen dieties; they appear to have kept the family safe for two and a half centuries.

William Errington was head of the family in 1713. He was a Roman Catholic and a Stuart sympathizer, but astute enough to keep out of trouble in 1715. He remained at home but sent his younger brother, Thomas to join the Jacobite rebellion; he was captured at Preston but eventually pardoned.

John Errington, William's grandson, inherited Beaufront in 1748. He had the reputation of being a "bit of a character" whose "many whimsical ways" endeared him to his neighbours. Henry Swinburne was less charitable when he said John was "as cracked as ever man was". However he quite sensibly contributed to the building in 1780 of Hexham's bridge over the Tyne; it was called 'Mr Errington's Bridge' because of this, and he was the first person to cross it, but in fact his contribution was less than the £3000 obtained by selling material salvaged from the previous bridge, and the £5000 granted by the County Council. The bridge collapsed during the floods of 1781. Undeterred, John spent a huge sum, reputed to be £20,000, on landscaping and creating gardens in his Beaufront estate. In 1779 John fancied he was the Duke of Hexham and applied to King George III for confirmation; all he got was a certificate of lunacy. He died, unmarried, in 1827, to end the direct line of the ancient Errington family.

Trustees sold Beaufront in 1836 to William Cuthbert of Redheugh, near Newcastle. The existing building was completed in 1841 by Dobson, who considered it to be his best work. It has been converted into several separate apartments.

Styford

L87   P548   NZ016622   3¹/₂ km, 2¹/₄ miles, south-east of Corbridge

In Anglian times both Styford and Bywell were components in a vast thanage belonging to the family of Waltheof, Earl of Northumberland from c995 to c1006. In the eighth century a monastery was established at Bywell which became so well known in ecclesiastical circles it attracted not one but two contiguous parishes, each of which required a parish church. Both were built at Bywell, St. Andrew about the year 1000 and St. Peter some sixty years later.

The two parishes made a convenient division of the thanage which was made use of by one of Waltheof's successors when his daughter married Hugh de Bolbec, a Norman who had crossed the Channel a few years before the Conquest. Hugh's dowry was land roughly coincident with St. Andrew's parish, and he and his bride made their home at Styford, a couple of miles upstream from Bywell. Hugh's land was inherited by his son, Walter, and King Henry I confirmed the grant as a barony in 1100. More precisely, it excluded Stocksfield but its boundary extended beyond Styford in the west, to Bearl (NZ055641) in the north-east and to Slaley and what was to become Blanchland in the south – plus, of course, the parish church and a bit of Bywell village.

Throughout the twelfth century the Bolbec's home and Styford barony headquarters was a motte and bailey castle. The mound upon which this was built, and about half its earthworks, are still to be seen some five hundred yards west of the nineteenth century Styford Hall. It has not been built on, and its moat along the northern side is still quite deep. It commands a clear view across a meadow to the river and the Styford – Broomhaugh ford.

Walter died soon after 1141 and was succeeded by his son with the same name. He made a lasting contribution to ecclesiastical history and tourism by founding a Premonstratensian abbey in 1165 in a very secret part of the Derwent valley called Wulwardshope. It was rechristened Blanchland.

The Bolbecs lasted only to 1262, in which year Hugh de Bolbec died leaving his worldly wealth to a bevy of married daughters. By this means Styford barony was divided between the families of Lancaster, Greystoke, Huntercomb and Delaval. Further marriages and dealings reduced this consortium by early fourteenth century to just two owners, John son of Roger de Lancaster and Robert son of Ralph, Lord of Greystoke. John gave his share to his son-in-law, Sir William de Herle of Little Harle, but when this man's son died the Greystokes were able to reunite the whole barony under their flag.

But not for long, for in 1403 it was confiscated by the Crown when one member of the family joined the Percys' rebellion against King Henry IV. In 1409 it was granted to Ralph Neville, Earl of Westmorland and baron of adjacent Bywell.

After four hundred years of divided existence, the old thanage was stitched together again – or nearly so: an area around Styford's motte and bailey, just a few acres at first although it was to grow, remained outside the union as the Earl granted it to his steward, John Swinburne of Chopwell, for an annual rent of £13.33. The motte and bailey had long since lost its usefulness and Swinburne lived in a house which had most likely been built by a previous owner or tenant. This house and small estate was not forfeited when the rest of the Earl's property was taken in 1569, but in 1583 the lease, now costing £40 a year, was taken over by Sir John Forster. It remained in his family until 1708, when it was sold for £5,500 to John Bacon.

John was the grandson of George Bacon, originally of Allendale, who became a lead mining magnate and bought Staward Manor in 1664. John never had Staward, and kept Styford only forty years before dying while taking a cure at Bath. Like the rest of the family, he had been a supporter of the Stuart dynasty and, while not actually joining the Jacobites, he had assisted them by sheltering the Earl of Derwentwater in September 1715 when bailiffs were trying to arrest him.

During the Forster and Bacon eras the Styford estate expanded and developed beyond the old feudal boundaries. The house was rebuilt and a village for its domestic and farm servants grew on the road to the ford. During the eighteenth century, however – probably after John Bacon's departure – the villagers were rehoused in Broomhaugh, across the river.

Bywell

L87   P548   NZ049617   6 km, 3¾ miles, south-east of Corbridge

Like Styford, Bywell was part of the Waltheof family's thanage before the Normans came. Wilfred, while Bishop of Northumberland between 665 and 677, built a church here and this developed into a monastery a century or so later. It became the third most important north of the Tyne after Lindisfarne and Hexham, and indeed it replaced the former for at least ten years after the island monastery had been destroyed by the Vikings in 793.

Because of its idyllic setting and great popularity, the Church dignitaries decided before the Conquest to create a parish centred on Bywell, and the monastic church was reconsecrated as the parish church of St. Andrew. Some sixty years later it became obvious that the parish was too large for efficient management, and part of it was hived off to form a second, the parish of St. Peter. It too needed a parish church so a second church, St. Peter, was built in Bywell a stone's throw from St. Andrew. Both have been restored many times since those days, of course, but both are still serviceable, redolent of past glories.

The thanage was split into two parts at about the time of the Conquest, the dividing line approximating to the parochial division. Hugh de Bolbec was granted St. Andrew's part as a wedding gift and he made his home at Styford. The St. Peter's was granted as a barony by King William II to Guy de Balliol in 1093.

Guy, a knight from Picardy, actually received quite a large barony, for not only did it include St. Peter's parish and church and the greater part of Bywell village but also Stocksfield and Newton Hall in the immediate neighbourhood and several isolated pockets of land including Marwood and Gainford in Teesdale.

The Balliols never actually lived in Bywell, preferring the Tees to the Tyne. Barnard de Balliol, Guy's nephew and successor, built a castle with a large round tower on high rocks overlooking the Tees at Marwood and called it Barnard Castle. This became the family's main seat, and remained so even when their property portfolio was enlarged by gifts from their royal friends – in Yorkshire, Cleveland and Hertfordshire from King Henry I and Stephen and in Scotland from King David I. Their Scottish associations never were allowed to usurp their loyalty to the English Crown, and indeed Barnard played a prominent part in the defeat of David at the Battle of the Standard in 1138.

The 1211 Pipe Roll states that Hugh de Balliol was holding Bywell for five knights fee, and was also providing thirty men for guard duty in Newcastle; he is known to have supported King John in his quarrel with the barons. His son John succeeded him and then, in 1233, made a momentous marriage to Devorguil, the heiress of Alan, Lord of Galloway and Constable of Scotland. Her mother, Margaret, was a granddaughter of King of the Scots William the Lion, so Devorguil held a high place in Scotland's line of succession. The early consequence of this wedding was that John got control of a lot more land, making him one of the most powerful barons on both sides of the Border, yet today he is remembered chiefly as the founder of Balliol College in Oxford.

John and Devorguil had three sons. The eldest two died early and it was the youngest, another John born in 1249, who entered the 'Competition' for the Scottish throne when both King Alexander III and the Maid of Norway died, and who emerged the winner in 1292.

Poor John had a miserable four years as king of Scotland, being squeezed between the growing nationalism of his subjects and the excessive demands of King Edward I, his 'feudal superior'. He revolted against this tyranny in 1296 but failed to get the backing he needed from his nobles, who instead signed a mutual help treaty with France, the 'Auld Alliance'. This was the start of the Scottish War of Independence; Edward sacked Berwick, defeated a Scottish army at Dunbar and appointed governors more amenable to his will to run the country. Balliol was divested of all his English property, imprisoned until 1299 then allowed to live out his last years in France.

Edward Balliol, John's eldest son, tried to make a come-back while King David II, Robert Bruce's son, was a minor. He strung together a modest army of rebels from Galloway and people who had been disinherited for opposing Robert Bruce, and with this he defeated a Scottish army under the Earl of Mar at Dupplin Muir near Perth in 1332. Three months later he succumbed to the pressures put upon him by the Scottish nobility and abdicated. King Edward III won a decisive battle against a large Scottish force at Halidon Hill near Berwick in 1333 and put Balliol back on the Scottish throne. Again he failed to establish any authority over the Scots, and in 1356 he threw in his hand. That was the end of the Balliol family in the military and political fields.

Bywell barony was granted in 1299 to King Edward I's nephew, John of Brittany, Earl of Richmond. He passed it on to his niece, Mary, Countess of Pembroke, who cared nothing for the barbaric North. The Scots, prosecuting their War of Independence in their own inimitable way, were making life in Northumberland well-nigh untenable, yet the Countess did nothing to protect her villagers or hinder the enemy. She died in 1376, and John Neville took over what by then had become a very rundown estate, worth only £26.66 a year.

John was the lord of Raby Castle in County Durham and only a few miles from Barnard Castle. His wife, Maud, was a daughter of Henry Percy of Alnwick. Their son Ralph was created the first Earl of Westmorland in 1397, and in 1409 he was granted Styford barony, thus becoming the master of the whole former thanage of Bywell.

Ralph's son, also Ralph, inherited the title and property in 1426 and almost immediately started to build a castle close to the Tyne. He completed the gatehouse, a tall rectangular building pierced by a ten foot wide vaulted entrance passage, but the rest of the castle, including its walls, never rose above the height of a man. It is not known why work was abandoned – cash flow problems, perhaps, or the realisation that cannon were being made which could laugh at stone and mortar, or possibly just lack of interest, we can only guess. Archaeologists have shown that the intended fortification was to lie north of the gatehouse – ie, the side furthest from the river where now there is a garden and entrance drive – but that its construction was arrested and eventually all that had been built except for the gatehouse was pulled down.

The gatehouse had its uses, even without its accompaniment. King Henry VI fled to it after his defeat at Hexham by Lord Montagu during the Wars of the Roses in 1464: he stayed only one night then left in such a hurry he left his helmet and sword behind.

At about this time the inhabitants of Bywell village began to make a name for themselves as manufacturers of metallic accessories for horse harnesses. Large oak forests in the vicinity provided plenty of fuel for their furnaces and they could not have wished for a larger market. The only trouble was that some of their customers were Border reivers who often fancied the villagers' personal possessions as well, and never paid for anything. These criminals became a serious problem, as a 1569 report for Queen Elizabeth by Crown Commissioners Edward Hall and William Homerston pointed put:

> "The town of Bywell is built in length all of one street upon the river or water of Tyne, on the north and west part of the same and is divided into two several parishes and inhabited with handi-craftsmen, whose trade is all in iron-work for the horsemen and Borderers of that country, as in making bitts, stirrups, buckles, and such others, wherein they are very expert and cunning, and are subject to the incursions of the thieves of Tynedale, and compelled winter and summer to bring all their cattle and sheep into the street, and when the enemy approacheth to raise hue and cry, whereupon all the town prepareth for rescue of their goods, which is very populous, by reason of their trade, and stout and hardy by continual practice against the enemy".

Apart from a few full-stops, all that need be added to this account is that the street referred to, part of the 'Auld Heeway' between Newcastle and Carlisle, is thought to have connected the two churches and to have been lined with workshops and two-roomed cottages.

This report, or 'inquisition' to give it its official name, was required when all the property owned by Charles Neville, the sixth and last Earl of Westmorland, was confiscated by the Crown; Charles had misguidedly joined the Rising of the Northern Earls, a futile attempt to restore Roman Catholicism. Charles fled to Flanders where he lived in exile for a further thirty years.

The unfinished castle was surveyed in 1571, when the gatehouse was said to be in good condition and "covered with lead". The surveyors were convinced that the builder had intended to complete the fortification and its wall had not been left man-height on purpose, simply to form a barmekyn. Thirty years later the lead had been stolen; obviously the leaseholders, the Lisle family who lived at Felton, had not been keeping a very keen eye on it.

The rest of the barony was leased piecemeal by the Crown until 1625. The Fenwicks may not have been the first purchaser, but certainly by 1630 Roger Fenwick was the owner. He was the youngest son of Sir William Fenwick of Wallington and his second wife, 'Mad Meg' Selby. Roger made a lot of money mining for lead on the Allendale moors, and in 1766 a descendant, William Fenwick, felt rich enough to commission James Paine to build Bywell Hall, a lovely mansion with grounds which sweep down to the river west of the village. In 1820 the Fenwicks sold their business and their mansion to the Beaumont family, the heads of whom were later elevated to the peerage as the Lords of Allendale.

Wylam

L88   P548   NZ111646   11¹⁄₂ km, 7 miles, east of Corbridge

Originally an isolated vill in the Bywell barony, Wylam and its tithes were granted by Bernard Balliol to the Prior of Tynemouth before 1158. The Prior had a house here from that date until 1297 when William Wallace, fresh from his victory over the English at Stirling Bridge, invaded Northumberland and wasted several villages including Wylam. To compound this injury, William of Ellerington cut down trees in the village and robbed its inhabitants to the tune of £200 early in the next century.

Prior Whethamstead built a new house in 1405. It was designed to resist future raiders and was described as a tower although it was not included in any of the usual surveys and was an exceptional shape, being three times longer that it was wide. The Prior called it his 'Sporting House' for he allowed his monks to go there to 'disport' themselves. The dictionary defines 'disport' as to frolic or gambol; the mind boggles.

After dissolution in 1539 Wylam Tower was leased to John Swinburne of Chopwell, whose family held it until 1604 when a coal mining consortium took it. Simple bell-pits, perhaps a drift mine, had existed at Wylam since the thirteenth century and there was still plenty of coal to take. During the 1660s or '70s Sir William Blackett bought the whole manor and opened a deep mine, Wylam Colliery. This was still being worked, on both sides of the river, in 1825, the coal won on the south side being conveyed beneath the river to the north bank, through what must have been the Tyne's first tunnel. It continued its journey to Lemington by railway, a great novelty, which was five miles and one hour away.

The Tower, thanks to frequent repairs, lasted well into the railway age, until it was cleared away in 1880 and Wylam Hall was built in its place. During its construction a splendid tunnel-vaulted basement measuring 60 by 19 feet was unearthed, confirming that Prior Whethamstead had indeed built a substantial fortification.

Area 9 Sub-Area C   River Tyne, South Bank

Dilston

L87   P547   NY975632   1¹⁄₂ km, 1 mile, south-west of Corbridge

When Aluric retired from the sheriffship of the royal manor of Corbridge in 1118, King Henry I carved the Dilston estate out of the manor and granted it as a barony to his former representative in lieu of a pension. The old man took the name of his gift – Divelston, as it was then – as his surname, and his descendants held the barony until 1290.

The last Divelston bequeathed the barony to a distant relative called Sir William Claxton, but the courts overruled the will and directed that a cousin, William de Tyndale should get the property. The Claxton family had to wait until 1416 before they could settle into Dilston. When they did they were quick to built a tower overlooking the Devil's Water, an L-shaped structure with a vaulted ground floor and a round turret sticking out on corbels at one end.

Sir Robert Claxton died in 1484 and left Dilston to his only offspring, Joan, the bride of a few months of John Cartington. Dilston remained hers and did not pass to her husband, so when John died their daughter Anne inherited only Cartington. In due course Anne married Edward Radcliffe, a younger son of Thomas Radcliffe of Derwentwater. Their son, Cuthbert, inherited Cartington when his mother died, and Dilston when Joan, his grandmother, died in 1521. Cuthbert's eldest son inherited Dilston and a younger son got Cartington.

The Radcliffes held Dilston for close on two hundred years. The first hundred was uneventful, the second quite the reverse. Sir Edward Radcliffe welcomed in the seventeenth century by building a hall on his estate which incorporated the old, but much altered, tower as a wing. In 1629 he purchased Alston's lead mines, a very lucrative investment which provided the where-withal to buy Langley barony in 1632. He lost this during the Civil War for supporting the king, but it was put on the market, bought by a London businessman, George Hurd, and sold back to the Radcliffes for £10,000. Sir Francis, Sir Edward's son, raised this huge sum by mortgaging some Yorkshire manors owned by his mother.

Sir Francis became obsessed by property ownership and during the 1660s he bought numerous estates in Northumberland, almost as if his aim was to surpass the Percys as top landlords. Property, however, was not enough: a grand title was needed as well. He achieved this by marrying his son and heir, Edward, to Lady Mary Tudor in 1687. She was fourteen years old at the time, the illegitimate daughter of King Charles II and Mrs Moll Davis, a stage performer whom Samuel Pepys considered more talented than Nell Gwynn. Next year Sir Francis became Earl of Derwentwater, Viscount Radcliffe and Langley and Baron Tyndale.

Edward inherited his father's estates and titles in 1696. He lived in London and played no personal role in Northumberland. An active supporter of both the Roman Catholic religion and the Stuart dynasty, he failed to see anything glorious about the Glorious Revolution of 1688, and when King James II was deposed he sent his son James to be educated with the ex-king's son in St. Germain in France. The two boys became close friends.

Young James Radcliffe became the third Earl of Derwentwater on his father's death in 1705. He returned to England in 1709 and, deciding that Dilston should be his home, he put in hand the complete remodelling of Dilston Hall, working to a plan which still retained the old tower wing. He married in 1712 Anna Maria, daughter of Sir John Webb of Canford in Dorset, and they lived in Canford a couple of years until Dilston Hall was habitable. The job was never completed, but the Hall provided a happy home – for just one year.

Northumberland at this time was ripe for Jacobite rebellion. Many of the influential landed gentry and business magnates wanted the Stuart kings back for religious or economic reasons, and secret plotting and scheming was the order of the day. The accession of George I, a Hanoverian who never even bothered to learn English, acted as a catalyst, and when in August 1715 the Earl of Mar and other Scottish noblemen proclaimed the Old Pretender as James VIII of Scotland and III of England there was an animated response south of the Border.

It was generally known that the Earl of Derwentwater's sympathies were with his old school chum, and the Government issued a warrant for his arrest. He evaded the law men and went into hiding, at first at Styford then at Newbrough, and did not emerge until all was ready to declare openly for James Stuart. The Radcliffes, James and his younger brother Charles, rode up and down the county during October, picking up what support they could find. They elected a Protestant Member of Parliament, Thomas Forster of Adderstone, to be their 'general' – for public relations rather than military reasons – and a few noblemen like Lord Widdrington joined them. But many others, especially Protestants like the Blacketts and the politically shrewd like the Capheaton Swinburnes, found reasons for staying at home, and the rising was not the unqualified success hoped for. Indeed, even after the Earl of Mar had sent troops under Brigadier MacIntosh, and Lord Kenmuir had brought men from Galloway, the total force numbered only two thousand. It proved to be no match for Government troops when they met at Preston on 12th November 1715. A handful of Northumbrians managed to escape, but most, including the two Radcliffes and Forster, were taken prisoner and marched into London gaols.

Charles Radcliffe managed, eventually, to escape and fled to France (he returned for the 1745 rising, only to be captured and executed). Forster also escaped, thanks to a clever trick played by his sister Dorothea. The Earl was kept in the Tower and resolutely rejected offers of freedom if he acknowledged the Hanoverian regality and changed his religion. His wife entreated the King and the house of Lords to no avail and he was executed in February 1716. His body was brought back to Dilston in secret by Frank Stokoe of Chesterwood and laid to rest in the private chapel which still graces the estate.

Not unexpectedly, the vast Derwentwater empire was sequestrated in its entirety, although Anna and her infant son John were permitted to continue to live at Dilston until the Government decided what to do. In 1735 an Act of Parliament decreed that everything should be granted to the trustees of the Royal Hospital for Seamen at Greenwich, to pay for the completion of their building programme and to provide for future maintenance.

It was a most handsome donation, especially as the Alston lead mines were still very profitable. The hospital was fortunate, also, in securing the services of John Grey as Northern Estates Manager; he was a conscientious and efficient agriculturalist who doubled the yield of the land in a few years.

In 1765 most of the Hall at Dilston was demolished, but the old tower, now roofless, was allowed to remain with just sufficient of the attached Hall to give it a couple of windows. This ruin still makes a charming picture but has no practical value and is retained purely for romantic reasons. The private chapel a few yards from it is perhaps of more interest to architects. A new Dilston Hall was built in 1835 on the south-western side of the grounds. In 1874 the estate was sold to W.B. Beaumont, who later became the first Lord Allendale, and today it is a centre for an Advanced Social Training Establishment.

Todburn Steel

L87   P560   NY987599   4¹/₂ km, 2³/₄ miles, south of Corbridge

An isolated farm on the fringe of Dipton Wood. The farmhouse is fashioned out of two bastles, the join made about two centuries ago. The operation required the roof of the western building to be raised slightly, and the opportunity was taken to block unwanted doors and windows, the outlines of which are still discernible.

Broomhaugh

L87   P548   NZ021615   4 km, 2¹/₂ miles, south-east of Corbridge

Until comparatively recently, Broomhaugh and Riding Mill were separate villages, divided by the Ridingmill Burn. Broomhaugh, on the eastern side, was a community of smallholders whose few acres faced onto a track leading to a ford across the River Tyne. The track is now a road called Styford Street, the smallholdings have been built on and the ford, while it is still there, is fit for nothing lower and lighter that a fairground traction engine. Track and ford led to Styford and must have been used a lot when Styford Hall's servants were rehoused across the river in the eighteenth century.

There are two, possibly three bastle derivatives served by this road, built during the smallholding days. One, at the river end, is called Broomhaugh

Farm House (NZ022616) and was a larger than usual bastle before being converted into a quite imposing two storey abode.

There are two adjoining cottages at the main road end, one called Stable End, the other Yew Tree Cottage. The latter is obviously old, but it is debatable whether it was ever fortified sufficiently to be called a bastle. There is no doubting Stable End, however, although it has been much altered. A date stone engraved 1699 probably shows when an extension was built onto its free gable end, hiding a still existing ground floor door.

Eltringham

L88   P548   NZ073627   8½ km, 5¼ miles, east of Corbridge

A small farming complex containing three houses and lying near the end of a lane which runs towards the River Tyne from Mickley Square, about a mile south-west of Prudhoe. The lane is clearly market 'Cherryburn', and the farms are quite close to Thomas Bewick's birthplace.

Eltringham House (pronounce the 'g' softly, as in Ovingham) is the most westerly building in the complex. From the front it looks like a pleasant two-gables stone house with two bay windows and a parapet-like decoration between the first floor and attic windows. This face, and probably the extension at the rear, are c1800 work, but the main house behind the facade is a fortified, early sixteenth century strong house with walls 4½ feet thick.

The gables give the game away, that facing west being the most revealing. It is constructed with rough, irregular stones but the outline of two blocked doors, one above the other, can be seen clearly. The east gable is similarly constructed and contains three small outlines of former windows which have been blocked rather carelessly.

Little is known about the history of the place, except that it belonged to a family called Newton from early sixteenth century. Seven year old John Newton inherited it in 1569.

Prudhoe Castle

L88   P548   NZ091634   10 km, 6¼ miles, east of Corbridge

Inspite of its twentieth century industrial surroundings, Prudhoe Castle is arguably the best, most revealing, Norman keep and bailey castle in Northumberland. The only thing which is alien to the archetypal layout is a house built between the inner and outer baileys. English Heritage, its guardian now, not only welcomes visitors but also invites schools to send whole classes for live history lessons, spending a day enacting a typical medieval existence.

Robert de Umfraville, son of 'Robert with the Beard', the first Lord of Redesdale Liberty, was awarded the barony of Prudhoe by King Henry I in

1133 or '34. He and his son built a motte and bailey on a ridge – mainly natural but with a slave-dug ditch part way round – which overlooks the Tyne. Recent excavations have revealed the probable positions of timber buildings and an enclosing palisade, and have indicated that the latter was replaced by a mud and stone bulwark. The Umfravilles probably moved to Prudhoe from Elsdon as soon as suitable accommodation was completed, for life there must have been more pleasant and safer than in Redesdale.

Odinel's son, Odinel II, spent much time between 1150 and his death in 1181 replacing the motte and bailey, section by section, with a stone keep and bailey castle. The curtain wall with the nucleus of the existing gatehouse was the first part to be completed, with the keep following either just before or just after 1173; the precise date does not matter as the curtain wall proved enough to restrain the Scots in that year, and again in 1174.

These raids were of a personal nature. During the 1140s, while Northumberland was a Scottish earldom, Ordinel II had been brought up at the Earl's court at Warkworth, where he shared this privilege with the future king of Scotland, William the Lion. The two boys were about the same age and became great friends, so later, after he had been crowned, William expected Odinel's support when he tried to regain Northumberland for his country. He had not counted on Odinel's loyalty to his king, which proved to be stronger than childhood ties. This so annoyed William that when Newcastle's defences frustrated him in 1173 he marched up the Tyne and besieged Odinel's castle at Prudhoe. Further frustration.

Next year, 1174, William went straight to Prudhoe, hoping to catch the castle unprepared. Once more the attack was unsuccessful, but in a show of pique William's army did manage to destroy the corn in neighbouring fields and to strip the bark off apple trees in the castle's orchard. Odinel had not been in his castle while this was going on; he was staying in Newcastle, keeping a close watch on events, and when William was homeward bound he force-marched a small army to Alnwick where it surprised the Scots and captured their king. William was kept a prisoner for a year, then was released after paying homage to King Henry II and promising never again to invade England.

The position and obvious strength of Prudhoe Castle lent it considerable influence in the control of the mid-Tyne valley. It was a psychological deterrent as well as a physical one, and few direct attacks upon it are recorded – and none that was successful.

The free-standing keep in the inner bailey was not large in area – only 41 by 44 feet – but it was tall and awesome. Two semicircular towers dominated the western corners of the wall. A grand hall was added to the bake house, brew house, soldiers' quarters and stables in the outer bailey: as at Warkworth, it would appear that the lord required more comfort than a keep could provide. The gatehouse was the pièce de résistance, however, and still is. Odinel's twelfth century building was single storeyed with a vaulted passage and Norman arch resting on two corbels carved as heads. During the thirteenth century another floor was added to carry a chapel, the lancet windows of which were corbelled out to make what is regarded as the earliest English oriel window. A guardroom on a second floor was added in the fourteenth century, as was an extra long barbican.

During the 1320s the constable of the castle was ordered to build a 'Peel Yard' beyond the outer bailey, presumably for the protection of villagers. This would have been a palisaded enclosure and there is no evidence of it now.

Odinel II's grandson, Gilbert, married Maud, Countess of Angus, in 1243, and their son, Gilbert II, who inherited the following year, assumed the title Earl of Angus. He also married well, taking Elizabeth, daughter of Alexander Comyn, Earl of Buchan, as his bride in the 1270s. They had no children so succession went to uncle Robert, who had four sons. One of these, Gilbert III, eventually inherited the titles and estates, and another, Ingrim, served as a commander in King Edward II's army at Bannockburn in 1314. A story is told about him which illustrates the healthy disrespect the professional soldiers held for their king's fighting capabilities. Just before battle commenced, Ingrim and the king saw Robert Bruce's men at prayer. "See, yon men kneel for mercy", said Edward, to which Ingrim replied, "You say truth; they ask for mercy, but not from you". Perhaps a little prayer on the English side would have helped; the king had to flee and Ingrim was killed.

Gilbert III produced no heirs although he married twice. His second wife was Maud de Lucy who had inherited Langley barony in 1367. The Earl of Angus thus had control of a large slice of Northumberland – Redesdale, Prudhoe and now Langley – as well as much property in Scotland. When he died, in 1381, Redesdale liberty was settled on a close relative, Thomas de Umfraville, but Prudhoe and Langley stayed with widow Maud until she died, in 1398, when they went to her second husband, Henry Percy, Earl of Northumberland. Other members of the family objected to this, and it was not until 1441 that the transfer was legalized.

Gilbert's death meant the end of the mainline Umfravilles, and Thomas's branch at Elsdon and Harbottle lasted only to 1436. Other cadet branches kept the name going, however – in ever reducing circumstances – to 1833 when Captain John Brand Umfraville RN, the son of a workhouse keeper, died childless.

The Percys neglected Prudhoe Castle, and from the end of the fourteenth to the beginning of the nineteenth centuries about the only work done was the building of a house between the inner and outer baileys in c1413 while King Henry IV's son, the Duke of Bedford, had a temporary hold on the barony.

During the sixteenth and seventeenth centuries the castle was leased quite often to people prepared to put up with a crumbling abode for the sake of a prestigious address. Thomas Bates was one until he got mixed up in the Rising of the Northern Earls in 1569. Lady Heron was another, and Reynold Heron was a third. His annual rental was £66.62, a sum he was loath to pay; he was evicted in 1627, having paid no rent for seven years.

Good times returned when Hugh Percy became the second Duke of Northumberland in 1786. He did a thorough overhaul of the castle, and in 1808 he built a mansion in Georgian architectural style to replace the fifteenth century house so that he could provide suitable lodgings for a relative. The mansion continued to be a home until 1966; now English Heritage have mounted a small exhibition in it.

Area 10
The South-East

Key Town: Newcastle upon Tyne
Sub-Areas:
A Greater Newcastle
B North Tyneside and
   South-East
   Northumberland
Note: Distances from
   Newcastle are from
   the Central Station.

A s well as the old heart of Newcastle upon Tyne, nominated here as
the key town, this last area includes the wide stretches around the city
which are controlled by the Newcastle upon Tyne City Council, the
Metropolitan District Council of North Tyneside and the Northumberland
County Council.

Key Town
Newcastle upon Tyne

L88   P549   NZ250638

In AD122 Emperor Hadrian built a bridge across the Tyne and a fort to
protect its northern end. He called both Pons Aelii, showing his pride in them
by giving them his first name, Aelius. The bridge linked the port and supply

base of Arbeia, South Shields, to Hadrian's Wall and its Military Way, which originally terminated at the fort.

The Angles, who began to settle in Northumberland a century and a half after the Romans departed, and remained with some Danish injections until conquered by the Normans, never really appreciated the military importance or the communications possibilities of Pons Aelii, but it is believed they built a monastery on the site of the Roman fort, perhaps in the eighth or ninth century. It acquired the name Monkchester, which suggests a monastery, and, while Bede made no mention of it, Anglian graves have been exhumed within the grounds of the present castle.

William the Conqueror seemed to regard Northumberland as a wild, untameable waste, useful only as a bulwark between the Scots and his kingdom. In this respect he could see that the River Tyne had an important role to play, especially if its lowest crossing point could be guarded by a castle. He ordered his son Robert Curthose to build a motte and bailey on the site of the Roman fort, presumably clearing it first of all traces of the monastery. The year was 1080.

This royal castle was intended to be the linchpin of the Normans' north-eastern defences. It was the 'New Castle' which superseded the 'Old Castle' of Bamburgh, regarded as being too close to the Border and too far off the main route to be effective. The replacement was well positioned for this responsibility, being protected on its north side by a deep ravine, now the Side, on the east by the Lort Burn and on the south by the steep banks of the river. Only on its west side was a moat necessary.

While it was in its timber state there are records of only one attack upon it, and that was by the king himself. The rebel Earl of Northumberland, Robert de Mowbray (1087 – 1095), had garrisoned the New Castle, also Tynemouth and Morpeth castles, when his relations with the Crown approached nadir. King William II took these strongholds before winkling Mowbray out of his Bamburgh hideaway. Any elation Rufus may have felt as a result of these successes was tempered by the feeling that the New Castle had not stood up to his army as well as a royal castle should, so he strengthened its ramparts.

Tradesmen and others who could make a living by supplying the castle's needs established a village at its gates, and called it Newcastle for obvious reasons. This grew while Northumberland was an earldom of Henry, Prince of Scotland, but peaceful prosperity was endangered when King Henry II reclaimed Northumberland as an English shire in 1157 and ordered the building of several stone castles in the county – including a replacement for the motte and bailey in Newcastle. As this was a royal stronghold, he felt personally responsible for its design and construction, and for its cost.

He did well to commission Royal Engineer Maurice to build the keep; he was the man who built the keep in Dover castle ten years later. He started work in Newcastle in 1172, and by 1177 he had completed a rectangular building of exceptional strength, incorporating a number of innovations such as a suite of rooms for the king, a plumbing system which delivered water in lead pipes from a ninety-nine feet deep stone-lined well to drawing points on all main floors, and stone slopes, or 'batters', at the foot of all outside walls to deflect stones dropped onto them into the enemy standing on the ground.

As the Keep cost a fortune – £911 – the curtain walls and buildings in the bailey were completed in stages during the following couple of years, as the royal purse would allow. Alterations and additional buildings were a continuing drain on finances throughout the thirteenth century. A barbican and gatehouse were built in front of the main western gate in 1247 and christened the Black Gate because the road leading to it was lined with houses built by a property developer called Patrick Black. A grand hall, the Hall of Kings, was mentioned first in 1292 when King Edward I and his vassal Scottish King John Balliol enjoyed their Christmas dinner there; it was built in the three acre, triangular-shaped main bailey, roughly where the Moot Hall and County Courthouse were sited much later. Its neighbours in the bailey were the usual requirements of a garrison – sleeping quarters, cook and brew houses, stables, farrier and probably a chapel.

While castle building was in progress, a new bridge was constructed between Newcastle and Gateshead; it had a wooden platform supported on the repaired stone piers of Pons Aelii. This and a beneficial town charter, granted by King John in 1216 when he was willing to do almost anything to gain urban support for his struggle with the barons, helped to develop Newcastle's trade, mostly in wool and hides and, increasingly, in coal. The town was still within the King's demesne, however (it was until 1618), and it acquired an important military role. Defence-wise it had little to worry about in pre-cannon days as the castle was too awesome for invaders to tackle, but in offensive terms it was well positioned to act as an assembly point where armies could be mustered for incursions into Scotland. It was within striking distance of the Border and had excellent supply lines by land and sea.

Fire in 1248 interrupted progress; it swept through the town, destroying several buildings and the bridge. Reconstruction began almost immediately, and the opportunity was taken to further strengthen the castle's vulnerable western approach. The new bridge was most impressive; the Roman piers were used again, but this time the arches between them were of stone, while the deck was wide enough to support buildings on either side of the road. It suffered some damage during a flood in 1339 and was repaired at roughly century intervals, but it served the riverside communities and the long distant travellers for over five hundred years until it finally succumbed to the 1771 flood which swept away all Tyne bridges save the one at Corbridge.

As the town grew in importance and size, several citizens found it pleasanter to live beyond the immediate precincts of the castle. Life was more congenial there, but also more dangerous when the Scots were on the rampage. In 1291 they petitioned King Edward I for money and licence to build a defensive wall. This was granted next year and building started almost immediately. Even before it was completed its psychological effect was sufficient to deter William Wallace in 1297, who halted his plundering and ravaging progress at Ryton.

The wall was completed in some fashion before Edward I died in 1307, but it was vastly improved during the reign of his grandson. In its final form it was 3740 yards long, between 12 and 15 feet high and about 8 feet thick. For much of its length it was fronted by a fosse the width of a cricket pitch. Nineteen towers were incorporated in it, with numerous watch turrets interspersed, and it was broken by six principal gates and two posterns.

Unfortunately none of the gates or their defences remain; all were demolished before 1824 because they interfered with the flow of traffic. The two most important were the West Gate, in line with Westgate Road, and New Gate, at the northern end of Newgate Street. Another on the north side of the town was Pilgrim Gate, while Pandon Gate and Sand Gate gave access to the east. Between the last two was Sally Port, which does not seem to rank as a gate; probably it was built much later, perhaps in the sixteenth century when troops were want to 'sally forth' on Border raids.

Nearly half the original number of towers remain, but not quite in their original form. Some were converted during the eighteenth century to serve as meeting rooms for trade guilds and companies. Morden Tower (Guild of Plumbers, Glaziers and Pewterers) and Heber Tower (Company of Armourers, Curriers and Feltmakers) along West Walls are good examples, while Sallyport Tower (Ships' Carpenters Company) near City Road and Plummer Tower (Guild of Masons) in Croft Street, although replacements, are very interesting. The Austin Friars' Tower, although not on the town wall, is worth a study. When the Augustinian friars were dissolved, King Henry VIII retained their buildings as an occasional meeting place for the Council of the North: he called it the King's Manor (hence Manors Station, etc.). In 1681 it was bought by the burgesses, its site mostly cleared and Holy Jesus Hospital built on it, but the friars' tower was retained and renovated and still stands to guard a multi-storey car park.

This new and complex defensive system proved its worth on two occasions in the fourteenth century. In 1342 King David led a major incursion which eventually reached Auckland, County Durham. On the way he had a good look at Newcastle but decided his best plan was to ford the River Tyne at Newburn. Then in 1388 Earl Douglas brought an army to the town's wall where he and Sir Henry 'Hotspur' Percy exchanged a few pleasantries. He did not attempt to gain admittance and left the real fighting for Otterburn. Commercially, the wall was a positive success, for it conveyed a feeling of security to those wishing to develop the town's coal and shipping potential. By 1384 Newcastle was the fourth most important town in England after London, Bristol and York.

King Henry IV granted Newcastle a charter in 1400 which made it a county outside Northumberland, with its own sheriff. The castle and castle garth were excluded and remained in Northumberland, an arrangement which pleased the burgesses of the day as it eliminated their maintenance responsibilities, but which in time proved to be a decided drawback as the area was beyond the reach of both the town's law officers and its trade guilds. Criminals took refuge there and tradesmen sought unfair advantages by selling their wares there. Queen Elizabeth put a stop to the first of these flaws in 1589 by granting the town's authorities permission to enter the castle garth for the purpose of making arrests.

The town wall made the castle virtually superfluous, and it was used for a long period as Northumberland's county gaol. The wall seemed so strong and impregnable there was no need for any defences behind it. But the stoutest wall does not last for ever, and when it was really needed it was in a sorry state of disrepair. The probability of a Scottish attack during the Bishops' War brought Lord Conway to Newcastle in 1639 on a tour of inspection. He found the wall dilapidated with some of the gates little more than holes in the stonework, and the castle no longer of military strength; he concluded that the town was not defendable and his only hope of stopping an army was to meet it in open country.

As anticipated, a Scottish army of about 30,000 men under General Alexander Leslie, Earl of Leven, entered Northumberland in August 1640 and headed south. Conway, correctly guessing that Leslie would try to take Newcastle from Gateshead and would cross the Tyne at Newburn, stationed all the men he could muster, about 3000, near the ford. His little band was annihilated and Leslie was able to walk into Newcastle.

The unwelcome guests stayed a full year and, by all accounts, behaved as occupying armies usually do. The citizens of Newcastle paid Leslie £60,000 to go home, and did not begrudge a penny of it.

John Marley, Newcastle's mayor, learnt his lesson well and saw to it that the town wall was not only repaired but also strengthened. He applied some urgency to the work for he could see how relations between king and parliament were deteriorating.

The Civil War, which started in 1642, was really an all-English quarrel between the Roundheads of John Pym and King Charles I and his Cavaliers, but the Scots were bribed by the promise of religious freedom to join in on the side of the Parliamentarians. Thanks largely to William Cavendish, the Marquis of Newcastle, the whole of Northumbria except Hull was a Royalist stronghold and thus the badly needed Newcastle coal was denied in the parts of the country which supported Pym. The Scots agreed to take Newcastle and free the coal supply.

So in January 1644 General Leslie was once again on the route to Newcastle. His passage was delayed by snow and the need to mop up elements of resistance on Coquet Island and in Morpeth, and this gave Cavendish time to bring reinforcements into the town. The Scots arrived in February, noted the strength of the wall and, after a few days of probing, moved on to more pressing business on Marston Moor. Cavendish made the mistake of following him and in July his army suffered a crushing defeat inflicted by the combined forces of Leslie and Cromwell. Cavendish was branded a traitor and had to flee the country.

Leslie returned to Newcastle in August with his army, estimated to be between 20,000 and 30,000 strong. Mayor Marley could only muster 800 soldiers now that Cavendish's force had been decimated, and to this he added some 700 armed civilians.

The Scots crossed the Tyne from Gateshead on a makeshift pontoon bridge and headed straight for a small outpost at Shieldfield, about half a mile north-east of the castle (NZ255646). This very vulnerable little fort must have been constructed hurriedly and manned by a few Kamikaze troops who, when they were surrounded by the enemy had but two choices, death or surrender. The structure was made of wattle and earth, yet its remains were still visible in 1859 when the site was cleared for the building of Christ Church. The historian Lithgow described it as a quadrangle with four-cornered bastions at the angles, "having the north-east side of one bulwark pallisaded, the rest not, save along the top of the works about they had laid masts of ships to beat down the assailants with their tumbling force".

Leslie's army was not beaten down and was soon able to give its full attention to besieging the town. Unlike the Elizabethan ramparts at Berwick, Newcastle's wall had not been designed to withstand cannon fire, and several breaches soon appeared. These did not give immediate access, however, so well orchestrated was the stubborn resistance of the garrison, and it took until October, an incredible ten weeks, before their defence was overcome. Their reward from the king was the proud motto, "Fortiter Defender Triumphans".

The Royalists suffered another defeat at Naseby in 1645, and a year later King Charles was captured by the Scots at Newark. He was taken as a prisoner to Newcastle where he refused to sign a document which might have secured his release – the 'Propositions of Newcastle', his opponents' conditions for peace which he saw as an apostasy of all his principles. The Parliamentarians then 'bought' the king from Leslie for £20,000, but eventually the wily monarch escaped from them and did a deal with his former captives. This led to a three day battle at Preston between Cromwell's Model

Army and the Scots; Charles was captured and, after a trial by a special parliamentary court, he was beheaded on the 30 January 1649. By this time Leslie and his army had left Newcastle and returned home.

The town wall was patched up after this but was never again asked to play a defensive role. The citizens got a fright in 1745 when the Young Pretender, Charles Edward Stuart, seemed set on bringing his Jacobites down the east coast route from Edinburgh, but nothing came of it. Some 15,000 men under General Wade were brought into Newcastle, and their presence persuaded the rebels to take the west coast route instead. When the Jacobites' cause was finally crushed at Culloden in April 1746 there was great rejoicing in Newcastle.

The slight damage sustained by the castle during Leslie's siege and occupation was repaired, but no one seemed interested in the old place. The Northumberland County Council stopped using it as a gaol in 1714 when a tower in Morpeth was converted for the purpose, and it was left to the not-too-tender mercy of a few traders and craftsmen who required cheap accommodation. The garth was used as an occasional market-place. In 1782 an advertisement appeared in the *Newcastle Courant* offering the keep for a modest rent and suggesting that "with the greatest convenience and advantage" it could be converted into either a windmill or a brewery.

Newcastle Corporation came to the rescue in 1803 and bought what remained of the castle for £600. The roof of the keep was repaired and the picturesque but out of character battlements and flag tower were added. In 1849 the Society of Antiquaries leased the keep and the Black Gate and they have looked after them ever since. They commissioned John Dobson to design new windows and doors for the Black Gate.

A lot of old masonry in the castle garth was cleared in 1810 to make room for the Moot Hall, a building replaced in 1910 by the recently renovated court house. A few fragments of curtain wall remain, as does the well preserved South Postern gate which heads the precipitous stair down to the river. From the postern a good view of the keep and its entrance is obtained, and the Newcastle to Edinburgh railway line, a less than happy Victorian contribution, is not too obtrusive.

Altogether quite a lot of medieval Newcastle remains and can be explored with the help of leaflets obtainable form the Information Centre in Newcastle's Central Library, Princess Square.   [**Plate 12**]

Area 10, Sub-Area A   Greater Newcastle

Elswick

L88   P549   NZ230637   1½ km, 1 mile, west of Newcastle

Now just a suburb of Newcastle, Elswick before 1835 was an independent township in Northumberland, separated from its large neighbour by the

Skinner Burn. It extended westwards to Benwell and northwards from the Tyne to Nuns Moor, taking in much of modern Fenham.

This important estate was awarded, with Aydon and other properties, by King John to Walter de Burum, Baron of Bolam, in 1204. The King, in fact, was merely confirming what had already passed into history, for James de Burum, Walter's grandfather, had owned the place from the early twelfth century, and had been able to grant it as a free gift to Tynemouth Priory in 1120.

During the period when Northumberland was a Scottish earldom, in 1147, Prince Henry granted the Priory fishing rights in the Tyne. Even this privilege did not induce the Prior to use Elswick as a residence, but he derived a considerable income by leasing it to farmers and, after 1330, by collecting coal mining licences and royalties.

Elswick coal, shipped from Tynemouth to London, initiated the lucrative Tyneside coal trade. Successive priors made money from it but were not averse to ploughing back some of their profits to develop techniques and to add to the safety of their tenants. Thus a fortified tower was built during the fifteenth century, although it was not mentioned until 1576.

When Tynemouth Priory was dissolved, in 1539, the Crown took over Elswick, but life there continued as before. Then in 1628 King Charles I sold the place in two parts, One to the local family of Ords and the other to the Newcastle family of Jenison, the latter taking the tower and a few acres around it for their home. A succession of later owners of this part built a mansion, then rebuilt it, then repeated this a few times more over two hundred years, all mansions being on the site of the tower and all called Elswick Hall.

The last Elswick Hall was built for John Hodgson in 1810, seven years after he became the owner. It was a noble building, designed by William Stokoe, with four large Ionic columns at its south front, but unfortunately its upkeep proved too expensive for the Hodgson family and they had to sell. Between 1877 and 1930 the Hall was an art gallery, while the grounds were purchased in 1881 by a group of business men and given to the council to save it from becoming a building site. The council established Elswick Park, still a pleasant oasis, but the Hall has been replaced by swimming baths.

Benwell

L88   P549   NZ210644   3½ km, 2¼ miles, west of Newcastle

The present day Benwell Tower is the fourth building to have graced the site. It is crenellated, but only because John Dobson, its architect, considered this a suitable decoration. In fact only the second of the four, built in Tudor times, was a true stronghold.

Between the reigns of William I and Henry III Benwell was a detached manor of Styford barony, held by the Bolbec family. Walter Bolbec built a timber hall house, the first structure on the site, at around the time he founded Blanchland Abbey, ie, about 1165. Its original purpose is not known, but a century later it was surplus to requirements and was given to Tynemouth Priory, to add to that fortunate institution's wide collection of Northumberland properties called Tynemouthshire. The Prior and his monks used the gift occasionally as a summer rest house, but for most of the time it was let.

One letting which proved to be a lengthy one was transacted in 1367. The tenant, called Scot, made an indelible mark on local geography by establishing a wooded park along the northern bank of the Tyne below his home. This became known as Scot's Wood, later 'Scotswood'.

Richard Scot, who styled himself 'Lord of Benwell', was the last of the family to hold the lease. During the early years of the fifteenth century his only daughter and heiress, Isabel, married William Heron of Ford and Cornhill. He was killed in 1428 while attacking Etal Castle, but he had lived long enough to have sired a daughter, Elizabeth, who inherited the lease of Benwell – but not of Ford or Cornhill which went to William's brother. Elizabeth kept Benwell in the Heron family by marrying her cousin John Heron, with papal dispensation, in 1438.

The house was very well maintained, but by 1500 it was due for replacement and building No.2 was constructed. The Herons were still tenants of Tynemouth Priory and it is not known who paid the bill.

King Henry VIII dissolved Tynemouth Priory in January 1539. The last prior, Robert Blakeney, accepted the inevitable peacefully so was awarded a pension of £80 a year and was permitted to retire to Benwell Tower, now Crown property. He stayed there until his death in 1549, then the Crown sold the property.

During its 260 years there is no record of the Tower's fortifications ever being tested, but it could boast of three further owners. It was an eminent structure, a gabled three storey mansion with a tower standing against one of the gables, and it attracted the elite. First to make it their home were the Ditchfields, then came a branch of the Delavals, and finally a family of Shaftos, chips off the Bavington Hall block. For a short period in 1739 the Shaftoes employed Lancelot 'Capability' Brown as their gardener.

In or around 1760 the Shaftoes demolished the Tudor mansion and tower and constructed Benwell Tower No.3. It was a long, many windowed, unfortified hall designed by James Paine. In 1779 it was sold to Andrew Bowes, a rather unsavoury Irish adventurer who had made a fortune and had married the widow of the Earl of Strathmore. By all accounts, he treated her most cruelly, refusing her permission to leave the house, even to walk in the garden, but she gained her freedom when Andrew was imprisoned for life for transacting some shady deal.

The Tower lay empty, save for the destructive elements of nature, for several years, although the rest of the manor, beyond the Tower's garden, must have been sold at about this time to builders of houses for the workers, for Benwell was fast becoming industrialised. In 1829 the Tower property was bought as a ruin by Thomas Crawhill, a successful Newcastle rope maker. He built the last Benwell Tower, which is still standing. Completed in 1831, it is obviously unfortified, but John Dobson felt it had to look impressive against its surrounds of mean structures associated with William Armstrong's armament factory on the river bank.

A Gothic-style chapel was added to the Tower in 1881, then, a year later, it was sold to a partnership of Sowerby and Pease. John William Pease, the senior partner, built Pendower Hall for himself and gave Benwell Tower to the newly formed diocese of Newcastle. It was the bishop's palace until a few years before the start of the Second World War.

From 1939 to the present day, the Tower has had a number of strange consignments. During the war it became a Civil Defence Centre and a fire station was built in its garden. In 1947 British Coal, or rather the National Coal Board, established a miners' training school there. This lasted until 1970, then it became a night club, to be followed after three years by an hotel, the Mitre Hotel, which traded successfully until 1989. Since then the BBC has been using it as a television studio.

Newburn

L88   P548   NZ168652   8 km, 5 miles, west of Newcastle

The 'burn' in the name does not refer to a stream but is a derivative of the Anglo-Saxon 'burh', or fortified town. Newburn, like Corbridge and Warkworth, was a royal burh when Northumbria was a kingdom, then, after 954, it became the earl's demesne until Earl Robert de Mowbray started to misbehave in 1095 and lost his property to the Norman kings. As if to atone in advance for his future sins, Mowbray had given the tithes of Newburn to Tynemouth Priory in 1090. The Priory did rather well from this sub-section!

In 1204 King John granted Newburn and other estates to Robert fitz Roger, the baron of Warkworth. It remained in the Warkworth empire until 1332 when the Crown seized it as settlement for debts, and it was granted to Henry, the second Lord Percy of Alnwick. Since then Newburn has had many occupiers and tenants, even a few owners, but somehow the Percys, whether barons, earls or dukes, have never been far away.

Newburn Hall was a fifteenth century tower with a sixteenth century dwelling attached to it. The Percys built both, and in 1530 Sir Thomas Percy, brother of the sixth earl, made the Hall his home.

Both the military and commercial importance of the town were due largely to its position on the River Tyne, for here was the lowest ford on the river yet it was navigable to this point by the seaworthy ships of the day. Several Scottish armies used the ford: King David Bruce, for example, on his way to Neville's Cross in 1346, and General Leslie who approached Newcastle in 1640 after crossing the river here and overcoming Lord Conway's meagre defences.

The presence of coal also contributed to Newburn's commercial success. A mine was in existence as early as 1367, and the ready accessibility of fuel was a factor in John Spencer's decision to start the Newburn Steelworks in 1822. At first it was merely a workshop producing files, but its products proliferated and soon springs and appliances for mines and railways were being made. In 1830 it became a steel manufacturing unit and rolling mill, and as such it prospered until 1924. The founder used Newburn Hall as his office, then later it became the pattern shop. It was demolished when the works closed.

Heaton

L88   P549   NZ267657   3 km, 2 miles, north-east of Newcastle

King Henry I granted a two-part barony in 1120 to Nicholas de Grenville. The barony took its name from its 'capital', Ellingham, two miles south-west of Chathill (NU171257), and this village with Newstead and Doxford formed the northern part. The southern part was rather scattered as well, and included Cramlington, Hartley, Jesmond and Heaton.

Nicholas's daughter married Ralph de Gaugy, who succeeded as baron before 1158. In due course Ralph's eldest son, Robert, became baron and, although he spent most of his time in the northern part, he had a town house in Heaton. This appears to have been a very grand edifice, a fortified palace, according to one report, and tradition has it that King John stayed there on one occasion.

Ralph's second son, Adam, established himself in Jesmond and initiated a new family line with the name 'de Jesmond'. His son, also Adam, did well, becoming High Sheriff of Northumberland in 1262, 1265 and 1267, but he was an unpleasant man, once described as bearing "an odious character for perculation and extortion". He was so disliked by the down-trodden proletariat he feared for his life, and applied to King Henry III in 1264 for a licence to build a crenellated hide-away, or camera.

The site chosen for this was down the Ouse Burn from Jesmond, in what is now Heaton Park. It was actually very close to Robert de Gaugy's abandoned 'palace' – so close in fact that the tradition attached to the old jumped over to the new, and the camera is still called 'King John's Palace' sometimes, although it was not built in that monarch's lifetime.

Adam went on a crusade with Prince Edward in 1270 and did not return. His widow, Christine, married Robert Bruce in 1275, one of the unsuccessful competitors for the Scottish throne in 1291 and the Bannockburn victor's grandfather. Adam's possessions were shared between two cousins, William of Stickelawe and Margory of Trewick, and their descendants held, and used, the Heaton camera until the sixteenth century.

By the early years of the seventeenth century the building had passed the point where repair was practicable. It and the area around it were acquired before 1617 by Henry Babington, who built Heaton Hall, an unfortified mansion, a few hundred yards south of the ruin on a site now hidden beneath Shaftesbury Grove. The Babingtons were owners for nearly a century, then in about 1713 the property was bought by a very young Matthew Ridley, who held it until 1755 when he moved to Blagdon Hall, having benefited by the will of his brother-in-law, Sir Matthew White. The Hall was left to waste away until the site was sold as building land and the open ground was bought by W.G. Armstrong in 1880 and presented to Newcastle Corporation who created a public park.

The ruin of the camera was stabilized in 1897 and remains an historic attraction within the park. Its north and east walls still stand to a fair height, and a feature is a large round-headed window which, presumably, is not original.

While in the Ouse Burn vale, it is worth recording that Castle Farm, near the northern end of Jesmond Dene (NZ255674), is neither medieval nor fortified. It was built in the eighteenth or early nineteenth century, then romanticized with crenellations by Dr Thomas Headlan, chief physician at the Newcastle Infirmary, when he built Jesmond Dene House in 1822. He did this simply to improve his view – just a garden folly – although the farm itself remained a working unit occupied by the Knox family until well into the twentieth century. Peter Knox was still doing a daily milk round in High West Jesmond and the southern part of Gosforth in 1935, his horse-drawn milk float filled with large churns being a common sight in those pre-war days.

Area 10, Sub-Area B   North Tyneside and South-East Northumberland

Tynemouth (with North Shields)

L88   P549   NZ372693   14 km, 8¹/₂ miles, east of Newcastle

The promontory at the end of Front Street in Tynemouth is a rock of magnesium limestone with sheer cliffs to the east and north, a steep drop to the south and a deep, wide ditch, part natural, part man-made, to the west. Access is by a causeway which replaces a drawbridge across the ditch.

Excavations carried out in 1968 revealed evidence of Iron Age and Romano-British settlements on the rock. A few Roman stones and a piece of Roman altar-stone have been found in old foundations, but these are thought to have been brought to the site as building rubble from Wallsend and do not indicate the former presence of the Roman legions. According to a twelfth century chronicle, the promontory was called 'Benebalcrag' at the time. This translates as 'Head of the Rapier Rock', a fair description.

From the seventh century to the fourteenth the rock was concerned principally with ecclesiastical affairs, and what warlike defences there were played only a supporting role and could not be classified as a castle.

Oswald, King of Deira and Bernicia between 634 and 642 and St. Aidan's royal benefactor, built a wooden church on the rock, then, a few years later, replaced it with one of stone. In 651 it received a gift which in later years was to bring it great fame and wealth – the body of King Oswin. He had been beloved by his people for his kindness and humility, and when a tomb was raised in his memory it commanded the devotion properly accorded a saint.

The Vikings were no respecters of saints or anyone else and they attacked the rock at least five times. According to legend, Halfdene, a Danish leader, made Tynemouth his headquarters in 875; if this be true than almost certainly he would have constructed strong defences around him, but nothing of this nature is recorded.

The little church must have succumbed for nothing more is heard of it. But a lay community did build up on the headland round a large hall house which became a favourite residence of Tostig, a protégé of Edward the Confessor and the much disliked Earl of Northumberland between 1055 and 1065. One of the reasons for his unpopularity was his drunken behaviour at Tynemouth.

Northumberland never settled down during William the Conqueror's reign, and its earls during that time were either rather useless or they got themselves killed by the populace. When William Rufus came to the throne in 1087, Robert de Mowbray was earl. He was the exception, a man of spirit. Inevitably he fell foul of the king, but before doing so he did a lot of good for Tynemouth by persuading the Bishop of Durham to allow some monks of Jarrow monastery to make regular visits there with a view to reviving Christian worship.

Jarrow monastery was closed in 1083 and its monks moved to Durham, which became a Benedictine establishment. The bishop built a church on Tynemouth's promontory and assigned a monk for permanent duty there. This was the beginning of Tynemouth's post-conquest monastic life. It was to have a great future, thanks to Mowbray's kick-start, but not under the auspices of the Durham Church; at the crucial time Mowbray and the Bishop were at loggerheads about some missing cattle, so the earl went to the Benedictine Abbey in St. Albans for assistance. The abbot there responded by sending monks to establish a satellite priory at Tynemouth.

Mowbray richly endowed the new priory and set a fine example of generosity which many other landowners, then and later, followed. The Duke, however, was a political as well as a religious animal, and in the former mode he managed to upset King Rufus, who brought an army north in 1095 to deal with his alleged treachery. In preparation for this, Mowbray had manned the defences at Tynemouth and had garrisoned his castles at Newcastle and Morpeth before retiring to Bamburgh Castle. The King captured all the strongholds and winkled Mowbray out of Bamburgh in order to strip him of all his property and honours before allowing him to retire as a monk in St. Alban's Abbey.

In contrast to Newcastle, which had been easy, Tynemouth Priory had been difficult to break into, probably because the huge ditch across the neck of the promontory was widened and deepened at about this time. Also there is a mound of earth in the south-west corner of the rock which could have been a motte dating from this period, but the idea cannot be substantiated.

Although the King had attacked Tynemouth, his quarrel had been with the earl and not with the monks who lived there. Indeed he was most generous to the latter and not only confirmed all the gifts of land Mowbray and others had bestowed on them but also he metaphorically collected these scattered properties together and conveyed them as a liberty to the Prior. The master of a subsidiary priory, the cell of an abbey, became the lord of Tynemouthshire.

The shire grew in importance and prestige over the years until dissolution. More property was donated and a few purchases were made by the Prior. By 1381 it included Tynemouth manor, North Shields, Preston, Chirton, Fleetworth, Murton, Whitley, Monkseaton, Hartburn, Dissington, Elswick, Earsdon, Backworth, Wolsington, Wylam, West Denton,, Benwell, Cowpen, Bebside, Hauxley, Amble, Eglingham, Bewick and several houses in Newcastle. All this property was revenue-producing for most of the time during the twelfth and thirteenth centuries, and the Prior was able to afford a new church during Henry I's reign, as well as a non-interference pledge from King David I when he invaded in 1138. There was even enough money to improve the defences when alarm bells started to sound at the end of the thirteenth century.

A licence to crenellate was obtained from King Edward I in 1296, and by the following year a strong wall and protected entrance was near enough to completion to deter William Wallace. This work still did not constitute a castle, but, when combined with what nature had contributed, it made the priory very secure. The priory also offered more comfortable accommodation than did the average castle or tower, so it was used as an hotel by visiting dignitaries quite often. As a rule the Prior was in favour of this as caring for travellers was in his brief, but he must have been just a little put out in 1312 when King Edward II arrived with his much patronised favourite, Piers Gaveston, hotly pursued by Thomas of Lancaster and Henry Percy, bearing between them all the justifiable wrath of the country's barons.

The post-Bannockburn period was a worrying time for Tynemouth, as it was for all the county. Both Robert Bruce and the Mitford Gang tried to take the priory and it became necessary to guard the place with eighty soldiers led by Sir Robert Delaval. While this saved Tynemouth, outlying manors of Tynemouthshire were not so lucky. Their inhabitants were bled dry and could contribute nothing to the priory. This loss of revenue, the expensive garrison and the cost of entertaining soon brought on a bad attack of financial hiccups. Appeals to King Edward II for help fell on deaf ears at first.

The Prior never closed his doors to harmless visitors, however, and in 1346 he received a rather special guest, King David Bruce no less. He invaded Tynedale that year with a large army, and while resting at Corbridge he sent a message to the Prior telling him to prepare dinner for him in two days time. This arrogance had an amusing sequel, for the king did indeed dine two days later in the priory, but not quite in the circumstances intended. David was taken prisoner at Neville's Cross and was conveyed to Tynemouth as a captive.

Whether or not this incident jogged King Edward's conscience is not known, but it was about this time that some funding came through, and Prior de la Mare immediately got to work repairing and extending both his monastic and defensive buildings. The result pleased the king, who called Tynemouth one of his strongest fortifications on the Border – yet it failed to resist for long the insidious battering of the sea or the ravaging of the Scots.

By 1380 the walls were being reported as ruinous once again. It took ten years after that to convince King Richard II of the need to contribute to their repair, but eventually he gave £500. His uncle, John of Gaunt, Duke of Lancaster, donated a further £100, and Henry Percy, the first Earl of Northumberland, chipped in with £66 and a thousand trees. All this benevolence Prior Whethamstede converted into strong walls with turrets, proper accommodation and facilities for a garrison and a large gatehouse-keep, the ruins of which still stand. The latter was an oblong building containing a great hall at one level, with kitchen adjoining, and a great chamber above it, and its entrance was guarded by a barbican still in a remarkable state of preservation. The new walls effectively closed the neck of the promontory by joining the gatehouse to the north and south cliffs. A tower called Whitley Tower, still discernible, terminated the north end. At last, in the dying years of the fourteenth century, Tynemouth ceased to be a priory with military defences and became a gatehouse castle protecting a priory. The place was equal in strength to Dunstanburgh further up the coast, which, incidentally, also benefited from John of Gaunt's attention.

The extra security and privacy the castle gave the priory was not totally good for its inmates and in 1536 King Henry VIII's commissioners found the moral standards there remarkably low. Serious charges were made against the Prior and about half his monks, but this mattered little for dissolution occurred three years later. On 12th January 1539 Prior Blakeney signed a deed of surrender. The long ties with St. Albans Abbey were broken and Tynemouth became a royal property.

Blakeney received a pension of £80 per annum and was permitted to retire to his manor at Benwell. The sub-prior got a pension of £10 and became the curate of Earsdon with Backworth. The other fourteen monks and three novices received annuities of between £2 and £6 and were told to look for pastoral work. The household goods and farm stock at Tynemouth were sold and the six church bells just disappeared. The famous shrine of St. Oswin was broken up. Most of the monastic buildings were destroyed or left as building material for possible future use, but the church itself was modified for use as Tynemouth's parish church, a function it performed until 1666. The priory land around Tynemouth was leased to Thomas Hilton, a prominent local business man who became sheriff of Northumberland in 1548. The widely scattered manors of Tynemouthshire lost their liberty status and became subject to state laws; they were leased or sold to local gentry. A constable was put in charge of the castle, which was retained for the king's use.

At first the king did not seem to know what to do with it. There was airy talk of a launching pad for attacks on Scotland and a central control of the marches, but it was left to the Earl of Hertford in 1544 to put his finger on a useful suggestion. In that year Marie de Guise, Scotland's queen mother, annoyed Henry VIII by repudiating a treaty he had signed with the Earl of Arran by which the infant Mary Queen of Scots was to marry the future King Edward VI. Henry's immediate reaction was to invade Scotland, and Hertford had the job of loading ten thousand soldiers and their supplies onto two hundred ships docked in the Tyne. While carrying out this duty, he saw much of Tynemouth Castle and became very impressed with its potential as a defence of the important port and seaway for coal from Newcastle.

He conveyed his thoughts to the Privy Council, and in 1545 Sir Richard Lee was commissioned to prepare plans. They were approved and put in hand without delay, and in fact the job was completed some three years before the Elizabethan Ramparts at Berwick were started.

Sir Richard did little to the keep and other existing houses which, one hundred and fifty years after their last face-lift, were in a fairly ruinous condition. His instructions were to produce a fortification which could both give and take artillery fire of Tudor sophistication, and he achieved this by constructing several gun emplacements on the edge of the cliff overlooking the mouth of the river, and by placing a completely new battery on the smaller and lower promontory south of the castle, on the far side of Prior's Haven (NZ373690). He was the first to realise that lobbing cannon balls from a height onto ships below was a very hit or miss business, and there was a much better chance of scoring with guns at a lower level which could sweep across the whole navigable passage of the river. To protect this battery and the old castle from possible land attack, he modernised the west wall, inserted some gun turrets and extended it southwards to the riverside near the Black Midden rocks.

The work gave employment to a thousand labourers but they did not make their fortunes out of it as the total wages bill was only £2118. Masons and other craftsmen were paid a further £233. Materials cost little as the old priory was used as a quarry. When the new battery was completed it was garrisoned largely by Spanish mercenaries – hence its name, the Spanish Battery.

This modern fortification was maintained in fighting condition until the Treaty of Edinburgh was signed in 1560 and the 'Auld Alliance' between Scotland and France came to an end. Queen Elizabeth could see no other possible enemy on the horizon so had the castle refurbished for use as a state prison. The consequent lack of protection for Tyne shipping caused considerable nervousness in the Admiralty and amongst Newcastle's merchants, especially after false alarms during the Rising of the Northern Earls in 1569 and the Armada in 1588. But neither Elizabeth nor her two successors were interested and they allowed the castle and its satellite to deteriorate until the 1620s when Sir John Fenwick, then captain of the castle, made it known that conditions had got too bad for him to live in the place. His complaint was supported by the Bishop of Durham.

Various schemes were put forward, including one in 1626 by Lord Clifford, Lord Lieutenant of the Northern Counties, for a low level fort at North Shields. This had considerable merit, and when it was shelved in 1636 as being too expensive, the Admiralty offered as a cheaper alternative a plan to build two small block-houses, one on each side of the river at North and South Shields. Still nothing materialised, and when General Leslie invaded in 1640 he was able to capture Tynemouth Castle and the Spanish Battery without any loss of life. He realised he needed to keep the Tyne open for the coal trade and his vital supply link with Scotland, so he refortified the castle, carried out the most necessary repairs and furnished it with effective ordnance.

Newcastle's year long experience of Scottish domination taught the city fathers and the Government the importance of keeping the port open. William Cavendish, the Marquis of Newcastle, was entrusted with the strengthening of the river defences, but all he was able to do was to implement an even cheaper version of the 1630 Admiralty plan. He abandoned the castle and constructed gun emplacements near the high water level at North and South Shields. Each consisted simply of baskets filled with sand and mortar with cannon placed between them. Not very elegant, but at least these guns could rake the entrance to the river, and could deal with any enemy ship which managed to make the Shields Narrows at almost point-blank range.

Come the Civil War and General Leslie's return in 1644. The old castle was garrisoned for the occasion at the start of hostilities, but most of the soldiers succumbed to the Plague and the Scots had little difficulty in taking the place. The gun emplacement fell in even less time.

When the war was over Cromwell authorized Sir Arthur Hazelrigg to spend £5000 on repairs to the fortifications of Newcastle and the port of Tyne. Most of this money appears to have been spent in Newcastle, for little was done further down the river. Tynemouth Castle passed the interregnum as an ordnance store and prison.

King Charles II got his castle back in 1660 and put some minor repairs in hand so that once more it could be garrisoned. A traveller in 1664 described it as being well fortified "with very good guns and good guard of soldiers". The latter lived in "convenient" houses within the castle and could enjoy the use of a bowling green, although their church was in poor condition. On the headland was also a "watch tower lately built where on every night of the year a great fire burns to warn shipping entering the port".

The Anglo-Dutch wars provided the Tyne with two alarms, in 1667 and 1672. After the latter a quite elaborate military station was built at North Shields (NZ363684). It was called Clifford's Fort after the Lord Lieutenant who first advocated its erection forty-six years earlier.

The threat from across the North Sea receded in 1674 but Clifford's Fort remained to shoulder the main responsibility for the safety of shipping in the Tyne. The old castle acquired a proper lighthouse and a new governor's house, but its fortifications were allowed to deteriorate. By 1681 they were ruinous.

Yet it refused to die! Unexpectedly, in the 1780s, it was given a new lease of life as an army barracks. New accommodation was built and what could be saved of the medieval building was crudely repaired with bricks and stucco. Not a pretty sight, but it held a thousand trainee soldiers and served the War Office well between 1783 and 1904. During the 1914-18 was it was used again by troops in training, and for many years afterwards artillery men fired their guns from the cliff-top emplacements in the general direction of targets towed by boats at a safe distance north-east of Tynemouth pier.

Fire broke out in 1936 and the opportunity was taken to remove the military unsightliness and to restore the castle to its eighteenth century condition. Further work in the late 1950s and early 1960s prepared the castle and the priory ruins for invasion by visitors keen to see this interesting example of our national heritage. What was left of the Spanish Battery was cleared away and its site was made into a car park.

Today the promontory is cared for by English Heritage and is open to the public most days of the year. There still remains a surprising amount to see – quite enough to set the imagination racing.

Clifford's Fort, a mile to the south-west, remained on active service even longer than the castle. During the Great War it was occupied by the Northumberland Electrical Engineers whose job it was to place, maintain and, if necessary, to detonate a string of remotely controlled mines laid across the river mouth. Then during the last World War it was used as a signalling station by the Admiralty who kept a tag on all ships entering or leaving the Tyne.

Not a lot is left of the original fort now, but its outline is still discernible as new buildings have been constructed on the old foundations. They are fish processing factories, and the site is in the middle of North Shields fish market. Two not quite so new buildings on the site are the 1727 'Low Light' and its 1808 replacement, the former now an old people's home, the later still operational in conjunction with the 'High Light' on the cliff top. Ships entering the Tyne have to get these two beacons in line to avoid the Black Middens and other navigational hazards in the river.

Whitley Bay

L88   P536   NZ357714   13 km, 8 miles, north-east of Newcastle

Whitley ('Bay' is a fairly modern appendage) was given to Tynemouth Priory by King Henry I, and thus became part of the fragmentary liberty of Tynemouthshire. The Prior had the power of a viceroy in most matters within his domain but one duty the king did not delegate was the granting of licences to crenellate. Accordingly, it was to King Edward III that Gilbert de Whitley applied in 1345 when he wished to fortify his manor house.

He got his licence and built a tower, probably demolishing the manor house and building on the same site. The 1415 survey lists the tower as the possession of the Prior, so it offers no hint about Gilbert's family, or what the man himself did for a living. So far as can be determined, the tower had gone before 1541 and has not been heard of since. There is certainly no trace of it today.

A couple of very ancient maps provide the only clue to the tower's whereabouts. 'Tower' is marked on them, but not with any great precision; it appears to be a little inland from Table Rocks, perhaps just south of the roundabout where the A191 road meets the A193 road, close to the old North Shields Waterworks.

Brier Dene

L88   P536   NZ336739   13¹/₂ km, 8¹/₂ miles, north-east of Newcastle

Gilbert de Middleton, cousin of Sir John Middleton of Belsay and field commander of the notorious Mitford Gang which caused so much distress in Northumberland in 1317, built a fortified manor house in Brier Dene a year or two before he plunged into a life of crime. Why he did this in not known; perhaps it was for a relative or some favoured servant, perhaps it was intended to be a safe retreat which might have been of use had not his capture been so cleanly done.

After his execution in 1318 the Crown confiscated all Middleton property, and this particular part of it went to Thomas de Heton of Castle Heaton and Chillingham. In 1329 Thomas settled it on his eldest son John and his heirs.

John died in 1335, predeceasing his father so a younger son, Alan, took over Brier Dene. But when Thomas died it was found his will had been changed and Alan had been left the main estates, so Brier Dene ended up in the hands of a third son, Thomas, allegedly illegitimate.

Just how long Thomas and his descendants held the manor house is not known, but at some time before 1613 it was incorporated into the Delaval estate, and a new farmhouse was built near it. The manor house was probably demolished at this time, yet an eighteenth century colliery plan shows an unidentified house a few yards from the farm, and it is just possible this was the manor house.

There is nothing to see today, but the manor house's position is known with fair certainty. It was on the north bank of the Brierdene Burn where a field road – now just a path – connecting Monkseaton to Hartley crossed it.

Seaton Delaval

L88   P536   NZ322765   15 km, 9½ miles, north-east of Newcastle

The Delaval family, a branch of which was associated with Seaton Delaval for over five hundred years, can trace its origin to Chateau La Val in Lower Maine, France, in pre-Conquest days. Guy, the first known member and owner of the Chateau in the eleventh century, married a daughter of King William's half-brother, Robert. This line soon petered out, however, and the progenitor of the Northumberland family was a distant relative of Guy's. Between 1082 and 1095 he was granted the Callerton barony, comprising Callerton Delaval (now Black Callerton), Dissington and Eachwick on the west side of Newcastle and Newsham and Seaton Delaval to the east. The feudal cost was two knights fee. The family's main seat for two hundred years was at Callerton Delaval, then they moved to the coast.

It was a straight line, father to son, descent until 1390, when Sir William Delaval died childless and the title and property passed to his cousin, John Delaval of Newsham. He also failed to produce sons and there was an interval of distaff descent before the Delaval name returned in 1471. A fortified tower at Seaton Delaval was mentioned for the first time in the 1415 survey, but probably it had been built by Sir William in the 1370s or '80s.

In 1606, a year before he died, Sir Robert Delaval had an inventory made of his possessions. It showed that he had added a Tudor manor house to his tower at Seaton Delaval, thereby extending his accommodation to include a buttery, larder, kitchen, pantry, dining room, parlour and stables on the ground floor, and a 'great bed chamber', five other bed chambers and several minor rooms on the first floor. His son inherited all this yet still felt claustrophobic so added 'a new long house' – presumably a wing – and made the tower more comfortable by inserting more windows.

The next in line, Sir Ralph, was a sharp-witted gentleman. In 1646 he married Anne, a daughter of the Scottish invasion leader, General Leslie, in St. Nicholas Church, Newcastle, which no doubt was filled with occupying troops. In 1649 he became the first sheriff of Northumberland to be appointed by the Commonwealth government, but by 1660 he had changed his allegiance to welcome King Charles II as a royalist. For this he was created Baron Delaval.

For thirty years before his death in 1691, the new Baron did much to help the Seaton Delaval community by creating industry and facilitating trade by constructing Seaton Sluice harbour. A bottle factory, a brick kiln and salt pans were amongst his enterprises, but what caught the public's imagination most was the clever way he kept the mouth of the Seaton Burn clear of sea-borne silt. He erected a sluice gate at a convenient narrow part of the valley, something like a lock gate but free moving so that the incoming tide would close it, trapping the fresh water, and the ebb tide would allow it to open to release the cleansing flood.

Alas, like many an entrepreneur before and after him, Ralph was careless with money. When his son John inherited he had to sell practically all his property to pay the bills. Last to go was Seaton Delaval, but here he had some good luck for the buyer was a kinsman and a Delaval!

Admiral George Delaval, retired, had made a fortune during a life spent partly in naval service and partly as a diplomat, and in 1719 he was looking forward to settling down in Northumberland and enjoying his remaining years. The property at Seaton Delaval was in poor repair, but the coast and surrounding country was superb, so he bought the estate and commissioned Sir John Vanburgh to design and build a new house. At about the same time, he also built Bavington Hall for his sister, Mary Shafto.

We know from Vanburgh's personal records that the extended tower was demolished and the new building constructed on its site, so we have the exact position of the old place even though nothing of it remains.

Work on the Palladian masterpiece started in 1720 and took eight years to complete. During that time both owner and architect died, the admiral in 1725 when he was thrown from his horse, and Vanburgh a year later, and neither saw the completed building.

Bad luck continued to dog the Hall. In 1752 the southern extremity was damaged by fire, and in 1822 most of the main house was destroyed, also by fire. It was reroofed but it was never refurbished and what impresses the visitor today so much is a central shell with useable wings.

A nephew of the admiral, Francis Blake Delaval of Dissington, took over the Hall, but he too was killed in a riding accident in 1752. His son and daughter, another Francis and Rhoda, the latter married to Sir Edward Astley of Melton Constable, inherited jointly.

Young Francis was a riot in London's artistic circles and was the main reason why the family became labelled as 'The Gay Delavals'. One of his maddest deeds was to make a wager with an actor friend, Samuel Foote, that he could build a castle in twenty-four hours. It is not known how long it took to build, but the product of the wager still stands above Holywell Dene, about a mile south-west of the Hall (NZ334760). It is classified as an eighteenth century Gothick folly now, and its name, Starlight Castle, suggest that part at least of its construction was done during the hours of darkness.

In spite of its asinine reputation, the line survived until 1814, then the inheritance passed to Rhoda's grandson, Sir Jacob Astley. He was elevated to the nobility as Baron Hastings in 1841, and his descendants have owned Seaton Delaval Hall ever since.

Seghill

L88   P536   NZ291744   11¹/₂ km, 7 miles, north-east of Newcastle

Quite a large fortified tower was built at Seghill in or about 1280 by Sir Adam de Selby, who had acquired the manor some forty years earlier. While he had no particular reason to be glad of his defences, they were much appreciated by his grandson, Walter Selby, when he inherited.

Walter was a wild sort of fellow, "both a robber and a warrier, alternately plundering and defending his country". He had married Katherine Delaval in 1304 or 1311 (records differ!) and the couple's main seat was at Biddlestone in Coquetdale, but Seghill was used often when Walter was in his plundering mode. In 1317 he joined Sir Gilbert de Middleton as a lieutenant in his infamous Mitford Gang, and for several months that year he led a shameful existence before escaping, first to Horton and then to Scotland, when the rest of the gang were captured.

The Scots seized the gang's former headquarters, Mitford Castle, in 1318, and King Robert Bruce, relishing the irony of it, put Walter in charge of the castle. This duty he performed until 1321, then he voluntarily surrendered himself and the castle to the English. His life was saved but he lost his freedom and both properties for six years, until King Edward III pardoned him after his coronation of 1327.

His experience behind bars did not dampen Walter's love of adventure, and he took an active role in the Scottish War of Independence – usually on the English side – until 1346, when King David Bruce captured him. He was forced to watch the execution of the two eldest of his four sons, then he himself was executed.

Son number three was with his father and elder brothers when they were captured, but he was spared the death penalty as he was too young to kill, and was imprisoned instead. The youngest son, who had been left at home, being little more than a boy, found it very difficult to manage two properties on his own, and in 1351 he sold both Seghill and Biddlestone to the Delaval family. The buyers were delighted, but son number three was horrified, and as soon as he was released from prison he tried desperately to have the properties returned to him. He was partly successful: Biddlestone was retrieved, but the Delavals held on to Seghill.

Thus the Selby connection with Seghill came to an end. The family continued to prosper at Biddlestone until 1914 and may have had some distant relationship with at least two other Selby families of some importance in Northumberland. These were the Selbys of Grindonrigg and Twizel and the family headed by Alderman William Selby, father of Mad Meg of Meldon.

The Delavals held Seghill until 1441, then sold to the Mitford family, who retained the place for close on three hundred years. John Warburton had this to say about Seghill tower in 1715: "The seat of Mich. Mitford Esq., seated on level ground, is an ancient well built pile consisting of a quadrangular tower with some modern additions, a large and well planted garden on ye south". It is known that considerable alterations and additions were made in 1673, and these are probably what Warburton was referring to.

The Mitfords sold to the Allgoods of Hexham in 1723, and they, in their turn, sold to Sir Francis Blake, the second of that name connected with Twizel, in or about 1790. He grew desperately short of money – in fact he died in a debtors' sanctuary in 1818 – and he had to let Seghill go in 1813, probably to creditors. He did leave a couple of memorials behind, however: the east end of Seghill village is still called 'Blake Town', and the public house there is called 'Blake Arms'.

This pub and its predecessor were built on the site of Selby's tower, and its vaulted basement was retained as the beer cellar. Its wall enclosed a floor area of $44\frac{1}{2}$ by $16\frac{1}{2}$ feet, and the vault was supported by circular ribs which sprang from the floor. There is evidence, also, that the tower had had three storeys plus a look-out at one corner. The modern pub is a conventional post-war building.

Burradon

L88   P536   NZ276730   10 km, $6\frac{1}{4}$ miles, north of Newcastle

This was a detached manor of Whalton barony, held during the second half of the twelfth century by Walter fitz William. Two of his knights were Umfrid de

Hogell and Bertram de Woderington and they were granted parts of the barony, Ogle and half Burradon going to the former in 1150 and Widdrington and the other part of Burradon to the latter in 1162. The Widdringtons quickly sold their interest in Burradon to Roger Baset, the sitting tenant, and the Ogles sold their part before 1290 to Peter Graper, mayor of Newcastle in 1304. Before the end of the century both had sold out to William Orde.

The Ordes were keen farmers but they had little success with the clay soil of Burradon. In 1441 the estate was valued at only 26 shillings, in 1482 only 20 shillings. By 1548 they had had enough and George Ordes conveyed his land to his nephew, Bertram Anderson. The Ogles of Causey Park bought it in 1626 and held it over two hundred years, selling it eventually to Joseph Straker of Benwell and his son John in 1857.

Interesting remains of a small tower exists in the yard of Burradon House Farm. It was built in mid-sixteenth century, either by Bertram Anderson or, more probably, by Oliver Ogle. Externally it measures 25'3" by 22'6", and it has a vaulted ground floor with three storeys above, reached by newel stairs. There were machicolations over the door. Lancelot Ogle repaired it in 1633 and left his initials above the fireplace he installed, but by 1715 it had been written off as "an ancient pile", and it was ruinous in 1769. It could use some preservation before it becomes even more ruinous.

Weetslade

L88   P536   NZ260726   9½ km, 6 miles, north of Newcastle

An estate in Dudley now but originally a manor in the Morpeth barony held, in 1170, partly by the Plessey family and partly by the sitting tenant who took Weetslade as his surname. The Plessey portion descended as did Plessey manor. South Weetslade remained a Weetslade family possession until John joined the Mitford Gang in 1317 and had his land confiscated. The Crown sold it to William de Haselrig.

A tower is listed without the owner's name in the 1415 survey as existing in 'Wittslad Juxta Mare', which is taken to be Weedslade although it is hardly next to the sea. There is no later record of a tower in the vicinity.

Appendices
A.   Some Jargon

Ashlar	Evenly dressed stones on the outer face of towers, castles and other important buildings.
Bailey Ward	area surrounding the motte or keep of a castle where the common soldiers were accommodated.
Barbican	Defensive structure in front of the entrance.
Bartizan	Small round tower protruding on corbels.
Batter	A slope at the base of an otherwise perpendicular wall of a castle keep or tower, to deflect stones, etc., dropped from the battlements onto the enemy.
Carucate	An area of land, probably about 100 acres.
Corbel	Stone bracket supporting an upper floor or a projecting parapet, window, turret or gardrobe.
Crenellate	Literally, to add battlements or other defences to an existing building to convert it into a fortification. Thus a licence to crenellate was the king's permission to do this. Most recipients built a new fortification from scratch.
Escheator	A bailiff who appropriated property when so commanded by the Crown.
Esker	Sand or gravel knoll formed by moving ice during the last glacial period.
Fitz	'Son of', used before family names became fashionable.
Gardrobe	Latrine.
Gothick	A nineteenth century flamboyant Gothic architectural style. Sometimes called 'gingerbread' or 'Strawberry Hill'.
Gravelkind	A form of land tenure by which a father's possessions had to be divided equally between all his sons when he died.
Grayne	See Surname.
Harl, harling	A rendering of lime and gravel, rather like stucco.

Haugh and Heugh The first is level, fertile ground left when a stream or river describes a wide sweep. The second is a hill or ridge with steep sides.

Hobelars Small, sturdy, sure-footed horses much used by reivers. Also called Hobby Horses.

Husbandland An ill-defined area of land capable of being worked by one man.

In Capite Land held directly from the king.

Insight Goods held inside the home, eg, furniture, utensils.

Kaim Mound of boulders and gravel deposited by moving ice during the last glacial period.

Machicolation Projection above a door from which hot tar, stones, sewage, etc., could be dropped onto the heads of unwelcome callers.

Messuage Property which included a dwelling house, outbuildings and demesne. Chief or Capital messuages belonged to the gentry and were usually fortified in the Border zone.

Motte As in motte and bailey castles: raised part within the bailey reserved for the castle's owner or representative.

Newel Spiral stairs or the vertical post around which they turn.

Oriel Projecting window supported on corbel and not resting on the ground.

Oubliette A prison cell with only one opening - in its ceiling. Also called 'bottle-neck dungeon'.

Preceptory Knights Hospitallers institutional buildings, including hostel, church and safe resting place for travellers.

Quoin Corner stone, usually larger and better dressed than adjoining wall stones.

Regulus Ruler of Cumberland when under Scottish influence. Often also the Tanist.

Shieling Sometimes 'sheiling' but 'shielding' is a modern catastrophe. A shelter on the moors used by shepherds and herdsmen who took their animals there to feed on the summer grass.

Springing Level at which an arch or vault rises from its support.

String course Horizontal stone ledge or moulding along the length of a wall.

Tanist Heir-apparent to the Scottish throne.

Vicus Civilian village outside Roman stations.

Windows Casement = side hinged; Dormer = projecting from slope of roof; Lintel = horizontal cross beam; Mullion = vertical member between glass; Transon = horizontal member between glass.

B.   Index of Places

C. *General Index*